COUNTERPOINT

COMPILED AND EDITED

BY

ROY NEWQUIST

LONDON

GEORGE ALLEN & UNWIN LTD

RUSKIN HOUSE   MUSEUM STREET

PRINTED IN GREAT BRITAIN
BY PHOTOLITHOGRAPHY
UNWIN BROTHERS LIMITED
WOKING AND LONDON

Dedicated to the Promotion Directors
of the many publishing firms
who arranged the majority of these interviews.
Without their kindness and co-operation,
COUNTERPOINT could not have been done

Foreword

At the risk of embarrassing Roy Newquist, the true maker of this book, let me say at once that whatever collective merit its sixty-three authors have is owing to his virtues as an interviewer. Anyone who has been interviewed a number of times will remember how certain questions, put in a certain way, can discourage conversation rather than promote it. They can, in fact, paralyze one's mind, such as it is. Some people we like to talk with, and some we don't. Roy Newquist is one of the rare souls in whose presence we prattle—without, however, ceasing to be serious. Indeed, it is in the endeavor to be serious with him, and so to tell him all we think we understand, that we find ourselves going on and on into disclosures we never made before. In the very best sense we become personal: not in order to show ourselves off, but in order to show how the subject at hand appears to us in the light of our actual experience, suddenly recalled and with his help made clear.

The subject at hand, I say. Roy Newquist in his Introduction has indicated what that was, yet I for one—of course I do not speak for the other sixty-two—was not aware of it during my own interview. I merely thought that he was interested in me and wanted to hear me talk: not necessarily about myself, but certainly about what I had done, was doing, and might still do, and whether in my humble opinion this made sense. The result is here and may be judged for itself. So too in all the other cases, which I find fascinating both for what Roy Newquist hoped they would reveal—I do not for a moment discount his hope, nor deny that it bore rich fruit—and for other quite accidental things revealed along the way. Which brings me back to his one indispensable virtue as an interviewer: purity of heart. No vanity, no itch to prove premeditated points. Simply—with smiles—a consuming interest in the person he happened to be facing. We never doubted this. And so, by a logic that would surprise him most of all, this is his book.

Mark Van Doren

7

Table of Contents

A*

Introduction

Q. So here you are, Newquist—sixty-three interviews with authors and columnists and publishers collected in a book. The title is COUNTERPOINT. Why?

■ *Newquist:* The original title, which made my editor shudder, was 76 *Variations on a Theme*. You see, there were going to be seventy-six interviews, and we had lots of variations but we had a terrible time establishing a theme. Besides, there was this thing about Meredith Willson's trombones. Don't you think COUNTERPOINT is a better title?

Q. It's shorter, but you mentioned variations on a theme—what variations, what theme?

■ *Newquist:* Originally I thought that the theme would be the author's desire—in fact, his emphatic *need*—to communicate. The variations would show the infinite approaches to communication and the equally infinite philosophical variations that underlie that intent. But all this added up to a terrible dust jacket and made the book seem much more literary and highbrow than it really is. My interviews haven't the depth, nor the prolonged analysis, that goes into the superb pieces on writers done by *The Paris Review*. This is no reflection upon my interviewees, whose depths certainly plunge deeper than my mode of questioning reveals. It's a matter of difference in intent. I hope to capture the working philosophies of the writer, his own life and attitudes toward life, his own work and the reasons for that work. Ideally, I would like to have the reader finish an interview, then dash out to beg, borrow, or buy books written by that particular interviewee. Preferably "buy." Authors live on royalties.

Q. You are begging the question.

■ *Newquist:* Not really. You see, the theme turned out to be themes, and the variations were endless. Admittedly, terms such as "truth" and "accuracy" and "work" keep popping up, and I don't think there's a writer I've talked to who doesn't feel an obligation to the public that buys his books and reads his words. But oh, those variations, the sense of individualism these people display, the pride of captaining one's own ship. Would you care to block a metaphor?

Q. Look, I'm just trying to find out—

◼ *Newquist:* They remind me, in retrospect, of what falcons in early training must go through. You know, allowed to soar free for a bit, then jerked back to the falconer's wrist. When you talk to writers you feel an immense insistence upon freedom, and yet, before more than a dozen sentences are out, you feel the conscience jerking them back to whatever defined or undefined responsibility they feel toward their work. It's a marvellous thing to behold because you know there's nothing to bring them back except the gravity of conscience. And this is invariably an overwhelming force.

Q. Do you think that writers are a superior group?

◼ *Newquist:* Since you put it that bluntly—yes, I do. At the risk of oversimplification, I think this superiority is based upon the vast amounts of knowledge accrued in the very process of becoming successful writers. (Or publishers or columnists, but to simplify things I'll call all the interviewees "writers.") They have learned a great deal, of course, about the inner and outer workings of man. But they have also concerned themselves with the world about them, with patterns of international and national conduct, the issues of our time, and the interplay of ethics and morals and beliefs that preoccupies our time. The writer, at the point when he can be judged "successful" has served a grueling apprenticeship that can't be determined in credit hours or degrees. Willingly or unwillingly, he is a student of contemporary history and a compassionate observer of whatever struggles intrude upon society. This provides the gravity of conscience I mentioned a few minutes ago. The writer, no matter what his mode of life in Connecticut or Beverly Hills, even if he is still slugging it out in an office, is a perpetual student in an enormous hall of learning called the world. He never feels totally on top of this vast spread of material, but you know after talking to him, that he feels compelled to stay with it. I cannot, frankly, think of another profession that requires such broad and constant study. Nor can I think of another profession that furnishes such willing students.

Q. But why the title, COUNTERPOINT?

◼ *Newquist:* Don't you want to know how these interviews were conducted? They were actually quite uncomplicated to set up and do. In the course of reviewing I read most of the books written by each interviewee. Appointments with the writers were arranged by letter or telephone, and often by the house publishing the writer.

Then I went to the writer, or he came to me, the tape recorder was started after a very brief warmup, and I asked short questions and hoped for long answers.

Q. Did you work with a set list of questions?

■ *Newquist:* No. There are certain questions I worked into almost every interview, but the actual course of the interview adhered to no pattern. For one thing, I wouldn't have gotten the breadth of information I hope I caught. For another, I don't think the writers would have appreciated pure mechanics. First, last, and foremost, they are individuals.

Q. How long were the interviews?

■ *Newquist:* I tried to get at least an hour's worth of tape—sometimes it ran a bit shorter, sometimes longer, but I think that an hour could be called the average length.

Q. Then what did you do with the tape?

■ *Newquist:* I had it transcribed, worked out portions to be used for radio and the basic information I wanted for newspaper use. The rough part came next: turning the raw transcript into a piece that had some measure of continuity, deleting stuff that wasn't pertinent, catching the inconsistencies in tense, person, etc. The spoken word differs drastically from the written, and this shows clearly in transcribing speech to print. Still, I tried to do a minimum of editing. Once this was done the transcript was submitted to the interviewee for any corrections, additions, or deletions the interviewee wished to make.

Q. Did they make many changes?

■ *Newquist:* Very few writers made more than a dozen word-changes. Three had been terrified by the tape recorder, and froze, and consequently dealt better with their material when they saw it in my badly-typewritten format. But there's remarkably little change between what was recorded and what is here served in print.

Q. Were the writers co-operative?

■ *Newquist:* Only two out of 252 interviews terminated in argument. All of the other writers were so co-operative, so congenial, that I finished up the series ten pounds heavier and a bit alcoholic.

Q. Where were the interviews conducted?

■ *Newquist:* Almost half of them were recorded at the Plaza Hotel in New York—a hotel I dearly love because of its nice, thick walls, its high ceilings, its general quiet, and the old-world standards of service that persist. (This is *not* a paid plug.) The other half, however, were recorded in hotels and homes and apartments and offices (and nursing homes and night clubs and hospitals) in San Francisco,

Los Angeles, out in Connecticut, in Chicago, London, Paris, adrift in the English countryside, and in Edinburgh.

Q. Did any of the writers you sought refuse to be interviewed?

■ *Newquist:* Only three out of the 250-odd I contacted.

Q. There are some rather big names omitted.

■ *Newquist:* There are many instances, of course, when arrangements with a particular writer couldn't be worked out. But I wasn't after a collection composed totally of big names—I was frankly more interested in gathering a representative group that would include many types of writers at varying stages of development. I sought a "composite," so to speak, of the active literary world. I hope that this balance roughly overrides the absence of any particular name the reader happens to find lacking.

Q. You mentioned that there were some questions you asked all of them.

■ *Newquist:* *Almost* all of them. Where I missed it was either through my oversight or because I knew the author was not inclined to consider these particular questions.

Q. What were they? The questions, I mean?

■ *Newquist:* The phrasings differed from person to person, so it might be more appropriate to list them in terms of subject. These are (a) the writer's obligation to his material and to his readers; (b) advice to a beginning writer; (c) the interviewee's attitudes toward, his opinions of, contemporary culture; and (d) the writer's ultimate ambitions insofar as his own career is concerned.

Q. Now, this title, COUNTERPOINT—

■ *Newquist:* Please. This is the last chance I'll have to talk at any length for hundreds of pages.

Most of the interviewees are also asked for a rough autobiography and for an appraisal of how they would like to be judged by posterity. Southern writers are asked why such a disproportionate number of America's most sensitive writers have hailed from the area south of Kentucky, and English writers are queried about items like "Angry Young Man" and "The Establishment" and "kitchen sink." Playwrights are asked about the state of theater, critics about the state of the art they are hired to appraise, journalists about the health of journalism, and the more serious writers about attitudes towards morals and ethics.

Q. But this title, COUNTERPOINT—

■ *Newquist:* It's so nice and short. At Rand McNally they were convinced that the *Variations* business would make people think this was a book about music, and I ended up feeling the same about it, but we had the devil of a time coming up with another title. Thus, when WQXR and I chose COUNTERPOINT as the title for the radio series made from these interviews, the Rand McNally people gradually decided that it would be a good title for the book, too.

Q. But what—

■ *Newquist:* In some respects I'd have preferred *Point Counterpoint*, but the late Mr. Huxley had used it.

Q. But—

■ *Newquist:* Actually, any title would have been either too long or a duplication or necessarily enigmatic. Now, "counterpoint" is basically a musical term, but even in a compact Webster's you'll find definitions that include phrases like ". . .the art of adding a related but independent melody or melodies to a basic melody, in accordance with the fixed rules of harmony, to make a harmonic whole. . ." The king-size Webster's gives me carte blanche by stating ". . .any artistic arrangement or device using significant contrast or interplay of distinguishable elements." COUNTERPOINT is really an appropriate title, because the author is asked to state his working philosophy—making highly personal points, then surrounding and explaining these points by presenting the life, and the approaches to life, that have brought him to his positions. Life is never played out in one thematic melody. It is accompanied by a constant interplay of other thematic material, some planned and orchestrated, others spontaneous and elusive. Perhaps God conducts the total performance, at times ignored by the all-human and the all-too-human chorus, but the writer must frequently leave this perpetual music festival to make his interpretations and signal his warnings to fellows preoccupied with singing or dancing or beating a drum or strumming a lute. As much as it aches him to withdraw, to insulate himself with lonely silence, the gravity of conscience forces him apart. This is inevitable, because it is his mission to provide the most permanent and revealing transcript that will survive the cacaphony of his time.

Roy Newquist

COUNTERPOINT

"Elsa's enormous sales . . . proves the hunger of people to return . . . to a world of genuine proportion, a world in which our balance and basic values have not been destroyed."

Joy Adamson
interviewed in New York, February, 1964

Joy Adamson

N. The most famous lion of our time—perhaps the most famous of all time—is a lioness named Elsa who successfully defies mortality by living on, years after her death, in the trilogy composed of *Born Free*, *Living Free*, and *Forever Free*. All three were best-sellers on an international level. From them the world has become acquainted with the unique relationship the Adamsons established with Elsa, and also the need to preserve at least a portion of Africa's once-abundant wildlife.

Joy Adamson, author of the moving Elsa books, is interviewed on her fund-raising tour of the United States. The deep-seated reasons motivating this tour will be discussed later and at length, but first I'd like Mrs. Adamson to fill in a history of herself.

■ *Adamson:* I'm Austrian-born, as you can plainly tell from my accent. In fact, there is so much accent that I've never been able to speak any language properly. I was born in the country—we had some estates near Vienna, but I was educated in Vienna. Still, my real roots were in the surrounding countryside. We had lots of game on the estates, and my family had lots of shoots. By watching the animals, I became interested in them. I shot my first buck when I was 16—but after this experience, I never shot again for sport!

My education started rather seriously in music, and I got a degree in Vienna. Then I became interested in sculpting, and after that in medicine, but before I got into medical studies I married. This ended the medical career. I went to Kenya to stay with friends when I was twenty-six years old. I fell in love with the country and have stayed there ever since.

Now, I had no training in painting, but when I came to Kenya I was fascinated by the native flowers and plants. Luckily, I was able to join an expedition—almost immediately after my arrival—an expedition financed by Mr. Campbell, an American who was associated with the Natural History Museum in New York. He gave the museum trustees the money to do research on the Chyullu mountain range which had never been visited by Europeans. Eight scientists were on the expedition staff, including my husband. I was allowed to join because it was actually our honeymoon.

In order to contribute something to the expedition, to justify my presence, I began painting the flowers. I became fascinated with this, and when we came back from the three-month expedition, I was asked to illustrate the next edition of a garden book on East Africa which marked the first attempt to present, in print, the indigenous flora of this country. This was a shock, because I truly was an amateur, but I did it. This was the beginning of my really extensive studies of flowers, and I ended up illustrating seven books published by the Royal Horticultural Society of East Africa.

While I painted flowers for fifteen years, I became especially interested in the alpine flowers in Kenya that grow on isolated volcanic mountains 17,000 to 20,000 feet high. I couldn't help but find many new species; everything I collected, I sent to Kew Garden in England.

My opportunities were unique, actually, because my husband was a game warden, and we had the privilege of going into remote and inaccessible areas on safaris with camels and donkeys as pack animals. It amounted to 360 days a year on safari, but for anyone interested in nature it was a challenge that couldn't be equaled. I collected on these trips everything I found of interest but I concentrated on flowers; I also collected anthropological tools and bones and insects and minerals. Then, too, I became interested in the coral fish from the sea. These beautiful fish lose their pigments two or three minutes after they're taken from the sea, so I took my paint books to the reef and painted them while their colors were still vivid. I would make a very rapid color sketch, and back on shore follow it up with a more thorough study of the fish, adding all the pigmentations I'd observed. It was fascinating. These paintings were bought by Mombasa municipality and they are at the museum there.

Later on I became very interested in the traditional life of the Africans, and for a year I painted them on my own because I thought their ornaments and costumes provided clues to the migration of the Kenya tribes (we have over one-hundred) as to where they came from and the routes they followed. Most of them originated in Asia, and a few in Egypt and Persia, and they concentrated heavily around Lake Victoria before distributing themselves. It is a challenging subject, only it is so vast that it would take an army of scientists to determine precisely what happened, but I thought that if I could make a small contribution by painting these tribes in their traditional costumes before the European influence did away with them, I might be of help. I was really stimulated by an ornament I found among the

Pygmys (who live in an area sprawled across the Uganda-Congo border, going deep into the Congo, of course). I found the identical
ornament among the Bantu Wakamba tribe close to Nairobi in
Kenya, and again on the Ethiopian border of the northern frontier in
Kenya. These belonged to Gabbra tribes of Nilo Hamitic stock.

Now, between the Pygmy, Wakamba, and Gabbra you couldn't
get a greater extreme in physical appearance and cultures, yet the
same ornament was common to all. This started me off. I thought
that they may have followed the same migration route, and that one
could probably find overlapping customs and similarities in ornaments. I carried on for a year on my own, and then the government
became interested in the project and commissioned my work.

The government assistance was invaluable, of course, because all
the money in the world wouldn't persuade the African to sit for
you unless the government supports you and organizes things. With
their assistance the various provincial commissioners, right down to
the last head man, tried to summon anyone who had authentic ornaments to come and sit for me and tell me all they knew about those
ornaments.

Well, to make a very long story quite short, I painted over 750
pictures; many were life-size to the waist and many were smaller. I
collected all the information I could. (The ornaments, when worn
correctly, can almost be used as a biography—station of life, marriage, circumcision phases, witch doctors, warriors, everything.) Actually, this will be the subject of my next book. I'm two-thirds done
with it, and would have finished it much sooner, but the present lectures on Elsa came along to occupy all my time. But as a book,
I hope—I'm sure—it will be valuable, not only to trace perhaps
some of the migration routes of the many tribes in Kenya, but to
preserve a record of the ways of life which have gone on for so
many centuries, but which will now be changed as Kenya is inevitably Westernized.

N. You mentioned that Elsa interrupted this project. How did
she come into your life?

■ *Adamson:* Again I must go to a beginning. The whole Elsa
story was so improvised from one day to the next that it must be reviewed as it happened, just as it had to be written the way it happened. You see, if we had known that Elsa would meet with this
tremendous success, we may perhaps have taken different photographs or treated her differently. As it was, without any inkling that
she would become world famous, our relationship with her was utterly genuine and simple and natural.

She came to us with her two sisters when my husband was hunting a man-eater. He was charged by a lioness, and only after he unfortunately had to kill her in self-defense did he find that she had attacked him because he had come near her three very young cubs.

He brought the cubs home, of course. All of them still had a blue film over their eyes and couldn't see. When they finally began to focus, we became their first impression, and automatically the imprint of their parents, and from that moment on they accepted us either as fellow-lions—or fellow-humans—I don't know which. Anyway, they treated us as they would treat other lions. Unfortunately, we couldn't keep all three. It would have been too much, having three lions in the house, so we had to send two away to lifelong captivity in the Blydorp Zoo at Rotterdam, which is a very nice zoo. We kept the smallest one, Elsa.

Now, I think that most lions are extremely intelligent and highly sensitive, but I believe that Elsa could sense by a kind of thought communication. I have no other word for it because it is totally different from having a dog or any other domestic pet who can read your mood. After all, those domestic animals have been in contact with man for thousands of years, and are conditioned from birth, and perhaps even before birth, to the environment of man. But a wild animal has much deeper integrity.

I feel certain that Elsa could understand my thoughts and act according to them. In so many cases I saw evidence of how she would answer my thoughts, so I knew that she was not merely responding from my mood or from physical signals. Elsa opened, for me, so many completely new and staggering insights into animal psychology.

We owe a great deal to Elsa. Perhaps this example will make this debt easier to understand. I have been told that every mammal is, in its first few days, weeks, or months, depending upon the species, a lump of meat that cannot register thought or display intelligence. In the case of a dog—he is mentally numb for nineteen days but on the nineteenth day something clicks, and from that moment on he is a complete, normally developed dog.

Now, Elsa and her sisters came to us much too young—anyone who picked them up during that vulnerable state would automatically become their foster parent, and so they accepted us as their parents, whether we were lions or humans. But how did Elsa—when she finally had her own cubs (and this was after four years of sharing her life off and on with us)—know that she had to conceal them from us for six weeks?

When she brought her cubs to us, these little animals were jolly well aware that they were lions and never allowed us to handle them. How did she know this safety period her young needed to establish their instinct of knowing their own species?

There are so many things we learned from Elsa, too many to discuss here. Despite our intimate relations she was never really domesticated or subdued. She voluntarily accepted us in her mind, yet she knew we didn't belong in her life. For instance, when she went hunting, or when she met a herd of antelope, she would encircle them and drive them up to us, expecting us to do the same thing a lion would do—kill them in ambush. Now, she knew that we never killed them, and she often showed her disappointment in us by knocking us down.

Elsa was never tame in the manner of being injured in her wild instincts, but she accepted us as being part of her. This may not have posed too many problems for her during her first four years of life— we remained her friends after all, though Elsa obviously knew the difference in specie. But then she had her cubs.

Elsa must have had to cope with, and think through, and understand, a great deal. Her cubs were wild, and did not accept us, and her mate was wild. I never saw him, but he was within a few yards of us every night, especially toward dawn. George almost fell over him twice. He was very shy, yet he never stayed too far away from Elsa and the cubs. How Elsa remained on good terms with us, at the same time managing her wild mate and her wild cubs, was remarkable. The cubs were never jealous of us (and when they grew big they could have been dangerous) because somehow Elsa managed a truce that was quite fantastic. One moment she would come up to me, if I became too familiar with the cubs and, by gripping me around my knee, told me to go away and leave them alone. The next moment, she would keep her cubs in place if they became a little too provocative in their games; she would sit on them and keep them immobile, until I had a chance to get away.

Elsa tactfully combined this double life—I should say triple life, because she had her own wild life, the wild life of her cubs, and life with us. This, in itself, was an important contribution to the knowledge of the psychology of animals. You see, I am convinced that all of these animals can teach us a great deal, far more than we even now suspect.

Before coming to Kenya I lived near Vienna, close to nature, and we had an abundance of animal life about. And I had, in my judgment, a very interesting, fascinating, rich life as far as culture and interests and friends were concerned. I traveled a lot and had the best Europe could give anybody. Then came Kenya and Africa. I know quite a bit about Africa, especially East Africa, and I soon discovered that there is a much bigger world than man can create.

The civilized countries seem to believe that the world was made for men and that only the values of a man-made world count. But man is only a part of the whole universe. There is a much, much bigger world outside him, yet all his civilization has separated or even divorced him from this real-life.

In Kenya I faced a great challenge in entering an apparently crude and uncivilized and uncultured life. But I found that I could carry my European heritage with me—books and correspondence and music, the mentality and the possessions of civilization. At the same time I gained a wonderful insight into that much bigger world of nature.

The animals can teach us so much. How to solve territorial problems, for instance, our wars, and problems like juvenile delinquency. These problems are rooted in power drives and frustrations, and these exist equally strong in animals. Only the animals have a much more constructive way of solving these problems than we do.

Now, man is certainly the most evolved, the most intellectual of all mammals. We can do almost anything now—give us another ten years, and we'll probably settle quite pleasantly on the other planets, or follow Cousteau to the bottom of the ocean. But clever as we are, we cannot refrain from two things: we cannot stop the inquiring mind which wants to find out what's going on around the next corner, and we cannot stop breathing.

The very small proportion of educated people who respect birth control is no match, unfortunately, for the millions of uneducated people who can't understand what birth control means and will consequently lead us to eventual annihilation. Suppose we destroy, for our benefit, every other living creature on earth? This will not solve our overbreeding. We can probably live on synthetic food, synthetic air, synthetic everything, but eventually we'd crowd out the production facilities for these synthetics. Man is the only creature who violates the balance of nature by his overbreeding and so does his best to annihilate himself by overpopulating his environments. Animals in their natural state, do a wonderful job of governing their populations. We could learn a great deal from them.

I am very interested in dolphins and try to visit every oceanarium where research on these challenging animals is done. Recently, in South Africa, at Port Elizabeth, I learned that man can hear up to

19 kilocycles of sound, a dog can hear 25, a bat can hear 80. (We learned radar from the bat, but only under the pressures of war.) Now, a dolphin can hear 120 kilocycles. This is one example of the superior senses other creatures have.

In the past thirty years, we have learned staggering things from and about other creatures. Vanity, fear, and self-obsession prevent us from learning more. I admit that I may get carried away by all ·this, but it seems absurd for man to think that animals are here only for his entertainment and utility, and that they should be removed from the earth because we cannot discipline our breeding. Does man have a monopoly to survive on earth?

Elsa certainly proved by her actions, reactions, and behavior that she knew many things beyond our conception.

N.   How did you come to write the Elsa books?

■ *Adamson:*   It is still rather puzzling. You see, I had never written a book before. A few articles, but never a book. I have a fairly detailed mind, and I do observe, but this didn't qualify me to write a book. But Elsa was so strong, and had so much to give, that even my utterly amateurish approach made an impact. Elsa has sold, up to now, almost 3 million copies—it is second to the Bible in sales. Elsa is translated into eighteen languages, with four or five to come, including those behind the Iron Curtain. Elsa has been transcribed into Braille. I think it's because Elsa has reached the *hearts* of people. I get this fantastic fan mail—thousands and thousands of letters, all written with love. There must be a reason for this, a reason that Elsa should have been given to all of us, whatever our background and language and education.

Perhaps Elsa makes us realize, consciously or unconsciously, how far we have come away from the basic things in life. Elsa reminds us of the logic in the balance of nature, the necessity for co-operating with nature, understanding, love. Nothing can be gained without love.

Now, please don't think I'm trying to be unrealistic about all this, or fanatical. It's just that the response to Elsa has been spontaneous and voluntary. It would have to be instinctive rather than learned. Unless things are given voluntarily they are not worth having. One cannot force or provoke real things that last. Elsa would do everything for me and I would everything for her because we loved each other. I wouldn't be doing this lecture tour, now, if I didn't think I was doing it for Elsa and her animals.

I think Elsa was given to everyone of us in the most crucial period of all—at a time when wild animals need all the help they can get to survive. In just the twenty-seven years I've lived in Kenya I've seen the enormous decrease of animal life. Africa, particularly East Africa, is the last stronghold of wild life we have in the whole world. You have only to look in your own country, or through Europe or Asia, to see how much is left of the indigenous fauna. The animals have been wiped out by man for his own exploitation, his selfishness. My husband and I, working in the Game Department, meet the thousands of tourists who come to look at what we have left. I ask people—especially those from the United States, who spend so much money to come to Kenya—why don't they stay in Palm Beach or the other lovely resorts in California and Florida and in the mountains? They come to Kenya, live in a tent, get drenched in the cloudburst, and stung by insects, when for a fraction of the money they could relax in America. They tell me, in whatever words they use, that they come to Kenya to feel, for a brief moment at least, in touch with real life. This is startling—it shows, again, the need of man to return to nature, to real life.

Elsa's enormous sales—her impact upon the entire world—proves the hunger of people to return, in whatever way they can, to a world of genuine proportion, a world in which our balance and basic values have not been destroyed. All this shows how important it is to preserve the animal life we have left. We cannot lose this last important link with what we really are, and I think Elsa has been given to all of us to help reestablish this link.

"If you know what you're doing and you've done it, you've accomplished something. Whether or not it's a work of art remains for somebody else to judge."

Louis Auchincloss
interviewed in New York, March, 1964

Louis Auchincloss

N. During the course of these interviews a prominent British writer ventured his opinion of contemporary American letters. "You're infinitely well off," he said. "You've got De Vries, Cheever, Updike, Baldwin, and Auchincloss, five writers who would make any literary period a healthy one. Your man Auchincloss, for example, is one of the few great stylists of the day—he's already written three books I know of, *Portrait in Brownstone*, *The House of Five Talents*, and *Powers of Attorney*, that will live in your permanent library of great works."

I couldn't agree more heartily with this appraisal of Louis Auchincloss. And in speaking with this master of two professions, I'd first like to ask him for a rough autobiography, and how his interest in writing developed.

■ *Auchincloss:* I was born in Long Island, lived in a town called Lawrence, and reared almost entirely in New York. They say there is nothing rarer than a New Yorker who has spent all his life in New York and its environs. There are actually a great many of us, but I'm rarer in that all eight of my great-grandparents lived in Manhattan. Apparently it was a family that had very little pioneer instinct; they came from Scotland and England and stayed right here.

I was privately educated in the Bovee School until 1929, when I went to Groton to stay for six years. I then spent three years at Yale and left without graduating because I decided that I would never be a writer so I had better become a lawyer without delay.

At Groton I wrote a story on the French Revolution (I was fourteen) for a thing called *The Third Form Weekly*. It was published in this boy's magazine and my interest in writing has never completely dissipated since. My discouragement at Yale came, by the way, after Scribner's had turned down a novel I had written—a very bad novel.

I went to Virginia Law School and took a pledge that I would not write any more, at least while I was there. I didn't write during the three years of the law school term, but I did write during the summer. However, I found, to my infinite relief, that I liked the Law very much, and it has never seemed to me a profession inconsistent with writing. In fact, I think it is a profession ideally married to writing because both deal with the written word and an emphatic need for probing and analyzing.

After graduating from law school, where I was editor of the *Law Review*, I went to New York. I worked there for just a few months when the war broke out, and I went into the Navy for four years. I was in the Atlantic and the Pacific, for the most part in amphibious warfare. I spent a year ashore, however, in the Panama Canal Zone in Naval Intelligence, and this period furnished me with the material for my first novel.

After the war I returned to the practice of law until 1952, when I resigned and spent two and one-half years living in New York and simply writing. Then I returned to the law and I expect to remain practicing law as lawyers don't retire. I married late, when I was thirty-nine, and live with my wife in an apartment in New York. We have three small boys.

N.   This is more or less jumping to the very present in your career, but you have a new book coming up in July, a Book-of-the-Month Club selection, I believe, and I wonder if you could discuss it.

■ *Auchincloss: The Rector of Justin* is a fictional biography of a New England headmaster, from what I call the great era of headmasters—Peabody at Groton, Drury at St. Paul's, and Thayer at St. Mark's. The fictional biography is written by a young minister who works under him. The headmaster would have been born in 1860 and died in 1946. He is represented in the book as being a very great man.

I draw material, of course, from the most vivid years of my life, which are those of childhood. It's been rightly said that childhood is a writer's whole capital. Fortunately, it's not a capital that can be used up in writing—it seems to be infinite, and writers go on using it throughout their lives.

My six years at Groton came when Endicott H. Peabody was headmaster; he was quite an old man and I had great admiration for him and quite an interest in the school. I was very unhappy at Groton for two years—got low marks and was unpopular. (Typical English public school novel material, by which we've all been bored.) Then for two years I was pulling myself together, and during the last two years I was very happy there—editor of the school paper and president of the school dramatic society and getting very high marks instead of very low ones. In fact, the gamut of my marks from the bottom to the top was considered a very remarkable graph in the history of the school's academic careers.

Now, everybody will say, when the book comes out—at least all my friends from Groton—that it's perfectly obvious that I've written about Endicott Peabody, and from what I know of readers it will be so impossible to dissuade them that I won't even try. Anybody who does not know me, however, would see no resemblance at all between the personalities of these two headmasters. Peabody was a great man, but in a different way than my headmaster is. He was a great, strong, serious, religious man—not a great intellectual, as the headmaster in my novel is represented as being. I suppose the book was born in the career of Dr. Peabody but came out as a book about a great headmaster who distinctly is not Endicott Peabody.

This is the first book in which I've dealt with a great man. I think it's the best thing I've done, and I've done a lot of thinking about why this should be. I had thought that my fiction improved as time went on, but I've come to a rather different conclusion. I had always assumed that the sacred twentieth century tenet that the subject of a book is completely and absolutely valid and can never be criticized, is correct. I'm not too sure, now, that it is. It seems to me that, assuming a certain capacity, if a writer elevates his material he will elevate his treatment. I think this is true of the French playwright Anouilh. I think it might be true of Tennessee Williams; if he would get a great theme I think he might be a great playwright.

N.   What do you feel about the obligations of the novelist—to his material, on the one hand, and to the public, on the other?

■ *Auchincloss:*   I suppose that a writer has an obligation to his material—to make good use of it. It never occurred to me that a writer had any obligation to his public. I don't see what that obligation could be. One certainly can't say, "The public ought to read thus and so, therefore I'll write it." Writing is too subjective. I don't think the writer can consider his public until his work is ready, and then, if it's good, it's there for the public.

I can speak only for myself, of course, when I say that I try to be very exact in my effects; I want everything to be just so. It bothers me to write about somebody I don't feel I could get inside of. I don't carry it to the point Ellen Glasgow did; she set her novels in Richmond, and she used to trudge around the city and be terribly worried if she described a house with two trees in front of it and found out that there was only one. She would alter the text until somebody pointed out to her that it made absolutely no difference whatsoever how many trees stood in front of that house. This can be called ultimate honesty, even though it was carried to a strange degree of intensity.

I like to feel that I must understand somebody completely. This is why the idea of writing a historical novel is inconceivable to me. How can I put myself in the position of a Tudor King or Queen and strut around the stage? I couldn't do it even if I spent years and years of research.

I did do one novel that could be called a historical novel (some events took place before my own birth) but it was still in the recent past of my family tradition, so I felt I knew something about it.

I may go too far: why shouldn't people let their minds run completely free? Shakespeare set his plays in places he'd never been to, in times that he never lived, and we certainly can't criticize him for that. Nobody would ever say that Shakespeare was dishonest in writing about Verona because he'd never been there. Yet, for my part, I can't write about Verona because I haven't lived there.

N.   Could you define your own objectives as a writer?

■ *Auchincloss:* I would like to catch chapters of the experience of living in the 1940's, '50's, and '60's—perhaps the twentieth century as a whole—chapters which are significant and which I want to re-interpret. I especially want to portray things into which I've been fortunate enough to gain insight—a front-row seat, so to speak.

When I first started writing I was deeply impressed by what I read. I was born of a generation that dealt very largely with subjective fiction, with what was going on inside the mind of the characters rather than what went on outside and around them. This sounds banal, but it certainly has been true of mid-twentieth century novels. So, at the start, I thought of myself as a writer of psychological novels, working within the mind of one or two principal characters. The first novel I wrote, *The Indifferent Children,* which was published in 1947, was entirely built around the problem of conceiving and creating the most ridiculous man in the world, then in trying to redeem him.

Well, as I dealt with different types in my novels I was again and again provoked and put off by the fact the characters were seen *not* internally, as I saw them, but as the product of a particular New York background. I felt myself being stamped again and again with this, as though I was writing a determinist novel in the tradition of Zola or Flaubert. In other words, Zola would take a character who was born in a particular year, in a particular family in a suburb of Bordeaux, and because his father was a drunk and his mother a prostitute, that character would end up in a certain way, and he would go this way step by step. That character would be completely tied into his fate, a thing Zola did very effectively.

I was not trying to do this because I did not believe that people were that tied into background, and the psychological problems I was dealing with in my early novels were problems I felt would exist in any class in any part of the country. Yet I got letters, for example, even my older brother wrote saying that he didn't see why one character would necessarily have ended up the way he did simply because he was born in a particular New York social circle. It had never occurred to me that this character was thus preordained. To me the things that were wrong with him were in his own mind, created by emotional factors and forces, in other words a purely Freudian interpretation independent of the background in which he lived.

As time went on I was again and again described as a student of New York moneyed groups. The outcome was a mixture of defiance and surrender—I thought, "Well, if that's what they say I am, I'll be it with a vengeance," and I turned, in 1958, to writing *The House of Five Talents,* a history of the expenditure—not the making but the expenditure—of a great New York fortune from the early 1880's until 1945. It was a subject I read a great deal about, knew a lot about, and I suddenly found that I rather enjoyed being the kind of novelist I was described as instead of being the novelist I had thought I was. Now I was a novelist who was observing a particular facet of the American social scene and trying to reproduce it.

I worked very hard on that, and I still think it's unique in that I don't know of another work of fiction that suggests what those families were like. A great deal has been written about the earning of the fortune, but very little about how it was preserved and sent down through the different branches. I like that novel.

Then you might say, "Do you like it as a work of literature or as a work of social history?" Well, at this point I don't care. I like it because it set out to do a particular thing and I think it did it.

You see, once the aim is right and the subject material is picked· and the two things mesh together, then literature will pretty well take care of itself. If you know what you're doing and you've done it, you've accomplished something. Whether or not it's a work of art remains for somebody else to judge.

N.   In looking at the status of creative arts today, what do you find that you most admire? On the other hand, what do you most deplore?

■ *Auchincloss:*   I don't do much deploring because I refuse to read, see, or hear what I deplore. There are better things to do with time. I don't read too much modern literature, but where I do read I'm usually very enthusiastic. I like Hortense Calisher, I like Jean Stafford, I like Norman Mailer.

There's very little theater to consider. It isn't a question of theater being bad, it's a question of theater hardly existing. In the last two years there's been Albee, and who else? Some good English imports and a tremendous number of musicals, and many of those revivals. I think there must be a theater around, but I think it's killed off by the ridiculous high costs. If the costs went down you'd probably have lots of good theater all over the place. When you look at an exhibit in the City of New York Museum of theater settings, theater settings in the nineteenth century, and see the sets Edwin Booth had when he put on *Coriolanus,* and see how none of them could be used today, even for a musical, all because of costs—well, it's no wonder we have no theater.

N.   Now, if you were to give advice to a young writer—the talented, serious, intent young writer—what would that advice be?
■ *Auchincloss:*   First, of all, I wish they wouldn't ask me. Do you think a good writer ever asks for advice? I don't think the young writer who asks for advice is going to be a writer. There are all sorts of people who want to write—except that they don't want to write, they want to be writers, which is a totally different thing. Norman Mailer wouldn't have asked for advice when he was nineteen or twenty. I don't know any first-class talent that would.

Once they know what they're going to do, they'll do it one way or another. It's a problem they'll work out for themselves. Even the good writers who teach in writer's schools can't teach writing—perhaps they can teach people to express themselves, but this doesn't necessarily make writers.

N.   I was thinking of so many youngsters I've encountered lately who say they have nothing to write about, no great cause or theme.
■ *Auchincloss:*   Here again, perhaps, they're not writers, if this is the way they feel. I suppose that even a very good writer can find it difficult to write, but it seems to me that throughout the history of the novel the major novelists were never at a loss for material.

It's inconceivable to think of Trollope or Balzac without material, and both Ellen Glasgow and Edith Wharton expressed in their memoirs their incredulity of the idea that a writer could be a writer who ran out of material, who didn't have a whole series of problems and figures and stories to tell. When they heard about "writer's block" or heard somebody say, "Oh, I wish I had a subject, I would write another book"—well, they couldn't conceive of such people being writers, and they expressed their disbelief, oddly enough, in almost parallel passages.

Everybody has the same amount to write about. What would you say of the young novelist who mutters, "Oh, I wish I had lived in France during the reign of terror, what marvelous things I could have written about—to see all those aristocrats having their heads cut off, what a wonderful day."

He isn't a writer at all who feels that his subject matter has passed.

"... whatever it is that simply *has* to be said is the thing that the writer should write. . . . This is his job, and it is the only way in which he will find his fulfillment."

Eileen Bassing
interviewed in Los Angeles, March, 1964

Eileen Bassing

N. Two novels—*Home Before Dark* and *Where's Annie?*—stand in the front rank of American works that are becoming classified, with high honor, as novels of compassionate realism. The author: Eileen Bassing, a young woman of charm and dignity that, at first meeting, both masks and dramatizes her intensity and depth of observation. At the time of this interview Mrs. Bassing was recuperating, in a Los Angeles hospital, from various ailments picked up during her long sojourn in Mexico researching and writing *Where's Annie?*. This might seem the ultimate degree of involvement in research.

The first question is the customary opening: Where were you born, reared, and educated?

■ *Bassing:* I was born in Boston, Massachusetts, and reared there and in the Middle West and in New York. But for the most part it was Boston—it was the place we always came back to, somehow. I went to college in California, but I personally think that my education as such really began when I was able to settle down to studying by myself. That is to say, when I was able to study, by myself, the things I was interested in, instead of the things other people thought I should study.

N. How did you first develop an interest in writing?

■ *Bassing:* That's a very hard question to answer because I can't remember ever having been interested in anything *but* writing. I learned to read very early, and loved reading; I had a rather solitary childhood in which I felt that I had many friends, and most of these friends were people I had read about.

Reading leads to writing, I think—and not from any lack of alternative, either. I started writing when I was about eight, and I've written ever since. It has never seriously occurred to me to do anything except write. There were other possibilities—I studied dancing and things like that, but none of the other things was ever as satisfying and absorbing as writing. It was part of me. It was something I was driven to do, and it gave me the greatest satisfaction—and perhaps the greatest dissatisfaction, both then and now—possible in my life.

N.   Could you outline your working procedures? Perhaps it's best to refer directly—if only roughly—to the production of *Home Before Dark* and *Where's Annie?*.

■ *Bassing:*   I'm glad you said "roughly" because I don't think I could give you a precise outline of any particular thing I write. I very much admire writers who can work from a neat, orderly outline, and I always feel that my method can only be called "chaotic." The complete outline isn't for me.

I do have a shadowy outline in my mind—as I did in *Home Before Dark,* for example. I knew what I wanted to say, and I knew a great deal about my central character. Once you have the character you're pretty well started, and I had done a great deal of reading in psychiatry. (The background for that novel is psychiatric. I don't mean that I had a psychiatric message—I didn't. It was the story in that setting which interested me.)

In any case I wrote the book, and I think that version came to four hundred and some pages. I read it and my husband read it. (My husband is a writer, and we do this for each other.) At any rate I didn't like it and he didn't like it and that was it—I tore it up and let the whole thing evolve over again. This isn't to say that all I had done was lost—indirectly, and even directly, a great deal of the first draft was used. Now, there are writers who do this in the mind, and don't put the first draft down on paper at all. I think best at the typewriter, however, and the only disadvantage to my system is that I have to do many drafts. I don't do much revising in an editorial sense. But I do a great deal of rewriting. I am actually more of a rewriter than a writer.

Now, *Where's Annie?* was a different kind of novel, very different in structure from *Home Before Dark*. It had multiple points of view, and told many stories from out of the past at the same time the main story moved along in the present. (The literary present.) The impingement of one character upon another moved the present story along, but in order to understand the characters you had to go back and learn a little about them. I found this fascinating to do. However, it did involve a great deal of rewriting and replanning and redoing. The outline, again, was very shadowy—I had the beginning, a kind of middle, a scene here and there, and maybe the end. I think I had the end in mind for a long time. Sometimes characters who never made it into the book were present in this shadowy outline at the beginning. I don't think it mattered that they didn't make it

B*

into the book because the mind supplies you with more characters than you know what to do with.

N.   In other words you don't really work from an outline at the beginning. You work from an idea, or some characters, and write a first draft—then make an outline and write it again. Is that right?

■ *Bassing:* Yes.

N.   Isn't that a very unusual way of working?

■ *Bassing:* Is it? I don't think so. It's true that I may have something of an outline in my mind, but I certainly don't put it down at the beginning. What happens first is a character. I get a character who wants to be told about, who demands to be told about, and that character begins to fill my mind. That character runs it, in a sense, from then on. I don't mean that you're at the mercy of the character—helpless. But I am following the character, and for me the action comes out of the characterization. Then I have to go back, everything has to be adjusted and worked out to make a story or a novel that (I hope) is interesting.

N.   What are you working on at the present time?

■ *Bassing:* I'm on another novel, and so far I've produced several beginnings which I don't like. I wouldn't say that I don't like any part of them, and I've probably kept a small part of each one. Now I've got what I think *is* the beginning, and I've got the character, and the character is beginning to "swing" as they say in music. When that happens the going is good—this is the most enjoyable part of writing. When a character begins to "swing" for me I very often feel like a spectator. I watch what it's doing, and what it's doing to other people, and I have a feeling of surprise. You know, the "I didn't know he was going to do that" sort of reaction.

N.   To turn to a more general subject, what do you most admire in the literary world today? We could embrace the theater, as well.

■ *Bassing:* There's a great deal that I admire very much, but to pin it down—well, it's like being asked, "Why do you love someone?" You don't really know—you can't count the ways. I admire the deeper and more profound characterizations we're beginning to get. I know many people don't agree, but it seems to me that man's first obligation is to know himself before he begins to run around in space, and so far we know very little about human beings and their natures. I'm interested in those novels and plays, poetry and motion pictures, which do profound character portrayals. The example that comes to mind is Eugene O'Neill's *A Long Day's Journey Into Night*, which I consider one of the most profound pieces of characterization, one of the most exciting things that has happened to me, in theater. I read a great deal, in what are called the classics as well as contemporary work, and there are many novels which have this depth of characterization, but it's hard to name those I like best. I could name a hundred, but it would be wrong to name three—and stop. I usually read a whodunit or two every week—they're fun for me, entirely different from life. I admire the fact that people go on writing what they consider good despite the condemnation which is periodically poured down upon the head of any writer who brings himself to national or international attention. For example, I think a great deal of Tennessee Williams is remarkable. And it's interesting to remember that each of his plays was denounced—though well-attended. Then he appeared on the cover of a national magazine and was not only accepted but was praised for the very things he had been denounced for all the way along. Writers should write what they feel they should write, no matter what anyone says. I admire most the writers who do this.

N.   Conversely, looking at literature and theater, what do you most deplore?

■ *Bassing:* I most deplore the precious, and I dislike the kind of writing that makes a virtue out of a lack of feeling. I call this the literature of repression. There is a vast group which feels that the only kind of writing which is correct or acceptable is the kind that examines some bit of minutia that carries no danger or threat to anybody, that will stir nobody up, and make no statement about what human beings are like. There's nothing of madness in this, there's nothing divine in this, there's nothing of art in this, in my opinion. This kind of objectification, or objectifying, so that the report on the minutia is very carefully and exactly written, is not only deplorable because of what it does not do for us, but because of what it does. This denial of the value of man's *emotions*, this infantile preoccupation with little safe elements in life, denies to human beings as individuals their value, their profundity, and their destinies. Sometimes Art has been called the mirror of life, and certainly when people read, they read to learn about themselves and each other and the world around them now and the world of the past. I do not mean to suggest that the task of literature is to instruct, although I believe it does instruct, by the way, incidentally, as it often, also incidentally, entertains. But literature in presenting a reality cannot continue to be literature and present a reality which denies—or represses out of consciousness—emotion and emotional thought. I like writers who not only look honestly at what they see and report their findings, but who naturally *include* in their

findings the emotions they find, too. It is, however, a risky business
and one I think many writers today are made to be afraid of, and so
they are encouraged to write safe stories about safe people, polite
marionettes whose concerns are pretty and exacting, rather than taking the big chance of violence and passion, beauty and nobility,
laughter and tears, and, in a word, drama. What I most deplore in
our literature of repression is the loss of drama.

N.   If you were to give advice to the aspiring writer, what
would that advice be?

■ *Bassing:*   First of all, I don't think I'd give advice, but if I had
to, I would say that the thing for a beginning writer to do is to write,
and to rewrite; to read; to avoid asking people what they think of
what he does; to follow what is intuitive within him. In other words,
whatever it is that simply *has* to be said is the thing that the writer
should write. It's very hard, you know, to be in touch with ourselves.
There are times when it isn't fashionable to write about something,
nonetheless it wants to be written, and this the writer must do regardless of whether it's going to sell or please people or make mother
happy. This is his job, and it is the only way in which he will find
his fulfillment.

I think that if a writer writes something that he knows is good,
that he has said what he wanted to say, he should stick with it no
matter how many people tell him it isn't good. People are often
wrong, agents are wrong, and editors are wrong.

Above all, he cannot be swayed by the judgments of people who
are not basically his peers. But if he has done the very best job he can
do, and is satisfied to some extent—nobody is ever altogether satisfied
—there will be editors who will find it and who will enjoy it.

I think the rule is this: If you like it enough to have written it,
and have done your very best by it, there's going to be someone who
likes it well enough to read it and probably someone who likes it
well enough to publish it, which in turn means that there will be
many more people who like it. Basically, one has to find the
publisher who likes what one likes to do.

N.   Do you feel that the writer has an obligation to the materials
he uses, on the one hand, and to the public for which he writes, on
the other?

■ *Bassing:*   Yes. The obligation of the writer toward the materials
he uses would be to present them in the best possible way, literally
speaking. In other words, he must do the best possible writing job
that he can. The obligation to the public is the need to communicate,
which is the essence of writing—one does not write for oneself. If

one did, he'd just write and put it on the shelf. The motive in writing is to tell someone about something, and your obligation to the public is one of communicating as clearly and vividly as possible without too much distortion.

Sometimes it is hard to write something which you feel people aren't going to want to accept. However, I think the writer must go ahead and do this, and do it if it is the truth, and do it as well as he can. He owes this to the public. He certainly doesn't owe it to the public to write down, and to avoid anything that might be provocative. The artist and the writer has always provoked society. This is part of his job. It happens automatically, anyway, whether he likes it or not, and his recognition of this is part of his obligation to society. I think this is quite important.

N.   To go from the work to the reaction to the work—what do you think of the state of criticism and reviewing at present?

■ Bassing: For the most part I'm not qualified to answer this question because I don't read criticism. I haven't devoted enough time to it to measure ours against the quality or the state of criticism in, for example, England or France. I'm inclined, when I'm working, to avoid reading criticism. They're two different functions, as you know, the creative one and the critical one. When I am engaged in creating something I do not want the critical function overdeveloped or in action at all. I want it to be delayed until the time comes to rewrite. Then, possibly, the critic has his day.

N.   Have you been affected by reviews? Do you think the writer should be affected by them?

■ Bassing: Yes, I have been affected by them—I think all writers are. But I don't think writers *should* be affected by them, for the reasons I just gave you. I don't think that reading reviews is beneficial to a writer who is creating and not thinking critically. Also, many reviews are destructive, and I suppose they do damage, especially if it is clear in the review that the critic did not know what the writer was talking about or trying to do. This is the most important single thing to the writer: "Did the reviewers understand, did the critics understand, what it is I was trying to do?"

If the critic has understood—then whether the review is favorable or unfavorable is beside the point. If the writer can read this criticism and realize that he has *reached* the critic, the critic has understood him, then he has the feeling that he will reach other people—which is precisely what he was writing to do. To get personal—yours was one of the reviews which understood perfectly what *Where's Annie?* was all about. It was a very complicated book in concept and complicated to write, although I do not think it seems complicated to the reader. Your understanding of *Where's Annie?*, and the understanding of all reviewers who got the point, was invaluable to me and a very nice experience. But it had nothing to do with writing.

The writer has to come back, basically, to his own thought: "Is this what I want to do? Have I done it? Am I pleased with it?" Not that the writer can ever be totally satisfied with what is done. But you know, in some measure, whether you did or did not make it for yourself. The critic within one's own mind is the one he really has to please.

N.   Could you outline your personal objectives as a novelist?

■ *Bassing:*   There's that word "outline" again, and I told you I'm not very good at that. But I think the answer is very simple. I want to keep writing books and experiencing the thing that is writing and feeling, and offering to people what amounts to what I see. I think the writer not only speaks for himself, but he speaks for other people, and this is one of the things I want to do and that I dare to do, although it doesn't sound very modest. I like to feel that I am speaking for a great many people who do not write, and who have experiences and would like to tell about them. I want to speak for those people, and I also want to tell how the world around us looks to me. I'm very concerned with our culture—our art and our literature—and I would like to feel that I made a contribution to it.

N.   If you could conceive of looking back at the present from a vantage point of, say, 2064, what would you like that far-off reader or critic to think of the work of Eileen Bassing?

■ *Bassing:*   Let's make it that far-off reader, because I've already spoken about being affected by the critics, though I suppose the critic is first a reader.

I would like what may sound like a peculiar thing. I would like—and I suppose in the year 2064 this might be possible—to be judged as a writer, not a lady novelist, not a woman writer, with no preliminary hyphenated prejudiced-remark qualification ahead of it. *A writer*.

You know, this just doesn't happen, now. Men are suspicious of women writers, men writers have, all this time, quite calmly gone ahead and written from a woman's point of view and assumed that what they were doing *was* a woman's point of view, without anybody getting very excited about it. I don't think that women are confined to a woman's point of view any more than men are limited to a man's point of view as writers, and I think that we've got to begin to leave the gender out of it. Especially when it is a matter of judging writing or enjoying writing.

But women have only had the vote since 1920, and in a way I suppose we are still second-class citizens. We certainly are when it comes to the arts. You might notice as you read or as you hear people talk—they will say that so-and-so is a lady writer, whereas I don't think I have ever heard anyone referred to as a gentleman writer, or a man writer. So I hope that in the year 2064 no one will refer to Eileen Bassing as a "woman writer" or a "lady writer." I hope to be referred to as a novelist. That's all. I might add that it's a rather heady idea—imagining that in the year 2064 people might still be reading me. In fact, I'll settle for that by itself.

"The humorist, as humorist has one obligation—to make the reader laugh. I think any other claim is sheer pretentiousness. But the humorist as satirist is another cube of boullion. . . ."

William Peter Blatty
interviewed in Los Angeles, August, 1963

William Peter Blatty

N. Almost every reviewer, at one time or another, deplores the fact that we are rearing few humorists and fewer satirists. Perhaps we don't take into account a general leavening of humor that pervades the works of De Vries, Updike, Cheever, and Salinger. Perhaps, also, we too quickly forget the advancing talents of young writers like Jules Feiffer and William Peter Blatty.

Blatty—a blue-eyed Lebanese—has turned out two rollicking books, *Which Way To Mecca, Jack?* and *John Goldfarb, Please Come Home!* In scene after scene he recalls the more carefree moments of Wodehouse and Thorne Smith, but a sharp cutting edge of satire does not let the reader dismiss these scenes too quickly. In talking to Mr. Blatty I'd like to begin the interview by asking him where the inspiration for *Goldfarb* came from.

■ *Blatty:* My most inspiring moments usually occur in the bathroom, but in this case I was in my living room listening to a symphony when, God knows why, the Gary Powers U-2 incident popped into my head. Suddenly I found myself wondering what would have happened if Powers had been Jewish and had crashed in Arabia rather than Russia. What wild international crisis would ensue? Eh? Yes. Definitely provocative. So I dropped my plans for a serious novel and explored this preposterous idea instead. What? Where did I get my characters? Where did I get an Arab King who falcons around his palace in an electric golf cart equipped with a Ferrari engine? Or my heroine, the daughter of a Jewish mother and a Spanish father and named Haya Condios? Or El Fego Gantry, the southern revivalist who is refused permission to pitch his tent at Disneyland after being told that "there are no atheists on the submarine ride?"

Who the hell knows! Side-vision, inspiration, I don't know what. I only know that each time I sit down to the typewriter I am petrified that whatever it is that happens there sometimes won't happen *this* time. Craftsmanship can take a novelist a long way; but humor is a thing that goes bump in the night; turn on the light and it isn't there. Am I making any sense? I hope so for my sake.

N.   Your first book, funny as it was, was nonfiction—

■ *Blatty:*   Yes. This was largely autobiographical, and sprang from my two years in Lebanon as a United States Information Agency editor. I was the blue-eyed Lebanese who—listen, there are *lots* of blue-eyed Lebanese. The Crusaders didn't spend *all* their time crusading. Right? Eh? My mother, yes, my mother was the book's central character, utterly Saroyanesque, and she hasn't changed a bit. She raised five children by concocting home-made quince jelly and selling it on the streets of New York—mostly on Park Avenue. I was dragged along as the "sympathy gambit." Yes, I could cry at will. You know, when I gave her that book I said, "Mom, here's a book I've written; see my name on it, here, the book is all about *you.*" Well, she took it from my hands and said, "Willy, you're thin, you're not eating enough," and put the book aside. To this day, she has never referred to its contents. Not even a "Hem!" or a "Fap!" My mad, wingy mother. She thinks television is two-way. Yes. I was on the Paar show a few years ago and when I came back I said, "Mom, I was on television, did you see me?" and she said, "Yes, did you see me? I waved!"

N.   But how could you get sent to Lebanon—speaking Arabic? I thought the government refused this kind of logic.

■ *Blatty:*   Actually, I was slated for Japan, but at the last minute they discovered that the man slated for Lebanon (who probably spoke Japanese) was Jewish, and though there are many Jews in Lebanon they thought it might not be a good idea to send him at that particular time. So they said, "What have we got left? I guess we'll have to send Blatty, even though he speaks Arabic." Of course. I spent two years with them, then came out to Los Angeles as publicity director for the University of Southern California. Then I published my first book, a motion-picture producer read it, hired me to write a movie, and I've been screenwriting, off and on, ever since.

N.   Could you go more thoroughly into your upbringing?

■ *Blatty:*   Well, my first years were spent weeping while Mom sold quince jelly. Then I went into the Air Force for four years, where I wept a little more, and (appropriately enough) they assigned me to the Nut Battalion. (That was the Psychological Warfare Division.) I was such a spectacular nut that they made me chief of the policy branch of the PWD. I was in command of several nut lieutenants and we wrote nut books—like manuals defining exactly what it was we were supposed to be doing. My job, my duty description, was to "analyze Soviet propaganda and tactics on a world-wide front and devise suitable counter-measures." My rank at the time was second lieutenant. Yes. This gave me a great deal of writing experience because we were commanded by a brigadier general and eleven lieutenants.

Every morning my commander—a brigadier general—would waft up a little memorandum for a project we should become involved in, based on some dream he'd had the night before. Here, now, no giggling. He was a guided missiles expert. Several of our group wound up at Bolling AFB getting psychiatric help. It was an illuminating experience. We were finally investigated by Congress, and they deactivated us. Rendered us harmless. Defanged us. Just prior to this our commanding general had purchased a yacht, and it was being shipped via flat cars to Washington; he was going to sail it on the Potomac. Well, the yacht arrived the same day he was assigned to Stillwater, Oklahoma, and ever since I've had visions of it lying on its side on the prairie beside the bleached bones of an ox.

From here I went to the United States Information Agency and was assigned to Lebanon. My formal education? An A.B. from Georgetown and a Master's Degree in English Literature from George Washington University. My post-post-graduate work is being done here in Hollywood.

N.   What do you think of the state of humor here in America?
■ *Blatty:* Humor is in big trouble. Remember James Thurber's piece on the Loch Ness Monster? It was called *There's Something Out There* and that about describes my feeling. There are some great, great humorists sniveling in the bullrushes of America, hiding from their natural enemy, all those unappreciative clods who never get the point of either wild or sophisticated humor. More Americans go to college than ever before, and yet fewer Americans than ever before have the necessary modicum of education and refinement of taste and wit to appreciate satire. In blunt terms, it means they don't get the joke so they don't buy the book so that not-so-dumb publisher stops publishing them and the geniuses either never get into print or they don't stay there long. We don't lack humorists—we *starve* them. Time was we had the Benchleys and the Thurbers and the Perelmans and so many others, but now there's little left for us but to reread these old greats over and over again. Jules Feiffer is coming up but where do we go from there? And whatever happened to Max Schulman? Don't answer, it was a rhetorical question. Schulman got rich. He may also have gotten his bellyful of idiots telling him, "Hey, you write real crazy, huh, Three Stooges stuff, but how about you should write something *good*, something *serious?*" God

knows how often I've been driven to contemplate writing "serious" novels because in this country humor and satire are considered the literature of unimportance. It does get under your skin.

Jonathan Swift was utterly mad in much of his satirical writing, but we don't have the large egghead audience that Swift had. It takes an egghead, these days, or the college wit, to appreciate high-level satire and off-beat humor because you need the frame of reference necessary to understanding the allusions.

I have a feeling that we are all heading toward subliminal universities, where the teaching will be done by teaching machines and a television professor teaches by using subliminal messages while running old "Gunsmoke" episodes. You know, with "*Twelfth Night* likes you, you like it" flashing across the screen. It's coming. Tomorrow. The day after. Next Tuesday.

N. Do you feel that the humorist has an obligation to the public beyond offering amusement?

■ *Blatty:* The humorist as humorist has one obligation—to make the reader laugh. I think any other claim is sheer pretentiousness. But the humorist as satirist is another cube of boullion. Mark Twain said we have one really effective weapon against foolishness and that's laughter. He said that only laughter can blow human folly and humbug to "rags and atoms at a blast. Against the assault of laughter, nothing can stand." A true rumor. Look at Jonathan Swift, and his exquisite use of irony, his effectiveness in combining the fury of a moralist with the farce of a harlequin. To call your enemy a knave is one thing, but to show him to be a fool is to destroy him. The common enemies of all satirists are, I believe, roughly folly, humbug, pretense, and the absence of charity. You can't preach them out of existence, but we can give you a good shot at laughing them into hiding for a while. The easiest way to perform is to mimic, to parody, to spoof, to make people laugh. The English satirists understood this. We don't.

N. Perhaps the lack of public response has cut down our quantity of humor?

■ *Blatty:* It may sound unseemly for me to say this, but good or great humor is far more difficult to bring off than "serious" writing. There is no such thing as a moderate success with humor and no such thing as a moderate failure. When you fail you fall on your face. You can learn to write, but you cannot learn to be a funny writer. This is something which is innate, is born in you, and you have to lose some of your inhibitions.

N. In working in Hollywood for motion pictures—

■ *Blatty:* I know what you are going to ask, and I can only say that I have an ambivalent point of view about it. First of all, most of the clichés about Hollywood are true. In fact, I have rejected the idea of doing a satirical book about Hollywood. The truth would be regarded as the wildest creation of my imagination, and would therefore be ineffective in a book.

On the other hand, even though we sometimes do screen plays by committee—working through the changes made by producer, director, and, sometimes, the star, and finally the film editor—there's satisfaction to be had. I have never, in the course of five screen plays, "written down." I keep to the same level of sophisticated humor found in my books, and if they want to take some things out, let them. But so far there have been few unreasonable changes by executives or producers. Yet it's a frightening thing for a writer because anyone can ruin your picture—the actor, the cameraman, the composer, the editor. So many hands are involved that a good picture sometimes seems a matter of extraordinary luck.

There's a thing called "hunger" that drives the writer to Hollywood. Few writers can make a living from novels. Meanwhile, don't knock writing for the movies. Little Billy Shakespeare would have gladly traded his rather extensive real estate holdings for cinemascope and a zoom lens!

N.   We spoke, a few moments ago, about the lack of humor and humorists. Could you elaborate, now, on the need for humor?

■ *Blatty:* We need it so badly, you know. That great big hydrogen mushroom cloud, we're living in its shadow, even when we're trying our damndest not to think about it. We may not consciously think about the possibility of nuclear war, but it's simmering in the subconscious, and we welcome the opportunity to laugh. Humor is one form of release, perhaps the best. But vicarious horror is a release, too. Why do teenagers enjoy horror movies so much? A psychiatrist told me that it's because they still believe in the possibility of things that go bump in the dark, in witches and goblins and vampires, and when they see them objectified on the screen they feel a great release from tension. Well, I feel that if we can talk about our political problems, our international problems, and laugh at them a little, we feel the same release from tension. One of the leading characters in *Goldfarb* is a nameless President who is last seen at the brink of crisis with his head in his hands muttering, "I wasn't satisfied with being rich."

N.   What advice would you give the youngster of ability who wants to make a career in writing—especially in humor?

■ *Blatty:* Mad, wicked child, why not wear a hairshirt for a living? No? Ech! Then read, read, read, read, read the very best in the field of humor, no matter how far back in time you must dip. And don't, under penalty of death, take any damn "creative writing" courses! Get a good grounding in the liberal arts, keep up with current events, and swallow tidbits of knowledge like a ravenous vacuum cleaner; they are the loom upon which you will weave your satire. This is magnificent advice, especially if you intend to write satire.

N. If you were able to look back upon one William Peter Blatty—say from the vantage point of 2064—how would you like to find him appraised?

■ *Blatty:* To begin with, being appraised in 2064 would in itself be a triumph. Beyond that, I'd like it said that I'm still good for a laugh, that I was a stylist as well as a humorist, and that what I had to say in my own time applies with equal force to 2064 and all that. I don't want much, do I? Just fame and glory and other humble aims of that kidney.

"I remember standing there in the moonlight waiting to get into our lifeboat . . . and I thought to myself that this was one time in my life when I had no idea of what was going to happen to me, I may live or die . . . it was then I realized that every normal person has great courage that's just waiting to be called on."

Margaret Bourke-White
Interviewed in Darien, Connecticut, July, 1963

Margaret Bourke-White

Note: At fourteen a youngster, no matter how sophisticated, is apt to dream of being Tarzan or President. I was fourteen when *Life* made its debut, forever establishing photography as a medium, not merely an adjunct.

I gave up Tarzana and the Presidency. For though I couldn't even handle a Brownie I wanted to be Margaret Bourke-White.

The greatness of Miss Bourke-White's work is apparent to even the casual reader who has watched the photo-essay develop as an art form during her years with *Fortune* and *Life*. Technically, of course, she performs miracles. But angles and lighting and composition are forgotten when we observe the miracle Miss Bourke-White repeats again and again in capturing the essence of a mood, an emotion, the soul itself. We feel the weariness of a GI, the quiet strength of Gandhi, the terror of death, the cruel grip of poverty, the exhilaration of victory.

But over the years, as though the immortality won with camera were not enough, Miss Bourke-White began writing. All her books—particularly her moving autobiography, *Portrait of Myself*—have borne the impressive Bourke-White signature in words and pictures. As most readers know, Miss Bourke-White has fought a long and noble and victorious fight against Parkinsonism.

When this interview was recorded, in July of 1963, she had recovered enough muscular control to show me about her stunning homesite near Darien, Connecticut, and enough control of speech to make this tape. Talking to this beautiful and determined woman, before, during, and after the interview, remains my most moving memory of time, place, and person involved in these interviews.

N. In talking to Miss Bourke-White I would like to use her autobiography, *Portrait of Myself*, as a springboard. In it, as I recall, you seem to dismiss your childhood far quicker than most writers do when they recap their lives. Was there a reason?

■ *B-W* Yes, it was a happy childhood on the whole, not at all dull or uneventful, and it probably provided a stable foundation

58

for all that has followed. I was greatly influenced by my father who had a great love for all forms of natural life, and a great respect for anything that walked or crawled or slithered or flew or simply "was." He probably taught me to respect the whole of life, and to observe. Yet other than this it was not a dramatic childhood, and I'd have bored the reader if I'd carried it beyond a few chapters.

N.   Oddly enough, despite this love of nature, you first made your reputation in industrial photography, didn't you?

■ *B-W*   Yes. I worked in Cleveland and Pittsburgh. Actually I first started touring factories with my father, and they never seemed dull to me. They seemed very beautiful. Then I made a series of steel-mill pictures that came to the attention of Henry Luce, at a time when he was about to launch *Fortune*. So I went to work with him eight months before the first issue came out.

N.   You had the first cover, didn't you?

■ *B-W*   No, that was on *Life*. But the photo essays we did for *Fortune* were very exciting, especially for that time. We even did the stockyards. In those days making a pig look artistic wasn't dreamed of.

N.   The idea of a young woman climbing ladders in steel mills wasn't dreamed of either, was it?

■ *B-W*   No. But all that was a part of the challenge—we were determined to do new and different and better things.

N.   Then you helped launch *Life*. Yours was the first cover and the first photo-essay.

■ *B-W*   Yes. This was when I really started working with people, with faces. I'd never done that before. The faces showed so much—in the Dust Bowl assignment, for example—that I couldn't ignore them any longer.

N.   This came to characterize your work, didn't it? I mean, it's the faces you shot—the range of expression—that we recall so well from your World War II assignments, for example, and your work with Gandhi. Did this become a conscious objective?

■ *B-W*   I know that with Gandhi this is a thing I wanted to do very badly—to probe as deeply as I could. He had such an extraordinary personality. He used to have a nickname for me. When I'd come with the cameras he'd say, "There's the torturer again." It was said in fun, of course. But he hated flashbulbs, and I'm a great flashbulb user. It was very funny with Gandhi, but before I had a chance to take his picture his secretary insisted that I learn to spin. I'd never used a spinning wheel, and it seemed like very peculiar preparation for taking a photograph. But later I saw why—the spinning wheel was a symbol with Gandhi. The homespun cloth that he and his followers wore expressed their fight for freedom. They were imposing a boycott against British textiles, and it was Gandhi's idea that if he could get all Indians to wear their own homespun cloth it would help their cause.

N.   During World War II, when you established some sort of record for experiences that women simply shouldn't encounter, you were torpedoed off the African coast. It's one of the dramatic highlights of the book.

■ *B-W*   It was a dividing time in my life. It wasn't only dramatic, it went much deeper than that. I had the feeling that this was bringing out the best in people. There was such extraordinary courage. I remember standing there in the moonlight, waiting to get into our lifeboat, which was flooded by the splash of the torpedo, and I thought to myself that this was one time in my life when I had no idea of what was going to happen to me, I may live or die. Then I noticed several nurses standing nearby, and the way they were trembling, and I thought, "This must be fear," and I had to admire their discipline because aside from the trembling they controlled themselves so well. I think it was then I realized that every normal person has great courage that's just waiting to be called on.

N.   What theaters of war did you travel into?

■ *B-W*   I was in Africa and England with the Air Force, and then I wanted to see ground warfare where I worked with the Fifth Army under General Clark. When we were beginning to move into Germany, *Life* pulled me out of that theater and sent me through the greater part of the German campaign. When the war ended I stayed on in Germany.

N.   Miss Bourke-White, the courage you mentioned in regard to the nurses on the torpedoed ship was something you caught on the faces of even grievously wounded GI's in Italy.

■ *B-W*   Yes. They went through so much. It was a dreadful part of the war—the Cassino Valley, especially. It seemed we moved just an inch a day. I remember how ironical it was to see the boys slogging their way through the mud and slush, and we'd see signs that would say, "10 Miles to Cassino," and there they were, moving just a slow step at a time.

N.   In Germany, as I recall, you added another career: you became a looter.

■ *B-W*   I was fascinated by looting, and finally succumbed to the fever. It may not be a very pretty side of war, but it's definitely there. You're in the land of the enemy and you're curious about how they live, and as far as the things in their houses are concerned, you feel they've stolen it from others. You have no morals about that. There is a curious moral code, however. It was all right to loot an empty house, but you never looted a house that had people in it. Or if a house was smashed flat it was all right to loot, as long as the owner wasn't there. We also had another unwritten rule, which was that only the persons who had actually been under gunfire had the right to loot. It seemed so strange to have a code of morals for an immoral act, but there it was. We used to joke about it a lot, and wonder, if we visited each other in peacetime, if we'd have to nail down all the valuables in the house.

I had one great haul—I got to Nuremberg and Munich with the Rainbow Division and they took over Hitler's private apartment as headquarters. Before I got there everything had been looted except a couple of statues of dancing girls that were too heavy for normal looters, but I wanted them. So some of the boys helped me wrap them in blankets and I sent them out by carrier plane. This was supposed to be inviolate, but somewhere between Munich and Paris the statues disappeared. I felt badly because these looters wouldn't know they came from Hitler's apartment—to them they'd just be heavy junk.

N. Before we were in World War II you spent a long stretch of time in Moscow, photographing the Nazi bombing of that city. I'd never realized the Germans had attacked Moscow so heavily.

■ B-W Yes, the first bombers came over on July 22, 1941, and the Germans were apparently determined to destroy Red Square and the Kremlin. Despite the number of pictures I took, the Russians just didn't want to admit there were so many planes over Moscow. No stories were allowed to go out concerning the bombing of the Kremlin. Actually, I know of one direct hit they made, right across the street from the little hotel where I was living. There was one very bad night when bombs and fire-bombs were falling especially heavily, and there was one direct hit that blew me and my cameras off the windowsill where I was working. I rushed back to the window when I could get to my feet, and a whole building seemed to be frozen in the air with stones and sticks and bricks falling out of it. It just seemed to hang there, and then it came down with a great crash. I learned later it was the palace that housed the Kremlin guard. Ninety-three men were housed there, and I don't know how many were killed, but the Russians would never let the story be released.

N. Now I'd like to back up to a question that can be called basic and theoretical, but I would like to know how you feel about the obligations of a news and feature photographer, particularly a photographer like you who works in depth, to the public.

■ *B-W*   I feel that utter truth is essential, and to get at that truth may take a lot of searching and long hours and the difficulty of analyzing two sides of a question, but I feel that that's our great responsibility. I had this feeling particularly strong in Germany, when we moved into Buchenwald, and the sights were so terrible I couldn't think about them. Still, I felt driven to report them because I felt I must record whatever concerns the course of history. There were at least eight hundred corpses in Buchenwald when we got there, a great pile of naked bodies and we could even see the pieces of skin to be made into lampshades. Many men still alive in the camp, even though we arrived to feed them, died before morning. It seemed to me that this was a sacred mission, that we photographers must get pictures of this because it was the ultimate in race hatred, and I knew, if the truth were shown, that humanity would not forget quite so soon.

N.   If you were to give advice to the aspiring journalist, what would that advice be?

■ *B-W*   Learn to look on both sides of the question. And most questions have *more* than two sides. This should become a firmly fixed habit of the journalist. He should never stop at the obvious. He should investigate just a little further than his job requires to get that plus-quality that characterizes the finest journalists.

N.   In looking at culture today, what aspect do you find most encouraging as far as the utilization of talent is concerned?

■ *B-W*   I admire people who are trying to use television constructively. I admire those who have used this new medium to good creative effect—Leonard Bernstein, for instance. And there are many others who are working through difficulties to put something fine on the air.

N.   Miss Bourke-White, in the last part of your book you discuss your battle with Parkinson's Disease, its onslaught, the operation, and the therapy I believe you're still undergoing. How did you first notice the disease coming on?

■ *B-W*   Just by dragging a foot. If I sat down, say for lunch, and I didn't get up for an hour or two I'd find that the first three steps were terrible staggers. Then I'd be all right again. I was completely mystified about what was wrong, and so were most of my doctors.

N.   It was some time, wasn't it, before the disease actually slowed you down?

■ *B-W* Yes. It was about eight years, and I feel so very fortunate that the new type of brain surgery had been discovered before I became a total victim. If it had been developed just five years later it would have been too late to help me. Yet, surgery, as wonderful as it is, is only 50 per cent of the battle. The rest of it we have to do ourselves. In my case it's been my very intensive and faithful physical therapy. One of the things I've always been grateful for is the fact that if this had to come to me, I'm so glad it's something I could work with—and I'm still working with it.

I've relearned walking, running, and I was so proud when I found out I could skip. I was practicing jumping rope, without much success because it took more co-ordination than I had. One morning I woke up early and grabbed my jumping rope and actually jumped. It all came back like a childhood dream. In fact, childhood games have helped me greatly. I can even play jacks—not all the fancy games children nowadays play, but I can play a straight game of jacks pretty well.

N. You've been working with speech therapy, too, haven't you?

■ *B-W* Yes. I've been doing everything from singing with Mitch Miller to performing facial exercises.

N. I never realized, before, that the onslaught of Parkinson's Disease is so total.

■ *B-W* It's a funny thing to discover that you direct your body to make a movement, and that you haven't made that movement at all—you've just been standing there. To bring the body back to obedience takes long, long practice. In my case I feel there are certain things I must do as health insurance. I always walk at least one mile a day and sometimes three or four.

N. You've got a rocky surface out here, too. I don't imagine that's been the easiest to navigate.

■ *B-W* It's been hard. For instance, I took you out to that little cliff this morning, and there was a time when I couldn't have made that short walk because the ground is so uneven. Now I make it easily, and I'm both glad and proud of it because it's a beautiful spot.

N. To turn back once more to your book—I'd like to touch on two episodes you handled so wonderfully well—namely, your marriages. First, what we might call the student union, and second, your marriage to Erskine Caldwell.

■ *B-W* I've always been glad that, even though my marriages broke up, I was married to wonderful men for whom I had great respect. I feel that each time was a notch in my growing process.

N. The first time you were the victim of a rapacious mother-in-law?

■ *B-W* Yes. She's dead, now, but she was a terror. She was very beautiful—she had masses of white hair, like a duchess, and if she'd given me half a chance I'd have loved her very much. But she was opposed to the fact that I was going on to school after marriage. She felt Margaret was indulging herself because she wouldn't quit college. It seemed the set of values I'd grown up with was completely foreign to her. Later I was glad because if I'd stayed married and had children, it would have changed my life completely. Not that having children isn't a worthwhile objective, but if it had happened to me I wouldn't have been able to see the world as a photo-journalist. I wouldn't want to change any of my life, even if I had the chance, because it's been the life I wanted.

N. Your marriage to Erskine Caldwell came after one of the most colorful courtships I've ever read.

■ *B-W* It was both funny and touching, the way he'd send cables to "Honey-Chile" all over the North Pole area. Actually, Erskine and I worked together in his Tobacco Road country, doing a book that was very important to both of us. It came at a time when I hadn't worked much with people, and wanted so badly to do more. He showed me that he hadn't exaggerated conditions at all, and he was such a patient and sensitive man that he taught me a great deal. He has a strong, instinctive feeling for the sufferings of others, and I respected this deeply and began trying to probe as deeply.

N. Then the inevitable problems of careers in conflict—

■ *B-W* It's a complex problem, of course—it always is. I thought everyone knew, as I did, that my devotion to the camera came first. Perhaps it's true, as someone said, that I have a lens for a heart.

You know, when a person digs into his life thoroughly enough to write an autobiography, it's possible to call so many things tragic and to rationalize errors. I think I've been particularly fortunate; even my two broken marriages and this illness have been important to my own growth and development. Probably that's the essence of the tragedies and triumphs in any person's life. Whatever happens signifies growth, if we're wise enough or fortunate enough to see it that way.

"A writer is obligated first and only to his material. Giving the public what it wants is good business if you are selling chewing gum; fiction is an art, not merchandise, and readers are moved by a writer's talent and not by his salesmanship."

Erskine Caldwell
Interviewed in San Francisco, August, 1963

c

Erskine Caldwell

N. Erskine Caldwell occupies a strategic position in the world of American letters. He entered the scene, over thirty years ago, with the subtlety of a dynamite blast. Novels like *God's Little Acre* and *Tobacco Road* established the fact that poverty and deprivation were universal problems, not exclusively the sad issue of the big-city slum. Many of the established critics were shocked, but since jarring the establishment has been part of any innovator's career, shock alone could not pronounce Caldwell's fame.

The gaunt and disturbing picture of life among the under-privileged was the framework upon which Caldwell built his sensitive and searching stories embracing compassion, humor, and irony. A bold simplicity of style, matched with a clean and virile story line, has made major works like *Tobacco Road* and minor opuses like *The Last Night of Summer* readable, memorable, and even significant. But in talking to Mr. Caldwell, I'd like to move to the very beginning, so to speak—to his own story.

■ *Caldwell:* My life is really rather dull. It would not make a book, and I would hate to have to read my own biography. My life is not typical, yet it's not extraordinary; it's mostly just dull. What I mean by dull is that I'm a writer, and the only thing I like to do in life is write. I've been writing now for the past thirty or thirty-four years and I'll probably keep going a little while longer. This is the way I live and breathe and work and believe.

When I began writing, all those years ago, I was more interested in the content of a story than I was in any technical derivations of a story or of a novel. What I did was to start at the beginning, without any background as a writer, without any knowledge as a writer. All I wanted to do was to tell a story, to tell it to the best of my ability —better, I hoped, than anyone else could tell that particular story. So I began when I was about seventeen by working on a newspaper. I think I learned a great deal about life and writing in those years of apprenticeship on a newspaper. It was a small newspaper, what you might call an intimate newspaper, a weekly. But I learned that there can be a story in anything and everything. Anything will make a story because everything has meaning in itself, and that meaning is always applicable to life itself. If it happens to one person it could happen to a million persons. So, when I wanted to write a story, and tried to write it, I was writing for myself—not for a million people—because I had to please myself first. If I was not satisfied with that story I would throw it in the wastebasket. If it didn't appeal to me, how could it please the million?

I was concerned with perfecting my own writing to the extent that its meanings were obvious. Not only to me, but to that audience of a million. They had to find a meaning. I did not add philosophy, or significance, but felt that any story of human life would find its own level of significance. Every reader would find a different meaning because every reader finds what he's looking for. All I do is to furnish the mirror, a mirror the reader can look into. This way he can see what he's looking for. If he's looking for a philosophy of life he can probably find it in some way, or if all he wants is entertainment he can find that, too.

N.   But along with "mirroring" there are elements of compassion so evident in works like *Tobacco Road* and *God's Little Acre* that I feel you must consciously dig to the heart of persons and the root of issues.

■ *Caldwell:* I think any work of fiction always has a basis in reality. We were just speaking of story content being a mirror—but actually, if we have to be serious about these things, we have to realize that fiction is more than entertainment. It is not a pastime, it furnishes something we can't get from life itself because fiction must concentrate, eliminate, add to life. People read to find out what they cannot find in their own lives or see around them. I don't claim to have any divine ability, I can't define any emotion or situation or thesis better than any other writer, but I can select my material with care and discrimination. In other words, I'm not interested in finding a plot on which to hang a story; I want to find out what elements of life move and motivate people. People make their own plot, if that's how the storyline must be defined. I've never known exactly what a plot is because I wouldn't know how to do one if I saw it. What I try to do is to help people themselves furnish the entire basis of a story.

If you are really deeply interested in people's lives and write about them, or even want to or try to write about them, they're going to furnish you with all the materials you spoke about a moment ago. You see, people themselves are compassionate by nature. Very few people—certainly not ordinary people like you and me, for example—have any great claim to being experts in psychology and psychiatry, and so on. What we do, what a serious writer tries to do, is to create people who have never really existed and make new people. These new people reflect everybody because they're composites of many persons. They are not re-created from life, like an extra-dimension photograph. In order to create something you have to make something which doesn't truly exist. In order to make this true and believable you have to know people themselves, and be able to believe in these people you're writing about. If you do not believe in them, if you think they're just characters to manipulate and turn into elements of plot, you end up with nothing. You have a book filled with words and nothing else. I think that all serious writing is something that's been created, that reflects people the author came to know and love and understand, with something of the author thrown in.

N.   To turn to the physical processes of research—could you describe the travel that went into the backgrounds for your various southern novels?

■ *Caldwell:*   I don't know whether you call it research or not. What I know is what I have done and seen and heard, and if this is research I'm guilty.

I grew up in the South and I happened to have been fortunate enough to live all over the South in my youth. I lived in every southern state, and I don't know how many towns and cities. When a person moves every six months or so from one place to another I suppose he gets a real cross-section of life by comparing life in Louisiana, for instance, with life in Florida. There are differences, and you recognize these differences if you have an opportunity to compare them, whereas if you live in just one place all your life you can't make such comparisons. I think that comparison has a great deal to do with understanding. No matter what the dialect is, or the racial characteristics might be, or their educational standards, you don't really recognize differences unless you can compare.

N.   The states south of the Mason-Dixon line have produced a disproportionately large share of America's leading writers. Why do you suppose this has happened?

■ *Caldwell:*   I don't know the real answer. In the terms of my own experience, because this is all I can talk about, I think it's that the South—until after the Second World War—was an agricultural region. It was not an industrial area, with concentrations of population. Life is always elementary when you are scattered far apart.

It isn't like a city slum, where you know people next door, above you, below you, on the street, across from you. In a sparsely populated region, such as in any farming country, you have to go and look to find something to write about. You don't find it out your back door because beyond your back door is nothing but a cotton field. There's nothing in that cotton field—so you travel around. You find that people who live these isolated lives are more intense than people who live in an urban society. People in an urban society tend to become similar, they have the same interests and they do the same things and they talk the same jargon. In an isolated community people are individuals. This individuality stands out, it's there for the writer to grab. Because a writer needs individuals, not prototypes, both to stir him and to give him material that makes stories, the writer in the South has an advantage. You can find uniqueness, wonder what makes a person what he is, why he talks as he does, what his social attitudes are, his religious attitudes. These differences, these elements of uniqueness, flourish in isolated regions. To me that's why there has been and is so much material in the South.

N. To turn to a recent book, *The Last Night Of Summer*, I wonder if you'd describe how the novel was born and evolved.

■ *Caldwell:* The setting is deep in the Mississippi delta country. I lived in this delta country many years ago, and I go back there every year, sometimes twice a year. This particular region is one of my favorite spots between New Orleans and Memphis, the border of delta country.

You might say this particular story could have happened anywhere, yet in my own mind it could only happen where it did— not in North Dakota or California or New England or in Europe. It had to take place in this one particular region, where the people I wanted in the book really are, where this story could be created out of individual lives, where the conflict could arise. In the delta region the heat can be almost unbearable, sometimes, and emotional breaks in people seem to grow naturally from the pressures that build up in them during a really bad heat wave. Toward the end of summer, when the heat breaks in a really wild night of thunderstorms, emotions break wide open, too. All these elements to me could take place in just one locality, and *The Last Night Of Summer* had to happen in the Mississippi delta.

N. To switch to a totally different aspect of your writing, what sent you to Europe during the years before we entered the Second World War?

■ *Caldwell:* I've always liked to travel, having grown up that way since the age of five. I wanted to find more comparisons in life. A few minutes ago I spoke about comparing people in different localities to expose the character of persons. The Old World, in my opinion, was a good place to go to compare the differences between life in America with the outside world. The Old World produced the people who came here; people in this country are derivatives. I wanted to find out what characteristics had been brought to this country, and what had been sacrificed or altered or changed. I wanted to learn the true character of various European peoples.

N. At least one of your books treated the Soviet war effort in detail, didn't it?

■ *Caldwell:* I suppose everyone would have a different impression of what happened in wartime. It all depends on where you are, what you're doing, all given circumstances. It just so happened that I was in Russia at the beginning of the war. What struck me was the harrowing fact that what happened in Russia could have happened nowhere else at the time, may never have happened before, may never happen again. This was the attempted assault by a well-organized war machine against a people who were essentially unwarlike to begin with, and who were not prepared for it, and who were not even industrialized to any great extent. They could only, in essence, retaliate with their own bare fists. It was a question of survival, not right or wrong, not politics or theory.

But perhaps people who are subjected to aggression are going to fight a little harder than people who face a less tangible foe. The Russians had everything to lose, their lands and their lives, and no matter how overwhelming the odds were supposedly stacked against them they were successful in their opposition to Hitler.

N. To change to the purely theoretical for a moment—if you were to give advice to the talented youngster seriously interested in writing, what would that advice be?

■ *Caldwell:* I'd probably give the same answer I would if you asked the doctor how to go about being a doctor. He'd tell you to take an apprenticeship for ten or fifteen years to learn the profession of being a doctor. You have to learn the trade of writing. You can't walk in the door and say, "I'm going to be a writer." Get yourself a typewriter and paper and write out your story? It doesn't work that way. Hundreds and thousands of people have been disappointed in life because they think they have a good story, or they're good oral storytellers. They think all they have to do is write it down. But writing is not a re-creation of the oral at all, because the oral is something you don't have to worry about in regard to grammar. You

can always make a little slip-up in English when you're speaking—
just as I'm undoubtedly doing right now—but when you write it
you have to know how to spell that word, you've got to know what
that word means, and although you can use maybe half a dozen
words to describe one particular thing you have to know which is
going to be the best word to do the job out of that half dozen.

It's elementary, I think, to say that you must understand what
you're dealing with. Words are tools or supplies or ammunition or the
fruit of talent or whatever you might want to call them. But if you
don't understand words, if you don't know the origin of a word,
what its original meaning was and what its application is today, I
think you are dangerously ill-equipped for the job of writer. You
simply cannot become a good writer until you learn the tools of the
business and the grammar. Anybody can learn to spell, I suppose,
with the use of a dictionary, but it's the definition of words, the
true meaning, and the implication of words that tell a real story.

N.   How much rewriting do you do in the course of turning
out a novel?

■ *Caldwell:*   This is hard to say, because I never actually write a
book, I rewrite a book. I wouldn't be able to set up rules for the
process; everything varies. I might write one sentence that will stay
put until the end, but I might go back and find an adjacent sentence
that I don't like and I'll fool around with that sentence for a whole
day before it comes out the way I think it should.

If you rewrite a book, say, ten times, I think you're most apt
to have a good book than if you rewrite it two or three times.
There's no limit to what you have to do to rewrite. It may take a
whole year's time, simply to get a simple story where it should be,
in a form that satisfies you.

So if I write a book ten times I think I've done rather well. If I
write it fifteen times I think it's going to be a little better, so I write
it sixteen times.

N.   Do you have a definite schedule of writing hours?

■ *Caldwell:*   Definitely. Just like everyone with a job, I follow a
schedule. I like my work; if I didn't like it I wouldn't be doing it. I
don't watch the clock in the sense that I put in two hours, or five
hours, or seven hours, and then quit. I suppose I have worked ten or
fifteen hours at a stretch, but as I've grown older I've gotten to the
point where I say, "Well, I've got more time to do this, now, than
I had twenty years ago, so maybe I'd better quit." So if the sun's
going down and it's getting hungrytime I quit with just seven or
eight hours under my belt.

The hours don't necessarily mean anything—it all depends on how much comes out of them. You may end up with only one page at the end of the day, or you may end up with fifteen pages. It's never merely a matter of gauging the words you write or the time you put in, but how successful you think you've been at the end of the day's work. If you're satisfied (and a writer has terrible problems satisfying himself) you've done a day's work.

N.   What works have you in progress now?

■ *Caldwell:* I always have something to do. I've been writing a book during the last summer. My wife and I finished about 25,000 miles of travel for a series of travel sketches. This will be a book that should be finished up soon. It will be called *Around About America*, and it will be a book about American life today. Non-fiction.

N.   In looking about you—at what is being written and published today—what do you think of the state of American letters?

■ *Caldwell:* I probably don't read nearly as much as you do, or a lot of people do. I've never been much of a reader—not because I don't like to read, but because I'd rather write than read. What I know about American writing is sketchy.

What I try to do is to read one book by every writer who has written as many as two or three books. I rarely read anybody's first book; I wait to see if he's going to do a second or a third. At this point I consider him a novelist or a short story writer, whatever he's attempting to do.

Of course, we constantly have trends, and even I notice these. But it isn't a matter of liking them—you live with them. If you were to say, "I only read Sir Walter Scott and I don't like these modern writers," you'd end up in a real bind.

I think that writing at the moment is comparable to other decades. It's different in one respect—we find a lot more sensationalism than we found even ten years ago, and a great deal more experimentation than we found then, but this is all to the good. Anything that's new might be good because it indicates an improvement over the old. Even if it isn't good, by itself, it means that an improvement is coming.

N.   Do you feel that the writer has an obligation to the material he uses, on one hand, and to the public for which he writes, on the other?

■ *Caldwell:* I am single-minded enough to say that a writer is obligated first and only to his material. Giving the public what it wants is good business if you are selling chewing gum; fiction is an art, not merchandise, and readers are moved by a writer's talent and not by his salesmanship.

N.   If it were possible to look back from the vantage point of 2064, how would you like the accomplishments of Erskine Caldwell judged?

■ *Caldwell:*   I would not know what to think about this in 1964—certainly not in 2064.

"The only obligation any artist can have is to himself. His work means nothing, otherwise. It has no meaning . . . the only really gratifying thing is to serve yourself."

Truman Capote
Interviewed in New York, March, 1964

Truman Capote

N. *Other Voices, Other Rooms* introduced one of the great literary talents of our time: Truman Capote. Without *Voices*, without *Tree of Night*, *The Grass Harp*, *The Muses Are Heard*, and *Breakfast at Tiffany's*—to mention only some of his fiction and reportage—contemporary American letters would present a far slimmer file in the valuable pocket labeled "quality."

In talking to Mr. Capote I would first, naturally, like to begin by asking him for the essential autobiography—where he was born, reared, and educated, and when his interest in writing developed.

■ *Capote:* I was born in New Orleans in 1924. (By the way, my name isn't Capote at all—I'll explain that later.) My father's name is Persons, and he was a salesman. My mother was only sixteen years old when they were married, and she was very, very beautiful—a beauty contest-winner type of child who later on in life became an enormously sensitive and intelligent person. But she was only sixteen when she was married—a normal, beautiful girl, rather wild—and my father was twenty-four.

My mother wasn't able to cope with the situation. She had a baby and she traveled with my father all around the South, and when she was eighteen she decided that she wanted to go to college. So I went to college with her, all the way through, and by the time she was graduated she and my father were divorced so I went to live with relatives in a rather remote part of Alabama. This was a very strange household. It consisted of three elderly ladies and an elderly uncle. They were the people who had adopted my mother—her own parents had died when she was very young. I lived there until I was ten, and it was a very lonely life, and it was then that I became interested in writing. You see, I always could read. I have the illusion that I could read when I was four years old, and I actually could read before I ever went to school. In first grade, reading was the only thing I liked to do, because I had this lonely childhood and reading took me out of it. I began to write, and also to paint—another deep interest I had. (I was also interested in music, but for various reasons I was not allowed to take music lessons.) Anyway, I started to write when I was eight years old and wrote a book when I was nine.

I spent every summer in that town in Alabama until I was sixteen. In the meantime, my mother had gone to New York and had remarried, so I came to New York to school for three years. I went to different boarding schools around New York, and when I finally left school I was seventeen and went straight to work at *The New Yorker* in the art department.

Originally I was to work for *The New Yorker* in the "Talk of the Town" department. This was during the war, and I had been sending them stories and articles, and I went to see the people I had been corresponding with; they were going to give me a job. It was during the war and they had lost all their staff. Well, I arrived, and they took one look—I was seventeen and looked about ten years old—and realized they could never send this child labor case out to interview anybody, so in the end I worked in the art department and turned out ideas for "Talk of the Town" every week and suggested personalities for "Profiles." I worked there for two years, then began writing my first novel, *Other Voices, Other Rooms*. When I really got into the novel I went back to New Orleans to finish it, and I've never set foot in another office. I must say that I really hate offices.

N.   You mentioned that your name really isn't Capote. How did you come to assume it?

■ *Capote:* My mother's second husband was a Cuban businessman named Capote, a name Spanish in origin. He adopted me, and my name was legally changed to Capote.

N.   Now, *Other Voices, Other Rooms* created quite a stir for a first novel, and certainly established you in the front rank. What was your reaction to its success?

■ *Capote:* So many things happened that were extracurricular to the work on the book that I mostly remember being shocked. There were so many cruel things written about me at the time, and a great deal of comment about the photograph on the back of the book (which was perfectly innocent). Somehow, all the publicity I read about it in the newspapers . . . well, I wasn't used to reading about myself. I was so shocked and hurt that I never got any pleasure out of it at all. Everything was different than I had always thought or hoped it would be.

Of course, the book was a literary success, and it sold quite well, but it has only been in the last six years that I could bear to think about certain things surrounding that book. I know it's a very good book, and it's coming into perspective and focus, and finally I feel no pain about anything connected with it. I just feel gratitude because, in a sense, it freed me to go on and do my own work. If I hadn't had that success, no matter what it was based on—publicity, notoriety, whatever it may have been—I would never have had the freedom to go on developing and maturing as an artist. (Perhaps I would have; I don't really know.) But I don't think it hurt me to have a success at that very young age because it wasn't really a success in my own eyes. If I had had any sense of fulfillment, or any of the things that go with that degree of success, it might have had a bad effect on me. But since I didn't get that satisfaction from it—in fact, got the exact opposite—it just sobered me up a great deal and made me realize on what paths I truly must go.

N.   There is a later book I would like to touch upon. What was your motivation in writing *The Muses Are Heard*?

■ *Capote:* This was the beginning of a long experiment. I've always had the theory that reportage is the great unexplored art form. I mean, most good writers, good literary craftsmen, seldom use this metier. For example, John Hersey is a very fine journalist and an excellent writer, but he's not an artist in the sense that I mean. Even Rebecca West at her best (and I think she's a remarkable reporter) doesn't do what I'm talking about. I've had this theory that a factual piece of work could explore whole new dimensions in writing that would have a double effect fiction does not have—the very fact of its being true, every word of it true, would add a double contribution of strength and impact. The "Porgy and Bess" piece, and one other piece I did for *The New Yorker*—a profile of Marlon Brando—were parts of this experiment. I originally did them just to see if I could do them. After I did the "Porgy and Bess" tour of Russia for *The New Yorker*, I wanted to see what I could do within the scope of something truly banal, and I thought, "What is the most banal thing in journalism?" After a time I realized that it would be an interview with a film star, the sort of thing you would see in *Photoplay* magazine. I decided that it must not only be with a film star, but that it must follow the absolute path of these things, in that they're always done as interviews that take place at one time with a person more or less on the fly. So I put a number of names into a hat and pulled out, God knows why, Marlon Brando. He was in Japan at the same time, so I went to *The New Yorker* and asked them if they'd be interested in this, and they were. So I went to Japan and spent just the prescribed time with Brando—an evening. I had actually known Marlon Brando before, so in a way I was cheating, but I didn't know him very well. I had dinner with him and talked with him and then spent a year on the piece because it had to be perfection—because my part was to take this banal thing and turn it into a work of art.

Anyway, I'm pleased with that piece. Lots of people can't understand why I wrote it, especially Marlon Brando. But it definitely had a point for me—an artistic one—and I moved slowly on this path because all the time I knew I was going to write a book, based on heaven knows what. I didn't know what the theme was going to be, but I knew it would be reportage on an immense scale.

I worked on other things, now feeling in complete control of myself within this form, becoming technically adept, just like one becomes technically adept at drawing skeletons to become a doctor. What I wanted to do, of course, was a great deal more ambitious than sketching skeletons; I was then going to fill it in, flesh it out, as it were. But it wasn't until five years ago that I knew what the subject would be.

One day I picked up a paper, and in the business section of the *New York Times* I found this very small headline that read, "Eisenhower Appointee Murdered." The victim was a rancher in western Kansas, a wheat grower who had been an Eisenhower appointee to the Farm Credit Bureau. He, his wife, and two of their children had been murdered, and it was a complete mystery. They had no idea of who had done it or why, but the story struck me with tremendous force. I suddenly realized that perhaps a crime, after all, would be the ideal subject matter for the massive job of reportage I wanted to do. I would have a wide range of characters, and, most importantly, it would be timeless. I knew it would take me five years, perhaps eight or ten years, to do this, and I couldn't work on some ephemeral, momentary thing. It had to be an event related to permanent emotions in people.

Now, there are thousands of crimes I could have picked, but I felt that this was mysteriously ordained. Why should I go to a small Kansas town? Why should I be interested in the murder of a wheat grower? I don't know, but it hit me head-on. The next thing I knew I got on a train and went to this little town in western Kansas. I was there for seven months that first time, and I've been back there many, many times since. I've been working on the book for five years, and it's almost finished.

N.   To turn briefly to a more general topic—since you, yourself, are southern-born, you might have some opinion as to why such a disproportionate number of our leading writers come from the South.

■ *Capote:*   I don't think this is true any more. During the last ten years the large percentage of the more talented American writers are urban Jewish intellectuals.

N.   But in decades prior to this—

■ *Capote:* Oh, yes, then a large number did come from the South and Southwest. I think one reason is that there is a definite code of values, of regional values, regional speech, regional attitudes toward religion, race, society. Rightly or wrongly, a whole code of behavior. I think all this is beginning to blur considerably, but in the South you knew where you stood and you knew where other people stood. If you lived in a southern town you could, from the time you were seven (provided you were reasonably bright), make a social chart of the whole town—morals, religion, social status. The rest of the country has rather lost this. It presented, for the artist, that "perfect prospect," as it were. In the sense that Jane Austen had a perfect prospect from which she could view life, southern artists, regionally oriented, have this—or did have it.

I, personally, have never thought of myself as a writer regionally oriented. My first book had a southern setting because I was writing about what I knew most deeply at the time. The raw material of my work usually depends on events lived ten years beforehand, (in fiction, not nonfiction). Now, of course, the South is so far behind me that it has ceased to furnish me with subject matter.

I don't think that *Other Voices, Other Rooms* can be called a southern novel. As a matter of fact it is sort of a poem, not a novel; it was a poem about an emotional situation. Everything in it has double meanings—it could as well have been set in Timbuctu or Brooklyn, except for certain physical descriptions. Actually, the only thing I've written that *depended* on its southern setting was a story called "A Christmas Memory" in *Breakfast at Tiffany's.* The moment I wrote that short story I knew I would never write another word about the South. I'm not going to be haunted by it any more, so I see no reason to deal with those people or those settings.

N.   Another question in the realm of theory: What obligation, if any, do you feel the writer owes the subject matter he works with and the public for which he writes?

■ *Capote:* I think the only person a writer has an obligation to is himself. If what I write doesn't fulfill something in me, if I don't honestly feel it's the best I can do, then I'm miserable. In fact, I just don't publish it.

The only obligation any artist can have is to himself. His work means nothing, otherwise. It has no meaning. That's why it's so absolutely boring to write a film script. The great sense of self-obligation doesn't enter into it because too many people are involved. Thus the thing that propels me, that makes me proud of my work, is utterly absent. I've only written two film scripts and I must admit that in a peculiar way I enjoyed doing them, but the true gratification of writing was completely absent; the obligation was to the producers and the actors, to what I was being paid to do, and not to myself.

The only really gratifying thing is to serve yourself. To give yourself free law, as it were.

N.   If you were to give advice to a young person intent on a literary career, what would that advice be?

■ *Capote:* People are always asking me if I believe that writing can be taught. My answer is, "No—I don't think writing can be taught." But on the other hand, if I were a young writer and convinced of my talent, I could do a lot worse than to attend a really good college workshop—for one reason only. Any writer, and especially the talented writer, needs an audience. The more immediate that audience is, the better for him because it stimulates him in his work; he gets a better view of himself and a running criticism.

Young writers couldn't get this even if they were publishing stories all the time. You publish a story and there's no particular reaction. It's as though you shot an arrow into the dark. You may get letters from people who liked or didn't like it, or a lot of reviews that really don't mean anything, but if you are working in close quarters with others who are also interested in writing, and you've got an instructor with a good critical sense, there's a vast stimulation.

I've never had this happen to me, but I know it must be so. I've given various readings and lectures at universities, so I have had some first-hand observation of it, though I never attended such a workshop myself, but if I were a young writer I would. I think a college workshop would be enormously helpful and stimulating.

N.   In looking at today's creative arts, literature in particular, what do you find that you most admire? Conversely, what do you most deplore?

■ *Capote:* I find that a very hard question to answer. I really don't deplore anything, because I like all creative actions just as actions themselves, whether I personally enjoy them or not. I can't deplore them just because I don't think they are right. Now, none of this "beat" writing interests me at all. I think it's fraudulent. I think it's all evasive. Where there is no discipline there is nothing. I don't even find that the beat writing has a surface liveliness—but that's neither here nor there because I'm sure that eventually something good will come out of it. Some extraordinary person will be encouraged by it who could never have accepted the rigid disciplines of what I consider good writing.

On the other hand, what do I most admire? Perhaps "admire" isn't the right word, but I think it's a fine thing that Katherine Anne Porter's *Ship of Fools* sold so well. Why? Because she's a remarkably good artist. And I think it's wonderful that her book was so popular and successful, whether people really read it or not.

I think it's fine that a young writer like John Updike can have a large success because he's an exceptionally gifted young man. The attention shown to young writers in this country is greater than anywhere else (except France) and this is encouraging. I suppose Russia gives their young writers more attention than any other country, but I don't happen to admire any of the young Russian writers. I like some of the Communist film makers, who do extraordinary work, but I don't care for the younger writers.

N.   What do you think of American criticism and review as a whole?

■   *Capote:*   I don't think the problem is as much a question of the level of American criticism as it is the outlets for it. I suppose the *New York Times*, commercially speaking, is the most influential of all book review outlets, and it's appalling. It's as middle-class and boring and as badly put together as it can possibly be. I thought it was interesting that the *Herald Tribune* started "Book Week." The way "Book Week" started out, it promised to be good, but it hasn't turned out that way. However, *The New York Review of Books* is excellent. This is really a step in the right direction.

As far as the little magazines are concerned, each seems to be in the hands of a separate fleet and is at war with all the other little fleets. You can't pay too much attention to them, if you're a writer. But then, I've developed a very thick skin about criticism. I've had to. I can read the most devastating things about myself, now, and it doesn't make my pulse skip a beat. You know, the writer is inclined to be a sensitive person, and he can read one hundred good reviews and one bad review and take that bad review to heart. I don't do it, not any more.

N.   As far as your own career is concerned, could you state your own objectives? Perhaps this should be placed in the perspective you would like applied?

■   *Capote:*   Well, I think I've had two careers. One was the career of precocity, the young person who published a series of books that were really quite remarkable. I can even read them now, and evaluate them favorably, as though they were the work of a stranger. In a way, they are. The person who wrote them doesn't exist any more. My metabolism, artistically and intellectually, has changed. I'm not saying it's for the better; it's just changed. The way one's hair changes color.

My second career began—I guess it really began with *Breakfast at Tiffany's*. It involves a different point of view, a different prose style to some degree. Actually, the prose style is an evolvement from one to the other—a pruning and thinning-out to a more subdued, clearer prose. I don't find it as evocative, in many respects, as the other, or even as original, but it is more difficult to do. But I'm nowhere near reaching what I want to do, where I want to go. Presumably this new book is as close as I'm going to get, at least stylistically. But I hope to expand from that point on in the multiplicity and range of characters I can deal with, because until recently I've been quite limited. Now I feel capable of handling all sorts of new and different characters which I couldn't approach before, and I think reportage has helped me. I think it freed many things inside of me—this opportunity to work with real people, then using real people under their own names. It has freed or unlocked something inside myself that now makes it possible for me to return to fiction with the ability to use a far greater range of characters.

"The quality I look for in any kind of writing . . . is that of complete sincerity and earnestness. The writer must have something he wants to communicate."

Bruce Catton
Interviewed in New York, March, 1964

Bruce Catton

N. It would not be presumptuous to call Bruce Catton our "official" Civil War historian, since this is what he has become, to a large audience. Few historians, official or otherwise, have combined the depth of perception and the vividness of presentation which constitute Mr. Catton's very special gift. Researched truth, illuminated by drama, can indeed become a powerful art form.

In talking to Mr. Catton I would like to start by asking for the most basic information of all—where he was born, reared, and educated.

■ *Catton:* I was born in Petoskey, Michigan, which is up near the tip of the lower peninsula, and I grew up a little farther down the shore of Lake Michigan near a town called Frankfort. Such education as I got I obtained at Oberlin College. I must admit that I never did succeed in graduating. I quit at the end of my junior year to become a newspaper reporter. I just didn't seem to be very much interested in higher education at the time. Oddly enough, I never did take a history course in college.

N. Where and how did your interest in historical subject matter arise?

■ *Catton:* It started strictly as an interest in the Civil War—probably because I more or less grew up with that war. The town I lived in (and this was many years ago) was filled with old Civil War veterans; it seemed that all the older men in the town had served. Every Decoration Day they'd march all the school children into the Town Hall. The old gentlemen would get up on the platform and talk about the Battle of Vicksburg, or some other battle, and we would parade out to the village cemetery to lay bouquets of lilacs on the graves of the departed soldiers. The Civil War fascinated us.

Then, a great many years later, after I'd spent time in the newspaper business and another ten years in government service, I decided that I wanted to have my say about the war that interested me so much and I started writing books about it. It never entered my head, at the time, that I was writing history. I just wanted to write specifically about the Army of the Potomac. Strangely enough, my first book started out to be a novel. I figured that if I were going to write about the Civil War it would have to be in a novel, because I didn't know enough to write anything else. When I got halfway through I realized that it was a perfectly terrible novel. Whatever I might be, I was not a budding novelist, and I had just sense enough to throw the whole thing away and start again. I thought, "I'm just going to write about this Army," and I did; eventually, the book got published. I wrote another, and another to follow that, and the first thing I knew I was writing Civil War history. But at the start I had no idea of becoming a historian. In fact, I'm still not quite sure that I have.

N.   Yet now you are firmly regarded as our official Civil War historian.

■ *Catton:*   It's odd, because it started just as I described. I simply began writing about something that interested me very much. I really did, however, become a student of the Civil War, not just a devoted amateur, because I found that the more I learned about it the more there was to learn. Thus I've spent a great deal of my time during the past ten years in libraries and museums, reading letters and diaries and old manuscripts to find out, as much as I could, what the war was like to the men who were actually in it.

I've always been more interested in the impact of the war on the ordinary soldier than absorbed in matters of strategy or tactics. I can't pretend to be a military expert of any kind. I do think that I have learned a great deal about the ordinary soldier who fought in the Civil War—what life was like for him, what he had on his mind, what he got to eat, how he had to sleep, what sort of medical care he received. I think everything I've done has simply grown out of that interest in the ordinary man.

N.   In writing about the Civil War, what do you consider your obligation to the subject matter you deal with and to the public for whom you're writing?

■ *Catton:*   It seems to me that my obligation all along has been the same obligation a newspaper reporter has—to find out exactly what happened, as completely as I possibly could, to tell the story without interjecting my ideas, and to give as good a picture of every situation as I could to people who weren't there and who might only know about it through what I tell them.

Perhaps the historian's job is the reporter's job. He has to be guided by facts as he finds them. He can't hope to find all of the facts. There will always be areas where his knowledge is incomplete, but he dare not launch out with a preconceived idea. He must start with a thirst for facts, a desire to know what it was really like and what actually happened, then he must tell his story in as unvarnished a way as he can.

His obligation to the public grows out of this. They expect him to provide them with a straight story, and this is what he must do.

N.   Then how do you feel about the historical novel, and the fictional dramatization of a historical sequence of events, that has become so popular in recent decades?

■ *Catton:* Well, since I started in this direction myself—before I discovered that I was no good at it—I must have thought the fictional approach admirable. My attitude, however, has changed, perhaps because it's something I can't do. Now it seems to me much better to treat history as straight nonfiction. I will admit that some of the finest glimpses of the past are obtained through historical novels that are good. Kenneth Roberts' books on the Revolution tell us a great deal more than we're apt to get from straight history about what disturbed and motivated and moved people at that time. As to the Civil War, Stephen Vincent Benet's *John Brown's Body* (poetry, but essentially a historical novel) is the most enlightening single book on the Civil War that has been written.

If it's done right I think that historical fiction can be useful and valuable. The trouble is, it isn't too often done very well and becomes next to useless. History is usually strong enough to stand on its own feet, you know.

N.   You spoke about the necessity for detachment. Have you ever become personally moved or involved in the issues or in specific incidents related to the Civil War?

■ *Catton:* I suppose you can't carry detachment too far. You do get emotionally involved, sometimes with individuals. For instance, you will get a set of letters written by a soldier. From day to day he is writing home to his folks, telling them what he's been up to, and you get to know and like him. Then, finally, there's the letter from his company commander saying, "Poor Joe stopped a bullet yesterday and we buried him on the battlefield and we're sorry he's gone." You feel a sense of personal loss when you read something like this, a far more personal loss than you feel through exploring the trials and tribulations of some general.

N.   Yet, as I recall, McClellan made you furious.

■ *Catton:* I'm afraid that McClellan does irritate me, and I started out as an admirer. As a matter of fact, my first book tries to show how this man managed to obtain and hold the admiration of the private soldiers who served under him. I thought he would prove to be a great man, but the more I learned about him the less I liked him.

On the other hand, a man like Grant—whom I approached with no prejudices whatever—came to fascinate me very much. But a writer is bound to run into this sort of thing, despite his insistence upon detachment.

If you're writing about a character you don't like, you can't permit your own feelings to come through—the reader isn't interested in your sentiments, he's interested in what the man was really like, and it's up to you to give a clear, fair, accurate picture.

You're bound to feel indignant about things that happened, too—take Andersonville. It was a horrible place, and you're bound to be upset by what happened there, with thirty thousand men confined in a sweltering camp where ten thousand of them died. But then you begin to look into other prison camps, both in the North and in the South, and you discover that they were all just about as bad; Andersonville may have been the worst, but only by a hair. Neither the North nor the South knew how to run prison camps.

I guess you get angry at war itself, rather than at individuals who might seem responsible for things that happened or the things themselves.

N.   Do you feel that in the general pattern of American education we neglected the Civil War until the Centennial came up?

■ *Catton:*   Actually, I don't think we neglected it. An enormous amount of material about the Civil War has been printed, starting before the war was ended and continuing to the present. We had a big gap that began at the time of the First World War. For twenty or thirty years little about the Civil War was published, though a few excellent things did come out. Freeman wrote his great biography of Lee in the early 1930's. Sandburg did his *Lincoln*. A spectacular historical novel, *Gone With The Wind*, came in the late 1930's, and Lloyd Lewis started his work, particularly on Sherman, at that time. Yet in general the Civil War did not get a great deal of attention.

I rather imagine that the First World War and the problems that grew out of it—the rise to prosperity, the disturbing international scene, then the Depression—took our minds off the Civil War. When my first book was finished, at the end of 1949, it was very difficult to find a publisher because they all said, "Oh, we just can't sell books on the Civil War; it's not a live subject any more."

The revival of interest belongs to the past fifteen years. I don't know just why that revival took place. I sometimes think that after the Second World War most of us were confused and unhappy. We didn't like the looks of the world situation, we didn't like some of the things that were happening in our own country, and I think a great many people subconsciously felt that we should look back into our own past to see if we could learn how to get out of the fix we were in, to see whether we'd ever gotten into so much trouble before.

Actually, interest in all phases of American history has picked up during the past fifteen years. Our magazine, *American Heritage,* is a testament to that. We started it in 1954, and I don't think that it would have been successful if it had been launched ten or fifteen years earlier. It's strictly a magazine on American history, addressed not to the professional historian but to the lay reader. Coming up in the early 1950's it seemed to strike a popular desire to know more about the American past—perhaps in the hope that we would learn a lesson or two by studying this past.

N.   Would you describe your work with *American Heritage?*

■ *Catton:*   Right now I'm Senior Editor. I'm sort of a Bernard Baruch—an elder statesman. I don't concern myself as much as I once did with the mechanics of getting the magazine out—handling copy, planning layout, writing heads, and so on. I've tried to divest myself of the daily routine to take a longer view. I don't know how I'd describe my job. I suppose it consists mostly of trying to help maintain a solid, interesting, and factually accurate magazine.

N.   To turn to the realm of theory—if you were to give advice to the talented young writer interested in nonfiction or journalism, what would that advice be?

■ *Catton:*   The first part of any advice I'd give would be to "Devote yourself to what interests you—really interests you—most." In other words, pick a field that you really want to study and write about. Then prepare yourself as well as you possibly can by learning all there is to learn about that field and proceed to write as clearly as the Lord will let you. Writing is not easy—it's a great deal of hard work. You write, then you go over it again and again, not only to polish style but to make sure that ideas are made clear.

It's easy enough to describe anything—a political campaign or a battle or a love affair—if you have unlimited space. But you never have unlimited space, so the trick is to make one word do the work of three. This takes practice, intense practice, and if you work hard enough you find that style takes care of itself. If you always try to clarify your subject, if you keep your preconceived notions out of your writing, and consider that you've got to communicate with a public that will dismiss you if you are inaccurate or deal in half-truths or in prejudices, you should succeed.

N. If you were to look at the creative arts in America today, particularly the written word, what would you find noteworthy, on one hand, and regrettable, on the other?

■ *Catton:* I won't answer this directly because I'm somewhat limited in what I read and see.

The quality I look for in any kind of writing—fiction, history, poetry, whatever—is that of complete sincerity and earnestness. The writer must have something he wants to communicate. He must have something on his mind. He must be dedicated to the idea of expressing himself as clearly and as completely as he can.

If he is simply writing to take advantage of some popular fad— if he's writing from cleverness rather than from depth—I don't think he is going to produce anything of consequence. He has to believe in what he is doing. He has to believe that it's the most important thing in the world, and approach it in that spirit.

In the field of fiction I don't pretend to any authority or opinion because I've read so little of it over the past few years. One thing I do notice popping up, and this I deplore, is the "once-over-lightly" person; the writer who spots a popular subject, a fad, a very current interest, and hurries into it—touches it superficially—and tries to get out with something on the subject before someone else mines the field. This seems to happen far too often.

N. I'd like to return to the Civil War, to one aspect of it which has interested me for some time. Have you discovered, as your research digs deeper, any general currents or specific incidents which have disturbed your original conception of the war?

■ *Catton:* That's a hard question to answer. The main outlines of Civil War history have been clear for some time. I don't think there were any great discoveries to be made, any disclosures that could change the general idea of what happened and why it happened.

But what you do find, by digging more and more deeply into the Civil War, is a growing awareness of how little you really know. A dozen years ago, when I started writing about the Civil War, I was confident that I knew just about all I needed to know about it. But each year I become more modest and humble because I realize that I've only looked at the visible part of the iceberg.

I don't know that you get any surprises—in some cases you confirm original ideas.

For instance, I don't see how anyone can study the Civil War in depth without coming back to the original conception of Abraham Lincoln as one of the greatest Americans who ever lived. Of course, you find faults; you find that at times he was a scheming politician, that he could be ruthless in his handling of people, that he frequently made mistakes. Yet your appreciation of his true greatness increases rather than diminishes.

The same thing has happened to me in connection with Robert E. Lee. He looked to me, at the beginning, like a postcard hero—too good to be true. Nobody could possibly be that high-minded, brilliant, and capable. Yet the more I find out about him the more I see that he was truly high-minded, brilliant, and capable. He lives up to his advance billing.

This doesn't often happen with great men. Usually your opinion of them goes down as you learn about them, but with Lincoln and Lee this doesn't happen. Then there's Grant, who turns out better than he's traditionally been depicted, and McClellan, who exposes less than met the eye.

But I don't think I've made any surprising discoveries or revamped original ideas substantially. I'm just a little less certain about the Civil War than I was fifteen years ago.

I've had a slight shift of interest. I become more and more interested in what happened in the Western theater of the war, an area that is too often neglected. We think about the war in terms of what happened in Virginia, but I'm coming to feel that the war was settled in the West—the blockade of the Mississippi, the use of gunboats, the way the Federal armies moved down the Mississippi valley and broke the Confederacy in half, then cut it again. While the events in Virginia were more spectacular and killed a great many more young men, they now seem less epic to me. I think that closer attention must be given Grant and Sherman, too.

N.   Earlier in our conversation you mentioned your interest in the ordinary soldier in the Civil War. Could you elaborate on your reasons for this interest?

■ *Catton:* The private soldier in the Civil War was more or less like all American soldiers. He was young, got into a big fuss that hadn't been his responsibility, and did his part pretty well. He was much less sophisticated, of course, than today's young man. He hadn't been around so much, he hadn't heard radio or seen television, and in many cases he hadn't read a daily newspaper very regularly. He had never been very far away from home; he tended to come from a rural background, a close-knit area background.

I think he had more romantic notions when he started off to war —noble purposes, good army life, and all that—and he was disillusioned very rapidly. In some ways I think he had a worse time in the army than the young man does today. His training was much less thorough. In many cases he had practically no training at all. He was shoved into action as soon as he learned to get into his uniform and do "squads right." There are even authenticated cases of soldiers to whom rifles were issued for the first time as they were on their way to battle.

The food was atrocious, or worse. The basic ration was hardtack, salt pork, and coffee. The hardtack was often stale, the pork frequently far from fresh. A great many men on both sides suffered from scurvy, strictly a deficiency disease. They suffered terribly from digestive difficulties due to bad diet. Medical care was poor; doctors at that time knew nothing about germs and very little about infections. It's amazing to learn that anybody who got wounded survived at all. The doctor would use the same knife on one patient after another without washing it.

His leadership, particularly at the company and regimental level, where it counted most, was apt to be very poor; there were no officer training schools. Most company and regimental officers were such simply because they were army politicians or were popular. Over and over you read that some of the brand-new regiments, if they had a West Pointer anywhere in the officer corps, were in luck because he could teach them how to pitch their tents, how to drain the camp, and how to look after themselves so they wouldn't die of pneumonia the first week out. But there weren't too many lucky regiments.

All in all, I think the ordinary Civil War soldier had a heavy load to carry, and the fact that he did as well as he did was a striking tribute to the innate solidity of the ordinary American. Without training, without good discipline, without leadership worth two cents, he made his way through such battles as Antietam, Shiloh, and Gettysburg and performed in a way that would credit soldiers properly trained and led. I think he comes off extremely well.

N.   If we were to look at the Civil War as a whole—the bloody struggle that it was and the bitterness left in its wake—do you think it accomplished anything of a constructive nature?

■ *Catton:*   Yes. I think the war established two things. In the first place, it determined that there would be one country rather than two—that when you lose a presidential election you don't turn to arms, you make the best of it. This was settled once and for all, and I think it was an important point.

In addition, the Civil War did end Negro slavery, which left us with a broader base for American citizenship than we'd ever dreamed of prior to that time. Once the slaves were freed there was little we could do but make full citizens of them. We've denied this citizenship for a century, but we've discovered that the denial doesn't work.

You see, there really isn't any halfway point between the ideals of Abraham Lincoln and those of Adolf Hitler. We can't have second-class citizenship in a democracy. I think that the difficulties we've been having in recent years, both in the South and here in the North, grow not out of the Civil War itself but out of the undischarged responsibility which we acquired in the Civil War. In other words, when we have these difficulties over integration and desegregation, we are not still fighting the Civil War but attempting to discharge the responsibilities the Civil War laid upon us. We haven't done too well at it, but we've got to keep grappling with it until we get it settled. I don't think there's any way out of it. In the end I think we'll resolve the issues and have a much better country than we've ever had before, and the basis for it will be the victory that was won in the Civil War.

War is a terrible, clumsy, unhandy way to settle things, but sometimes it marks a turning point in a nation's destiny. I think our Civil War did that for us.

"I keep telling young writers I meet that if they want the sure road to success . . . write something that will make people laugh."

Bennett Cerf
Interviewed in New York, July, 1963

Bennett Cerf

N.   Bennett Cerf is undoubtedly the best-known publisher in the
United States. Not only is he familiar as president of that successful
giant, Random House, but his keen abilities as raconteur and humorist have attracted a vast television audience, his anthologies have been
best-sellers year after year, and his lecture tours draw crowds that
are automatically and magically turned into Cerf fans.

Mr. Cerf is also the champion of the pun, taking an affirmative
stand in the question as to whether or not the pun is the highest form
of humor. He not only collects them, he invents them. And while
we're relating to humor, the most appropriate question to open this
interview involves the nature of humor and its state: Mr. Cerf, do
you share the opinion of so many that humor is in decline, that
there's a notable lack of it and an even more notable lack of real
humorists?

■ *Cerf:* I wouldn't say there's been a decline in humor, but I do
think there isn't as much of it around simply because our times are
not conducive to the development of humorists. The young man of
today who's in college and would be training his steps in the direction of humorist, is the young man who's concerned with our world
of nuclear bombs and what's going to happen to him when he gets
out of college. The most serious persons I've encountered in years
are the undergraduates. That's where the humor always came from.
So I would say that there are fewer people turning out humor today
at the time when we need it most. I keep telling young writers I
meet that if they want the sure road to success, for heaven's sake
write something that will make people laugh.

N.   In other words we stand a slim chance of reproducing a
Wodehouse or a Thorne Smith, even though we are turning up a
major half-sardonic, half-humorous talent like Jules Feiffer.

■ *Cerf:* The Jules Feiffers and the Mort Sahls and the Walt Kel-
lys and the Shelley Bermans have a note of cynicism, sometimes of
fear that's just beneath the surface. Now, this has been true of lots
of humorists in the past—I think even Mr. E. B. White has always

had a very sad undertone in the humor he's written. James Thurber was often a bit sad and caustic, too. But today I think it's more noticeable than ever—humor has a negative side that's barely hidden, sometimes not even hidden.

N.   We keep hearing, too, that fiction is suffering.

■ *Cerf:* It's not the fault of anybody, it's the times we're living in. Fiction today is having trouble competing with nonfiction. The world around us has become so fabulous, so incredibly exciting, that it's almost impossible to create anything that will rival the news of the day. Because of all this excitement nonfiction outsells fiction in nine cases out of ten, whereas a short time ago it was the other way around.

N.   A thing I'm curious about, Mr. Cerf—between the intense amount of work you do at Random House, your lecture tours, the books you put together, and your television appearances—exactly when do you not work?

■ *Cerf:* I have lots of time to myself. I've always explained, when this question is asked, that everything I do is keyed into everything else. In other words, every job I perform has some relationship to the other parts of my life. Now, the main part of my life is devoted to Random House—to publishing. I'm doing exactly what I've always wanted to do, publishing the best darn books I know how to publish, the best I can get my hands on. The lecturing I do is very often at colleges where (a) I meet the students who are taking advanced writing courses, (b) meet the heads of the English Department who are using our Random House and Modern Library and Vintage books in their classes, and (c) meet the people who are running the college bookstores. It's those people who give me ideas for new titles for our Modern Library and Vintage books.

The television show which is done live on Sunday night—one of my times off—is a pure diversion. I love it—it's lots of fun, brings out all the ham in me. But even when it's valuable because often Arlene or Dorothy will introduce me as Bennett Cerf of Random House, and whenever Random House is mentioned on a show that has that vast listenership it ends up as a free ad. Maybe this is why a great many people in the United States who don't know the name of another publishing firm do know the name of Random House. It's an intangible, but it's valuable, I think.

The books and columns I write are tied up with my life in the literary world. It's the stories I hear from authors and people in the book world that I often use in my columns. So, you see, everything ties up together. The man to me who is really in trouble is the man

D

who takes jobs that are completely disassociated from one another, making him jump from one world to another. I won't allow that for myself.

N. In that direction lies ulcers and heart attacks and sessions with a psychiatrist.

■ *Cerf:* Luckily, I'm born with a nonulcerous disposition. I've always managed to see the best side of life. In fact, I've a partner named Don Klopfer who's been wonderful to have with me all my professional life because he holds me down when I go off on wild fits of optimism. He keeps me at a happy balance.

N. Your frequent contact with students, with the staffs of colleges, must give you a clear idea of what's coming up—of talent on the rise. Could you comment on what you think is forthcoming, and on what the young person interested in writing should be doing to groom himself?

■ *Cerf:* There are some superb writers coming along—and thank heavens, because we need them. So many of our top writers have died off in the last few years—Faulkner, Hemingway, Wolfe, Edna St. Vincent Millay, Willa Cather, Sinclair Lewis, Eugene O'Neill, and so many others. When I went to college these were the great names, the people who led the literary and theatrical fields. Now we've got to replace them, and I think we've a wonderful crop of young writers coming into their own—if they're not a little too cynical, a little too apt to look at the sordid side of life.

N. Is there any advice you'd give them?

■ *Cerf:* I would say—as I said before—that people who can write humor should try to do it. Furthermore, I don't want to sound like a Pollyanna, but I'd like to find more young writers who are writing about the decent people in this world and the nicer things in life. We've got so many who can treat the other side, and I don't think we should neglect it, but we've already got a full quota of writers who can fill us in on juvenile delinquents and squalid surroundings. I like a book on the order of *To Kill a Mockingbird*. The overwhelming success of that book just proves what I'm trying to say— that if you give people a story about decent and attractive and lovable human beings the book will take off.

N. But *To Kill a Mockingbird* had guts—it wasn't all sweetness and light.

■ *Cerf:* But it was about real people—the father in that book, and the kids, made you feel happy that such people existed. I'm talking about a competitor's book, now, so I'm not just plugging a Random House book, but I dare say that *To Kill a Mocking-*

bird was one of the most hopeful signs in the literary world today.

N.   Mr. Cerf, having gone through college nurtured largely on Modern Library books, I'd like to hear about the origin and development of Modern Library and what you've done to bring it up since its founding.

■ *Cerf:* The Modern Library wasn't started by me. It was launched by Horace Liveright and Albert and Charles Boni with the firm named Boni and Liveright. When I was in college I began seeing Modern Library books. At that time they were bound in imitation leather. It was really cloth treated with some kind of castor oil, and though the smell was supposed to have been removed from the bindings, on a hot day the Modern Library warehouse could be smelled five blocks away. I never dreamt I would own the series, though I admired it from the start. When I got out of the School of Journalism, after a brief trip down the path to Wall Street, I got a job with Boni and Liveright. Within two years I managed to beg, borrow, and steal enough money to buy Modern Library.

Then Don Klopfer, who I mentioned before, pitched in with me to launch our own firm. Just the Modern Library. The first thing we did was to throw out those smelly bindings. Then we got Rockwell Kent, who was *the* artist of the day, to redesign the books for us.

N.   Is the running figure—the Modern Library trademark—his?

■ *Cerf:* Yes, he did the running figure. He was also a close friend of ours in those days, and when we decided to launch the new and larger firm he happened to be in our office. I came in saying, "As long as we're going to publish some books at random, why not call it Random House?" And Kent said, "That's a beautiful name, I'll draw you a trademark," and he sat down at my desk and in about seven minutes drew the house that's been the Random House trademark ever since.

N.   A question about a personality: Knowing that you and the late William Faulkner were very close friends, could you define his position in American letters and also describe him as a person?

■ *Cerf:* I would say that Bill Faulkner was one of the three or four finest gentlemen I have ever met. Doing business with him was an unalloyed pleasure. He was a gentle and wonderfully warm man, and it broke my heart when he died.

As far as his standing in the literary community is concerned, I think that William Faulkner, Ernest Hemingway, and John O'Hara are the three biggest names in American literature in the past ten years, maybe even twenty years. I think that John O'Hara is one of the least appreciated writers of our time. His short stories are masterpieces.

N. His short novels are apt to be masterpieces, too.

■ *Cerf:* I think his new book, *Elizabeth Appleton*, is a typical O'Hara novel, and I'm glad to say that it's selling wonderfully well. In fact, it is today number two on the national best-seller list, within two weeks of publication. The only thing ahead of it is Morris L. West's book about the Pope which came out with a spectacular sense of timing that's never been duplicated in publishing history. These two books are runaways.

I think O'Hara belongs in the same league with Faulkner and Hemingway. These are the very top spots.

N. Another general question—what do you think the obligations of the publisher are, both to his writers and to the public as a whole?

■ *Cerf:* The first thing the publisher must do is to be satisfied with the authors on his list. Once you publish a writer you owe it to him to bring out his book as efficiently as you can. We at Random House and the associated firms of Knopf and Pantheon have always tried to make our books look as handsome as possible by putting a little bit extra into the typography and bindings and design. It may not sell extra copies of the book, but it gives both publisher and writer a sense of aesthetic satisfaction. Then, with the authors we publish: We don't always agree with a philosophy, social or political, the writer espouses—some have views we can't agree with—but it doesn't stop us from publishing them if they're good authors. We're very proud to publish Ayn Rand, for example, whose views differ greatly from James Michener, whom we're also proud to publish. In other words, I can't ask authors to write to suit me—I'm asking authors to write the best books they can turn out, and if they give us the proper books it's up to us to publish and promote them in a way that will make the public discover them.

N. In looking back over the successful history of Random House do any particularly dramatic or humorous incidents come to mind?

■ *Cerf:* I could talk about books and publishing all night—it's the most fascinating business in the world.

One or two things do stand out in my memory, and I'll try to trim them to fit on this tape. The first is the day we legalized the publishing of James Joyce's *Ulysses* in the United States. We went to see Joyce at a time when copies of *Ulysses* had to be smuggled into America. At that time the book was published by Sylvia Beach of Shakespeare & Company in Paris, and it was a big, fat book with light blue paper covers. Many tourists came back from Europe with a copy smuggled in the bottom of the trunk, because coming back with *Ulysses* was the thing to do—it was forbidden. Very often books that are forbidden sell ten times as well simply because they're taboo. Censors should remember that when they start hollering about a book, they do the opposite of what they want to do—they increase public interest and consequent sales, often beyond the merits of the book.

At any rate, I visited Joyce in Paris and persuaded him to let me take on the fight to legalize *Ulysses* in America. We signed a contract and paid him an advance with the understanding that if we fought and lost the case he'd keep the advance. This was the first money he'd made from *Ulysses* in America, although thousands of copies had been smuggled in before that. We then came back home, and I persuaded Morris Ernst to take the defense of the case for us. We had the good fortune, plus the good planning, to bring the case up before Judge Wollsey who made the historic decision freeing *Ulysses* for publication in this country. I think this was a landmark in American literary progress. Ever since then, *Ulysses* has been a consistent strong seller on the Random House list. That was an exciting episode.

Another thing that stands out in my mind is the publication of the American College Dictionary. We didn't have the faintest idea of what it would cost, but I came into the office one day and said, "Let's do a dictionary," and on that happy note we proceeded to spend a million dollars—which we didn't happen to have at the time. But we did bring out one of the finest college dictionaries in the business, and it's still a great backlist item for Random House.

N.   How do you feel about the discovery of writers?

■ *Cerf:* Some writers we call "discoveries" can thank their lucky stars that their book came out at the right time, with sales often exceeding merits. But it's exciting to have a new writer burst on the scene. For example, when James Jones' *From Here to Eternity* came out everyone knew that an important writer had made a debut. It was the same with Salinger's *Catcher in the Rye* and Philip Roth's *Goodbye, Columbus*. When that book came on the scene, it was obvious Roth would be big and important. When Truman Capote's *Other Voices, Other Rooms* came along, he was only twenty, with the darndest penchant for getting free publicity I've ever seen. He had a full-page picture in *Life* before a single one of his stories was published in a magazine. Today Capote is one of our truly great writers, and we're proud to have him on our list.

N. He has grown, almost incredibly.

■ *Cerf:* Outside of the new collection, the last Capote novel we published, *Breakfast at Tiffany's*, became a successful movie and had a great deal of charm. But you'll see how very much Capote has grown again as a talent in a new book, the story of a famous murder case in Kansas, which may turn out to be one of the most important nonfiction books ever published in America. This will be ready next year, and titled *In Cold Blood*. A great part of it will appear in *The New Yorker*—they seem to be planning to throw everything out of three or four issues in order to run this incredibly wonderful book.

Capote is the true writer. He works very slowly, and may spend a whole day searching for a particular word. This is in rather sharp contrast, of course, to the incredible output of John O'Hara who writes for five or six hours every day. Both Capote and O'Hara are real writers who simply cannot be dissuaded from their work by movie offers or television offers. They're intent on writing. Too many writers, nowadays, spend their time wandering across the country or around the world, skiing or going on the beach and taking time off for lucrative film or television jobs instead of spending their time developing the sense of purpose and craftsmanship that turns a good writer into a great one. Their literary work suffers an immediate and disastrous decline, both in quality and in quantity. I can't blame them, in many ways, because it's fun to get rich, and it's fun to have fun, but I wonder if they realize how often they assassinate their own prestige.

The young writer coming up can be tragically sidetracked by diversions. There's still an enormous temptation to settle for Hollywood money or television money or advertising money, but the talent seldom grows while they're glittering away at big prices. It takes a person with real guts to withstand these temptations.

What pleases me tremendously is the fact that at Random House we have a great number of splendid young writers under contract. Their books may be hard to sell now, but I think we're betting on the right horses. Within the next five years we'll be coming out with names that will flash across the literary heavens like some of the writers we've just been talking about.

I'm being the eternal optimist, but this is the heart and soul of publishing and the joy of being a publisher.

". . . Simplicity, honesty, clarity, grace. Put down what you want to say to the best of your ability. If it can be a little gay along the way, so much the better."

Ilka Chase
Interviewed in New York, April, 1964

Ilka Chase

N. *Past Imperfect, In Bed We Cry, Always in Vogue, The Carthaginian Rose, Elephants Arrive At Half Past Five*—these are just five of the informative and highly entertaining books written by an author who has won equal fame as an actress: Ilka Chase. Because she has acted, written, and traveled with an intensity that sometimes seems to wrap three lives into one, I'd like to begin the interview by asking her where she was born, reared, and educated.

■ *Chase:* I would say that I'm unique in only one respect: I live two blocks from where I was born in New York City and I don't think many people can say that. I was born on East 59th St. and I live on East 57th. I've made a big loop of course; I've lived in Hollywood, I've lived in Europe, but I've always come back to New York.

As far as my education was concerned I should say that my schooling, while expensive, was sketchy. My husband sometimes says there are gaps in my education. He's right, there *are* gaps. My parents were divorced when I was very young and even when they were together they both worked. After the divorce, my mother went on with her job. She spent a lifetime at *Vogue* and was editor-in-chief of the magazine for thirty-eight years and sent me off to boarding school. I was about five at the time—that may seem a bit young, it did to me, but mother did it because she couldn't stay home and she couldn't afford a starchy English nanny or a dictatorial Fraulein.

I went to a convent in New York although none of my family has ever been Catholic nor am I myself. My mother's background was Quaker and my father was from New England, and his relationship with God was a personal one. They got on without interpreters. I was sent to a convent because only the nuns would take a child as young as I was then. It was the order of The Holy Child Jesus. Poor darlings, I'm afraid they were gypped. I expect they hoped to convert me. That part didn't work out, but they were wonderfully sweet and kind and I loved them dearly.

By the way, I learned to play pool in the convent. That was because the order owned a house in the country that had been given to them by Thomas Fortune Ryan, the financier, and it had a pool room in it, and the sisters didn't see any reason to convert it into anything else and we all used to have grand times playing. Mother Mary Agnes was a whiz.

When I grew a little older I left the nuns and went to other boarding schools, and when I was sixteen my mother gave me the choice of college—always supposing I could pass the entrance exams—or of going to school in France. Well, college just seemed to be boarding school all over again, but all my life, ever since I was a small child, I had had a passion for Europe. I can't explain it any more than I can explain why I wanted to act ever since I was little. Those desires are born in us but anyway, feeling as I did, I leaped at the chance to go to France.

I went to three French schools actually—all of them near Paris—and I learned to speak French the easy way by hearing it all around me and going to the theater and the opera and attending lectures in museums. My love affair with France began at that time and lasts till this day. Like most love affairs it isn't always smooth sailing, but to me France is an enchanting land.

My husband prefers Italy and it's true the Italians are far more tolerant of one's attempts to speak their language. The French become deliberately obtuse and behave as if one had insulted their mothers as well as their mother tongue if every accent and trilling R isn't in place. Also, when they say you don't seem at all like an American they consider they're paying you a compliment. I know all that about them, and I realize it infuriates many people, but it makes me laugh and frequently they are courteous and almost always intelligent and they have grace. Nor do I think them as money-mad as some do. They are demons about closing their shops for the lunch hour—a long one—and the month of August is sacred to vacation, and whether they are losing money or not interests them not at all. They love it all right but they have other values too.

Well, anyway, after two years in France, I came home. I was eighteen and mother felt I should make a debut the way other girls of my age were doing. I did but it wasn't a very happy time for me. Just when I would have been making friends and above all getting to know boys I had been out of the country. I often felt like a wall-flower and was very sorry for myself. My other problem was that I always liked older men better than boys of my own age. Now of course I find those callow youths quite charming.

But even when the "debutanting" wasn't too bad, the only thing I really wanted to do was act so when I finally did get started in the theater I thought it was heaven. Some of my experiences I now realize were on the scruffy side but I was learning something about the job I loved best.

N.   In your opinion is a formal education necessary to a success in the theater?

■ *Chase:* Education is vital, of course, and today in most professions and businesses any young person does better with a college background because of the keen competition, but in the art world I should say that talent, skill, determination and, of course, training in your own particular field are more important than a college degree. You may have graduated *summa cum laude* but if you can't develop a sense of timing you'll never make a good comedian, and if you haven't got a sense of form and color you probably won't paint a very good picture.

Curiously enough my own mother, who was an extremely successful career woman, had only an elementary education. She attended a country school as a girl and that was it but she had a mind and unswerving loyalty and a passion for her job. Also she was of her time. I doubt that a young girl today with no more education than mother had when she started would have the same opportunity.

N.   You've spoken of your love for the theater and acting. Before we turn to writing could you discuss the roles you've most enjoyed?

■ *Chase:* I've never played a role on Broadway I was really crazy about. In summer stock, yes, because I've played masses of the good parts but hardly anything I've ever liked on Broadway. Two shows I had fun in were musicals, *Revenge With Music,* and a revue, *Keep Off The Grass.* This may sound rather strange because I can't sing a note but the rest of the cast took care of that. I just had to act.

The biggest success I was ever in was *The Women* by Claire Booth Luce. We ran a year and a half. I thought my part, Sylvia Fowler, was a real monster. She was everything I dislike, catty, shallow, self-centered, totally without compassion. A dreadful woman yet funny because the framework of the play was comedic, if acid. I thought all that when I first read the script but I wanted to play the part because I was convinced the show would be a smash. It was one of the few times I was right. Of course, if a part is meaty an actress is bound to enjoy it to some extent even if the character is a horror. Take *The Little Foxes,* for instance, or *Who's*

Afraid of Virginia Woolf? And I'm sure Judith Anderson revels in *Medea.* Nobody says with a fond smile, "Look at that dear girl devouring her children," but it's a great role and Dame Judith is superb in it.

Still, despite the fact that I've only occasionally played a woman I warmed to personally, I do love to act and if anyone came up to me right now and said, "Here's a good script with a good part for you," I'd jump at the chance. As it happens I've recently finished writing a play myself. Whether I've pulled it off and whether I'll get it produced I don't know but I think it has something to say, Lord knows it's timely and only slightly more controversial than *The Deputy.*

N.   Is it a comedy or a drama?

■ *Chase:* Something of both. You know there did used to be a form called comedy-drama and that's what this is. To me it's a satisfactory form because it's lifelike. No one laughs all the time or weeps all the time. Life is a stew, a potpourri if you like—rough and smooth, funny and sad, depressing and occasionally, very rarely, exalted. I don't mean to imply that I've mastered all that—I haven't of course—but I've tried to be honest and I think with good actors the play could be engrossing to an audience.

N.   Is there a part for you in it?

■ *Chase:* If an actress sits down to write a play, it's unlikely that she won't think of a part for herself. My part is a good one but the play is in no sense a star vehicle. There are eight characters and they are all important.

N.   How do you regard the current theater in general?

■ *Chase:* I think it's doing reasonably well. It seems to me to have health, vitality. Oh, we've had resounding flops, of course, but they're perennial, and we've also had plays and musicals of quality and great variety in the last few seasons. I don't know why people moan over the theater so. The good, the outstanding, is the exception in any field. The mediocre and the poor are never with us. But *A Man For All Seasons, Who's Afraid of Virginia Woolf?, Beyond the Fringe, Dad Poor Dad, Dylan,* those two zany delights, *Barefoot in the Park* and *Any Wednesday;* a while back *A Taste Of Honey, Becket*—those are just the ones that pop into my mind, oh yes, and of course, the incomparable *My Fair Lady;* for my money they're top flight theater. And I think theatergoers deserve a pat on the back too. Some of those plays, notably *Virginia Woolf,* require real stamina on the part of the audience. I think for the most part the American theatergoer is game, willing to accept the new and controversial, willing to give it a whirl, so to speak.

N. What's your reaction to the Lincoln Repertory Theater?

■ *Chase:* It's got a long way to go. But we all have to creep before we can walk and at least it's a beginning. The one thing that does disturb me about it is that it seems to have a sanctimonious, pretentious air, a lack of humor that's unfortunate. If you compare it to the Old Vic or Jean Louis Barrault's company, it's a pretty poor relation but it is after all a very young relation. Let's give it time. Personally I prefer the APA, the Association of Producing Artists. They seem to be having a lot more fun and they're equally dedicated. Ellis Rabb is a splendid young director.

N. Do you think the theater has a duty to uphold moral standards?

■ *Chase:* I certainly do not. To begin with whose morals are under discussion? I am unalterably opposed to censorship of any kind in any part. Occasionally something I may consider dirty or degrading gets public presentation. The actual harm it does is highly questionable and usually transitory, but censorship can lead to real trouble. To my way of thinking the only test to which a play should ever be submitted is extremely simple. Is it interesting? When you are sitting in the theater are you amused or thrilled, fascinated or moved or frightened? On rare occasions inspired? If you are you've got your money's worth and that play has admirably fulfilled its duty.

Mind you, I am not unaware of the very real problem posed by television when a cataract of violence and crime and stupefying vulgarity comes pouring into your living room to be witnessed by children and young people, but even then I do not think that government or church or self-appointed censors are the people to stem the tide. If networks and stations themselves have no taste or shame, and obviously they haven't, then it is up to parents to exert control over their children's viewing habits. People say that's very hard to do and people are right. Bringing up children so that they develop into self-sufficient, happy, useful individuals is hard work and men and women should be willing and, let us hope, prepared to tackle the job or else not bring children into the world.

Also I think the citizenry as a whole should demand an educational system that makes sound values, fine achievements in every field of living so interesting to young people that they will turn of their own accord from trash and sensationalism. If that happened, the television people would see the light in an instantaneous blinding flash. If the money stopped, so would the garbage.

N.   Do you think there's much hope of that?

■ *Chase:*   No.

N.   Suppose we move on to books for a bit. Did you have a burning urge to write, just as you had to act and travel?

■ *Chase:*   No. Some years ago Ken McCormick, who is now the editor-in-chief of Doubleday and who was in the firm at that time also, came to me (I had a radio program, "Luncheon At the Waldorf." In its day and way it was successful. I did interviews with people and held forth on any topic I wanted to and discussed parties or the theater or whatever) and Mr. McCormick said to me, "So you write the show yourself?" and I said yes I did—except for the answers of the people being interviewed naturally, and he said, "Has it ever occurred to you to write a book? Maybe an autobiography?" Well it just happened that two or three other publishers had the same idea so I was rather feeling my oats and I said grandly, "Oh other publishers are after me too." And he said, "But we'll give you an advance." I thought to myself, "he's crazy," but I thought I'd be crazy not to take it so that's how I came to write a book. Filthy lucre. No burning urge, no message that wouldn't be denied, just money. It was money that made me finish it too whenever I began to run down. In those days I didn't realize that an advance is the publisher's gamble. The author doesn't have to pay it back and the publisher hopes to heaven he'll recoup on the sale of the book. I felt if I didn't finish the job in honesty I should give the money back, and I didn't want to do that. Also I found I was having fun. More than I do now when I'm working on a book. I knew less. As it turned out I had beginner's luck. *Past Imperfect* was an autobiography and it sold well. Then I got an idea for a play, but no producer had his tongue hanging out waiting for a script from me, but Doubleday did want to follow up *Past Imperfect* with another book, so I turned my play idea into a novel, *In Bed We Cry*. That went over very well indeed but, there again, I was lucky because it was during the war and oddly enough the book business was booming.

N.   Have you noticed that recently a good many people are writing books who aren't writers by profession?

■ *Chase:*   Lord, yes. Of course I suppose I wasn't either when I started, but it's true that nowadays there does seem to be a strong tendency on the part of publishers to commission books from people who have achieved success or at least some kind of celebrityship in fields other than writing. If you're a military man or a politician, an actor or the divorced wife of an actor—provided he's well enough known and the divorce was notorious enough—why, the chances are an editor will come knocking at your door, check in hand. Once the first salvo has been fired, however, it gets more involved. Somewhere along the line hard work has got to set in. I can't speak for other writers; maybe they wait for the mood to strike them, or the Muse alights on their brow like a pigeon, but for myself, the only way I know how to do it is to put a blank sheet of yellow paper in the typewriter, apply the seat of the pants to the seat of the chair and go ahead. And never mind the weather or the time or the mood or the state of health.

N.   How would you define your objectives as a writer? I know this is complicated because you've written autobiography, fiction, and travel. You've covered a wide range.

■ *Chase:* Well, perhaps I have, but as far as my objective goes the same one holds for any kind of writing. The older I grow, the more I write, the more I strive for simplicity, clarity, and precision. However, I think anyone who is recounting something in a book— I'm speaking now of nonfiction—if you're relating something that's happened you're sometimes faced with a problem. I think as a matter of fact I spoke of it in *Past Imperfect* because that's when I was first confronted with it. Should you tell *exactly* what happened or should you make it interesting? Sometimes by a tiny omission, a wee addition, you can add a fillip and a flourish to what might in actuality have been on the drab side. It is in moments like these that an author and his conscience are alone in a quiet room wrestling it out to the ultimate throw. Who comes up on the side of the angels? Speaking for myself, within what I like to think of as a framework of decency, I've got my conscience pretty well cowed.

On the whole, I'm a big truth addict but in the circumstances we're talking about I think a teensy weensy manipulation of fact is permissible if it's going to make the story more vivid to the reader. If it gives him more fun, go ahead, gussy it up a bit. However, if fact and objectivity are in play, such shenanigans are the blackest of crimes. For a newspaper reporter or a historian, invention or shifting of emphasis is inadmissible. In pursuing those professions one must be scrupulous since, being human, with the best will in the world, one is bound to make mistakes and errors of judgment, but one is duty bound not to do so deliberately. Also, of course, not only is truth stranger than fiction, it is often more engrossing. It pays well, too.

Newspaper publishers are usually quite rich—and look at all the "As Told To" books . . . "The Story of My Life" . . . sales are brisk. Content is vital but style runs it neck and neck. A fresh turn of phrase, an unexpected word, humor, compassion, irony, the author's own quality and observation brought to bear on a story; the sorriest or most threadbare of truths appear in new and evocative garb. For example, I have only recently read John Steinbeck's *Travels With Charley*. I'm ashamed of myself for getting to it so late but what a heart-warming book that is and, despite all the states he passed through and all the people he met, he and his poodle were by far the most interesting characters. I'll probably be tarred and feathered for saying this, but if you're traveling through the United States you have to brace yourself for a good deal of tedium. I'm not talking about our superb natural features, the Grand Canyon, The Great Smokies, Yosemite, some of the fabulous private gardens that are occasionally opened to the public, but there are a good many miles of nothingness too. Outside of the geographical marvels there is an all-pervading sameness. The same scrofulous housing developments spreading like cancer over the face of the land. The houses are woundingly ugly, jerry-built, and totally lacking in privacy. Where once there were potato fields and stands of corn, we now have cement parking lots. Forests, of course, have long since been razed to make room for skyscrapers and city slums. Ponds have been filled in, rivers polluted, fish and birds are being destroyed by the millions because of pesticides, and expressways and superhighways, where hundreds of people are killed every year, band and bar the scarred countryside.

I've traveled a good deal over my native land in the course of lecture tours, fashion show commentaries, road tours with plays, and I assure you it is tragic. Furthermore, it's often very difficult to differentiate one city from another. They have no characters. Food is the same every place. Deplorable. I'm not talking about dining in private houses where one may be served delicious and memorable and civilized meals, but our average restaurants and hotel dining rooms are pretty mediocre. New Orleans, even San Francisco are to a considerable extent coasting on their old reputations rather than on their present actual fare.

I know the government wants to do all it can to persuade foreigners to travel through the United States but, frankly, I shall be surprised if there is any great mass movement in this direction. There might be an influx of people coming here to live—on a much smaller scale something like the mass immigrations of the last century—but I doubt that because working conditions and pay all over Europe are getting to be pretty good and look at Japan, booming. If they don't come here for jobs I certainly can't think many of them are going to come for pleasure.

To begin with, our high standard of living means that our prices are terribly high. To be sure they are in France too and that's one reason the French won't travel. It costs them so much to live at home they haven't anything left over. Another reason they won't travel is because they think they have the most beautiful country in the world and what can you offer them that's better? They're not far wrong. Italy is pretty lovely too, and so are Greece and England and Scandinavia, and they've got those marvelous ancient buildings.

One thing of course that Europeans and Asians might come to look at is the magnificent European and Asian art that fills our museums, but I suppose they figure they've got plenty of that at home too. Good heavens, why don't you stop me? I've wandered as far afield from your original question about my objectives as a writer as though I'd actually toured the U.S.A.

N.   That's all right. What are the objectives?

■ *Chase:* As I've said. Simplicity, honesty, clarity, grace. Put down what you want to say to the best of your ability. If it can be a little gay along the way, so much the better.

"You want a sense of reality in what you're writing. It's terribly easy to deceive yourself, you know. . . . But 'have I said it' true. . . ?' "

John Ciardi
Interviewed in New York, March, 1964

John Ciardi

N.   John Ciardi belongs to an unusually large audience not only
by virtue of his immense and pleasing talent, but also because of
his unusually widespread theater of operations. He is Poetry Editor of *The Saturday Review*. He is an instructor and a lecturer.
He has recorded records for children, published verse for children,
and a greater quantity of verse for adults. He is an essayist. His
principal role is, however, that of poet; and in this interview we'll
use this stand as the springboard for all he discusses and assays.

In talking to Mr. Ciardi I would like to plunge first into the
facts of life, where he was born, reared, and educated, and when
his interest in poetry arose.

■ *Ciardi:* I was born in Boston in 1916 and when I was about
three years old my family moved to Medford, Massachusetts,
which was then a somewhat rural town about seven miles out of
Boston—it's now a rather dreary row of dormitory boxes that could
be called a bedroom town. I was graduated from Medford High
School, then went to Bates College in Lewistown, Maine, for three
semesters. I ran into various difficulties up there—some to do with
emotions, some with cash—so I transferred to Tufts, which is in my
back yard, and was graduated in 1938. After this I went to the
University of Michigan to take my master's. I started in on my
doctorate, but got a job, then got a book published, and never went
back for it.

As closely as I can remember, I've always fooled around with
one kind of writing or another. Things that would get stuck up
on the classroom bulletin board when I was in third grade, stuff
like that, but I never took writing seriously until I got to Tufts
and ran into John Holmes, certainly the greatest teacher I've met.
He was a fine poet, and he seemed to possess, as a person, all the
things I was hungry for. There were a lot of excellent men on the
faculty of Tufts who could talk about the history of ideas and
source works, and all the attendant disciplines, but Holmes knew
the insides of a poem; he knew the management of it. He was not

an art historian; he was a painter, that was the difference. I worked with him, and then, on his recommendation, went out to the University of Michigan to compete in the Hopwood Awards. Avery Hopwood, as you know, made a fantastic amount of money writing Broadway farces back in the twenties, the *Charlie's Aunt* sort of thing, and when he died he willed a great amount to the University of Michigan for annual awards in various kinds of writing.

Luckily, I won, because during the course of the year I got myself deeply in debt. I had no money, but in the brashness of youth assumed I would win a Hopwood Award. Thank God I did, because a large share of it was pre-spent.

N. You were first published while you were still a student, weren't you?

■ *Ciardi:* Actually, it went by stages. The manuscript I submitted for the Hopwood was drastically revised before it appeared. The substance of my first book, *Homeward to America*, which Henry Holt published in 1940, should be called the signal effort. In 1942 I signed up with the Army and wrote some poems while I was overseas. They were war poems, mostly, and they were collected in 1947 by Atlantic-Little, Brown and titled *Other Skies*. After the war I worked for Twayne Publishers, adding an anthology list and a little personal nepotism by doing a book in 1949, one in 1950, another in 1951. There may even have been one in 1952—I'm not sure.

Then I went to England, followed that with a year at the American Academy in Rome. My *Inferno* translation came out in 1954, but a year earlier I started teaching at Harvard, then went down to Rutgers. By an odd coincidence I had sold my *Inferno* to Mentor Books and they shopped around for a hardcover publisher, ending up with Rutgers Press. I was not at Rutgers when they accepted it. One department accepted the book, another department accepted me, and they've been publishing my senile poetry ever since. My juvenile poetry has gone various places.

N. In looking back at all the work you've done, is it possible to pick any particular poem or a collection as your own favorite?

■ *Ciardi:* I don't know how that could be done. As a matter of fact, not long ago Joseph Langland and Paul Engle brought out an anthology called *Poet's Choice*, and they asked contributors to pick out the poem they liked best. I thought this would be intriguing to do, so I went through my poems. But how do you decide? It's like trying to pick a child. I hope some are better than others; I like to think some will stick around. It's damned hard, so I finally said something evasive about poems I might have picked and chose a different one.

Another thing—Harcourt, Brace is doing an anthology, and they wanted me to choose poems for it and I told them I wouldn't—I wanted to see what they would pick. They surprised me. They picked a poem I never would have selected, and I read it, and I thought, "Yeah, I'm glad they chose it." It's fun to see what someone else will choose. Maybe another person has better judgment.

But I can refute that statement, too. I've got a book of poems on the press. I sent the manuscript to a very good friend, whose criticisms I generally value, and he decided it was a disaster. He didn't like it. I walked the floor with that damned manuscript for three weeks, just reading it to myself, trying to decide whether I should or should not take his advice, and finally I decided that it was not my poems he disliked—it was my lousy character. Every one of the poems expressed my character.

N.   You mentioned your translation of Dante's *Inferno* which was a major project. How did you get caught up in it?

■ *Ciardi:*   To begin with, I could not speak Dante's Italian. I could hardly read it, but the text had been very carefully annotated, and all one really needs is a knowledge of contemporary Italian, a few guides, and a text that is annotated for an Italian university student to explain the shifts and the phrasing. You see, at times Dante was simply using fallen Latin. (He uses "caso" for the past participle of "cabuso," or "fallen," but in contemporary Italian "caso" means "case" and "caduto" means fallen. You wouldn't know it unless somebody annotated it for you.) But the poem can teach you a language. I got into snarls, I still get into snarls, but there were and are notes to straighten me out.

N.   To come closer to the office we're sitting in—how do you describe your work with *The Saturday Review?*

■ *Ciardi:*   I wish there were a reasonable explanation. Physically, what I do is to come in on the average of one day a week. I have a secretary who sorts things for me, and it takes a certain amount of time to run through the submitted poems. There are usually a pile of them that have come in during the week, but they're rather lowgrade, so it doesn't take long to reduce a three-foot stack to a two-inch stack. But the two-inch stack takes a lot of reading. Usually I slip it into my briefcase and take it home with me.

Then there's the mail to be answered—in my case, to (mostly) be looked at and thrown away. A bit of it is answered, but I use the wastebasket as an assistant to my secretary. The point is this:

I've got a part-time arrangement here, I've a column to write, and if I answered all the mail that came in I'd be at it all week. If I throw away 95 per cent of it I can get back to New Jersey and get my own work done.

N.   As far as the column is concerned, what would you say your objectives are?

■ *Ciardi:*   I don't know—at least, not yet. I haven't particularly tried to formulate it. I want to keep it entirely free-wheeling. I suspect it will strike some pattern sooner or later.

During my first five or six years with *The Saturday Review* I did nothing but critical literary articles. Since I began the column I practically stopped doing those, but frankly, the column is more fun. Every blessed thing you know or see or hear is potential subject matter, and in a sense it's a matter of rediscovering what I, at least, call the "familiar essay"—a neglected and wonderfully usable form.

N.   Which is hardly practiced any more.

■ *Ciardi:*   There are a few doing it. Many who lament the decline of the great essayists seem to forget that one of the great masters, E. B. White, is still functioning. Bernard De Voto wrote what might be called the familiar essay, and Thomas Hornsby Farrell was often brilliant in *The Rocky Mountain Herald.* It's fun to work with—formless, if you want to call it that, yet you can make it do so much.

N.   You mentioned sifting through a great deal of submitted poetry to find some worth considering. How do you find the general level of poetry being written today?

■ *Ciardi:*   There's a terrible sameness about the amateur poetry we get by the ream. Some sweet person somewhere is moved in the spirit, but not moved to language, so she puts down the unenacted language of whatever moves her and sends it in as a poem. Actually, it's an aesthetic disaster. It contains a human feeling, a perception, a reaction, but usually it's a stereotype.

There's just no way of explaining to people who have never heard an orchestra, the difference between an orchestra and an ocarina. So I refuse to engage in correspondence regarding these poems because it would take forever and yield nothing.

Basically, if we get something like five or six hundred poems a week (which is average), it's seldom that we end up with twenty that are worth a quick glance. I'm glad I'm an editor, which means that I can stop reading as soon as I know a poem isn't for us. I'm not a teacher who has to suffer through. When I get to "baby on

my mammy's knee" or "June, spoon, moon," I don't care how
many pages are attached—I stop. Nobody who commits this will
commit a poem.

Yet I don't suppose we'll know for years what's really being
written now. Literary reputations flash and go. Supposing you had
asked, thirty or forty years ago, to name the important writers?
You'd have listed Joseph Hergesheimer, Pearl Buck, James Branch
Cabell, Sinclair Lewis—and come up with a strange list of per-
manences. Edwin Arlington Robinson looked like a major poet
back in those days. But you wouldn't have listed F. Scott Fitzgerald. It takes time to see backward. I don't know what we're writing.
Look over a best-seller list of twenty years past, and see if you can
recognize one name or title, unless, of course, you were involved
specifically with a name or title. The best sellers have a habit of
disappearing.

As far as poetry is concerned, I don't think this is a time for
substantial major poetry on a big scale—yet I know that we can put
together an anthology of half a dozen poems from one, ten from
another, three from another, all contemporary poets, that will equal
any of the Elizabethan miscellanies.

N. If you were to give advice to the young poet what would
it be?

■ *Ciardi:* There isn't any real advice. You can't map a route—
every person has to find his own way. I'd like to give my advice,
if any, to the teachers. They keep encouraging students to express
themselves creatively (as they put it) but all they encourage is
outflow. They never encourage them to discipline. Well, a horse
can express himself, a mule can express himself, but my God—I
once did a piece for the *Saturday Evening Post,* and I find myself
sticking to its title—"The Act of Language." Whatever else a poem
is, it's an act of language, a discreet use of the medium. Language
in a poem is not used in the same way language is used outside of
poems. The words are more demandingly, more searchingly used.
It's as if they were X-rayed and their inner structures were considered in their inner relationships. This is the language plastically
used rather than informationally used, and sometimes it takes time
for a poem to assert itself, sometimes it does so instantly.

Our problem here at *The Saturday Review* is mathematical. We
publish a little over a hundred poems a year. Now, where are we
going to find a hundred great poems a year? I doubt that they're
written in that quantity. Supposing that the seventeenth, eighteenth,
and nineteenth centuries produced poems at the rate of 100 great

ones per year—you'd have to go to college for twenty-five years to become an English major. And *if* a hundred great poems were written during the course of the year, they all wouldn't come to us. We have to publish some stuff that is not the final distillation—sometimes there's a passage, an image, a catch in the poem, that's good enough to overcome a weakness.

Advice? I can only say there's a hell of a lot more to being a poet or a writer than simply "expressing yourself creatively." Somewhere there should be a thought.

N. You mentioned the word "discipline" from the teaching standpoint. Do you think——

■ *Ciardi:* I think poetry and nonpoetry have become confused because of the lack of discipline. The beats have rejected it outwardly—oh, they keep a kind of loose cadence measure. There's a demoniac impulse in poetry; it can go, too. Students, as I watch them, all seem undisciplined. They're all screechers of their feelings rather than shapers of the language.

N. Do you think this is truer of our day than of past eras?

■ *Ciardi:* I don't think so. Perhaps what confuses it is the general confusion that has resulted from semiliteracy. Not long ago a man who was ignorant knew it. Now we have a school system that doesn't educate people, but does succeed in camouflaging their ignorance. It turns them out in a semiliterate state, able to read a newspaper, and assures them that because they can read a newspaper they can understand anything. Everybody is a critic.

N. Can you elaborate on this?

■ *Ciardi:* Let me put it this way. How many people read John Donne in his own time? Basically, only the people who went to the university, which was 1 per cent of the population, if that. Of those, not all were readers of poetry, so you got a fraction of a fraction of 1 per cent as your audience in poetry.

I'm not sure that we do that well. Think of the Lincoln-Douglas debates. Farmers hitched up their buckboards and drove forty miles, drove all day long or even two days, to hear some real speechifying. They knew they couldn't sling the language, they knew they couldn't understand all of it, but they felt joy in hearing masters of the orotund. Take Bryan, the silver-tongued orator. He came out with enormous rhetorical statements that sound terribly funny to us, now, but—well, even my parents respected him. My mother had no education—but mind you, she had an enormous respect for mine.

What I think happens today is that we turn out semiliterates.

They've got a diploma, the diploma says they're educated, and they think they are educated. But if you listen to some of them reason, or see some of them write, or ask what reading they've done, you quickly discover that they're illiterate and ignorant. They may be technically proficient at certain jobs, they may be good salesmen, but they know nothing of their own language or its achievements, and I think this knowledge is one of the true marks of an educated person. They're ignorant about music, about the arts in general, yet they feel free to have opinions about them. They had a course somewhere. They probably got a "C" in the course, but the grade system seems to tell them that "C" stands for "competent."

The savage, you know, is a human being who has not received enough news from the human race. Well, the school system says that these semiliterates *have* received enough news from the human race, but the poor slugs don't know how much they *haven't* received. Now, if they hadn't gone to school they'd know of their ignorance; it would be obvious to them. I'm not even talking about the public school system. The colleges do this. After all, the insistence of a college on education is finally defined by its minimum requirements, and there's no school that doesn't have its minimum requirements set too low. I taught at Harvard for several years after the war. I don't know if they've changed things now, but at that time the minimum requirement was three "C's" and a "D," keep your name out of the newspapers, and you'll get that golden diploma after four dreamless years. Let's put it this way. I don't know of any college where it is impossible to get an education, but you get it by exceeding the minimum requirements and your own drive. You don't get it because the college insists upon it. The college only insists upon its minimum requirements. I'm happy to say that this may be changing because of the pressures of enrollment. I'm hoping, frankly, that this squeeze—Rutgers, for instance, will have to turn down about 4,500 qualified applicants next year—will do something to raise the standards generally.

I can recognize the general argument that it serves the good of the country to have even the dumb ones and the mediocrities exposed to a college education. They're perhaps more socially useful after four years in college, even if they've just dragged along on the bottom, than if they hadn't gone. But the argument never considers what the presence of these democratic slobs does to the standards of the college.

N. What about the technical or professional skills taught?

■ *Ciardi:* I think that our technical education—on many levels, at least—is quite demanding simply because the market imposes its demand. It's our liberal arts education I find myself worrying about because there's no objective measure. A doctor has to go through a lot of physically verifiable checks. He has his internship; he must prove he can accomplish certain things. By the time his first five thousand patients have died we know he may not be a very good doctor.

The liberal arts college has no such yardsticks. Think of the number of courses, the number of combinations of courses, that can be taken in a liberal arts college. It's possible, assuming that two thousand courses are offered, that no two liberal arts students will have exactly the same curriculum. They might have to go to gym, and take a few science courses, but there's no exact measurement of what they've learned or accomplished when diploma-time comes around. At least doctors, dentists, lawyers, etc., can be measured— they're like Wheaties, all going down the same chute and fitting the same package.

N. I'll go from the training period now, to the liberal arts as practiced. In looking at the present cultural scene, what do you find that you most admire? On the other hand, what do you most deplore?

■ *Ciardi:* I suppose it's typical of the age when I admit that I deplore more readily than I admire. I think there's a kind of—well, I won't give it a name since I disagree with it so totally.

In the American theater everybody seems to be damned busy finding out who he really is. This seems almost to be the formula for our theater, and I have a notion that all these seekers really know who they are. It isn't the finding-out that bothers them, it's the knowledge, and they don't like what they've found out, so they reject it and try to find out that they're really something else. Maybe I'm too mechanistic and too materialistic, but I don't think I've got a soul that is going to soar up into the heavens; I think life is an engaging trip with some pleasant interludes, but it comes to nothing, and getting there is *all* the fun. Perhaps my pragmatic view is too little to settle for, and not very dramatic, so all our soulful writers keep seeking their image and their identity. I have a feeling that their images and self-identities are pretty damned apparent; they're just not willing to settle. They've got a chimera complex and want to be something else.

I'm afraid this embraces the current novel, too. Again, this incessant search for identity. Now, I'm not saying that we shouldn't have a search for identity, but suppose you find it and you don't want it? Then you're forced into inventing an identity that you really aren't, then baying at it as though it were hanging up there like the moon. I find myself observing this in so much theater and so much writing. Poets are prey to it, too. I think the thing I deplore most is the general attitude, along with this soul-search, of feeling sorry for themselves—the poets, for example, who brood over the fact that life hasn't made them millionaires. (I'm not talking about the good poets, who have assurance in themselves, but the bad poets.) In particular, I'm thinking of the psychic situation of the person who is ambitious, decides to be a poet, gets himself a job at a university, the advancement is not immediate, the kid's tuitions have popped up, and life is a grind. The material regards are inadequate; he's not free to spend time with his poetry. This is to be regretted, but it's no qualified reason for feeling sorry for himself.

On the positive side, I find poets with a certain solidity and substance. And I don't mean that they're solid, substantial corporation executives. A man like Roethke, a man like Lowell—men who have even flirted with the edge of madness, and gone over it now and then, but have always engaged themselves and made something of it. They've loved the act of making. Roethke found his poems were his way of dancing out of madness. Lowell, I think, found his poems a kind of serenity that brought him back to assurance and a base. It's a dramatic thing to watch. I think there's a certain stability and assurance about Karl Shapiro and Richard Wilbur, and there are others I could mention, Stanley Kunitz, for instance. They're rewarded by their own going, and it's good going. It's talented, it's engaged, and its made. Theres no substitute for talent—a man can be an utter stinker as a person, but if he's got talent, he's set.

N. If you would, I'd like you to read a few of your poems and comment on them—how they happened to be written, perhaps, or what you were driving at.

■ *Ciardi:* You're asking for lies. It's inevitable. I've been asked to do this over and over again, and lies come out.

Let me put it this way. The least a poem can be is an act of skill. An act of skill is one in which you have to do more things at one time than you have time to think about. Riding a bike is an act of skill. If you stop to think of what you're doing at each of the balances, you'd fall off the bike. Then someone would come along and ask you to rationalize what you thought you were doing. Well, you write a poem. And somebody comes along and asks you to rationalize what you thought you were doing. You pick out a theme and you're hung with trying to be consistent with the theme you've chosen. You have to doubt every explanation.

Nobody has worked harder than Valéry, the French poet, in trying to explain how he produced certain poems. He answers with every qualification in the world—touching this and that but ultimately lying. You have to end up lying. You know that you had something in your mind, but you can never get it set straight. In some cases you can remember where you were when you wrote it, and also which form you are talking about. Suppose the thing had gone through fifteen or twenty drafts in fifteen or twenty places. Why did you change it? Actually, you've forgotten most of the changes, and you'll be astonished to find an old worksheet and see what you had in the first place.

You don't know where a poem gets started any more than you know what you say in a conversation. You don't stop to think, "My God, what was the source of that? where did it come from? how did I come to say that?" Somebody says something to you and you say something back. You don't say, "Hey, that was a pretty good remark." (Besides, the good remarks are the ones you think of on the way home.)

I've been flipping through this book trying to find a poem I thought I could say something about, and the fact is that I can't find any. What I believe happens is this: an idea gets going, whatever starts it, and then you're involved in answering what you've started. The form exists in the act of writing it—you're trying to get a balance. This is what I meant by the language we use plastically. I once said to a musician, "You can't write a piece of music backward." He said, "Oh, that's one way of writing it." Maybe it works for music, but you can't write a poem backward. (Somebody might just decide to do it to prove I'm wrong, but I don't think so.)

A simple poem like this, now—it's called "Good Night" and I know I made some changes in it.

An oyster that went to bed X million years ago,
Tucked itself into a sand bottom, yawned, so to speak
and woke a mile high in the Grand Canyon of the Colorado.
If I am not here for breakfast, geologize at will.

This one's kind of a joke. I don't know what started me thinking about oysters and the Grand Canyon. I certainly hadn't meant to put it that way, but having got that much said I found—if I put in a pause and thrust the last line against it—that it came out as a kind of a quip and epigram. (In this case almost an epitaph.) Now, some of my themes are identifiable. I seem to have written a great many poems about my father, all of which are too long to read aloud, partly because I became identified and confused when I was a kid. My father died when I was not quite three. I was the only son in the family. I had three sisters, and I was supposed to bear a special resemblance to my father, and my mother sort of adopted me as a replacement for her husband, and in a way I became my father. It made a theme that comes out in so many ways, so many paths of exploration. I don't really know what I feel about my father except that I think I get closer to him after reading twenty or thirty poems that concern him.

I recall something of a poem I wrote when I was overseas on Saipan—an elegy. I was a gunner on a B-29, and I found myself writing a number of elegies for friends who took off and never came back. Somewhere I got started writing an elegy for myself. I guess it seemed prudent; I'd been writing them for other people and I thought it would be nice if I had one, too, but I couldn't seem to find anybody in the Army I could trust to write it, so I decided to do it myself. I called it "Elegy Just in Case." There was probably some connection with the fact that Jonathan Swift had written an elegy for himself very jokingly. He was in Ireland, and he reports the news of his death reaching the card tables of London, and the great line comes when the lady at the card table says, "The Dean is dead? and what is trumps?" I think I borrowed some of the tone from this, and made it a kind of quippish elegy just in case, and decided I'd better give myself a sort of Viking funeral to do it up right. Vikings used to have a dead dog at their feet when they were sent out to sea on a burning ship, and I thought the colonel would do very nicely for that.

When I first wrote it, it was about six stanzas longer than it is now, and about every two years I found myself cutting a few more stanzas, stripping it down, changing it here and there for one reason or another. You see, you start something, a theme comes to you, and all you have in the theme is a sense of possibility, and then you explore it, and sometimes it works out. You have a feeling that you've used it all up and it comes to rest. Other times it seems to start off well and then boggles and that's it.

So chances are, when you discuss the reasons or the themes or the motives behind a poem, you lie.

N. I'll change the subject to your children's poems, which

you've carried through records as well as several books. What do you think a child gains from the reading of poetry—whether it's a matter of silent reading, or the reading of poetry aloud in home or classroom?

■ *Ciardi:* I think it's one of the finest things that can happen in the home. It's a basically desirable interchange of ideas and interests between parents and children. I don't think there's any such thing as a kid who's not joyous in his engagement of poetry. They're born with a love of poetry. It's a pity to see them lose it as they do—when the school system grinds them down into examination answers, and they begin to get wary of poetry as a form.

Poetry is a joyous thing. Kids have fantastic imaginations, a fantastic readiness to respond to language. It even tickles them into thinking. But they do it for fun—they do it in their games, in their football cheers, in (a debased way) the recordings they buy. I also feel that language is one of the most deeply shaping forces upon any individual. (I can't save my kids from damnation, but I'd like them to go damned with a little language flair.)

Basically, just think back, let anyone think back upon his own life, and ask him what he thinks he would be without language in him, how much of his awareness, his presence, his sense of identity, to quote a dirty phrase, would be lost if he didn't have languages as a medium. The other thing, for what it's worth, and I'm not sure I know, is the fact that there seems to me an enormously high correlation between general intelligence and language skills. This might be because language is the general medium for the test, but basically, I.Q. and vocabulary go very close together. An interesting thing about it, and there might be later findings, but I recall that when I was in school we learned that children of whatever age tend to have their vocabulary by blocs—words of a certain difficulty, then words of a certain conceptual status, so that you can make groups—Groups A, B, C, Q, and so forth. It's likely that if the student has any of the words in Group Q he has them all, and probably none from the next group unless he happens to be a foreign student. Many of the words that are difficult in English might be native to his language and be cognate in English, you see, and upset this balance. For example, every Italian child says antipatico, which is "anti-pathetic." These are nursery words, but if an Italian exchange student comes over here, antipathetic is an easy word for him. Otherwise only English professors use the word, and damned few of them at that.

N. In surveying poetry today, who would you pick out as

the most valuable poets of our time, and what poems would you single out similarly?

■ *Ciardi:* Well, the obvious senior poets are clear enough, you know—Frost, of course. I don't know what time will do to Eliot's reputation, but some of it will be left. I suspect that Wallace Stevens and William Carlos Williams are candidates for the long run. I have a feeling that Carl Sandburg is not: But these are only feelings, and time will prove me right, wrong, or indifferent.

Aside from this very senior lot I think that E. E. Cummings will grow in reputation. I don't see any such growth in store for Hart Crane, who in a real sense was his contemporary. Behind them is a whole generation—Roethke, I suppose, is a senior in that particular age group. Actually, it's partly my own generation—within ten years or so—but as I said earlier, if you'd asked for a list thirty-five years ago the list could have been furnished and it would have been wrong. Whatever happened to Robinson Jeffers and Edwin Arlington Robinson? Now it's the lyric poems of Robinson we remember, not those great dinosaurs of Freudian retellings or the Arthurian legends that took up all that space in the *Times* review section.

Dylan Thomas is certainly an undiminishable poet. I suspect the man who is yet to come into his own is W. H. Auden; I don't see that anything can happen to him except growth.

N. Now, if you were to put yourself in the position of a critic many years hence, how would you like him to look back upon John Ciardi?

■ *Ciardi:* That's a hard one. Let me put it this way. I only hope that my work, or part of my work, could stand the test Emily Dickinson used to ask. She would send in her poems and her question always was, "Have I said it true?" She never said, "Have I said it pretty?" or "Have I said it beautiful?" but "Have I said it true?" I think this is the test. You want a sense of reality in what you're writing. It's terribly easy to deceive yourself, you know. You love all your children. Even when they're blind in one eye you try to make astronauts out of them. You only look at the good eye. But "have I said it true. . . ?"

"Any anthology done without enthusiasm is like a TV dinner, frozen, tasteless, and quickly forgotten. . . . I would like to write with life—life in each sentence."

William Cole
Interviewed in New York, November, 1963

William Cole

N.   In recent years William Cole has become both extremely well-known and highly praised for a number of anthologies. From the popular standpoint, he is one of the few anthologists who manage almost unerringly to please by virtue of choice. From the critical standpoint, he is (again) one of the few whose taste and judgment regarding selection, and "point of order," receives a favorable nod. Perhaps, today, the need for intelligent anthologizing is at a peak. With more material to choose from, and (because of the constant presence of television) less time to read "in total," the public seems to favor digests, excerpts, and anthologies—preselection, in other words.

In starting to talk to Mr. Cole I'd like to ask him where his anthologizing began—and what his motives as an anthologist actually are.

■ *Cole:*   Since I could most appropriately start with a few paragraphs from an article I wrote for *The Library Journal* a few years ago (about what qualities an anthologist should possess) I'll be lazy and quote:

"The first requisite for an anthologist should be a crusading enthusiasm for his subject. He should be a practitioner of literary buttonholing continually exclaiming through the medium of his compilation, 'Hey, take a look at *this* one!' Any anthology done without enthusiasm is like a TV dinner—frozen, tasteless, and quickly forgotten. He should have a large library, scissors, paste, and an abiding conviction that if he likes something, other people will—or should. Where research is concerned he should love his subject so much that he would have been wallowing around in it anyhow, even if there had been no ulterior anthologistic purpose."

This is a good start in defining how I feel about anthologies. But let me just hark back for a second to something you said in your opening remarks which tied me in with "digests, excerpts, and anthologies." I loathe digests; I loathe *The Reader's Digest*. As the man said after seeing himself in that scruffy little magazine,

"In digestion I feel sick." I have on occasion excerpted—I recall Carroll's "The Hunting of the Snark" in a children's anthology—and I still feel vaguely guilty about that, but there simply wasn't room for the whole poem."

N.   How did you first become interested in becoming an anthologist?

■ *Cole:* Strangely enough, I had no idea of ever being one, but I was working at Knopf about twelve years ago, doing publicity and a little editorial work, and I had the idea that somebody should do a collection of the best material from *Punch*—cartoons and prose and poems. I had been reading *Punch* ever since I was in the Army in England, and I cast about for somebody to do it, checked with a few people who had done anthologies, and they simply weren't interested.

Then one evening, lying in bed trying to get to sleep, it came to me with an incandescence Edison never dreamed of, that I could do it myself, by God! So I did.

N.   Where did *you* begin? As far as birth, rearing, education are concerned?

■ *Cole:*   Well, I really wasn't educated. I was born in Staten Island, which is an oddity in itself. That island, a little south of New York City, laughingly referred to as "The Gem of New York Bay," was where I began. I grew up there and in the suburbs of New York and didn't go to college. I was a terrible student—I could only make any sort of grades in things that interested me, and the curriculum didn't offer too much of interest. I'm glad it went that way—it seemed to work. I'm happy doing anthologies, and I'm doing what interests me. I've never done an anthology just for the dough. Each one starts with some enthusiasm all my own.

N.   But you did work, first, in publishing?

■ *Cole:*   Yes. I was in the Army, as everyone my age seems to have been, and then I got a job working at Knopf as a publicity man. I stayed in that field for fifteen years—until a few years ago, in fact, when I launched out on my own doing full-time anthologies and introductions to things and bits of this and the other.

N.   What do you feel the obligation of the anthologist should be toward the material with which he's working?

■ *Cole:*   I feel he should never put something in a book just because his publisher would like it there, or because he thinks the readers of the book expect to see it there. He should suit his own interests and tastes and enthusiasms. It's a very selfish art, if you can call it an art.

E

N. You mentioned his concept of the public—

■ *Cole:* He should never feel a duty toward the public. He should be an enthusiast. He wants to show something, he wants people to see something that gave him pleasure, and here it is. If they don't like what he offers, he misses the boat, of course, and perhaps he fails.

N. To get technical—could you describe the blood, sweat, and tears through which you put an anthology together?

■ *Cole:* Well, let's first count up the twenty-two anthologies I've done so far. About fifteen of them are poetry, mostly for children, though there are quite a few for adults. Obviously *Erotic Poetry* is for adults, as is another big one called *The Fireside Book of Humorous Poetry*.

When I feel an anthology coming on I start in my files. I keep voluminous files of everything—I'm something of a pack rat—I carry things to my nest from everywhere. So I start in these files and isolate everything that might be applicable to this anthology. Say it's *Erotic Poetry*. I go through voluminous files of poetry I've clipped from magazines and newspapers and start with that.

Then I dig into my library at home which contains about a thousand books of poetry. I go through everything from Dannie Abse to Marya Zaturenska. Then I go through the hundreds of other anthologies at hand and mark lightly, in the back of each book, the page numbers where there are poems that might do for my anthology. When I've finished this I go to the public library and look at the complete works of some poets whose works I don't have at home. In fact, in the *Erotic* anthology, I went through the complete poetry stacks of the New York Society Library—a very good library. (It has nothing to do with society, nor have I.) But I went through the entire stacks and looked through every book that I hadn't seen before.

Now, by that time, I have an idea of how much material there's going to be and how far down I have to winnow it. Then I go through and re-read everything, making little check marks next to the ones I know I want typed out. Then I hire a girl to come in in the afternoons and type madly for a couple of weeks. By that time I have twice as much material as I can use, so it becomes a process of winnowing and winnowing some more. I check to see where duplications come in. Then I figure out how the book will be divided.

The anthologist can divide a book chronologically, or alphabetically by author, or he can invent categories. Each way has its advantages—for instance, the alphabetical-by-author is very good for children's books because they can read four or five poems by one author. If they like the author we hope they'll go to the library and take out a whole book and get to know the poet.

In the *Erotic Poetry* I decided that the best way was not to do it alphabetically by author because there are many one-shot authors who've written good erotic poems. Also, the chronological approach didn't seem advisable because I'd end up with about fifteen ballads in thick Scottish dialect in a group, and this is very difficult for the reader to work his way through. Or I would end up with a bunch of folk songs from eighteenth century England, and there's a deadly sameness when they're all stuck together. This is why I did *Erotic Poetry* by categories. A section on "Incitement and Desire" and a section on "Deviations"—seven sections on all the aspects of love, the erotic aspects, that seemed to work out.

Once I have the manuscript in shape what happens next is it goes to the editor at the publishing house, and he promptly calls to say, "Everything is marvelous except that you've got too much material, you've got to cut some more." I'm an easy bleeder, but I know I've got to do it, so I cut some more. Then the big problem of clearing the permissions begins. On some books I've done this myself, from home, but on others I've managed to bludgeon the publisher into writing all these clearance letters to the copyright holders of the various poems. This is a matter of sending out 300 letters and waiting to see what comes back. Often they say, "Okay, pay me so much and you can have it." Other times letters never come back, and I end up checking, checking, checking. Some authors can never be found—they've died, they've disappeared. Then there are those publishers who write and say they want a $100 permission fee for a four-line poem, and you have to call them up to tell them the facts of life. (They're usually delighted to hear them, as most people are.)

Once this is done you sit back and wait for galleys to come through. You correct your galleys, inevitably overlooking a couple of horrifying misprints. Then you wait for the book, and then you wait one hell of a long time before you make any money because the permissions fees go against your royalties, and the royalties, as you know, are on a scale extending from 10 to 15 per cent. Ten per cent of a $5 book is 50 cents, and if your permissions fees run five to seven thousand dollars you have to sell an awful lot of books before you make a buck. But it's worth it.

N. Do you feel—from the standpoint of presenting anthologies—that you spur the reader to read more in a given area?

■ *Cole:* Absolutely. This is the idea—I want them to read the particular poets. Very few people read single volumes of a poet, and I hope that if I present enough of the work of a good poet the reader will go on and look up that slim volume in a library, or better yet, buy it. I'm afraid this doesn't happen as often as I'd like to see it happen, but the dream is a nice one.

N.   A few minutes ago you mentioned misprints. Are there any that stand out in your mind as being particularly absurd or significant?

■ *Cole:* Odd things can happen to a poem on the way to an anthology. I remember a poem by Hilaire Belloc, a very amusing poem called "The Frog," and once, a long time back, an anthologist printing this poem misprinted a line to read "And do not call him names/ as slimy skin, or polly wog,/ or likewise Uncle James." "Uncle" was picked up from that anthology by a second anthologist. (Anthologists don't always go to the original sources, which is the same great mistake historians seem to make.) The misquotation proliferated, ending up in at least five books that I know of, and perhaps more people now associate the frog with "Uncle James" than with "Ugly James."

You must, of course, always check original sources. Yet as I mentioned before, no book shows up without some embarrassing typographical errors. I remember David Daiches, an English poet (critic, really) did a very good light poem about Jane skating with her date, etc., which I ran in the *Fireside Book of Humorous Poetry*. I got an immensely irate letter from him after the book reached his doorstep, saying, heatedly, that the poem had the word "expiate" rather than "expatiate." He said this ruined (1) the meter, (2) the meaning, and (3) his reputation. He was one mad poet, but luckily we had a second printing where we expiated or expatiated the error. I wish I knew, right now, exactly what these words meant.

N.   I'll look them up. To get a bit specific, now, about three of your books in 1963. I'd like to discuss *Erotic Poetry* in terms of how Random House brought the anthology to market.

■ *Cole:* It started as they all do. I do a lot of poetry reading—some for ulterior anthologistic purposes, some for pleasure. I'd noticed, over the years that there are a great number of poems about the joys and displeasures of love—of sex and love together—and I one day thought, "Maybe there should be a book." I recalled a Theodore Roethke poem, and a couple of poems by the Earl of

Rochester, and I put them together in my mind and said, "That's the beginning, the nucleus of a book." Then I really dug in and put together an outline of what this book might be, and took it to three publishers because I thought that it was such a good idea it deserved to have three publishers bidding against each other. It worked. Three bid, and Random House got it.

Also in 1963 I put together an anthology of Animal Poetry for Young People. The phrase "Young people" is an odd one, but I don't want to say "children." It's really aimed at nine to fourteen or even older. This is titled *The Birds and The Beasts Were There.* It emerged simply because I knew that no good anthology of bird-and-beast poems existed. I had an amusing time finding a title; I'd earlier done a book called *I Went To The Animal Fair* which was an anthology for very young children—only about thirty poems were included. I was casting about for a title for the second book of animal poetry when it came to me—"I went to the animal fair/ the birds and the beasts were there . . ." The logical extension is that I will next have to do a book called *The Big Baboon By The Light of The Moon.* I can't imagine what *that* book might be, but one wit suggested that it would be a good title for my autobiography.

N. I'd like to switch from your role as an anthologist for a moment, if only because you're caught up in the literary world as a whole. I wonder what views you might have of American letters at present—trends or specifics you most admire or deplore.
■ *Cole:* To start off negatively, I would say that what I most deplore is *Catch 22* and the spawn of books that are naturally following in that same jazzy, mixed-up style—Elliot Baker's *A Fine Madness* and all—I think *Catch* is the most overestimated book in the last twenty years; it's really a series of five jokes with variations; it's all on one level, there's nothing to get your teeth into, and O.K.—so War is Hell and People Are No Damn' Good.

On the other hand, I don't think my enthusiasms are exceptional—I always keep in mind one of my favorite quotes, from A. T. Quiller-Couch: "The best is the best, though a hundred judges have declared it so." I think Mailer is the big man—he can think and he can write, and he'll tackle anything. And he's never been afraid to change his mind. After that, in any old order, come James Baldwin, Philip Roth, Updike, Styron. Nabokov is such a fantastically good writer that I'm sure other writers hate him. Herbert Gold is an odd case—up and down. He has a great short story, *The Heart of The Artichoke,* and a fine early novel, *The Man Who*

Was Not With It. I think it is his very best book, a book about carnival workers that is very funny, very vulgar, very moving.

This summer I had a delightful experience. I was stuck out in the country without many books around. I was in a house where there was a small collection of Calder Willingham, so I read one or two of them. I was amazed. He is the funniest writer in America today, with a wild ear for dialogue. Delightful, but with something to say. I got as much pleasure from him as I get from Peter De Vries, which is plenty.

N.   How do you feel about the amount of introspection that seems to have crept into our writing over the last few decades?

■ *Cole:* I never think about introspection—to coin a De Vriesian phrase. Oh, well, if it isn't too self-indulgent I don't mind introspection. As to Salinger, I'm one of the few people in the world who's indifferent. I think he's good light reading—I read him with some pleasure and occasional revelations, but I can't take him very seriously. He's got his little world, but it ain't mine and it ain't much of anybody's.

N.   To return to the world of anthology—what are you planning or working on at present?

■ *Cole:* Right now I'm working with a cartoonist friend, Mike Thaler, on a collection called *The Classic Cartoons*—a bit off the poetry beat—that will contain all the cartoons that people have ever talked about—the ones that have made them say to friends, "Did you see that Arno last week . . ." or that Feiffer, or that John Held, Jr., or perhaps, that Gibson Girl. It will start with Daumier and those chaps back there, and come right up to some of the young cartoonists of our day.

I've also just put together a *Punch* collection for American readers—the *Punch* editors had started it, but they'd put in too much about cricket and that "Oh, Mumsy!" cute stuff that only the English can bear.

I am also doing a book I enjoy very much—a labor of love, actually—a number of publishers have already turned it down with unheard-of promptness because it's a collection of short, short poems by modern poets, all eight lines or under. Called *Poetry Brief* for the moment. I don't know why I like this idea so much, but it seems to work. There are some wonderful poets who can say so much in so little.

And I'm just finishing an anthology for children—poems about bad children called *Beastly Boys and Ghastly Girls.* And I have plans for an enormous collection of humorous prose from the

English-speaking countries—a two-volume thing, one from America, the other from England, Ireland, etc.

N.   Predating your work as an anthologist, you must have been aroused to poetry and prose at a fairly young age.

■ *Cole:*   As I mentioned before, I didn't get to college. I barely got through high school and spent a year after that looking for a job—it was the Depression. So I lived in a suburb with my mother and my brother, and I did my own educating, in a way. I found a list that Somerset Maugham had made of books everyone should read, so I started reading. A lot of it was mighty dreary, but I plodded through. Then I started reading voluminously in all directions, buying books in thrift shops and Salvation Army shops. I sort of found myself. I couldn't help marking things. First I'd scrawl boldly, "How true!" in the margin, as most people do when they're seventeen or eighteen. Then I started marking page numbers discreetly, in the backs of books, referring to pencil dots by paragraphs and things like that. I've been doing this for some thirty years now.

Thus my library is really one large uncollected anthology. My years in publishing helped—you get a lot of free books. Publishing offered me access to these books, and it still does. There are times, however, when being an anthologist offers quaint disadvantages. Some time ago the *Times* had an article about *Spoon River Anthology*, a Broadway show, where they finally decided they had to drop the word "anthology" from the title because a lot of educated people didn't know what the word "anthology" meant.

I was at a luncheon, also not too long ago, when I was introduced to a man as ". . . this is Bill Cole, editor and anthologist." The man started talking to me about anthropology almost immediately. Another time, even weirder, somebody thought I was an ontologist, and I had to go to the dictionary to find out what an ontologist is—"the science of being, as such!"

N.   In addition to your work as an anthologist you also do a fair amount of creative writing. What are your objectives in this more general area?

■ *Cole:*   Well, I don't think of it as creative writing. I wish I did. I think of it, at best, as high-class journalism. I would like to write with life—life in each sentence. I would like to think that I wrote a tenth as well as Dwight Macdonald, or a twentieth as well as H. L. Mencken. Their ideas are not always ideas I share, but the verve, the life, the poetic flair they have for putting a word to work for them!

Liebling had that spirit; Joseph Mitchell, a marvelous *New Yorker* writer, has it. I would really go along rather firmly with Kenneth Rexroth, who said, in *The Nation* a number of years ago, that it had taken him twenty years to learn to write as he spoke, to learn to write a relaxed, conversational style, and that's what I would love to be able to do.

"In America, where everything is cast on the soap-selling level, there's no hope for quality. I've always felt . . . that the American audience itself has a much higher level of taste and comprehension."

John Crosby
Interviewed in London, England, October, 1963

John Crosby

N. For many years John Crosby has been one of America's most literate and entertaining columnists. His acerbic views of television—from individual programs to his pronouncements on trends within that industry—are still recalled with anger by some persons, with delight by a much larger audience. More recently, his columns from Europe have added freshness and insight to the American's understanding of specific events as well as national frames of mind. The first question for Mr. Crosby: How has all this come about?

■ *Crosby:* You want me to start from Year One? Well, I've been a newspaperman for twenty-eight years, and this is a mighty long time. I started with the *Milwaukee Sentinel*, which was a Hearst newspaper leased to Paul Block. It was fascinating, working in chain journalism. I covered courts, politics, police, almost whatever there was to cover. It was a very poor newspaper—poor in the sense that it didn't have much money—so we, as cub reporters, did a little bit of everything, which turned out to be invaluable experience.

In 1936 I went to New York for a temporary job with the *Herald Tribune*. This became permanent, another of the good things that have happened to me. I worked on space. For a while I was a police reporter. Then the *Tribune* discovered that I liked to write plays, so they threw me on a beat that isn't covered much any more—the show business beat—that included opera, movies, music; anything that lived and kicked. My opposite number on the *New York Times* in those days was Jack Gould, who later became my opposite number in reviewing radio and television.

I did this until the war, then served five long years in the Army. When I got out in 1946, the *Herald Tribune* didn't know what to do with me. The place was stamping with reporters who had come back from the wars, and they had a large staff of replacements who had been there for five years or more and couldn't be fired—not ethically, anyway. Thus, they more or less

invented a radio column and asked me if I wanted to do it—simply
because, as I mentioned—I had an interest in show business. At the
beginning, they didn't know what kind of column it should be—
gossip or otherwise. I told them I wanted to write criticism. So I
did, and it was fairly successful, right from the start. They started
to syndicate the column within three months, which is just about a
world's record for syndicating something. When television came
on the scene, it became a television column.

   N.   Until you had what is called a bellyfull.

■ *Crosby:* That didn't happen all of a sudden—I'd had a bellyfull
for five years before I quit. Actually, I'm lazy. It was an easy job,
but I should have made the move into wider spheres much earlier
than I actually did.

   The first five years of television were enormously interesting.
There were new things, new people. There was a period around
1945 when television was livelier and more interesting than any
other medium. It made movies, and even theater, look rather pallid.
They had young playwrights like Paddy Chayefsky and magnificent young directors like Arthur Penn and Johnny Frankenheimer.
All these fellows have gone into the movies or the theater, now.
But that was a golden age, and it's a pity it lasted only a few
years.

   N.   What caused the decline in quality?

■ *Crosby:* I used to have a lot of theories but I've discarded most
of them. One that prevails is the advertiser control of television—
the insistence upon being innocuous, or offending no one—I think
this is a disastrous thing. As a consequence, television gives mild,
harmless, mindless semipleasure to a majority.

   You know, in the United States we're always worrying about
"government control," but when you come over here you're absolutely bowled over by the BBC which is totally government-
controlled. (I can't say this, either, because actually the BBC is
above the government—they wouldn't dare tamper with it.) The
BBC gets money straight from the viewer, a perfectly wonderful
system. Perhaps the BBC got rather stuffy until a commercial
channel opened in competition, but they livened up with great
shows like, "That Was the Week That Was." They did things of
startling boldness and originality.

   Many of the BBC programs are slanted to the higher mentality.
"That Was the Week That Was" was considered high-level stuff,
yet it had an audience of thirteen million. Now, thirteen million in
a small country like England would be the equivalent of about fifty

million in the United States. To put it mildly, this is success, and it's a success that accedes to higher tastes, and doesn't cater to the lower.

In America, where everything is cast on the soap-selling level, there's no hope for quality. I've always felt (and I still do, for that matter) that the American audience itself has a much higher level of taste and comprehension than the advertiser gives it credit for. The operation of the BBC here in England proves that people want better programming and are even willing to pay for it.

N. But we have ratings—

■ *Crosby:* And the ratings knock hell out of decent programming. An audience of two or three million is considered minute— now, this isn't a small audience. Any play that had an audience like that would be a smash hit. Ratings are murderous. In the first place, I don't believe them. I thought so before Congress investigated ratings, and I still do. Remember, Congress turned up the fact that ratings were hideously inaccurate. Even if they could be accurate, I think they're immoral. Being inaccurate there's no excuse for them at all, yet the advertisers continue to fall for the trumped-up Nielsen sort of thing. The public has every right to feel grossly insulted.

N. Have you had any regrets about leaving the TV review field?

■ *Crosby:* God, yes. The world is such a big place, and suddenly, when you're turned loose with a total carte blanche, it scares your pants off. I probably still wander around too much—I should settle on some aspect, and yet. . . .

I thought, when I first became a general columnist, that I would emphasize culture—books, plays, opera, the gamut. But I've discovered myself getting into such things as architecture and politics. I've listened to Home running for reelection up in Scotland—fascinating, hearing the then acting Prime Minister lecture to the sheepherders.

N. Could you describe your column more fully?

■ *Crosby:* Well, the title is "John Crosby Abroad" and it's simply an American-abroad sort of thing. You see, so many Americans are going abroad, living abroad, and getting rather hip about it, that there's a place for this sort of thing. When I first came to New York, that city was the center of the universe for journalists. Now the four-hour jet flight to London makes it not only possible but advisable for the journalist to wander abroad whenever he can. And since so many Amercians do this—entertainers and just plain ordinary people as well as journalists—we seem to be founding an alert, floating population that embraces every class, that is (at the same time) classless. This is an important development, and it must be widening the horizons of the American newspaper subscriber.

N.   How would you define the objectives of your column?

■ *Crosby:* My objective now—and for that matter, the same aim guided my television columns—is to broaden the horizons of my readers. I say this with the utmost humility, though it may not sound very humble. I think that Americans tend to get into terrible ruts. Perhaps all people do, but I'm more conscious of the Americans because I am one and it's the audience I write for. We get into ruts about viewing things as right or wrong, black or white, desirable or undesirable.

For instance, every European nation has socialized medicine. The Conservative government in England is actually further to the left, as far as all forms of socialism are concerned, than the Democratic party in the United States. Now, things like this aren't generally known, and I think they should be known. I think Americans should know how the average European lives, and what he thinks.

Coming to England with a pair of fresh eyes, eating English food, meeting the English, listening to the language as it's used by the English, is stimulating. It provokes a lot of ideas.

I like the way culture is treated over here. In Europe you find subsidized theaters, subsidized operas, subsidized motion pictures. We Americans have strong feelings about any kind of subsidy—we think everything should be a matter of private enterprise. The American in Europe is astonished to find that the mixture of socialism, subsidization, and state ownership has produced a healthy climate for all forms of creativity, for all forms of culture. This is just one small area in which I hope to pass on at least some shreds of knowledge.

There's another reason, too, why I think and hope my sort of thing is important. We're so accustomed, in the press, to crisis journalism that it's hard for the average American to picture any foreign country as it is in its more average moments, in its daily life. For instance, when Berlin was hot, there were over 800 correspondents on hand; Algeria had 1,500. Now, neither of these places are really that important. We become overanxious about one thing, and the press exaggerates that anxiety still further out of proportion.

I don't want to grapple with people getting killed. I want to write about them living, the way they live, because their lives are important today and tomorrow and the day after tomorrow. As far as I'm concerned, the hell with revolutions and wars. I want to present them doing ordinary things, eating, making love, attending the theater. But peace and prosperity are the hardest things to write about, and this is my beat. I'm glad it is.

N. I don't want specifically to change the subject, but this relates to your move from Paris to London. My introduction to Europe came by traveling to Paris, then to London, and my own rather corny observation is that Paris, lovely as it is, is only a love affair, but London is a marriage.

■ *Crosby:* You're saying something that seems to be increasingly felt by a great many people. A very witty friend of mine said, "I can't stand Paris since the French started acting as if they owned the place." And it's true. The French are getting very rich, now. They're almost richer than we are, but for years they were the waiters, the lookers-on. Now they can eat their great food, make passes at their beautiful women, buy good seats in their own opera houses and theaters. This must amount to an unmitigated pleasure for the Frenchman. Now, I like the French a lot, though I know many people who don't—including the French. The French complained to me about my column, and often, because I was too nice to them—too sugary. The French are more complex than most Europeans, and the visitor should not feel disgruntled if he doesn't understand them right away.

Someone once said that while the Italian is like a puppy, the Frenchman is like a cat. He holds you at arm's-length for a while. He doesn't rush to embrace you the way the Italian does (and, for that matter, the Spaniard, and even more startlingly, the Englishman, who, contrary to popular belief, is the soul of friendliness). But once you gain a Frenchman's confidence, and he becomes your friend, he's your friend forever.

The French criticize us because they claim that when they come to America, they are overwhelmed with hospitality the first week and can't be found the second. The French are the opposite—they don't rush into anything. They want to look you over, and they want you to look them over. But once a friend——why, I go back to France and meet people I haven't seen for twelve years, and they march you straight into their homes, fall all over you, show you the new children, and it's wonderful!

N. I'm going to turn to your book, now, the collection of Crosby's best, to comment on one article—the poignant piece you did on Marilyn Monroe. Could you go into that?

■ *Crosby:* Well, I only met Marilyn once, and that was near the beginning of her career. She was twenty-four. She was making a picture with a very close friend of mine, Nunnally Johnson, who now lives in London. I think it was *How to Marry a Millionaire.* She met me at the Polo Bar in the Beverly Hills Hotel. She came in slacks. She was a tall girl, a big girl, and she apologized for the slacks and said she'd just finished a dancing sequence. What struck me, as we sat there and talked and drank up a storm, was her utter candor. You could ask her questions that brought answers you couldn't possibly print: about her sex life, about everything. She was starting to be psychoanalyzed, and I told her I couldn't understand why—she was a big star, beautiful and young, with everything at her fingertips, including Joe DiMaggio.

Then she told me about her parents. She said, "My mother is in an insane asylum; my father died in one." I think she had some uncles who were committed, too; the mental history of her family was terrible. She said that it worried her terribly.

I think she was a better-adjusted girl at that time. I saw her from a distance, in later years, sometimes said "hello" but never talked to her again in any depth. But Billy Wilder, another good friend of mine, made a movie with her, *Some Like it Hot,* and he swore he'd never go through another film with her. He said she couldn't memorize the simplest lines.

Now, when she was twenty-four, she was a pro—she could do dance sequences, dialogue, fine subtle comedy. What happened in the next ten years is somewhat obvious, but not altogether. She went so terribly to pieces, but even then she must have been a wonderful person. I never met anyone who didn't like her, man or woman, and in the Hollywood cat-factory this is something. I get quite peevish about this whole psychoanalysis bit when I think about it. I wonder if Marilyn wouldn't have been a hell of a lot better off without it. When I met her she was friendly, outgoing, even happy. At the end she was lonely and couldn't communicate with anyone.

N. In your book you also included some pieces about the theater—about playwrights in particular—that involved great depth.

■ *Crosby:* Well, I wrote plays—I still do, for a hobby. As a matter of fact, I was a member of the Playwright's Studio which was affiliated with the Actor's Studio. Inge was a member, Tennessee Williams, and Arthur Miller. They'd all read bits of their plays—scene by scene—and then we'd sit and criticize. Sometimes we'd use Studio actors, who were the best in the world.

On the subject of theater, a quite unnoticed recent trend promises real excitement. Theater is moving away from the great population centers. It's happening here in London. Fascinating things are being done in places like Coventry and Stratford; then the plays come to London. I think we're going to have that same situation in the United States. I think Tyrone Guthrie in Minneapolis will be doing more interesting things on a broader scale. With Broadway costs what they are, this is vital.

N. Now, if you were to give advice to the youngster who wants to make a career of journalism, what would that advice be?

■ *Crosby:* I'd advise anyone with a thirst for journalism to get into television. They have the money, the audience, and the fun right now. It's not an easy thing to get into—but then, journalism has never been awfully easy to get into. This is one of the bulwarks—the difficulty of getting in. If you can't surmount it, you don't belong in it.

N. What do you admire—and what do you most deplore—in the cultural world of today? And what would you hope for?

■ *Crosby:* I am most struck with admiration by the way motion pictures are becoming an art form, a true and original and vital mass art form. I think people like Fellini in Italy, Jean-Luc Godard in France, and Stanley Kubrick in America, are doing vastly more interesting things in movies than are being done in theater.

I deplore almost anything painted on canvas in the last twenty years. I consider contemporary art the most appalling nonsense, and all forms of art appreciation of action-painting a form of idiocy.

What I would like to see in the United States is the growth of a genuine regional theater in some of the new playhouses I mentioned before. Cities like Dallas, Madison, Milwaukee, and St. Louis all have theaters, actors, directors—everything but playwrights and local plays. The development of regional playwriting would add tremendous cultural vitality to American theater.

"What is art, but a way of sharing experience. . . . As for the humorist, he does not laugh so much at mankind, as he invites mankind to laugh at itself."

Peter De Vries
Interviewed in Westport, Connecticut, March, 1964

Peter De Vries

N. "Peter De Vries, in my joyfully partisan opinion, is the most reliably funny comic novelist now at large." (Orville Prescott, the *New York Times*.) I think that this simple statement sums up the outward presence of Mr. De Vries in American letters. I would like to elaborate on the verdict slightly, however, to point to the sharp edge of satire De Vries employs in pruning the tangled roots of exurban living, and the compassion which made *The Blood of The Lamb* an unforgettable poignant experience. So powerfully developed are the De Vries talents that Harper Lee, in regarding him as the natural successor to Evelyn Waugh, quickly establishes his status.

In talking to Mr. De Vries I would first, of course, like to ask him where he was born, reared, and educated, and how his interest in writing first developed.

■ *De Vries:* Is this one of those chances you get to prove that your childhood was as unhappy as the next man's?

I was born in Chicago in 1910 into a Dutch immigrant community which still preserved its old-world ways. My origins would have been little different had my parents never come to America at all, but remained in Holland. I still feel somewhat like a foreigner, and not only for ethnic reasons. Our insularity was twofold, being a matter of religion as well as nationality. In addition to being immigrants, and not able to mix well with the Chicago Americans around us, we were Dutch Reformed Calvinists who weren't supposed to mix—who, in fact, had considerable trouble mixing with one another. We were the elect, and the elect are barred from everything, you know, except heaven.

I wasn't allowed to go to the movies, to dance, play cards, go to the regular public schools or do anything much that was secular, even on weekdays. On Sundays we went to church (usually three times) and in between services we sat around and engaged in doctrinal disputation, in which we became adept at a very early age. It was said about us, "One Dutchman, a Christian; two Dutch-

men, a congregation; three Dutchmen, heresy." We accepted and
even repeated this without any apologies or any suggestion that
there was anything wrong with this religious pugnacity. We were
the product of a schism, and we produced schisms.

I wrote a reminiscence story about a young man like myself
that says a good deal about my background, I think. The young
man was saying to his father, "Why do we have to wrangle and
have all these fights forming new sects all the time? Why can't we
emphasize the central truth on which all Christians can unite?"
And the father saying, "Stop talking like a crackpot!"

N. This sounds like what might be called—without exaggeration—a minority group.

■ *De Vries:* Indeed. With me a dissenting voice within that; a
splinter group of one, you might say.

To go on with what I take to be the purpose of your original
question. I did have the full Dutch Calvinist upbringing, from
parochial schools right through college, which was Calvin College
in Michigan. Good schools they were, too—I should say, "are"—
for the Dutch Christian Reformed still maintain their own institutions and keep themselves unspotted from the world.

N. Do you think this background has determined the actual
nature of your work in any way?

■ *De Vries:* Oh, I suppose biographical or psychological analysts
could make the case that my fascination with the sophisticated and
"worldly" world is a vicarious escape from this (in many ways)
painful immigrant childhood, with its sense of exclusion and in-
feriority, and that my satirizing of the upper crust is, well, a
simultaneous appeasement of the household gods being flouted, etc.
Who knows? Who cares? I don't. One just sits in the corner and
secretes the stuff. Don't ask a cow to analyze milk.

N. At what point in the upbringing you described did you
first begin to secrete the stuff? Did you make a living from writing
at an early age, or did you have to do other things?

■ *De Vries:* I did many, many things on the side. I may not be
able to recall them all. After graduating from college at the height
of the Depression (I should say the "depth" of it, I guess), I got a
job editing a Chicago community newspaper at a salary of twelve
dollars a week. I worked there for a year or so, until in one of my
"Personality of the Week" sketches I described a local businessman
as being a member of both the Masons and the Knights of
Columbus.

Next, still writing stories and bouncing sonnets off the moon,

I went to work operating a candy-vending machine route. After a few years of that I sold some poems to poetry magazines (if you can call nothing-to twenty-five cents a line "selling") and I simultaneously became part-time associate editor of *Poetry*, without relinquishing the precarious living afforded by my two days a week on the candy route.

Without relinquishing either of these two jobs (listen carefully; this is where the going gets tricky), I took on a taffy apple route from a man who was going into another line of work. That added a few more days a week, making six in all (the editorship also took two days). In those years I also picked up money as a free-lance radio actor, lectured to women's clubs, and worked as a furniture-mover on one of my father's trucks. That was his business. I also tucked in a few dollars writing a rhymed table of contents for an advertising magazine. The editor of that periodical telephoned the editor of *Poetry* one day, asking if he could recommend a poet for this job. I said yes, I'd send one right over, and hot-footed it down there myself.

N.   With all this going on, how did you manage to get any writing done?

■ *De Vries:* Your guess is as good as mine, but I did get it done. As a matter of fact, I finished a novel.

N.   That would be *But Who Wakes the Bugler?* Now, in line with all this, what would be your advice to young writers?

■ *De Vries:* Go and do thou likewise. Do something else, don't just write. It's dehydrating. Don't do all the things I did, or even any of them, but do something besides write. Unless, of course, your background, your past, has already fed you from some vitally human source, or supplied you some personal color.

Don't take a cozy post teaching English at some college. Drive a truck, run a filling station. I sometimes take a dim view of these grants and awards they give writers left and right nowadays, although I did get one myself, from the American Academy of Arts and Letters when I was safe in *The New Yorker* editorial offices and didn't need the money. I have a friend who is on a committee for one of those foundations dishing out money, and I kid him about it. When I visit him, every time his phone rings or he leaves his chair for some reason, I say, "As long as you're up, get me a grant."

N.   Could you define your objectives as a writer? For example, does the label "satirist" suit you completely?

■ *De Vries:* I don't think about what I am or what I'm trying to do, except to amuse an intelligent reader with what I hope is some truth we both know about life. "Who of you, by taking thought, can add one cubit to his satire. . . ?" Anyway, call it satire, humor, or comedy—I don't care.

I'd say roughly that the difference between a satirist and a humorist is that the satirist shoots to kill while the humorist brings his prey back alive. Swift destroyed the human race; Mark Twain and Thurber enabled it to go on. We human beings are all absurd variations of one another in any case, and this is what comedy of all kinds puts down on paper. I don't think I pursue any conscious "purpose" or "motivation" so much as an unconscious instinct of, and for, the absurd. I simply follow a comic scent where it leads, and if I seem occasionally to meander, I do it like the beagle who rambles in a strict attention to the trail. I couldn't possibly explain the concoctions of my books in any other way. The result must be banked on in terms of the validity of the instinct in question— this instinct for the ludicrous. A given theme may be psychologi- cally or sociologically worthy of pursuit, but the result will be sounding brass or tinkling symbolism unless it actually excites the writer's imagination and hits him where he lives. Right through his blood and down to his toes.

N. You've been regarded by many critics as a commentator on what might be called "the Ordeal of modern woman." Could you comment on that?

■ De Vries: I think the term is a misstatement. It should be "the modern Ordeal of woman," for it is but an acute inflammation of a chronic woe. Shaw put his finger on its eternal core when he said—I think it was in Back to Methuselah—that woman resents the burden of creation being so unequally divided.

I think that is only half the story. She further resents the fact that the life she has produced is organized and ordered by the sex having least to do with its creation. The urge to correct this mani- fest inequality shows itself on those petty levels familiar to us as the nag, the battle-ax, and the back-seat driver, but on worthier levels we see her spreading her wings in art, government, and business. Woman is educated for the latter, to find herself oftener on the local zoning board than in the halls of Congress, her pic- tures staring down at her from a bedroom wall oftener than hang- ing in a national gallery.

Now, those odds are exactly the same for the male of the species, but her disillusionment has been parlayed into this ordeal with a capital "O" from which man is excluded, and with a powerful lobby of anthropologists and journalists putting her case for her. But isn't it about time this lobby were dissolved and women recognized the general human ordeal, with her husband as full partner? Maybe he is trapped in an office when he wants to write, just as she is in a kitchen when she wants to paint.

What we need is not submission of the one to the other, but a joint submission of both to the hard facts of life, or we shall soon see a counterlobby with the slogan, "Equal Rights For Men" (or perhaps more appropriately "Equal Wrongs for Men") and then the jig will be up. It's nearly up now, I'm afraid. There's so much sand in the matrimonial gears that the old machine can hardly function any more. And each spring, down from Radcliffe and Bennington, swinging brief cases and paint kits, comes a fresh crop that can hardly be expected to ease matters.

The problem of the sexes is coexistence, and it is the same as for the two great political powers: Not to let rivalry become enmity. I would advise all newlyweds to make a sampler of that and hang it over the kitchen sink. This way the husband will see it as often as the wife.

N. Now, since you've been so strongly identified with *The New Yorker*, I'd like to ask a question which might involve a conditional answer. Could you describe your work for *The New Yorker*, and then could you evaluate that magazine's past and present position in American letters?

■ *De Vries:* Anybody who can clearly describe his functions on *The New Yorker* is regarded as a freak, so I'll content myself with saying simply that I go in a few days a week to finger pieces of paper having to do with comic art. As a reader of the magazine, I think it is incubating literary talent at the same rate as ever. Who better?

N. But what about the charge that there is not as much humor in it as there used to be?

■ *De Vries:* I like all this carping about *The New Yorker*, because it shows where people look for new talent, and where they really most expect it to turn up, so in a way it's a tribute to the magazine. Any new car coming down the pike will most likely round the bend into view in its pages. The editors are watching just as wistfully as you. Meanwhile you can't blame the editors for any momentary shortage of prose clowns. People doing that always amaze me. All talent is pure happenstance. When the accidents of nerves and glands and environmental torment that go into making a humorist combine in a given person he will write humor. He will

scratch where it itches just like a poet. He is not produced by edict
of Ross or Shawn, and it will do you no good to holler, "Louder and
Funnier." That's one thing. The second thing I might point out is
that, if there are fewer comics today than in the heyday of
Benchley and Company, or if they seem less funny, the "serious"
writers are more so than their ancestors in the short story. There
is more wit and humor in Cheever and Salinger and Updike than
in a comparable clutch of serious writers of a generation ago—and
there was damn plenty of it in the late Joe Liebling too. So I would
say that this precious commodity hasn't disappeared from the store,
it's just on another shelf. And I think the customer is still getting
his money's worth.

N.   To turn to the writer in the more general state—do you
feel he has, on the one hand, an obligation to the material he uses
in his work, and on the other hand an obligation to the public for
which he writes?

■ *De Vries:*   Sure the artist has an obligation toward the material
from which his stories are created, but the obligation isn't a literal
one. He may have to exaggerate an environment he's delineating in
order to portray it effectively—select, omit, even distort. Didn't
Picasso define art as "a lie that tells the truth?"

As for an obligation to the public, he discharges it best by
honoring his obligation to himself. I write for myself. That statement is the exact opposite of the priggish or egotistical remark it
may seem on the surface. I try to satisfy myself not on the assumption that I'm special, but that there are thousands more out there
just like me with my tastes who are amused by the same things I
am, touched by the same things I am, and who will therefore
enjoy reading what I've enjoyed writing. What is art, but a way
of sharing experience?

As for the humorist, he does not laugh so much at mankind as
he invites mankind to laugh at itself. There are levels on which to
do this, and the point is best illustrated, I think, by the story that
is told of Shaw. He was once taken to the theater where he
laughed his head off without really thinking much of the comedy
that was being performed on the stage. The whole experience irritated him, in fact. "I don't want to be jostled into laughter," he
explained to a friend afterward, "I want to be moved to it." I know
that I have sometimes sinned in this regard, but I hope to go on
from book to book, each time realizing a little better, may it be,
that high ideal.

N.   We hear so much comment these days on the decline of the novel—for the past decade it has been ostensibly dying. Do you feel this way about it?

■ *De Vries:* I think we should put away the stethoscope and leave the patient alone. The novel seems to be becoming what the theater was a generation ago—a fabulous invalid. Maybe it's not an invalid at all, but a hypochondriac who's been taking his own pulse too much. What are we waiting for, another Hemingway or Faulkner? That's all well and good. In the meantime, what's wrong with Anthony Powell, Nabokov, Salinger, John Cheever; but each reader can make his own list.

N.   I'd like to turn to your most recent novel, *Reuben, Reuben.* What were you trying to prove in that book?

■ *De Vries:* That I could be funny for a hundred and eighty-thousand words. Rather than the seventy-five or eighty-thousand to which I had been previously accustomed. I hope that *Reuben, Reuben* represents another small step in the direction of the ideal I mentioned a short time ago. And I'd like to hope that it's my best book to date. God knows this is little enough to ask.

N.   In looking at today's creative world—fiction, nonfiction, perhaps even theater, what do you most admire?

■ *De Vries:* What I most enjoy. I'm past admiring anything I don't enjoy. I have given up the grisly business of Appreciation. I've got too many creases in my neck to waste my time cork-screwing my attention into something I really don't enjoy. I don't read for anything but pleasure, and God knows that's a rigid enough task, if the person to be diverted is one of any intelligence or subtlety himself. Didn't Eliot call poetry "a divine form of entertainment?"

On the basis of that yardstick I'll take Anthony Powell, Scott Fitzgerald, Proust, Faulkner, Elizabeth Bowen, Kingsley Amis, as of the moment, Lardner and Thurber. You can have James. I read his fiction as Oscar Wilde said he seemed to write it—"as though it were a painful duty." Hawthorne, Jane Austen, Trollope, the others the critics are always reviving—well, after ten pages of them I'm in need of reviving myself. I guess I can't read anything but what's contemporary, and that's about the size of it.

N.   As long as we've got you in a deploring mood, what else would you like to beef about?

■ *De Vries:* Mainly this, divorce of appreciation from enjoy-ment, which is the curse of academic literary analysis. Think of all those miles of interpretation and the analysis of the contents of a book without one word about whether the critic had a good time with it, experienced the entertainment for which it was written in the first place. It's as though you told what you had for dinner by giving the recipes for what you ate—or worse, a chemical analysis of the food.

Reviewers at least perform the function of reporting whether a novel provides the pleasure for which it was originally intended. For myself, I hope the charge of readability can be brought against me as long as I live.

N.   Recently—I believe it was in *The Saturday Review*—I came across a review of *Reuben, Reuben* that elaborated on the fact that you "lacked cohesiveness." Can you comment on that?

■ *De Vries:*   That is because of my influences.

N.   You mean literary? You've been compared to Thurber, Benchley, Lardner, Lewis, Marquand——

■ *De Vries:*   No. I don't derive from any of them. I would say my main influences spring from two sources: Debussy and Sibelius. From one the emphasis on the individual nuance rather than the melodic whole, the chord being its own justification quite apart from any duty to a supporting continuity. From Sibelius, carte blanche to be as free-form as I please. Anyone wishing to call that "lack of cohesiveness" is welcome.

N.   No Bach?

■ *De Vries:*   I agree with Colette, who called Bach "a golden sewing machine."

N.   What is your evaluation of the resulting work, however it happens to be derived? One frequently-quoted remark now states that you consider yourself a serious writer.

■ *De Vries:*   Oh, I never said any such thing. Doesn't it sound out of character? I hope so! I don't use words like "serious." They're like "cultured." You know, "She was a cultured person." Anyway, it's false to life to separate elements from counterparts with which they are inseparably mingled in reality. You can't talk about the serious and comic separately and still be talking about life, any more than you can independently discuss hydrogen and oxygen and still be dealing with water.

I think good writers reflect this basic fact. Nobody has been funnier than Mark Twain or Thurber. Robert Frost understood (and exemplified) this principle beautifully, I think. He says somewhere—I think in a preface to a book of Edwin Arlington Robinson's—something about how if we want to be charming or bearable the way is almost rigidly prescribed: if it is with outer seriousness it must be with inner humor; if it is with outer humor it must be with inner seriousness. Neither one alone will do without the other, is the gist of Frost's remark.

So let's scotch any misquotation about seriousness. There are writers—and you can have them—who think that all you have to do to write a serious book is to lack humor. They are sorely mistaken—as mistaken as those benighted cut-ups who think that all you need to write nonsense is to lack sense.

N. Since you won't be pinned down, could we try a capsule summary? If it were possible to put yourself in the position of looking back at the career of Peter De Vries—say, from the year 2064—how would you like yourself to be evaluated?

■ *De Vries:* My needs are modest. A good artist predicts as well as reflects, and all I ask is that they say, "We know now what they couldn't see then. He was six months ahead of his time."

". . . one current trend—and I'm not altogether happy about it—is the comic novel. I can't see growth or justified continuation for the arch and somewhat phony comic novel."

Maurice Dolbier
Interviewed in New York, March, 1964

Maurice Dolbier

N. Maurice Dolbier is one of the most frequently-read and highly-praised literary critics on the American scene. As senior daily book reviewer and as columnist for the *New York Herald Tribune*, he combines reviews with interviews in a manner that not only evaluates, but often humanizes, the book and author he is dealing with. The Dolbier standards are high, yet the wide respect he has won is for his unequivocal fairness and for his refusal to "play games" at the expense of book or author.

In talking to Mr. Dolbier I'd first like to ask him where he was reared and educated, and how his interest in books came into being.

■ *Dolbier:* I was born in Skowhegan, Maine, in 1912. I was educated—first of all in the Skowhegan public schools. Then I went to a dramatic school in Boston because I didn't intend to be a book reviewer. (Does anyone intend to be a book reviewer?) I intended to be an actor, so after dramatic school I performed on the road in New England, mostly in Shakespearean companies.

In 1930 or 1931 I decided not to try to make a living as an actor. It was difficult, then, to make a living at anything, and impossible to keep fed as an actor. I went back to my home, settled down, and did some writing that didn't sell. Then I went into radio in Bangor, Maine, first as an announcer, then as almost anything and everything—program director, educational director, script writer, commercial writer, history dramatizer. As I recall, we covered the French and Indian War in a year's time. I wrote some radio plays that were done on the Columbia Workshop in New York. One of these, a play called "The Bust That Nobody Loved" was picked up and done by the BBC, and I received a telephone call from Random House wanting to know if I could turn it into a juvenile. (The play was an adult fantasy.) I did, and this started a sort of side career, that of writing children's books. I did this off and on up until the last six or seven years.

I went from the station in Bangor to a job as news announcer for the *Providence Journal* in Providence, Rhode Island. With the retirement of their radio editor I became radio editor of the *Journal*. I also did some book reviews at the time. Win Scott was the literary editor and I was his Asia expert. I hadn't been to Asia—I haven't yet—so I was an unlikely choice to represent that great land mass. But when I came to ask him if I could do some reviewing for him he said, "Well, most of my categories are filled—I have a Civil War man, I have a Revolutionary War man, I have a science man, I have a historical novel man, but I just lost my Asia man. Would you like to take his place?"

So I began reviewing books about Asia, but gradually worked my way East, finally coming to the United States and reviewing American books for him. Then, with the retirement of (this becomes monotonous—I seem to move ahead via retirements) Mr. Scott, I became literary editor of the *Providence Journal*, and when Lewis Gannett retired in New York as a daily book reviewer for the *Herald Tribune* I came to New York, and here I am.

N. How many books do you read and review each week?

■ *Dolbier:* Ordinarily I review three a week. Some columns will cover two books at a time, but ordinarily each column is on a single book.

N. Do you read a great many more in the process of culling?

■ *Dolbier:* Yes, but it's more culling than extra reading. I haven't really got time, on this schedule, to say, "Come, now, this wasn't as good as I thought it was, so I won't review it. Instead I'll do something else." I have to make my choices and stick with them.

N. In looking at literature in general terms, covering your span of years as a reviewer, I'd like to ask this three-pronged question: What trends have been obvious during this time? What do you think of the state of letters at present? What would you hope to see develop in the near future?

■ *Dolbier:* There is going to be a long pause in the tape while I try to remove the prongs one by one.

In the first place, my career as a reviewer covers the last twenty years, but whether this is a good twenty-year span or not is rather a question. I'm avoiding the question of trends principally because I think of myself as a book reviewer, a daily book reviewer at that, rather than a critic. I know the two should mesh, but literary critics ordinarily have more time to sit back and discover more things about trends and parallels and things like that.

The daily book reviewer is not quite drowned by, but must swim bravely against, the torrent of new books pouring out from the presses every day. I can only tell you what kind of a trend we

had this week. But I'd be hard put to define what trends we have
had in the past twenty years. The last real trend I can remember—
and this came before my time as a book reviewer—was the proletarian novel of the 1930's. In the 1940's we ran heavily to the self-
analysis novel, but then we have always had self-analysis novels—
first novelists writing about themselves, and sometimes second
novelists and third novelists writing about themselves. This is a continuation, a thing that's been with us ever since Rousseau, whose
confessions were not a novel (or so he said.)

But what are the trends this week? It seems to me that one current trend—and I'm not altogether happy about it—is the comic
novel. This didn't necessarily start with Amis and *Lucky Jim*, but
about that time young authors began looking, not into themselves,
but at all the miserable people around them. They began writing
funny, bittersweet, angry books. Now, there have been some good
comic novels. I think Heller's *Catch 22* was one of the brightest,
but it stands almost by itself. I can't see growth or justified continuation for the arch and somewhat phony comic novel.

This may be a picayune thing to bring up, but I think that
authors are now more interested in grammar and style than they
were, say, a decade ago. There is less carelessness in the work of
novelists, old and young, than there was then. And I could be
wrong. I could go back to the office and pick up five novels that
just came in and find that we have returned to stammering, un-
grammatical, unstylized terms. Needless to say, I hope this doesn't
happen.

I do regret the fact that we haven't more promising young
novelists coming along. (I hate that word "promising," but there's
no exact synonym.) It seems that every three or four years there
are three or four young novelists who appear, and you say to yourself, "Ah, this is the new generation, these are the people to watch!"
Well, you watch and you keep watching, but there they stay, with
perhaps another novel or two that show very little progression.

This is an unhappy situation, because you're not getting much
progression from the older generation of novelists, either. I still
have my eye on Ralph Ellison. I think he's a promising young
novelist, and I keep waiting for that second novel (as everyone
seems to be waiting).

Perhaps one reason for the lack of young novelists is the lack
of enthusiasm that is generally shown when a good young novelist
comes along. I can think of two or three novels I found to be the
best things written in the United States for a long time, but they

died in the bookstores. Some of them weren't even mentioned in book reviews.

N. From the twenty-year span—your twenty-year reviewing span we're talking about—what books would you pick as outstanding?

■ *Dolbier:* I think the last American book (we're talking about novels, now) that really excited me was *Catch 22*. *The Invisible Man*, well before that, was magnificent, of course. There were two first novels I delighted in—*The Gay Place*, by a young Texan named Bill Brammer, a Houghton-Mifflin Fellowship novel. It seemed as though Gore Vidal and I were the only two reviewers in the country who thought that this was about the best novel of American politics ever written. Authors seem to have steered away from that subject, but this man knew politics and knew how to write. Incidentally, we're still waiting for Brammer's second novel, too. Then there was *A Place Without Twilight*, by Peter Feibleman, that appeared about six or seven years ago. It should be regarded as a modern American classic.

What other novels? Twenty years is a long time; would *Guard of Honor* come into this period? I think it's the highlight of Cozzen's career to date. Of course, I like the Faulkner trilogy, and I'm afraid that this about wraps it up.

From Europe there've been some impressive things, of course. In England, the two extremely opposite kinds of writing—Durrell, with his *Alexandria Quartet* and C. P. Snow with his *Strangers and Brothers* series—both are great. I understand that the two authors don't much care for each other, and that their admirers usually don't like the other writer's books, but I'm in the middle. I like them both. I admire the ambition of the English, the writing of the two long chronicle novels I just mentioned, plus Powell's *Music of Time* series. I don't know why Americans don't go in more for this. Some of the English and French series-novels seem to go on forever, and everyone's the richer for them.

N. From this same personal time span can you choose books that were disappointing to you because they did not live up to high expectations?

■ *Dolbier:* I suppose James Gould Cozzens' *By Love Possessed* would be my keenest disappointment. As an admirer of Cozzens I hoped (and expected) that this was going to be a very fine book. I suppose, too, that I was affected by the promotion—we are, you know, whether we want to be or not. But when a book is talked about and written about for a year prior to publication, some sort of expectation is built up. *By Love Possessed* was being hailed as one of the masterpieces of the twentieth century (this is always dangerous to say or imply) and it wasn't.

I try not to anticipate a book. I don't sit around and say, "This is what I've been waiting for" when I read the announcement of a forthcoming book. It isn't fair to anyone, and it has an unfortunate tendency to make a little disappointment seem like a catastrophe, and the catastrophe may be confined to the reviewer's mind and not present in the author's work.

N. Now, if you were to give advice to the young writer who starts off with a given talent and ambition, what would that advice be? Perhaps, as a reviewer, you'd want to speak in terms of the end-product you'd like to see him produce.

■ *Dolbier:* I'd first say that advice is dangerous. I could advise a young author to read, read, read, because it is wonderful to have a wide background of reading. But on the other hand, if he has not already read and launches a long reading program he may spoil whatever was good in him to begin with—freshness, imaginativeness, the bold approach.

I could say, "You've got it, kid, just stick with it—write what's in your heart and in your mind, especially in your heart, or even in your guts," so he goes ahead writing what is in his heart and guts but has no background knowledge of what has taken place in other guts and minds and hearts, so there may be no reason to read his outpouring.

I hate to give advice. It seems safe to say, "Don't write so much," or perhaps this advice should be given oftener to publishers rather than writers. I have a feeling that authors ordinarily know what they can do best. I've seen so many instances when a young, good first novelist has written a regular-size book, and the publishers say, "Oh, no, that won't sell, expand it." So it's expanded, and a very bad novel is made out of a very good novella, and the critics write the man off.

N. I thought that happened after the second novel.

■ *Dolbier:* I think it's true that most writers are written off after their second book. Sometime I have a feeling that we sit around waiting to pounce on that second book. But the heart of that matter is, we're usually generous enough to dismiss the first novel as an interesting failure if it is a failure rather than a success. The second actually asks for closer appraisal. Sometimes the appraisal is too acute, but more often it's fair. Even Mailer was nailed on his second novel, and I'm not going to argue, now, as to whether or not *Barbary Shore* should have been attacked as it was, but I think we rather expected more from Mailer. Actually, the book may outlive *The Naked And The Dead*—it's a good piece of work—but critically it was shot to pieces.

N.   What do you think of American reviewing and criticism?

■ *Dolbier:*   Well, I have sometimes thought about writing a piece about this very thing that would be titled "Please Don't Shoot the Piano Player, He's Doing His Best." The trouble is, as the music goes on I begin to wonder if he is doing his best. Perhaps the piano player *should* be shot. I haven't made any vocal comment on what has become the traditional criticism of American book reviewing—that it's too bland, especially in contrast with British reviewing—and I'm convinced that the critics of critics who have been reading only bland reviews haven't been reading British reviews at all during the last few years.

The whole business of standards is a tricky one. I read somewhere, not too long ago, a complaint that criticism has not yet established a vocabulary of enthusiasm. It has a vocabulary of denigration, but if you enjoy the book it is difficult to say that you like it in terms that aren't larded with clichés or blandness. Well, I do think that the chief purpose of book reviewing—especially book reviewing for daily newspapers (I'm staying away from a discussion of book sections or Sunday magazines) is to call attention to books that have interested or pleased or delighted you, books you would like to tell other people about. I presume this is the standard, if there is a standard, of any good general reader, one who is interested in many subjects. If you like only one or two kinds of books you're not valuable to a large audience. I've always thought that the general reader was neglected in reviewing and criticism, even though the reviewer sometimes feels there's nobody out there. Well, what is called "the paperback revolution" proved people are out there—out there waiting for good books on almost any subject.

I don't know if I'm making my position clear. I wish I were writing this, right now, instead of talking it.

N.   You didn't want us to shoot the piano player.

■ *Dolbier:*   Right, because I'm playing the piano.

N.   Could you elaborate on what you feel the objectives—perhaps even the obligations—of the book reviewer should be?

■ *Dolbier:*   Yes. I wouldn't want to leave this with me saying that the sole responsibility of the book reviewer is to recommend an interesting book to someone. This is an objective, and an important one, but another is to warn the reader against meretricious work, either by blasting it in his own sweet and bland way or by not reviewing it at all.

I'm afraid that the latter is my mode of handling. When a big, best-selling novel comes out, and I think it's dreadful, I ordinarily don't touch it because I don't want to read it. In the first place I don't have time to read it. (Maybe I should somehow warn people that they don't have time to read it, either.) But considering what has happened in the past, when I've delivered these warnings I've only served to bring more readers to the thing.

If I may bring up an example—somewhat akin to Paul Revere's horse, it happened so long ago. I thought that *On The Beach* was a perfectly dreadful book, badly conceived, badly written, badly carried out. Despite the fact that I ordinarily liked Nevil Shute's books I jumped on *Beach* on publication date. The next day the publishers took almost a full-page ad with a line at the top that said, "In All Respect to Mr. Dolbier," and followed this with a list of quotations about people who had found the book absolutely smashing, starting with, I think, Adlai Stevenson and going through half the members of Congress, five or six prominent book reviewers, and maybe even Shakespeare.

I still thought that *On The Beach* was a terrible book, but by reviewing it I gave the publisher a chance to run a very attention-catching ad. Well, they spelled my name right.

Yet the duty of the book reviewer is to say why he doesn't like particular books. Perhaps I shouldn't like so many in my bland way—I'm sorry. I've been reading all these critics on critics, and I've come to the horrible conclusion that if you like P. G. Wodehouse on one hand, and Proust, on the other, this has nothing to do with a fine catholic taste. It shows you have a weak intellect. Maybe you shouldn't like Proust.

N. You mentioned, before, when we were talking about advice for young writers, that you'd rather pass on advice to publishers. What would that be?

■ *Dolbier:* This is also of a contradictory nature. One piece says, "Let the author alone." The other says, "Get a good editor in there to start working with your writer." Publishers need both pieces of advice, and they're not quite in contradiction. It depends upon which author they're working with, I suppose, but ordinarily I think that (just as there is a lack of good critical writing in America) there's a lack of good editorial supervision in American publishing houses. I don't know how this can be corrected, because good editors are hard to find. But I think that many books are spoiled by bad editing or by a lack of editing. In other words, back at the factory something should be done to the product before it appears on the desk for review and on the shelf for purchase. This does not consist of turning a good novella into a bad novel—it has more to do with trying to turn a good novel into an excellent one. Do I confuse the issue properly?

N.   If you were to look at the general run of writers now at work, from whom do you expect the potential of growth, the product, that might make the next decade more exciting?

■ *Dolbier:* Let me make all the brave young writers angry. In America here are the people I look forward to seeing doing fine things in the next ten years: Ralph Ellison, Saul Bellow, James Gould Cozzens, people who have been writing and are writing and are continuing to write. Among the younger writers (and I don't know where "young" ends with writers because I see Saul Bellow often mentioned as a young writer, which makes me feel good, having reached a certain age myself), Philip Roth, Peter Feibleman, and Bill Brammer; Shirley Ann Grau, John Updike, John Cheever. Can't think of young playwrights and only a few young critics. Norman Podhoretz would probably head that list.

In England I'll start at the other end again. Compton MacKenzie keeps turning out very good books—he's over eighty, and I think his list of published works is also over eighty. Ivy Compton-Burnett, Charles Snow—fine young comers. In the middle group, John Braine, John Wain. (They've taken to rhyming.) Wain, I think, is a man to keep an eye on. I've never thought much of his novels, but as a poet and critic he promises to become the thing he dreads—a "grand old man of letters." I won't complain. We need a few.

N.   I wanted to ask you about this business of the American writer starting strong and fading so quickly into repetition. Can you think of a reason for this?

■ *Dolbier:* I wish I could match this question with an interesting and erudite answer, but I can't. When you say it I immediately ask myself if you're being accurate—and I guess you are. The danger in this observation, however, is the fact that ordinarily an American writer's last work is not as bad as the critics usually say it is. In other words, Sinclair Lewis never reached the heights that he achieved with *Arrowsmith* and *Main Street,* but his closing novels were nowhere near as bad as the critics made them out to be. Both Faulkner and Hemingway went strong, right to the end.

Perhaps writers, American writers, don't grow and expand as they should. Perhaps they're discouraged by critics who wait to pounce on that second novel. Maybe American writers should go out to face the voters instead of themselves and their publishers and their critics. They need something to keep them on their toes, their mental toes. Early success doesn't. Heaven knows early failure doesn't, either. I have no real answer—it's not as simple as a matter of drink and the devil, though these two flaws have affected some writers I know.

N. My final question concerns what you would like to see evolve in American writing—the type of writing, its depth, the subject matters utilized, the sharpening of talent.

■ *Dolbier:* I would like to see—and I think this is one of Charles Snow's big complaints—I would like to see a closer relationship between the subject of fiction and the actual social life of the American community. In one respect I suppose this would bring on a whole batch of new novels about Madison Avenue advertising agencies. (Who knows—there might still be room in that area for a good novel, peoplewise.)

The American political scene, as I mentioned, has been skimpily explored except on the level of fantasy. I hope Allen Drury won't mind, though I'm sure he will, when I suggest that *Advise and Consent* lies in the area of fantasy and melodrama. *Seven Days In May*, *Fail-Safe*, the presidential convention novels coming up, all are rather on the fantastic side. Between Henry Adams' *Democracy* and the Brammer book I mentioned earlier there doesn't seem much to fill the gap.

American business (I don't know much about it, myself) is apparently one of the wonders of the world, but few American novels have dealt with it with any degree of competence. There is a wide gap between American writers and American business.

This whole area, the mixture of science and government, has been investigated in England by C. P. Snow. Heaven knows as much is happening in this area in the United States, but few novels deal with it.

I don't even think the American home is covered particularly well. Perhaps it's because the novelist resents home, in the first place, which is true of some of them, but somewhere between the nest of vipers in the angry plays and the angry novels (the possessive mothers, the impotent fathers, the rebellious and sexually confused sons and daughters) and the simpering domestic comedies of television, there are whole areas of American living that writers are not writing about. Perhaps some writers are, but I would have to go back to the office to look in the files to see who they are.

We also don't have novels that deal with Americans in relation to the world. I mean in real and actual and thoughtful terms and situations. We've had the exposé novels, like *The Ugly American*, and some novels about diplomats abroad, but this is another area to explore because Americans are all over the globe in or out of relationship with other people.

There are all kinds of subjects waiting for the writer. And we're waiting, too.

"When a novelist writes about a world he knows, when he describes particular events which (by the nature of his craft) should be interesting, entertaining, diverting, he is producing a protracted metaphor. . . . The novelist expresses universal truth through his metaphysical illustration of his story."

Maurice Edelman
Interviewed in London, England, October, 1963

Maurice Edelman

N. Maurice Edelman combines two remarkable careers in a manner that hasn't been duplicated since Disraeli. He is a Member of Parliament and a writer of great stature. If only one of his books were to be chosen as an example of his literary accomplishments, the novel *The Fratricides* would come to mind for its superb blend of realism and invention. The painful personal and political aspects of the complex period in Algeria just prior to the French withdrawal are utilized in a book that deals compassionately with persons and bluntly with the gravely difficult time and place in which these persons lived.

In talking to Mr. Edelman I would naturally like to examine, first, how he succeeded in molding two lives, two careers, into one.

■ *Edelman:* Well, I was born in Cardiff in South Wales in 1911 and spent the whole of my early life there. I went to school in Cardiff and was brought up under the influence of the Welsh nonconformist liberal tradition. I went on to Trinity College, Cambridge, where I read modern languages. I think the languages—French and German—influenced me rather strongly. I studied the literature of both France and Germany in some depth and, though it didn't result in any sort of commercial qualification, it enlarged my literary horizons. My favorite author at the time, I recall, was Heinrich Heine, and I believe his prose style greatly affected my own.

When I came down from Cambridge with a degree in Modern Languages in the slump of 1932, I had some trouble finding a commercial outlet for that specific qualification. There were about two or three million unemployed in England. But eventually I went to work for a lumber firm and was able to use my languages traveling abroad for them. Specifically I was in the plywood industry, and at the outbreak of World War II I was working on the application of plywood to aircraft construction. But this wasn't my true metier.

In the meantime I had been writing a great deal. In fact, the direct occasion for my leaving my plywood job was a book I wrote called *Production For Victory, Not Profit,* which wasn't very popular in the circles in which I moved at the time.

Thus I was left to look around for something to do in the war. It happened that I was invited to join *Picture Post* as a war correspondent, which I did. I went to North Africa for them, developing a close acquaintanceship with Algeria, a country I've written about a great deal since, both in fiction and nonfiction. I went on to France after the landings and established relationships—indeed, in some cases, strong friendships—with many of the leading figures in French politics.

By coincidence, on my return from France, I was sent to cover the Labour Party convention in 1945—this was before the great general election which swept Labour into power. There, quite fortuitously, I was invited to present myself for a selection conference to choose a Member of Parliament—or, rather, to choose a candidate. Of all things *I* was chosen and to my great surprise found myself elected.

I had always been a supporter of the Labour Party and although I had never had any tangible political ambitions, I was elected to Parliament in 1945, and I've been there ever since. For five years, you remember, the Labour Party formed the government of Britain, but for the remaining thirteen or fourteen years we've been in opposition. Being the opposition can be a rather sterile and unrewarding activity, and in order to live at capacity I took the opportunity to devote myself to what you call my "parallel career" of writing.

N.   I'd like to discuss the political novels you've written. They seem to deal with truths—sometimes, almost clairvoyantly, with truth before it happened.

■ *Edelman:*   Let us say as a kind of preamble that I believe every writer should write about the world he knows. I think one should use the imagery, almost the metaphor of the life one knows best to represent more general truth. I write about the Westminster scene, about Parliament, a sort of Court of Versailles, because that's the world I know best. It's the institution in which I spend the most significant hours of my life.

A dominant thing which struck me very quickly about this scene is the contrast—indeed, the conflict—between the private and public personalities of politicians who must present a certain standard face to the world no matter what private inner conflicts are going on.

F*

My first British political novel was called *Who Goes Home*. The theme concerned a young and rising minister who committed a peccadillo and found himself in frightful public and private difficulties. It expressed my feelings about the deep inner conflicts which I think all public men have.

Parliament, in a way, is like the navy. Everybody knows about it but no one really understands its intimacies, its expertise. The navy is a great institution in England, yet there are very few naval novels. Likewise, there are few political novels. Very few writers have interpreted Parliament in fictional form.

You mentioned Disraeli, who wrote *Coningsby*, perhaps the greatest political novel of all time. Then there's Trollope and his parliamentary novels, and one titled *The Prime Minister*. But Trollope (and I say this with great respect because on the whole I admire Trollope) was a rather disgruntled journalist and a candidate who had failed. He tried to get into Parliament, he didn't succeed, and I think a certain portion of his rather dim view of politics sprang from his own private frustrations. In other words, I regard Trollope as an onlooker rather than an inlooker. By looking on from the outside his objectivity was invalidated by romanticism.

Now, I've written about politics because it's the world I've inhabited for many years. I have a great deal to learn about politics, but it's been fascinating to me, particularly the activities in the Chamber where you have the dramatic confrontation between the two sides. This is a place where one can study human nature very closely, because people—even in their public manifestations—expose themselves. They're surrounded by 600 critics who know all the rules of the game, all the tricks, and because of this you get (in a curious way) the paradoxical combination of the public man concealing himself while inadvertently exposing himself. It's a paradox, but I think it's the essential thing about parliamentary service.

Hypocrites can succeed in politics—they can and do—but I don't think they put much over on their cynical colleagues. Exposure is revealing to the mind that has vast acquaintanceship with both the bold and the subtle bits of political gamesmanship. On the other hand—and perhaps this is because I'm a "liberal"—though it does sound like a conservative view at the surface—I believe very strongly in tradition and in the value of institutions. In effect the institution of Parliament (and I'm quite sure this applies to your Congress, too) is one which tends to elevate people to the level of the institution even if they, themselves, are very ordinary or even inadequate people. This is what has been happening in Parliament and I find it a dramatic thing in itself. In short, people—very ordinary people—will come to Parliament, but in the discharge of their public duties, they become elevated to the level of their institution. Sometimes they fall below that standard, but if they do so consistently, or flagrantly, they are almost invariably returned to private life.

N. In dealing with the political world—where you are actually on the inside, as a participant, then on the outside, as a writer—do you feel a moral or ethical commitment to the material you use and the public for whom you write?

■ *Edelman:* Very much so. I do, first of all, because while I'm certainly a participant I'm not a committed politician in the sense that I'm a committed partisan. I certainly support my party wholeheartedly in its programs and policies, but on the other hand I think that by its very nature, by the way politics forces people to say "yes" or "no" or regard as "black" or "white" any given problem we take a crude approach to in search for truth. Perhaps this is the only way we can have "applied approximate truth." It's a rough and ready answer to the problems of the day, and it's probably the logic that must be applied to circumstances. But the writer is much more capable of dealing with the various aspects and facets of truth.

To me the novel is a means of looking at a given problem from all sides to find the all-embracing truth. I'm conscious of the multiplicity of the aspects of truth because only by accepting that multiplicity can we also experience compassion, the moral quality which is missing from the rough and tumble of party politics.

You see, political life is really a case of the survival of the fittest. A constant tooth-and-claw battle goes on. It's a battle that involves intrigue, strategy, tactics—usually within the rules, although the rules are broad enough and flexible enough to include all sorts of moral violence. We saw this happen in the Profumo affair. All the hounds were baying after this unhappy man who committed the mistake, perhaps the fault, of misconducting himself. It was extraordinary how everyone pulled their skirts away from him, just left him to fight it out on his own.

Personally, I think that in the whole of civilized life the most important moral quality is that of compassion. Perhaps it embraces most of the other virtues. But because compassion is missing—at least on the surface—from politics, I feel that I as a writer must present it in the very real and human position it takes beneath the surface of campaigns and votes and "yes" and "no" and "black" and "white."

N. Didn't this desire for perspective, for emotional perspective, underlie the complex Algerian political background of *The Fratricides?*

■ *Edelman:* Actually my on-the-spot research in Algeria was fairly extensive. Then, my deeper involvement lay in understanding the people concerned. Perhaps you remember the character of Dr. Hassid, the old neurosurgeon, a civilized man who really wanted everyone to be happy and devoted his life to serving other people. A fuddy duddy, in a way, a man who didn't understand the apparatus of politics. I certainly wanted the reader to get involved with him. I mention him only to underline the point that my basic research consisted in finding a model for him. The model was a neurosurgeon I knew in Algiers during the war, but I also know a man in Britain who specializes in paraplegia and furnished added insights into the person Dr. Hassid would be.

I'm trying to say that a writer establishes his universals through an interpretation of local and topical individuals and circumstances. Whether I'm writing about Algeria, or Westminster, or the House of Commons, I'm really concerned with what I call universal metaphors. When a novelist writes about a world he knows, when he describes particular events which (by the nature of his craft) should be interesting, entertaining, diverting, he is producing a protracted metaphor. Just as a poet can use the simile "My love is like a red, red rose, that's newly sprung in June" to tell you about his love, the novelist expresses universal truth through his metaphorical illustration of his story.

N. Do you find a concern for truth obvious in today's fiction?

■ *Edelman:* It's hard to say. As far as I can see certain novelists, especially in England, are exploring areas of activity that have been long neglected. For example, writers like Alan Sillitoe are dealing with working-class activities which had almost vanished as the subject-matter of novelists. Yet I must be cautious; I think one must make a proper distinction between the excitement of novelty and the reality of discovery.

Any human activity is justifiable raw material for the novelist, but the ultimate worth of that novelist will depend upon whether or not he has transmitted that raw material to the realm of universal experience. It's all very well for people to come along, throw up their hands in delight, and say, "Isn't this wonderful? The working class people go to bed with each other, use rough, raw language, and have mothers and fathers." This was a great discovery, you know, for the middle class and some of the so-called upper class. But this can be a form of inverted snobbery, a throwback to the naïve concept of the noble savage and the noble working class. I say this as one who has spent much of his life among the working class. The word "noble" is as out-of-place here as it is with the savage. There are noble people, certainly, just as there are at any level of life. But when critics go slumming and praise the working-class novel simply because it is a working-class novel, they are doing literature a disservice.

N. To go a step further, what is your most serious criticism of the novel of today?

■ *Edelman:* Let me deal first with this continental thing, the so-called "antinovel." I think it's perfectly proper to experiment with the form of the novel because no one has ever been able to define what a novel is. I remember E. M. Forester's lectures on the novel in which he began saying that there are so many definitions of a novel that we must settle for an all-encompassing definition, and he quoted a French critic who said, "A novel is a prose work of some length." That isn't a bad definition, and it leaves a great deal of room for experimentation.

The antinovelists in France who have tried to remove the plot and even the author's identity, substituting a self-revealing state of mind, have performed some exciting services in their experimentation, but they have often gone to extremes in denying the place of plot, characterizations, and form. Isn't there a great deal of room for variety of treatment within the *accepted* framework of the novel?

I hope this doesn't sound intolerant, but I think one of the real problems in fiction today is that there's too much of it. An enormous amount of fiction is being written because there has been an enormous increase of literacy. Superficially, the novel seems to be the easiest form for a literate person who wants to express himself. He may not have anything to say—he may use the novel as a stream-of-consciousness type of therapy that's cheaper than the psychiatrist's couch—and he may be justified in locking himself in his room and pouring his soul out on paper. It makes the job of the critic vitally important; he must decide what is a novel and what isn't.

Unfortunately, the problem of the superabundance of novels is paralleled by the decline of criticism. I won't go into this too thoroughly because our problems in England undoubtedly differ from those in America, but I don't think a youngster who's trying to make a name for himself should have the week's huge lot of novels thrown at him for review, nor do I think novelists should review each other. The road to a show-off type of criticism, on one hand, and to private-ax criticism, on the other, is all too obvious.

On the other hand the flood of novels means that a great many will go uncriticized. This creates a problem for the reader, but the problem will exist as long as publishers hope that somehow, if they throw out enough of a novel crop, one will turn out to be a best-seller. I think encouragement should be given to anyone who wants to write; I think it's proper that people should want to express themselves. But it's a pity that publishers don't exercise the function they once performed—of being the pre-critic who gives advice and guidance to people writing fiction. Thus what is written today, published, bought, or not bought, is *merely* produced—not conditioned, as it should be, into disciplined and purposeful form.

N.   If you were to give advice to the talented young person who is intent upon becoming a writer, what would that advice be?

■ *Edelman:*   I can't remember who said it, but I don't think you can escape that very tired old maxim, "If you want to be a writer, write." It's no good escaping to a sanctuary in Cornwall or Cape Cod; it's no good planning and daydreaming; the thing to do is write. Only the heat of discipline and effort will let the person know whether he should or should not go on wanting to be a writer. And only such discipline and effort will produce a writer of real merit. The second thing I think a writer must do is to involve himself in the stream of life, take part, do a job—too many youngsters feel that a job is beneath the dignity of a writer. Perhaps the time does come, when the writer has accumulated enough resources, that he should go off and write exclusively. But to write about life one must know something about it, and the demands of a job, working with and for a variety of persons, is an important way to develop this knowledge.

N.   I'd like to talk about your most recent work—your biography of Ben-Gurion.

■ *Edelman:*   This has been quite a departure for me. It was commissioned both in America and England, and I started off with great enthusiasm. But my enthusiasm has been rather qualified by the backbreaking work involved. I've always admired Maurois' *Life of Disraeli*—a romanticized biography, yet scholarly without being drily academic. I feel there is room for the novelistic biography.

Thus in writing *Ben-Gurion*, I've enjoyed it not only as one who has interested himself in his political audience, but as a novelist concerned with characters and delighted when they come to life.

In another way writing *Ben-Gurion* has resembled working on a novel. It was interesting how my mood, my reaction, my judgment of the characters changed as I went along. As in writing a novel I began with a certain picture of my characters—but gradually, as I went along, my concepts changed and the characters changed. I do hope, however, that in the end it became a homogeneous work.

N. Are you returning to the political novel?

■ *Edelman:* Yes, there's one which has been germinating for a long time—a sequel to the novel titled *The Minister* in England and *Minister of State* in America. It will be titled *The Prime Minister*. Now, I know that Trollope wrote a novel called *The Prime Minister* about a century ago, but I think there's room for a modern novel about a prime minister. Although it will be a sequel to my last political novel it will also be a development. I want it to be much more detailed—in a way, much more elaborately developed—than any novel I've written in the past. Now, I've always believed that a writer should not spell everything out, that he should write allusively, by means of ellipses. He should make the reader do a bit of work. That is how I've tried to write in the past, and I've always found it very rewarding when a few people have understood the technique I've applied. On the other hand it's been a disappointment when readers haven't bridged my gaps. Whom to blame—them or me?

I will still be allusive, but at the same time I'll spell some things out in detail. I think there is room for more spelled-out detail in the political novel. I'm not thinking of *Advise and Consent*, a novel I do not particularly admire despite its success in America. Despite its length I did not find it an acute enough interpretation of politics, and so many of the politicians—including those of my acquaintance —seemed to be fashioned of pure cardboard. It was anything but a definitive political novel. Now, I'm not saying that I will or can write anything like a definitive political novel—I don't think there can be such a thing. The most I can do, and hope to do well, is to apply my experience, the knowledge of politics I now have, to a very large canvas that portrays the movements and interactions of politicians in England.

N. My final question is a broad one, but I'm asking it because of your political experience and because of your obvious concern for moral and ethical conduct on the private as well as the public level. What obligation does the individual, as an individual, have toward himself, and toward society as a whole, to live constructively?

■ *Edelman:* This is a significant and fundamental question and I'm delighted that it's been raised. It's something I ask myself constantly, and I hope it's a question that occurs to enlightened people throughout the world.

We are living on a nuclear brink and everyone is dancing more and more frenziedly on that brink. Some seek material advantages and stimulation, others try to procure for themselves, by hook or crook, benefits to which they are not entitled—this is reflected in our rising crime rate.

It's easy to be pessimistic, too easy, but if one can calmly look for historical parallels one goes back to climacteric points when civilizations were decaying. And if one can see the parallel it's entirely possible to apply corrective measures. It's not without significance that the most frenzied period of luxuriousness, of self-indulgence, or eroticism, was in the time of Plague. The plagues of medieval times were always accompanied by this frantic spree of self-indulgence. In primitive societies, when the end of the world seemed near, everyone hurried out for a jolly good time. When Hitler was in his bunker under fire, it is well-attested that the whole bunker system became the scene of an incredible orgy. I'm not saying this in any narrow moralizing sense because I think that our world is one in which the material, the moral, and the social must find a proper balance in view of the nuclear dangers that confront us all the time. Not too long ago our Prime Minister pointed out that the world had come to the brink of nuclear war three times within twelve months. Such crises make people—young people, especially—try to encapsule all the potential joys of living in a very brief period. Thus you have a breakdown of conventional morality, the obvious examples of people rushing to gather the greatest sensual and material advantages for themselves. What should the individual do when he is conscious of this temptation? It's an enormous question.

People who have conventional, traditional attachments to established religious faiths and ethical systems have a relatively easy solution. But for people without firm faiths or convictions things aren't as easy. The younger person is particularly afflicted. He argues that "Morality's fine—you've lived your life, you're now thinking of the possibilities of another life, but we haven't lived ours at all, so what are we going to do about it?"

As a politician and writer I feel that my first duty is to try to state a problem because many persons are conscious of the *effect* of the problem but not the problem itself. To provide an answer or solution for other people is impossible, except in the way that one's personal solution can serve as an example or a guide for other people who are looking for guidance.

Personally, I'm in favor of total nuclear disarmament in whatever way it can be achieved. I've stated so in my political life as well as in certain of my writings; but even if the bomb were removed from our conscience, we'd still have the problem of instilling in our children and grandchildren a belief in progress. What we lack today is the Victorian belief in progress, of the perfectability of man. We lack this belief simply because too many of us feel there is nothing to be gained. In short, I think our first solutions are necessarily political—political on the national and international level. It's no good thinking that we can do away with juvenile delinquency by beating or constraining the young. This won't help. In our acquisitive society we do not intimidate train robbers by sending other train robbers to jail for twenty years. Crime follows the general pattern of society. If we have a society that is acquisitive, that bars nothing, that regards the tycoon as a hero and the takeover as an heroic act, we will find the so-called criminal classes imitating the tycoon in their own fashion.

If one wants to improve the moral health of the so-called criminal classes—if one wants to remove the singular and collective threat to morality and life—one starts working on the moral health of society as a whole.

"The practice of creative writing is the practice of an art, an ancient and rich art, and regardless of the skill or lack of skill of the writer, he cannot escape this definition. . . . He is an artist and his only obligation is to the truth."

Howard Fast
Interviewed in New York, February, 1964

Howard Fast

N. The twenty-odd books by Howard Fast include a great number of titles we might call "standards" in the American repertoire. With imagination, style, and an eye toward significance, he has woven his major works from threads of historical, social, and political events. Nor has he stood free of the currents of time, even when controversy and censure became his due. *Citizen Tom Paine, Freedom Road, Spartacus, The Winston Affair, April Morning,* and *Power* are some of the major titles of works by Fast that cannot be excluded from the library, but in talking to Mr. Fast I'd like to touch first upon a quite unusual work, the screenplay for *The Hill* released as a book in 1963.

■ *Fast:* I think we must begin with the concept. This book, or rather, this screenplay, is a modern miracle play—which means that it is conceived in the manner of the miracle plays of the Middle Ages, telling the story of the passion of Christ in terms understandable to the audience that witnessed its performance. In my play *The Hill* I tell the story of the *passion,* in terms of the current situation in Harlem and New York. The Hill of Calvary is the hill that gives the screenplay its title. An improbable mass of rock, it literally looms over the ghetto of Harlem. My Christ is a carpenter, and he is crucified at the top of this rock. Two thieves move through the story with him and die with him. All of the elements that exist in the Gospel according to Mark are here in modern terms, in modern dress, with no attempt to explain incongruities or anachronisms.

I would hope, as one incident piles upon the next, that by the time we reach the crucifixion, the total impact is so dramatic and believable that the audience no longer doubts that this is precisely how the crucifixion took place.

N. I'd like to go back, now, into your own life and career—where you were born, reared, educated.

■ *Fast:* I was born in New York City, reared both in the City and upstate in Green County. The milestones in my life were the great Depression, the war in Spain, and World War II—three convulsions that had so much to do with shaping and conditioning almost all men of my time.

My formative years were in the 1930's, and I suffered from all the good and all the evil components of life in the 1930's in these United States. Perhaps the most memorable factor that molded my thoughts was the desperation of the Depression years, this and the rise of fascism in Europe. I became a radical, because as a radical I lived with hope and purpose. But such was the manner of my time.

N. When did you start writing?

■ *Fast:* My first novel was published in 1933, so I began professional writing more than thirty years ago. I already have had to renew the copyright on three of my books. This has the effect, of course, of making a long time seem longer. Still, it remains a very long time indeed.

N. In the 1930's a great percentage of America's front-running intellectuals embraced communism, and, as I recall, you were one of them. Could you explain how this happened? How so many writers, artists, educators, and intellectuals swung so far to the Left?

■ *Fast:* It's as difficult to explain all the reasons for this as it is to explain to any young man of today precisely what the 1930's were like. The condition of the 1930's is understandably unreal to the American who lives today and whose years of maturity came after that era.

The 1930's were essentially a period of despair, a period without hope, and people cannot live without hope any more than they can live without bread. The thirties were a time without hope or bread, and during this time of despair—and of hunger for so much of the population of the United States—hundreds of thousands of people turned to communism.

Intellectuals turned to communism because they were sensitive people who had to believe in a cause. They had to find hope somewhere, and they found answers to their problems nowhere else even if communism's answers were less than ideal. There was no great movement for civil rights then; there were no jobs; there was no great labor movement. The world of the thirties was so different from the world of today that it is almost impossible to describe it convincingly. Physically, its trappings were the same— we had automobiles, airplanes, and most of the things we regard as modern conveniences, but in terms of social structure it was very different. Think of millions of Americans living in shacks, of millions of tons of food being burned or buried or dumped while people starved to death (there were thousands of deaths due to starvation).

Think of a labor movement without influence, industries without any unionized workers, wages being endlessly lowered. The world of the 1930's was a world where no one held out a hand of either promise or authority. In this gap, an untenable vacuum, the left wing grew.

The left wing movement of the 1930's was not comparable to anything that exists today. It had little or nothing to do with the Soviet Union. It was a movement of militant mass forces that responded to the needs of the time.

N. Now, if you were to look back at your career as a whole, what would you choose as landmarks or highlights?

■ *Fast:* This is very hard to say. The book I wrote which has sold best—in fact, its sales exceed that of all other works of fiction in modern times—is *Freedom Road.* Internationally, this book has sold over twenty-five million copies; so in terms of importance I'd have to place it at the top of the list as both an achievement and an incident. On the other hand, the book which seemed to me most to fulfill my own objectives is one called *The Last Frontier,* a story of the Cheyenne Indians. I even think it will survive for a while—but who can ever know how long a work of art will live?

But of all my books, the one that seems to be taken closest to the country's heart—in that it is read for pleasure and also used as a textbook in thousands of schools throughout America—is a short novel I wrote called *April Morning.* It never achieved the flambuoyant notices that put a book on best-seller lists, yet it has already gone through eight printings and shows every sign of being a permanent part of our literature—partly because, as I mentioned, it has been adopted as a textbook. Very likely it will be my best-remembered book.

April Morning is as good a book as I have ever written, as nearly perfect a book as I could hope to write. And I doubt whether I will again equal the balance, the mood, of *April Morning,* and personally I like it better than most of my work.

N. To turn to the contemporary scene as a whole—the novel and perhaps even the theater as points of discussion—what do you find that you most admire? And, on the other hand, what do you most deplore?

■ *Fast:* Well, not being a critic I don't applaud and I don't deplore. I don't have to—and I'm very pleased that I don't have to.

I would say that the biggest difference between the literary product of my youth (I go back 25 years) and the works of to-day is the difference between an attempt to entertain the public and preoccupation with oneself. Twenty-five years ago novels and plays were conceived of as entertainment. The art of story-telling was highly respected and ·enshrined. Today the art of story-telling in its grand sense and tradition, the art of such masters as Steven-son, Conrad, Clemens, to name just a few—is lost. Instead of story-telling we have psychoanalytical analysis and fairly dull introspection. Digestive problems, private neurosis, the inside of the outside dominate. This prevails in both so-called fancy fiction and class theater, and as a most regrettable counterpart we have enormous, poorly written novels which tell a story, but tell it badly, with poor English and little art.

The novel to be read for sheer pleasure is very rare today. There are few writers in today's America who write literate and intelligent work that can be read for pleasure. British writers do this—at least a few—but in America even the Dashiell Hammetts, Raymond Chandlers, and James Cains have passed from the scenes. John Steinbeck and John O'Hara are brilliant, talented writers, but how many others?

N. If you were to give advice to the young writer of today—the talented youngster determined to make a career of writing—what would that advice be?

■ *Fast:* "Should I be a writer?" When I'm asked this I say, "No," and the person who asked the question is hurt and horrified.

Why do I tell him that? If a person has to ask this question there is sufficient doubt present to negate any hope of success. To be a successful writer requires devotion and fanaticism. You dedi-cate yourself to an apparently impossible task and stick to it until it either destroys you or until you succeed.

The only sound advice I can give the young writer is to tell him to have faith in himself. Whether he is talented or not, he must have enough faith in himself to disregard all advice and all criticism, and to think only in terms of learning what he must learn and accomplishing what he must accomplish. If I were to advise a young writer as to where he should work, I think the answer would be "Wherever you can make some money, whether it's on a news-paper or as a free-lance writer for films or television." There are vast opportunities for writers today. Thirty years ago there were no opportunities for writers. To set out on a writing career then was to court every kind of disaster—social disaster, mental disaster, and physical disaster.

This is not at all the case today. Today society has a need for writers. Television, the great medium of the future, is in imbecilic infancy and needs good craftsmen. It rewards its craftsmen richly. In other words—it's a good time to be a writer. Try it.

N. I'd like to return to your most unusual screenplay, *The Hill*, to ask you how you came to write it.

■ *Fast:* The first reason is the physical existence of Mount Morris Park. Add to this the distaste with which I observed the film industry's efforts to tell the story of the life and death of Christ.

Now, it is said that every serious writer will, in his own time and in his own way, put down his version of the Passion of Christ, not simply because of the compelling dramatic content of this story but because—regardless of religious conviction—each generation relives the moral dilemma and agony of a man who dies for other men. For the same reason the story demands an approach that is holy in its veracity and truthful in its artistry.

Now, both of these demands have been ignored by the film industry, and the endless spate of Biblical films that pour out of the dream factories of Hollywood and Rome is largely dreadful. I've seen pictures like *Barabbas*, films of such cruelty, such sadism, such vicious and barbaric bloodthirstiness it seems obscene that they should be presented as religious documents. I've seen *The Ten Commandments*, which is little more than a study in sexual titillation. *This*, mind you, is presented to kids as a religious document. I feel that what Hollywood does is to sell dull pornography and sadism in religious trappings as an art, or a nonart form. Nowhere is there an element of truth, of belief, of reality. These are the things I try to inject into *The Hill*.

N. Do you feel that the writer has any obligation to the material he uses? Similarly, do you feel he has an obligation to the public for which he writes?

■ *Fast:* When you ask what a writer owes his material, you pose a curious question indeed. My answer would embrace the next question as well. He owes nothing to his material, nothing to his public. He is neither a debtor nor a parson; good, bad, or indifferent, he is an artist, and his only obligation is to the truth.

If you sense any mystic overtones here, they are not intended. I am wholly down to earth and practical. The practice of creative writing is the practice of an art, an ancient and rich art—and regardless of the skill or lack of skill of the writer, he cannot escape this definition. What of art? Does it imply obligations? I think not. Like life and history, art has its own remorseless and built-in punishment—and it rewards those writers who attempt to honor the truth as they see it. Not as an absolute, but as a measure of the reality and anguish and hope of mankind. Conversely, it withholds the mark of excellence from the liars, the cheap running dogs of fad, fashion, and sentimentality. Of course, this is merely an introduction—the kind of dogmatic denunciation that can irritate the hell out of people. Rightly so, too. Yet when one is asked a question whose implications are as wide and deep as the ocean, what is one to do? Even as a foolish question deserves a foolish answer, a highly philosophic question always ends up with one small part of an answer. Perhaps the crumb is better than silence. I don't know.

N. How do you feel about our standards of criticism and review?

■ *Fast:* Sad. They who can do, will not make a life of criticism, and the noble critic who approaches the work of workmen with honor and respect as well as critical facility is not among us. I have little love and less respect for the critics—but what creative writer would say otherwise?

N. If you were to stand at a future vantage point—say, 2064—how would you like to have the work of Howard Fast appraised?

■ *Fast:* Honestly, I neither know nor care. I am a workman—all artists who are not dilettantes are workmen—and I do my work as best I know how and earn my daily bread. Sometimes a lot of bread indeed, sometimes less. I have done well. I have no complaints—except that I never wrote that book I go on dreaming of writing. But the future? I leave that to the critics—who honor neither reality nor common sense.

"Humor has to be based on something, but what it's based on is up to its creator. There aren't any rules. The only obligation the humorist has is to develop a line and remain faithful to it."

Jules Feiffer
Interviewed in New York, July, 1963

Jules Feiffer

N. Jules Feiffer has risen to front rank as humorist in a remarkably short time, both because his talent is great and humorists are few in number. The scarcity of humor is mentioned almost constantly by the personalities I have interviewed; over a dozen have said that we take ourselves and our times far too seriously, foregoing the pleasures of amusement.

Feiffer—now a novelist as well as a cartoonist—has confirmed one of my private fond beliefs; working in longer forms he has enlarged upon all his abilities, moving from "pieces" to full-length works with the full fire of his satiric wit. My first question: Where and when did your work first appear, and how has it progressed?

■ *Feiffer:* I'd like to respond to something you said in your opening statement first—I disagree with the opinion that we're taking ourselves too seriously. I think the problem is, we take ourselves too grimly, but not seriously enough. There is very little seriousness in our discussion of what is happening to us—there's a lot of pretense, but very little real seriousness. Whether we dig at the root of our problems in a light way or a heavy way I doubt if there's much real honesty in our efforts to come to grips with the problems of our society. Now I'll answer your question.

I began the cartoons for *The Village Voice* in 1956—almost eight years ago. When I began I was sure I couldn't do this sort of thing more than three or four years—even though the schedule was light, only one cartoon a week. My terms were that I could do anything I wanted, in any form I liked, and their part of the agreement was that they wouldn't pay me. But it worked out well for both of us, I think. It re-taught me a value I had developed contempt for, mostly because my peers had contempt for it—and this was the value of being an "amateur." All my advisers advised me to never do anything for free—get paid for everything, they said. Before I started doing the cartoons in the *Voice* I got paid for everything; I was doing more and more work and earning less— probably because I was doing things I hated to do—things I got

188

no enjoyment from. I was quickly turning into a hack. I'd wanted
to become a cartoonist since I was a child. I loved to draw, I loved
to invent fantasies, and I loved to combine words with pictures.
But after being a professional for several years the word "love"
went out the window. I was doing it because I *had* to, because it
was the only way I could make a living, the way most people do
their jobs—because they know of no way to get out.

Becoming an amateur again—going to *The Village Voice* and
saying "I just want to get in print somehow"—re-created the element of love in the work, and revived the pleasure of being an
amateur, of doing something for the hell of it. It was easily the
most valuable lesson I've learned in my career.

So—be warned of the good advice of others. Be warned when
they tell you that your attitude is immature. Be warned against
all *good* advice, because *good* advice is necessarily *safe* advice, and
though it will undoubtedly follow a sane pattern, it will very likely
lead one into total sterility: one of the crushing problems of our
time.

N.   Thoreau's "quiet desperation" again—

■ *Feiffer:* A tense, frightening phrase, and it's probably more
apt now than it was at the time of Thoreau. I've also read a magnificent description of modern society written by Tolstoy—
seemingly the problems have always been there, and all we're doing
today is compounding the felonies.

N.   It's alarming enough to watch the effects of the 40-hour
week—the waste of time, the boredom, the restlessness that's laughingly called "leisure."

■ *Feiffer:* Is it any wonder that we have a leisure problem?
From birth we are taught the sanctity of work—that we must make
use of everything. The word "use" can be an ugly word—we must
use time, *use* leisure. There's something vaguely suspicious about
looking at a sunset for a long time; there's nothing suspicious if
we're using a camera to photograph that sunset.

N.   From your *Village Voice* beginnings your cartoons have
gone on to appear in over forty papers in the United States, and
you have a healthy foreign distribution.

■ *Feiffer:* After *The Village Voice* began using me, the second
paper to pick me up was the London *Observer*. After a year of
London exposure I was better-known to the English audience than
the American audience. I discovered when I went to England that
I was thought of as an English cartoonist; as a matter of fact, a
number of Americans thought I was English, and at New York

parties when they heard my Bronx accent, they were shocked.

N. As far as translations are concerned, your work now appears in nations like Sweden, Japan, and Italy. You probably can't read them back directly, but how do you think the flavor of your American background comes off in the other languages?

■ *Feiffer:* The expectancy has always been, that the cartoons were so privately New York they couldn't have any meaning elsewhere in the country. When that was proved wrong we thought they were so privately American they could have no meaning outside the United States. But the English picked up the cartoons faster than the Americans. When they went on to Italy the old hesitancy came up again. We could explain the English interest, because they've become more and more Americanized, but what could the Italians possibly see in my work? I don't know what they see, but the books do very well in Italy and in all the other countries they've invaded via translation. The best way I can explain this is to suggest that for better or worse the world is becoming Americanized and *our* problems are becoming *theirs.* For better or worse we are the vanguard of the future, simply because we were the first rich country, the first affluent society, the first country with a burgeoning middle class, the first country where mass poverty disappeared as an issue. Now these positive values, along with all the negatives we know so well, are becoming part of all national cultures.

N. In reviewing *Harry the Rat With Women* I made one observation which may or may not be right, and I'd just as soon be corrected if I'm wrong. I said that the book gave pleasure for two distinct reasons—first, because it was wildly funny in itself, and second, because it was a telling satiric study of our youth and beauty cult and various forms of pseudo-intellectualism.

■ *Feiffer:* I would make it broader than that, and say that it struck at the uncertain worship we give ourselves. Much of what we do in life, in guises like social work or charity, are outlets for our private drives. Some of these are good, some are terrible, and some are neither. Harry, however, was clearly interested in nothing on earth except himself and he was so naked about it (not aggressively naked, because all he had to do was stand there and all things came to him, so there was no need for aggression) that he offended those people who *disguised* their self-interest. That's part of the book, and it's about a number of other things, too.

N. There's a quality creeping into your work which reminds me very much of Max Beerbohm, and I have an idea that as you grow older your work will have even broader Beerbohm touches.

■ *Feiffer:* I had never read Beerbohm, but after finishing *Harry* a friend read it and said that some of it reminded him of *Zuleika Dobson.* I promptly got the book from the library and fell in love with it. Any comparison with Beerbohm I consider a lavish compliment.

N. Let's take up the Feiffer discord. For every three people I know who read and like your work, there is one who simply can't take you—at least, among my friends and acquaintances. They say you make them uncomfortable. Do you find this reaction elsewhere?

■ *Feiffer:* I've heard this from people. I'd rather have this reaction than have people love my work who are continually its targets. One of my chronic complaints is how easily I become accepted by the people I try so hard to wound. Instead of my wounding *them*, they wound *me* by loving me to death while I'm expressing my hostility.

We've reached that age where we like to hear about ourselves; especially when it's negative—a new cliché: "I don't care what you say about me as long as you spell my neurosis right."

N. We have a capacity for rationalizing away all our sins and misdemeanors, haven't we?

■ *Feiffer:* Freud and sociology have helped us considerably. We think of our sins emanating, not from us, but from society. We're just not to blame individually. How many of our television programs or message plays end where the defense attorney looks around the courtroom and says, "It is not *this man* who is at fault, it is *all of us* who are at fault?" While this may, in part, be true it's nonetheless a marvelous cop-out—because if I don't have to blame *me* or blame *you* but can make some general indictment of *society*, I end up blaming nobody.

N. I have a friend under analysis who is firmly convinced that every mistake she ever made in her life, and all her deficiencies, can be traced to the fact that her mother rejected her at the age of five days.

■ *Feiffer:* What did her mother do on the seventh day?

N. I don't know—I've gotten so I run when I see her coming.

■ *Feiffer:* It's frightening to contemplate what kind of mothers these people make. Possibly because we're about to have a baby I've created two new characters in a series of cartoons. These are two pregnant women, and in each strip they discuss the futures of their unborn children, and all their worries and doubts. In one they discuss the fact that they don't want to be like *their* mothers; they don't want to be manipulative because they realize this makes a child a mess. They discuss what messes they, themselves, have become, all because of manipulative mothers, and yet they decide that while they *are* messes they're a lot better off than other people they know because they're at least, *interesting* messes. The challenge is "How do we make a child an interesting mess instead of a stable nothing?"

N. Now, as far as American humor as a whole is concerned—to be outrageously demanding with a question—what do you think about it?

■ *Feiffer:* I think as far as the written word goes, until recently it's been fairly depressing. However, in the last year or so some good funny books are cropping up: Elliot Baker's *A Fine Madness* for one. Kurt Vonnegut, Jr's *Cats Cradle* is the best satire I've read since *Handful of Dust.* In other areas humor is in the best shape it's ever been. In terms of a connection with reality, the nightclub satirists have been wonderful, beginning with the Chicago operations; groups like Second City, people like Mike Nichols and Elaine May and Lenny Bruce, a film like *Dr. Strangelove* have made us aware of what's been happening to us in the post-World War II period. These people are much sharper, much better than any of their predecessors, particularly when we think of entertainers like Will Rogers.

N. But the nightclub comedians you've mentioned have changed the route of humor, haven't they? The warm, folksy stuff that Rogers so often pulled has disappeared.

■ *Feiffer:* A lot of folksiness used to be a disguise for things much deeper. Probably the best example was Mr. Dooley, who had a rural accent but was fairly sharp. Twain wrote bitter things in a folksy style. I'm down on Will Rogers since I saw a televised biography where he was seated with President Hoover telling all his fans to stick with the President and not worry because Hoover would get us out of the depression. I doubt that he intended that as satire. Satirists should stay away from Presidents.

N. I'd like to go a little deeper into the content of the big hardcover *Feiffer's Album.* How would you break it apart?

■ *Feiffer:* There are seven pieces. The introduction is a review of satire involving several nightclub satirists and how they see themselves—they claim they're constructive, not destructive, but it's wonderful to watch them tear each other apart. It's a very nasty piece, and I'm very fond of it.

The next is a fable—I've always wanted to write a medieval fairy tale in a gothic style so I did it. It's called *Excalibur and Rose*, and it's about a man named Excalibur who couldn't help being funny, who delights everyone in his village, but who has no serious side and feels a lack because of it; so he goes off in search of his serious side. On his quest he meets another questor, a girl named Rose who's always crying, who's constantly grave and sees only terrible things in the world. Her search is for perfection because she sees such a terrible lack in everything. She wants the perfect society, the perfect man, etc. So the two of them go off together to seek their fortunes—in glorious color.

Another story, called *Harold Swerg* is about a little man who could do anything better than anyone else—throw a ball farther, run faster and all that—but the problem is that he doesn't *want* to. He enjoys being a filing clerk. When all the moguls of the sports world get after him to get him to play baseball and football he simply sends them away. This becomes a major problem with his refusal to enter the Olympics. The Soviets have the best team ever. The only man who could hold up our end is Harold Swerg, and he doesn't *want* to.

Then I have something I call *Superman*—a review sketch about what happens when Superman saves a lovely young lady from a mugger, and rather than being thankful, as distressed heroines always have been, she wonders why he has this compulsion to go around saving people while dressed in those effeminate blue leotards. What's he trying to prove?

There's a story that appeared in *Playboy* called *The Lonely Machine*—about a man named Walter Fay who doesn't get along with *other* people. *Other* people take things away from him, don't give him the love he wants and the companionship he needs. So he invents a machine called the Lonely Machine that gives him all the attention he's never had. Then of course terrible things happen. Terrible things happen in all these pieces.

The longest piece in the book is a one-act play called *Crawling Arnold*, the story of a young man named Arnold Enterprise who, at the birth of a new baby in his home (his parents are seventy, so the news comes as quite a shock), reverts via sibling rivalry to crawling. The only problem with this is that Arnold is thirty-five years old. The playlet also involves other disparate themes, which I hope in some way or other are connected: Civil Defense, air-raid tests, Negro nationalism, psychiatric social workers—maybe I left something out.

The book concludes with a twelve-page pantomime about two people watching the growth of a flower. It's called *The Relationship*. It's very dirty.

N. What do you think the obligation of the satirist or humorist is to his time and his public?

■ *Feiffer:* I think the relationship of any humorist or writer or artist of any type is precisely what he wants to make of it. I don't think he has an obligation beyond presenting his best work; work that satisfies him and proves to him that he's using his talent correctly. Me, I'm a propagandist. If I can't think of a theme whose reputability I'm trying to either establish or demolish, I can't do a story; I'll have nothing to write, nothing to say. But that's my particular framework.

Humor has to be based on something, but what it's based on is up to its creator. It can be zany, like Perelman, whimsical and light like Thurber, or dead-serious like Mencken. There aren't any rules. The only obligation the humorist has is to develop a line and remain faithful to it.

"My advice would be to write—never to stop writing, to keep it up all the time, to be painstaking about it, to write until you begin to write."

Gabriel Fielding
Interviewed in Maidstone, Kent, England, October, 1963

Gabriel Fielding

N. Gabriel Fielding has become one of the best-known and respected novelists in the Western world. A case in point—and a very high point it is—*The Birthday King*. This novel was a best-seller on both sides of the Atlantic, a critical success in the lasting sense of the word (by this I mean it was a book that reviewers and critics came back to cite again and again) and the winner of the British Commonwealth's most exalted literary prize. Amazingly, *The Birthday King* dealt with the Nazi-Jewish relationships that could easily have been "old hat" by the time Mr. Fielding's novel was released. The vigor of his approach and handling proved, to the contrary, that no subject matter is stale when it is treated creatively and conscientiously.

In talking with Mr. Fielding I would, of course, like to go back to the very beginning—to his growth as a person, his evolvement as a writer.

■ *Fielding:* To go all the way back I'd have to say that I can only remember my childhood as a beautiful golden blur. I remember things like silver birch trees, just as Robert Frost mentions them, and pools in the grass, and happiness with teeth. Then I remember a terrible separation when I was sent away at the age of eight to a snob preparatory school in the south of England, where everything and everyone, from the masters to the hens, seemed hostile. I think that this, in a sense, was the beginning of the pain out of which I write.

I do write out of pain—I believe most writers do. But from that experience onward I became extremely introspective, extremely frightened of life, particularly frightened of people. Whenever, as I grew older, I came across (in other people's books) the analysis of pain I was immediately interested. Perhaps it was in that early period that I decided that I would one day use my pain and the insight it gave me in a career as a writer. I decided that I was nothing if not a writer. I didn't want to be morbid about this, but pain, to me, was of surpassing interest, and its reconciliation with life the mainspring of writing.

N. But first you became a doctor—

■ *Fielding:* My parents were reluctant to let me undertake the risks of reading English at Oxford. I had two brothers there who didn't do terribly well, the money was running out, and they said to me, "Many doctors have become good writers. The practice of medicine is an ideal apprenticeship." They said this quite rightly, and I suppose the element of pain entered in again because they noticed that I was extremely sympathetic to anyone in pain of any sort, to anyone suffering from disease or injury.

For instance, there was one occasion when there was a terrible motorcycle accident. We were coming back from a picnic in the car when we saw three drunken figures coming down the road with great scarlet bibs of blood all over their chests. One man, whose eye was hanging out, turned out to be the local vicar, but all were staggering, in frightful condition, along the road. Well, everyone else in the car was ill, but I wasn't. I got out. I wanted to see, and see closely (not just morbidly), but I also wanted to know what I could do. I wanted to be involved. Since I did get close to the men, and it fascinated me and affected me, it became one of the examples my parents quoted (when I was older, of course) to convince me that medicine was a sympathetic career for me.

Thus, on the understanding that I was going into medicine as a preparation for writing, I went numbly, almost dumbly, through the medical course. It's taken me years to realize how little I liked it. Throughout the five or seven years of the course I went along like a hen with its beak on a chalk line, through the classes, two years of anatomy, and the traumatic experience of hospitals because it seemed that I had to do it. It didn't occur to me to feel that I could be brave enough to say to my parents, "This is not for me."

One of the things that kept me going during that time was the writing I was doing. I joined the Philosophical Society in Trinity College, Dublin. Oscar Wilde had been a member of it, as well as President Mahaffey, so I was able to satisfy that important side of myself through more appropriate interests. Medicine, to me, was the sentence I had to fulfill in order to be free to write; one might say it was like working seven years to get Rachel, then being landed with Leah, as in the Bible. By the time I emerged from medicine I had more or less succeeded in convincing myself that I was a doctor. I honestly didn't think the other dream, the vision of being a writer, could come true.

Quite honestly, I'm a pessimist; I don't expect much from life. I'm astonished when things go right. I'm astonished when words like "open sesame" are spoken and a door opens, as it has opened for me—but to get back with the story.

I got through medicine, and I was a doctor, but through the stresses of practice I began to realize that I didn't want to be one. The yearning to be a writer opened up again; then I fell ill. The desire to write grew, the dream came back, enlarged. I was not a romantic, but I saw that I had my chance and I took it. I started writing. That was only twelve years ago; actually, all of my writing has been done in these twelve years, after my thirty-seventh birthday.

N. One American critic has commented that writers should throw away everything they write prior to the age of forty, then start their professional career.

■ *Fielding:* Possibly. Yet I go back to some of the things I wrote as a very young man, even as a child; they always attracted attention. But since these things were only extracurricular, it was a bit like having an enormous love affair with a woman who had been walled up in a tower. Occasionally she would drop a message from the tower, or you would get one to her, but most of the time she was locked away while you battled with the dragon.

N. But when you did start writing as a career, and success came, how did you react?

■ *Fielding:* I think I could put it this way. As a doctor I know that we use only a fraction of our organs. We use about 30 per cent of our kidney surface, a small percentage of the lung. All the time I was unable to write due to the demands of medical training and practice I felt like a man who has a large lung which he is not using. I knew I had this lung, I was conscious of the ability to use it, but conscious that I was not using it.

Once I started writing seriously I had an extraordinary sensation of total use. I suppose it was euphoric and I don't think it's unusual for the writer to experience it. To use another metaphor, it was as though I was driving a car and suddenly discovered that the machine had a supercharger. Or it may have been what Aladdin felt when he first went into the cave with the old lamp. (I think I describe this in my novel about Dublin.)

Essentially, because of my experience, the variety and the pain of this experience, I felt that nothing had been wasted. I realized that what I'd stored up and had not so far used, formed a rich deposit. Once I started writing I could use this, not from a sense of morbidity or self-pity, but for some larger objective. I felt I'd gained insight into lust, into passion, into despair, into everything by which men are wooed. Thus the very act of writing seemed to release the energy of those organic areas which before had been stored in unused reservoirs.

Perhaps all writers feel this release, this accomplishment, to some degree. I know that when I'm writing well I have a feeling of having come into my own, everything seems justified. Otherwise the act of writing, and its success, involves the expected satisfactions: vanity and the excitement of being in the limelight. When one has a product to sell, one wants it to be discussed.

Now, the other thing of enormous satisfaction—and this I've discussed with many other writers, including Muriel Spark—is the conviction that when one is writing one is about to discover something which has existed for a long, long time, but which has been hidden from knowledge. Writing to me is a voyage, an odyssey, a discovery, because I'm never certain of precisely what I will find. I don't know what will spring from my own memory, from five or ten years back, and will appear again with enormous illumination—with new and significant meaning—not only to me, but (if I serve and express it properly) to the reader. But on bad days, on days when things just don't come, I'm in worse shape than I was as a doctor. Then I can look at things I've written which are good, and think despairingly, "Where could it have come from? How could I have done it? Will I ever be able to do it again?"

N.   To turn to *The Birthday King*. How did the theme of the novel, the actual plotting and writing of it, evolve?

■ *Fielding:* It evolved very slowly and from a very early stage of my life. I was a war child, born at the time of the First World War, and I grew up with the knowledge of death, of suffering, of pain, which very early in my life became associated with the Germans. We used to play Germans and English. My father's health was crippled by that war— he contracted sleeping sickness as a result of his service in Italy. One of my uncles was lost in the war, and my mother, who had a strong psychic sense, suffered more than did most women at home because she was so often aware of what was going on and what would happen.

I grew up with this idea that if man could become monstrous he would be a monster in German form. He would wear a gas mask and commit unspeakable atrocities and unleash clouds of poisonous gas.

Later, when I entered my own war, it became a private obsession not to incriminate the Germans for what they had obviously done but, from my own sense of humanity, to explain and resolve it. I had, in other words, become more mature. We have to do this. We have to find a fear, identify it, and later resolve it. When I set out to do *The Birthday King* I felt that if I could explain all the involved issues with a pure and clinical detachment I might also succeed in resolving and exorcising the Germans for a great number of other people.

Now, it's very interesting that when the prize was awarded, the Germans who actually helped me with the book came over for the presentation and sat on the platform with my first publisher, Erica Marx, who is Jewish. The fact that I had the Germans and the Jews on the same platform with myself—that we could openly discuss the disease that had this particular nation in the presence of one of their victims—made my book something of a diagnosis, and also, perhaps in a very small sense, something of a healer.

N. Is it true that your novels sell better in the United States than in England?

■ *Fielding:* Yes. To date they've sold a great deal better—I'm using this in the collective sense, because some have only sold slightly better whereas others have gone far ahead in America.

N. Is this because our market is larger?

■ *Fielding:* I don't think it's just because of that. Of course, it's a factor, but I think the real reasons are more subtle and harder to explain.

When I meet an American—and I suppose there are really two kinds, "open" and "closed" Americans—I find it easy to establish rapport, a sense of excitement. Perhaps I've met only the "open" Americans. Somehow the American maintains the permanent adolescence which I value so greatly, which I assume is intrinsic in my character. I think that this quality is essential to the creative artist: his sense of wonder, his ability to speculate, his freshness and daring. I feel at ease with the Americans I've met; I can behave as I like, say what I like, explore any idea because nothing will be shocking, nothing will be a closed issue. The only unforgivable sin to an American is to be boring or bored.

In England things are quite different. If you want a real discussion, the kind I most enjoy, you've got to pick your man carefully. (Ninety per cent of them are not so much dead as so cautious they might as well be dead.) Even then, instead of rapport, you're apt to frighten the Englishman or fill him with distaste when you come up with anything beyond the conventional.

Now, the American loves to taste and explore and speculate about anything new. If this is immaturity, then I'm immature, but I think it's a wonderfully forgivable immaturity. Perhaps all this helps my books in America.

N. I'd like to shift, now, to a still more speculative area. If you were to look at the literary world today, closely and critically, what elements, what work, would you most deplore and what would you admire, and again, what would you hope for?

■ *Fielding:* This is difficult. I've just been trying to sort out these ideas for an article for the Sunday *Times,* and I think I might repeat much of what I said.

I believe that the novel is presently in decline, and for a very paradoxical reason: the world is awakening to reading and to thinking. In other words, mass education, automation, the forty-hour week, and a neutral kind of leisure, is converting mass populations to reading, to watching television, to absorbing (or at least hearing and seeing) more. A surprisingly large segment of the audience convinces itself it can write too. Now, the reason that the novel is falling is because these people are turning out first novels—I know writers who are working on their sixth, numerically, but who are still writing their first. They're subjective novels, full of boredom, frustration, sexual fantasy. The new public I'm talking about has its own frustrations, its own sexual fantasies, and eventually feels damned if it's going to read about someone else's.

In other words I believe that until the novel returns to its original function—which was only a bit lower than prophecy and poetry—it will not be read.

My past twelve years, both as far as reading and writing are concerned, have been devoted to what I call "the classical novel of obsession." I think that the writer who is most worthy to be published and read is the writer absolutely and totally obsessed with what he has to say. He's not writing from mere fantasy of fruitless frustration; he's working from obsession. This applies to James Joyce, who was an obsessed man, to Dickens, to Tolstoy, Dostoevsky. Many contemporary novels are as satisfying as the copy on a cereal package (and perhaps should be as brief).

Now, I will only read the obsessional, but with this qualification: the energy must be so concentrated that the writer will achieve enormity out of the narrowness and perfection of his obsession. Until the novel gets itself off the psychiatric couch and away from the kitchen sink and down from the steps of the brothel it will be neither entertaining nor rewarding.

N. You've partially answered the next question, which concerns your advice for the talented youngster who wants to make a career of fiction.

■ *Fielding:* My advice would be to write—never to stop writing, to keep it up all the time, to be tremendously painstaking about it, to write until you begin to write. This is what I've had to do, so I may be speaking from a vantage point too close to personal experience. I've had to write so much in order to write so little.

The mere habit of writing, of constantly keeping at it, of never giving up, ultimately teaches you how to write. It's the practice of writing that makes you a writer. Yet if you should find, after a certain length of time, that you don't want to write, that the burden of it erases the joy of it, then give it up. I believe that all writers who make the grade do so because writing, and only writing, is absolutely essential to them. No amount of talent will do the job if it isn't backed with compulsion.

N. To take compulsion one step further: What do you feel the writer's obligations are to the public he is writing for, on the one hand, and to the material he uses, on the other?

■ *Fielding:* First of all, I think the writer must entertain. For example, Colette, whether she described a slice of tart with a bit of red currant jelly on it, and a wasp gently digging a little quarry in the jelly, or whether she described, as in *The Cat,* an effeminate young husband more in love with his cat and himself than with his bride, she gave you the true quality, the intrinsic quality, which made these things glow, brought them to life. The same quality a great still-life artist gives an apple or a pear.

I think the first thing the writer must do is to illuminate whatever it is he is writing about. This is the poetic function of the writer.

The next duty that springs from the function, the exquisite function of his craft, is to instruct. The nicest compliment ever paid to me about my novels came when someone said, "I didn't like your books when I started reading them, but I find now that I have read them over the last ten years and they have altered a tiny fraction of the pattern of my thought regarding my own life." Now, when I read the classical obsessional novelist, I'm being instructed. I'm instructed by sympathy. One of the loveliest things about this is when you say or feel, "Ah, I, too, knew this. I knew it without knowing it, but now I know it." This is a marvelous thing, what Claudel called "the delicious pulp of words." In short, the writer must reconcile himself and the reader to life.

The final function of the writer is, I believe, his insistence upon being a wise man—asking a wise question. Now, if ever I feel that I am not a wise man, that I am not continually progressing in my attitudes, in my knowledge, in my life, then I should be like Thomas Merton. I should plump for elected silence, but unlike Merton I would keep this silence. I do think these three things— the function of entertaining, with its accompanying poetic function; the function of instruction, and finally, the function of wisdom, must distinguish the writer.

Of course, I take novel writing very seriously. At the moment I am writing a novel which is alarming me terribly, because every single one of the things I just said is totally violated. It's the study of lust, it's unedifying, it's light, it's vicious, it's horrible. I'm breaking all my rules, but, somehow, I may ultimately observe them. I have a feeling that the reason I'm finding this novel so difficult is because I am breaking all my rules, yet I suspect that some magic will enable it to ultimately fulfill my canons. Yet, if I discover that I am not truly fulfilling my rules I simply shan't finish it.

I'm taking quite a risk with this novel, you see. I'm trying to explore the corruption in England at this moment. This is a dangerous thing, an almost sacrilegious thing, in light of my own principles. I'm exploring corruption by means of corruption, but there we are. And yet, if the magic doesn't happen, if it turns out to be only corruption, I shall have to abandon it.

N. You've mentioned your own ideals as a novelist, and the problems you face in working beyond your rules. If we enlarge this to look at the world as a whole, what do you think the individual should do to live constructively with this world and in peace with himself?

■ *Fielding:* That's a difficult question to answer; it almost has to be divided into parts or sections. The first is "How is a man to live most profitably to himself and to others without any specific relationship with religious belief or philosophy?" and the other section would be based upon my particular convictions as a Christian. Yet in essence the answer, my answer at least, has to be combined.

The most important part of living is loving. For me—as a man, a doctor, a neighbor, and a father, loving surmounts all. When I have been unable to accept other people, to care for them, to love them, I am somehow diminished.

As a doctor it isn't always possible to love a patient. As Eliot said, "The surgeon plies . . . the bleeding hands." The doctor is treating himself when he's treating a patient. When sympathy is lacking, instinctive or intuitive sympathy, I must find some compassion in myself, some pathos in the patient which relates to me and enables me to treat both of us.

Now much of the medical work over the past twelve years has been in a prison where I've had to deal with people suffering from enormous hatred, enormous sin, enormous crime. Yet I have, in dealing with these people, had to find a point where I could accept them. (Not for me to forgive them, of course, but somehow, imperatively, to accept them.)

Sybil Thorndike, the great actress, said that whenever she drives past Wormwood Scrubs, one of our big London prisons, she waves her fist and says, "You boys in there, not one of you has done anything that I haven't done on the stage or in my heart. In order to act my part I've had to do just about every crime and commit just about every sin under the sun. I have done them, too, with you."

In a way this is what I mean, what I was trying to do in *The Birthday King*, what I try to do in life. I try not to be isolated from people. I try by empathy, by empathic exercise (and it's a rather instant kind of exercise) to reconcile my fellows to myself and myself to my fellows so that we're all one and everything is understood and forgiven.

This is the first answer; insofar as the private individual has areas of fear and hatred inside him for any other creature, for any other man in particular, he is crippled. What I consciously try to do is to diminish my private areas of hatred and fear and prejudice. I hope, by the time I die, that they will have shrunk into very small areas, a minute part of the whole of me.

To put it into a cliché, I'm preaching tolerance, but I find that its counterpart, the positive aspect, love, is the most important part of life.

Now I come to the religious side of life, to ideas. Ideas are what make or kill philosophies. They make a man or they kill a man. For instance, a few years ago I had an opportunity to hear and meet Sir Oswald Mosley, a man whose every word and action as a thinking man has been abhorrent to me. That night a lot of people walked out; they refused to meet Mosley. But I was with a Catholic priest, and I said to him, "I don't think I can face it, Father. I don't think I can meet this man." And he said, "Doctor, the first part of a fish to go rotten is its head. Let us see what is in his head."

Well, I listened to Mosley for two hours and everything that came out of that man's head was as stinkingly dead as old fish. It was revolting, and I felt myself at liberty to attack the man's ideas. In this sense I'm extremely intolerant. I'm like Mary McCarthy; ideas I think are wrong, that go against my central philosophy, I will attack with everything I've got. For example, I'm not against Communists, but I'm against communism. I feel myself at liberty to destroy the Communist idea, but not to destroy Communists, unless, of course, they're seeking to destroy me and force the matter to one of self-defense.

But coming back to religion. After about ten years in childhood in which I was a Christian—because my parents were Christians—I endured a spell of twenty years when I was nothing. I was just the typical secular pagan of today. I got along with life, I found medicine had most of the answers for me in the philosophical sense, and I didn't worry about the supernatural. I didn't worry about religion. It was of very little interest to me, but gradually, after I had read a bit of Buddhism I became very "left-wing." For a time I thought all the world's evils were materialistic in origin. Then, gradually, I discovered that neither medicine nor materialism nor even the finer reaches of Buddhist mysticism explained my world, solved my problems. So I began seriously to investigate Christianity, just as I had seriously investigated communism when I was a medical student. I came to the astonishing conclusion that it might be true.

Now, this was a very strange time for me when I suddenly began to consider that possibly the whole of the central Christian message was true, namely, that God made the world, that He found it going wrong, that He therefore became man and that He suffered crucifixion and death at the hands of His own creatures in order to redeem them. When I got behind it, having begun to accept this simple story as possibly being historically, allegorically, and mystically true, it was a wonderful thing to investigate the subsequent happenings in Christianity as a product of this single event. This is what we call "revelation," and I was like Jacques Maritain, the French philosopher. Maritain was asked why he became a Catholic late in life and he replied, "I am a philosopher. If truth is in the dung hill, to the dung hill I must go." This was much of my attitude when, after reading and thinking and discussing at great length, it became apparent to me that if Christianity was true, then the truth of it still abides in the authority of the Roman Catholic Church.

Now, you might say, "What difference does that make to you?" I can only reply in words that would paraphrase Dame Edith Sitwell. She was asked why she became a Catholic, and she said, "For three reasons. I wanted fire, I wanted discipline and I wanted authority." As Muriel Spark said to me, "I would always ask a man of his actions, 'What is your authority?'" She also became a Catholic, and so, of course, did Evelyn Waugh and Graham Greene and many other intellectuals. (I loathe the word "intellectuals" because we're all intellectual; call us "professional" intellectuals if you like.)

You might ask, "Did it make any difference to you when you became a Catholic?" Well, I made my obedience to the Church of Rome and I did it wholeheartedly. For one thing, I had only two children, had had none for eight years and was ill; I didn't relish life very much. I had a lovely marriage, but outside of my marriage life seemd to me to be a jungle. When I became a Catholic I proved my sincerity because we had four more pregnancies in nine years. We lost one of these, but we did have another three children, and this year I adopted a sixth. This you might say is "basic."

You might also ask, "How does it work?" and I can say, arrogant as it may sound, that when I told Evelyn Waugh I was going to become a Catholic he congratulated me in a letter by suggesting that the Catholic Church was the beginning of intellectual and spiritual development. I thought this was extremely arrogant of him at the time; in fact, I think it delayed my conversion by a month. But I have to confess now that for me, as a person, it has proved true. My entry into the Catholic Church has resolved, for me, an enormous part of my personal difficulties.

I have found that insofar as I use my Church and the sacraments it gives me, I profit beyond all description. Insofar as I fail to use them I drift back into all kinds of moral and intellectual confusion.

Not everyone in God's province needs to become a Catholic. Faith is the gift of God, and God has His own dispositions. For me Catholicism was my gift of faith, but it does not mean that God fails to love non-Catholics, and that men and women cannot live profitably without Catholicism. I can see many other people making good sense of their lives without becoming Catholics, but I have never seen a man make a success of his life without loving his fellow creatures. Love, again, is the essence.

This is the most vicious and terrible thing about communism, that it destroys the idea of the mystery and holiness of the individual and puts the State in front of him. We must never do this in our own lives. We mustn't put our family in front of people, nor our income, nor our interests, nor our ambitions. We mustn't, you see, be "little Communists." This is why I say, "Cling to love and expand your personal affection for all people insofar as you can, every day that you can, and destroy the coldness within you that entertains fear, hatred, and disapproval."

"I'm glad to see a return to romantic writing—at least a swing toward it. The story with a beginning, a middle, and an end seems to be returning to favor, and this should be good for everyone."

Ian Fleming
Interviewed in London, England, October, 1963

Ian Fleming

N. In 1952 James Bond was born—full-grown, suave, dashing, with a taste for fine food, women, and liquor. Since then he has become a giant in the world of contemporary letters, changing little from the day of his spectacular birth, though claiming an ever-widening audience. Perhaps no single character in the loosely-defined area of the suspense novel has captured a market so boldly and held it with such consistency. (Sherlock Holmes is the only counterpart that springs to mind, but he was a sleuth, not an adventurer, and we never did really know whether or not Mr. Holmes ate, drank, and bedded down.)

In speaking to Ian Fleming, the creator of the fabulous James Bond, the first natural question would be the origin of Mr. Bond. Who is he?

■ *Fleming:* Well, he's almost entirely a product of the imagination, though I've used various people I knew during the war, spies and commandos and even newsmen, because I was working in Naval Intelligence and came across unusual characters quite a lot. By "unusual" I mean people who really dealt in or with espionage, which is a bizarre world of its own, far away from any norm.

Now, I didn't want Bond to be a glamorous figure at all. I merely sought to create an interesting man to whom extraordinary things happen, but I didn't want him to be a paragon, a freak of quality. This is why I chose the very dull name "James Bond." When you think of it, it *is* a dull name. (I could have called him Peregrine Caruthers or Trevor Carr, something exciting or romantic.)

The name I borrowed, without his approval, from a very famous American ornithologist named James Bond who wrote *Birds Of The West Indies*. This book is one of my bibles when I am out in Jamaica, where I write every year, and it occurred to me that it was a properly anonymous name for my hero.

Now, you'll notice that the James Bond of the first book was a straightforward man who didn't really possess a total personality.

In fact, in the first several books you'll find absolutely no discussion of his character, few of his mannerisms, no character study in depth. The closest to this comes when the Russian Secret Service, the KGB scrutinizes him rather closely in *From Russia, With Love.* But I kept him quite blank, in a way, at first, giving him no quirks, no particular morality or immorality, not even a definite detailed personal appearance.

As the series has gone on, however, James Bond has become encrusted with mannerisms and belongings and individual characteristics. This is probably a natural outgrowth of getting to know him better. I don't know if this is good or bad, and I don't know where all the elements that compose Bond come from, but there they are.

N. Do you think you've put any of your own personality into him?

■ *Fleming:* I couldn't possibly be James Bond. First of all, he's got much more guts than I have. He's also considerably more handsome and he eats rather more richly than I could possibly manage to do. As to quirks and tastes, likes and dislikes, bits of me probably creep in. But not important bits.

N. The only real criticism of your books I've come across, made some reference to the fact that "James Bond novels are studies in sex, snobbery, and sadism."

■ *Fleming:* I don't think they are studies in anything, not even in those quite proper ingredients of a thriller. Sex, of course, enters all interesting books and all interesting lives. As to snobbery, I wonder how much it isn't a very common motivation, perhaps a spur. Wouldn't all of us like to eat better, stay in better hotels, drive faster motor-cars, write better books? James Bond is lucky; his life is both cushioned and exciting. As for sadism—frankly, the old-fashioned way of beating spies with baseball bats and truncheons became obsolete during the last war. It's quite permissible to give them a rougher time than we did in more gentlemanly days. But as to "studies in sex, snobbery, and sadism," I'm certain they are nothing I attempt, want to attempt, or could do properly should I attempt them.

N. In considering both the character of James Bond, and the general pace of your novels, can you think of any writers who have influenced you?

■ *Fleming:* Two splendid American writers, the great masters of the modern thriller, Dashiell Hammett and Raymond Chandler. I was influenced by these writers, by their extremely good style and

the breadth and ingeniousness of their stories. I suppose, if I were
to examine the problem in depth, I'd go back to my childhood and
find some roots of interest in E. Phillips Oppenheim and Sax
Rohmer. Perhaps they played an important part.

N. In creating the situations in which Bond finds himself, do
you pay a great deal of attention to the authenticity of background?

■ *Fleming:* Yes, I do. I don't think I've ever written about a part
of the world which I myself haven't visited. But you see, I was
a reporter for a long time. I have a reporter's eye and sense of
locality, and I add to this by taking notes and buying road maps
wherever I happen to be.

N. Could you describe the ascent of James Bond on best-
seller lists?

■ *Fleming:* I'm still puzzled as to why and how it happened, but
the sales of the books go progressively upward. They've taken a
sudden leap in the past two years in both England and America,
but that's partly due to the first film being made and released, now
followed by the second. The paperback publishers have taken advantage of the films to increase their prints. I see that my total
American sales now exceed eight million, and in England about
seven million. But I'm still very much surprised that an Englishman
should have been chosen by the Americans as a popular hero. It
doesn't often happen.

N. I think there are a few twists that make James Bond seem
very American. Likes and dislikes, brand of cigarettes, and his
rather full sex life.

■ *Fleming:* There is some American detail. Of course, three or
four of the books are set in and around America, and there's a
subsidiary hero, an American named Felix Leiter who's with the
CIA and later with a detective agency.

But I do get into trouble with my Americanisms. People write
in and say I've got things wrong here and there. Recently, in fact,
I got an assistant librarian at Yale who passes on all my American
scenes. I give him the book, and he very kindly goes through it and
suggests where the American language could be improved. So I try
to catch everything, but still—well, it annoys me as much as it
must annoy Americans to find America so clumsily depicted in
English books. Similarly, the English are annoyed by mistakes
American writers make about England. As an author, one should
try to get the lingo totally correct. This applies most strongly to
the gangster idiom (of which we have an exaggerated idea, perhaps largely due to Damon Runyon). Gangster language changes

with the times, just like beat language, and it's very difficult, if one isn't living in America, to keep up with it. But I try my best, and I'm pleased to find that too many Americans don't complain.

N. I still have a feeling that throughout your stories you use Bond, or other characters, to take verbal potshots at certain people or institutions you, as a person, have negative feelings about. Are you aware of this?

■ *Fleming:* Oh, yes, I take potshots at a lot of things, including American food, which I find frozen to tastelessness, and Swiss ethics, which are very strange indeed. I often let a subsidiary character express my prejudice or quirk. And I unashamedly rag the Russians. They are still up to their old tricks. Not too long ago we had that big spy case in Stuttgart in West Germany where a Russian assassin, sent by their Secret Service, confessed to the murder of at least two West Germans with liquid cyanide. The cyanide was fired, from water pistols, into the faces of men who were going upstairs. When they fell dead immediately—and cyanide is quick—no traces of it were found on them, and the verdict in both cases was "heart failure." As long as the Russians keep on with that sort of thing I'll have to go on ragging them about it. I think it would be a wonderful thing if we turned off the whole espionage heat. We'd save a lot of money. But that's neither here nor there.

N. Do you think you'll ever tire of James Bond?

■ *Fleming:* Unfortunately, it isn't a matter of tiring of James Bond. It's a question of running out of inventiveness. One can't go on forever having blondes and guns and so forth in the same old mixture. I do try to find a different milieu for each story and a very different plot. I hate the idea of short-weighting my public by giving them the same jazz all over again. In fact, I'd be too damned bored to write it myself.

Somerset Maugham, who is a great friend of mine, once said: "I'm amused by your stories, but your great trouble will be in running out of invention." I think that's probably correct, so how long it will keep going I just don't know. When I feel the situation slipping, I'll simply stop writing James Bond stories.

N. Last year—in *On Her Majesty's Secret Service*—I finally became annoyed with your disposal of a heroine I liked. Bond actually married her, then pffht—she was dead. How important is his bachelorhood?

■ *Fleming:* Well, James Bond couldn't really be married. I can't have him settling down. His wife would be irritated with his constantly going abroad, she'd want to change his way of life and all his friends, and Bond would worry about the measles epidemic back home and his own faithfulness and—no, it can't be done.

This same problem faced Raymond Chandler. In the last book he started to write, just before he died, he was going to have Marlowe marry a French countess. Well, he was very amusing when he told me about this, about how it really would be the end of Marlowe because she'd change all his habits and friends, he'd take to the bottle, and between her wealth and his faults the personality of Marlowe would be quashed. So in *Majesty's Secret Service* I took the easy way out. Tracy is no more.

N.   To turn away from James Bond for a bit. Your career obviously started long before James Bond took it over. Could you outline it?

■ *Fleming:*   Eton and Sandhurst make up the early part, and then I went into Reuters, the international news agency, and had a great deal of fun there for three or four years. Then I went into the City to try to make some money, but I wasn't very good at just plain making money. The city of London is a wonderful club to belong to, but it's altogether too diverting.

I went back to Moscow, where I had worked for Reuters, but now with the *Times* of London. From there I was more or less drafted into Naval Intelligence, as they wanted somebody with languages and some knowledge of the city, though my choice because of Sandhurst would have been the Army. I was stuck there throughout the war, personal assistant to the director of Naval Intelligence, until I was demobilized. Then Lord Kemsley, who owned the *Sunday Times,* and a very long string of provincial newspapers, asked me to come along and organize his foreign service. This was great fun, and I was at it until about two years ago— Foreign Manager of the *Sunday Times* was the title. I'm still on the editorial board, but journalism is now completely subsidiary to running the James Bond factory.

N.   You've more or less incorporated, haven't you?

■ *Fleming:*   I've had to. I am a company, and it's perfectly legitimate, but it's the only way to keep all ends straight and to save some money from the tax people. However, I am British, and proud of being British, and I'm not going to dodge fair payment by making a dash for Switzerland or one of the other tax paradises. I'll continue to divide my time between England and Jamaica and save a bit less. But even if the tax thing wasn't in the picture, I'd have to be a company. There are always too many Bond projects at hand.

N. In the realm of theory, when you're writing the Bond stories, do you feel any definite obligation to the hero you've created, the situations you employ, the public for which you're writing?

■ *Fleming:* I think I find more of an obligation to myself. I write the sort of books that I, personally, would like to read if somebody else would write them for me. They are the type of books that while away the time on an airplane journey, when one is ill in bed, and do away with boredom, or worry.

I set out to entertain and stimulate the reader through all his senses, right down to the taste buds. In most books, you know, the hero has a meal, but you never know what he eats and how much he enjoyed it. In English detective stories people are forever drinking cups of tea or pints of beer and that's the end of it. It has amused me to put together good food and things I happen to like myself and have James Bond eat them for me.

As far as locations and logic are concerned, I think we discussed these before. I try to make everything credible, as related to what I know about the rather improbable world of espionage and the parts of the world I've visited. A glaring inaccuracy, or a stretching of plausibility, would bother me more than it would any reader.

N. Again, theory: What advice would you give the talented youngster who is seriously concerned with making a career of writing?

■ *Fleming:* Well, I would tell him to write more or less as he speaks. To try to get an accurate ear for the spoken word and not, so to speak, put on a top hat when he sits down at his typewriter. He must not think that literature has to be literary. I talked over this very subject with Georges Simenon not too long ago, and he made the same point—not that we should write in a less than literate manner, but that we must avoid pretentiousness. This may be an oversimplification, but I'd tell the youngster to learn to type well and to avoid literary myths.

N. In looking at literature and theater at the moment, what do you find that you most admire, and what do you most deplore?

■ *Fleming:* I've gotten very tired of this "kitchen sink" period. In fact, the boiled cabbage school bores me to tears. It isn't necessary to wallow in filth to know what filth is. Things go altogether too far when filth is viewed as beauty and obscenity becomes accepted communication. The world is drab enough, and sometimes horrifying enough, without having this desolation monopolize our theater, books, and films.

I'm even old-fashioned enough to disagree with the findings of the *Lady Chatterly* case. I think it would have been much better not to push that work out into the world, though I dare say the world will digest it and get used to it as it's absorbed Miller's erotic excursions to the tropics. We'll take any four-letter word without a flinch, and I suppose that those words will ultimately lose their shock, then their meaning. I think that they rather strike an attitude on the page, however, and I refuse to use them.

On the other hand I'm glad to see a return to romantic writing —at least a swing toward it. The story with a beginning, a middle, and an end seems to be returning to favor, and this should be good for everyone.

"To me, any novel which doesn't have something to say on the subject of whether and why the characters are authentic or unauthentic is difficult to take seriously. It is merely an entertainment."

John Fowles
Interviewed in London, England, October, 1963

John Fowles

N. *The Collector* was one of the most successful novels published in the United States in 1963. Virtually flawless in form—in the bold yet subtle handling of a unique plot—it was also distinguished by a polished and mature style. The suspense involved in a basic, horrifying predicament became all the more gripping as the perversities of time, place, and person maintained a relentless reality. The success of *The Collector*, both in the critical and popular sense, is all the more astonishing in view of the fact that it is a first novel by a young British writer we might call "unheralded." In speaking with John Fowles, I would like to begin by asking him how *The Collector* came into being—how he originated the macabre situation upon which it is based?

■ *Fowles:* It's complicated story, but basically I think of *The Collector* as a parable. You see, I have always wanted to illustrate the opposition of the Few and the Many (*hoi polloi*). I take these terms from the pre-Socratic Greek philosopher Heraclitus, who's been a major influence on my life. For him the Few were the good, the intelligent, the independent; the Many were the stupid, the ignorant, and the easily molded. Of course he implied that one could choose to belong to the Few or to the Many. We know better. I mean these things are hazard, conditioning, according to one's genes, one's environment, and all the rest. Because of this element of hazard, the proper attitude of the Few to the Many is pity, not arrogance. I wanted to explore this inevitable but very complex tension in the human condition.

I also wanted to attack—this is saying the same thing, really—the contemporary idea that there is something noble about the inarticulate hero. About James Dean and all his literary children and grandchildren, like Salinger's Holden Caulfield, and Sillitoe's Arthur Seaton (in *Saturday Night and Sunday Morning*). I don't admire beats, bums, junkies, psychopaths, and inarticulates. I feel sorry for them. I think "adjusted" adolescents are better and more significant than "maladjusted" ones. I'm against the glamorization of the Many. I think the common man is the curse of civilization, not its crowning glory. And he needs education, not adulation. The boy in *The Collector* stands for the Many; the girl for the Few. I tried to make them individual, so they both have individual faults. But behind them are the faults and complexities of the greater situation.

But to get back to the girl-in-the-cellar situation. How did I come on it? Well, some time during the 1950's, I went to see the first performance in London of Bartok's opera, *Bluebeard's Castle*. It wasn't a very good performance, but the thing that struck me was the symbolism of the man imprisoning women underground. It so happened that about a year later there was an extraordinary case (again in London) of a boy who captured a girl and imprisoned her in an air-raid shelter at the end of his garden. She could have gotten away earlier than she did, but she was—if not mentally deficient—not very bright. In the end she did escape, but there were many peculiar features about this case that fascinated me. And eventually, it led me to the book.

N.   I'd like to go into your own rough autobiography—the life that actually preceded *The Collector*.

■ *Fowles:*   I went to an English private school. Then I went to Oxford. Before that I did some service in the Marines. I was a lieutenant—and hated it. Perhaps this was because I had been head boy at my school, and head boys at English public schools have a lot of power. You run the school's discipline. At the age of eighteen I had had power to judge and punish 600 to 800 other boys, and this gave me a distaste for power that has grown and grown and grown. (Incidentally, if I have any criticism of America, it would be that everything there tends to be judged in terms of power and potency.)

After I left Oxford, I taught at a French university for a year. I studied French at Oxford and came deeply under the influence of French existentialist writers. I've never shaken this off. From France I went to Greece to teach at a boys' school. Then I returned to England and taught for a year or so in an adult education center. Since then I've been teaching English to foreigners in a large London college.

N.   Are you still teaching?

■ *Fowles:*   No. I gave up my job in April of this year. I've always taught in order to be able to have time for writing. It's one of the great advantages of teaching. I think teaching is a noble profession. I have nothing against it, but I've wanted to write, and teaching is the best means to the end. In any case, for me, writing is a kind of teaching.

Well, I've been writing, off and on, for twelve or fifteen years. I haven't written with method, that's my trouble. I started seven or eight novels, wrote twenty stray chapters of each, put them by—and they never got finished. But with *The Collector*, I knew I had the story I wanted. I felt sure of the novel from the start. The few friends who were told about it didn't share my enthusiasm, but I felt intuitively that it could be made into something.

N. If you were advising the young writer on a course of action—training and development, more or less—what would this advice be?

■ *Fowles:* First of all, read and think. All good books are distilled experience. Stay away from creative writing courses. Perhaps these courses are useful for people who just want to make a profession of writing: journalism, literary journalism, script-writing or stories for the mass magazines. These people can learn something from creative writing courses. For me, writing is part of my existentialist view of life. It's an attempt to make myself wholly authentic. I think the serious writer has to have his view of the purpose of literature absolutely clear. I don't see that you can write seriously without having a philosophy of both life and literature to back you. Some philosophy of life is a property of all better writers. It may be an anarchistic one, but it's there, part of the writer, part of his work. Ultimately he writes for his view of life—not for money.

N. What do you think of the state of British writing at present?

■ *Fowles:* I would say, not too healthy. I think a viable blanket criticism is that we're too insular, too privately embroiled. This may be bound up with the fact that at the moment most of the British Left—the intelligentsia—are anti-European. And there's certainly far too much satirical writing. When everyone "does" satire, it loses its point. Some of our best younger writers belong to the so-called "provincial" school, which is sympathetic. We also have an even worse flock of heavily symbolic novelists. Some of their work makes one fall on one's knees and pray for a Zhdanov. Of course, we also have a literary Establishment to deal with—all the usual incestuous and nepotal features. We need a return to the great tradition of the English novel—realism. English is a naturally empirical language; I suppose that's why realism haunts all our arts.

I think the publishers in London are partly to blame. Far too many novels are published—everyone agrees on that. And the publishers too often seem incapable of seeing beyond their noses—or rather, beyond whatever was successful last year. I mean they're too influenced by vogue. Some of them are very amateurish at their jobs by American standards, incapable both of launching a book properly and of giving a writer the kind of editorial sympathy most of us need. I'd better add that my own English publisher is generally recognized to be an exception to all this.

N. What do you think of allied fields in England, of the theater, for example?

■ *Fowles:* If I were to name the field that is healthiest, it would be the theater. We have some good dramatists—Osborne, Harold Pinter, John Arden, Arnold Wesker. They may not always have much to say, but they say it interestingly and well.

N. What about criticism?

■ *Fowles:* I think that serious academic criticism is quite good in England, but many of us are unhappy about the state of journalistic criticism. There's too much subjectivity and maliciousness in it; too many of the weekly reviewers are more concerned with showing off than with criticizing. The thing I hate especially in England is the way novelists so often review other novelists. What I would like to see grow in England is a body of independent novel reviewers who are not practicing novelists themselves. We don't find painters criticizing other painters, or pianists reviewing other pianists, so why should one novelist be allowed to review another?

N. How do you feel about American criticism?

■ *Fowles:* I think your criticism is healthier, more open. I've gathered, since I've been in New York, that you feel British criticism is more sophisticated, and attains a more serious level. But I smell a whiff of fresh air in your criticism. It's franker, more open, possibly more naïvely expressed, but actually, more serious.

In England my novel was reviewed as a crime novel by three of our most "intellectual" newspapers. They gave me good crime-novel reviews, but I was shocked that this could happen. It hasn't occurred in America. Some reviewers have criticized the book, but at least they've taken it for something more serious than a mere suspense story.

N. I wanted to ask you about the reception of *The Collector* in England.

■ *Fowles:* I can't complain. It might be interesting to mention that the novel sold eight thousand copies (as of September 1963) and these days that's a lot for a first novel in England.

N. It's far ahead of that in the United States, isn't it?

■ *Fowles:* It's over forty thousand copies now. And it was published later, of course. It was very skillfully launched by my publishers, Little, Brown. That undoubtedly helped a lot.

N. What work do you have in progress?

■ *Fowles:* I'd better say first of all that I'm more interested in poetry and philosophy than I am in the novel. If I were to specify my aims in life I'd first of all like to be a good poet, then a sound philosopher, then a good novelist. The novel is simply, for me, a way of expressing my view of life.

However, I am writing another novel, set in Greece. It won't be the same as *The Collector,* but I hope it will also contain a very strange kind of situation. I'm certain that I must write in terms of strict realism. I'm a great admirer of Daniel Defoe—what I admire most is his creation of the extremely unusual situation, such as we find in *Robinson Crusoe* treated scrupulously in terms of his talent and honestly in terms of life. I hope this sort of approach will underlie my next novel, the Greek one. I also hope to have some philosophical ideas, mainly existentialist ideas, published in 1964, under the title *The Aristos.*

N. Then you are deeply interested in philosophy?

■ *Fowles:* Yes, indeed. This is what I admire about the French school of novelists. Sartre and de Beauvoir and the others. Although I don't necessarily share their points of view, I absolutely share their serious view of the writer's function. I feel I must be committed, that I must use literature as a method of propagating my view of life.

N. To turn to a basic question—what do you feel the obligation of the novelist is to the public as a whole?

■ *Fowles:* I'm afraid I'm going to give you an unsatisfactory answer. I don't feel that's a fair question. You can't generalize like that. I think we need novels that provide pure entertainment—novels to read, to enjoy, to put down, to forget. I happen to write novels for more serious reasons, but personal reasons that I have no right to impose on literature as a whole. If any writer says novels should be written *only* for entertainment, parroting the worst of our reviewers who say, "If it's fun it's good," or *only* for didactic reasons, I'd say to hell with him.

N. Conversely—and this may strike closer to your approach— what obligation do you think the writer has to the characters he creates or borrows?

■ *Fowles:* Once again, I don't think I can answer that because it depends upon whatever is the case. For *me* the obligation is to present my characters realistically. They must be credible human beings even if the circumstances they are in are "incredible," as they are in *The Collector*. But even the story, no matter how bizarre, no matter what symbolisms are involved, has to be possible.

N. You accomplished this in *The Collector*. The horror grew as the story progressed, but no matter how nightmarish it became, it was still believable.

■ *Fowles:* For me, that's a great compliment. William Golding, an English writer who, for other reasons, I admire very much, has to my mind one consistent fault: he doesn't treat his characters realistically enough in the extreme situations he invents. There are times when the credibility begins to wear thin. The same thing mars Kafka. I'm only stating this criticism because it helps explain my own view of life and of the function of the writer. Believability must dominate even the most outlandish situation.

N. In the world of writing, British, American, even the product from the Continent, what do you most admire, and what do you most deplore?

■ *Fowles:* Here, I think, I most deplore the stress on purely clever writing—the mere manipulation of words that American writers seem to practice more than writers in England. The danger of this, I think, is that you breed a sort of rococo cleverness which may be interesting to literary cliques and other stratospheric elements of the literary world, but which basically says nothing about the human condition, which teaches nothing, which does not touch people's hearts. I believe in the heart. In other words, I think that writing tends to be too cerebral, both here and, by imitation of you, in England.

In other ways, of course, your characteristic preoccupation with technique pays off. Young American writers often have all sorts of professional virtues young British ones haven't—cleaner descriptions, neater dialogue, a sharper eye for inessentials. But these virtues may be spoilt by the admixture of what seem to us artificial made-to-recipe symbolisms and deeper significances. I mean, I think we retain certain amateur virtues. Your writers have better eyes; ours have sincerer minds. You are, in general, pragmatists, believers in the sales figure. We're in general romantics; we believe in the muses, in writing as a vocation rather than writing as a career. Of course there are exceptions galore. But I think this explains *characteristic* faults and virtues on both sides. After all, it's a good polarity to have in the house of our common language. What's finally important is that it is the same house, not that we're all different in it.

N.   How do you feel about Salinger, and the cult he's attracted?

■ *Fowles: The Catcher In The Rye* is a master book, but after that I feel he fell into an over-cerebral way of writing. We always have to have some cerebral writers. Salinger is a brilliant writer, and it's ridiculous to say he shouldn't have gone his route. He's still writing so far above the level of lesser novelists that I can't include him in my general complaint about the trend. He's not responsible for his imitators.

N.   What English writers do you most admire at the present time?

■ *Fowles:*   I admire William Golding very much. I admire Evelyn Waugh and Graham Greene. Their philosophies of life horrify or bore me, but I think that, technically, they are both masters, especially in narration, which is the key to good novel-writing.

N.   Is there any trend in writing you anticipate? I mean, speaking generally and on a world basis, do you feel that any particular school of writers, or type of writer, is going to become dominant?

■ *Fowles:*   I think the existentialist trend will increase. We're going to get more extreme-situation novels. (Of course, extreme situations go back to Defoe and even before him.) Books like Golding's *The Lord Of The Flies*, and my own, will come more frequently. We'll have more of the key existentialist notion of authenticity in life. One is unauthentic largely because of the pressures of modern society, pressures that change from year to year. We'll have, I hope, more penetrating analyses of characters under pressure from society. I would like to see more of this serious and didactic approach. We've had enough escapism and satire.

N.   How would you define existentialism as an influence on the novel? What do you think existentialism as a philosophical force *should* bring to the novel?

■ *Fowles:*   One interesting field is the problem of free will. This is the question of whether you can discover enough about yourself, whether you can accept enough about your own past, to become what we call an authentic character; someone who is in control of his own life, able to withstand all its anxieties.

To me, any novel which doesn't have something to say on the subject of whether and why the characters are authentic or unauthentic is difficult to take seriously. It is merely an entertainment. A very existentialist novelist, in this sense of defining authenticity, is Jane Austen. Most of the time she was writing about a moral tradition, attempting to establish what authenticity was in her particular world and circumstances. This, of course, is Lionel Trilling's approach to Jane Austen, and I am sure he is right.

But I can best answer your question by saying that I think existentialism is going to infiltrate all our arts because its ideas are slowly affecting society as a whole. You know, you become an existentialist by temperament as much as by reasoning. You *feel* it as much as think it. Your life is harried by constant anxieties, fears of things, nauseas, hatreds of things. Life is a battle to keep balance on a tightrope. To live authentically is not giving in to the anxieties, not running away from the nauseas, but solving them in some way. This giving of a solution is the wonderful thing about existentialism, and why I believe it will take the place of the old, dogmatic religions. It allows you to face reality and act creatively in terms of your own powers and your own situation. It's the great individualist philosophy, the twentieth century individual's answer to the evil pressures of both capitalism and communism.

The girl in *The Collector* is an existentialist heroine although she doesn't know it. She's groping for her own authenticity. Her tragedy is that she will never live to achieve it. Her triumph is that one day she would have done so. What I tried to say in the book was this: we must create a society in which the Many will allow the Few to live authentically, *and* to teach and help the Many themselves to begin to do so as well. In societies dominated by the Many, the Few are in grave danger of being suffocated. This is why the Many often seem to me like a terrible tyranny. *The Collector* is a sort of putting of the question. *The Aristos*, I hope, will be a direct existentialist answer. My answer, anyway.

"I think of this as my obligation: to present the subject with as much honesty of fact and integrity of person as possible."

Gerold Frank
Interviewed in New York, September, 1963

Gerold Frank

N. It would not be unfair to state that Gerold Frank—until 1963—was known as the most skilled and resourceful ghost writer of American letters. *I'll Cry Tomorrow; Too Much, Too Soon; Beloved Infidel*, and *My Story*, brought to print the private lives of Lillian Roth, Diana Barrymore, Sheilah Graham, and Zsa Zsa Gabor, respectively. With the release of *The Deed* Mr. Frank emerged as quite another writer. His incisive study of the assassination of Lord Moyne—an act surrounded by political and emotional ramifications —presented Frank totally on his own. A solid, critically successful book, it seemed to mark such a departure for Mr. Frank that I'd like to begin the interview by asking him how he came to write it.

■ *Frank:* Actually, this book has been ticking away like a time bomb in the back of my mind for at least eighteen years. I should begin by saying that a foreign correspondent meets three or four shattering experiences in the course of his duties. Usually he can walk away from stories, because he's always the observer, never the participant. His heart may be moved, and his conscience touched, but it's just one more story and he goes on to the next.

There were three or four times when I could not walk away from a story. The first was when I saw a man die in the electric chair. I was sent to Sing Sing. Now, this is a private and awful moment because you're sitting ten feet away from a man, looking into his eyes, a man who knows he is going to die, who knows you will watch him die. You are linked together with this stranger, this fellow human being, in the final, irrevocable moment of his life; and when your eyes meet, it is a terrible confrontation. You are overcome by embarrassment, pity, terror, infinite tenderness, swept by emotion. Death enters that room, silently, unseen, and suddenly you are staring at a dead man sitting in a chair. A shattering experience! It is reality as implacable as anything you will ever know. When you leave that room, you are a little changed, humble as never before, perplexed, wondering what is life, what is death, what is good and evil, what is our responsibility for our brother.

The second memorable experience came when I attended the Nuremberg Trials. I entered the courtroom to see seated before me the dozen or so Nazi makers and shakers of the world, the men responsible for so much human suffering, for death on such a scale. And this was the arresting fact—that they looked like you and me; not monsters with horns protruding from their heads, but everyday men with the faces, the anonymous faces of the thousands you pass on the street without looking twice. But by some dread magic of destiny, they had been seized by an incredibly evil virus, they had been given power, and the result was evil incarnate. The power they obtained not only corrupted them but corrupted the world until the world purged itself of them.

The third time this happened was when I attended the trial of Adolf Eichmann in Jerusalem three years ago. I felt the intensity and bitterness and suffering of the Jewish people concentrated in that little courtroom where it seemed twenty centuries—no, fifty centuries—of Jewish history beat down on us, and the voices we heard might have been heard again and again through those centuries: at the Inquisition, at the Crusades, at the pogroms and massacres that mark that history.

The fourth time came when in a courtroom in Cairo I watched two boys from Palestine, Eliahu Hakim and Eliahu Bet-Zouri, defend themselves for having committed the Deed. They had killed a man coldly, with premeditation, but they killed him for an ideal. The ideal was the freedom of their people in Palestine. The act underlined the ancient question of evil means for a good end. Of course, most revolutionaries are ready to give their lives for what they do: these two—the younger was 17, the older 22 (the younger was a high-school student, the older, a brilliant college student who translated Saroyan into Hebrew, was studying for a Ph.D. in Semitic Languages, a popular, extraordinarily gifted youth) had wanted to shake the world with an act that would call the world's attention to the struggle for Jewish freedom in Palestine in 1944–45, three years before Israel achieved its independence. They had not known each other until they met in Cairo, though both were members of a secret terrorist group, the Stern Gang, made up of some 200 boys and girls. The two Eliahus killed Lord Moyne, British Minister of State in the Middle East—he was Walter Edward Guinness, of the well-known brewing family—as a symbol of what they considered intolerable foreign rule over the Jews of Palestine. They believed freedom could be won only by fighting for it and they considered themselves at war with Great Britain, the mandatory government in Palestine. They were convinced that their act would change the course of history, and they were prepared to give their lives as payment.

They could have escaped the death penalty by pleading temporary insanity; a lawyer besought them to do so. They were young, they had been driven out of their minds, he suggested, by the daily reports of growing Jewish massacres in Europe. The boys refused. "Such a plea reduces the Deed to an emotional accident. It was not that: it was planned, a political act carried out for high moral purposes," they insisted.

As an American correspondent, I was touched by the two boys —every correspondent was. Their bearing, in the very face of the gallows, was magnificent. Yet they had committed an act of murder. They were noble in death, still convinced that their Deed was that of dedicated patriots sacrificing themselves for human liberty. Indeed, the Egyptian hangman wept as he carried out his task. The interplay of morality here is complex and enormous, and it affected me so that it simply had to become a book, a book that could be written only eighteen years later when time added to my perspective and when I'd had the opportunity to return to Cairo and Jerusalem to talk to the boys' families, friends, fellow terrorists; to read the books they read; to listen to their teachers; to speak to the Rabbi who had accompanied them to the gallows; and then put together the entire heartbreaking story as it came to conclusions and yet evaded conclusions.

This is a long answer to your question. But it does explain how a writer comes to do such a book. He writes it because it is the logical sum of everything he's done, known, experienced, up to the moment of writing it. I have no idea what my next book will be. I think that in maturity and interests, if not in substance, it will in some way flow from *The Deed*. I think this is the natural function of the writer: to absorb the world about him and give it back, subtly changed by whatever strange sea-change he has caused it to undergo.

N. To turn, now, from *The Deed* to your other books, the ones on which you worked as a very live ghost. How did you collaborate with the ladies involved?

■ *Frank:* The collaboration was in the gathering of material: I wrote the books. Each talked to me for about a year, and I suppose I obtained perhaps 75 per cent of the material in this fashion. This meant an almost psychoanalytical unfolding of their lives—endless interviews in depth, day in, day out. The remaining 25 per cent I got through research, interviewing all who knew them, from child-hood playmates to present-day intimates, from reading their diaries and letters and everything written about them.

In working with Sheilah Graham on *Beloved Infidel* (the story of Sheilah and F. Scott Fitzgerald, whom she knew in the last years of his life), I did a great deal of research on Fitzgerald. I found the doctor in Los Angeles who pronounced him dead; I talked to those who had known him best, Buff Cobb, Sr., Dorothy Parker, Nun-nally Johnson, his fellow writers, his psychiatrist in New York, and brought all this to Sheilah. It opened doors in her memory and helped make the book, I like to think, a third-dimensional auto-biography.

With Lillian Roth, I spent day after day talking—it was, again, almost like lay analysis, although obviously I am not an analyst and don't wish to make the analogy too precious. I began by saying, "Look, there will be no secrets between us. There are things that cannot be put into a book, but so far as it is humanly possible, so far as it falls within the limits of what is germain to the unfolding of your story, this must be honest and complete. To blur it would do a disservice to you and to those you want to understand you."

The same process was used with Diana Barrymore, night after night. I interviewed her friends, her father's friends, her mother's friends. I found her baby nurse (of whose existence Diana knew nothing). I talked to her doctors, to her analyst. Diana confided to me in hospitals when she was recovering from alcoholism, on trains, in her apartment, in moods and in situations when she scarcely knew whether she was on earth or in Hell. When she died a few years ago, at thirty-nine, I was called upon to deliver the eulogy at her funeral—bringing her story to its tragic full circle.

Now, none of these people would be in books unless they wanted to tell their stories. Diana Barrymore had been trying for years to write something entitled, *What's wrong with me?* She would wake up to see that grinning, drunken face of hers on the front page of a tabloid, and think, "My God, what did I do now? What's the matter with me—why can't I make sense out of my life? Every time a door is opened for me, I fall through it; every time I'm on the stage, I show up drunk; every time I get a second chance, and a third, and a fourth, I throw it away!" She once said to me, "I ought to be horsewhipped for what I've done, yet God knows I didn't want to do it."

The essential neuroses of many people, the most powerful and most painful, is when they are compelled by themselves to do things they don't want to do. This was what Diana was doing. I became convinced that behind that grinning drunken face, was imprisoned a frightened child, who hid her fear by arrogance. Was I naïve, thinking so? No, for psychiatrists agreed with me. She was frightened because she felt inadequate to live up to the name Barrymore. Here was the daughter of one of the greatest actors, one of the handsomest men of his time, John Barrymore, and of an enormously magnetic, beautiful woman, poet and dramatist, Michael Strange; and she, Diana, was not beautiful, nor magnetic, nor intellectual, abjectly ashamed of herself because she bore a fabulous name and felt unworthy of it.

When she was little, there were literary soirées at her mother's home, with guests such as George Bernard Shaw and Michael Arlen, and when she was announced: "Miss Diana Barrymore," and ushered into the illustrious company, she suffered agony. "I was yellow-faced, I was bow-legged, I had matted hair, I had just come down from hiding in my bed reading some trashy love-story magazine instead of Tolstoy. Someone like Cecil Beaton or Noel Coward would say, 'Well, Diana, what have you been reading?' and I would blush all over and not know what to answer."

One can understand why as she grew up she turned to alcohol, because with alcohol she *was* Diana Barrymore. With the magic of liquor she could become the darling of society, the beautiful, talented Diana, chip off the Barrymore block, Michael Strange's outrageous, brilliant daughter. When she was sober, none of this was true: the princess' carriage changed back to a pumpkin. We don't know what makes people drink, but she gave one reason when she would tell me at a certain point in her drinking, "I'm all right now. I feel no pain."

It was all so sad because she was inherently capable. Brooks Atkinson said there was an actress in her if she'd let the actress out. She tried very hard toward the end, but it was too late.

Lillian Roth spelled out another compulsive tragedy. She was a talented singer, at the top of her profession. Then she became an alcoholic in her twenties. She descended into that nether world and remained there for seventeen years, yet was able to come back and tell us of that strange land. Very few can return after seventeen besotted years, but she made it back from hell and could describe it. *I'll Cry Tomorrow* gave courage and hope to thousands. Again, I was fascinated by a woman struggling against whatever these devils were. Perhaps, if she'd been analyzed earlier, she would not have had these problems. We don't know. But all people who have problems, whose lives have importance or significance——

N. I'm afraid I missed any importance or significance in your book on Zsa Zsa.

■ *Frank:* Well, Zsa Zsa is an unusual person. My interest in her, my approach—I should not say approach, because in no instance did I approach them to tell me their stories, each came to me—my interest in Zsa Zsa was an interest in the anatomy of glamor. Millions of women seek to achieve glamor: what is it, what does it mean to those who possess it? What does a glamorous woman think of herself; what are her fears, her hopes, her fulfillments? What does it mean to be beautiful and pursued by men? (Aren't these the dreams, regardless of sex, of the Walter Mitty in each of us? To be irresistible to the opposite sex?) What had Zsa Zsa to say to this? Perhaps if she told what it was like, it might not be what we expected. Perhaps here would be solace for women who are not glamorous. And what coinage had the male in her eyes? If men everywhere sought her, had men any value at all? What did life, success, the future, look like from such a vantage point?

The fact is that Zsa Zsa, whatever her place in the hierarchy of values in the world, exists, is wondered about, and plays a rather unusual role in our contemporary society.

N. We didn't go into *Beloved Infidel*, and I'd like to, because I thought this was a superb book.

■ *Frank:* I'm glad to hear you say this, because that story has a warm place in my heart. Here is Sheilah, born a cockney girl on the wrong side of the tracks in London, reared in an orphanage, consumed by fantasies of beauty, fame, and wealth, of being presented at court, of becoming a great lady, of finding herself transfigured by a great love. All these, to one degree or another, came true. She met Scott Fitzgerald—she was in her twenties, he in his forties. He was an alcoholic, tubercular, in debt, with an insane wife in an institution, a man who woke at twenty-three to find himself famous but was now, in middle age, all but forgotten—and this beautiful girl became his companion. I once asked Sheilah what Scott did for her that made her turn from younger, handsomer, wealthier suitors, and she said, "He taught me that I am valuable." Probably no person can do more for another, ever. She, on her part, gave him the warming, deeply important knowledge that he could be loved by a young, vibrant, beautiful girl; that he had won her love, not because he was a writer, but because he was a man, loved and admired for himself. Each gave to the other what each then desperately needed—the special security, sustenance, support.

H*

So it was a great love story, so simple and authentic that it over-comes our tendency to look rather cynically on real-life love stories.

N. How would you define your obligation to the material you work with, composed, as it is, of the fabrics of actual lives?

■ *Frank:* Jean Jacques Rousseau, writing his autobiography—and here I must paraphrase for I don't have the book in front of me—said he would astonish the world by presenting a man as he really is. I think of this as my obligation: to present the subject with as much honesty of fact and integrity of person as possible. At the same time to help the subject, so far as I am able, to understand the drives, impulses, and conflicts in his or her life. I think of both of us as searching together to discover who and what he is, what led and shaped the direction of this special journey he is taking through the years, and then mirror this exactly; hoping that because I am there at once removed from the subject I may be able to correct distortions, some of which the subject may be unaware of; hoping that together we can achieve the accents of truth.

As to why I do this, write such books—every novelist becomes each of his characters. Flaubert could say of the fictional woman he created, "Madame Bovary, c'est moi." Like a Dybbuk, the writer inhabits his characters: they speak with his voice, they become him. I settle for one character, but the character is a real human being—that is the overwhelming fact, the character is real, not a figment of imagination!—and I live through him or her. When I was very young, I had dreams—what writer has not?—of being another Dostoevsky. Failing this, I seem to have discovered characters who might have been invented by Dostoevsky, or some other tragic writer. They have lived lives that have fascinated me. Perhaps these lives were lives I secretly wanted to live myself. Who is to say what a writer truly seeks to communicate?

N. How, on the other hand, would you define your obliga-tion to the public for which you are writing?

■ *Frank:* I see no difference in these obligations, for I am the public.

N. In looking at the literary and theatrical world of today, what instances or trends excite your imagination? Again, on the other hand, what do you most deplore?

■ *Frank:* Since I am Freud-oriented, I am excited by books that probe into the why and wherefore of the human condition. I am intrigued by such plays as *Who's Afraid of Virginia Woolf?*, *After the Fall, A Man For All Seasons, Waiting For Godot, The Deputy*. I deplore little in the literary or theatrical world of today.

All of it, even that which appalls us, is necessary, I think, to our development, save perhaps the omniscience of critics, and their insufferable arrogance in some weekly magazines.

N. What advice would you give the talented youngster who wants to make a career of writing?

■ *Frank:* Don't. But if he won't listen, then consider everything he does as an apprenticeship for writing, knowing that in the end he must write himself out and away from every other endeavor and into the job of writing itself as a way of life.

N. If you were to put yourself in the strange position of looking back on the work of Gerold Frank (say in the year 2064) how would you like to have Gerold Frank appraised?

■ *Frank:* It seems to me that the experience of viewing life through the living subject is far more immediate—perhaps far more real and therefore genuine—than trying to re-create it through the memories and letters and histories of others. This is what he tried to do, searching forever in others for himself.

N. And finally, why don't you do your own autobiography, having been so successful at chronicling the lives of others?

■ *Frank:* I am working on it, but I desperately miss someone like myself to help me. Who am I, if there is not someone like myself to see me and tell me?

"[The novelist's] view of the human race ought to be a charitable view. I don't mean he should never be savage, but the writer who hates his fellow man shouldn't try to be a novelist. A mortician, perhaps, but not a novelist."

Pamela Frankau
Interviewed in London, England, November, 1963

Pamela Frankau

N. *Sing For Your Supper*, by Pamela Frankau, stands as one of 1964's most successful novels. Sensitive, important, and "spatial" in the sense that time is observed with uncanny relevance to human life and growth, it is a high point in the career of a novelist who has built an enormous audience on both sides of the Atlantic. Since Miss Frankau's career is so long and notable, it's only fair to start with the broadest question of all: a rough autobiographical outline.

■ *Frankau:* If you don't mind, I'll skip birth and all that, since it happens to everyone, or at least I assume it does. But my personal writing history begins so far back that there are no surviving records. I wrote my first novel in a black, shiny exercise book when I was thirteen. The title was the *Primrose Way* and it was a very sad piece of work. (Sad meaning melancholy, and probably sad meaning terrible.) I was determined to have the heroine die. She did this nobly, by turning her car into a hedge in order to avoid running over a dog. I bade her farewell in the last line—in an absolute bath of tears, of course—with the brilliantly lucid phrase, "So the road runs, Sally, into the sunset."

N. Did you coin that phrase "into the sunset?"

■ *Frankau:* I hope not. It seemed to me, at the time I wrote it, the most beautiful phrase anyone had ever written. But there's no record of that first book, nor of the next two or three. They weren't even typed. One remained unfinished, partly because it was about killing my father and partly because I had to take an examination.

Then I left school and got a job in Fleet Street with a woman's magazine. My first published novel, *Marriage Of Harlequin*, was written largely on the commuter train between Windsor and London. I would recommend this as the ultimate test in concentration: to write in a third-class carriage with your elbows jammed into your sides with people peering over your shoulder to see what on earth you are up to. Then there were some equally unrestful circumstances at home. We were a devoted family. There was only one large living room, and to ask to have the gramophone turned off would have been unthinkable.

After *Harlequin* I wrote regularly, speedily, and lovingly, but not—repeat *not*—well. Still, I *was* a natural writer. I turned out a great many short stories on the side. But I don't think I realized what a novel ought to be until 1930. That was the year I wrote a book called *She And I*. I don't quite know what had happened. Looking back I can see I'd begun to read more. I was growing up a very little, and I'd met some real writers. Rebecca West was one of them. She was my introduction to better taste and better judgment. She opened a lot of doors for me and I'll always be grateful.

She And I, although it's by no means a good novel, was a point of departure. I mean that then, for the first time, I wanted to write well, really well.

Well, I'm either being arrogant or forgetful, but I couldn't honestly say how many novels I turned out in the nine years between *She And I* and 1939, when the war put a stop to writing. Around fifteen, perhaps. They did improve, I think, mainly because there was more story in them and less talk. (When I began I didn't care a hoot about telling a story. I just liked people to go on and on and on talking.)

The first literary success I had in England wasn't with a novel at all, but with an autobiography. I was twenty-seven and the only reason I wrote an autobiography was because a publisher offered to pay for it. He paid me; I spent the money, and a year later found myself facing the horror of writing the thing. I owe the success of that book to John Van Druten, the playwright, who was a great friend of mine. I told John, "I can't stand these books that go on 'I, I, I' all the time, and I'll never be able to write it." John said I should take a part of my life from which I was now completely detached and write about it as though it had happened to another person.

So I wrote the autobiography in the third person and called it *I Find Four People*. I did the autobiography of a schoolgirl; another of a young girl growing up on Fleet Street; a third of the arriving novelist; a fourth of the copywriter. (From 1930, through 1931, I was working as a copywriter in an advertising agency.) The reason the book was good, was because all those periods of my life were finished. I was miles away from them, and could look at them with absolute detachment. Sometimes I think

I'd rather like to do another one. Taking various versions of myself again, past versions, far away versions. Maybe I'll wait till I'm
sixty.

N. After the autobiography, did you return promptly to the
novel?

■ *Frankau:* Yes, until the war came. After that, I didn't publish
again until 1948, by which time I'd matured a good deal. (I don't
mean I'm really grown-up even now. I don't believe I ever will
be—not if I reach the age of ninety-nine, which seems remarkably
unlikely.) Still, those nine hideous years, with death for company,
made a great difference in the person who sat down to write
again, when they were over. The books I've written since, aren't
books to be ashamed of. This is more than I can say for some of
the early ones.

A Wreath For The Enemy was something of a goal in my
literary life. I am still pretty fond of it. After it was done, the
characters stuck around and haunted me. This gave me the idea
that I'd like one day to do a whole series of books about the
same character. At first, I thought Penelope in *A Wreath For The
Enemy* was going to be the one. But she wasn't. She faded out and
nothing came of the idea for ten years, until it finally launched
itself with *Sing For Your Supper*.

You see, *Sing For Your Supper* is the first volume of an intended trilogy, the life story of Thomas Weston, whom we first
meet when he's ten years old. I have a strong belief in magic, magic
of all sorts, orthodox and unorthodox, and it's the magical element in Thomas that makes him the right sort of companion for
me. From childhood up, I have had the gift of extrasensory perception. I don't do much about it. I'm not a medium, nor a
spiritualist, nor do I spend my time gazing into a crystal ball. But
my "psychic wavelength"—and I hope I don't sound too pompous—has led me down some strange paths to some strange experiences. Thomas, who has the gift, but to a far greater extent,
is the person I want to follow from his childhood to his old age.

The background of *Sing For Your Supper*—what the Americans
might call a carnival background—was easy. I could draw on
memories of an uncle whose Pierrot shows we used to dote on
when we were kids. I had the most fun with the book (frivolous
fun, not serious writer's fun) inventing all the lyrics and jokes.
I was out to make them as vulgar in fiction as they'd been in fact.
And I fell in love with the job. I went much, much too far. At
one moment I wrote the entire lyric, even the bridge refrain and

every variation in the chorus, of a song that took up five excruciating pages. Then I burst into tears and cut it out.

That particular background belongs only to *Sing For Your Supper*.

But I'm dealing with Thomas now in the second volume, *Slaves Of The Lamp*, when he's in his twenties.

N. You've spent a considerable amount of time in America, haven't you?

■ *Frankau:* I've conducted my own private love affair with America since I went to visit there during the war. Now I'm the victim of transatlantic schizophrenia. I can get homesick for America when I'm here, and homesick for England when I'm there. My favorite place for writing in America is Martha's Vineyard, where I once lived for a whole year, right through the winter. No telephone, no friends, just the perfect isolation I'd always wanted for writing. I've written several of my books on that beloved island.

N. To turn to the theoretical, I wonder if we could discuss the novelist's obligations—a two-headed affair. First, from the standpoint of the public for whom the novelist is writing; and second, from the view of the novelist's obligation to himself or herself.

■ *Frankau:* First, before you start thinking about the public at all, you've one enormous priority obligation; to the work itself. I share Kipling's belief that you can only write what is laid on you. It's absolutely fatal to try to beguile the public. Fatal, because it's dishonest; it's all against the creative instinct; it's a salesman's operation. And (let us mix the metaphors) it's putting the cart before the horse.

You start by falling in love with your story. Then you write it. Then you want someone to read it. With the reader in mind, you aim for clarity. You also aim for liveliness and pace. And if you think I can tell you how to get them, I can only say, by doing it all wrong for years until you learn your craft.

As a reader, I want certain things from a book. As a writer I try to provide them. When I read a novel I want to be involved in the story, I want to believe it's happening, I want to feel as though I'm living in it. The moment I feel I'm just being told a story on paper, then I feel let down. The people stop being alive, and this is no longer an adventure I'm sharing. This usually happens when I can hear the author talking to me. So when I write I keep myself off the page as much as I can. It's the characters who do the talking, the thinking, the living. The reader (I hope) will feel he's walked into the room and found the action going on.

That's why I always write a scene over the shoulder of just one character. When I read a book where the author darts from one person's head to another, giving the thoughts of each, I cease to believe any of it. In life, we are incapable of darting from one psyche to another. As a reader, I can't stand hopping around inside three or four heads, and when I'm writing, I don't give my readers that kind of unreal exercise. But I shouldn't really sound so dogmatic about it. I know anyone can break all my rules and still write a better novel than I can.

N. Also in the realm of theory: if you were giving advice to the beginning writer, the beginning novelist in particular, what would that advice be?

■ *Frankau:* I'd start by telling him, with a sob, that he couldn't have chosen a worse moment to try fiction. Two-thirds of today's fiction shows itself on the television screen. Sales of novels are slumping down and the poor darling can't expect to make money. So much for my awful warning. Then, I'd remind him of the importance of pleasing himself, a tip I owe to Jack Priestley. He's right—you *must* be in love with your idea and write it to your own highest standards. This way alone you'll be truthful, you'll be a maker, doing a maker's job.

Then I'd tell him that the two most difficult things a writer must learn are stamina and self-discipline. (I said earlier that my own first lessons on concentration came from writing in thoroughly adverse conditions.) Anyone who is going to make writing a career has got to protect his work and himself for as many hours a day as he can manage. If he's doing another job in order to keep himself—which he probably is—he should set himself a minimum of two hours a day for writing. And even that requires stamina. If he neglects this minimum, he'll never get anywhere.

An awful lot of people have said to me, "I imagine you can only write when you feel like it." The answer to that one is "bosh." If you left it till you felt like it, you'd never do it at all. Writing is a demanding, exacting, lifetime labor. It can never come easy. The writer as a person. . . . As a novelist he must have an imagination, an observing eye, and—in my view at least—a liking for people. His view of the human race ought to be a charitable view. I don't mean he should never be savage, but the writer who hates his fellow man shouldn't try to be a novelist. A mortician, perhaps, but not a novelist.

N. What are your own working habits?

■ *Frankau:* When I was young, ideas for novels followed each other so quickly, I worked in a high fever, writing with nonstop concentration, always longing to get on to the next thing. This doesn't happen any more. Ideas come slowly. I have to keep my ears and eyes open and wait. Once the story has moved in and begins to grow, I apply several hard-and-fast rules. The first: "Don't talk about it—not to anybody." The novel you talk about—Hemingway said this—is the one you don't write. When I'm roughly able to see beginning, middle, and end, I'm ready to write. The characters at this stage are like people seen through a fog. Sometimes the fog will part enough to reveal them, then it will swirl over and hide them. I can only clear the fog by sitting down to write my rough draft. I write four to six hours a day, though I might go quite crazy and work ten hours one day and none at all the next. (See? I'm violating my own rules already.)

I can never set myself a definite period for the completion of the rough, but even if it takes eight or nine months, I still try not to talk about it. While I'm writing, I can see mistakes, gaps, characters changing themselves over my dead body, every kind of chaos, but I don't rewrite. I just go charging on, making notes for revision when I stop for breath.

Once the rough draft is done, I can mop my brow and say, "We're safe, here's a book." I have a terror of unfinished work, a lifelong fear that I won't get it done. But now I'm safe. I spend the next few weeks brooding, arranging my notes, setting up the whole scheme in its final form. Then I sit down and write it all over again, usually working six hours a day. Every single word is written by hand (as it was in the rough, so now in the smooth), while I'm polishing, tidying, and changing. But at this stage, I *can* talk about it. Once, only once, I talked too soon and blew a novel sky-high.

N. You mentioned, before, a fallow period when you did no writing. What did you do through the war years?

■ *Frankau:* First of all, I went into the Ministry of Food, where I wrote my only authentic best-seller, (unsigned, alas . . .) a cookbook for the wartime housewife, telling her how to make the best of the rations. I didn't write the recipes, not being that inventive a cook, but it was my job to put it into English. None of the recipes were written in anything remotely resembling English until I got at them. The book was called *Food Facts From The Kitchen Front* and sold more than a million copies. I wrote every word, including the foreword by the Food Minister. After about a year as a civil servant, I joined the army, the A.T.S., as a private. I think I was probably the oldest private in the British Army at that time, but I graduated to become an officer and went into the Army Education Corps. I stayed in the army until the end of the war. As I've said, I grew up in the process, but it was torture to return to writing. My months of work on the first novel after the war felt more like an illness than like the process of artistic creation.

N. What opinions do you have concerning today's trends in fiction?

■ *Frankau:* Oh, dear. I'm afraid I *do* like a story that has a beginning, a middle, and an end. If it's just one long scream of anguish about internal misery, I feel very sorry for everyone concerned, but it doesn't hold my attention.

On the other hand, I feel that contemporary writing style is pretty good. Today's style is a great improvement on that of yesterday. If I tried publishing my first novel now, I doubt any publisher would take it. The actual way with words is a better way. I don't know why. But seven or eight years ago I was reading for the book society and all the time I could see how much better the writing was. The stories on the other hand didn't exist. The whole knack of storytelling seemed to be on the way out. And this made me quite cross. Incidentally reading for a book club is another thing authors must avoid. I couldn't write a single, solitary word while I was doing all that reading.

N. How do you regard the current state of literary criticism and reviewing in America and in England?

■ *Frankau:* Well, I think American critics are much better than English. And that, you'd never guess, is because I get much better reviews in America. But even if I didn't, I'd still think much the same. You see, the American reviewer has one enormous advantage—far more space. He also appears to read the book, which is more than can be said for his English counterpart. In England the reviewer is badly paid, he's short of space, and he's determined to be a smart-aleck. I don't think it's the critic's job to be brightly destructive. If you can't create, you mustn't destroy and, on the whole, a reviewer's a eunuch rather than a creative person. And, of course, I could go on for hours about critics, aside from the fact that in seven years I haven't read a review of one of my books except by mistake.

N. Now the novelist's job begins with producing a novel.

This involves conception, gestation, and heavy labor. From here it goes to the publisher and all the various aspects of the publishing business, from preliminary editing to final advertising and marketing, are brought into play. In general, what have your experiences been with the many publishers you've had in England and in the United States?

■ *Frankau:* Since I began, I've seen a great change come over the publishing business on both sides of the Atlantic. When my first novel was accepted, I was, naturally, amenable to suggestions from the publisher. I remember all the words they wanted out. Harmless words in this day and age; I mean "damn" was rationed. I took the "damns" out. I took some other things out too. At nineteen I was fairly humble.

It's different today. I now know that an author has to keep a very wary eye on the editor. Incidentally, I don't remember that there was such a thing as an editor in the old days. In America particularly, the functions of the editor and copyeditor can be a menace. Particularly to young writers. I've known some of them to send portions of a book to the editor and get his suggestions. I'm dead set against this. In fact I think it's iniquitous. Surely an editor shouldn't be sitting around waiting to see what's wrong with a half-finished work. Authors don't need interference while they're writing. Writing's a lonely business, and has to be. Of course, there comes a moment when you would love to hand six chapters to someone and say, "What do you think of this?" provided you could be assured of a favorable reaction. But that's a temptation to be guarded against and, in the United States particularly, the editor doesn't help the writer to guard against it. On the contrary.

Mind you, I've suffered relatively little from this sort of interference. I was already in my forties when I first made a name in America, and I said very loud and clear, "No editing—above all no copyediting." Being a person of firm convictions (I'd call them prejudices if anyone else popped up with them) I've gone on saying this for more than ten years. I don't expect the editor to rewrite, repunctuate, or reparagraph any book of mine. These things are my business and nobody else's.

N. So I suppose you refused all editorial suggestions on *Sing For Your Supper?*

■ *Frankau:* Well, unfortunately, the answer there is "yes" and "no." Let's take the copyediting first. Here I acted true to type. When Random House sent me a batch of edited copy, I screamed like a badly-wounded eagle, downed a double scotch, rushed to the telephone and sent the longest and most expensive cablegram in history, daring them to change so much as a hyphen.

N. And, where does the "No" come in?

■ *Frankau:* Well, you see, when the manuscript first went to Random House, Joe Fox, my editor, wrote me a long letter containing three extremely intelligent queries. These, by the way, had not been raised by the English publisher. They pointed out omissions which—much against my will—I admitted, took up, and changed on the galley proofs. So, after all my raging against editors and the editorial functions I must, in a glorious burst of British fairness, credit Joe Fox with making three discoveries that greatly improved the end of the book. And if there's a moral to this story I suppose it is that those firm convictions of mine turn out to be prejudices after all.

"The literature of the past ten or fifteen years has been marked by . . . the very curious American cult of personality. Writers are concentrating on individual psychology, individual problems, individual pathology . . . to the exclusion of the social framework that is present in great writing and great art."

Maxwell Geismar
Interviewed in New York, October, 1963

Maxwell Geismar

N. America is seldom given to literary controversies. We stood fairly to the sidelines while France rocked on existentialist heels, and, more recently, we calmly observed the fuss in Britain over C. P. Snow's "two cultures." Even the occasional storms aroused by Salinger, Mailer, and Gold fail to bring us to our feet.

But in 1963 Maxwell Geismar—a critic of real stature—created turbulence with *Henry James and The Jacobites*. Learned howls of anguish were heard in ivy-smothered halls extending from Harvard to the University of Southern California. And all of our major literary magazines and many newspaper supplements carried articles and letters faintly tinged with blood.

For Geismar did something no gentleman would do. He assulted the cultists who had erected a shrine to perpetuate the adoration of Henry James. I'd like to ask Mr. Geismar, first, exactly how the book evolved.

■ *Geismar:* Actually, the content was scheduled to be in the fourth volume of my *History Of The American Novel*, the volume which includes Edith Wharton, Mark Twain, and William Dean Howells. James was supposed merely to be another chapter in that book, and I usually take about a year to do each of the essays. At the end of a year of working on Henry James, I was absolutely bewildered. I was stunned to find that—at least, in my view—the critical commentary on James simply did not match up with what he wrote.

N. In what way didn't it match up?

■ *Geismar:* The criticism piles itself upon itself. Each Jamesian critic outdoes the last in admiring everything that James wrote. One example: Stallman, the most recent of these critics, says that next to *Moby Dick, The Portrait Of A Lady* is the greatest American novel he has read. This, to me, is sheer nonsense, and I couldn't resist inserting in my book the line, "Oh, what a mate for Ahab would Isabel Archer be." She's a rather thin, pure, sterile, charming, young American maiden.

But this was James's concept of women. They had to be pure, young, beautiful, and rich. When they are all these things but one, the missing element is supplied. Isabel is simply given money, for example, to be "complete." This is the basis of the Jamesian kingdom, of what I call his "leisure class kingdom." *The Portrait Of A Lady* is a charming, old-fashioned, sentimental romance of a young American girl who goes to Europe—to England, first—to experience life. To James, from the age of eleven onward, life meant Europe.

This is just one of the curious things I discovered about the person called Henry James. One of the more obvious things, I must admit. I would like to say here that I rather admire the old artificer. I'm rather attached to him; he is a curious specimen. My book is not biased in the sense that I dislike him. The queerer he gets—and he gets very queer, indeed, in the late novels—the better I like him, in an odd way. I simply don't consider James to be the major writer he is now claimed to be. I don't think he is a major writer at all. I think he is something else: namely, a major entertainer. He's the master of a curious sort of literary entertainment, of trickery which is nonetheless very pleasant to read.

N. It always struck me—during a too-intensive study of Henry James all through college—that James was always completely detached from what we call the human predicament.

■ *Geismar:* He was very far from the human predicament. Henry James had very little connection with the human race. He dealt with an imaginary leisure-class world where money always existed, but never earned money. Seldom did a Jamesian character earn money. James shared the typical American snobbery of that period regarding people who made money. One had to inherit wealth—inherited wealth was infinitely superior to the earned kind. Old money was better than new money.

All this becomes comic, once you find the key. If you start to tell the story of a Jamesian novel, and you begin to laugh, how can you regard it as great literature?

Now, as to women. Money and women are connected in the sense that money and sex are connected. James could not abide sexuality in a woman. His heroines had to be pure, young American girls. Isabel Archer rejects the two men who really want her and marries the one man who will ruin her life, but he possesses the Jamesian virtue of not caring for her physically. Caspar Goodward, the American millionaire who is (for James) definitely sexual, is thrown out of her life immediately. He terrifies her.

Now, somewhere during his late maturity—around the 1890's, actually—James had a kind of "Jungian" breakthrough. All his repressed sexuality broke through in a series of books, most of which (like *The Turn Of The Screw*) dealt with small children who are snooping around to discover what sex means. James, in this sense, is a child innocent of sex, ignorant about it, and he suddenly wants to find out what it is. In these books we find children who hear the sounds of sexuality about them—of gaiety. The adults in these books are having some kind of fun which excludes them. They are driven from the scene. This period reaches some sort of climax in *The Sacred Fount*, when the "Observer" tries to guess the sexual secrets of the other characters. He invents a series of lurid romances, until he is finally told he's crazy, and he's thrown out of the castle. *What Maisie Knew* falls in this category, as well as *The Turn Of The Screw*.

In the later years James became preoccupied with sex in a voyeuristic sense. In my book there is a section called, "The Psychology of the Keyhole." Like a child, James looked through keyholes to see what older people were doing, as Max Beerbohm realized at the time. This is almost incredible in terms of modern fiction. It is certainly singular in the whole history of literature. And when he portrays sexual women, they are always poor and criminal.

N. As though sex must be associated with the unclean——?

■ *Geismar:* There's no question of that. In *The Wings Of The Dove*, we have Kate Croy who is sexual, in the sense that she spends one night with her lover illegally, but this was as far as James went. One night, one embrace, was all, but that was quite daring for James. Yet she does this in order to make her lover marry the rich girl. Sex is usually associated with crime, or duplicity, in the land of James. But what more can we expect from Kate Croy, who comes from a dubious, lower-class background?

N. How and when did the Jamesian cult come into existence?

■ *Geismar:* It has existed, in some degree of strength, for a long time. At the end of his own life, James felt that he was a disgrace, an exile. People laughed at his books; most people, that is, laughed at most of his books. They did not understand him. Yet he had a small, loyal, articulate cult of followers even then. This was in 1915, 1916.

In the 1920's James was being collected by a sizeable group of intellectuals. He was becoming a property. My wife has a whole set of first editions of Henry James which she bought in the 1920's.

A small group, but growing in size and strength, was making James important.

In the 1930's he was obviously "out" because his world had no connection with the harsh and bitter events of that decade. The cult, as we know it, started in the 1940's, and I think it significant in relationship to that period. It was actually launched by the Harvard professor, F. O. Matthiessen, a critic I respect who, nonetheless, went "haywire" over James. He discovered the notebooks and became the Jamesian specialist. But it's interesting to note that at the end of his life, at a point where he could not help being committed to the Jamesian vogue, he was working on a study of Dreiser. Dreiser, as we know, is the polar opposite of James. This, to me, has significance. Perhaps Matthiessen was trying to escape his own trap.

In the 1950's James became a cult for those who absolutely outlawed Dreiser. These are the two poles of American literature, you know. Dreiser is the master of modern realism, James (to me, at least) the master of modern romance. The latter is a type of literary entertainment, fascinating to read, but with little relationship to his world or ours. I somehow cling to the old-fashioned notion that great novelists reflect the human condition. This forces me to ask myself, "What condition does Henry James reflect?"

N.   And you find no valid association with life as a whole?

■ *Geismar:* James did not share his life with others; perhaps this is why he had no real life of his own. Aside from his friendship with Edith Wharton (and those two were very cozy), he had small contact with women. As far as we know, he had only one curious love affair, this with a woman who committed suicide. James rushed into her apartment to gather his letters. I think he was afraid some of his secrets would be exposed. That was his first concern—not so much grief over the woman, but fear that the letters would make some part of himself public knowledge. This is the basis of the story called *The Beast In The Jungle*, a very good story indeed. James almost admits the truth about himself and the woman.

N.   In the technical sense James was often superb. Yet I've never felt, in reading James, that the people he presented, and his plots, bore any relationship to truth.

■ *Geismar:* They didn't—they didn't at all. Because of this a British lady commented at his death, "Poor Mr. James. He never did know the right people." He was an outsider in England, and

he knew very little about America, the nation he "deserted in
his imagination," as he puts it in his memoirs, at the age of eleven.
At the age of eleven, his overwhelming ambition was to become
a famous author. A famous author, to him, meant someone like
Thackeray, a British aristocrat who lived in an English castle, for
James' childhood reading had been largely confined to the British
Victorians. He could not stand the thought of Paris, which was
too emancipated. London was his focal point; the London of
Thackeray and, to some extent, of Dickens; the London of medieval
culture.

He constantly used the term "the British race." Now, "race"
in his sense is related to snobbery more than to biology. The
British race was different from and superior to the American race
because they had more money; they had better homes; they had
a past. James constructed this imaginary romance, a private world
where the superior British race was compared to the vulgar
American.

N.   Didn't some other rather definite prejudices play a role?
■ *Geismar:*   Indeed, yes—but, in a way, they were also literary
prejudices. He was always anti-Semitic. He had no use for the
working class. In fact, the lowest level he dealt with in his writing
was the sort of "working class" typified by English butlers—like
the famous Brooksmith, who somehow learned to understand what
books were by carrying them from the library shelf to his master.
Just feeling the cover of these books had educated Brooksmith. He
is used as James' proletarian hero. Actually, Brooksmith worships
his British master.

In the world of James the lower class had only one ambition:
to ape the upper class and Henry James. Thus, when his master
died, Brooksmith's life was destroyed. He disappeared, vanished
into a void because he would never again work for such a cultivated man. I think this example illustrates James's understanding
of a lower class man.

His political world was just as peculiar. In *The Princess Casa-
massima* he deals with a British anarchist. This novel was written
when James first came to London. He walked around the streets,
read some of the scary, sensational headlines, and developed a romance in which the European anarchist movement was threatening
the British world. His hero, the anarchist, is a bookbinder named
Hyacinth Robinson. (Even revolutionists have to deal with culture.) Hyacinth is a bookbinder, and an anarchist, but he has a
noble father. Most of James' heroes have some nobility included

in their background. Hyacinth, this fierce anarchist, also has a small inheritance from his noble father. But then, all of James' people have inheritances or are given fortunes. Hyacinth goes off to Paris on his small inheritance and discovers what true culture really means. He's never known, and suddenly he realizes that this anarchistic plot is simply a dastardly attempt to destroy everything that is precious to him in British culture.

Now, this is called James' great revolutionary novel. Certain critics, such as Lionel Trilling, rate James with Dostoevsky as a consequence. Dostoevsky, mind you, really knew what anarchists were like. But in the Jamesian world, Hyacinth passes over to the leisure class. He can no longer abide anarchism, and when he's given a mysterious order to assassinate somebody, he shoots himself. This is a great revolutionary novel?

N. You also mentioned anti-Semitism——

■ *Geismar:* I'm coming to that. In a volume called *The American Scene* (which has been hailed, again by critics like F. W. Dupee and W. H. Auden as a significant work, a "great documentary" this time) James returned to America to revive his memories of the American scene. This was around 1904. Well, he liked Albany, which was somehow rather feudal. But in Boston he felt the awful impact of democracy. James was completely antidemocratic, a fact which may explain some basis of his current vogue. (At least, it tells something about the critics who are defending him so strongly.) James was a royalist. He called America "The Lost Colony"; the American Revolution, "The King's War." He saw everything from this medieval English outlook, so how could he ever understand what the United States was all about?

In Boston he revisited Harvard. He was impressed by the handsome young men he saw there, but he asked himself, "Whose sons are these?" and he couldn't answer. He did not know their family names, nor their family backgrounds. Therefore, they were suspect.

He wandered down to New York and was overwhelmed. He was rather like an absentee landlord in a country which had been taken over by aliens. The aliens in *The American Scene* are mainly Jewish, and when he descended into the East Side—at that time alive with the great flowering of Jewish culture Van Wyck Brooks so glowingly admires—he was shocked. The East Side was exciting in those days. The Yiddish Art Theatre was famous. It was the first development of Jewish culture in America. James could make nothing of it except that he saw these greasy faces, heard this alien language. He became quite vicious, and compared these strangers to certain low forms of biological life—to worms. His latent anti-Semitism came out very strongly because these untidy aliens were taking over his country, the country he had abandoned, the country in which he had rights as absentee landlord.

Then a worse thing happened. He went South and saw the effects of the Civil War. His father, the marvelous Henry James, Senior, had been a supporter of John Brown, the strong abolitionist. (Henry had not served in the Civil War. Two brothers served, but not Henry.) This was another intriguing personal episode. He had incurred a most peculiar accident. The accident, as described by James himself, was a Freudian dream, but nobody knew what the accident was.

When he went South he saw these terrible, ignorant, lazy darkies who stood around the station and looked at him. They didn't get out of his way and they didn't know who he was. They were not well-trained servants. So James mourned for the southern aristocracy because their servants were trained so badly. This is the kind of commentary we read in *The American Scene*. This is a great documentary?

N. Could you describe your own research that went into preparing and writing *Henry James and The Jacobites?*

■ *Geismar:* As I mentioned, a year of study normally puts me "on" my subject, but a year of Henry James left me baffled. He was an enigma to me. My evaluation of him and his writing was opposed to a great weight of critical opinion that proclaimed all of his works—novels, stories, essays, and documentaries—to be unique masterpieces. James had taken rank over Melville, a great American writer. Dreiser was in the doghouse, another great American writer. In short, James had become almost the only writer of consequence.

I didn't, at that point, know enough about Henry James, but I knew something was wrong. I knew something was phony, but I couldn't put my finger on it. So it took me another year of reading Henry James to fit things into a pattern that made sense. This is a pattern that Jamesian scholars ignore or deny. If they acknowledged it, they would destroy the praise they have heaped upon him.

At the end of a third year, I almost began to laugh. I saw, I thought, the kind of person James really was, and what he was writing: a weird class-entertainment, technically skilled but lacking any relationship to human history or human society, to all the things with which great literature deals. Incidentally, I was so deeply perplexed in dealing with James that I have thousands of pages of notes that sprang from an attempt to see every side of each of the Jamesian works. One set would deal with what was supposed to be there, the other, with what I ultimately found. Toward the end of the third year, I decided that I'd better start writing because if I really let myself get overwhelmed by these notes, the book would never get done.

N.   I wonder, to leave Henry James at this point, if you would outline your total career.

■ *Geismar:* I suppose my actual career began when I was teaching contemporary literature at Sarah Lawrence in the mid-1930's. I had written a novel which I can't bear to look at, which I never sent out. It was the quick way to discover I wasn't a novelist. However, I'm not embittered—I don't want to be a novelist. I became a critic, 'way back then, and I've always enjoyed it. Perhaps my criticism differs from others because I am closer to the novelist. I try to read the novel as though it's my first exposure to the writer at hand, then consider the novelist as though nothing has been written about him. I try to see everything from the novelist's point of view *first* (and this includes all the works by Henry James). I'm pleased that some contemporary writers feel that my criticism springs from this level.

The first book I did, of what has become a series, was *Writers In Crisis*. It was published in 1942 and dealt with the generation which included Hemingway, Faulkner, Dos Passos, Ring Lardner, and Thomas Wolfe. It was fairly successful, sold quite well, so I continued.

I had left F. Scott Fitzgerald out of the first book, simply because there hadn't been room for him, so I put him in the next book as a link between the generation of the 'teens and the so-called "lost generation." This second book, *The Last Of The Provincials*, was published in 1947. It included Fitzgerald, of course—the link—plus Sherwood Anderson, Willa Cather, Sinclair Lewis, and H. L. Mencken. With the obvious exception of Fitzgerald, these were somewhat older people. They formed the background for Hemingway's generation, even though Hemingway had disowned Sherwood Anderson as his literary father. There's a great difference between Mencken, Anderson, and Cather, say—and the oncoming Fitzgerald, Hemingway, and Faulkner. A definite break. Willa Cather reports that her world broke in two in 1925, and I think there's a great deal of truth in this.

Sinclair Lewis was caught. He tried to be sophisticated, like the new generation, but he was at heart a member of the older generation. This was one of his great problems.

Five or six years later the third volume appeared, *Rebels and Ancestors*, which dealt with the beginnings of modern realism. Theodore Dreiser was the pioneer figure here, but the cast also included Stephen Crane, Jack London, Frank Norris, and Ellen Glasgow. These were really the ancestors of a modern school which came to a climax with Hemingway, Scott Fitzgerald, John Dos Passos, Tom Wolfe, and Faulkner. Dreiser opened the trail for those who came after him and often repudiated him.

I am working on the fourth volume, as I said earlier, which deals with Edith Wharton, Mark Twain, and William Dean Howells, and was to include, Henry James. Then the James book came along and spoiled everything. It had to be a book in its own right. Because I got so caught up in the James thing, disturbing the planned sequence, I realized that I had to fill the time-gap with something (it hurts to have too many years elapse without a book), so I collected some of my articles and reviews and wrote some new essays on contemporary figures like William Styron, Saul Bellow, J. D. Salinger, James Jones, Howard Griffin, and Norman Mailer. This became *American Moderns*, now in its sixth printing. It has done much better in sales than the more serious volumes, which proves something.

N. What are your feelings toward recent trends in American writing, toward the last two or three decades in particular?

■ *Geismar:* My feelings are at the heart of both *American Moderns* and the Henry James book, you know. I think the whole cult of Henry James is an evasion on the part of American intellectuals who are playing, what James himself called, "the game of literature." Before this, we took literature very seriously, particularly as it dealt with contemporary society.

But in the period of the Cold War (roughly), there was a general withdrawal of American intellectuals from contact with the world. The world was too scary, too dangerous. It was easier to pretend that America was a great, powerful nation without problems; except maybe that of getting a baby-sitter or a new refrigerator or a new car. The rest of the world happened to be in a highly revolutionary state, and I think that our concentration upon figures like Henry James is a direct reflection of cold war panic, a fear of facing up to the world around us. I think, without getting political, that this cultural view is one reason why we find ourselves involved in so many dubious propositions. We don't want to understand the rest of the world.

N. What do you think of literary metaphysics? Salinger, for example, started off with a bold, forthright first novel, and now seems to get more curiously mystic with each book. Does this seem to be the temper of the dominant writers of today?

■ *Geismar:* The answer is "yes" and I'm very glad that you brought up Salinger. He is typical of this sort of thing.

The literature of the past ten or fifteen years has been marked by—if I may use the term—the very curious American cult of personality. Writers are concentrating on individual psychology, individual problems, individual pathology (as in Tennessee Williams) to the exclusion of the social framework that is present in great writing and great art.

Tolstoy, for example, writes about the Russia of his time, and we know Russia after reading Tolstoy. Balzac wrote about the France of his time, and we know that France. Or take the marvelous case of Proust! By contrast, Salinger has retreated into an absolutely weird world of Eastern mysticism and an equally weird world of the self-enclosed family—the Glass family. (The name seems to be very symbolic, and Salinger must be aware of this.) The Glasses are involved exclusively with their personal problems and with each other, a small "inner" group. They represent the prevailing tendency of American literature, a very bad one, I think. This is associated with the cult of Henry James, because in his own way James did exactly the same thing—he created an imaginary world. Apparently we do not like to face the real world today in our literature or in our politics.

N. For the young writer coming up—the neophyte novelist, poet, playwright, or critic—what advice would you give as far as preparation is concerned, and what hopes would you have for them as far as the kind of work they eventually produce?

■ *Geismar:* I'm pleased to answer this one. Everything I say reflects, of course, from the entrenched position of the English departments in our universities. Here we find instructors conditioned in the 1940's toward the new criticism which is purely formal, toward the cult of James which is purely imaginary leisure-class writing—entertainment, perhaps, but little more.

Thus my advice to young writers would be to stay out of the English classes. Left to themselves they will have more sense, more reality, but if they indulge in the training and discipline provided by most of our universities today, they won't have a personal or professional chance until they break away. Even James Baldwin started out in the same way. He was nonpolitical, he was anti-revolutionary; he wished to be considered as a "pure-art artist," not an American Negro writer. He was a disciple of Richard Wright. If anyone could have been more involved with the Negro scene in America than Wright, I don't know who he was, or what he did. That's why Wright's books are great—he dealt with those realities.

Baldwin broke with him, broke with what he called the novel of social protest. He claimed this was obsolete—that art had to be pure. Now, it's a very interesting commentary that he has become a most eloquent spokesman for the whole Negro Civil Rights movement in the United States today. Baldwin has traveled the whole circle from what he was taught and trained to do, to what he is doing today. And today he's right.

Thus I would advise today's young writers not to go to college. I think they may be better off without this particular discipline until things change in our universities. Maybe the anecdote regarding Sinclair Lewis at Yale is not far off. When he came in to face a creative writing class there, he said, "I understand that all of you want to write." The class said, "Yes," and Lewis said, "Well, go home and write."

As to more positive advice for young writers, this is a difficult thing. In one sense, either they have it or they don't; and if they have it, they must find their own way, as they do. No reputable critic would try to establish a set of "rules," "laws," or immutable "principles" for all young writers to follow. This is just what I object to in the Jamesian code of "good taste" and "correct writing" now being taught in many universities. I have reviewed some of these "Jamesian" novels written by aspiring young professors—God help us, and God, in His infinite mercy, should help them! But what a critic can do, and what I believe the function of criticism to be, among other things, is to help and encourage young writers of talent simply to have the faith to continue working in whatever their own chosen path of work is. That is to say, criticism, using the perspective of the past, of history, of the best things in our literature, should also be directly involved with the contemporary scene—as, for example, such figures as Van Wyck Brooks, H. L. Mencken, and Edmund Wilson were in the 1920's— and as the New Criticism of our own period, concentrating on a little list of "classics," has not been.

At least one of the most rewarding aspects, personally, of my own work has been the friendships I have had with contemporary writers like James Jones, Bill Styron, Howard Griffin, Truman Nelson, and others, many others, less well known. I have a large correspondence, and letters from writers are usually a pleasure to get.

N. Who do you think our most important writers are at present?

■ *Geismar:* The best writers, today, are those neglected by the academic quarterlies because they obviously don't fill a particular literary or critical view. James Jones, I think, is a marvelous writer. *The Thin Red Line* is among the best books written during the last ten years. It's been scarcely noted in high and serious quarters because Jones is concerned with the common man. He works with a military framework. He is highly radical in an unconventional way, very critical of modern society. He thinks that no society can stand the kind of warfare we have been indulging in. Jones doesn't fit the Jamesian cult in any sense; he's a polar opposite. Jones is usually described as a low-brow, but I think he's a genius.

William Styron is another fine writer who is finally—seven or ten years after his first novel—being taken up somewhat by the colleges. It could be his undoing.

I think that John Howard Griffin, a Texan, is a remarkable young writer. He did the documentary *Black Like Me*, you know. He traveled through the South as a Negro. The good novelists keep on behaving like novelists, thank God. They don't obey critics, they don't even know who critics are. But the academicians —the bright boys who go through college—have got to have something against them, to begin with, if they heed what they're being taught. Griffin also wrote a splendid first novel, *The Devil Rides Outside*, and a fascinating second novel called *Nuni*. Talented as he is, he was virtually unknown until the recent success of *Black Like Me*. I would place these as the talents I admire most.

N. What about Updike or Cheever?

■ *Geismar:* They belong to what I call *The New Yorker* school, of which both Salinger and Philip Roth are also products. *The New Yorker* school reflects our period, which deals with the tormented sensibility of the author. There is usually a wound in childhood from which the protagonist never recovers, never really understands, and never resolves. This is the pattern of *The New Yorker* writers in general, and it seems to me to be another kind of game which we are playing and which reflects a reluctance to face up to the traditional responsibility of the novel.

N. It's odd, but as much as I admire the techniques of *The New Yorker* fiction writers, I seldom recall an individual characterization or scene.

■ *Geismar:* I've so often debated this subject on television and radio with people who don't understand what I'm trying to say. I know I'm in a critical minority, but the whole thing seems obvious. Yet they are so caught up with figures like Salinger and Roth they don't attempt criticism; they regard these writers as being above it all.

I kept reading Roth's *Letting Go* even though I knew, at midpoint, that nothing, absolutely nothing, would happen. I knew then that the people were not going to be important, that their human relationships would not be important, that the novel would end absolutely nowhere, which it does. Still, I kept on reading it.

This is the quality that Henry James has, too, you know. James is really superior to these people but he shares the identical social and cultural tendency, a form of isolation. Readable as they are—Salinger, Roth, Updike, Cheever—they have very little to say. Roth's problem is how to use his talent, which is good, and his technique, which is marvelous. He's like Herman Wouk—long on ability, but lacking in something worth saying.

N. What about Mary McCarthy?

■ *Geismar:* I hate to debunk our First Literary Lady—which is what Mary McCarthy is often called—but when I think of Edith Wharton and Willa Cather, Ellen Glasgow or Simone de Beauvoir, I simply cannot place Mary McCarthy on this level.

The Group is not a very good book which is being highly publicized. Mary McCarthy is "in" with the right critics, and it will consequently take a few years to assess the quality and value of *The Group* more correctly.

N. During my college career most of my "Lit" courses consisted of a very heavy diet of Henry James—reading him, even rewriting some of his plots. Have we ever had a cult like this before? Do you foresee the time when the present Jamesian cult will come to an end?

■ *Geismar:* First, I think the James cult is something very special. We've always had small cults dedicated to this or that writer, but never a cult which, in effect, dominated all our critical and literary values like the James cult. I don't know what this means. Perhaps we are reaching a period of some sort of decadence, where a cult can establish itself so firmly, and so powerfully, that it can dominate taste. This, to me, is unique. In my own writing and evaluation, I include James and Dreiser basically as equals. They are equally important to American literature. They are also the two extremes.

My feeling, as an American critic, is that I want every part of our tradition to be incorporated. I don't want anything left out, and I don't want to be biased about any section. I would like to be fair and accurate about every phase of our tradition, but the cult of James makes this impossible until the cult expires. I find myself in the position of a trust buster. Until we get rid of this cult, we cannot have a proper sense of our whole and entire tradition, which includes a splendid conservative writer like Hawthorne and a radical like Melville. They represent opposite extremes of our past. But we have never had a cult which, say, glorified Hawthorne and ignored Melville, and this has happened now.

The cult of James simply means that the whole tradition of contemporary realism, which is our great tradition, which has made our literature a world literature, starting with Dreiser and his contemporaries, extending to Hemingway and Faulkner and Thomas Wolfe, is ignored. Henry James was a social fantasy.

"But too much American writing—perhaps too much writing done everywhere—is self-absorbed and precious and almost private. We encounter mental convolutions which are neither edifying nor emotional. So much is written, so little said."

Genêt
Interviewed in Paris, France, November, 1963

Genêt

N. Janet Flanner is familiar to the millions of readers who maintain *The New Yorker's* vast readership, generation after generation. Better known as Genêt, her letters from Paris are richly literate, compounded from vital subject matter, couched with style that serves to constantly remind us that "letters" are more than a, b, and c. The French persist in complexity—in their cultural as well as their political life—but the magic of Genêt is such that readers of *The New Yorker* are inclined to understand the clouded why, what, when, and where of life in France better than other Americans.

In talking to Genêt I would like to begin with the essentials of biography—how Janet Flanner as a person has become the "institution" we so fondly know as Genêt.

■ *Genêt:* I was born in Indiana, and now, at this time of life, I look out of my hotel window onto the Gardens of the Tuileries. It is a magnificent view, including a carved corner of the Louvre, a distant patch of the River Seine, the golden dome of the Invalides where Napoleon lies entombed, the spires of several churches, the Obelisk on the Place de la Concorde and the Eiffel Tower. I can list them by heart. It is a view quite superior to anything I might have found in Indiana and is one of the reasons, one of the permanent reasons, I am here.

N. Where were you educated in the States?

■ *Genêt:* I went to the University of Chicago for two years after I had lived abroad with my parents for a year and a half. I had a sister who studied piano in Berlin with Ossip Gabrilovitch, son-in-law of Mark Twain. We didn't know where to go then, except to follow her. Berlin was then the center of piano study. Dresden, at that time, was for voice. I was seventeen years old, what the Germans call a *backfisch*, meaning one so immature as to be hardly worth catching. I had never been abroad; for that matter, none of us had. I have a younger sister, Hildegarde Flanner, who is a very good poet. My mother equipped her with a large doll which she didn't love very much but which she dragged about. We spent the winter in Berlin and the summer in Munich and around Munich, on Starnberger See, which was Wagner country. Then we went to England and Scotland. We were going to spend a year in France, but my father's money ran out so we returned to America. A year or so later I went to the University of Chicago. It was cheap and excellent, especially strong in writing. I had known from the age of six that I wanted to be a writer.

N. When did you first start working?

■ *Genêt:* I suppose if *The New Yorker* hadn't been created in 1925 I would never have managed to start. I had known Ross, who was the editor and founder, and his wife Jane Grant. They were friends of Alexander Woollcott, Dorothy Parker, and Frank Adams, of the famed Algonquin Hotel Roundtable group, to which I did not belong. I was too provincial. But I knew them all. After I decided in 1922 to live in Paris, Jane wrote to me in 1925 and said, "Ross and I have a magazine called *The New Yorker*. We wish you would write us a Paris letter, the kind that you send me to tell me what's going on there." So I wrote back and said, "Is your magazine any good?" and she replied, "No, but it will be." So I wrote a double letter from Paris in the summer of 1925. *The New Yorker* had been founded on St. Valentine's with a cover picture of Eustace Tilly, with butterfly and holding up his monocle. My first two letters were published as one in September of that year. They were a bit confused because they had been combined. I've been writing for *The New Yorker* ever since.

N. It's been a long and a rich career.

■ *Genêt:* It became a little richer after I got Ross to pay me more. He started me at $35 a letter. At that time, with a small income from my family plus the extra $70 a month, I lived over in the St. Germain des-prés district. My raise made an important change, though I didn't move to a better hotel. I simply ate better, drank slightly better wine, bought one or two better suits, and traveled more. I was fascinated by the churches and cathedrals of France, particularly those analyzed architecturally by Henry Adams in his great volume called *Mont St. Michel and Chartres*. I traveled by rail, second class, excepting for the short trips, by third class. I stayed at the little provincial hotels. If they had a bathtub they kept coal in it. I visited the principal Romanesque and Gothic churches described by Adams and after years of appreciation came to know those churches better than many of the French. This was rather special for an American who traveled the

1*

hard way and was not even Catholic—I was brought up as a semi-Quaker. Incidentally, the French know what a Quaker is because of Quaker relief in this last war. They admire them rather strongly. There are quite a few Quakers in France, mostly down in the port city of La Rochelle on the southwestern coast, the Protestant part. They even have an annual meeting.

N. I didn't realize there were enough Protestants left in France after the Huguenot business to hold a convention.

■ *Genêt:* That was a mistake made by Louis XIV and his wife Madame de Maintenon. Many of them were wool weavers who escaped and fled to Holland where they vastly increased both the quality and quantity of their goods. Many went to England. Chanel, the famous French dressmaker, came from the center of France, called the Auvergne, a very poor part. She had been a shepherdess as a child. She became, of course, very wealthy and famous as the first modern Paris style-setter, but she always returned to her own part of France to buy her wool. She bought it raw, just after it had been sheared from the sheep. Then she sent her wool to England for weaving. In this way she really introduced English tweeds to France and made them highly popular. She was quite an extraordinary person. She always did everything the French hadn't thought of doing, except make money. The French had thought of that already.

N. Turning to what might be called the theory behind your own work, do you feel a sense of obligation to the material you use in your pieces for *The New Yorker?*

■ *Genêt:* Do you mean would I mislead my small part of the U.S.A. reading public by being overly-polite about the French? No.

Ross, when he gave me the only information he ever did give me, about what I was to report on in Paris, said, "I am not paying you for what you think, I'm paying you for what the French think."

He was quite right. Naturally I should report their interpretation and their notion of things French. Once in a while, when I am perfectly sure that my thought about some French event is indubitably right, I will say, "Most intelligent Frenchmen think," and then say what I think. In the end I satisfy both of us—the French and me.

Actually, I am very honest and very honorable about what I say. One has to be a disciplined and responsible journalist in dealing with foreign affairs or even foreign news. All the good international journalists worth their salt are very careful, very precise. No hysteria, no faking of scoops—there aren't any scoops any more. Generally the background of the news is too well known.

N. Can you pick out any particular incidents that have occurred during your stay in France that stand out vividly for one reason or another?

■ *Genêt:* Heavens. You're covering a lot of territory. Well, there was one awfully important moment. I was standing on the curb, like any other member of the French crowd, one noon in 1938. It was in front of Maxim's, Lehar's "Merry Widow" restaurant, and we were waiting for Daladier, then the Premier of France, who had been to Munich with Prime Minister Chamberlain to deal with Hitler. They had accepted Hitler's terms which would supposedly avoid war. Daladier had been so frightened by his own weak-kneed acceptance of Hitler's terms that when he got out of his plane at Le Bourget and saw a crowd of people waiting for him he was terrified. He thought it was an angry mob, that he was going to be attacked. When he entered Paris he discovered, to his astonishment (he was a rather slow-thinking fellow) that he was being hailed as a hero for saving France from another war.

I was watching him, as part of the crowd, when a woman standing next to me held up her good-looking little baby boy, perhaps a year and a half old, screaming at him in French, of course, "Look, my little one, there he goes—the man who will save you from being a soldier and ever having to go to war to fight Germany!" A year later, France was fighting Germany.

This was a moment that marked the two epochs—the end of the first, the beginning of the second. Between 1921 and the beginning of World War II, life was fantastic in Paris—the most brilliant modern epoch of taste and modernistic creation. Then came this last war, with all its dimness and horror and floundering, followed by the rejuvenation that came with de Gaulle.

Alas, I wasn't here to see de Gaulle march down the Champs Elysées. Time goes very quickly, yet I distinctly remember the first time I heard de Gaulle mentioned.

I had gone to England during the summer of Munich, passing through a small town called Abbéville. In the window of a famous antique shop I spotted a wonderful bed of the directoire period with a lady's head and bosoms carved at the top of the bed posts and her little bare feet at the bottom. I took a fancy to it and bought it, bringing it back to Paris with me three weeks later.

Alas, after the war began in earnest, France fell in six terrible weeks, and France's only victory took place at Abbéville. The forces there were led by an almost unknown colonel who had been quickly advanced to the post of brigadier general. His name was Charles de Gaulle, and afterward, when I tried to reassure the French by saying, "But you had a victory, you had Abbéville with Charles de Gaulle" they would say, "We had what? Who's he?"

N. Not too long ago, a very dramatic day in France saw the deaths of Edith Piaf and Jean Cocteau. France seemed to undergo a period of national mourning. In fact, the reaction in France was so strong I think most Americans were rather puzzled. Could you explain why their deaths were felt so deeply?

■ *Genêt:* This is a fascinating subject. Perhaps it begins, as far as any rational analysis of an emotional subject can be analyzed, with the fact that the French like their entertainers old. Male and female. Piaf, poor creature, wasn't as old as she looked. She was only forty-seven, but illness and poverty made her look a dilapidated fifty-five or sixty. Cocteau was seventy, and as I mentioned, the older they are the better the French like them. Look at Maurice Chevalier at seventy-five—he's still splendid. He's like an old bottle of humorous brandy to the French. They love him.

I think the French are critical and skeptical of youth in any person, but when they get used to their entertainers, after the first half-century, they become very devoted to them. Both Piaf and Cocteau are what the French call *des monstres sacres:* the closest translation, "a sacred monster," meaning a phenomenal personality. I don't know whom the English accept this way today except, perhaps, the Sitwells, and in America we are afflicted with a maniac feeling generally only toward youth.

Now, both Piaf and Cocteau were sacred monsters by birth as well as brilliance. Madame Piaf had been born in wretched circumstances, on a sidewalk, actually, with a couple of policemen who had been passing by serving as midwives. She was brought up by her grandmother, who ran a house of ill-fame, and she began singing in Montmartre at the age of thirteen or fourteen for pennies tossed to the sidewalk. She had an enormous voice, a tremendous voice, and she sang about the class she belonged to. It's the oldest class in Paris, the poor class, and the largest. They've always had their own songs, what we now call torch songs, about defeated trampled love, women's songs, about how, "I danced with him, he was curly haired, I loved him, and he never spoke to me again." Piaf began singing in music halls, which were much like our old vaudeville houses, and she rose quickly. Her records were tremendously popular, and her last song, her last great hit, contained the lines, "No, I regret nothing. Everything has been swept away, love with all its tremolo, I'll start again at zero." It was tremendous because everyone knew about her private life. She had had lots of tremolo.

Piaf's voice was either loved or loathed. The former were in the vast majority, but there were those who couldn't stand her. It was an authentic loud Paris shout about the disasters of being a female, French, and poor. She was a great artist within her means.

Another thing that struck the French fancy for dramatics that day was the fact that she had died at seven in the morning. Cocteau heard about her death at eleven and said, "Ah, the boat is beginning to sink," meaning that the people of his generation were beginning to perish. He died at one o'clock, more or less as the result of the shock of her death.

Cocteau was a dominating figure in the French entertainment world. He dominated by his talent and by his role in the great innovations of the twenties and thirties.

These changes were drastic, and actually began in Paris with the Russian ballet just before the First World War. Nijinsky and other great dancers swept Paris; *Petrouchka* and *Firebird* and Stravinsky's *Sacre du Printemps* became famed. To this shock was added cubism and Picasso and Braque. New drawing, painting, shapes, music, ballet. No one had seen ballet like this; they were used to young ladies in white skirts tipping about on their toes, and then, from Russia, came the vivid new carnal ballet. This, for France, was the beginning of the Russian Revolution. For the Russians themselves it became sadly political, but for the French it was aesthetic. It began with ballet.

Cocteau plunged himself into all this. He was a young man of a rich family. His mother was a widow, and this probably gave him a chance to expand—no father to restrain him. He was enormously gifted and strange, and he had a taste for many things which were forbidden by law, and he had artistic appetites with a great creative function. He was certainly one of the first to make extraordinary movies, wild melanges of mythological and classic and contemporary qualities. His plays, especially his first plays, like *The Young Married Couple on the Eiffel Tower* were similar; elaborate and difficult, they shock the imagination. Creations we now associate with Beckett, such as *Waiting for Godot*, are creations of surprise.

An interesting thing about the experimental, the daring, the creative, is the fact that it immediately begins taking on qualities and losing some. By the time the public can truly understand it, it has become less worthy of understanding. That may sound cynical, but I believe it is true.

Cocteau's whole life, his whole career, was productive and creative in the dramatic sense of the word. Until the last moment he was a part of public life. He belonged to France, and when he died, just these few hours later than Piaf, France was impressed, even thrilled as well as saddened by the close drama of both deaths as well as moved by the loss. Two sacred monsters made exquisite exits almost together.

N. I hope this isn't too sweeping a question, but I wonder if you could analyze the general and specific changes that have come to Paris during your years here.

■ *Genêt:* First I must point out that Americans have furnished the greatest changes in France. Most of us are of foreign blood, which blood we don't really know, unless we can find out who our great-grandfather was. Few of us are Indians, so our origins lay in Europe.

Well, few of us knew anything about Europe, and when we began going abroad we found things we had never had at home— aesthetic beauty, elegant buildings, tremendous rich museums, wine, different kinds of food. No fried chickens but rewarding sauces. Beginning in 1921 Americans came over in droves. We continued to come, of course, until the Depression brought travel to a halt in 1931. But by that time we had left a lot of evidence of ourselves in France. The French fought it off at first. They didn't like Coca-Cola. Oddly enough, the only place that Coca-Cola was immediately successful was in the Mohammedan countries—Algeria, Tunisia, Morocco—where the consumption of alcohol is forbidden. The Arab populations found Coca-Cola delicious on a hot day, and they paused a great deal to refresh. But the French didn't like it at first. They said it had a peculiar American taste. They didn't wish to be Americanized; but later in the 1930's, when tourist trade revived, the inevitable had begun to happen.

The first evidence came, as it always does, in advertising—types of advertising plus neon lights and large billboards which began to invade the Champs Elysées. But, in the meantime, the Americans had changed, too. We had almost become semi-European, at any rate broader in tastes and sophistications.

Look how "foreign" we are now compared to our way of life in the early twenties. Look at today's entertainments, the books, our taste for elegance, the snobbish gracious living motifs advertised in America. Why, our grandfathers would have turned over in their graves if anyone had mentioned "gracious living." They were still struggling in the cornpatch.

After World War II the French accepted Americanism with a vengeance. It was what they wanted; it was what they needed. For four years they had been occupied by the Germans. They began being preoccupied by American ideas and tastes. Look at the snack bars all over Paris. They're called "le snack." Paris also has quick lunch spots that are called "le quick." Sometimes they're written "queek." Then Paris got a little further along and opened what we call cafeterias. These they call "le self," for self-service. They began borrowing American words and phrases which they sandwiched in among their French, leading to the hybrid language. They disliked Franglais and now can't rid themselves of it. All over Paris you can get little hot dog sausages grilled on toast; you can get fried egg sandwiches to go along with your Coca-Cola; you can get tomato juice, which the French had never bothered with—they only put tomatoes in salad. There is an enterprise called the "le drug store" on the Champs Elysées near the Arc de Triomphe. I hear it has a soda fountain, and I must find out because I adore chocolate sodas.

The French love American snacks and gadgets, especially the young French. The young people are extremely susceptible to the American influence. They've made our things their own, so they don't necessarily feel as though they're being unpatriotic. All the boys went through the blue-jeans and sandals period. Over on the Left Bank, where I used to live, one boy I knew came from an awfully good French family and attended the Sorbonne. He used to hurry over to the Deux Magots Café before classes opened, go down into the men's rooms where he stored a sweater, a pair of jeans, and a pair of sandals. He would change out of the very good suit his father had had made for him in London and dress in this mock-American outfit so he wouldn't feel "out of place" while obtaining his classic French education.

Today the jeans have gone from the scene to a great extent. The French youth has discovered that Italian clothes are even tighter. In fact there's so much Italian influence that, near the Champs Elysées, the young greet each other with *ciao* which is Roman slang for "hi" and "good-bye" and so on.

All this stands in contrast to the fact that the French have never before been a nation of people to accept foreign inventions or ideas. They have had enough of their own. But the creative function of French art declined after the 1930's. Earlier innovations were no longer innovations, and new motifs or forms failed to appear. Art became utterly abstract—not even the shape of cubism was left.

To examine this decline would be a long and intricate process. A nation that had flourished throughout the eighteenth, nineteenth, and the first portion of the twentieth centuries with its truly fantastic creations of the novel, of art, and later of cinema, suddenly failed to beget a new supply of creative talents, of creative minds.

This leads to another enigma—the mystery of creative births. No one understands how a perfectly ordinary couple, prosaic and even dull, can produce a child that turns out to be André Gide or Renoir or Cocteau. This is something great scientists might fiddle with for a while and leave the heavens and the explosives alone. For two or three centuries the French had great creative births. Children were born with enormous talent and ambition and daring. Then, like an omission in French destiny, that kind of child ceased to be born.

France has gone downhill, of course, but we've not done too well, either. We are not making Hemingways constantly. Faulkner has come to his end. We had Henry James but didn't greatly appreciate him. Of course, he was no giant of his times like Hemingway, to change the very art of contemporary fiction. Ernest created a style of sentiment and masculine pessimism that will last, meaning it will outlast his present drop in popularity. It will continue to last even in France.

An astonishing thing was the way the French turned to Faulkner, in the mid-1930 years. They became fascinated with him. He was popular in France before he was in the U.S.A. The first of his books to be translated was *Sanctuary*. I'd had difficulty reading that book in English, but I was energetic enough to plough through it in French. I do not understand how they understood it, but they did. But then, the French have always known a great deal more about our Civil War and thus our South than we did. The recent popularity of books on the Civil War answers an enormous emptiness in American education. But the French had always known a great deal about it because Lee's campaigns were highly regarded as great military strategy, and they were taught at Saint Cyr, the French equivalent of West Point. Also, the French—by the nature of their own national makeup—were sympathetic to an agrarian aristocracy. Until the Revolution they raised great families, lived on their lands, made their money from their lands. Thus they understood the agrarian attitude of the South. Not until the 1930's, in fact, did France succumb to big business, big factories. Yet in many aspects of mechanization—those that really count, to me—France has often led the United States. Take railroads, for example. We used to think we had the fastest and the best. Well, we didn't. Even before the New Haven line became a tragic joke for commuters, French trains have been faster, more comfortable, more practical, for decades.

The European railway systems—the French, Italian, and British in particular—offer a startling education to the American who travels from Darien, Connecticut, for example, to New York, or from Lake Forest to Chicago. Or who takes what used to be crack trains from New York to Chicago to California. Today they are wretched. Of course, now we all fly like angels. No one except me wants to ride a train, but I enjoy them. I love to sit in a train and look. I can't find anything out about a country landscape by riding up in the sky—the sky is a universal affair. I think I'm perhaps monkey-minded, very simian-minded. I like to look. I think one tastes a country's qualities through the eyes—it's one of the ways we learn. How people look, how they dress, how they think. These things you can see.

N.   If you were to comment on the cultural world of today—literature, theater, music—which aspects do you most admire, and which do you most deplore?

■ *Genêt:* In America or in France?

N.   Wherever you travel, whatever you're acquainted with. For you this becomes rather extensive.

■ *Genêt:* I've got to comment on the Italians first, because they've come up recently with extraordinary literary talent. Their new novelists, their modes of the novel, are fresh and exciting. They learned from America. Their films have been equally good. I'd like to spend some time on this subject, because films have become the great unifier of talent—a truly international medium.

This is something we see immediately in France, because the French are very critical-minded. By this I mean that they have a sense of the critical faculty, the appraising faculty. They know *why* they like and dislike, not merely *what* pleases and displeases them—even the young people, the French girls with hair like haystacks and the men in tight Italian trousers. Their first concern about a film is "who directed it?" and "how was it directed?" Why, there isn't a fan in Hollywood who knows the names of directors. Several of his wives and local gentry may know how much he paid for his house but they can't appraise his talent.

In France they realize that the director is the person who *makes* the film; his imprint is on every foot of it. If he's talented and strong he'll even maneuver the stars so often used for boxoffice draw, not for ability.

Right now, in Paris, American Westerns are enjoying an enormous vogue—re-vogue, we call it. One theater presents a new old American Western every day. The French youth didn't get to see them before. They haven't got anything like our plains and mountains over here. In France there simply isn't that distance, that vast space, that freedom for movement. The young Frenchman won't grow up to ride a horse—he'll go into business, but this doesn't hurt the vicarious pleasure he gets from an American Western. American literature is enjoying a vogue in France, too. Hemingway and Scott Fitzgerald are big. In a movie which made a big hit here, *Le Feu Follet*, which literally means *Will of the Wisp* (rather silly, since it's a suicide film) the hero—just before he kills himself— picks up *The Great Gatsby* in English and finishes it. Fitzgerald, of course, was a part of Paris during that romantic expatriate period; unfortunately, he made champagne a necessity, like bath water. Ernest Hemingway still has an enormous influence here— excites great admiration. They can't apply his themes to their lives, but they admire him technically. Perhaps this receptiveness toward work from outside France reflects the fact that they themselves haven't been too gifted lately. But I don't think we can complain— let them lie fallow for a while. The two or three centuries of creativity the French writers and minds gave us can be savored and absorbed while they rest.

N. What do you think of the state of the American novel?

◼ *Genêt:* Quite bleak, isn't it? I don't see any great emergence of talent. Mary McCarthy has come as close as anyone because she applies a very instructive and thoughtful, very academic knowledgable mind, to her work. She was convinced of the necessity for recording the truth of 1933, for example, in *The Group*. It *was* the truth, too—I'm old enough to remember that period, am much older than she is. Perhaps *we* didn't talk as much about sex as her "Group" did, but don't forget that women were emerging, then, and all American women with the vote thought we were going to do important things. Well, we did some things that were important and a lot of things that weren't. *The Group* is an almost uncanny illustration of what we hoped for, as brave new world intellectuals, and how much we failed, as human beings. But too much American writing—perhaps too much writing done everywhere—is self-absorbed and precious and almost private. We encounter mental convolutions which are thoroughly extraneous, and sexual elements which are neither edifying nor emotional. So much is written, so little said.

N.   I'd like to turn to the evolving talent, the young writer or poet or playwright with talent and ambition. What advice would you give him for preparing himself, for shaping his talent?

■ *Genêt:*   I suppose you mean an American?

N.   Since we seem to be growing so much alike, either American or French.

■ *Genêt:*   No, it could not be either American or French. The same advice could not cover both. The French still receive a semiclassical education, though their parents complain that it is not nearly classical enough. The Americans no longer have a classical education. When I went to Tudor Hall as a girl at prep school I started Latin in seventh grade like the English children. (I might add that I was terribly weak in mathematics; I had to take geometry three times and I still didn't understand it.)

I think the first thing the American who wants to write should realize is the fact that a college course called "Creative Writing" does *not* enable you to write. All writing is creative, unless you're making out a grocery list—and that might be creative, too, if you decide to have cabbage instead of brussels sprouts. But we've got the notion that we can teach anything . . . that two semesters makes one proficient and three semesters makes one an expert. This isn't true. No one should write who hasn't got talent. No one should write who hasn't got something to say and isn't willing to work very hard. The great difficulty with young American writers is the meanness and poorness of the vocabulary in America. In my time I've seen the vocabulary, the working vocabulary, diminish appallingly. Some of the American slang is awfully good, downright irresistible, but it's only slang—a simplification of language, or a substitute, not an enlargement.

I think that pronunciation is the key to the downfall. I do not think that Americans can lay a fair claim to being the leaders of a new world when they pronounce so badly and when so many speak with such ugly accents in such ugly voices. It doesn't sound to me —with my Indiana upbringing, mind you—like the voice of the master or the leader of the Western world.

The most pleasing American accent comes from San Francisco.

It is an unaccented English, and nice to hear. Boston is nice, as are parts of New York. Maine, with its twist, I like very much. Ohio still has some pleasing accents. From there on out you get some ugly sounds. Unfortunately, many Americans have the notion that any man who speaks with a pleasing accent is a sissy. I don't know how they invented this confusion. Freud and Kinsey should have informed them to the contrary.

A failure in phonetics is the thing which has torn down our language. We never pronounce vowels any more. "Has he come into the offus yet?" The word is "office" and should be pronounced "office." But any final vowel which is an "e" is reduced to a "u" or an "uh." This, I believe, has had a crimping and crippling effect upon the use of our language.

Of course, grammar has gone to pot, too. It's being picked up again, and this pleases me, because grammar is basic and useful. It's like the electric lights to help you go up the street or down or around the corner. Today's students are not too likely to know what an adverb or a verb is or what the difference is or that a noun is the name of something, of anything, and I wonder how they can be expected to write a sentence properly let alone creatively if they don't know how it is constructed.

This lack of preparation shows up constantly at *The New Yorker* office. Very nice girls turn up there from the female Ivy League colleges. We have probably let it be known around town that we need a few good stenographers. So we get these young ladies who say, "I would like to write and I would like to start with *The New Yorker*." We usually say to them, "Would you write something right now, please?" and, delighted, they ask what we want them to write. "Why don't you describe how you came into the office this morning, who was on the street and in the elevator?" (I'm making this up, but this is the sort of thing that constantly happens.) The girl's almost invariable reply is, "Oh, I don't remember" or "nobody interesting." So you see, they're not prepared for writing even if they could write; they're not observant, they don't look about them. And what they do turn out is usually wretched. They don't have the faintest knowledge of the grammar and construction that makes E. B. White so superb. He wouldn't like this being mentioned but he does turn out beautiful eighteenth century English. By the same token Thurber wrote beautifully, even when he wasn't being funny. But the grammatical preparation that leads to thought and style and eloquence has been eliminated from the younger generation's education.

Assigned reading is a haphazard proposition nowadays, too. What do you expect from a youth whose exposure to American literature consists, for example, of capsule digests that explain the plot of Henry James' *The Golden Bowl* and *What Maisie Knew*. There are differences between these stories that simply can't be capsuled—but between Kinsey reports and creative writing courses the students haven't got time to read a great writers text. They might know that Henry James was an expatriate, and a peculiar bachelor, but why complicate the little student mind by making it read and comprehend his genius by reading his style in a full story?

Not long ago I spoke to a young man who was a senior in a California high school, and I asked him which of Shakespeare's plays they were reading. He said, in a shocked voice, "Shakespeare? We don't read him—we'd never stand for it." We can't have writers who are not familiar with the processes of writing and the great books that have been written.

Vocabulary and grammar and knowledge and curiosity provide the foundation for a writer. Without these things writing is a costly waste.

N. In writing your letters from Paris—which obviously involve a great deal of preparation—how would you describe your own working processes?

■ *Genêt:* For one thing, I read enormously. I work alone, I wouldn't know what to do with an office staff, and I portion out my own time. I read eight French papers a day, from the Communist morning daily *Humanité*, to the august evening paper, *Le Monde*. I also read two English papers, the London *Times* and *The Manchester Guardian*. I select the news I want to use, cut it out, put it around my desk, and lose part of it. This is all very complicated. When I decide what I'm going to do I've got to get a start. This isn't easy. I can't begin my sort of piece in the middle—I have to launch myself the way you start pedaling a bicycle. I fall off repeatedly. I write very painstakingly. While I'm not a very disciplined person in a physical sense—my room, for example, is usually disorderly—I'm a disciplined and hard worker. A Paris Letter, which runs about 2,500 words, takes four to five full days to write—and one or two of those days extend to twelve hours of work. I love to write, to find the exact word, the balance. So often it isn't enough to say "a red frock." You need a word with a double meaning. There are crimsons like the sunset, like sunrise, like blood. The reader can be touched by all three qualifications of the word "red." I usually work with three or four dictionaries at hand—French and several English dictionaries. Certainly the Larousse French dictionary, which gives root origins, is very useful to me when writing about French subjects. So many French words have Latin or Greek origins, and lead to subtle nuances of meaning one would not expect. I cable my letter so as to include the latest news if it is useful or fit to print.

De Gaulle has been good for all of us here, whether we are French or American. He is highly educated: writes almost pompous high class literary French and speaks it with such laudable rich vocabulary and style, that all of us have pulled up our bootstraps to extend our own vocabularies and style. He has been a great education for most of us. It takes thought to write about a phenomenon such as he is.

N. The final question I have concerns the origin of the name "Genêt." How did it come about?

■ *Genêt:* I've never been able to settle that—nor to change or improve the story. When Ross founded the magazine in 1925 he had planned to use articles which would be signed with nom de plumes as the English coffee house writers used—"Spy" and so on. For a while Bob Benchley signed some of his short profiles "Searchlight." Dorothy Parker signed her reviews "Constant Reader." To my astonishment, when I received the slim issue of *The New Yorker* that contained my first piece, I discovered that it was signed "Genêt" with a circumflex over the final "e." So I wrote to Ross and said, "By the way, would you mind telling me who Genêt is, or which Genêt you mean, or what type of Genêt am I being called?"

I gave him a choice of three. I told him that there was a Genêt who was a representative of the French Revolution, sent to Washington as a publicist to help establish good relations with America. Washington didn't take to him very well, and asked for his recall, but I think this Genêt settled down somewhere in America. He was *Citoyen* Genêt, or Citizen Genêt as all French were called at that time. I asked Ross if I could be that one.

Then there is the genestra Genêt which is a big weed with spikes on it and large, lovely yellow flowers. It grows on hillsides and heaths. I said, "It's a very high-class weed, but it is still a weed, this Genêt." The third application would be still more painful. Genêt is what is called in English the Jenny, the female of the ass family. Now, which one am I supposed to be?

Ross's answer was very characteristic—complete silence. So I never knew which one he had in mind.

"The best thing an American writer can do is to describe the world that he sees and not worry about other writers or critics, not even worry too much about the readers."

Herbert Gold
Interviewed in San Francisco, August, 1963

Herbert Gold

N.   Few American writers are as strong an influence upon our world of letters as is Herbert Gold. He has taken a rather dour look at modern man, working in depth to establish both the positive and negative poles of this outlook while gradually synthesizing a philosophy. He has also championed writers favoring new modes of expression.

Two recent works, the novel *Salt* and the anthology *First Person Singular*, have met a vivid press. Praise for the latter is almost unanimous, but *Salt* seems either violently liked or violently disliked. The first question I'd like to ask Mr. Gold concerns the creation of *Salt:* why it was written, what he expected it to accomplish, and what he feels it has accomplished.

■ *Gold:* You've sprung the whole world at me. I wanted to give, in a sense, what it is like to live in a big city in America at a time when people don't trust their work, their love affairs, their marriages. Friendship is suspect and politics make little sense. I wanted to show people—some of good will, and some of bad will—trying to deal with that set of issues.

Also—and it sounds odd after putting it so sourly—it seems to me that this is a time when there's an enormous amount of freedom simply because we are on the ledge of history. We have the freedom to jump off or to crawl back in or to wave violently from our ledge. It's a time in which there can be a great deal of fun. So I wanted, to become a man of few words, to write a tragedy comically. It seems to me this is a comic problem—people have everything, yet don't get the good out of it.

In *Salt* our limitation, our confinement to the narrow view, is summed up in a hero who wants to find true love. This is not a proper ambition for a man. True love is a complete abstraction. What you do when you find true love is to find a specific girl who has a certain smell, a certain kind of hair, certain kind of muscles and weaknesses, a whole set of specific attributes. If you want "true love" you don't find anything, so the hero has to adjust his ideal to

280

meet reality. He also wants to find perfect work. He wants to find
that which will fulfill his creative capacities to the utmost. Well,
you can't do that in the United States today. During a war, perhaps,
a man can use himself utterly, but war has become impossible. So he
has to live in New York and adjust to the possibilities of love and
the possibilities of work which are available. This is a very sad situation to be in—not to be able to use yourself to the utmost. At the
same time it has comic possibilities. It's the identical situation
Don Quixote is in—except that, instead of charging windmills, the
protagonists of *Salt* charge New York women. New York
women sometimes seem to have more arms than windmills, and tilt
as badly.

N. For some time you've championed specific writers, sometimes with, and sometimes against, the grain of general critical
opinion. Could you single out any individuals, now, from whom
you expect great things?

■ *Gold:* It's impossible to say who is going to do what. You
can't tell about novelists, even bad novelists, until they're dead,
and even then they can leave posthumous works to revise every
verdict. It's very hard to predict who will develop. I would think
that a writer who has shown steady development—and he's no
longer in his youth—is Saul Bellow. Other writers who have developed very steadily, and have the gift of intelligence required, are
George P. Eliott and Bernard Malamud. There are younger writers
with great potential like Leon Litwack, Warren Miller, Thomas
Williams, and Walker Percy. I would read anything new that
Nelson Algren writes. He certainly isn't a new or younger writer,
but he always has something to say.

Now, I've always been very hard on Kerouac, but in his next to
the last book, *Big Sur,* he suggested the possibility that he might
become a real writer. He's given up being what Clancy Segal has
called "one of nihilism's organization men" and he's writing about
the dilemma of being a middle-aged, balding beatnik. There's a
possibility of his truly finding his metier, but not in the dilemma of
a man who is over forty and still the leader of youth!

N. Now that there's some chance of retrospect, how do you
view the beatnik cult?

■ *Gold:* Well, it was always sort of fake, a new kind of conformity. I wrote a piece on Kerouac before *On The Road* came
out. I saw an advance copy of the book, and the beatnik thing
seemed dead to me, then. It reflected a very small, edgy, itchy side-
movement in American letters. It was part of the Eisenhower

epoch, part of the isolation from anything meaningful, part of the days of the McCarthy chill.

Time went backward for the creative person during the Eisenhower era. There was no sense that anything was to come. I can give you an example based upon a young man I know who is a typical potential beatnik. He wasn't a writer; he was an engineer who had the chance to go to Ghana to build roads. He would spend three years in Africa to find out about a new society, but he said, "I can't do that, I'll get behind all the men in my class. They'll all have wives, they'll all have incomes of $20,000 a year." He simply couldn't leave.

Fortunately, the temper of the times has changed a little bit. I don't mean to exaggerate the importance of the Peace Corps, but that kind of spirit, or the spirit of these people who march on Washington, or Freedom Riders in the South, these things indicate that the people who once merely played the bongos and read Zen to express themselves can now do something. They can sell their guitars and do something effective.

N. In other words, something positive is happening.

■ *Gold:* Just the fact of action is important, but something *is* happening. It may not be a clear-cut victory, but then Nietzsche said, "If you analyze a victory it becomes a defeat." Something is happening, and it may not be terribly important, but at least it's a vital step removed from the self-involved frolicking in the psyche that the public beatniks indulged in.

Still, a man like Kerouac has talent. Certainly a man like Ginsberg has talent. He has the ability to arouse people, he has a rhetorical gift, but the beat movement was ridiculous. It attracted a lot of people who just wanted the chance to wear heavy eye shadow and play chess in coffee houses.

Perhaps the ultimate display in the ridiculous was Mailer's part in the beat movement. To him, it must have looked exciting. Norman Mailer is an unhappy man who is constantly looking to have an experience, whether it's sex, drugs, hysterical explosions, or getting his name in the paper. The beatniks looked as if they were doing something. He's in the position of a deaf man who yells because he thinks other people can't hear him. Actually, it's he who can't hear other people.

Mailer has had a history of catching on to movements when they were over. He was a Trotskyite when that was over, a beatnik when that was over, a Freudian when that was done as a mystique. He's perpetually looking for a cause, for another war to fight, but

I think he is symptomatic of something that is peculiarly American: we're all looking for heavy experiences.

Mailer became very popular all at once because he did some wild things in public which were really the simplest expressions of a neurotic, but because he had written a best-selling novel ten years or so before, he became very exciting to a lot of other people —people who were, shall we say, incapable of stabbing their wives. I remember that when that happened the *Chronicle*, here in San Francisco, ran a headline that read, "Naked and Dead Author Stabs Wife."

N.   With quotation marks in the right places, I hope.

■ *Gold:* Typical, also, was this incident. An editor in New York called me, knowing that Mailer and I are the opposite of friends, and said, "Would you write an article about Norman Mailer?" This was just after he was in terrible trouble. He had stabbed his wife; he had been declared psychotic by a psychiatrist; he was coming up for trial. The implication was, "Will you write an article because you can get back at him now?" What a scabby desire for sensation the newspapers and magazines are after! They make a man like Mailer indulge himself because they are constantly rewarding him.

In other words, if you have any temptation to get your kicks out of publicity, the media are there waiting for you. For example, I'm talking to you now. I know that if I say something especially scandalous I have a better chance of being listened to than if I just sit and talk to you.

N.   I'm afraid I have to agree. But to turn back to you again, I wonder if you could retrace your own steps as a writer—more or less put your own career into chronological order.

■ *Gold:* Let's see. I was in the war, studied philosophy, then went to Paris to write a dissertation on philosophy. I bought a bicycle and found that it was easier to write fiction while riding a bicycle than it was to be a philosopher under the same circumstances. So I wrote a first novel called *Birth Of A Hero* which I'm not terribly proud of, but it did teach me something about being a writer.

Then, while I was still in Paris, learning French and studying a whole new society, something happened which could be called an awakening. I wrote a story called *The Heart Of The Artichoke* which was, for me, a turning point. I started being my own man. I think my first novel was very derivative from what I had read before of Tolstoy, Henry James, the writers I most admired. After that I was writing what I had to say. I blush a little when the word "vanguard" comes up. I don't think I'm an institution or a leader. I have some interest as a writer, but it"s because I have a special, personal point of view. I wish, actually, that I could be a political leader. I wish there were a politics possible in this country.

My argument with others has always been against forming schools—instead, to cultivate one's own garden. The writers who want to be leaders in this country find that they're just following one of the laws of thermodynamics that says hot air rises. They rise, but they don't do anything, they merely spread hot air. The best thing an American writer can do is to describe the world that he sees and not worry about other writers or critics, not even worry too much about the readers.

N. Getting back to you, what followed *The Heart Of The Artichoke?*

■ *Gold:* Well, I spent two years in Paris. Then I decided I was an American, not a transplanted American, certainly not an expatriate, so I came back to the United States with the recurrent idea: to get to know a society is to work in it. So I went to work first in a hotel, then for the Regional Planning Commission in Cleveland, which is the city in which I grew up. Then I became a college teacher, which I've been off and on—more off than on— ever since.

I wrote *The Prospect Before Us* and *The Man Who Was Not With It* (which dates before the beat movement and came out of private experience.) At the age of seventeen, I spent a year on the road, while all my high school classmates were working in defense plants. Anyway, after the Cleveland re-experience I lived in Haiti for a year and wrote *The Optimist.* Then came *Therefore Be Bold* and a collection of stories called *Love and Like,* which I'd been doing over the years, and a collection of essays titled *The Age of Happy Problems.* Then the book which I think is my best—and which has gotten the worst reviews—called *Salt.*

N. Have the reviews been that bad?

■ *Gold:* The book has enraged a lot of people. I think it's a sign of doing the writer's job when he outrages the critics. I have the feeling that with *Therefore Be Bold* I had written the book which was going to please the greatest number of critics and from then on it would be downhill. In other words, the better I get the fewer people I'm going to please. Fortunately, *Salt* has had more readers than any other book I've done.

N. I've got to admit—*Salt* has a certain shock value.

■ *Gold: Salt* shocked people. I was attacked both personally and as a writer. As a writer I was delighted by the attacks, but some of them were so personal that I felt grieved as a human being. Writers are human beings. It's painful when you hear a critic say, "I don't like you—you're vulgar, you're obscene." So, as a person, I am bothered by assault, but as a writer I am pleased. I think that the more I am my own man, the more any writer is his own man, the more the critics (who are by nature conservative) are going to be outraged by his work.

Some of the ironies of this situation are, of course, self-evident. You often find in literary history that when great books were published, when books we now call great were published, everyone was shocked by them. After such a book survived ten years it became a classic and it was read in a different way. This is one of the reasons why you have to go on reading and writing new books. You can't just read the classics because in many important respects they've been assimilated. The new book, which represents the green growing tip of the best thought of the time, will be shocking. It will get under people's skin.

Oddly enough, both Shakespeare and Dostoevsky make many rather harsh points about society which are as true today as they were back then. But what a difference in the acceptance of critics—for example, in *The Possessed* a man says, "What was he drinking?" and someone answers, "vodka." Then the man says, "Well, that will be the last glass of vodka he ever drinks." In the next beat of the book the man is found dead.

Well, we don't think of this as brutal. We think of this as art. We say, "What an artistic way of expressing that idea, what a lovely way to express brutality." You see, the book is one hundred years old, and we see it, now, as a classical means of writing, as a problem in form beautifully resolved. But if we say—well, in *Salt* I describe certain sorts of brutality that abound in today's New York. But people are insulted. They don't say, "This is a formal problem" or "This is an artistic problem." They say, "I don't like the way he's talking about me."

N. To turn toward the general scene, now, I wonder what you find most hopeful in the literary world at present.

■ *Gold:* I think something has replaced the big social novel of the thirties. The "inside," "dopester," or "big picture" novel has enjoyed a vogue for good reasons. Sometimes these novels are misleading, but at other times they ring with basic truths. You can discover that homosexuality rules Congress—one of the silly notions of the book clubs—or find out what's going on in Hawaii or Texas. The novelists are tending to take upon themselves, unasked, the role of politician, preacher, or moralist, partly because the politician, preacher, and moralist aren't fulfilling their roles. A great many novelists are first telling a story, then giving a view of life, and in a very conscious way saying something about how they think human beings should live. I don't know what term we should use for this—the "moral novel" or the "metaphysical novel"—but it's as though the novel is doing what Donne, in his *Meditations* tried to do in his time, to express the moral consciousness of the age.

Writers like Saul Bellow, Bernard Malamud, George Eliott, R. V. Cassill, Thomas Williams, and a great many others, are not just telling a story in a specific style—which is characteristic of them—but they are also presenting a point of view, a contemporary version of Lutheranism, for example, as in the case of George Eliott, or a matter-of-fact Jewish romanticism as in the case of Saul Bellow. I think that each of these writers could be analyzed from the point of view of a metaphysical or philosophical position being taken.

I think this is hopeful, not because it's an ultimate perfection, but because the writer is assuming a larger role.

N.   Conversely—what do you most deplore in today's literature?

■ *Gold:*   Bad books. Display for the sake of display. Time-serving in the guise of expressing the time. Following of fashion, even the original fashions of Nabokov or Ginsberg or Bellow or Mary McCarthy. Planting of symbol and manner out of some meek graduate-student hope of approval from Teacher. The axing and grinding and jockeying for position of the literary life. The new power that writers have—to speak, to get their names in the papers, to be interviewed, even to make money—has to be taken comically. I was sitting with James Baldwin at Cyrano's in Los Angeles when a banker rushed up with a dozen copies of his books and a pen, saying, "Here, Mr. Baldwin, will you endorse these?" For deposit only. Bernard Wolfe is sitting down there plotting a book entitled, *Down and Out in Hollywood and Palm Springs.*

N.   Now, as far as the young writer coming up is concerned, the serious aspirant who wants to write well, what kind of advice would you give him in regard to living and learning?

■ *Gold:*   First—and many writers either laugh at me or feel indignant when they hear it—I would say, "Don't write." At least, do something else. The great problem for American writers is the fact that they don't know anything—they don't have any experience. They may know about a family, love, marriage, being a child, being a husband, being a father. They may know about sex. They know a few or some or all of these things in personal detail.

What happens is that a lot of very talented young people write a first novel about their great love affair, or their unhappy childhood, or the one traumatic experience they've had, or about the war. They are established as writers and can go on writing because they have a certain technique and training.

Then they find that they have nothing to say. This means that they do the peculiar things that we've noticed in so many writers. They flee toward a ridiculous vulgarization of, say, Zen; they try the drug or sex exits; or they run away toward public madness. If they're of more prudent temperament they retreat into a kind of stylistic exercise. Thus we get writers who produce a good first novel, then do increasingly fine imitations of it.

Typical, at the most successful level, is the *New Yorker* novelist, the *New Yorker* short story writer, who tends not to imitate good models, but to imitate himself.

The best thing I think a writer can do—a young would-be writer—is to learn to do something besides write, to get some experience in the world, something as romantic, perhaps, as the Peace Corps, or something as practical as being doctor, lawyer, or Indian chief.

The American writer is an isolated man; he's morally isolated from other Americans. He needs a sense of cause or responsibility to others. He's caught in a life which, if he makes a living by his writing, means that he doesn't run in rush-hour traffic, he had no responsibility to staff. While he is undoubtedly doing something of importance, something socially useful he has a sense of isolation. The result can become, as one novel follows the next, the hollow echo of words, not the resounding echo of life.

I think it's a vital refreshment for an artist to live and work in the world of people. The danger to the writer is the trap of self-absorption. He becomes absorbed in his own psychology and in his own little family problem. He's not going to know what's inside those high buildings downtown.

This problem is partly a new one and partly a very old one. It's an old one in that there's always been the institution of the man of letters, but not in the United States. Certainly the French man of letters exists and has existed, but he's a phenomenon in literary history. The American writer must accept his position of being anarchically outside society, and also must pay for it by finding a productive place in the world. He should aim to earn his critical rebellion. If he crows like a cock, he should be sure he has surveyed the barnyard.

". . . we do feel very strongly that one must picture life as it is, but that's no reason for overemphasizing sex or violence. They have a very definite place in life, and consequently in literature. . . . I think it's up to the writer to use some restraint; blueprints aren't essential in depicting evil."

Mildred and Gordon Gordon
Interviewed in Los Angeles, August, 1963

K

Mildred and Gordon Gordon

N. Novels by the Gordons have sold phenomenally well. They are expert blends of suspense and characterization, and they are never without an element of fun. Each of the twelve in print at the time of this interview is thoroughly professional, tailored to capture the wide market that awaits any mystery offering suspense, entertainment, and intrigue.

In speaking to Mildred and Gordon Gordon I'd like to begin by asking them how they came to work together as a team.

■ *M. Gordon:* I started us off in our life of crime by writing a little whodunit—strictly a bit of fluff—when Gordon was with the FBI in Chicago. We had always been writers but had worked exclusively with nonfiction until this time. Gordon was busy and told me that this was my chance to take a crack at fiction—so I did.

I chose the mystery field because I felt it was the most stylized area of the novel and would be the easiest to work in. I wrote my first mystery while waiting for Gordon to come home nights—the FBI creates many lonely evenings for a wife. Perhaps we didn't realize it then, but Gordon's work with the FBI brought us a world of material—not only the feel of suspense and people in suspenseful situations, but the effect of danger upon the criminal and the victim and the victim's family. Since we were and are as interested in characterization as we are in plot, all of Gordon's work was grist to the mill, and after my first book we turned to collaboration.

N. How long were you with the FBI?

■ *G. Gordon:* For three years—and most of that time in Chicago. I think I know every dark street in Chicago—all the interesting spots on Clark Street, etc. Actually, Mildred and I started out as newspaper people, then did magazine articles. After the interlude with the FBI we've pretty well stuck to fiction.

I'll emphasize what Mildred said about characterizations because the people in our books are very real to us. After we finish a book we feel as though we'd spent time with dear friends or relatives or someone we've helped through a trying situation. Perhaps we should feel that way because all of our characters are drawn from people we know—and this includes the criminals.

■ *M. Gordon:* We also plot very carefully. We plot everything from the beginning because we belong to the school that feels you should start building to a definite climax. We believe that anything not essential to the plot, that does not contribute to suspense, should be omitted. There's another school that believes this robs you of spontaneity, but since we both work on the same book at the same time we must plot a story to the very end.

N. How do you work, by the way?

■ *G. Gordon:* Well, it's a rather confusing process. Theoretically, we plot a book through to the finish, then divide the chapters. Mildred will take a chapter that happens to appeal to her, I'll do likewise, and then we exchange copy. If I don't care for what Mildred has done I may rewrite it. If she doesn't care for what I've done she may do the same. By the time it's in print we seldom know who has written what.

N. But you stay married.

■ *G. Gordon:* It never gets personal with us because of our start on newspapers. We grew rather well accustomed to having our copy marked up.

■ *M. Gordon:* We still listen to any advice we get that seems legitimate. We often give a section of a book, or a completed book, to someone we believe can give us an honest appraisal if we're in doubt about the effect we're striving for. We listen to each other, and also to Isabelle Taylor (our editor at Doubleday) because we realize that we certainly don't know everything there is to know about writing, and she certainly knows a great deal about what people want to read and what will sell.

■ *G. Gordon:* I don't think that any writer can keep an accurate perspective on his own work.

■ *M. Gordon:* We have a great advantage, I think, over one person writing a book because we have two points of view. We don't argue—arguing takes too much work and too much time and rarely gets you anyplace—but we do discuss both sides of a question or a plot angle. Frequently, one of us is sure he sees it correctly, but when we stop to analyze it we get different views. The fact that we do differ in our opinions and in our attitudes is invaluable.

■ *G. Gordon:* It's easier, too, because if I get in a jam, if I can't see my way through a chapter, I toss it over to Mildred and she approaches it with a fresh perspective. Within an hour or two she's solved what seemed (to me) an insurmountable problem.

■ *M. Gordon:* And vice versa.

N.   Turning to one novel, *Undercover Cat*, because it's the most recent suspense story by the Gordons I've read, could you describe how the novel evolved?

■ *G. Gordon:* Yes, it sprang from a black cat we owned. We bought him from the SPCA for all of two dollars.

■ *M. Gordon:* We had him in Chicago, and he kept us out of some of the best apartments.

■ *G. Gordon:* Many of his adventures are actually included in *Undercover Cat.* We had this story in mind for quite some time, but we always hesitated to write it because the field seems so crowded with animals and humor and, to be specific, humorous animals. So we waited a few years, but I should mention that it isn't a cat story, actually; it's a Doris Day type of comedy. At least Walt Disney hopes so because he's bought the film rights to star Hayley Mills, who will be eighteen by the time it's filmed and a sort of junior Doris Day.

■ *M. Gordon:* Our cat was a twenty-five pound monster, the same as in this story. People would look at him and not believe their eyes. They thought he was some species of small black panther. He literally stopped traffic when he rode in the car; we would slow down in a business area and he'd pop up to look around and a crowd would gather.

■ *G. Gordon:* But where would Disney find a twenty-five pound cat? We've reduced him to fifteen pounds for the movie.

■ *M. Gordon:* Then there's the problem of photographing a black cat at night, so now he's a Siamese.

The idea of the FBI having to follow a cat to solve a crime occurred to us some time ago. Anyone who has ever had a cat knows of the humorous and difficult situations that can arise. And it's fairly simple to incorporate suspense because you can never predict what a cat will do. They don't follow orders, like a dog, and the fact that the cat must be followed by some rather literal FBI agents invites all sorts of consequences.

N.   Now, to take all of your books into consideration, do you know what the sales totals are, and where they've been published?

■ *G. Gordon:* Doubleday tells us that our books have sold over eight million copies, including reprints, in seventeen countries. We're helped, of course, by the way American suspense stories have become so popular everywhere, even in Europe. American writers are doing very well in France, Germany, Italy, and the

Scandinavian countries. In West Germany, suspense novels by Americans lead in mystery sales. Perhaps one reason for it is the fact that we live at a fast tempo, the American stories are fast-paced, and many people won't take time to read the delightful English mysteries that create such fine mood and atmosphere. Personally, we enjoy them immensely, but now you'll notice that the English writers are following the lead of the Americans. Ian Fleming is as American as any American writer could be.

N. To turn to the realm of theory, what do you feel the mystery writer owes his audience, his characterizations, and his craft as a whole?

■ *M. Gordon:* I think it depends upon what target you're trying to hit. If you're doing a fast-paced story, or the Erle Stanley Gardner type, you don't have to emphasize characterization. You simply haven't time. But we produce only one book a year, and we spend a great deal of time on characterization.

■ *G. Gordon:* We especially enjoy realism. By this I don't mean the hard-boiled or the sordid. So often people confuse realism with the sordid. Actually, realism gives believability to suspense and we need it in our kind of novel. The reader can't be caught up in a sense of danger and excitement unless he believes what is happening.

■ *M. Gordon:* In this same sense we never write about a place we know nothing about. Some of our books have foreign settings, but we've been there and studied those settings. We don't try to interpret the economics or politics of a country, but see it as the casual visitor or tourist would.

■ *G. Gordon:* One of our most successful books was *Case File: FBI*, which was set in Chicago. The places and the people are actual.

To get back to your question about responsibility—we do feel very strongly that one must picture life as it is, but that's no reason for overemphasizing sex or violence. They have a very definite place in life, and consequently in literature. But they should be handled with the same degree of taste and restraint that newspapers use. I think it's up to the writer to use some restraint; blueprints aren't essential in depicting evil.

N. Do you find your own tastes and preferences, perhaps even characteristics, entering your books?

■ *G. Gordon:* No matter how much you try to get out of yourself and into another character I suppose some of you carries over. You do get a chance to air an opinion about one of your favorite beliefs or eccentricities. It's wonderful in the suspense field because if we really don't like somebody we can put him into a book and murder him. It gives us a vicarious sense of something. Perhaps it's good therapy.

N. How do you feel about the contemporary suspense stories where the author persists in killing off almost all the good guys?

■ *G. Gordon:* In the first book we did in collaboration we killed off the heroine at the end—a woman with whom we had great sympathy. We felt we had to murder her to be realistic, but this was the only time we ever did it and we'll never do it again. We had hundreds of letters from people who complained bitterly—not mildly—calling us every name under the sun. We're not going to kill off the good guys or good gals any more often than we have to.

N.   In looking over the past few decades, what would you pick out as notable trends or developments in the suspense field?

■ *G. Gordon:* Well, Erle Stanley Gardner is a trend which goes on indefinitely, but he's the master of a particular type. In the early 1950's we had the sex-and-sadism thing which came to a climax with Mickey Spillane. Since then there's been a swing in the other direction, and right now there seems to be a preference for books that will take you somewhere behind the scenes—the cloak-rooms of Congress or a brokerage house. People are interested in backgrounds—this is the reason for the great success of books by Helen MacInnes and Mary Stewart.

■ *M. Gordon:* Another trend has been in the construction of books. The trend is toward suspense rather than mystery. We refer to our books as suspense stories rather than mysteries because frequently the writer and the reader know precisely who the villain is. You see, there can be no mystery whatsoever, but there can be a great deal of suspense, so the reader is just as involved in the tracking down of a bad guy as he is in the figuring out. But people still like to be frightened, to enjoy some vicarious danger, and as long as they do we won't go hungry.

N. Could you discuss a few other books you've written in terms of how they evolved?

■ *M. Gordon:* Well, we had a lot of fun with *Operation Terror* because it was about our neighborhood and our neighbors. The book opens with the heroine driving into a dark garage. This was my own experience. We lived in an old Spanish house, and the garage was separated from the house by twenty feet of dark, gloomy shrubbery. Every time I drove in I thought, "What if someone is lurking here?" so I would get out very quickly and run to the house. It became a perfect background for suspense.

■ *G. Gordon:* There must be quite a few such garages throughout the country. Women wrote us from everywhere saying that after reading the book they refused to enter dark garages alone.

I think another of our favorite books was *Captive*. This was set in the Indian—Navajo Indian—country, almost a foreign background because the Navajo way of thought is so contrary to our own. We had lived in Arizona for many years—it's one of our favorite states and favorite backgrounds, so we used a suspense story based on a Caucasian schoolteacher who is seized in the Navajo country by two criminals and held hostage. We brought in the FBI and, of course, the Navajo police.

Incidentally, the Navajo view—the old Navajo view—on crime and punishment is fascinating. They feel the Caucasian view of punishment is all wrong. If I commit murder, society should not send me to prison because nothing is accomplished. Instead I should be forced to contribute forevermore toward the welfare of the victim's family. This is quite unique, and who knows—it might work as well as our penal system does.

■ *M. Gordon:* We enjoyed doing a book called *Menace*, too— it was set in the Orient, in Japan, Hong Kong, and Thailand. We had made a trip through this area, and we were struck by the fact that when you travel abroad you have almost no protection against danger, particularly the type of danger you can't put your finger on. You can go to the police, but the police (if the heroine is an American, as ours was) don't want to get involved in an incident that smacks of being international. You're quite vulnerable, so this gave use the basic idea for *Menace*.

■ *G. Gordon:* Our heroine was the type of girl who seems to go all over the world now to take jobs with oil companies, construction firms, and the like. I understand that there are one hundred thousand American girls now working in far places, most of them as secretaries. We came across a few in the Orient, and we were fascinated by the sort of problems which could come up but which (fortunately) don't happen with regularity.

N.   My final question concerns your name, Mr. Gordon. Is it a pseudonym or your given name?

■ *G. Gordon:* It is a ridiculous name, isn't it? Most people think it's a pseudonym, but it isn't. It's real. When we wrote our first book for Doubleday and set it forth, as writers do, "By Mildred and Gordon Gordon." Doubleday wrote back and said, "For heaven's sake, we don't know what we're going to do about this, but we can't use that 'Gordon Gordon' because people will think we've made a typographical error."

■ *M. Gordon:* People responded to our wedding invitations by sympathizing with us for the misprint.

■ *G. Gordon:* So this is why we write under the name of "The Gordons." We run a risk that way, too—people think "The Gordons" might be a night club act from Las Vegas, and they're terribly disappointed when they find out we're just writers.

"If you want to go into the theater because you think it's lovely fun to stand up in a spotlight and be admired by everybody, and then go to Hollywood and make a lot of money, you may end up awfully bored. Once you've made the money, once you are a celebrity, who wants to have their clothes torn off . . . who wants sex-mad fans and all that? This is something you outgrow, if you're normal, by the time you're eighteen. . . ."

Tyrone Guthrie
Interviewed in Minneapolis, Minnesota, April, 1964

with an afterword by Bradley Morison, Public Relations Director of the Tyrone Guthrie Theatre.

Tyrone Guthrie

N. No theatrical director of our time is better known than Sir Tyrone Guthrie. It is also safe to say that Dr. Guthrie is frequently the most controversial figure in the vast world of theater. With genius, taste, and profound respect, Sir Tyrone has performed large and small miracles with most of Shakespeare's tragedies, and with other plays as various as *Cyrano de Bergerac*, *Oedipus Rex*, and *The Matchmaker*. At Sadler's Wells and the Metropolitan he has mounted powerful productions of *La Traviata*, *Carmen*, *Falstaff*, and *The Barber of Seville*. His searching new look at what are too often mere "standard" properties has enlivened theater in London and New York. He brought the brilliant Stratford, Ontario, theater into being. Most recently he has molded the Tyrone Guthrie Theatre in Minneapolis into exquisite form, an event of profound significance because it proved that theater in America, contrary to prevalent diagnosis, is not dead, not even indisposed, provided enough is ventured.

In talking to Sir Tyrone Guthrie I would like to go back a bit, to trace his entry into theater.

■ *Guthrie:* I was fortunate enough to get an offer to go into the theater while I was still an undergraduate at Oxford. I made my first appearance when I was twenty-three in, of all things, the leading role—the part of Captain Shotover in *Heartbreak House*—a drunken sea captain, retired, eighty-eight years of age. I lasted until lunchtime of the first day of rehearsal when I was taken aside and told very kindly but very firmly that I could either leave that minute or stay on to clean the lavatories at a considerably reduced salary. I'm glad to say that I stayed on to clean the lavatories.

N. What major roles did you play before you became a director?

■ *Guthrie:* I didn't have any major roles. I played Charles, his friend, and second footman, and things like that because I was with a small company and somebody had to play them, even me. But I never played big roles, and I realized that being nearly six-foot-five in height, and no beauty, my chances of getting roles were extremely slim. Anyway, I really wanted much more to direct than to act. My goal was always to become a director, so one way and another I struggled along and kept myself going until I got to be a director.

N. What were your first directorial assignments?

■ *Guthrie:* I was with the B.B.C., sent to work on their staff in Belfast. This was in the very early days of radio, way back to the early 1920's, and one of the things I had to do was to choose and direct the dramatic material which was then being broadcast. (There wasn't really very much of it.) But as a result I was asked by the Ulster Literary Theater—a group comparable to the Abbey Players but much less eminent, though dedicated to the same ends—to direct one of their productions. This was my first effort. You could scarcely call it a fully professional assignment, but I was at least asked by somebody to direct, and I think this is the only way to begin. You've simply got to find somebody who's ignorant enough, or stupid enough, or poor enough, to put up with you until you begin to learn.

N. How long did you work in the British Isles before you did anything in Canada?

■ *Guthrie:* For above twenty-five years altogether, though I had been to Canada earlier. It was on a radio assignment for the Canadian National Railways. This again was in the early days of radio, and our group was some sort of subsidiary department— I'm not sure if we belonged to express or parcels, but it was something incongruous. It was a pleasant project, though probably not of blazing importance.

N. How did your work on the Stratford, Ontario, project, come about?

■ *Guthrie:* I got a telephone call at home in Ireland. I was out when the call came, and the postmistress (ours is a very tiny village) answered and said, "Who's calling?" The voice said, "Tom Patterson," and she said, "Who's Tom Patterson? Where are you calling from?" He said, "Toronto," so she promptly hung up because she thought it was a joke. She went out to feed her hens and wasn't available for four hours. The call came again and this time she thought perhaps it might be serious, so she put him through, and this Canadian voice from the far end of outer space said, "I'm speaking from Stratford, Ontario. We want to do a Shakespeare Festival. Will you please come out and give some advice?" So I said, "When do you want me to come?" and he

said, "Tomorrow." I said, "Are you going to pay expenses?" and
he said, "Yes, and we can offer a small fee." So I said, "Expect me
the day after tomorrow."

N.   How many years, now, has that association continued?

■ *Guthrie:* I've been professionally associated with them for
quite some years, but we're still on the friendliest and closest
terms. I haven't worked there for six or seven years. I helped
them to start it, and I stayed three years, then cleared out. I'm a
very strong believer in clearing out while the clearing's good—
before they've tumbled to your two or three dull tricks. I think
that if you're going to be the head of anything, however important
or unimportant it is, your responsibility is to find the successor and
give way to him pretty soon—not to hang onto the job until you're
really past it.

N.   This is a digression, I know, but it's an interesting subject
in itself. What are you doing in jams and jellies—it seems so far
from theater?

■ *Guthrie:* This village I was talking about is very small—there
are only about 250 people. When I was a kid it was twice as big,
but the young people, especially the cream of the crop, are drain-
ing away to other parts of the world. This problem isn't peculiar
to Ireland, it's happening all over the world as people go from
rural to citified areas.

But if you live in and are fond of a place that is being decimated
like this, it's a terrible thing to see. So a group of us in the village
(all quite unaccustomed to manufacturing or commerce) decided
that if we didn't pull ourselves up by our own bootstraps the village would fade away. So we formed an association and beat our
brains trying to think of what we could do. The manufacture of
jam seemed the most sensible thing because in short term it offers
a choice of employment other than just helping mother and father
on the farm, and in long term it could diversify the agriculture in
the growing of fruit for the jam. Our first year of production is
over. We made, with voluntary labor, three thousand pounds of
samples just to see if we could make the stuff and what the
quality would be. We had to convince somebody else that it was
worth buying; it's in the luxury category, you see, pure fruit and
sugar. Most of the popular-priced jams are made of preserved
fruit and aided with a lot of preservative and coloring matter and
flavoring matter, and many of them have nothing more closely
resembling fruit than turnips. Anyway, our jam turned out to be
quite good and we have found markets. Last year we employed

between thirty-five and forty-five people for the whole of the year from the beginning of the fruit crop. Now we're increasing the factory premises and making improvements. I think this year's production will be rather up.

N.   Another digression: I have often wondered, while reading Irish novelists and poets and playwrights, if the Irish have a more finely developed lyric or poetic or dramatic sense than other peoples—say, the English or the Germans or the Russians. Since you are Irish, and have worked with theater in Ireland, what do you think?

■ *Guthrie:* Well, yes, I think perhaps we have. Rhetoric, story-telling, phrase-making comes very easily and naturally. Don't ask me why. Perhaps its the climate. Perhaps, like Jews or Negroes and other people who have had to endure a good deal of bullying and suppression, the Irish have taken refuge from the harsh realities in a dream-life of high-colored, fanciful events, with phraseology to match. Anyway, it seems we sort of have the gift of the gab.

N.   To return, now, to the world of contemporary theater. What do you find in today's theater that is admirable and encouraging? What, conversely, do you think constitute our evils and problems?

■ *Guthrie:* The good thing it seems to me is, paradoxically enough, the way the theater is beginning to come to terms with the fact that it is no longer the primary means of distributing theatrical or dramatic entertainment. (It's taken fifty years for this to happen.) The mass-distribution job has been taken from theater willy-nilly, and I think it is splendid to have set the theater free to concentrate on more important things than the sale of tickets.

The big sale is always going to be through the mass production media because it's so much easier to see a play by just sitting down in front of a box and turning a knob—the quality of the stuff you get is not necessarily of the highest. I'm not saying that all television drama is bad; it isn't. Occasionally it's excellent, but, necessarily, the good things are rather few and far between, particularly in America where the sponsor has to be considered more deferentially than he does in Britain. Then, too, the experience itself calls for a different kind of drama. It's prefabricated. The audience contributes nothing creative to it. It merely opens its mouth and sucks it in as a goldfish sucks in algae or whatever in hell goldfish eat. I don't think this is as interesting—what you might call as strenuous—as being part of the theater audience where you yourself are one of the people who are creating the performance. A live play isn't just made by the actors and received by the audience; the audience influences the actors and vice versa. Live theater is therefore a more creative experience—admittedly a more strenuous one—and since most of us are lazy most of the time, and some of us are lazy all of the time, one obviously settles for the easiest thing—pouring out a bottle of beer, sitting back in a deep chair, and watching the box.

Now, I don't think this means that there isn't a very large public that is prepared now and again to make considerably more effort if they can be shown that they will thereby get considerably more reward. This is the good thing, the best thing. I could easily say it's hopeful that there are so many good actors—but there have always been good actors. And I could go into the interestingness of some·of the good modern playwrights, but there are always a few (strictly limited in number, of course) good modern playwrights.

It's the business aspect that I find most significant and interesting and hopeful.

The dark side of the picture is—in my opinion—the fact that Broadway has made it impossible at present, and in the foreseeable future, to allow management to have a policy longer sighted than next Thursday. There is no alternative to the smash hit or the smash flop and having a smash hit is as much a matter of luck as of skill or judgment or knowledge or even art. The costs are absurd and they become more absurd every season. What would happen to Broadway if investors weren't willing to take chances—well, I'm afraid Broadway would no longer have theater. Of course, the investors do get an enormous return if they're backing *My Fair Lady*—and they continue to invest because, like all gamblers, they're hopeful of more hits of this nature. But the smash hit comes once in seven or eight times. Now, I don't think that the kind of person who backs theater only to make a killing is necessarily a creative or tasteful patron—he's out for the flutter. But I don't think he's completely greedy. It pleases him that the flutter may also be represented as a kind of artistic flutter, that he is indirectly doing a bit of good as well as earning a possible dividend of 1,000 per cent.

But the costs—the actual costs of production—are really something of a nightmare.

N. So often we read about and hear about the effect of the critics on theater, that four or five men can make or break a

Broadway play, and that in other cities, particularly in Chicago, the virulence of criticism diminishes theater.

■ *Guthrie:* I do think that the critics carry an influence out of all proportion, but I don't think they can be blamed for that. The public is to blame, and in long terms the management is to blame because the price of theater tickets is so high.

If people are going to be asked to invest many dollars for an evening's entertainment, they are going to insure themselves of being entertained by being guided by somebody who ostensibly knows more about it than they. It's too expensive to go just for the fun of saying, "I don't agree with Mr. Taubman."

As to the virulence in cities like Chicago—well, in Chicago I think the criticism is disastrous. One critic in particular is extremely bilious—a very able writer, and all, but it's sad to see able talent wasted on psychopathic malice and prejudice.

N.   Is it possible to state your objectives as far as your entire career is concerned?

■ *Guthrie:* I'm glad to confine my objectives to here and now. If I considered my whole life and career in general terms I'd probably be less than truthful. Like anybody else I've been a victim of changing goals, and like anybody else I'd rationalize what has happened from a standpoint of self-interest, taking on some rather unconvincing idealisms.

N.   To come down to particulars, could you explain your objectives as Artistic Director of the Tyrone Guthrie Theatre?

■ *Guthrie:* We set out here very rigorously to formulate a policy which can be stated in one short sentence: To do a classic program. This necessarily excludes American plays because the American theater hasn't been indigenously American long enough to develop any classics. O'Neill would really be the first playwright who expressed America in the theater, and that was only forty years ago, and forty years isn't long enough to let a play find its classic or non-classic status.

At any rate, here we are doing a classical program of four plays each season offered in repertory. One of the four must be an American play of potential classic status. It would be very silly to say that because there hasn't been time for Americans to develop dramatic classics that there haven't been many *potential* American classics written since O'Neill began. There are ten or twelve American plays written fairly recently that don't look wanting in comparison with the world's greatest, and each season we will include one of these in the program.

You may say, "Why the classics? Why not new plays?" and my answer is that in our opinion new plays get a good showing. (Contrary to popular opinion, the desks of producers and agents and managers are not stuffed with unproduced masterpieces.) I think that the new playwrights in this country get a better showing than the great ones of the past. Also, if you are launching any sustained cultural effort—an art institute, a symphony program, or a theater—you base the program upon the classics. Taste has to be formed by the audience and the performers on the basis of the classics.

N. What are your convictions regarding the advantages of repertory theater?

■ *Guthrie:* First of all, I think it is good business. It costs just a little bit more to change programs every day, but there are substantial advantages for the public. It's much more fun for them to see the actors in different parts in different plays in quick succession. It also enables the management to cash in on a success and to eliminate, rather inconspicuously, a flop (and the best management has its quota of flops.)

Above all, I think you get a better standard of acting and interpretation from a group of people who know one another, and who know one another's shortcomings and longcomings. This is proven by the fact that all the greatest periods in the international theater have been under such a regime. The Greeks were writing for a specific public and in a comparatively small city, and the people knew the performers quite well. If they didn't know them personally they knew the author, and the performers knew the tastes and habits and minds and beliefs of the people they were playing to.

This same thing happened in the golden days of the Elizabethan theater. The companies knew one another. When Shakespeare was writing a play he wrote the parts with specific actors in view; the actors knew their author, and above all, they knew their public. They knew what to expect, they knew what to give, and yet they dared to take risks. The same thing came again in the third great theatrical period, that of the Comedie Francaise. This was a permanent company. Moliere was not only the playwright, he was the leading actor and almost a part of the company as well as the manager. Again, not only was the company a tightly knit group, but it had a tightly knit group relationship with their public.

In general these seem to be very important precedents which one ignores at some peril.

N. Could you discuss how you chose the four plays you are presenting this year?

■ *Guthrie:* Yes, and quite simply. You just can't arbitrarily say, "I think the finest play of all is *King Lear* and we're going to do *King Lear*." That is, unless you know you've got on hand somebody in whom you've got great confidence—not only that they can perform *King Lear*, but that they can convince the public that they are performing it well.

You can't choose plays without reference to who's going to act in them, and the availability of actors to a great extent governs the program. It's maddening, because it's like trying to do a jigsaw puzzle on the deck of a ship in a high sea. Just as soon as you think you've got the last bit of the puzzle put into place the deck tips up and the whole damn thing slides every which way.

You choose a program and then it all falls apart because X, who said he would be available, tells you that he's just signed up to star in a Hollywood movie and he's so sorry and could he come next year instead? This will happen three times before your list is settled. Then, too, one must see it all from the actor's point of view. They are casual laborers, and it's very difficult for an actor to say, "Yes, I will be available for nine months in Minneapolis" at theater wages which are not quite even with Broadway wages. We don't pay our people badly, but as you know, star actors expect very high pay indeed. The star actor can command from television and movies, and often from Broadway, wages which make the pay of archbishops and prime ministers look like peanuts.

N. Do you think the star salary situation has hurt theater?

■ *Guthrie:* I don't think it has. It's quite a good thing. It frees them very often from complete dependence on managerial whims, and the actors who are really good are not cheapened by this. They don't just go whoring off to the big money all the time. They realize that in order to get anywhere near the top of the tree they have to, somewhere along the line, get a number of the great roles under their belt and in their subconscious.

N. In looking at the total role of the theatrical director, what do you think his obligation is toward the theater, on one hand, and to the public, on the other?

■ *Guthrie:* Well, I don't think we have any obligation to the public. Theater, simply by doing its own job, has got to create its own public. This is why I think it is so important to formulate a policy. You won't get anywhere, in my long experience, if you say, "We're just going to do good plays." That means you're going to do the plays you like and everybody won't share your taste.

You've got to follow a consistent policy, and collect around you the people who agree with that policy and who like the kind of thing you do and the way you do it. So I don't think that you've got to consider the public too much. We are their servants, but we've also got to lead them, and certainly we've got to consider the theater—the well-being of the theater—and subordinate our own private tastes to that of the group.

But again, there must be leadership, and if you are the artistic director of the theater you've got to say in the long term, "The plays will be done because I think they conform to our policy and I think that at this particular moment we can cast such and such a play and do it well." You'll often be mistaken, of course, but this is the risk any leader has to take.

N. I'd like to ask a question which smacks of naïveté—I love theater but I'm not well versed, and I'm rather like the person who likes a certain piece of art but can't say—

■ *Guthrie:* Which, by the way, seems to me a senseless apology. "I know what I like" is the ultimate in taste.

N. Unless one hasn't followed through to evaluate or deepen taste—

■ *Guthrie:* That's true. I suppose you should take some trouble to develop and improve it, but again this is the point of a classical program. We try to induce people to base their taste on what the best minds of previous generations have agreed to regard as the ultimate in taste.

N. What I was going to ask—stumblingly—is that if, in the three modern-dress productions you've done of *Hamlet*, you don't encounter some inconsistencies in the tenor of the action. In Hamlet's time, personal matters were resolved with a great deal more violence. Now it is illegal and inadvisable to settle a grudge by murder, and it's illegal to duel—

■ *Guthrie:* Yes, I do think some incongruities develop, just as I think if you do it in modern dress you either have to cut the celebrated lines or simply rise above the inconsistency when Ophelia says, "His doublet all unbraced his hose down-gartered . . ." If the man isn't in doublet and hose she is, for a moment, talking complete nonsense. Though incidentally, nobody thinks that she is talking complete nonsense when the play is performed, as it usually is, in Renaissance dress, when he's not in doublet, either, but let that pass. There is some inconsistency, but I think the inconsistency is of relatively slight importance because basically, in my opinion, human nature hasn't changed. Human institutions have changed slightly; and there was more overt violence in the Renaissance period than there is today, but I don't think that we are actually less violent.

I think *Hamlet* still holds up splendidly as a psychological document, but I think one is better off facing those possible incongruities than in placing the play back in the romantic past where a series of romantic stereotypes are going over over-familiar lines. I think there is a great danger, with Shakespeare, of being totally romantic and totally removed from real life. This treatment works to Shakespeare's detriment. This romanticizing is often concealed under the term "respect," but I think it is rank sentimentality that brings no fresh thought whatever to bear on what the text means in modern terms.

N. Still pertaining to *Hamlet*, last year you staged *Hamlet* not only in modern dress but at full length. What do you think has been lost in the cuttings of *Hamlet* that have been more or less standard for a long time?

■ *Guthrie:* What has mainly been lost are, first of all, the passages which quietly lead up to the main climaxes. When it's heavily cut you simply leap from climax to climax without an adequate story and without factual preparation or emotional preparation of the characters who are going to take part in the climaxes. Secondly, the only intelligent way to cut *Hamlet* is to leave the great soliloquies intact; thus Hamlet's part dominates the whole, enormously more than the other characters. The King becomes almost totally meaningless in the heavily cut versions, and Fortinbras often goes out altogether, and so on down the line. Everybody gets cut to pieces except Hamlet, who remains, but who plunges in a rather psychologically unacceptable way from climax to climax. The story is unintelligible, and the play is robbed of an immense amount of richness.

We did *Hamlet* last year almost totally uncut. I don't think that very much time was wasted—none on scene-changing. It took four hours of close attention, which puts a heavy strain on any audience. But one reason we did it this way was to make it implicitly clear that because we were in Minneapolis, in a city that hasn't had much theater in the past forty years, we were not condescending. We had to assume that the audience was unsophisticated, but we did not therefore assume that it was unintelligent. Nor was it. The degree of concentration was remarkable.

N. What has your reaction been to the acceptance of the theater in Minneapolis?

■ *Guthrie:* I've been enormously impressed with the quality of audiences here, not just at our theater but at concerts. The symphony audience is marvelous, people turn out for lectures on the most unlikely subjects, and both quantitatively, and far more important, qualitatively, people are prepared to take trouble over something they think will interest them—energetic, intelligent, hearty trouble.

I don't know whether this is because the weather is so tough that you can survive only if you're a very energetic person, or whether it's a sort of serious Scandinavian, Lutheran manifestation. I won't pretend to psychologize about this, but the fact is that it isn't only in the theater, but in all forms of congregation, that this great responsiveness can be seen. I've attended several churches here, and the participation is terrific. They attend to the sermon, they say the prayers with great punch and as though they meant them, and they turn out.

N. To turn to an area of theory: If you were to give advice to a youngster who wants to make his way in theater, what would that advice be?

■ *Guthrie:* In a sentence or two the advice would be so general as to be almost meaningless, but I would say this: If you want to go into the theater because you think it's lovely fun to stand up in a spotlight and be admired by everybody, and then go to Hollywood and make a lot of money, you may end up awfully bored. Once you've made the money, once you are a celebrity, who wants to have their clothes torn off every time they go into the street? Who wants sex-mad fans and all that? This is something you outgrow, if you're normal, by the time you're eighteen—though maybe not.

A lot of us stay stage-struck. I'm madly stage-struck at sixty-four, but with no desire to be A Star. I'm absorbed in joining with a group of other people to "make" something in the supremely vivid terms of the theater, for which the supreme penalty is the fact that you're writing on water. A theatrical experience can't be captured. It is absolutely of the moment, and for me that is one of its great charms. I *like* to think that we're writing on water for this vivid moment. I would hate to feel as an architect must—that posterity is going to stand up and say, "Look at the mess he made on this street corner."

N. My final question is also in the realm of theory. If you

were to assume a vantage point in 2064, and you could look back
to what happened now, how would you like to have the career
of Sir Tyrone Guthrie appraised? What would you like to have
accomplished?

■ *Guthrie:* I would like to feel that the work I've done for the
Old Vic and Sadler's Wells, helping to start the Shakespeare Festival at Stratford, helping to start this Minneapolis theater, were
part of a break into a new phase of theater—that these were all, in
their separately unimportant ways, steps toward a more contemporary, a more progressive view of what the theater ought to be,
and which distinguishes them from the conventional regard for
artistic achievement or failure.

It is the aim of using the theater as a means of public service—
not simply as a means of making profits for private shareholders.

*Because of the merit, the significance, and the success of the
Tyrone Guthrie Theatre in Minneapolis I am including this conversation with Bradley Morison, Public Relations Director of the
Tyrone Guthrie Theatre. This material serves as a broad background to what has been accomplished in Minneapolis in terms
that apply to the state of American theater as a whole.*

N. This is a complicated question, but I wonder if you could
explain what the reaction has been to the Tyrone Guthrie Theatre
in Minneapolis—what anticipated and unanticipated results have
occurred?

■ *Morison:* The response to this project has been fantastic. I feel
very strongly, at this point, that the reason we were somewhat
successful at the box office last season (our first) was not due to
anything we did as far as promotional activity was concerned, but
should be credited to the fact that the audiences in the Midwest
had a cultivated interest. They had been prepared by an enormous
amount of educational theater and community theater, and they
were ready to accept this sort of thing.

I sincerely feel that you could have taken the same project, the
same building, the same cast, the same plays, the same promotion
plans, and set them down anywhere else in the country and they
wouldn't have come anywhere close to working as well as they
did here. These audiences are ready. Look at the way we raised
money—the entire $2,300,000 needed to build the theater was raised
from the Minnesota community, the largest donor being the

Walker Foundation. But the contributions ran all the way down to high school classes that presented plays as benefits for the Guthrie Theatre, and there was a Sunday School class in Mankato, Minnesota, that donated $6.37 to the building fund.

I've been doing a lot of traveling in Iowa, the Dakotas, Minnesota, and Wisconsin, getting to know the area and, more importantly, trying to find out what kind of theatrical activity is going on at the community level and in various high schools and colleges. One reason for this is to find out what we should be planning as a theater organization to help theater wherever it exists and to take on the responsibility of being a true regional theater.

The term "regional theater" has been bandied about quite a bit, but I don't think there really is a regional theater in this country in the true sense of the word. It seems to me that it is our responsibility to be more than a mere building in Minneapolis where a group of actors come and put on plays in the summertime. We have got to strive to become a Midwest community institution, an institution rather akin to a library that contains theatrical talent, information, and ideas upon which anyone in the Midwest who is interested in the theater can draw.

Exactly how you put this into practice, how you develop this sort of program, I don't know; it's without precedent but it is something we are seriously exploring. How can we work with colleges, universities, high schools, and community theaters, helping them to reach new people, helping them take on more ambitious projects? We're exploring.

Right now we're giving a certain amount of assistance to the Sioux Falls, South Dakota, Community Playhouse in mounting their season-ticket drive. We've worked with their art people on the design of a brochure, given them counsel and advice on their promotion, and I'm going to Sioux Falls to preach hellfire and damnation to their volunteer workers. This is an experiment to see if we can get new people into their theater; in the end this will get new people into *our* theater. We have experimented this year with a sort of study kit on *Henry V* and *Saint Joan* which we've distributed free to every high school English teacher in the state of Minnesota. This, again, is experimental, to get their reaction to this sort of thing, to see if they are interested in having background material, photographs from us to help them teach dramatic literature and interest their students in theater. In broad strokes this describes some of what we are trying to do. Of course, putting on the plays is our first responsibility.

N. You mentioned that you thought that the Tyrone Guthrie Theatre did better here than it would have elsewhere. Why?

■ *Morison:* I don't really know what is responsible for the inordinate amount of theater activity that exists and thrives in these five states. I do know, for instance, that in Iowa a great deal of the interest in theater and the actual theatrical activity can be traced back to the University of Iowa Theater Department.

Professor Mabie organized their theater department some twenty-five or thirty years ago. He had some truly interesting ideas about theater, and about what the responsibilities of a university theater department should be. He felt there were two particular directions to be taken. The first was to put on plays, the second was to work with theater in communities throughout the state of Iowa. Wisconsin developed an interesting plan in the same direction. Consequently, in both Wisconsin and Iowa and to some extent in Minnesota, the universities have been active in giving aid and support to community theaters and high schools.

Another thing Mabie did at Iowa was to make the theater free to all students. Thus in a four-year period the student will have been exposed to Oriental drama, Greek drama, to the theater of the absurd, to the broad cross-section of the world's theater. Now, since many of the graduates from the University of Iowa remain in Iowa, you develop a high percentage of the population who have been exposed to all kinds of theater, then gone back to their communities to participate in or attend theater.

These things may not be unusual in themselves, but this combination of things in this area has aroused deep interest in theater. In 1946, when I got out of the Navy, there were in operation in the Twin Cities area three theater groups. Today there are twenty-five, all operating successfully, all theoretically supporting themselves very nicely. Now, another thing that makes this area unique for theater is the fact that the Twin City area, plus the state of Minnesota as a whole, is a brain-industry area. There is not much heavy manufacturing here. There are a lot of companies that use a high percentage of highly-trained engineers and other well-educated people. I think we are one of the highest areas in collge-trained population. This can't help but be good for the arts. And the University of Minnesota, with its 33,000 enrollment, second only to all the University of California campuses, helps a great deal.

N. In tracing the origins of the Guthrie Theatre, how did it come to Minneapolis?

■ *Morison:* It all began with Oliver Rea and Peter Zeisler, who are our managing directors. Both of them worked in the professional theater in New York, and what it came down to is that they got fed up with the New York Broadway commercial theater and the restrictions they suffered. Together they had produced a musical called *Juno* based on *Juno and the Paycock* with Melvin Douglas and Shirley Booth. It was a fine musical; it played the Winter Garden Theater, and closed in four weeks. Oliver and Peter bemoaned the fact that you got together a group of people, actors and production personnel, and through the whims of fate they disperse after ten weeks, never to see each other again, never to work together again. This is not conducive to truly great theater, where you need a company that plays together and becomes an ensemble.

At any rate they decided, after *Juno* closed, that the only path to better theater in this country was to take the bull by the horns and put together a permanent company to do the classical plays that don't get a break in New York. They further decided that the only way this would work outside New York was to find some person so well known in the theater that an actor would not feel that he was losing out by going to Detroit or San Francisco or somewhere else to play in a company. You see, actors are inclined to feel that they have to be in New York to get important parts, to come to critical and popular attention. The hinterlands mean nothing; the good notice in Seattle is without significance, etc.

Anyway, Oliver and Pete decided that there was only one person in the theatrical world who had enough stature to make a credit worthwhile for an actor *out* of New York—Sir Tyrone Guthrie. Both of them had worked with Dr. Guthrie previously, so on the spur of the moment they flew to London and asked him if he was interested in starting a major repertory company somewhere in the middle of the United States. His answer was "yes" so Oliver Rea and Dr. Guthrie proceeded to fly around the countryside talking to people in different communities.

They started with Boston, Detroit, and Milwaukee, and I think they visited Chicago. I know they visited San Francisco and a number of other communities; they hadn't even intended to come to Minneapolis-St. Paul, but Dr. Whiting at the University of Minnesota theater department wrote them a letter and said that they should at least consider the Twin Cities, so they came into Minneapolis-St. Paul and had lunch with a group of people from the community who were interested in this sort of project. After this luncheon these people formed a steering committee and made up their minds they were going to get this theater. Well, Guthrie and Rea eventually narrowed their choice of sites to Detroit, Milwaukee, and the Twin Cities. They were looking for three things, actually: for a community that could raise the money to build the rather unusual kind of theater they wanted; for a community that had a large university with a sizeable theater department (they wanted to explore the opportunities for professional and university theaters to work together); and for a community that would enjoy having this kind of theater in its midst and that could support it.

At first the Twin Cities had difficulty finding a location and raising money. Zeisler and Rea had rather narrowed things down to a choice between Milwaukee and Detroit when the Twin City people decided they were not going to let it get away. They made a presentation to the Walker Art Center suggesting that the theater be built behind Walker, and that Walker could then use the theater in the winter as an auditorium. Walker responded with a grant of the land plus a half-million dollars, so the Minneapolis-St. Paul committee flew to New York and made a new presentation—at the eleventh hour, so to speak—saying in effect, "We want this theater, we've got the land and we've got the money." So the Twin Cities was chosen.

Dr. Guthrie will tell you it was largely a matter of hunch —he liked the people here. Perhaps that was it as much as anything; they liked the people and felt that the people wanted and would support this kind of theater.

It happened, the theater's here, and the fact that it exists, and the fact that it's here, is probably one of the most important events in American theater in this century.

"Write something every day, though it may be poor; write something even if it's only your diary. Just get into the habit of putting words down, and try not to miss a day . . . it's important just to write, consistently, persistently."

Emily Hahn
Interviewed in New York, March, 1964

Emily Hahn

N. Emily Hahn possesses a broad yet exacting talent which is obvious in her frequent pieces of reportage for *The New Yorker*, and in books like *China To Me* and *China Only Yesterday* that reflect a depth of research and historical analysis. At the time of this interview she is involved in no less than three books that stand in varying states of readiness, something few authors can say at any given time of life. In talking to Miss Hahn I'd like to leap from her present state of business to the earliest years—asking for a sketch of autobiography and the origin of her interest in writing.

■ *Hahn:* I was born in St. Louis and went to public schools until I was fifteen when we moved to Chicago. I finished high school in Chicago and went to the University of Wisconsin, where I started off with the usual arts and science courses.

I didn't want to go to college at all. I had wanted to be an artist, a sculptor of animals, but my mother made me promise to try college, and if I still wanted to sculpt animals after a year I could quit. By that time I had been caught up in my private war with the University of Wisconsin Engineering Department who didn't want me to study in their halls. I was the first girl to do it, and I was so busy fighting them I completely forgot everything else until—well, four years later I graduated in engineering.

I'm a writer like most other writers, I suppose, because I was always a reader. Everyone in the family was, and I never meant to be a writer—I just took it for granted that I would write on the side. We all did. But as I said, I took my degree in Mining Engineering, then went to Columbia for a term. I was disappointed with all this, somehow, and I just left it. I drifted around for a while and suddenly realized that I was writing—earning my living writing. And that's how it began.

N. How did you gain your deep insight into China? So many of your articles and books deal with China from the historical standpoint as well as in matters of contemporary life.

■ *Hahn:* Well, I had been studying a bit of anthropology at

Oxford. (I had gone to the Congo during my most restless phase and became interested in anthropology.) I was on my way back to the Congo and I thought that this time I would get there by going around the west coast of the continent.

This sounds as though I was a very rich young woman, but I wasn't at all. I was always living from hand to mouth, but in those days it didn't cost much to go places.

My sister came with me as far as Japan. She said, "Let's just stop off and look at Shanghai." So we stopped; I think it was to be for a weekend. Nine years later I was shipped out by the Japanese. Nobody could live in China that long—it was an unbroken period, mind you, with no return to the West—without learning to speak Chinese. This was not easy for me. You also cannot live in a place, any place, for nine years, without being caught emotionally and trying to understand it.

That was when I began to write seriously. I also began to write for *The New Yorker* at that time. I had done one or two of those little things of one-column length they used to run in *The New Yorker*. Then, when I started my pieces on China, Mr. Ross liked the work very much and one thing led to another. I read omnivorously about China, though I'm certainly not an expert. To be an expert in something you have to spend your whole life at it, and you have to know a great many more things in a lot more depth than I do regarding China. But I am fond of it, and perhaps this substitutes in some measure for the expertness I lack.

In writing *China Only Yesterday*, for example, I had to push my way through a lot of personal weaknesses. I was strongly prejudiced for the Nationalists, but I thought, "This is no good. People are always writing propaganda, that's understood, but it isn't fair to let obvious prejudice sink into a book like this, that someone might use as a source or for reference." So I tried to keep personal feelings out.

N. Didn't you sort of climax your long stay in Asia by becoming involved in a really powerful scandal?

■ *Hahn:* It was a scandal, wasn't it? Yes, I had a baby out of wedlock and I had it on purpose. I think it was my purposefulness that scared people so much. I wanted the baby and I went ahead and had it. I'm now married to the baby's father, as everybody who read a certain *New York Times* editorial knows. We've been married a long time, and have another baby, but I suppose I did shake people up a bit at the time.

N. Could we discuss the three books you're simultaneously

involved in? The first book is just about finished, isn't it?
■ *Hahn:* The first is done—proofread and all that, and it comes
out in June. The title, I'm afraid, is *Africa To Me*, obviously taking
off from my first best-seller, *China To Me*. It's a collection of
various long pieces I wrote from material gathered from my four
or five trips to Africa.

The first time I visited Africa I went to the Congo, went
broke, and stayed there for two years, willy-nilly, and I wrote a
book about that. (You can't stop a writer from turning everything into a book.) But there was one piece, infinitely better, that
I wrote many years ago and was kept here at *The New Yorker*
office and never used. Now it's being put into this book.

Then I went to Lagos, Nigeria, for the Independence. I wrote
something about that, and it's included, and then, over these last
two years, I've been working a lot on pieces about East Africa,
Central Africa, and South Africa, where I made my last trip.

The book is written from the standpoint of the observer noting
changes in Africa—how primitive everything was when I first
went, and how (goodness, how we fall into clichés!) Africa has
emerged. No, I don't want to use the word "emerged." It would
be better to say that we're listening to Africa, now, which we
certainly weren't at the time of my first trip.

N. You're also doing a comprehensive book on the Bohemian
movement for Houghton-Mifflin?
■ *Hahn:* Yes. It involves a great deal of research, but research is
reading, and this I like best. I'm afraid the word "comprehensive"
is a bit strong, though.

What this will be, actually, is a study of Bohemia in America,
and the things I'm reading and the paintings I'm studying go back
to the earliest days of the Bohemian movement in the United
States. I'm halfway through with the book, but it's a puzzling
subject. I'm still searching for a satisfactory definition of the word
"Bohemian." Everybody has his own idea of what the word means.

Actually, the movement began in Paris in the middle of the last
century. The word "Bohemian" was made into world currency by
Murger in his famous *Scènes de la Vie de Bohême*. Yet the movement has always existed, hasn't it, in the wandering, artistic type,
the nonconformist?

N. From the standpoint of definition I should think that
"gypsy" would be a better word. Bohemia is a region, a part of
what is now Czechoslovakia—
■ *Hahn:* Oh, but it meant the same thing. The reason they

called the movement "Bohemian" was because they thought—erroneously, of course—that gypsies emigrated from Bohemia. The gypsies in France did come through Bohemia. "Gypsy" and "Bohemian" are the same word, as far as the French are concerned. I still have to explain to people who discuss the book, "No, I'm not writing about the Czechs."

N. *La Bohême* could never have been written about the Czechs!

■ *Hahn:* Puccini took it from *La Vie de Bohême*, years later. But it's still odd, defining the word. To you and me it means, essentially, a person who breaks away from conformity and chooses a career in the arts or on the fringe of the arts. Yet there's a preface to a children's book, one of those cut-down versions they do now, of *The Moonstone*. In the preface it says "Wilkie Collins was unmarried, and so lived a Bohemian life." Now, this is certainly a very sweeping version of the word's meaning.

I started by reading the people who can be regarded as the originators of the Bohemian life in America. I'm very carefully leaving out France, since if I included France I'd never finish the book. Besides, if I included France then I'd have to take in the whole Western world because Bohemia has existed and exists everywhere, and this would take two lifetimes, so I'm concentrating on the United States.

One argument we had to settle at the very beginning of the book, my editor and I—and it still isn't quite settled, for that matter —is whether or not Edgar Allan Poe was a Bohemian. I say he wasn't because he tried to conform. He may have been a little nutty. The fact of genius has nothing to do with being a Bohemian, by the way; we're not appraising their gifts, we're talking about attitudes toward life. Poe is alleged to be the first great Bohemian in America because, for one thing, he lived in Greenwich Village, but that's silly because in those days everyone lived in Greenwich Village or further south. It was simply another cheap residential area.

Poe struggled hard and conscientiously to make a living—a lot of people don't see that; they see him as a drunk or a dope addict sleeping it off in a gutter somewhere. Even this is not necessarily being Bohemian, and Poe probably didn't drink a lot. Huneker's father said that one thimbleful of brandy was enough to make him quite drunk; apparently he had an allergy to liquor. And he did try to conform. He would refuse to attend a dinner party, even though he needed the food, unless he had a decent suit to go in. That is not being Bohemian. Still, I don't leave Poe out. I argue him through one chapter.

N. Would you associate Bohemianism in America with a general desire to elude responsibility, or the desire to live a free life?

■ *Hahn:* It's both. We've got a lot of Bohemians who don't produce anything. We've got people producing works of art who are not Bohemians at all, who live like regular businessmen. It's simply the basic matter of attitude, the nonconformist attitude. I think this is it in a nutshell.

N. What about the third book in prospect?

■ *Hahn:* This is another one for Doubleday, and it's going to be about zoos—not a book for children, but for the general audience, for everybody who likes zoos. It will be about the outstanding zoological gardens scattered throughout the world—I'm not going to work zoo by zoo, because that would make tiresome reading, but I'm going to take some significant ones and point up what is interesting. Our zoos, of course, grow more and more important as a means of preserving wildlife which, it seems, will otherwise disappear.

I'll also show how zoos are tied up with education. In London for example, the Regent's Park Zoo has a remarkable program. Every week during the school term they place a certain animal— say, a raccoon—by itself in a special cage. The teachers bring their children to see this animal, and study the animal's habits, its history, its significance, the country it comes from, and in this way learn a great deal through real association. The whole London state school system works together on this. But of course the British are wonderful about animals anyway; they like them better than people.

N. To turn to more general areas—fiction, nonfiction, theater— what do you find now that you most admire? What, on the other hand, do you most deplore?

■ *Hahn:* I think I like all this breaking-down of meter and rhyme. I don't always like reading the results of it, but I like the tendency to find something new. It isn't only an American search; we have it in Europe as well. This breaking-down freshens things.

As for theater—it's funny about that. You can get an awfully bad year when there's nothing to excite you at all, and then you see something you like a great deal. I was disappointed in *Marco Millions*—such a beautiful bore, and that's too bad, because I remember being thrilled reading it when I was a child in the Midwest. But *Who's Afraid of Virginia Woolf?* was a very exciting play. I felt, at the end, as if I'd sat up all night in that room myself. The people were horrible; you told yourself you couldn't identify with any of them, yet I was so scared by it that I must have been identifying with that wife.

As for television, I loathe the bad grammar and folksiness they use in the commercials, and one can't get away from commercials, so I get cross. Still, I do watch it sometimes, though not a lot.

In writing, I simply can't keep up with the new stuff. There are so many more people in the world today, and so many of them are writing, that you can't get even a fair sample of what's going on without working at it day and night. Instead, I read what I want to when I take time off, and try not to think in terms of trends except when my mind's on Bohemia.

N. If you were to give advice to the talented youngster who wished to write, what would that advice be?

■ *Hahn:* Write something every day, though it may be poor; write something even if it's only your diary. Just get into the habit of putting words down, and try not to miss a day. I don't mean to say that anyone should stick at something that isn't going right —I often have to put a piece aside and come back to it later after I've switched to something else for a bit. But it's important just to write, consistently, persistently. Reading is probably just as important. Read everything you can lay your hands on and have time for.

N. In dealing with serious subject matter, such as you do, what do you feel your obligation to the material actually is?

■ *Hahn:* To set down the truth as clearly and conscientiously as possible.

N. What do you feel your obligation to the public is?

■ *Hahn:* To be readable.

N. Those are short answers—

■ *Hahn:* Well, there isn't much to be said about those things. There might be if I felt I was someone great, a superb artist, but I don't think of myself that way. I can only give my theories, my rules.

N. If you were to project yourself into the position of surveying the career of Emily Hahn—say, from a century away— how would you like her to be regarded?

■ *Hahn:* I would like people to say that she was a good reporter, that she set things down as they were and made them readable.

L

"Writers, like other people—congressmen or doctors or housewives or clerks in the A&P—are unwilling to take a stand about good and bad, right and wrong. This is particularly bad for the writer, because if he is not taking a stand about right and wrong, he has no conflict."

Margaret Halsey
Interviewed in New York, August, 1963

Margaret Halsey

N. Margaret Halsey possesses a two-edged talent, both ends kept admirably honed. Her wit and powers of observation became apparent in the best-selling *With Malice Toward Some*. On the other hand, the depth of her concern for the conduct, the ethics, the morals of our time dominate *Color Blind* and *The Pseudo Ethic*. I'd like to begin by asking her where she was born, reared, and educated, and how her interest in writing developed.

■ *Halsey:* I was born and raised in Yonkers, New York, as my parents were before me. I went to the public schools in Yonkers, and then got a B. S. degree at Skidmore College in Saratoga Springs and an M. A. at Teachers College, Columbia University. As to writing, I could always write. When I was in some such lofty intellectual position as the sixth grade, I wrote an essay on a thunderstorm which the *Yonkers Herald-Statesman* published with a little box over it saying it was the best essay by a child they'd ever seen.

N. I'd like to discuss your most recent work first, *The Pseudo Ethic*, in terms of how you came to write it.

■ *Halsey:* I can't answer that in any perfectly-manufactured well-rounded sentence. I simply wanted to. This whole matter of ethics is a subject very much on my mind. I have a daughter, fifteen, and I constantly come across the questions each parent must encounter: "Why should people do things right if they can get away with doing them wrong?" and so forth. They're constantly confronted with the evidences of cheating at exams and on income tax. I simply started thinking about these things, the ambiguities of what is taught and what is done, the chic business of getting away with something, so I felt it was a book that had to be written.

I don't think I'm a lone crusader or anything like that. There are lots of magazine articles on this subject. For instance, not too long ago *Look* had a piece that in bold type at the top said, "We need a new moral standard, our morals have collapsed." But I take the opposite view—that we aren't going to have a new moral standard, that we can't have a new one. We must go back to the old one; therefore it isn't our morality that is going to change but our behavior.

In other words, we must return to the Judeo-Christian ethic—"Thou shalt not steal," "Thou shalt not lie," "Thou shalt not bear false witness." All these things provide the lubrication for our human relationships. We can't change these things to fit with what we're doing. We must change to fit in with them.

For example, during the bomb scare a few years ago, some rather weird interpretations of morality came up. There were actually a few ministers who said that it is justifiable to shoot your neighbor in the doorway of your bomb shelter to protect your family. Now, the old Judeo-Christian ethic is exactly the opposite. It says, "Love thy neighbor as thyself" and "Greater love hath no man than this, that he lay down his own life for his friend." This is the exact opposite of bomb-shelter morality.

Perhaps the chic violation of Prohibition, and the chic cheating on income tax has had something to do with our letdown in standards, I don't know. I think there have always been elements in a culture which try to pull down morality, simply because people tend by nature to be self-indulgent, to do what they want. There must always be at least a small group of people working on morality to keep standards up.

One of the major things that happened in this country to account for the spectacular collapse of morality (and I think this is more important than the Robber Baron ethic of the late nineteenth century and Prohibition and Income Tax) was the fact that our real speaking, teaching moralists were intimidated by the whole McCarthy fiasco we went through after the Second World War. The people most affected by him were artists, performers, liberals, intellectuals, distinguished teachers, distinguished ministers, the very class that sociologists call "the carriers of our morality." McCarthy frightened them into silence. They didn't dare say anything with *Red Channels* operating against them, and if they weren't frightened into silence they were simply, if they had access to the public, not allowed access to the public. These people are essential in keeping up our moral standards, and it's important that they should come back strong.

One of the things I would like to see would be a force in the field of morals or ethics like the SEC. Remember, after the Depression, when the American people felt that terrible injustice shouldn't happen again—their savings wiped out and their livelihoods wiped out? They set up the Security Exchange Commission to regulate the handling of money and the investment market so (economists tell me) a thing like the crash in 1929 couldn't really happen again. I think a code like this governing congressional investigations would be a great contribution. That way people couldn't be questioned as they were during the years of the witch-hunt. They were questioned without lawyers. Congressional committees acted, although they had no legal power to do so, like courts, and the people being questioned were up for trial, so to speak, without legal protection.

But I've gone too long about this. As I said, the book had to be written, or at least I had to write it.

N. I'd like to go back to the beginning of my acquaintance with your career, *With Malice Toward Some*. How did you come to write it?

■ *Halsey:* Well, that was a peculiar thing. I feel odd discussing that book, now, because it was done so many years ago it's like bringing back my lost youth. I was living in England and my husband was teaching at the University of the Southwest in Exeter. We lived in a little village eight miles away, a really pre-World War I English hamlet with the thatched roofs and the pub and the vine-covered cottages and the immemorial elms, like something out of a picture book, but there wasn't very much for me to do.

England, before the war, had more of a caste system. There were the gentry to which we belonged because my husband taught. We belonged as much as Americans can belong to the gentry, which, needless to say, isn't all that way. They rode to hounds, and I'm afraid of horses, so there was very little for me to do. I had worked for a publisher in New York, and in my idleness I wrote lots of letters home to people explaining what I thought of these English riding after hounds and foxes over the assorted hills and dales, and the publisher for whom I had worked collected these letters and sent them back to me and said, "You have a book here."

Naturally, I was delighted to put them together into a book because I had time on my hands. It's the last time I ever did have time on my hands, as a matter of fact, but this is my lost youth speaking from twenty-five years back. Everybody in the publishing house said the book wouldn't go—"All this stuff about the English has been done before"—except the publisher himself. But he said, "I have a hunch, I feel it will go." So he published it, and it went— it was a runaway best-seller. Male intuition is a wonderful thing.

N. Then, in *Color Blind*, you became altogether serious. What actually provoked your interest in the subject of Negro-white relations?

■ *Halsey:* Superficially, as a writer, I like to alternate light and serious subjects because the change of pace is enormously refreshing. I don't want to be "typed," and I certainly don't want to "type" myself, and I don't want to make the reader think I'm altogether predictable.

But more than that, *Color Blind* grew out of a personal experience, an especially poignant one. During World War II, I went through a nurse's aid course. Everybody did something for the war effort, and I tried this bit, but I discovered I was too squeamish for the nurse business. A girl fainted in the course, and my impulse was not that of Florence Nightingale or the Good Samaritan. My basic reaction was fright and a strong wish to go away from there.

Obviously, nurses' aiding was not for me, so I went to work as what they called a captain of hostesses at the Stage Door Canteen. The canteen, as you may remember, was run for enlisted men by theater people and it was located in Times Square.

Now, the theater has always been much in advance of other professions in the area of race relations. The theater didn't discriminate against Negroes, but you'll remember that World War II was fought on a segregated basis; the Army was segregated. The Stage Door Canteen was one of only two canteens in the country that was open to Negro servicemen on exactly the same terms as granted the white. It was a bold social experiment. It got most of its publicity in the usual way—theater people went there and had their pictures taken—and only occasionally would anything get into the papers regarding the fact that this was a racially integrated canteen.

The climate of opinion in those days was, on the part of Caucasians, solidly against mingling with Negroes. Race relations weren't publicized, so we had a job of education on our hands. We talked to our junior hostesses, we wrote them letters, we had meetings in which they were told that they must treat the Negro serviceman the same as the white. They must sit with them, talk to them, make them welcome, dance with them. It was an interesting and unusual and challenging opportunity.

People said, "Oh, you'll have trouble," and "You'll have race riots," but we didn't. We didn't because we made up our minds to make it work. Besides, the Army had one little gimmick which turned out to be helpful. In the Army there's a rule that any man who's wearing a United States uniform must stand attention if he hears "The Star-Spangled Banner." We had a phonograph with a record of "The Star-Spangled Banner" and any time we thought there might be trouble, on it went. But in four years (and I think this speaks well) we only had to play it twice. Once it didn't have anything to do with the fact that a white serviceman got sore because Negroes were there.

But you asked me how I wrote the book. Well, the war ended, and it seemed a pity that all this material should go to waste, so I really wrote the book to make our experiences available to other people who were interested in doing something. I think one thing World War II accomplished, perhaps spurred by Mrs. Roosevelt, was to make people aware that this was a war for democracy, and that a whole segment of our population whose pigmentation was "wrong" were being excluded from democracy. I think the war contributed toward breaking down the barriers, but a lot remained to be done, and that's why I wrote Color Blind.

N.   What obligation do you feel toward your material?

■ Halsey: If something needs to be said, particularly if it's something as vital as the subject matter of Color Blind, then I feel an immense obligation to get it into print, to make it as readable as possible. It's a combination of a sense of moral obligation and a desire to communicate.

N.   What are your impressions—I should say the things you like and dislike—about the literature of the present day?

■ Halsey: Of recent years I think there has been a deterioration of literature which unconsciously reflects the deterioration of morals. People, because of this moral collapse, are unwilling to commit themselves to take a stand for right or against wrong. There is a new false morality which is based on popularity. Perhaps this is the result of the mass market, nationwide media, and so forth, but there seems to be a feeling nowadays that anything you can make a nationwide audience condone must be all right.

There's so much uncertainty in moral attitudes. Writers, like other people—congressmen or doctors or housewives or clerks in the A&P—are unwilling to take a stand about good and bad, right and wrong. This is particularly bad for the writer, because if he is not taking a stand about right and wrong, he has no conflict. If there's no gulf between good and bad, how is the writer going to carry his reader along and keep his attention?

The writer has substituted, but one of the devices he's substituted—I'm keenly sorry to say—has been the element of violence, increasing descriptions of violence and sex, putting them into detail to attract the reader as a substitute for the conflict that isn't there. It's a fake substitution and I'm frankly tired of the novel with the high sexual content. As a matter of fact I told my husband just the other day that I want to write a novel with all the old-fashioned reticences and silence about sex and title it, *I Stayed Out Of Bed For The FBI.*

As to theater, well, I got caught up in the big fight about *Who's Afraid of Virginia Woolf?* I'm one of the group that doesn't like it. In fact I walked out on it. I was bored.

Here again there was no conflict. You know, because of the lack of conflict between good and bad, the lack of suspense, the novelist or playwright attempts to attract the audience with scarifying language, violence, and sex, and as a result the plays and novels are rigidly confined. *Virginia Woolf* is an excellent example. Here's a history professor who talks steadily from two in the morning until dawn, and there isn't one mention of a student, curriculum, faculty, dormitory, or campus. There is no mention of political events, which is very strange for a history professor. The professor talks only about one narrow little aspect of his rather unbelievable wife, and I got bored. I didn't find all the "layers of meaning" in the thing so many of my friends did. Sex is certainly a part of life, but it isn't sound art to make sex stand for everything.

N. Now, if you were to give advice to the talented youngster who wants to write, what would that advice be?

■ *Halsey:* For one who is starting to write now I think I'd very gravely give this warning: the pendulum is beginning to swing back. I would not recommend that the young writer take *Who's Afraid of Virginia Woolf?* or the plays of Tennessee Williams as models, because I wouldn't be a bit surprised if they very rapidly became obsolete.

You know, the Negro movement in this country has given morality a shot in the arm. Here are people who are not out for the main chance, who are not opportunists, who are fighting for human dignity and fighting for it (on the whole) with great dignity and restraint. I think the Negro movement may help affect a change in the direction of a more conscious morality, of a return to the old-fashioned virtues the Negro leaders are exemplifying.

I think the young aspiring writer or playwright should get back to the complex, many-layered novel or play which has more in it than sex or violence. I don't mean that he should dive into the

L*

socially or politically conscious novel of the 1930's—that became as one-track as sex is now—but the realistic heart of people and issues, the things that make Joseph Heller's *Catch 22* or Doris Lessing's *The Golden Notebook* novels that will last after most of the sex-and-violence epics are off the shelves.

He must know more than sex, you know, because sex is after all narrow. He must know the environment in which he lives, and put significance into his portrayal of that environment.

"We've got to take a good look at the society in which we live, and wonder if there isn't something wrong with a social system that seduces people, both men and women, into consumers."

Sterling Hayden
Interviewed in Chicago, December, 1963

Sterling Hayden

N. Sterling Hayden's *Wanderer* was one of the great hits of 1963. The element of surprise cannot be discounted as a factor in its success, for here was an autobiography turned out by a Hollywood personality that had true literary quality, guts, and astonishing honesty. It was not gossip; it was not a blue-sky appraisal of the cult and art of movie-making; and it was written entirely by Mr. Hayden.

Now, most writers make it obvious that with them writing has been an obsession from a very early age and a practiced craft for only a few years less. But since we were totally unaware of Sterling Hayden as a writer until *Wanderer* burst upon the scene, I'd like to keep the first question very elemental and ask him how and why he wrote it.

■ *Hayden:* I think I wrote it because I wanted to leave behind something of value, something of which I could be proud. Perhaps every man wants, essentially, to do this. I've always respected writing more than any other form of activity a man could indulge in. Perhaps there are many arts on a par with writing, but outside of being a powerful figure in a revolutionary movement (if things were ripe for such a movement, which they certainly are not in this country), I'd like most to be remembered as someone who produced a work of literary merit.

Your remark about the long submergence, if it can be called that, of my own literary interests, raises a question I've pondered a great deal. I've always wanted to write, and I have written. When I was a kid I'd come home after fishing on the banks and write a story, but it was poor, very poor. I collected some rejection slips, back in my teens, from *Harper's*, *The Atlantic*, *The New Yorker*. Then I quit submitting stuff until I started *Wanderer*. During the last few years I was in Hollywood I worked on some screenplays, but they were always adaptations of someone else's original work. In a way this is a dodge in itself. It's relatively easy to write a screenplay when you're not carving out the story, the characterization, the point of view.

332

When we get right down to it, I guess some of us mature very late in this country. This has been the story of my life in an intellectual sense, even in a political sense. Perhaps the man who starts writing in his early teens or early twenties is conscious of the struggle that exists, very early in life, for recognition or social justice. I was never aware of these things. This is another reason why I thought *Wanderer* would have a strong and deep appeal to a wide range of readers because it can't help but mirror the frustrations of so many Americans whose lives don't make sense.

Thoreau said that we lead lives of quiet desperation. Mine was a life of flamboyant frustration, but I still think the reader often will see himself in the book even though I'm the protagonist.

I had, in fact, picked a quote from the 1853 preface to *Leaves Of Grass* to use on the title page, but Knopf inadvertently left it out. Whitman says, in one beautiful, little, terse sentence, everything I hope can be synthesized from my book. He said, "You shall stand by my side and look in the mirror with me." I guess this sums up how I hope *Wanderer* will be both enjoyed and regarded.

N. Although *Wanderer* contains your autobiography to date, I wonder if you would roughly outline your life.

■ *Hayden:* I think the first thing I'd have to say is that I always had a feeling of being different, even when I was six or seven years old. I remember standing in front of the lily-white house we lived in, in a lily-white suburb, twelve miles from New York, watching the commuters go to work. Every morning they would step out of their doors simultaneously, throw a kiss to the wife, march down to the depot, come back on the 5:23. And every Saturday afternoon they'd wash the car and on Sunday they'd go for a drive. I remember thinking then, "God damn it, something's wrong. Is this all there is for a man?"

This permeated all of my thinking, all of my life. I did very poorly in school; I don't think I got a decent mark in my whole life. I didn't care. I always felt, somehow, I was destined (and this doesn't sound very modest, and I apologize if it isn't, but I don't think it's necessary to apologize, so the hell with it) to find a different road. I don't know how or why I felt this way because the family I came from was certainly unimaginative. Nothing was ever discussed; they had all the smugness, all the fears. There was no depth, no probing, very little reading, and words like "union" and "Democrat" were frowned upon.

That household broke up very quickly when I was nine, and the next act read: "Enter, Stepfather." He was a barnstormer, a self-styled promoter. He might have done very well, but this was in the depths of the Depression. We just hit the road-to-nowhere-sure. I enjoyed the travel because again it carried out the feeling I had, or the theme, that I wasn't like anybody else. I reveled in the vicissitudes that accompanied those years when we drove from town to town and stayed in boarding houses or in some hotel that he was allegedly about to take over and develop into a monstrously successful situation. This was never realized, of course.

In the winter of 1930, we ended up along the coast of Maine on a tiny little island. My parents were broke. The fancy car had been impounded and sold; they had one whole dollar; and we had a hard time dragging through the winter. While my mother and stepfather colored postcards, I was exposed to the world of ships.

This was in Booth Bay Harbor, Maine, where there were still three-, four-, and five-masted schooners as well as fishing schooners, coasters, draggers, and trawlers. Suddenly this became my world. I really don't know why, unless it was pure escape. But that world of ships was full of beauty to me, and I responded to it. I remember realizing then that there was sadness, too, because the great age of shipping had passed and the ships gradually ceased sailing, and the boys who should have been shipping out were working in service stations or leaving the town. The frontiers vanished in the East, too, and the conformities crept in.

Anyway, I went to sea, and the sea offered a viable world directly opposed to life ashore. On a ship you felt that you were men working together; you had a feeling of belonging. I guess you have to belong somewhere. I loved the sea and felt that it was my element. I worked hard and I did well. I learned then, I guess, that no matter how implausible a situation might be, or how difficult the odds, if you take the plunge and work hard, you'll come out on top. So I went to sea for a long time, and it was a good life. Then I lost a ship off Cape Hatteras, and at this low ebb of fortune, the opportunity came to enter the Hollywood scene.

I drifted with it. I guess I was somewhat enamored of it and curious about it. The money was attractive (though it wasn't the main factor), but I soon found myself enmeshed. I made a couple of false starts in Hollywood. I started at the top, and over the years I worked my way down. I did two pictures before the war, then took four and one-half years off. I had quit after the second picture. I drove back to Boston and threw my license plates into the harbor with a fine flourish. This was duly recorded in the press, which pleased me.

After the war I went back into pictures but, by this time, I was conscious of what I felt was the struggle for social justice. This was a result of what I had seen in Yugoslavia. I had also been exposed to a man in San Francisco, allegedly a member of the Communist party, who started me reading and thinking about socialism.

I joined the Party and got out of it in six months. I was never in it, actually. I'm not excusing myself at all—I don't feel I have to. Curiously, I feel more radical in my beliefs today than I did when I was a member of the Party. This poses a question in view of the witch-hunt affair: Is it a Party, or is it the presence of injustice, which presents the real problem?

In 1949, three years after I'd gotten out of the Party, I realized that I had nowhere to turn. I had tried everything and I was always what they called a "ninety-day wonder." I could always make a splash, but I had no staying power. I guess this is the situation with most men who are misfits or loners or wanderers, whatever you want to call them. The next real solace, the next real promise, lies in the next ship, the next port, the next job, the next girl. "Next" is a powerful word to some of us and, for the first time, I realized I had no "next" left.

Through a chain of circumstances, I became involved—thank God—in deep analysis. During the analysis period, I had married for the second time, had three or four kids, and a custody fight was looming. So I sat down and worked out, in a very calculated way, a plan to keep the kids in one house for three or four years to give them a chance to stabilize. They'd been through a lot. After this I would write, really write. I first intended to write a novel, but I realized that it would be an autobiographical novel, as most first ones are.

In 1956 I bought a schooner, bought it the way I think most men build an estate or gather annuities or buy insurance, for a feeling of protection. The schooner represented the lever by which I hoped to blast myself free of the ruck of Hollywood. It amounted to just that, because in 1958, rather suddenly, I got ready for a voyage that was not to be a play voyage. I had it in mind to make a series for television in which the voyage and the sea, the ship and the lagoons, would be the sugar-coating on a pill. (God knows, you can't give the American public a mere conversation show.) I wanted to build a show examining the values by which people live, the things that make them feel and fight, the essential truths life should revolve about. The voyage was to do that.

The idea went to hell in a handbasket. I got into trouble with the court, the lawyers, the ex-wife, and everything, and the results made headlines. I just took off with the kids and went to Tahiti. I began to write down there, but I realized I couldn't stay in Tahiti indefinitely—too expensive, with a ship and a big crew. So I took my time, fired my crew one by one, and replaced them with an all-alien crew, the smallest and best I've ever had, and came home in forty-three days to San Francisco. I sold the ship immediately, but I'm still heavily in debt, thanks to the voyage and the custody fight.

Then, providentially, I met a girl and was married for the third time. This is the first time I've ever felt really married; the first time I've ever loved anyone; the first time I've had the capacity to love anyone; the first time I've possessed enough stability to take a little office in an old freight station and go to work on the book. I began writing *Wanderer* in the spring of 1960, and two years later it was done.

So that's me up until now.

N.   I'd like to return to one point in your career that stands out sharply in *Wanderer*, and also plays strongly in my own memory. It's your performance in *The Asphalt Jungle*. What made this movie so different from the others—the ones you loathed?

■ *Hayden:*   I can answer that in two words: John Huston. I had known of Huston, of course, even though I knew very little about the industry all the time I was in it. I had no particular respect for Hollywood, and no real ambitions as an actor, so I ignored it as much as I could. This was unfair for a fellow who came to Hollywood raw, and ten days later was assigned the second male lead in a technicolored affair that starred Madeline Carroll and Fred MacMurray. But as I said, I started at the top and worked down.

To get back to *The Asphalt Jungle*. No one likes to do inferior work in an inferior operation, and most of the pictures I had done prior to Huston were very inferior. (To digress: I got a lot of money and spent it, and the pictures I made were highly regarded by a certain segment of Hollywood and, obviously, by a rather large portion of the populace. In fact, people still see some of these monstrosities on television and come up to me—people who should know better—and say that they saw such-and-such a picture and that I was great in it. And I think to myself, "You poor son-of-a-bitch, what the hell's the matter with you?" But I can't say that, of course, so I smile and evade further discussion.)

Back to *The Asphalt Jungle*, (I'm wandering all over the place and I'm sorry.) I realized that *Asphalt* was going to be a good film, and for the first time I had the feeling that I'd better make a real effort. Oddly enough, I saw the film a few months ago on television, and I looked at myself closely, as anyone must, and didn't like what I saw. I was carried by a brilliant director, a very able cast, and a good story. It is regarded as a good film, and I know it is a good film, but I don't think I contributed a hell of a lot. When the filming had been completed, I remember going to Huston and saying that this was the first time in my acting life—or in my Hollywood life, I can't flatter myself as an actor—that I had any real interest in the business, and that maybe I'd better learn something about it. He said, "Ya, I think you'd better. You're running the risk, when this comes out, of having people say, 'Ya, Hayden can act as long at it's in a Huston picture.'"

This was true, so I went to work with a coach. I never could get myself to work in a drama school. This to me was an acutely embarrassing sort of thing, so I went to a private coach and horsed around, went through the motions for a few months, until one absurd day when I found myself acting in the basement with a Western hero, and I thought, "This is ridiculous!" and I walked out. And that, my friend, was the function of *The Asphalt Jungle*.

N. But after swearing off acting you made a movie in 1963, didn't you?

■ *Hayden:* This is embarrassing. All through the book I keep reiterating that I will never act again; I'm finished, done; and yet I did do another movie. In 1962, in fact. I'd been working on a novel for eight months, and was absolutely flat broke. So I sold a Volkswagon bus I had and came East to New York. I took a room in the old Chelsea Hotel on 23rd Street and was waiting for an advance, when the phone rang one afternoon. It was Stanley Kubrick, with whom I'd worked on a movie called, *The Killing*. Kubrick was calling from London, and he outlined very quickly a film entitled *Dr. Strangelove, or, How I learned to Stop Worrying and Love the Bomb*. He said that it was a picture that would deal with the cold war situation and the threat of nuclear holocaust. It would treat the business as a nightmare comedy. He told me that Peter Sellers was going to play three parts in it, and he thought there was a role I could handle: the part of a psychotic SAC general whose name is Jack D. Ripper and who, for reasons of his own, would trigger World War III.

I sensed immediately that my resolve to abstain from acting was going out the window because I believed this was a picture that should be made. I had then, and have now, confidence in Stanley Kubrick's ability and guts. I would have done the picture for nothing, and almost did, but I got a good deal in a fine film. It infuriated the right wing, naturally, because it milked a few sacred cows, but I hope it made a lot of people sit up and realize how stupid and how dangerous the arms race and the nuclear standoff really is.

N. *Wanderer* was an exceptionally frank and open autobiography, and you must have felt some pain in writing it. Were you aware of any obligation as you were writing it?—toward your material, on the one hand, or the public on the other?

■ *Hayden:* Well, I mentioned that I originally planned to do a novel, but that it would be so autobiographical, it would obviously be a raw and amateurish first novel. So I wrote an autobiography, certain that I could be more blunt and ruthless with myself.

In the first place, I felt that if I was to be critical of society, it was incumbent upon me to be critical of myself. And I had to be all the way critical, to attain some depth, because all the superficial crap was too well known. A lot of my life has been on the surface, some of it in headlines. To be worthwhile, I had to go deep. I had to show what triggered my life, what fouled it up at times, what pleased me, and what made me sore. If I succeeded in doing this, I felt I could really make a contribution—the reader would see himself in it, at least in fragments of it; and to me, this is what a book has to be.

Perhaps my tastes are different. I read almost no novels, and I find very little nonfiction that moves me very much. Part of this is due to the fact that I've been trying to educate myself, late in life, and I've had a tremendous amount of reading to do in areas I should have covered long ago—particularly in terms of history and relations between the working stiff and the bosses, and the whole world of economics. (Back to the late-blooming Hayden again. Makes me sound like some goddam variety of flower.) But I've tried to do all this in recent years, and to some extent, I've succeeded in educating myself.

But, as I started to say, I felt that if I was totally honest with *Wanderer*, I would produce a book that people would feel. This is what I wanted to do, and this is what I hope the book does. I know it's doing that to some extent, though I'm a bit appalled at the lack of capacity of many people who appear, on the surface, to be able to feel and sense and respond to the human condition, but who really are blunted. I don't say this critically; I think it's a very deep tragedy.

That was the motivation behind what has been called "a searing reexamination and delineation of my own particular, peculiar life."

N.   Acknowledging the fact that you have started a bit late as a writer——

■ *Hayden:*   Even Conrad beat me; he started in his late thirties, and I was just over the forty-mark and felt older. Sorry.

N.   . . . what advice would you give the neophyte, the young writer who wants to make his way?

■ *Hayden:*   I should respond quickly and say that I don't feel in a position to give advice on that subject. But hell. I haven't been asked these questions before—you have no idea of the damfool questions interviewers toss at a Hollywood character—and it's a good feeling to get down to the bowels of all these issues.

There's this saying about "Everybody has one book in him and it's the story of his life." Well, I'm cognizant of that, but I feel that in a way my first book isn't just a job of writing. It's a blast, a burst, an explosion of emotion and feeling and conviction and regret and sadness. Out of a whole life it suddenly let go.

I think I'm at some advantage, assuming I express myself well. Let's face it; I have a great deal to say by this time, I've had long talks with my editor, a wonderful man named Angus Cameron at Knopf. I remember Angus saying to me that one reason for the deplorable caliber of writing turned out in this country today is that the young writers haven't lived enough.

This is why some wonderful books came out of World War II, though most of these same writers have gotten bogged down, with the exception of Mailer. And I guess James Jones is doing all right; *The Thin Red Line* is powerful. But the young writers I've read haven't seen or been or done enough to sustain their talents.

Generally speaking, the young writers I meet, certainly in San Francisco, talk a lot and don't follow it up with much that's worth shouting about. Half the time I don't know what the hell they're saying.

N.   Then you may well be at an advantage, with a lot of living behind you.

■ *Hayden:*   I certainly think so. Let's face it; we're living in a rough time. The chaps I see who are now in their twenties or early thirties have lived in a period when the individual has been under wraps. This has not been a dynamic period in terms of the country's development. The country has been poised at a certain peak of affluence. I think we're in a great deal of trouble, and that we'll be in deeper trouble, unless there's some radical change. I don't mean "radical" in a purely political context, either.

I think the Negro movement is an extraordinarily exciting thing, not because of the horror of it, but because of what it offers. The Negro movement makes me hope that (unless some idiot gets into office and starts throwing bombs around) there's some slim chance that this country might get back on the track it was originally intended to ride. We might get rid of this worship of material success and security which no country, no culture, has been able to survive.

Maybe a country can't change its ways—I don't know. But if there is any chance, I think the Negro problem, as it's called (and I agree with Baldwin that it is not so much a Negro problem but a national problem and the white man's problem) yields substantial promise for the future. But it's a rough road.

N. To go back to *Wanderer* again, to another theme you handled frankly. This dealt with the American male's loss of manhood; not so much his ability to make love as his ability to live an assured life for himself.

■ *Hayden:* Now we're back to the beginning of the interview, when I was talking about being seven years old and watching the commuters, the poor bastards doing the rat-race routine.

It's no different, now. These past weeks have kept me jumping around the country, speaking, making all sorts of appearances, being interviewed, and I'm convinced the situation has grown worse. I sit on plane after plane, usually loaded with executives or businessmen of some sort, and I talk to them, or try to, or watch what they're reading. What are they reading? Company documents and graphs and pages of percentages and figures. One guy the other night couldn't tear himself away from the merchandising of soup. Soup is fine, but this happens to be his world; this is his life.

And I notice, when I sit in bars, or airport lobbies, or on limousines and buses, the same graphs and statistics, the perpetual business dialogue I feel—well, Jessica Mitford writes about the American way of death, but the American way of death isn't the burial ritual (silly as that is), but the way the average man lives. When you consider the beauty there is in this world, the rapture that can be known, the excitement and exaltation there is for the taking—the things to look at and feel and read—

Look at the state of book-selling in this country today. Some time ago, I read a comparison of the United States and Holland.

In Holland, 863 books are published each year per mil'' on population, and in America we get 80. There are less than 300 real book stores in the United States.

Now, I realize that everyone can't haul-ass to Tahiti. I'm the last advocate of that, actually. But what does the American male do for recreation, once he's finished studying those bars and graphs? He may get loaded, but joylessly; and he may make love, probably just as joylessly; or he may sit in front of the idiot box and watch lousy old movies. Probably *my* lousy old movies, and God knows, there are few that are any lousier.

We've got to take a good look at the society in which we live, and wonder if there isn't something wrong with a social system that reduces people, both men and women, into consumers. The only God I see now is the ratio of production-to-consumption-to-profit. Unless we are blessed with some arrogance, enough to negotiate our way through this cannibalistic wilderness, the rights of the individual are nonexistent. We're trapped in the cycle to produce, consume, and profit, and that fellow who is so devoted to marketing soup isn't a person, he's a digit.

N. Speaking of rapture—this was something the reader felt in *Wanderer* whenever you stepped aboard a ship. Could you elaborate on your feeling toward the sea?

■ *Hayden:* For me the sea is an escape; it's a way of life; it's a world far away from the biznik. Maybe I should have slugged it out the normal way for the acquisitions that spell security. Yet the sea doesn't spell quite the escapist route as the person falls into when he gets out of schools and goes to work to bury himself in a safe job with a regular paycheck in order to acquire his damned little cars, his house, his patio, and his little outboard motorboat. I don't mean to sound disparaging toward this individual because I feel an immense compassion for him, the poor, trapped, miserable son-of-a-bitch. At sea—call it escape or a deeper reality— I found a microcosm of life, an oasis of honesty where there wasn't room to be phony, where the common enemy was a storm in peacetime, or the wrong guns in wartime. Sometimes nerves wore raw, and sometimes we didn't smell too good, but we knew each other and what went on with each other—heart, soul, guts, the works—and there were no paper heroes or cardboard villains. We were good, bad, and indifferent for real.

I remember, while I was still sailing, being dressed down by a prosperous uncle who owned a perfume company. He was wealthy and successful, and he used to sit in the New York Athletic Club and talk to me about "finding myself." Well, I'd listen to him, and all the plush advantages he was painting for me, but over his shoulder I'd see the tugs going down the river and hear the ferries whistling, and I thought, "Don't talk to me about success, you don't know what the hell you're talking about."

I agree with Lewis Mumford's *The Golden Day*. If I had the money, I'd like to take this book around, this and *Walden,* and read them to every biznik who'd listen. Including that poor jerk who's merchandising soup.

N.   That man bugged you.

■ *Hayden:* Only because he's one of so many millions of the living dead.

N.   The final question: What are you going to write next?

■ *Hayden:* Immediately after completing *Wanderer,* I went to work on a novel that has been in the back of my mind for years. Now I'm almost through the first draft. It deals with what I regard as a pivotal point in this country's history; namely, the period of the middle 1890's. I'm beginning the book in 1893, and I'm going to carry it through 1906. To me, the country could have gone one of two ways at that point. It could have gone as it has, toward materialism, or it could have done a left-face, placing people ahead of gold. This was the day of the first big strikes; of Cripple Creek and the Coeur d'Alene Mountains in Idaho; of the Homestead, and Carnegie, and Pullman strikes. It was the day that just preceded the "wobblies"; the day when the seamen were beginning to organize; the day of our real class struggle. What I'm trying to do is tell a story of this vast confrontation of forces.

The story is actually played out on the decks of the big Cape Horn sailing ships. These were massive steel vessels that came around the Horn from Philadelphia or New York or Baltimore, bound for the West Coast or the Orient, usually laden with coal. They were terrible ships. Men worked under appalling conditions. These men had come out of the mines, the mills, the lumber yards, hobo jungles, and off the road—men who had tramped the land and were lost—and they didn't land on these ships of their own volition; they were shanghaied.

I'm using the ship as a catalyst again because on a ship you have society in microcosm. All of society's forces are involved within the 320-foot length of steel deck.

N.   Have you any further writing plans?

■ *Hayden:* Yes, there's another novel in me, in the note stage right now. This is about a guy who feels the frustration I spoke about, the desperation of this materialistic life, and literally burns everything he's accumulated, severs his relationships with wife and children, and tramps the world with a ten-pound rucksack to find out what's going on. But this comes later.

Back to the novel I'm working on—it's a big one, and I want it to be an important one, a good one, and I want to finish it. I guess a guy like me has to go on the assumption that when you smoke three packs of cigarettes a day while you're writing, and you drink half a quart of whiskey every night, you're not going to live as long as that benighted bastard who's out merchandising soup.

"I don't think today's writers know what guts are. They think it's a string of dirty words, I guess. . . . The deviates expose their problems with considerable gusto. Baldwin, Rechy, all their tiresome breed. This isn't guts or even gusto, really—it's like getting sick in public. And not even cleaning up the mess they make."

Ben Hecht
Interviewed in New York, September, 1963

Ben Hecht

N. Ben Hecht performed, for many decades and in many roles, as one of the pivotal figures on the American literary scene. As a journalist he made an indelible impression with works like *1001 Afternoons In Chicago* and *Gaily, Gaily*. As a playwright he gave us *The Front Page* and *Twentieth Century*, and as a motion picture writer or writer-producer the powerful *Spectre Of The Rose*, *The Scoundrel*, *Crime Without Passion*, *Wuthering Heights*, *Notorious*, and many others. And he wrote a vast collection of short stories. If, in a coloring book, Hecht should appear, the only suitable direction that could be given would be to color him "vivid." For this is the impression he has left on all the written and performing arts he has commanded. How did it all begin?

■ *Hecht:* I was precocious. I figured out, as a kid, that I never wanted to work for any boss. I disliked authority when I was twelve or thirteen, and I wondered how I could make a living without coming into contact with authority.

The answer, at that time, came from an uncle who was a liquor salesman. He picked me up in front of a vaudeville theater in Chicago and asked me what I was doing. I said, "Trying to figure out what to do with my life." So he took me to a newspaper publisher named John Eastman and I became a reporter. I ran errands for about four months, but I found that my dream was more or less realized. There was no authority. It wasn't that there was no authority in the newspaper; there just wasn't any in my head. I think I'd have been the same if I had landed in a boiler factory or a steel mill, but it seemed more reasonable for there to be no authority on a newspaper than in a packing plant.

I decided, when I was very young, that I would enjoy myself no matter what I did. I've managed for fifty years to do that. I don't remember having any problems that a child of fifteen couldn't solve. I never remember having to do things I didn't want to do. Even the money I've made in movies was money I wanted, so the making of it wasn't altogether gruesome.

I found that because of the fact that I didn't like authority and didn't like bosses and didn't like crystallized ideas I was related to all sorts of literary types. I wrote for H. L. Mencken's "Smart Set" when I was about seventeen or eighteen, and for the *Little Review* in Chicago about that same time. There was an awful lot of competition, then. About one out of five writers in those days was a bit anarchic, opposed to authority of all sorts. Mencken was not the leader—he was a symbol of the type of individualism versus anything, anything that smacked of conformity. So I was one of a crowd, but I continued to survive while the crowd didn't. The crowd gradually dwindled down to the individual writer—that is, the writer who isn't impressed with the politics of his country, who doesn't care much who is President or what the President does, who has no interest in foreign intrigue or power politics, who is not inclined to be a kibitzer at some distant chess game where he is not allowed to make any move or even see what the moves are. This individualistic sort of person, this type of writer, is almost gone from my country today. I find hardly anyone who isn't more interested in everything outside them than in what goes on inside.

Nearly all the writers I read, with very few exceptions, are terribly concerned with events in Asia, Africa, Europe—places they've had no contact with. The politicalization of our so-called intelligentsia has been amazing. In my day, in the 1920's and 1930's, politics was as forbidden a subject as discussing incomes. Politicians were looked upon as a necessary nuisance and we didn't care who was in charge.

Today, of course, there isn't a newspaper that isn't filled with politics—the President, his dull family, his duller friends. If it isn't them it's the latest blurred news from Viet Nam. It can't be that there's no other news to print.

Maybe this obsession with politics is a way of marking time. People have had their God taken away from them, they have no faith, and they are incredibly confused by science because science is doing things that only Jules Verne was supposed to have done. This era of confusion, without goals and spiritual obsession, leaves a drifting people who can be grabbed by any bait thrown at them. This is why they're interested in European and Asiatic politics—it doesn't concern them even though it costs them a lot.

The thing that has truly astonished me in this country is the way America won a war to do away with militarism and power politics—this was the First World War—and now we have become the greatest militaristic and power-politicked country on earth. In doing so the citizens of this country have allowed themselves to be taxed exhorbitantly. In 1910 or 1920 a tax rate such as we have now would have resulted in the impeachment of the President and every member of the Cabinet. There would have been rioting in the streets.

This indicates the slow breakdown of American morale. Obviously the objectives of our politicians are to turn us into Russians as painlessly as possible—people who are ruled by the state and contribute all their efforts to the sustenance of the state. They are doing it rather well—nobody thinks of protesting. A protest would be looked upon, not as an attitude, but as treachery. But that's enough about politics. I loathe them and I resent the way they've ruined the Press.

Another amazing thing, however—along with this empty-headed concern about political matters—is a thing I've seen happen since I first started to work in Chicago. When I first launched myself, rather feebly and confusedly as a writer, there was one great enemy. He was called morality, Victorianism, hypocrisy. Censors were strangling literature, strangling theater, ripping "September Morn" out of the window because she was nude. We all fought against Victorianism, morality, and hypocrisy as if this was the greatest enemy of mankind.

Well, I've lived to see that enemy laid by the heels and almost removed from the United States. I was arrested by the federal government, a long time ago, for writing a book that was supposed to be lewd, obscene, lascivious. The book could be printed in a ladies' magazine today. In fact, it might not be accepted because it's so gentle and sweet.

The disappearance of the censor has really rattled me—I no longer know which side I'm on. I don't like books with dirty words. I don't like books with unrestrained physiological attitudes toward the heroine. Sex is something everybody knows—there's no reason to draw a blueprint every time it comes up. On the other hand, I feel that it's wrong to oppose these writers because they are the result of the victory that we fought to win.

I hear things in the theater in New York that literally shock me, and I'm not easy to shock. They're the same words I heard in brothels and when I was a kid in drops and joints. Language not merely profane, but language from the bottom of the pack, drunken two A.M. language. The new playwrights are so busy with dirty words you'd think they'd discovered a new plot. But as I say, I don't know which side I'm on—we fought for this freedom and we got it.

Another source of confusion comes with the so-called "modernists." I wrote the first article about James Joyce that was written in Chicago. I thought he should be defended, that change or development should never be opposed. What I see now of the modernists convinces me that they've gone all fake; they were partly fake, way back then, but now? Music is all the way dissonant; art is utterly abstract; poetry is full of dots and odd symbols; drama is upside down; and audiences have become so artistic they don't enjoy anything they can understand. We helped this along, too, back in the 1920's and 1930's when we thought freedom of expression and innovation and change and lack of repression were everything. Now I'm not so sure we should have fought the good fight.

But to get back to my career—it's gone every which way. I've written twenty-eight books, eighty movie scenarios that reached the screen, about ten scenarios I directed and produced myself, ten or twelve plays (eight of them produced), three or four musicals that were produced and three or four hundred short stories that were printed. I've just kept scratching away and jumping from one thing to the next. This started when I was a kid.

I was scheduled to be a musician—and I was a good one. I gave a two-boy concert in Orchestra Hall in 1908; I was thirteen, I think. I played the violin. But somehow I didn't stick with it. I was also a circus acrobat. I ran away with a circus, Harry Costello's one-ring show. I lived at his house in Racine, and he taught me routines on the trapeze and bars. So for a long time I didn't know whether I wanted to be a musician or an acrobat. I compromised by taking up magic when I was fifteen, giving shows in Racine and Kenosha, nickel admission.

When I arrived in Chicago I had exhausted several professions at the age of sixteen, so it was natural to start being a writer. I never liked what they called being an "artist" although I was a member of the art group in Chicago. The "artist" to my journalistic mind was the combined fake and cult-leader who sent rich old ladies into raptures. I never appreciated the fakery. This is why I've never cared for Faulkner, Hemingway, or any writer who went out of his way to ostentatiously turn the simple to the difficult and back to the simple again. (Faulkner couldn't pull the last bit.)

My first literary friend in Chicago was Sherwood Anderson because he couldn't write. Writing was totally impossible for him for years. He didn't know the English language. He would begin his story, "Down the street ran George Willard." Then he would change it to "Coming down the street was George Willard." It would take him a week to get the first sentence done because he was illiterate, and this was *Winesburg, Ohio*, he was working on. I, also, was illiterate, but not that bad. But this crowd turned their illiteracy into some kind of superiority.

Those years of newspaper work in Chicago were great. They even had a different breed of criminal, and it's a cinch that the standards of reporting were different.

N. In what respects were the criminals and the reporters different?

■ *Hecht:* Well, the crime we had then wasn't necessarily bigger or better, but it was like everything else; it was less commercial. Criminals in those days weren't part of the general look of the country—they weren't materialists. They were adventurers; there were no syndicates. Why, before Capone organized the big $150,000,000 per year combine, a criminal was usually a fellow without much money. He was a criminal for the same reason that the Midwest and Southwest had produced outlaws. They liked to live without working. But they didn't rob and slug people in alleys —they held up jewelry stores, places like that. One heist would give them enough to live on for three or four months. They weren't enemies of the public. They usually shot each other because of dandyish quarrels over girls, over money, over territory. In many respects they reminded me of the nobility of the Middle Ages—they thought work was soiling, and honor was a thing that had to be defended with a gun. Being called a name meant somebody died.

The criminals we had in those days weren't hired, either. Today a hood who goes out and kills somebody is like a waiter or a messenger boy. He's hired by the syndicate and looked upon as the lowest member of the organization. He's not given any social applause, he isn't allowed to dine with the boss, he's just paid his $1,000 or $2,000 to rub somebody out.

There was no boss. The criminal was an entrepreneur. He strutted and swanked like a fellow who had won a lot of jousts. He had no interest in money—when he'd make a score he'd throw it away so fast you wanted to stop him. I'm remembering them too fondly, perhaps—we had some of the dirty ones, too. Yet it's amazing how terribly well read some of them were, how observant, how ready to talk about life with a capital "L" or even philosophy. Of course, the stretches in prison helped. The prison libraries weren't very extensive, and sooner or later the guy in the clink would have to read Montaigne.

They were colorful, then—not cruel, not twisted, not full of "dese," "dems," and "dose." But then, Freud hadn't gotten to them and they hadn't read Mickey Spillane.

N.   After your newspaper days in Chicago you went on to New York, didn't you? Wasn't that when you and MacArthur wrote *The Front Page?*

■ *Hecht:*   I found myself in New York in 1927. I'd always hated New York because I thought it was the most commercial town in the world. But nowhere else—in Chicago or Des Moines or San Francisco or New Orleans—could you find a publisher. There was nobody to buy your stuff.

When I came to New York I found the grand bazaar for the so-called artists. The cash registers clicked away, and people were buying plays. I'd known MacArthur; we'd been friends in Chicago when we were eighteen. I told Charlie that I had a plot for a play. He was mad about theater—I never was. So we started talking.

MacArthur and I had something in common. We had opposite friends, read opposite books, had completely opposite personalities, but we both refused to grow up. We remained the same people we'd been in Chicago, kept our hats on in a room, dropped ashes on the floor, kept a veneer of uncivilization. So we pooled our memories of the town and we wrote a play using actual characters and keeping their names. One or two characters we made up, but we didn't have to make up very much because we had the richest, the most colorful personalities in the world right in our hands.

The newspaper man at that time was irresponsible, uncontrolled, red-blooded, and fun. He was between twenty-five and forty, he'd been around, he was going to get around some more, and his job was to divert the public. In those days the newspaper was the big entertainment—no radio or television to distract from it or compete with it. So these men were responsible for entertainment as well as news, and they dug it out and brought it in. Today's newspaperman may be just as bright, and he may make more money, but he's way behind when it comes to diverting the public. This is probably the newspaper's fault, not his.

But it seems funny to hear *The Front Page* called "exaggeration." If anything, we underwrote.

N.   Isn't the change in journalism part of the pattern of the times? The standardization or conformity or whatever we wish to call it?

■ *Hecht:*   It's not as simple as that. Journalism's tamed down, sure, because newspapers have become big business. But on the other hand the theater and fiction have gotten wild and dirty. And not with any real guts.

I don't think today's writers know what guts are. They think it's a string of dirty words, I guess. Tell them to write a book with verve and gusto and you'll get something like *City Of Night*. The deviates expose their problems with considerable gusto. Baldwin, Rechy, all their tiresome breed. This isn't guts or even gusto, really —it's like getting sick in public. And not even cleaning up the mess they make.

If I had a boy of seventeen who wanted to write I would deprive him of all newspapers and books, never let him hang around with people who were making more than $30 or $40 a week. I'd do this so he might get a smell of human beings instead of editorial-ized opinion and too much education. Most of the youths who come to me for advice have been through college and taken postgraduate courses. They'd have been just as well off if they'd done nothing.

It may have something to do with the inroads women have made on the male world, too. Males today haven't changed into females, but there isn't much difference between a male and a female. The women are standing at your side, working in the same profession, using your same vocabulary, drinking your drinks, telling your dirty stories. Beards have disappeared, moustaches have gone out of style, and ladies have strong hands. Women today are a bit mascu-linized—even those malnutrition cases in fashion magazines look like boys.

All this may have something to do with the lack of gusto. The sexes have lost their mystery for each other. The double standard is practically gone. The double standard made you full of gusto—you had to lie all the time, you had to be a lively hypocrite. Great mental activity. You also had to outwit the good girls. This was difficult, because in those days if she outwitted you just a nickel's worth you had to marry her. Most of the people I knew left Chicago about the same time for the same reason. They were running away from women they'd married only because they'd kissed them once too often and gotten hooked. They were escap-ing. MacArthur was escaping, and Anderson, and Bodenheim, and Floyd Dell, and me. We left town to get easier divorces.

N. You mentioned the young writer in light of what you'd not want him to do. What actual advice would you give him?

■ *Hecht:* The first and most vital thing a young writer must do is to decide to be himself and find the cause that carries only his name. He must be his own cause—he must not shop around for things to join up with, ideologies to hook onto. He must answer back to everything around him as a human and an individual. Even if his answers are crude and rather dumb as long as they're his answers—and not echoes of the journalistic dust storm blown through our heads constantly—he can begin. He must imitate only himself, or he'll never get anywhere. The good writers—whether I personally liked them or not—began this way.

These writers have had another thing today's youngsters don't realize—the fact that writing is the most horrible form of discipline, the most constant discipline there is. You never learn, from writing four books, how to write the fifth. It's not like violin study. After you've studied the violin for four years you can play it. After you've written for five years you still can't write. After twenty years you still can't write. Each piece of work is brand new—you make the same mistakes and have to do the same number of re-writes. You never get smart, you never get a technique, if you're expressing yourself.

On the other hand, if you're making up an entertainment purely to please others, you do get a technique. I can write a movie script of any kind in two weeks. But here you're merely carving a toy for others to play with. You're using their attitudes and desires. It's difficult, in this medium, to express yourself in a way that makes you admire yourself, so it's better to call it "business" rather than "art."

So the two things are: Find out who you are and make your own answers. Be influenced by nobody, including God. Then, work every day. The writer who doesn't work five to eight hours every day isn't a writer. I don't think I spend more than an idle week during a year. Writing has become a habit to me, like narcotics—I just can't be idle.

Now, I'm not knocking movies. I've been at them too long. You don't write, direct, and produce something like *Spectre of the Rose* without coming out with some satisfaction. You may not make much money, when you're that committed, but the satisfaction remains. The same goes for *The Scoundrel, Crime Without Passion, Wuthering Heights, Scarface, Kiss of Death, Notorious,* and *Spellbound.* There's satisfaction, of course, in a script that's well done. But unless it's your own story to begin with, the satisfaction has to be limited to money because you're a technician, not the creator. The real part of creation—the origination and follow-through—is the big thing, the important thing, the hard thing. The young writer is playing a tough course—but if he names his own cause, and works like hell, he gets the biggest reward of all."

M

"I wish there was more comedy in the theater today. . . . When you stop to think of how little genuine comedy is written now, it's really frightening. You wonder if we have lost all sense of humor."

William Inge
Interviewed in New York, February, 1964

William Inge

N. Any selection of plays written over the past few decades—
the best, the most significant, the most enduring—would inevitably
include several by William Inge. The choice is a broad one, with
four, at least, that cannot be separated from American theater:
Picnic; Bus Stop; Come Back, Little Sheba; and *The Dark At The
Top Of The Stairs.* I'd like to ask Mr. Inge, as a beginning, for a
rough outline of his life and career.

■ *Inge:* I was born in Independence, Kansas, in 1913. It's a town
of about 15,000, a very prosperous town up until the time of the
Depression. In fact, it was an extremely wealthy town. One felt, as
a consequence, that it presented a microcosm of small town life in
its extremes. Life in Independence was competitive, with a brisk
social life that offered young people a lovely environment in which
to grow up. Unfortunately, if in any way you ran against the grain,
it furnished a very troubled environment.

I have very fond memories of Independence, and I'll probably
feel nostalgic about it all my life. But then, I suppose one is nostalgic about any home town from New York to Timbuctu. I first
wanted to be an actor, and at the age of seven I acted spontane-
ously. I used to listen to my sister recite pieces and monologues
she learned in a little private acting class, and found that I was
unconsciously memorizing her pieces. In the third grade, one day,
I offered to give a recitation, and very bravely did so. I had myself
a career. I was a kind of prodigy actor in the town and in that part
of the country, and I gave recitations until I was old enough to go
to high school and college where I could actually appear in plays.
I acted with a few summer theater groups, and for a period with
the Kansas Tent Show, with a sort of old-time Toby show, and
also in summer theater in Indiana. I loved acting, and built my life
around the premise that I was going to be an actor.

Then I found, upon graduation from college, that it was going
to be difficult to bring this dream into reality. I feared going to
New York—I had no money and no acquaintances there—so I began

to flounder. I went on for a Master's Degree at George Peabody Teacher's College in Nashville, Tennessee. I had taken my undergraduate work at the University of Kansas, but I thought that I'd get my Master's so that I'd be able to teach in case my other plans fell through. Of course, once you prepare yourself to fail, you fail. After a year of working on my Master's, I found that I no longer had the courage to act. I don't know if I became too introspective or what, but I felt that I was no longer an actor, even though I wanted to act. I didn't feel that I had the guts to stand in front of an audience.

I did some radio work at a Wichita, Kansas, radio station, announcing news and writing some continuity. I had never thought of myself as a writer in any sense of the word, yet I found that (when called upon) I could write continuity and commercials. But I still don't think of myself as a writer, didn't plan any sort of career as a writer. As a matter of fact, I didn't know what to do. I hated teaching, but I went on and taught in a Kansas high school, then taught five years more at Stephens College for Women, a junior college in Columbia, Missouri. For three years of that time I taught with the late Maude Adams.

At the end of this five-year stretch I felt I was getting nowhere, that it was time to leave. So I went to St. Louis and became drama, movie, and music critic on the *Star-Times*. This lasted until the end of the war, when the man I was replacing—a friend—came back. So I went back to teaching, this time at Washington University in St. Louis. I hated it, but it was a job, and teachers were needed rather desperately to handle the influx of ex-GI's.

While I'd worked for the *Star-Times* I had written my first play—more out of desperation than anything else. Actually, a doctor had once suggested, rather idly, that I try my hand at playwriting; he thought I might make a go of it. The suggestion stuck with me, and when I was thirty-two I did start writing. It was called *Farther Off From Heaven*, and I sent it to my friends Tennessee Williams and Margo Jones. They liked it, and Margo wanted to produce it in her Dallas theater, so this was great encouragement. From then on I considered myself a playwright, and while I was teaching at Washington University I wrote *Come Back, Little Sheba*. (I had written two or three others but they were rather half-hearted attempts; I was struggling with the craft.)

Sheba was written in the fall of 1948, purchased by the Theater Guild in February, 1949, and produced the following September in Westport, Connecticut and the next February in New York.

Sheba had a modest success on Broadway, but certainly enough to give me the encouragement I needed, so I continued writing. I dug an old play called *Front Porch* out of a trunk—a play I hadn't previously been able to realize fully—and got to work on it. It came out, of course, as *Picnic*, which was very successful, the most successful play I've had. It won the Pulitzer Prize and the Drama Critics Prize. Then came *Bus Stop*, which I actually developed out of a short story I tried to write about an actual incident I had seen happen, some years before, when I was taking a bus from Columbia, Missouri, to Kansas City.

I've always thought of *Bus Stop* as something of a fantasy. I guess it falls into the realm of naturalistic comedy, but it's more of a fantasy than people realize. I think it has something of the fable about it. At any rate, after *Bus Stop* I wrote *The Dark At The Top Of The Stairs*. All of these plays were successful.

Then came *A Loss Of Roses*. This was not successful. It was my first real failure, and (naturally) it was very discouraging. However, for the first time in my life I encountered serious misunderstanding during production with practically all the people I was working with. I don't think any of us really sat down before the play got underway to decide what kind of play we were doing. I learned a very serious lesson from this. However, with my last play, *Natural Affection*, I had to learn it all over again.

In all modesty I really don't think *A Loss Of Roses* is all done. Certainly I never saw, on stage, the play I wrote. There was too much trouble during production. We cut and mended, and I got myself into a situation I didn't know how to handle.

N.   As far as current theater is concerned, what do you most admire and what do you deplore?

■ *Inge:*   Well, although I'm considered a rather traditional writer I'm quite taken by the avant-garde. I highly admire Pinter, and I get a great deal of stimulation and excitement from Beckett and Genêt.

I find that now, when I go to the theater, I tend to be bored by something that is merely a well-made play. After the first twenty minutes I know all that the play will be about, I know how the conflicts will be resolved, and I'm simply too restless and impatient to sit around and watch its predictable course.

I want to be surprised—I don't want to know what's coming. I think that innovations are creeping into the new theater that will prove immensely rewarding. More and more, this new theater is becoming an expression of the unconscious. You don't know what is going to happen next. I don't want to go to see the plotted play any more. I don't insist upon Beckett or Genêt, but I do want to be kept alert and surprised.

I'm not fond of plays on ideas, either. When I went to see Ionescu's *Rhinoceros* I found it to be a play of ideas. After fifteen minutes I wasn't interested enough to continue watching it. Ideas, it seems to me, are better suited for books.

I think Albee is a very exciting writer. He's somewhat traditional, but he keeps you constantly alert and interested. His plays are well made, but they are not predictable. There's a freshness, a great freshness, in *Who's Afraid Of Virginia Woolf?* I liked that.

N. How do you feel about today's drama criticism? Do you feel that plays are really being evaluated upon their own merits, as products of our time, or do you find that criticism is lacking in judgment?

■ *Inge:* I think it's rather hard, right now, for critics to function. We're in a period of transition, and when you read the critic's comments you can see that they don't always know how to react. It's difficult to know how to respond to new things, and too often the critic thinks of the politic thing to say—not necessarily in favor of the play, but the politic thing with his readers.

I do think that the three decades of destructive criticism—and it's been with us since the 1920's—can now be seen in terms of cause and effect. We have to admit, whether we like it or not, how really harsh and absurdly vicious much theater criticism has been. Fashionable criticism has always been vitriolic; drama critics have always sought to say the clever thing rather than the true thing. If we want to think that this has not hurt drama, we're crazy, because it has. We sacrificed the theater itself for the sake of personal writing reputations. The theater, if it's going to be an art, has to be respected even when it's ridiculous. We have to respect it as an institution, and write about it in terms of what it might be rather than terms of what it is.

Chicago is a choice example of criticism gone wrong. It's no accident that there is scarcely any theater in Chicago, now, that this city of five million people has never had theater of its own, that it has always been dependent upon road shows, many of which don't bother with Chicago any more. Criticism in Chicago is and has been, from almost all quarters, preposterous, not only vicious but unlearned. I don't think that the would-be Chicago theatergoer knows how actors and producers and managers feel when they go into Chicago, sometimes to open, sometimes to close, and have ridiculously vindictive things said about them that border upon personal insult. I could name a dozen shows that would have opened in Chicago in the past fifteen years but haven't done so because they just didn't want to enter this climate.

Most theater people do not fear genuine criticism. I myself have always felt that I could take honest criticism. But we shudder from vindictiveness, from affront, and I think we have to admit that most criticism, over the past thirty years, has been vitriolic. Its effect has been to inhibit us. The press is powerful, after all. So powerful that the gentlemen of the press should act like gentlemen, and the ladies like ladies, and not take an unfair advantage of the power they have. Think of *Time* magazine—powerful and widely distributed—saying the snippy, adolescent things it says about the arts, not only theater and cinema, but the plastic arts as well. Isn't it possible for Americans to be generous in spirit, to be kindly about things that don't live up to the highest expectations? Can't criticism act in the sense of trying to illuminate experience instead of destroying it?

I think that this blatantly destructive criticism is a great shortcoming in our national character.

N.   Could you define your overall objective as a playwright?
■ *Inge:* I'm sorry that I can't give you an immediate answer; perhaps I honestly don't know. I know, in both theater and film, that I try very hard to reconcile and unite man's physical nature with his spiritual. This problem consumes me at times, but it's an old, old problem. And in a more immediate way I want to express something of what I feel is contemporary in people. What this is I don't really know, except that I find myself observing things and remembering things I want to perpetuate.

N.   Put it this way: If you were a critic in 1995, looking back to the fifties and sixties, how would you like William Inge to be appraised?
■ *Inge:* Well, I'd like them to find, in my plays, something appealing and humorous and sad and kind of lyrical, something that has the power, even after time has elapsed, to please their sensibilities. I have never wanted to be a disturbing writer, though I may have been, once or twice. (My movies have disturbed people, though I haven't meant them to.) I think I've always wanted to warm people more than to warn them. I've never been moved to write of social issues, and I know—despite the fact that I've enjoyed some plays with a social message very much—that I hate to write of people as members of any particular group. I want to see human

nature more purely in terms of itself. I'm probably closer to some of the Irish playwrights, like Sean O'Casey and Synge. I'm not as lyrical as they are, but I think I'm about as lyrical as my Kansas background affords me.

I like to get some of the quality of song in my plays. I also like a play that's both sad and funny because I don't think, in this day, we can look at any issue in a purely tragic or purely comic light. I wish to God there was more comedy in the theater today— and in films, too. When you stop to think of how little genuine comedy is written now, it's really frightening. You wonder if we have lost all sense of humor. This year I went to see a new comedy titled *Barefoot In The Park* and I adored it because I found myself laughing uproariously for the first time in years. I was relieved to sit in a theater enjoying myself.

We've almost ceased to think of theater as entertainment. We approach it self-consciously. We are trying too hard to be significant, and we don't feel that we've gotten our money's worth of the theater unless we're kicked in the pants with some social blame, unless we leave the theater feeling guilty and full of misery.

I think one of the mistakes we make is in thinking of the theater as an educational institution. At one time, centuries ago, the theater had an educational function because it was one of the few public meeting places. But now we have compulsory education—people can go to school for a remarkably long time, even adult night school if they want more. They have both radio and television, both of which are much better educational media than the theater.

I'd love to see the theater relax and do and be something that is fun, something that's attended for pleasure. Maybe I haven't always practiced what I'm preaching, some of my plays haven't provided much fun. The last one in particular, I guess. But still I believe what I believe, and if, sometimes, my plays don't live up to this, it's my own shortcoming.

N. I've noticed, in reading back over your plays, that you never seem to be truly finished with one, you go on rewriting, enlarging, revising. Is this compulsion of yours a private one, or is it a tangible expression of most playwrights' insistence upon improving what has been done?

■ *Inge:* I can only speak for myself—but I do think other playwrights work things over, though whether they work them into production is something else. But I want to leave the play behind— in published form—as the best possible piece I can write. Now, quite often I'll be disappointed in some aspect of the play as it is produced, but when I get the play ready for the publisher I attempt to make it as nearly perfect as I can.

The expansions of my one-act plays is something else. Quite often I write my one-act when the idea for a play is just beginning to germinate and I want to put it into some quick form. I'll turn out a one-act that may be very deficient, but it's a substitute for note taking.

N. Looking back at the succession of plays you've written, what would you pick out as highlights? Individual evenings, sustained performances, notable events of any sort?

■ *Inge:* Well, there was always the extraordinary performances of Shirley Booth and Sidney Blackmer in *Come Back, Little Sheba.* These were constantly satisfying. I will always remember Eileen Heckert's proposal in *Picnic,* and the opening night of *Bus Stop.* I think this was the most beautifully successful opening night I'd ever had. We tried out in Philadelphia, had been two weeks out of town, and the play had never really crystallized out of town. It began to come together when we put Albert Salmi in the cast (rather late). I think he got to play the role for only four performances in Philadelphia before we opened in New York, but the play was still finding itself and people in Philadelphia didn't know how to react to it. There were some serious elements in the play and the audience was a bit reluctant to laugh.

Bus Stop could never call itself a comedy until it opened in New York. I think we played to three preview audiences before we opened, and they all hated the play. Then came opening night— and the great reward for the fact that we had all been able to retain our faith in the play throughout the series of negative experiences. Opening night all our dreams materialized. The play was performed exactly as Harold Clurman, my director; Bob Whitehead, my producer; and I felt it should be performed. It was a brilliant opening night. The response was marvelous, and I think I realized—for the first time—what that New York opening night does for a play. It crystallizes it. Often you don't really know what your play is until it passes that crucial test. You have perhaps the sharpest audience in the world sitting in judgment, and theirs is the viewpoint you will get from no other audience—more critical, more appreciative, more knowing. It's the test. Sometimes a play will show itself in facets it had never shown before that opening night.

As far as *Loss Of Roses* is concerned it's just a blur in my memory—I try not to remember it. But I cannot forget Kim

Stanley's wonderful performance in *Natural Affection*. I think that if I had nothing at all to do with the play, if I'd happened in on it unknowing and unexpecting, I would have been moved by her performance. I think it was the best piece of acting I've seen since Laurette Taylor's *Glass Menagerie*. She was thrilling.

N.   Now we move to the realm of theory. If you were to give advice to the young writer or playwright on working procedure or ambitions, what would this advice be?

■ *Inge:*   I don't think I'd give any advice. I really don't feel that I have any advice to give to a young playwright unless he has some particular question he wants to ask himself. I don't think you can give advice in the theater. For one thing, you don't know if the theater will last much longer. It's a very antique institution—quite old-fashioned. It's really the only social institution left for which you have to make arrangements in advance. It's harder and harder, in life as it is lived today, to make those arrangements. It's hard to plan two weeks in advance, make all the necessary preparations to go to the theater, babysitter, train, all the paraphernalia of our supposedly simplified life. For example, if the play runs longer than a standard timing you have to dash to make your last train—and miss the ending.

The theater is a bit cumbersome in today's life, and in the future it might well exist only in an intimate way. I suppose there will always be some kind of big theater for big cities—by subscription, on one hand, for transients, on the other—but I think the serious theater will get more intimate, the houses smaller, the theaters littler.

I could be wrong. I can't predict what will happen. But with things as unsettled as they are, any advice would sound trite. Things like "Write what you feel, not what someone else expects you to feel . . ." or "Satisfy yourself first with what you write before you expect to please anyone else" will always be good advice, whatever form theater might take. The good playwright does not go out to his audience—he lets his audience come to him. The audience has to come to the theater, to good theater, to work for the experience they get. You can't hand them mush on a platter. The theater has to remain integral, honest with its own values, and let the audience reach for those values.

"Much of the time we're preoccupied with the morally ugly, the deeply pessimistic. Then we veer off to sheer hilarity, verging upon nonsense. It's better to sit in the middle of this see-saw than to commit yourself to either of the ends."

Pamela Hansford Johnson
Interviewed in London, England, October, 1963

Pamela Hansford Johnson

N. In actual life she is Lady Snow, the wife of Lord Snow, who, in turn, is very popularly known as novelist C. P. Snow. But a wide and discerning audience credits such works as, *The Unspeakable Skipton* and *Night and Silence, Who Is Here?* to the incredibly gifted Pamela Hansford Johnson. Her style, her wit, and an unerring sense of characterization, inevitably bring cheers from critics on both sides of the Atlantic and, as I mentioned, from a large and vital and growing public. I would like to ask Lady Snow the origin of *Night and Silence*, since it is her most recent work to appear in both England and America.

■ *Johnson:* To tell you the truth, it was sheer perversity. I once wrote an article for the *New York Times* Book Review in which I explained why I wouldn't write about America. My point was that unless I had lived in a place for three years flat I should feel that it was impudent to write about it. (By now, I must have spent three years in America, but only in bits and pieces, not three years running.)

You know, it's fatal to write a statement like that. The article had hardly appeared when the thought came to me, "But what fun it would be to write about America!" So I did. I was really quite careful, however. I chose an English hero; a luxury-loving, self-indulging Englishman abruptly thrust into the kind of life with which—because of his background—he could not cope. I was extremely cautious to get as little wrong as humanly possible. Oddly enough, we're supposed to speak the same language; yet our differences are either so bold that you can't make mistakes, or so subtle it's hard to avoid them. So I had this book read, as soon as it was finished, by at least three Americans. I hope it is altogether right, but I have had letters saying, "No, this is wrong, no American would say that!"

N. I didn't find any goofs.

■ *Johnson:* I really don't think one ought to. I certainly took enough pains to avoid them. Still, with the best will in the world, these things happen. But my impulse in writing *Night and Silence* was simply to produce a comic novel; it's a pleasure to write one occasionally. I thought I might have some fun, harm nobody, and add to the gaiety of nations. Not many people are trying to do this.

N. There is a dearth of comedy.

■ *Johnson:* There's a great deal of comedy of a sort, but it's black comedy. Some years ago I myself wrote a black comedy called *The Unspeakable Skipton.* To tell you the truth I'm rather pleased with it. But I think *Night and Silence* is what you call a pure comedy, a *piece rose,* if you like. It has no purpose more important than to give the reader pleasure.

N. This can often be as important as comedy that bears a driving purpose.

■ *Johnson:* Well, comedy can also be socially conscious. In fact, I suppose it must always, as opposed to force, have some measure of significance. The reason we laugh is because somebody has tickled us on the nerve. It's the kind of nerve which makes us jump, just like the reaction to a dentist's drill. (Only a nicer reaction, we hope.) If comedy has no relationship whatever to life as it is lived, then it is bad comedy and won't achieve its purpose.

N. I'd like to turn to your career as a whole—a rough sketch of your writing history.

■ *Johnson:* Well, I've written all my life. I think most writers have; it is a compulsive occupation. I was born in a rather prosperous South London household with a strong theatrical background. My grandfather was treasurer to Sir Henry Irving, and I think I am the only member of my family on the maternal side never to have been on the stage. For many years, this was a source of regret to one. Suddenly, for various reasons, it became very unprosperous indeed, and at the age of ten I was a member of a poor family. I couldn't go on to a university—it simply wasn't in the cards. No grant in those days would have compensated for the fact that I could bring no money home.

For a long time I did office work—in fact, for quite a time I worked in the office of an American bank in London. I was always writing poetry for minute sums of money (extremely valuable to me then) but I suddenly thought I might do better writing a novel. You see, I had published a book of my poetry, and it wasn't until I saw it in hard covers, that I realized what deplorable stuff I was turning out. An idea for a novel came to me. I wrote it, and had a lot of luck; it was taken at once and caused quite a stir in its time. This was in 1935.

N.   Which novel was that?

■ *Johnson:* It was called *This Bed Thy Center*, and was regarded as an extraordinarily daring book. It wouldn't be now, I can assure you; things have changed drastically. Then I got off the track, somehow, for many years. I wrote a good many novels during that period, but respect few of them. It was not until 1947 that I really began to consolidate my ideas in my experience, and to decide just what I wanted to do.

N.   In surveying the literary scene as a whole, what do you think of the temper and quality of work that's appearing?

■ *Johnson:* I don't think any country, at the moment, is in a very striking stage of literary development. We're not doing anything particularly dashing in England. If we were I'd immediately throw out names without having to think, but I can't immediately pin a name to anyone who arouses deep and abiding admiration. It's very much the same in America, and also in the Soviet Union though they are producing some poetry of interest. I can't read it—I have to rely on the translation—but I suspect some of it is uncommonly good.

On the other hand, isn't the whole history of literature rather like that? We go through periods when no country seems to be doing very much; and then suddenly there's a great outcropping, a great flowering of Art. It may happen any place at any time, (I think it has been happening with painting in Australia) but at present I don't find much to cheer about.

To our positive discredit, we are producing a great deal of work that is morally ugly and, to a degree, are encouraging people to think that the morally ugly is the only interesting and desirable thing. This is not only nonsense; it's dangerous nonsense, both morally and aesthetically.

N.   Aesthetically?

■ *Johnson:* Let me put it like this: We are in process of encouraging people to believe that only the pornographic, the sick, and the sadistic, are real for our time, but literature of this sort satiates very quickly, and blunts the taste. The reader brought up on it isn't going to find the slightest charm in, say, *Ce'billon fils*. He will have ruined his literary palate even for sexual pleasure and delight.

N.   In light of· this—the absence of notable work—what advice would you give the younger writer starting off on a career?

■ *Johnson:* First of all, he should try to achieve emotional balance. We seem to seesaw. Much of the time we're preoccupied with the morally ugly, the deeply pessimistic. Then we veer off to sheer hilarity, verging upon nonsense. It's better to sit in the middle of this seesaw than to commit yourself to either of the ends.

I think it's a great mistake for a writer—especially a young writer—to say, "This life is no good, we're all going to hell, blackness is all and blackness is descending." On the manic end, it's equally bad to go off in a burst of hilarity, to say, "Everything's all right, there's nothing to worry about." To take your stand on either is to achieve a literary imbalance. Either way means falsehood.

At present the largest number of falsehoods are emerging on the side of blackness. Now, the world is not quite so bad as a lot of young writers think. (But maybe it's part of being young to find everything appalling.) Later on life begins to seem a little brighter, if only because there's less of it ahead.

N. In looking back over your own career, which of your books emerges as the most satisfying to you? That is, if you can pit one against the other.

■ *Johnson:* I think one can do that. I think one does it, in fact, and at times it can be discomfiting, especially if you don't like a recent work too well. Writers are always supposed to progress, you know, according to people who don't understand literary history.

My first novel, *This Bed Thy Center,* wasn't a bad job for a girl of twenty-two. You must realize that I now feel entirely disassociated from that girl; she was a different person. Life does that; we can't escape some degree of compartmentalization, some degree of real change in ourselves.

In more recent years both of my comedies—*The Unspeakable Skipton* and *Night and Silence*—plus a rather neglected book published in 1956 gave me great pleasure. It was called *The Last Resort* in England, but because Cleveland Amory had already used almost the same title I had to call it *The Sea and The Wedding* in America. As I said, it was virtually neglected, but that doesn't stop me from being fond of it. So if I were asked to keep just three of my novels those would be the ones. If I were allowed four I'd include the first one.

N. This may be difficult to do, but is it possible to explain the genesis of any novel—the source of the basic desire to write it and the characters you ultimately use?

■ *Johnson:* As far as I'm concerned—and I think every writer is highly individualistic about this—a novel must spring from three sources.

First there must be a theme—something important you want to say. And this *must* come first.

Second, there must be a character—a character you want to work with.

Third, there must be a place. It may be a place like Bruges, where I spent some time in my youth, a place I wanted to say something about. What never occurs to me is a story as such, a plot in any formal sense. I have always had difficulty with plots.

As I mentioned, every writer treats this genesis in an individual manner. My method, my approach, might be quite wrong for other writers.

N. Since you and Sir Charles do travel a great deal, and since you've recently spent considerable time in both the United States and Russia, I'd like to go into your observations regarding the strengths and weaknesses of literature in each nation.

■ *Johnson:* Well, our most recent Russian journey began in Moscow. As we had come to know many Russian writers both in their own country and in London, we were met by old friends. We talked with writers in Moscow—fortunately, we know the literary circles fairly extensively there—then went down to stay with Sholokhov at Vyeshenskaya, which is right on the Don (about 125 miles from Volgograd) and is very exciting. Then back to Moscow for continued talking.

My overall impression is that their literary life is active to a degree. There is reader-participation to an extent I wish we found in America and in England. It is quite startling. Having just had my first novel published in Russia, I found readers everywhere. They not only wrote to me from all parts of the Soviet Union, but when we had a meeting with our readers in Russian in the Baumann district, at a perfectly ordinary branch library, three hundred people turned out. About eighty of them spoke, all giving something like brief book reviews, and the audience seemed to have read our work with an intimacy I wouldn't expect to find anywhere else. The Russians are passionately interested in literature—this, of course, isn't new. They always have been. Now, however, the interest extends to a much larger segment of the population.

In America on the other hand, you find more work being produced. Perhaps this is the result of widespread creative writing courses. (I don't think a creative writing course is necessarily good for a young writer. I reserve my judgment on this because I've seen it taught badly and I've seen it taught well. Nevertheless, it does interest masses of young people in writing.) I should think that in America, where there's such an enormous desire to work creatively in one form or another, that something important is bound to be produced if only by the sheer mass of production, which seems to me inevitable in the long run.

In England we fall between the two stools. Our readers presumably care about us, or we'd starve; but a great number of our writers make most of their income through the B.B.C. or through some kind of teaching or reviewing. In England we're narrowing our ambitions. We're beginning to think that there's one very small circle of endeavor into which everything must fit. The only thing that really counts, in other words, is "angry young man literature" (which I call "the literature of trivial protest") but it doesn't draw (except in a few cases) very large readership. I am taking the theater into consideration here, as well as the novel.

Now, I don't want to be misunderstood. You can write the most awful trash and have an enormous readership. You can write trashy plays that run for years and years. But, conversely, if you write books that no one wants to read, and plays that nobody wants to see, something is wrong. I'm inclined to think that something is wrong in England at this moment. Perhaps things are wrong in America, too, and in Russia, but I talk with more knowledge of my own country. Here, for some reason or another, we are exalting a minority literature because we've developed a sort of claque system to cheer it on.

N. I'd like to turn again to theater, for a moment, because I feel something extraordinary is happening that involves both England and America. I think it can be summed up in a play of debatable merit called *Luther* and an actor of unquestioned merit named Albert Finney who has become the most talked-about and probably the most popular actor in the United States. In fact, Broadway as a whole has almost been dominated, in recent years, by British plays and British performers. How would you evaluate this?

■ *Johnson:* I think I must be more general about this, and a bit nationalistic. England produces extremely good actors. We have always done this, and at some levels—the middle-aged character actor, as an example—we are supreme. We grow them as easily as poppies.

Finney is a very attractive, very intelligent actor. I saw *Luther* and feel as you do; I don't think it's a very good play. Finney did what he could with it. I don't think it was a good play because, when I reached the end, I didn't know what made Luther tick.

Finney is an attractive and intelligent actor—but I think that we are rather good at producing his kind. There are others, and there have been others, of his caliber. For example, I shall never forget the young Richard Burton in 1951 in the tetralogy of history plays at Stratford-on-Avon. I felt then that we were going to have an actor of the very highest rank—not simply to rank with our Oliviers, but with our Irvings, Keanes, Garricks. But he seems to have left us, and his great potential, behind. I hope I am wrong about this.

N. British theater seems very exciting—

■ *Johnson:* It is. The only trouble, right now, is the way it's becoming so curiously divided. On one side we have the purely commercial theater which is kept going by the "coach parties" which come in from all over the British Isles for an evening at the theater. This will keep certain plays going, plays that may have no artistic value whatever, for years.

On the other side we have a narrow range of plays which are appreciated by a very small audience, but simply cannot break through to a vast public lying in the middle. Not wanting the purely commercial stuff, on one hand, and not wanting the extremely narrow stuff on the other, we end up with a great vacuum in theater that needs to be filled. What's going to fill it I don't know.

N. The final question reverts to your own career. Could you state your primary objective as a writer? Your ultimate goal of attainment?

■ *Johnson:* I suppose this is so personal—yet so common to all writers—that it hardly seems worth saying; but I have always felt that what I really wanted to do is to write a novel in which I can say something in a way that will make people think, "Why, I've always thought that, but never found the words for it." This is my greatest interest—to try to dive down into characters as deeply as I can—characters in relation to society. I am not interested at all in the study of character in vacuum. That is purely narcissistic literature. "This is all about me, I'm the important figure, nothing else matters, I'm apart from society." This interests me no more than if I were to see a painting that had a central figure with nothing whatsoever behind it, which would, in terms of visual art, be an absurdity.

I don't want to read that sort of thing, and I don't want to write it. I distinctly recall the pleasure I found in Russia by talking to a group of Don Cossack women who told me that when they were growing up, through adolescence to maturity, they had felt as my heroine felt. All the miseries, joys, shames, despairs, satisfactions. I was glad of this; because the difference between girls in a Don village and girls in the 1930's in the suburbs of South London could scarcely seem greater; yet I had rather hoped that what I said about my girl would be essentially true of any girl; and in Russia they found identification.

In the main, of course, one always struggles to do something important and to do it well; and no writer can ever feel totally satisfied even when a job is done. The only flick of triumph is when one can say, "I have achieved just a shadow of what I set out to do."

"Too many of our current American writers give way to the pushing of time, the quick answers, and they push for solid answers, thinking they can't afford vagueness."

James Jones
Interviewed in Paris, France, November, 1963

James Jones

N. *From Here To Eternity* and *The Thin Red Line* are two of the most distinctive novels to spring from World War II. James Jones has written other novels of equal merit, but most readers, when they consider Jones, think of these two immediately, perhaps because they are the most revealing works of fiction to emerge from the grueling Pacific theater of war. Since it's a long route back—from Mr. Jones' present life in Paris to the Pacific in wartime to a Midwestern origin—I'd like first to have him fill in the chronology.

■ *Jones:* Well, I was born in Illinois in 1921, and I grew up to be a Depression teen-ager—a little too late to get into the McCarthy troubles (fortunately for myself, because if I'd been able to I would have). My family was middle-class—my grandfather was first a sheriff, then a criminal lawyer, in the little town of Robinson. He had one of the biggest houses in town, set up his four sons very well, and died in 1929, a month before the crash, whereupon we discovered that everything was in Insull stock. So I had a childhood that was at first fairly safe and secure, but from 1930 on I lived in a very insecure sort of world. Most of us did, at that time, not only in Robinson but everywhere.

About the only thing I remember of high school that had any significance at all, as far as the future went, was the fact that I used to write some way-out English themes. I realize now that I got a peculiar emotional release in this theme writing because it was closer to fiction than essay. After I was graduated from high school I worked on construction jobs, then went into the Army because my father couldn't afford to send me to college. I didn't think of working my way through school—I guess I was pretty much at loose ends. I joined the Army in 1939, when I was eighteen.

When I enlisted I had a choice of where I wanted to go—and I wanted overseas. I had read too much P. C. Wren in my youth, and I thought it would be adventurous to see the tropics. My choice lay between the Philippines and Hawaii. I chose the Philippines, but my request was beyond the quota by three men, so I was sent to Hawaii, which was very lucky for me. My father had originally suggested the Pacific because, as he said, "If you're out in the Pacific you'll be safe when we get into the war. We'll be sending troops to Europe to die, but you'll be safe in the Pacific." Instead, of course, I was in the thick of it when the United States got into the war.

N.   When did you start writing *From Here To Eternity?*

■ *Jones:*   Well, it was a long time after that. I started writing in 1940 when I was in what we then called the Air Force. I was stationed at Hickam Field, the showplace of the Islands. Whenever Dorothy Lamour or Bing Crosby came over they were always brought to Hickam Field to be photographed. This was to help build up the services. Anyway, they had to have very good grass, so they had about two thousand men pushing lawn mowers. I was one of them and I didn't like it. The adventurous army I had pictured wasn't equipped with a goddam lawn mower. So because of this I eventually transferred to the Infantry, which was an unheard-of thing. I ended up at Scofield Barracks. Again, I was lucky, because had I still been at Hickam Field on December 7, I might have gotten killed.

While I'd been at Hickam, I had read Thomas Wolfe's *Look Homeward, Angel.* That boy, Eugene, and his dreams seemed so much like myself that I decided I had been a writer all the time without realizing it, so I started writing. I wrote odds and ends the rest of the time I was in the Army, but I was discharged in June of 1944. I went to New York University for a while, and it was there in New York on the GI Bill that I wrote a first draft of a novel that has never been published. I took it to Maxwell Perkins at Scribners. He turned it down, so I quit school and went to Florida and spent a year and a half working on fishing boats. I could work on the fishing boats at night and write in the daytime, sleeping part of the night on the boat so I wouldn't be too tired to write. We'd go out in the evening and lay our nets, then sleep until dawn, then haul in the fish and bring them in. I'd have the rest of the day to write, so I rewrote the book twice again. The second time Scribners turned it down less forcefully, and the third time, after I sent it in, I left Florida and went home to Illinois. On the way I stopped off at Tallahassee to see my brother who was working there in the Red Cross, and while I was there I wrote Perkins a letter about an idea I had for a new book. I summed it up in a very small four-line paragraph, but when I got home to Illinois he had sent me a wire which said, "Would you consider laying aside the first book in preference to beginning a second if we give you a $500 advance now, with further advances to come later?" This was pretty much of a gamble for a publisher, you know, but he was good at taking these gambles. He'd done this same thing with Scott Fitzgerald's first novel. I decided to go along with the deal. The first book never has been printed, and when I looked at it, later, I realized it would have to be an entirely different book if I tried to rewrite it.

So I began *From Here To Eternity* on the strength of that wire and the advance.

N. How did you react to its critical reception, and to sales?

■ *Jones:* I didn't realize it was as important at it was. Critically, I don't care very much, and as far as sales are concerned I didn't realize it was as big a best-seller as it turned out to be. I was pretty green. I just accepted everything without question.

N. Now, after four successful novels, you're living in Paris. Can you explain what drew you here—and what keeps you here?

■ *Jones:* Well, my wife and I were living in New York when I finished *The Pistol.* I wanted to spend some time in Europe—just curiosity, I guess, and a vague idea for doing a novel. I was very much in love with Django Reinhardt and his music, and I got an idea for a novel using Django, or the spirit of Django, and American jazz men living in France, a lot of whom I talked to after they came back to the States.

We decided to come over here for a year or eighteen months, just to get background material for this book. But we stayed on after that. We were here for two years, loved Paris, and then we had our baby. So we had a choice of either finding a new apartment or buying a place (which meant committing ourselves to a long-term stay). I stumbled onto this place on the Ile-St.-Louis, probably one of the most beautiful parts of Paris, and the only way we could get it was to buy it. So we talked it over and decided to stay for an indefinite period, probably ten years at least. After buying it we knew we wouldn't have enough money left to go home, so even if we didn't like it here we'd be stuck.

Paris is a magnificent place. They put up statues of authors and name streets after them. Can you imagine Hemingway Avenue in New York? Paris is like walking through a perpetual painting that's on rollers. You never look—it comes to you. There's something about the light of the *Ile-de-France* (the section of which Paris is a part) that makes it almost necessary for painters. They come here, live here, work here.

Writers don't have to come to Paris. Yet there's a special joy in living here, a camaraderie. You know that other people are getting up to go to work laboring over typewriters or canvases, and this is helpful.

Socially, there's another great thing about Paris. If you're a success in New York as a writer you sort of leap bodily from one group to another. The two don't merge—the successful and the unsuccessful. Here you go to an artist's dinner party or buffet, or just to spend an evening, and you see six or eight guys who appear to be half starved, in blue jeans and old leather jackets, rubbing elbows with people in evening dress. It doesn't make much difference here—the success factor, I mean. They know that one year Smith will be on top and somebody else will be down, and the next year that somebody else will be up and Smith will be down. There isn't the success grouping in Paris that there is in New York or most any place.

There isn't any real group sense in Paris, now—not like there was in the 1920's. There's no group of Americans or comingled Americans or other nationalities who share the same philosophy about art or life like there was in the 1920's. This group was anti-bourgeois, and they were attacking the cheap mentality of the American bourgeois. This doesn't exist any more. We've all grown out beyond that—now everyone is on his own. You meet the writers only socially. You don't philosophize about the arts, and the Philistines like they did, at least from what I've experienced.

N. In looking at the current literary scene, could you pick out trends or individual books or events you find helpful—and similar elements you deplore?

■ *Jones:* I'd probably have to reflect everything through the view of my personal prism. I've become pretty "sot in my ways"— pretty fixed to my own style. When I write I like to get in a lot of the meat of life, how a town looks, how it smells, how things feel and taste. To do this you've got to have extra space to work in. This makes the book longer, and it cuts down 'somewhat on the theatricality, the theatrical dramatic sense of the book. But to me it's part of living, and when I read a book it's what I want to read, along with the characterizations and the problems and the emotions that form the actual structure.

It seems to me that this is an American thing, or at least it passed from England to us. Proust was the exception in France, but with us it's passed from the early English novel (it sort of got lost in the middle English novel) to America. You can call it realism, but it's something we've lived and worked at for a long time. It seems to me that it isn't being done any more in American literature. I don't know why. Maybe there isn't time, either for the writer or the reader, and I think it's a shame. However, I intend to go on working this way.

In connection with the same thing—this sense of the press of time—we get involved with the philosophy of today, which involves the business of symbolizing life in easily apprehended capsules. We end up with books which make symbolic—in a very overt fashion—the problems of the world and the problems of society. I think this is dangerous. It's too easy to make up symbols and construct a book before you write it.

In my case I start with a theme which I can more or less state in a fairly simple sentence, a group of characters, and a milieu in which I want the book placed. I throw all of these into the pot and let them sort of stew and write their own book. I feel that in this way the symbolisms which grow as the book and the characters grow are more subtle and more true to what life is really like. You can't get this by imposing on life an attitude, either symbolic or nonsymbolic, which outlines and determines all the factors in life. At bottom I find my method the true heart, the true depth, of what we so sloppily call "realism." Too many of our current American writers give way to this pushing of time, the quick answers, and they push for solid answers, thinking they can't afford vagueness. Well, life is vague, you know, and every time you come up with a solid answer about a vague life you get an ideology which doesn't include all the factors.

Right now I'm starting a book in which I'm not at all sure of what will happen. I have a rough idea, but it's very rough. It's not in continuity with any of my other books. It's totally different. This is scary, in a way, but I find that my brain isn't capable of creating—before I start writing—everything about a group of characters, the essential situations, the symbolic meanings. These will emerge as the book goes along. Whole new avenues and facets of characterization and events will spring up that I can explore. If I line it out too completely and begin with a plot which contains certain immutable symbols that represent what I believe about life and people, then I've limited myself in such a way that I can't explore those new unanticipated avenues that will open up later.

N. One of your novels, *The Pistol*, was quite different from all your others. It was less physical than metaphysical. How did you come to write it?

■ *Jones: The Pistol* was an exercise, actually. A deliberate attempt to write that type of novel. It began with an idea, an event that happened to myself, this business of getting a pistol by accident on the day that Hawaii was bombed. I was doing a number of short stories at the time, and suddenly it occurred to me to use the pistol as a symbol of human salvation, the lengths to which people would go to acquire this symbolic salvation. They would rob, steal, cheat, beat somebody up, to get it—and once they got it, to keep it. It seemed such a perfect symbol to me, philosophically, related to all human salvation, whether the particular religion is a matter of Catholicism or the Democratic party or communism. (It doesn't make any difference; they're really all the same.) I used the pistol, and the series of events built around the pistol, to develop and elaborate upon this theme. *The Pistol* is more of a European novel, the French novel in particular, and I enjoyed doing it but I'd feel frustrated if I had to do it all the time. I would probably feel safer, but I'd be frustrated in the sense that I wouldn't be working with the real meat of living. I wouldn't be getting the subtle qualities of symbolization. They're what I'm striving for.

N. How do you feel about the beat movement that flourished for a while recently?

■ *Jones:* Well, I think that like any group orientation it had a tendency to take a great deal away from the individual's view of life. I think that all these kids were looking at life with the same pair of eyeballs. Mel Brooks, on one of his records where he's imitating a beat singer, says, "We're all singing, everybody's listening, we're all singing, but I have the mouth." You know—one pair of eyeballs for several hundred people. I think the same thing would apply to Madison Avenue and any other group of organized thought. It's a typically American organizational thing. Which is strange, because the beats wanted to be anti-organizational.

N. If you were to give advice to the young American who's serious about writing as a career, what would that advice be?

■ *Jones:* Well, I'd first say to read everybody you can, everything you can, whether it's in your own field or not. Of course, read mainly in your own field, but study on your own. Stay away from theories which other people have created about writers and work five solid hours a day on your own work. That's about all I can say.

N. Not too long ago I pulled a boner in reviewing your book *The Thin Red Line.* I read it hastily and dismissed it as just another war novel. Then I felt uneasy about my opinion so I went back and read it again and found an immense vitality and richness that made it an outstandingly fine book. (The denouement of the homosexual situation, for example, is one of the most original and hilarious incidents in modern fiction.) Now, if a reviewer can make a mistake like this, and in all good conscience, I wonder what a writer in your position thinks of the state of literary criticism in the United States at present.

■ *Jones:* I think there are two different things we're talking about. True criticism in American letters is generally confined to very small magazines and pays very little. It's done by very dedicated college professors who make very little money and have too many kids. About 150 people will read the piece of criticism, and it will come out anywhere from one to four years after the book is published.

Now, the book reviewing business, which can make or break books, is an entirely different thing. I'm afraid very few of our true critics work at reviewing. I could name three or four, but your major book reviewers are people who have to read eight or ten books a week, which is pretty hard on them. The reviewer isn't told to take a book away for a month to see what he thinks about it. It should work that way, but it doesn't because of time and pressure. So I don't think, all in all, that American criticism is in a great state at the moment, but I think it's in a better state than book reviewing.

In the book reviewing end of things somebody seems to be sitting at a desk saying, "Well, now we must cover this and we must cover that" and he portions it all out—somebody, usually just anybody, gets this, and his matching nonentity gets that. If the editor of a particular newspaper happens to have met me at a cocktail party and says, "Gee, that guy isn't as crude and horrible as I thought he would be," he'll give my book to somebody who might treat it favorably. On the other hand, if I meet somebody at a cocktail party and he says, "What a horrible bore that man is!" he'll give it to somebody he knows damn' well will pan it.

It's all very strange. It doesn't mean very much except that it helps or hurts sales, but fortunately, the book reviewing business isn't quite as devastating as the field of theater criticism, where the critics can actually close a play in a few days or a few weeks.

N. Since you're a young novelist, with a great deal of constructive time left, could you outline your own plans and ambitions?

■ *Jones:* Well, I've reached the age now where I'm pretty sure

I've got more novels laid out in notebooks than I'll ever be able to finish. But I guess I'd like to get deeper into what makes people tick, people of our age; what makes them terrified, or brave, or bloodthirsty, or whatever they are. We've got a very hard world to live with, most of us. The way we try to cope with it ought to be of interest to future generations.

I've got one further novel planned with a war background which is based (naturally) upon my own experience—with the period of a year or so while the war was still going on, when I was in a hospital in the United States, the kind of wild, crazy life everybody was leading. It seemed like everybody was working as a welder, all the girls were riveters who spent their nights with us veterans at the Peabody Hotel in Memphis. I wonder how many rivets they missed the next day, how many short-fused grenades went out. It was a weird time. I think five of those books would make a set—I guess you'd call it a pentalogy.

The pentalogy would begin with *From Here To Eternity* and end with *Some Came Running*. This new book would be somewhere in the middle, right after *The Thin Red Line*.

Now, *The Thin Red Line* was a book I wanted very badly to do, and for a long time. The one I'm working on right now, however, is totally different. Ostensibly, it's about skindiving. I've done quite a bit of it, have gotten fairly good at it. Skindivers are a strange breed of men—fascinating. Why they seek the danger they go out for, I don't know, and I'll probably have to write the book to find out. I may be wrong, but I think this type of physical courage is—for men of my time—very much involved with odd sexual frustrations. This is what I'd like to explore in this book, but it has nothing to do with my other books except that (philosophically) it carries over from the preoccupation with physical courage. I'm also a little irritated with people saying that I'm not capable of writing a love story, so I want to do a real love story in this book, too.

N. My final question concerns *Some Came Running*, which had what could be called a mixed reception from critics and reviewers. Can you recall your own reactions to the press at that time?

■ *Jones:* Well, as you might remember, *From Here To Eternity* got its share of bad reviews, but it was such a runaway best-seller that the bad reviews were forgotten, and I think a lot of people were waiting to lower the boom on my second novel. Or maybe the bad reviews weren't forgotten, and the reviewers were so irritated at having the book sell in spite of them, that they lowered the boom. I don't really know.

Some Came Running was a long novel, and it had about ten major characters. It got panned, but the critical reception didn't bother me because it sold well and made money. The money was important because it enabled me to go on writing.

I still think *Some Came Running* is the best book I've written. *The Thin Red Line* did what I wanted it to do—there were no loose ends .or unresolved qualities about it—but it was an easier book to write because I didn't attempt as big a job as I did with *Some Came Running.* In that one I tried to dig deeper into people, and what makes them tick, and why they are what they are, than in anything else I've written. So I really don't care about the critical reception. I only hope the book I'm working on now comes off as well. Even though it may have fallen short of perfection, it attempted more, succeeded with more, and regardless of the criticism it got it still dangled itself in front of me—like a donkey is led by a carrot on a stick—as an incentive.

"... to define a publisher's obligation is to state his goal, which is to publish good books ... books that have a lasting value."

William Jovanovich
Interviewed in New York, October, 1963

N

William Jovanovich

N. The prominence of Harcourt, Brace & World as a publisher of the first rank (both in the quality of books issued and in the ever-important sales figures) is inseparably linked with the ambition and direction of its president, William Jovanovich. His firm —now the third largest in the world—is perhaps most readily identified with such titles as Mary McCarthy's, *The Group*, Helen MacInnes's stories of suspense, Joy Adamson's *Elsa* books, and a glittering miscellany by such outstanding writers as Kingsley Amis, Erich Maria Remarque, and William Golding. In talking to Mr. Jovanovich I'd first like to ask him what he has sought to accomplish during his years with Harcourt, Brace & World.

■ *Jovanovich:* Actually, our means of growth has been both internal and external. We've grown by developing our basic list, but at the same time we've acquired other companies. The latter phase of our development is probably complete, now.

The question is always raised: "How big can a publishing house get?" Generally speaking, I think people really mean, "How large can a publishing house become and still maintain the criteria and standards of good publishing?" I'm not sure I know the answer to that question—whether direct or implied. I suppose the answer really lies in not trying to publish too many books of one kind. We, as you know, publish trade books (books of general interest), children's books, elementary textbooks, high school textbooks, college textbooks, and educational tests. We are diversified in a sufficient number of fields so that we can't really become "overpublished" in any one.

The question of size in publishing is misunderstood, in any event. There is a feeling that "distinguished" is an adjective that can only be applied to a small publisher. I think this is a mistake. I know some distinguished large publishers and I know some not-so-distinguished small publishers. But rather murky opinions and attitudes take over here, so I won't pursue the point.

N. In the area of relations that exist between publisher and author, how do you define the publisher's obligations to his writers?

■ *Jovanovich:* Well, I think that to define the publisher's obligation is to state his goal, which is to publish good books. By good books I mean books that have a lasting value—books that are well written, sound in thought, serious in content. The publisher really bears the obligation to tell an author whether or not he believes the manuscript falls into the category of a good book. Now, if he disagrees, I assume that the author finds another publisher. Certainly the author has his own standards and his own aims, just as the publisher has his standards and aims, and when these coincide I think you have a good publishing relationship.

Publishers are sometimes timid with their authors—usually, I'm afraid, to the disadvantage of the author. On numerous occasions we have persuaded an author to put aside a particular book, for his benefit (we believe) as well as our own. At other times we have, in common discussion, created ideas for books that an author proceeds to write. Essentially, it is the publisher's role to make public—not himself to create—and it is a great mistake for a publisher to get himself confused with his authors. He is the purveyor of good works—not the creator of them.

N. In line with this, what types of books, what types of writers, are of the greatest interest to you?

■ *Jovanovich:* Again we'd have to make a distinction between general books and educational books, though I don't think the distinction is as broad as it once was. Generally, of course, one looks for new writers who have something creative and original and imaginative in them. One has to nurture these qualities in writers.

One of our problems today as book publishers is that many of the media that used to assist us in nurturing writers have disappeared. A young fiction writer, for example, can't find the market for short stories that was available thirty years ago. Magazines now carry almost all nonfiction and little fiction. Faulkner and Hemingway used to appear in *Esquire,* Faulkner and Cozzens in *Collier's* and *The Saturday Evening Post.* This is largely a thing of the past.

One of the results of this market decline, incidentally, is that in our desire to encourage and nurture young authors we sometimes encourage them to stretch material to book length when we shouldn't be doing this. I don't know the answer to this problem—perhaps no publisher knows the answer.

However, I don't think that book publishers ought to start magazines solely as an answer to this particular problem. I'm afraid this takes more expertise than most book publishers have.

Essentially, a publisher looks for the qualities in a writer he would appreciate as a reader. Perhaps this suggests that a good publisher is an amateur—in some ways I think he is. Once he becomes too professional about the problems of publishing he may forget the source of his enterprise—this being the writer himself.

N.   By turning to look at the other side of the coin, what do you think the publisher owes the public?

■ *Jovanovich:* Obviously the book publisher has specific great obligations to the public because book publishing is, by its nature, the freest form of expression in America. We don't have the pressures from advertisers that magazines and newspapers encounter. We don't have the elements of censorship that other media, such as radio and television suffer. I think the publisher incurs a serious obligation to make proper use of his great freedom. Some of the most important controversial ideas of the day find their way into books. Publishers should have both the courage of their convictions, and a respect for freedom of expression, in publishing books that may be contrary to general opinion.

I think, on the whole, that American publishers fulfill their obligations quite ably. Perhaps we don't reach as many people as we might—we need a better distribution system, but this is another subject, involving problems which may be largely insoluble. In fact, perhaps we expect too much. I don't think that book publishing will ever reach audiences comparable to those reached by magazines, radio, or television. Perhaps we shouldn't try, because when we do we often end up doing a rather poor job of publishing, and produce the "made" or packaged book which is often heavily promoted and often not worth publishing.

N.   Granting freedom of expression, do you think there is an obligation to publish or refrain from publishing works that violate your own moral or ethical stand?

■ *Jovanovich:* This is fundamentally a difficult question, for the reason that the publisher must rest on his own judgment and not pretend to represent the public in making judgments. The fact is, however, that if you use a criterion of serious writing, serious purpose, I think you have no difficulty in recognizing works that are, for example, licentious or salacious in intent. You have no difficulty recognizing works that are lacking in taste and in serious motive.

I haven't found this to be much of a problem, and we've never suffered serious censorship problems regarding our own list. Occasionally you get pressures and resentments from certain groups, religious or political, but this sort of thing can be withstood if you are patient—particularly if you don't become too aroused immediately. One thing I've learned is this: Never let authors answer the criticisms or censorships from such groups. They invariably cast more oil on the random fires.

It doesn't really take very much divining to judge which works are valid and of serious importance, if you yourself are serious. It's a sort of cycle. You invariably come back to what your own goals are. Of course, if your goals are to publish pornography, your judgments will be doubtful.

N. I'd like to turn to your own career—you've come so far in a remarkably short time that it can't be an average success story.

■ *Jovanovich:* There's a book called *Growing Up Absurd*, and the title should belong to any autobiography I write, actually, because I did grow up absurd—following a career so Horatio Algerlike as to resemble stock fiction.

I was born in Colorado in a coal camp. My father was a Montenegrin immigrant, my mother was a Polish immigrant. I went to public schools in Denver, won a scholarship to the University of Colorado where I was a major in English literature. I won a fellowship to Harvard, later went into the war for four years, came out, and started working toward a doctorate at Columbia University. I finally ran out of money, and this is what led me into publishing. I needed a job very badly. I joined Harcourt, Brace in 1947 as a college traveling salesman.

Now the truly absurd element comes in. Seven and one-half years later I became president of Harcourt, Brace. That was nine years ago—I became president of a publishing house at the age of thirty-four. Perhaps it's all somewhat like what Somerset Maugham says somewhere—that it's better to be lucky than skillful.

N. You're also writing a book, aren't you?

■ *Jovanovich:* Yes, I'm writing a book about publishing and writing and learning for Harper & Row. I'm afraid it's been a rather disastrous experience, because I'm beginning to understand the point of view of an author. For a publisher this is not practical knowledge nor a salutary form of enlightenment.

I've found myself being evasive with Harper over my writing and my delay in writing, and I've finally come to the point where I don't answer their letters at all. This suggests to me that authors do have a reason for their basic antagonism toward their publisher. But I think, once I finish the book, that I'll regain my perspective.

At any rate, I'm having a great deal of fun writing this book because I'm trying, in effect, to suggest the concepts of book publishing in the United States—indeed, in the world—without writing a textbook. Whether I'll succeed, I don't know. It's a series of eleven essays, and I don't know who my audience will be, though I presume it will consist mostly of people in publishing. But I'll let Harper worry about that.

N.   When you look at the publishing industry today, what do you think of the promise and quality of young writers coming up, as opposed to what we could see a decade ago, or two decades ago?

■ *Jovanovich:*   I think it would be foolhardy to suggest that we have—in America, at any rate—as large a number of promising writers at present as we had (for instance) in the 1920's. But perhaps numbers aren't significant—one good writer may make up for twenty mediocre ones, and there are some strong, vigorous writers today.

I think that writers are affected by the almost cosmical problems of our world in that so many haven't been able to apply imaginative ideas in a meaningful way, and a sense of politics, of social problems, seems lacking in so many. Writers today tend to write in a very restricted way, but this doesn't mean that they are totally unimaginative.

It's difficult to generalize about a generation of writers—I suppose we must wait until the generation has passed. This may be a more fertile period of writing than I acknowledge. Ask me this question twenty years from now, and I'm sure I can speak with more assurance and less hesitation.

N.   If you were to speak to the younger writer, what sort of advice would you give him regarding his own grooming and preparation?

■ *Jovanovich:*   Obviously, the first thing a young writer should do is write. This seems a very simple statement, but it's serious. He should write, and write, and write some more, and try to find a market for his writing, wherever that market may be. I don't think that magazines and newspapers and radio and television are bad influences on the young writer. If he can be published or heard in any media I think it's good for him, and it's good for refinement of his craft.

The main piece of advice I'd give the young writer is simply to finish things. In most writers I think there is a logical development, a sequence of growth, but I don't think he develops or grows unless he finishes one piece of work before moving on to another, preferably another piece of quite a different sort.

There is an opposite tendency that's almost as dangerous as flitting about from one piece of unfinished business to the next. This is the tendency to prolong a work, through grants and fellowships or aid from publishers (perhaps all three), and live with it far too long. This may amount to a type of specialization that isn't illuminating, in the long run, or profitable in the short run.

Perhaps what I'm really trying to say is that in our time we ought to develop more men of letters, men whose profession is writing, writing in a variety of media on a variety of subjects. Whether this is sensible or illogical, I don't know—but it seems to me that the only way to develop a craft is to encompass as much of that craft as one can.

"I believe that my critics have a right to voice their opinions, and I'm not simply being a 'good guy' about this. I've blasted the other guy, and he has a right to blast me. This is a free society and everyone is entitled to express an opinion. The only thing I ask of my critics is this: read the book."

Victor Lasky
Interviewed in New York, July, 1963

Victor Lasky

Note: Recorded in July, 1963, this interview preceded the assassination of President John F. Kennedy. This interview, dealing with depth and breadth in matters of research, is of value as a documentation of method, quite separated from the tragedy which occurred later.

N. *J. F. K., The Man and The Myth*, by Victor Lasky, added a great deal of excitement to the summer 1963 book season. The big, expensive book, published by Macmillan, became an immediate best seller, spurred by mixed reviews that emphasized its controversial nature. Perhaps never has an American President and the tenor of his administration, been so critically examined during the administration's reign. Some critics condemned the book as a totally negative view of Kennedy. Others praised it as an exceptionally honest study that refused to heed accepted taboos. Yet in all fairness it must be stated that *Man And Myth* deserved its best-seller status for the depth of its analysis and the quality of Lasky's writing performance.

In talking to Mr. Lasky I would first like to ask him how he came to write the book.

■ *Lasky:* The easy answer would be to say that I wanted to make a dollar; but the truth is that I was first seized with the idea during the 1960 presidential campaign when Norman Cousins, editor of *The Saturday Review,* asked me to review a book by Arthur Schlesinger, Jr., *Kennedy Or Nixon, Does It Make Any Difference?* This was one of those campaign quickies in which Mr. Schlesinger attempted to get liberals excited about the then-Senator Kennedy, who was the candidate on the Democratic ticket.

In reviewing the book I had the feeling that Mr. Schlesinger was overlooking many of the facts underlying Kennedy's rise to power and his grab for the nomination. I also felt that he adopted a double standard insofar as he questioned Mr. Nixon's ability to change without being motivated by opportunism. What I'm trying to say is that the thesis of the book, in my humble estimation, was that

Mr. Nixon could not change his position without being labeled an opportunist by Mr. Schlesinger, but that Mr. Kennedy could change positions, as he did, on every issue of our times. He did it, according to Mr. Schlesinger, out of idealism because he was— quote—maturing—unquote. Mr. Schlesinger found ambition a horrible thing in Mr. Nixon but a great thing in Mr. Kennedy.

So, at that time, I wrote a rather strong review at the height of the campaign, which I later broadened out to become the best-selling *J. F. K., The Man and The Myth*. I hope I explained this sufficiently.

N.   For the sake of background I'd like to go more into your past, bits of autobiography and accomplishment.

■ *Lasky:* Well, I was born in New York, brought up on the streets of New York, went to New York City public schools, and was graduated from Brooklyn College. I went to work for the *Chicago Sun* at an early age. I didn't know better—I'm kidding. I was a reporter and rewrite man on the *Sun* for several years. Then I went off to war, became a combat correspondent for *Stars and Stripes* in the European theater of operations.

After the war I returned to Chicago, served a stint as New York correspondent for the *Chicago Sun*—this was before it became the *Sun-Times*. Then I went to work for the *New York World Telegram*, joined the Scripps-Howard organization, spent some time as a Washington correspondent and traveled a great deal.

In 1950, with Ralph De Toledano I wrote a book called *Seeds Of Treason*, a book about the Alger Hiss case that won some modicum of fame. Following this, as with most writers, I went to Hollywood for a few years and made a lot of money. I don't know what happened to it, but I made it. I made a picture with Dore Schary, a full-length documentary called *The Hoaxsters*, an expose of Communist infiltration tactics, which I'm proud to say was nominated for the Academy Award. Unfortunately a better documentary, *The Sea Around Us*, by Rachel Carson, beat us out. (I have so much admiration for Rachel Carson that I'm not really unhappy about it, but because I was all prepared to accept the Oscar in New York I felt rather overdressed that evening.)

Following this I spent about ten years as a free-lance writer in and out of politics. I edited anthologies, I wrote for magazines, then I joined the North American Newspaper Alliance where I am at present, a syndicated columnist appearing in about 125 papers.

In 1960, when I became interested in the campaign, I took a leave of absence to go to work for the Republican campaign. The

outgrowth, of course, is this book, and for the past three years—
except for doing my column and making some fast trips here and
there—I've produced this gigantic monster. I don't know how many
pages it is, but I can't lift it, and I'm a pretty big boy.

N. In some quarters it's regarded as a king-size hatchet job.

■ *Lasky:* I consider it the story of John F. Kennedy, told fully
and truthfully, so the "hatchet job" accusation surprises me. I was
amused by the way the *Chicago Tribune* labeled it a hatchet job.
I love the *Tribune*, and feel I know its editorial stands well, and
consequently this was the last paper I expected to criticize the
book this way. It was like carrying coals to Newcastle. The *New
York Times* didn't like it, but a lot of people did. Roscoe Drummond liked it, the *Herald Tribune* liked it—with reservations. (I'm
talking about John Hutchens, who unfortunately is leaving criticism to go with the Book-of-the-Month Club. Wonderful critic,
but like I said, he had reservations.) Arthur Krock seemed to like
it, the President himself has indicated that he read the book and
that he didn't think it was as brilliant as Krock and Drummond
seemed to think it was. The truth is, I don't think either Krock or
Drummond really thought it was brilliant, at least, they didn't say
so. At any rate I am grateful to the President for his plug.

N. How have you felt about some of the adverse criticism?

■ *Lasky:* Well, I feel this way: If you're going to dish it out
you've got to learn to take it. I've dished it out all my life, and you
don't find me writing letters of protest to editors when someone
lands on me. Perhaps my attitude is influenced by the fact that
adverse criticism isn't affecting the sale of the book. I'm a controversial guy—I'm not boasting about it, but I believe in controversy.
I think that the trouble with our civilization—at least in the United
States right now—is that there's a blandness in political life. I like
guys who say what they think. I don't care if they don't like me,
if they don't like the Republican party, or if they don't like the
Democratic party, at least they're read or heard if they speak up. I
had my say in six-hundred-some pages. I believe that my critics
have a right to voice their opinions, and I'm not simply being a
"good guy" about this. I've blasted the other guy, and he has a
right to blast me. This is a free society and everyone is entitled to
express an opinion. The only thing I ask of my critics is this: Read
the book. Don't go by what you think about me personally. I have
the feeling that some critics just glance at a book (not only mine)
and then turn out a profound analysis.

N. In writing a book as important as this—a book that even

could have political influence—what do you feel your obligation is to the general reading public, and to the material you're using?

■ *Lasky:* I don't believe I've written a political book in the sense that I am advocating any particular candidate as an opponent for President Kennedy. It's a funny thing, but a lot of people have labeled this a conservative or right-wing book, a right-wing hatchet job, and so on, but I don't believe it is. I was trying simply to set the record straight. Kennedy, himself, was a conservative, or a neo-conservative (in my estimation) until comparatively recent years. He contributed $1,000 to Mr. Nixon's campaign against Helen Gahagan Douglas in 1950, a fact which I disclose in my book, although it has been fairly common knowledge. Why it never came out in the 1960 campaign I'll never know.

But to get back to my main point, I don't consider Kennedy a liberal or a conservative—I consider him a politician par excellence who will trim his sails to win power. On every important issue of our time—foreign aid, for example—Kennedy has turned a full circle. At one time he was opposed to foreign aid. He felt, and I quote him in my book, that "You can't take care of every Hotten-tot in the world." He said that—I didn't. I give this as an example because today he is criticizing those opponents of foreign aid in both parties who have his old idea, that we cannot go on forever supplying the world with dollars, that people abroad must start doing things for themselves. He said these things eight and ten years ago, and voted consistently to slash foreign aid. I cite this as only one example of his turning full circle.

To get back to the point that you raised: I'm not advocating a candidate, I'm examining a President. My job is that of the reporter, reporting facts as best I can. People can say that while my facts are right, the overall impression is wrong, but I don't believe so. In John F. Kennedy we have, I believe, a man who has achieved eminence because of his great professional skill in the art of press agentry. Take his administration thus far—compare his deeds with his 1960 rhetoric. I don't believe he has demonstrated the great leadership he claimed to have. Look up and down the country, look around the world—where have we really bettered ourselves? Even Pakistan, one of our most loyal allies in Southeast Asia, seems to be going down the drain. Charles de Gaulle and Konrad Adenauer seem to have their misgivings, and they express them openly. De Gaulle refers to our President as (in French) "Jack the Infant." Of course, de Gaulle has his own problems, but I'm saying a lot and getting away from the point.

N. I wanted to go into the research you employed in turning out this book.

■ *Lasky:* Well, I worked on the book for many years, of course. I sent my wife on many chases through my dusty files, picked up the phone and called newspaper libraries from here to San Diego, visited newspaper morgues in many cities. Incidentally, one of the most interesting criticisms raised against me by Tom Wicker of the *New York Times* was that I relied a great deal on newspaper reports. This struck me as very funny, because the *New York Times* prides itself on being a newspaper of record. I went to the record, to the newspaper of record, and I relied a great deal upon published materials.

Why did I do this? People have said, "Mr. Lasky wrote a very interesting book, but he didn't go to pick things up first-hand, he didn't talk to the President, or to whosis." The truth is, I talked to many people. I didn't talk to Mr. Kennedy for obvious reasons; he was well aware of what I was up to, and I wouldn't embarrass him. I wouldn't embarrass the White House. I wouldn't ask for an appointment.

But I did talk to many people, and one of the strangest things I came across in doing the book was the fact that many people were frightened. They were unwilling to be quoted for the record. While they gave me good stories I couldn't use them for the simple reason that they wouldn't go on record, so I was forced to go to *the* record.

For instance, I remember talking to a prominent Democrat in Boston who told me about an amusing episode during the 1952 campaign when Mr. Kennedy was running against Mr. Lodge. The Kennedy slogan at that time—"Elect me, I can do more for Massachusetts." At the very time he used that slogan he was using non-union and non-Massachusetts labor to print his various propaganda posters. Now, this man told me this story—I checked it out and it was true—but he wouldn't let me quote him.

Now, I've got some amusing sidelight stories in my book, but I had to go and dig them out of the files. My responsibility in writing this book was first to seek out all the pertinent material on record, then to document every piece of evidence on a fact-by-fact, word-by-word basis. As you can see in the back of the book there are at least thirty to forty pages of solid documentation which my wife spent a month in compiling. This was at the suggestion of Macmillan, my publisher, and it was a terribly valid suggestion.

I understand that the Democratic National Committee has obtained every one of these sources. I have seen a copy of the memorandum they prepared. I didn't read it, but the stack looks immense. But my verifications and documentations are solid—they must be, because people are entitled to know where I obtained my material, and on what basis I made my—quote—outrageous—unquote—conclusions.

N. I was surprised not to find more on Cuba.

■ *Lasky:* I thought I spent more time on Cuba than I should have; perhaps it's a matter of opinion. The most interesting thing about the Cuba issue is the controversy as to whether or not Mr. Kennedy, as a senator or as a candidate for the Democratic party, was informed by the CIA as to the upcoming invasion that had been organized by Eisenhower. I try to give both sides of that question. I give the White House press releases in full, and I give Nixon's position. Herb Klein was Nixon's Press Secretary, and he is quoted at length. Fred Seaton, Secretary of the Interior under Eisenhower, played a role in this whole business. I have my own conclusions. At that time I was indirectly involved. I didn't know of the invasion, it was kept from me, but I knew something was up. I know how angry Nixon got when Kennedy started to demand that we invade Cuba, when he screamed and fussed all over the country about the Communist Menace ninety miles from home. I present both sides of the affair and let the reader draw his own conclusions.

As far as the Bay of Pigs, I devoted twelve or fifteen pages to it, and included some new material. I relied basically on the *Fortune* article by Charles Murphy—an article Kennedy felt was not entirely accurate, though I felt it was. Mr. Kennedy and I have a difference about the Bay of Pigs. I include that wonderful story about Bobby Kennedy going to the President the night the disaster at Bay of Pigs became evident and saying, "Those black-hearted Communists, they can't do it to you." I often wonder whether those black-hearted Communists were supposed to have co-operated with the American-backed invaders.

Actually, the Cuban thing needs a book all its own—a book to be written when passions have cooled, when historians can start nit-picking to find out what really happened. We never really did get the whole story.

N. I'm going to turn now to the area of theory, and ask you for your evaluation of current journalism, books by journalists, and your opinions of trends and events in the other arts.

■ *Lasky:* I know more about the field of journalism, and what we would call topical books, than I do about novels. I hate to concede this, but one of my favorite novelists is Ian Fleming. I was reading James Bond long before Kennedy heard of him. Mr. Fleming, you know, is Promotion Manager of the London *Sunday Times*. Now, about topical books: I would say that one of the great tragedies of today's publishing world is that topical books aren't as popular with publishers as they were at one time. In Europe you'll find many more topical books—the analysis of fast-breaking developments. One reason is the time involved in book production. For example, my book was finished in August of 1962. My publisher decided to postpone it, so I updated it as far back as the next March and April. It takes six months to really get out a book. I don't only mean physically, but to prepare the salesmen, gear all the operational procedures of a large publishing firm. Expense, the high production expense, is another factor working against topical books. They have a tendency to die very quickly. I'm thinking, now, of several books written by friends. One, a very nice guy now on the *Washington Post*, wrote a book on Kishi and he worked on it for three years. Kishi, the Prime Minister of Japan, resigned just a month before the book was published, so three years' work went down the drain.

Another friend of mine, Wells Hangen, formerly with the *New York Times* and now with a radio or TV network, wrote a book about the men and leadership in India. A very good book—but before he finished it Mr. Menon was out of office. Several other leaders in the Indian political world were out, so the book itself was dated at publication time.

This probably won't happen to my book because it can be updated. Furthermore, much of it goes into the background of Kennedy, his political and social evolution.

Now, while television brings events to a person at a moment's notice, a large public wants to know more than television can show. Thus a topical book is important. For example, people may want to know what Jack Kennedy is really like, or what goes on in the integration trouble-centers in the South. Television can show them some background, newspapers can show some, but they're apt to be confusing. The weekly magazines do a better job of co-ordinating all this material, but in the final analysis a book can pack the total perspective between covers. And the public needs this perspective very badly.

As far as novelists and the literary world are concerned—I know very little. I buy a novel occasionally. Right now I'm reading *The*

Collector, by John Fowles, a terrific book. The literary world must be an exciting one, all in all, and though I know very little about it I'm pleased to have a feeling that I'm helping it by putting a best-selling book on the market.

N.   If you were to advise the student, or the aspiring journalist, interested in journalism or the topical book, what would your advice be?

■ *Lasky:* Well, I'm one of those purists who feels that a good student will make a good newspaperman. In journalism today you have to know something about almost everything. I personally feel the lack of knowledge in the field of science; I don't know what's being said when scientific discoveries are discussed. I also wish I knew languages better. I talk a lousy Spanish and a worse French. Today's journalist should be proficient in several languages, at least two. It's true that you can get along with English all around the world, but it's so much better, when you're interviewing a personage, to be able to converse with him in his own language. I've interviewed people like de Gaulle and Juan Peron. I've interviewed every dictator except Khrushchev and Hitler. With Castro I spoke in English, and there was no problem, but with Peron I had to speak in my atrocious Spanish. A journalist can't capture the full flavor of a man's thinking unless he speaks his language. I've always found this my major handicap, so I'd advise anyone who seriously wants to get into journalism to put real time into languages and to bone up on the sciences. The man who wants to succeed in journalism today has to learn a great deal about this big, wonderful world we live in, not only by study, but by living in different parts of it. Travel is important, living abroad is important; just a few years away from home, really away, can add so much perspective. You see, there are no set courses for an aspiring journalist. I'm not arguing against journalism courses. There are fine journalism schools and fine instructors, but they can't really make a journalist. They may give you some of the jargon of journalism, and tell you what a printing press looks like, and how to edit a piece of copy, but in the final analysis the more a student knows about the basic subjects the better off he'll be in the world of journalism. Big chunks of knowledge, all types of knowledge, should be absorbed. Then he should get curious as hell about everything he doesn't know 100 per cent of the way, which means, in short, he's got to go around wearing a question mark at all times.

N.   What works have you in preparation right now?

■ *Lasky:* Well, my agent is very interested in a sequel to this book, a quick analysis of the New Frontier in operation. If I do get to work on it I'll have to take off for Bermuda with all my material and spend a few months writing it, then hope to have it out for next year's political campaign. The title would be *While America Slept*, the story of the Kennedy years. For some time I've been working on an examination of what's wrong with the American position abroad—not from a partisan standpoint, because several administrations must be considered. But what's wrong with foreign aid? Why is it that we're not able to beat the Communists at their own game? On the other hand, are the Communists really beating us? I'd like to examine the question of prestige, to see how much reality and how much nonsense is involved. I'd like to do it in real terms, not in a Burdick treatment.

In short, I don't want to do an "anti" book about our position in the world—I'm not against foreign aid, I'm not against intervention, per se—but I feel that thorough analysis and research and honest exposure is our only road to strengthening and improving ourselves. Without this strength, and without certain improvements, this big, wonderful world of ours may not be around much longer.

"I want to do the best I can with the talent God gave me. I hope to goodness that every novel I do gets better and better. . . . In other words all I want to be is the Jane Austen of south Alabama."

Harper Lee
Interviewed in New York, March, 1964

Harper Lee

N. Throughout the course of these interviews, in those conducted in Europe as well as those completed within the United States, the name of one author and one book have popped up with amazing frequency when the hopeful aspects of the literary present and future are discussed. The author: Harper Lee. The book: *To Kill A Mockingbird*. No present-day reviewer can forget the summer storm that came, in 1960, with the release of this novel. High praise was almost unanimous, both for the excellence of the book itself and for the welcome draught of fresh air that seemed to come with it.

In talking to Miss Lee I'd like to first explore her own background—the particulars of birth, rearing, and education.

■ *Lee:* I was born in a little town called Monroeville, Alabama, on April 28, 1926. I went to school in the local grammar school, went to high school there, and then went on to the University of Alabama. That's about it, as far as education goes. There was one peculiarity, however, aside from my resisting all efforts of the government to educate me. I went to law school, the only odd thing in a thoroughly American stint of formal learning. I didn't graduate; I left the university one semester before I'd have gotten my degree.

N. When did you first become interested in writing?

■ *Lee:* That would be hard to say. I can't remember, because I think I've been writing as long as I've been able to form words. I never wrote with an idea of publishing anything, of course, until I began working on *Mockingbird*. I think that what went before may have been a rather subconscious form of learning how to write, of training myself. You see, more than a simple matter of putting down words, writing is a process of self-discipline you must learn before you can call yourself a writer. There are people who write, but I think they're quite different from people who *must* write.

N. How long did it take you to write *To Kill A Mockingbird?*

■ *Lee:* I suppose I worked on it in elapsed time of two years. The actual span of time was closer to three, but because of many family problems and personal problems I would have to quit at intervals and pick it up again. Two years would be it.

N. I know this is an almost impossible thing to do, but could you bare any of the roots of the novel? Of where it began in your own mind, and how it grew?

■ *Lee:* You're right, this is very hard to do. In one sense, I think that *Mockingbird* was a natural for me, at any rate, for my first effort. In its inception it was sort of like Topsy—it just grew, but the actual mechanics of the work itself were quite different.

Naturally, you don't sit down in"white hot inspiration" and write with a burning flame in front of you. But since I knew I could never be happy being anything but a writer, and *Mockingbird* put itself together for me so accommodatingly, I kept at it because I knew it had to be my first novel, for better or for worse.

N. What was your reaction to the novel's enormous success?

■ *Lee:* Well, I can't say that it was one of surprise. It was one of sheer numbness. It was like being hit over the head and knocked cold. You see, I never expected any sort of success with *Mockingbird*. I didn't expect the book to sell in the first place. I was hoping for a quick and merciful death at the hands of the reviewers, but at the same time I sort of hoped that maybe someone would like it enough to give me encouragement. Public encouragement. I hoped for a little, as I said, but I got rather a whole lot, and in some ways this was just about as frightening as the quick, merciful death I'd expected.

N. Are you working on another novel at present?

■ *Lee:* Yes, and it goes slowly, ever so slowly. You know, many writers really don't like to write. I think this the chief complaint of so many. They hate to write; they do it under the compulsion that makes any artist the victim he is, but they loathe the process of sitting down trying to turn thoughts into reasonable sentences.

I like to write. Sometimes I'm afraid that I like it too much because when I get into work I don't want to leave it. As a result I'll go for days and days without leaving the house or wherever I happen to be. I'll go out long enough to get papers and pick up some food and that's it. It's strange, but instead of hating writing I love it too much.

N. *To Kill A Mockingbird* was turned into a film with what I felt to be an unusual degree of integrity. How did you feel about it?

■ *Lee:* I felt the very same way. As a matter of fact, I have nothing but gratitude for the people who made the film. It was a most unusual experience. I'm no judge, and the only film I've ever seen made was *Mockingbird*, but there seemed to be an aura of good feeling on the set. I went out and looked at them filming a little of it, and there seemed to be such a general kindness, perhaps even respect, for the material they were working with. I was delighted, touched, happy, and exceedingly grateful. I think this kindness and respect permeated everyone who had anything to do with the film, from the producer and the director down to the man who designed the sets, from Greg Peck to the peripheral characters, the actors who played the smaller parts.

It impressed me so much I asked people if this was the way filming generally ran, and they said, "Only when we're working on something we can respect." It was quite an experience, and yet I assume actors must have feelings, private feelings, of course, about material given them. They can't really be happy with something they don't like. But all of us connected with filming *Mockingbird* were fortunate to have the screenplay done by Horton Foote. I think this made a great difference.

N. I thought the casting of Gregory Peck was another brilliant move.

■ *Lee:* I did, too. You know, Greg is a very youthful man, a very elegant gentleman, a lot of fun. The first time I met him was at my home in Alabama. Greg and his wife and Bob Mulligan, who directed the film, and his wife came down to see me and to see the countryside down there.

I'd never seen Mr. Peck, except in films, and when I saw him at my home I wondered if he'd be quite right for the part. The next time I saw him was in Hollywood when they were doing wardrobe tests for the film. They put the actors in their costumes and slam them in front of the camera to see if they photograph correctly.

They did Mr. Peck's test on the lot on the little street where the big set had been erected, and the first glimpse I had of him was when he came out of his dressing room in his Atticus suit. It was the most amazing transformation I had ever seen. A middle-aged man came out. He looked bigger, he looked thicker through the middle. He didn't have on an ounce of makeup, just a 1933-type suit with a collar and a vest and a watch and chain. The minute I saw him I knew everything was going to be all right because he *was* Atticus.

N. A quick transition from Hollywood to your home country
—why is it that such a disproportionate share of our sensitive
and enduring fiction springs from writers born and reared in
the South?

■ *Lee:* Well, first of all you have to consider who southerners
are. We run high to Celtic blood and influence. We are mostly
Irish, Scottish, English, Welsh. We grew up in a society that was
primarily agricultural. It was not industrial, though it is becoming
so, for better or worse.

I think we are a region of natural storytellers, just from tribal
instinct. We did not have the pleasure of the theater, the dance, of
motion pictures when they came along. We simply entertained
each other by talking.

It's quite a thing, if you've never been in or known a small
southern town. The people are not particularly sophisticated,
naturally. They're not worldly-wise in any way. But they tell you
a story whenever they see you. We're oral types—we talk.

Another thing I've noticed about people at home, as opposed,
say, to people in New England small towns, is the fact that we have
rather more humor about us. We're not taciturn or wry or laconic.
Our whole society is geared to talk rather than do. We work hard,
of course, but we do it in a different way. We work in order not
to work. Any time spent on business is time more or less wasted,
but you have to do it in order to be able to hunt and fish and gossip.

I think first of all our ethnic background, then the absence of
things to do and see and places to go means a great deal to our
own private communication. We can't go to see a play; we can't
go to see a big league baseball game when we want to. We
entertain ourselves.

This was my childhood: If I went to a film once a month it
was pretty good for me, and for all children like me. We had to
use our own devices in our play, for our entertainment. We didn't
have much money. Nobody had any money. We didn't have toys,
nothing was done for us, so the result was that we lived in our
imagination most of the time. We devised things; we were readers,
and we would transfer everything we had seen on the printed page
to the backyard in the form of high drama.

Did you never play Tarzan when you were a child? Did you
never tramp through the jungle or refight the battle of Gettysburg
in some form or fashion? We did. Did you never live in a tree house
and find the whole world in the branches of a chinaberry tree?
We did.

I think that kind of life naturally produces more writers than, say, an environment like 82nd Street in New York. In small town life and in rural life you know your neighbors. Not only do you know everything about your neighbors, but you know everything about them from the time they came to the country.

People are predictable to each other simply by family characteristics. Life is slower. You have more time to look around and absorb what you see. We're not in such a hurry that we can't do anything but go to the office, come home, have a drink, settle down, and collapse for the evening.

I don't know if there's any real explanation for our number of writers and the way we write beyond the rambling I've done. I think it's a combination of our heritage and the way time runs at home.

Of course, this kind of South is becoming a thing of the past. We're becoming industrialized; we're moving away from the small towns; we're beginning to concentrate in the cities. But it will take quite a while to take the small town out of the South—we're simply a region of storytellers. We were told stories from the time we were born. We were expected to hold our own in conversation. We certainly don't have literary conversations, we have conversations about our neighbors. Some of it's straight fact, some of it's a bit embroidered, but all of it's part of being tellers of tales.

N. How have you adjusted to living in New York?

■ *Lee:* Well, I don't live here, actually. I see it about two months out of every year. I enjoy New York—theaters, movies, concerts, all that—and I have many friends here. But I always go home again.

N. Here's another large order. When you look at American writing today, perhaps American theater, too, what do you find that you most admire? And, conversely, what do you most deplore?

■ *Lee:* Let me see if I can take that backward and work into it. I think the thing that I most deplore about American writing, and especially in the American theater, is a lack of craftsmanship. It comes right down to this—the lack of absolute love for language, the lack of sitting down and working a good idea into a gem of an idea. It takes time and patience and effort to turn out a work of art, and few people seem willing to go all the way.

I see a great deal of sloppiness and I deplore it. I suppose the reason I'm so down on it is because I see tendencies in myself to be sloppy, to be satisfied with something that's not quite good enough. I think writers today are too easily pleased with their work. This is sad. I think the sloppiness and haste carry over into painting. The search, such as it is, is on canvas, not in the mind.

But back to writing. There's no substitute for the love of language, for the beauty of an English sentence. There's no substitute for struggling, if a struggle is needed, to make an English sentence as beautiful as it should be.

Now, as to what I think is good about writing. I think that right now, especially in the United States, we're having a renaissance of the novel. I think that the novel has come into its own, that it has been pushed into its own by American writers. They have widened the scope of the art form. They have more or less opened it up.

Our writers, Faulkner, for instance, turned the novel into something Wolfe was trying to do. (They were contemporaries in a way, but Faulkner really carried out the mission.) It was a vision of enlargement, of using the novel form to encompass something much broader than our friends across the sea have done. I think this is something that's been handed to us by Faulkner, Wolfe, and possibly (strangely enough) Theodore Dreiser.

Dreiser is a forgotten man, almost, but if you go back you can see what he was trying to do with the novel. He didn't succeed because I think he imposed his own limitations.

All this is something that has been handed to us as writers today. We don't have to fight for it, work for it; we have this wonderful literary heritage, and when I say "we" I speak in terms of my contemporaries.

There's probably no better writer in this country today than Truman Capote. He is growing all the time. The next thing coming from Capote is not a novel—it's a long piece of reportage, and I think it is going to make him bust loose as a novelist. He's going to have even deeper dimension to his work. Capote, I think, is the greatest craftsman we have going.

Of course, there's Mary McCarthy. You may not like her work, but she knows how to write. She knows how to put a novel together. Then there's John Cheever—his Wapshot novels are absolutely first-rate. And in the southern family there's Flannery O'Conner.

You can't leave out John Updike—he's so happily gifted in that he can create living human beings. At the same time he has a great respect for his language, for the tongue that gives him voice. And Peter De Vries, as far as I'm concerned, is the Evelyn Waugh of our time. I can't pay anybody a greater compliment because Waugh is the living master, the baron of style.

These writers, these great ones, are doing something fresh and wonderful and powerful: they are exploring character in ways in which character has never been explored. They are not strictured in the old patterns of hanging characters on a plot. Characters make their own plot. The dimensions of the characters determine the action of the novel.

N.   Now, if you were to give advice to the talented youngster who wants to carve a career as a creative writer, what would that advice be?

■ *Lee:*   Well, the first advice I would give is this: hope for the best and expect nothing. Then you won't be disappointed. You must come to terms with yourself about writing. You must not write "for" something; you must not write with definite hopes of reward.

Young people today, especially the college kids, scare me to death. They say they are going to be writers. Their attitude is, "I'm going to write it, and because I write it, it's going to be great, it's going to be published and make me great."

Well, I've got news for them. (You must think I regard writing as something like the medieval priesthood—and sometimes I wish our government could see its way clear to support our writers on bread and water and shut them up in a monastery somewhere.) People who write for reward by way of recognition or monetary gain don't know what they're doing. They're in the category of those who write; they are not writers.

Writing is simply something you *must* do. It's rather like virtue in that it is its own reward. Writing is selfish and contradictory in its terms. First of all, you're writing for an audience of one, you must please the one person you're writing for. I don't believe this business of "No, I don't write for myself, I write for the public." That's nonsense. Any writer worth his salt writes to please himself. He writes not to communicate with other people, but to communicate more assuredly with himself. It's a self-exploratory operation that is endless. An exorcism of not necessarily his demon, but of his divine discontent.

Of course, he gets his material from the world around him. He's on the inside looking out, yet at the same time he has to stand away from it and look inward.

I'm making no sense, I'm sure. But writing is the one form of art and endeavor that you cannot do for an audience. Painters paint, and their pictures go on the wall, musicians play, actors act for an audience, but I think writers write for themselves, and this attitude of "I'm going to write and be great just because I write" is where most young people fool themselves.

Another way they fool themselves is when they study to be writers. They are training themselves, in colleges, to be writers. Well, my dear young people, writing is something you'll never learn in any university or at any school. It's something that is within you, and if it isn't there, nothing can put it there. But if you are really serious about writing, if you really feel you must write, I would suggest that you follow the advice the Reverend John Keble gave a friend who asked him how to get his faith back. "By holy living."

N. What are your impressions of those cross-pollinated fields of criticism and review?

■ *Lee:* Well, I think that we really have no literary critics in the sense that they exist (for instance) in England. We have reviewers. We have many, many book reviewers, but we have few or no critics who write consistently. I can think of only three offhand, and this is bad.

Just the way your book pages are operated in your big New York and Chicago and Los Angeles newspapers spells the trouble. These people have to work at a furious pace. They have to read heaven knows how many books a week, then they have to write something. Like our theater critics, they have to rush out to make a deadline. This is one of the most destructive things that can happen, one of the most depressing things.

Look at it this way. A writer has spent years turning out something that deserves more than a hasty appraisal, but that's all he gets. Ironically, it's just as hard to write a bad novel as it is to write a good one—just as backbreaking, just as formidable a series of crises. But so many good novels come out today that are more or less born to blush unseen. They are hastily dismissed or they are hastily praised.

We really have no tradition of criticism. (Here we go, back to tradition.) The thing that has made it worse is the mass media—television, radio—that dominate time with less than a full creative effort. Reading gets confined to a quick grab for the latest bestseller as the commuter dashes for the train.

I think the American public is the worst-informed public in the world about its own literature. We have few journals that begin to compare with English periodicals like *The Spectator* and *The Economist*. But then, books are published in England in a more leisurely fashion, and the judgments on them are better simply for that. In general, American criticism is in a very poor state, and I think it always will be.

N. How would you define your own objectives as a writer?
■ *Lee:* Well, my objectives are very limited. I want to do the best I can with the talent God gave me. I hope to goodness that every novel I do gets better and better, not worse and worse. I would like, however, to do one thing, and I've never spoken much about it because it's such a personal thing. I would like to leave some record of the kind of life that existed in a very small world. I hope to do this in several novels—to chronicle something that seems to be very quickly going down the drain. This is small-town middle-class southern life as opposed to the Gothic, as opposed to *Tobacco Road*, as opposed to plantation life.

As you know, the South is still made up of thousands of tiny towns. There is a very definite social pattern in these towns that fascinates me. I think it is a rich social pattern. I would simply like to put down all I know about this because I believe that there is something universal in this little world, something decent to be said for it, and something to lament in its passing.

In other words all I want to be is the Jane Austen of south Alabama.

"You should write . . . to please yourself. You shouldn't care a damn about anybody else at all. But writing can't be a way of life; the important part of writing is living."

Doris Lessing
Interviewed in London, England, October, 1963

Doris Lessing

N. In *A Man and Two Women* the enormous talent of Doris Lessing can be seen in full bloom. Few writers dig to the emotional heart of human involvement better than Miss Lessing, and several critics have observed, in one phrase or another, Miss Lessing's almost uncanny grasp of human relationships: the actual, the artificial, and above all, her command of the vast area where the real and the contrived are blended into the bulk of our lives. To go back to the beginning of things I'll ask Miss Lessing where she was born, reared, and educated.

■ *Lessing:* I was born in Persia because my father was running a bank there. He was in Persia because he was fed up with England. He found it too narrow after World War I. Unfortunately, I remember nothing about Persia consciously—though recently, under mescaline, I found that I remembered a great deal, that it had influenced me without my knowing it.

Then my father went to Southern Rhodesia on an impulse (which is how he ran his life), to farm. He had never been a farmer, but he took a very large tract of land—thousands of acres, in American terms—to grow maize. Thus I was brought up in a district that was populated sparsely, very sparsely indeed, by Scottish people who had left Scotland or England because it was too small for them. I spent most of my childhood alone in a landscape with very few human things to dot it. At the time it was hellishly lonely, but now I realize how extraordinary it was, and how very lucky I was.

After this I went into town—a very small town that had about ten thousand white persons in it. The black population, of course, did not count, though it was fairly large. I married in my teens, when I was far too young, and had two children. That marriage was a failure and I married again. Let's put it this way: I do not think that marriage is one of my talents. I've been much happier unmarried than married. I can't blame the people I've been married to—by and large I've been at fault.

N. When did you start writing?

■ *Lessing:* I think I've always been a writer by temperament. I wrote some bad novels in my teens. I always knew I would be a writer, but not until I was quite old—twenty-six or -seven—did I realize that I'd better stop saying I was *going* to be one and get down to business. I was working in a lawyer's office at the time, and I remember walking in and saying to my boss, "I'm giving up my job because I'm going to write a novel." He very properly laughed, and I indignantly walked home and wrote *The Grass Is Singing.* I'm oversimplifying; I didn't write it as simply as that because I was clumsy at writing and it was much too long, but I did learn by writing it. It focused upon white people in Southern Rhodesia, but it could have been about white people anywhere south of the Zambezi, white people who were not up to what is expected of them in a society where there is very heavy competition from the black people coming up.

Then I wrote short stories set in the district I was brought up in, where very isolated white farmers lived immense distances from each other. You see, in this background, people can spread themselves out. People who might be extremely ordinary in a society like England's, where people are pressed into conformity, can become wild eccentrics in all kinds of ways they wouldn't dare try elsewhere. This is one of the things I miss, of course, by living in England. I don't think my memory deceives me, but I think there were more colorful people back in Southern Rhodesia because of the space they had to move in. I gather, from reading American literature, that this is the kind of space you have in America in the Midwest and West.

I left Rhodesia and my second marriage to come to England, bringing a son with me. I had very little money, but I've made my living as a professional writer ever since, which is really very hard to do. I had rather hard going, to begin with, which is not a complaint; I gather from my American writer-friends that it is easier to be a writer in England than in America because there is much less pressure put on us. We are not expected to be successful, and it is no sin to be poor.

N. I don't know how we can compare incomes, but in England it seems that writers make more from reviewing and from broadcasts than they can in the United States.

■ *Lessing:* I don't know. When I meet American writers, the successful ones, they seem to make more on royalties, but then they also seem to spend much more.

I know a writer isn't supposed to talk about money, but it is very important. It is vital for a writer to know how much he can write to please himself, and how much, or little he must write to earn money. In England you don't have to "go commercial" if you don't mind being poor. It so happens that I'm not poor any more, thank goodness, because it's not good for anyone to be. Yet there are disadvantages to living in England. It's not an exciting place to live, it is not one of the hubs of the world, like America, or Russia, or China. England is a backwater, and it doesn't make much difference what happens here, or what decisions are made here. But from the point of view of writing, England is a paradise for me.

You see, I was brought up in a country where there is very heavy pressure put on people. In Southern Rhodesia it is not possible to detach yourself from what is going on. This means that you spend all your time in a torment of conscientiousness. In England—I'm not saying it's a perfect society, far from it—you can get on with your work in peace and quiet when you choose to withdraw. For this I'm very grateful—I imagine there are few countries left in the world where you have this right of privacy.

N.   This is what you're supposed to find in Paris.

■ *Lessing:*   Paris is too exciting. I find it impossible to work there. I proceed to have a wonderful time and don't write a damn thing.

N. To work from *A Man and Two Women* for a bit. The almost surgical job you do in dissecting people, not bodily, but emotionally, has made me wonder if you choose your characters from real life, form composites or projections, or if they are so involved you can't really trace their origins.

■ *Lessing:*   I don't know. Some people I write about come out of my life. Some, well, I don't know where they come from. They just spring from my own consciousness, perhaps the subconscious, and I'm surprised as they emerge.

This is one of the excitements about writing. Someone says something, drops a phrase, and later you find that phrase turning into a character in a story, or a single, isolated, insignificant incident becomes the germ of a plot.

N.   If you were going to give advice to the young writer, what would that advice be?

■ *Lessing:*   You should write, first of all, to please yourself. You shouldn't care a damn about anybody else at all. But writing can't be a way of life; the important part of writing is living. You have to live in such a way that your writing emerges from it. This is hard to describe.

N. What about reading as a background?

■ *Lessing:* I've known very good writers who've never read any-thing. Of course, this is rare.

N. What about your own reading background?

■ *Lessing:* Well, because I had this isolated childhood, I read a great deal. There was no one to talk to, so I read. What did I read? The best—the classics of European and American literature. One of the advantages of not being educated was that I didn't have to waste time on the second-best. Slowly, I read these classics. It was my education, and I think it was a very good one.

I could have been educated, formally, that is, but I felt some neurotic rebellion against my parents who wanted me to be brilliant academically. I simply contracted out of the whole thing and educated myself. Of course, there are huge gaps in my education, but I'm nonetheless grateful that it went as it did. One bit of advice I might give the young writer is to get rid of the fear of being thought of as a perfectionist, or to be regarded as pompous. They should strike out for the best, to be the best. God knows we all fall short of our potential, but if we aim very high we're likely to be so much better.

N. How do you view today's literature? and theater?

■ *Lessing:* About theater, well, I'm very annoyed right now by that phrase, "kitchen sink," that is being used so frequently. I don't think it means very much. There are two kinds of theater, and I don't think they should be confused. People who want to see a roaring farce, like *Sailor Beware*, should enjoy it. It's perfectly legitimate, and there's nothing wrong with the theater of enter-tainment.

The cathartic theater, theater that moves people in such a way that they or their lives are changed, or they understand more about themselves, is a totally different thing. The phrase, "kitchen sink," comes from critics who don't know their jobs, or theatergoers who are being bullied into seeing things they don't want to see. They should never go if they don't want to. There's nothing wrong with a minority theater and a minority literature.

N. What about the recent trend toward introspection?

■ *Lessing:* Well, I haven't been to America, but I've met a great many Americans and I think they have a tendency to be much more aware of themselves, and conscious of their society, than we are in Britain, (though we're moving that way). By a coincidence I was thinking, this afternoon, about a musical like *West Side Story*, which comes out of a sophisticated society which is very aware of

o

itself. You wouldn't have found in Britain, at the time that was written, a lyric like "Gee, Officer Krupke." You have to be very socially self-conscious to write *West Side Story*.

N.   What do you feel about the fiction being turned out today? Does it share the same virtues and failings as theater or can it be considered separately?

■ *Lessing:* Quite separately. You want to know what contemporary writers I enjoy reading? The American writers I like, for different reasons, are Malamud and Norman Mailer—even when he's right off center he lights rockets. And Algren. And that man who wrote *Catch 22*. And of course, Carson McCullers. But I only read the books that drift my way, I don't know everything that comes out.

N.   How do you feel about critical reactions to your own works?

■ *Lessing:* I don't get my reviews any more. I read reviews if they turn up in the papers I get, but I go through them fast and try to pay little attention to what is said. I think the further I'm removed from this area—reviews, the literary squabble-shop, the better. I got angry over reviews of the *Golden Notebook*. They thought it was personal—it was, in parts. But it was a very highly structured book, carefully planned. The point of that book was the relation of its parts to each other. But the book they tried to turn it into was: The Confessions of Doris Lessing. I remember I went down to my publishers' office to look through the reviews, because they said I'd had a lot of good ones and I should see them. Well I remember thinking: Its surely not possible that all these reviewers should have minds like gossip columnists. Because of the shape of the book, and the point of that shape, and what it meant, they weren't interested.

You see, the literary society in London is very small and incestuous. Everyone knows everyone. The writer who tosses a scrap of autobiography into an otherwise fictional piece (which writers always have done and always will do), he's not credited with any imagination. Everyone says, "Oh, that character's so and so," and "I know that character." It's all too personal. The standards of criticism are very low. I don't know about American critics, but in this country we have an abysmal standard. Very few writers I know have any respect for the criticism they get. Our attitude is, and has to be—are the reviews selling reviews or not? In all other respects, the reviews are humiliating, they are on such a low level and it's all so spiteful and personal.

N. Do reviews sell books in England?

■ *Lessing:* My publishers claim they help build a reputation and that indirectly they do sell books. This is probably true. But in Great Britain everything is much more cumulative and long-term than in America. One simply settles in for what you call the long haul. But "reputation"—what are reputations worth when they are made by reviewers who are novelists? Writers aren't necessarily good critics. Yet the moment you've written a novel, you're invited to write criticism, because the newspapers like to have one's "name" on them. One is a "name" or one is not, you see. Oh, it's very pleasant to be one, I'm not complaining, I enjoy it. But everyone knows that writers tend to be wrong about each other. Look at Thomas Mann and Brecht—they were both towering geniuses, in different ways, and they didn't have any good word for each other.

Ideally we should have critics who are critics and not novelists who need to earn a bit to tide them over, or failed novelists. Is there such an animal, though? Of course, sometimes a fine writer is a good critic, like Lawrence. Look at something that happened last year—I wrote a long article for the *New Statesman* about the mess socialism is in. There was a half-line reference to X. To this day, people say to me, "that article you wrote attacking X." This is how people's minds work now. At the first night of one of Wesker's plays, up comes a certain literary figure and says, his voice literally wet with anxiety, "Oh, Wesker is a much better playwright than Osborne, he is, isn't he?" He felt that someone's grave should be danced on. He was simply tired of voting for Osborne. Tweedledum and Tweedledee. In and out.

You're going to say the literary world has always been like this. But what I said about the theater earlier applies—nothing wrong with the audience who likes *Who's for Tennis?* and the critics who do. It's all theirs. But they should keep out of the serious theater. Similarly, of course, the literary world is always going to seethe with people who say, I'm bored with voting for X. But writers should try to keep away from them. Another bit of advice to a young writer—but unfortunately economics make it almost impossible to follow: Don't review, don't go on television, try to keep out of all that. But, of course, if one's broke, and one's asked to review, one reviews. But better not, if possible. Better not go on television, unless there is something serious to be said (and how often is that?). Better to try and remain what we should be—an individual who communicates with other individuals, through the written word.

N. To return to *A Man and Two Women*. Which stories in this collection would you choose as personal favorites?

■ *Lessing:* That's very difficult. I like the first one, titled "One Off the Short List" because it's so extremely cold and detached—that one's a toughy. I'm pleased that I was able to bring it off the way I did. Then there were a couple of zany stories. I'm attached to. The story about incest I liked very much—the one about the brother and the sister who are in love with each other. Not autobiographical at all, actually; perhaps I wish it were. And I like "To Room 19," the depressing piece about people who have everything, who are intelligent and educated, who have a home and two or three or four beautiful children, and have few worries, and yet ask themselves "What for?" This is all too typical of so many Europeans—and, I gather, so many Americans.

N. Perhaps life without challenge or excitement amounts to boredom.

■ *Lessing:* Life certainly shouldn't be without excitement. The Lord knows that everything going on at the moment is exciting.

N. But hasn't boredom become one of our most acute social problems?

■ *Lessing:* I don't understand people being bored. I find life so enormously exciting, all the time. I enjoy everything enormously if only because life is so short. What have I got—another forty years of this extraordinary life—if I'm lucky? But most people live as if they have a weight put on them. Perhaps I'm lucky, because I'm doing what I want all the time, living the kind of life I want to live. I know a great many people, particularly those who are well off and have everything they are supposed to want, who aren't happy.

N. Right now a great many criticisms are leveled against bored Americans who have a surfeit of what they want. Is this true of England?

■ *Lessing:* I think that England is much more of a class society than America. This street I live on is full of very poor people who are totally different from my literary friends. They, in turn, are different from the family I come from, which is ordinary middle class. It isn't simple to describe life in England. For instance, in any given day I can move in five, six different strata or groups. None of them know how other people live, people different from themselves. All these groups and layers and classes have unwritten rules. There are rigid rules for every layer, but they are quite different from the rules in the other groups.

N. Then perhaps you maintain more individuality.

■ *Lessing:* The pressures on us all to conform seem to get stronger. We're supposed to buy things and live in ways we don't necessarily want to live. I've seen both forms of oppression, the tyrannical and the subtle. Here in England I can do what I like, think what I like, go where I please. I'm a writer, and I have no boss, so I don't have to conform. Other people have to, though. But in Southern Rhodesia—well, there one can't do or say what one likes. In fact, I'm a prohibited immigrant in South Africa and Central Africa although I lived in Rhodesia twenty-five years. But then, the list of people who are prohibited in these areas is so long now.

I am not as optimistic as I used to be about oppressive societies. When I opened my eyes like a kitten to politics, there were certain soothing clichés about. One was that oppressive societies "collapsed under their own weight." Well, the first oppressive society I knew about was South Africa. I lived close to it, and I was told that a society so ugly and brutal could not last. I was told that Franco and his Fascist Spain could not last.

Here I am, many decades later, and South Africa is worse than it was, Southern Rhodesia is going the same way, and Franco is very much in power. The tyrannical societies are doing very well. I'm afraid that the liberals and certain people on the Left tend to be rather romantic about the nature of power.

I'm not comparing tyranny to conformity. The point is that people who are willing to conform without a struggle, without protest to small things, who will simply forget how to be individuals, can easily be led into tyranny.

N. But isn't there strength in the middle road? In the area that lies between fascism and communism?

■ *Lessing:* I don't know. I hope so, but history doesn't give us many successful examples of being able to keep to the middle. Look at the difference between British and American attitudes toward communism right now. Sections of America seem absolutely hypnotized by the kind of propaganda that's fed to them. Now, if it is true that communism is a violent threat to the world, then Britain—which has a different attitude—has been eating and working and sleeping for twenty years without developing ulcers, but America has ulcers. I would say that we are doing a better job of keeping to the middle of the road. You've got some rather pronounced elements who would like to head for the ditch or force a collision.

Hasn't America been enfeebled by this hysterical fear of communism? I don't think you sit down to analyze what the word

"Communist" means. You end up in the most ridiculous situations, as you did in Cuba. When you see what a great nation like America can do to muddle this Cuban thing you can only shrug your shoulders. Please don't think I'm holding out any brief for my own government, but we're in a lucky position. I mean, England is. We're not very important, but America holds our fortunes in their large and not very subtle hands, and it's frightening. When I went to Russia, in 1952, I came to the not-very-original conclusion that the Americans and Russians were very similar, and that they would like each other "if." Now I see you moving closer and beginning to like each other, so now both of you are terrified of the Chinese, who will turn out (given fifteen years and not, I hope, too much bloodshed and misery) to be just like us, also. All of these violent hostilities are unreal. They've got very little to do with human beings.

N. And very little to do with the arts?

■ *Lessing:* The arts, nothing! I was talking as a person, not a writer. I spent a great deal of my time being mixed up in politics in one way or another, and God knows what good it ever did. I went on signing things and protesting against things all the while wars were planned and wars were fought. I still do.

N. To get back to your career, what are you working at now?

■ *Lessing:* I'm writing volumes four and five of a series I'm calling *Children Of Violence*. I planned this out twelve years ago, and I've finished the first three. The idea is to write about people like myself, people my age who are born out of wars and who have lived through them, the framework of lives in conflict. I think the title explains what I essentially want to say. I want to explain what it is like to be a human being in a century when you open your eyes on war and on human beings disliking other human beings. I was brought up in Central Africa, which means that I was a member of the white minority pitted against a black majority that was abominably treated and still is. I was the daughter of a white farmer who, although he was a very poor man in terms of what he was brought up to expect, could always get loans from the Land Bank which kept him. (I won't say that my father liked what was going on; he didn't.) But he employed anywhere from fifty to one hundred working blacks. An adult black earned twelve shillings a month, rather less than two dollars, and his food was rationed to corn meal and beans and peanuts and a pound of meat per week. It was all grossly unfair, and it's only part of a larger picture of inequity.

One-third of us, one-third of humanity, that is, is adequately housed and fed. Consciously or unconsciously we keep two-thirds of mankind improperly housed and fed. This is what the series of novels is about—this whole pattern of discrimination and tyranny and violence.

N.   At the beginning of the interview you mentioned becoming involved with mescaline. Could you describe this in more detail?

■ *Lessing:* I'm not involved with it. I took one dose out of curiosity, and that's enough to be going on with. It was the most extraordinary experience. Lots of different questions arise, but for our purposes the most interesting one is: Who are we? There were several different people, or "I's" taking part. They must all have been real, genuine, because one has no control over the process once it's under way. I understand that experiences to do with birth are common with people having these drugs. I was both giving birth and being given birth to. Who was the mother, who was the baby? I was both but neither. Several people were talking and in different voices throughout the process—it took three or four hours. Sometimes my mother—odd remarks in my mother's voice, my mother's sort of phrase. Not the kind of thing I say or am conscious of thinking. And the baby was a most philosophic infant. and different from me.

And who stage-managed this thing? Who said there was to be this birth and why? Who, to put it another way, was Mistress of the Ceremony? Looking back, I think that my very healthy psyche decided that my own birth, the one I actually had, was painful and bad (I gather it was, with forceps and much trouble) and so it gave itself a good birth—because the whole of this labor was a progress from misery, pain, unhappiness, toward happiness, acceptance, and the birth "I" invented for myself was not painful. But what do I mean, we mean, when we say "my psyche"—or whatever phrase you might use in its place?

And then there's the question of this philosophic baby, a creature who argued steadily with God—I am not a religious person, and "I" would say I am an atheist. But this baby who was still in the womb did not want to be born. First, there was the war (I was born in 1919) and the smell of war and suffering was everywhere and the most terrible cold. I've never imagined such cold. It was cold because of the war. The baby did not want to be born to those parents (and remember the baby who was also its own mother) and—this is the interesting thing, it was bored. Not the kind of boredom described in my story "To Room 19." But a sort of cosmic boredom. This baby had been born many times before, and the mere idea of "having to go through it all over again" (a phrase the baby kept using) exhausted it in advance. And it did not want, this very ancient and wise creature, the humiliation of being smothered in white flannel and blue baby ribbons and little yellow ducks. (Incidentally I'll never again be able to touch or look at a baby without remembering that experience, how helpless a baby is, caged in an insipid world of comfort and bland taste and white flannel and too much warmth.) This creature said to God, Yes, I know that boredom is one of the seven deadly sins, but You created me, didn't You? Then if You gave me a mind that goes limp with boredom at the experiences You inflict on me, whose fault is it? I'll consent (this baby said) to being born again for the millionth time, if I am given the right to be bored.

But as the birth proceeded, the pain, the boredom, the cold, the misery (and the smell of war) diminished, until I was born with the sun rising in a glow of firelight.

Yes, but who created all this? Who made it up?

It wasn't me, the normal "I" who conducts her life.

And of course, this question of I, who am I, what different levels there are inside of us, is very relevant to writing, to the process of creative writing about which we know nothing whatsoever. Every writer *feels* when he, she, hits a different level. A certain kind of writing or emotion comes from it. But you don't know who it is who lives there. It is very frightening to write a story like "To Room 19," for instance, a story soaked in emotions that you don't recognize as your own.

When I wrote the *Golden Notebook* I deliberately evoked the different levels to write different parts of it. To write the part where two characters are a bit mad, I couldn't do it, I couldn't get to that level. Then I didn't eat for some time by accident (I forgot) and found that there I was, I'd got there. And other parts of the *Golden Notebook* needed to be written by "I's" from other levels. That is a literary question, a problem to interest writers. But that creature being born wasn't a "writer." It was immensely ancient, for a start, and it was neither male nor female, and it had no race nor nationality. I can revive the "feel" or "taste" of that creature fairly easily. It isn't far off that creature or person you are when you wake up from deep sleep, and for a moment you don't recognize your surroundings and you think: Who am I? Where am I? Is this my hand? You're somebody, all right, but who?

"I can't read some of the moderns—I'm never quite sure of whether they're being experimental, careless, or lazy. . . . I think that the state of literature today is rather healthy. I don't know if your best-seller lists are any criteria, but some contemporary literature of quality shows up on them."

Arthur H. Lewis
Interviewed in New York, September, 1963

Arthur H. Lewis

N. *The Day They Shook The Plum Tree* was not regarded as a potential best-seller by its author or by its publisher. Yet since its 1963 publication it has gone through nine editions to bring a total of more than 50,000 copies into print—quite pleasantly matching an enthusiastic critical reception with public response.

In talking to Arthur H. Lewis, the happily surprised chronicler of the Hetty Green story, I'd first like to ask him how he came to write the book.

■ *Lewis:* Actually, a member of the New York Bar had read my preceding book, which is about an attorney. He had this book with him at a luncheon in Philadelphia when he asked a friend of mine if he knew the author—that he had an idea for a book he would like to discuss with me. A meeting was arranged, and as a result this attorney turned over a great deal of fascinating material on Hetty Green. I consulted with my editor, Julian P. Muller at Harcourt, and from that time on we worked together to develop the book.

The lucky part for me was to be able to go over four million words of testimony in this attorney's office, testimony that had not been made available before, and it was made available to me only because the fortune is entirely dissipated. The last lineal descendent of Hetty Green died in 1952.

Since childhood I had been intrigued by this strange woman. But then, I'm interested in eccentrics. My books are essentially about eccentrics, and certainly Hetty—she and her whole family, including her son and daughter—fit into the category of eccentrics more obviously than any family group I know. I did a great deal of research in addition to reading the material in the attorney's office, traveled a lot, talked to a great many people, and out of it all came *The Day They Shook The Plum Tree.*

N. And it was not expected to be a best-seller.

■ *Lewis:* Emphatically not; it's definitely an off-beat book. In fact, a piece in the *New York Post* written by Martha McGregor said this: "Arthur Lewis' book about Hetty Green is a surprise best-seller. Even the publisher is surprised. 'This is what makes horse racing' says Harcourt. If the publisher had anticipated such a large sale they would have priced *Plum Tree* lower."

Well, I wish it had been priced lower, but it did very well. In fact, I think that unless a writer is in the category of O'Hara or Cozzens or Shirer, writers whose books reach best-seller lists automatically, he's surprised when a book is a best-seller.

N. What is your analysis, if one can be made, of the things that make a best-seller?

■ *Lewis:* It can be attributed to a lot of things; not all of them are repeated in any pattern. I think good promotion is important; I think the enthusiasm of the salesman for the firm is important. What the book dealer and the salesmen in the store think of your book is extremely important. I'm not at all certain of how important advertising is; I know that ad budgets for books are very low. Television and radio help, particularly if you have a literate listening audience, as so many radio stations have today. All these things help. I'm not mentioning the quality of the writing, and this is deliberate. I don't think the writing matters very much. Too many badly-written books reach best-seller lists.

Now, I'm not saying that all books on best-seller lists are badly written. A majority are well-done, but there are an appalling number of best-sellers that are drivel. But then, these lists are not trying to appraise the book for its literary values; they're only reporting national sales. I clipped a piece from the *Miami Herald*, written by their book editor, Beatrice Washburn. She's made a study of best-sellers and I was amused by what she said. She asked herself the question, "What makes a best seller?" (By the way, she had no answer.) But she replied, "Publishers don't know or they wouldn't bring out anything else. Book sellers and critics are puzzled by *Oh Ye Jigs And Juleps*, Virginia Cary Hudson's contribution to western culture, which might reasonably be enjoyed by little girls, very old-fashioned little girls, or people with an I.Q. of about 78."

I'm curious about this, myself, and whenever I'm in a city, speaking or doing business, I stop in at book stores. I talked to a book dealer not so long ago about *Juleps* and another book and asked how it happened that these books—without sex, without the other factors normally attributed to a best-seller—were selling so well. She said, "Well, the books are funny, they sell for $2 and they can easily be put into your pocket without ripping your pocket." I would hate to think this is criteria for American literature.

This is contradicted, of course, by the fabulous success of Shirer's *Third Reich*, a $10 book that wouldn't fit in any pocket. I don't know what the basis of a best-seller is. I think that luck might have a great deal to do with it—and I mean just plain luck. I was fortunate, for example, in having the producer of a national television show read *Plum Tree* and like it. Luck played a major role in this because the producer was going to Bermuda for a weekend and he asked one of the girls in the office to hand him something to read. There must have been 500 books in his office— every publisher automatically sends producers of national shows a review copy of every book—but my book just happened to be on top of the pile. He grabbed it, read it, and sent me a telegram after he got back, asking me to appear on the show. From that time on everything moved.

I think another big factor is in having a good director of publicity working for your publisher. I have this at Harcourt. But they tell me that sometimes everything can work right and the book will still lay an egg, so I guess I return to the point where I don't know what makes a best-seller.

N.   Could I turn to your own life, now—in rough auto- biography?

■ *Lewis:* I was born in a small town in the hard coal regions of Pennsylvania, a town called Mahanoy City which I'm sure nobody ever heard of. When I went to school the population was close to 17,000. I've been away for forty years and the population is now about 8,000. I was just up there for a centennial. It's a very sad part of the country, though the people are not.

I left to attend school at Franklin and Marshall, and Columbia. I was awfully close to a degree, but I wanted to become a newspa- perman. I didn't do well at school, yet my degree was in sight when a newspaperman from Philadelphia, on the *Inquirer*, called to tell me there was a job open—a job I could have if I came down in the morning. So I packed up my books, five weeks shy of graduation, and went down. I worked on the *Inquirer* and other papers for a number of years. I was press secretary for four governors of Pennsylvania, did some radio programs for Westinghouse, wrote a lot of magazine pieces and television shows, taught at the Uni- versity of Pittsburgh, and came here to Madison Avenue where I worked (while commuting to Philadelphia) for a number of years as a huckster. I sold a book to the movies, and this enabled me to quit. I'm married, have a daughter and a granddaughter, live in surburban Philadelphia, and that's about it.

N. How do you feel regarding your obligations as a biographer, to the public, on one hand, and toward your material, on the other?

■ *Lewis:* I think that, utter and forthright honesty must be the principal objective of the biographer. I try to be as objective as I can, to avoid letting my own prejudices creep in. What I'm passing on is information. It's up to me to make this information as readable and entertaining as I can, but if I distort facts then I'm not performing honestly as a biographer.

Now, I'm not saying this applies to people who write fiction. But I know it applies to my field. In certain instances one must glide over some things for the sake of good taste, and sometimes one is inclined to drag in facts which do not move the story at all but are interesting in themselves.

I overwrite horribly. A book of 100,000 words will have to be cut out of 175,000 words of manuscript. Fortunately, it's the extraneous things that are cut out; the important things, which should make the book, are (I hope) left in.

I hate to use the word "integrity" but I think it's important. I think that integrity must be basic in any writer. But along with this —applying to newspapermen or novelists or biographers—the writer must have an intense curiosity. Unless he has a high degree of intellectual curiosity regarding people and places he just isn't going to be able to write.

N. I'd like to turn to research—using *Plum Tree* as an example of the way a biographer works with fairly contemporary material.

■ *Lewis:* Well, my first job was to peruse these four million words of testimony. This took about seven weeks. I'm a pretty fast reader; I made heavy notes, but in going over these notes I ran across a great many names of persons who had been witnesses at the trials. This testimony evolved from three trials, and they were recent enough to assure me that some of the witnesses would still be living.

My next problem was to find someone who had known Hetty Green. She had died in 1916, and this was tough because there weren't apt to be too many people alive who had known Hetty. I ran across a surgeon who operated on Hetty in 1912; he was still practicing in 1962. He was helpful.

Then it was important to find out everything I could about her character. I wanted to know if she had been badly maligned by the press of her day—she had a terrible press, you know. But she hadn't been maligned; they told the truth about her.

I went into the newspaper files in a number of cities and dug up material not only about Hetty and her two children, the Colonel and Sylvia, but about people who were mentioned in major or minor roles. Then I began a tour from Maine to Florida, talking to people who had known Hetty and to some of the recipients of Sylvia's largesse. All this consumed about seven months, and was really the fun of doing the book. The rest was just plain hard work.

I have a rigid writing schedule which I don't break. I write from five-thirty in the morning until twelve-thirty every day, and I don't miss a day. It takes me about five months to do a book. I write and rewrite each morning, so that the copy that accumulates is fairly clean. (This goes back to newspaper training, I suppose.) I have another advantage which I think many newspapermen or ex-newspapermen have: I don't argue with my editor. This may shock many writers, but when the last word is in I agree with my editor, just as I once had to agree with my city editor. This may sound like compromise, but it isn't—he knows his job.

In the Hetty story there was quite a lot of material which I felt had to be deleted. One of my characters, the Colonel (a courtesy title) had a libido which was rather wild. At first I wanted to put it in, because I thought it gave the book more spice, but then my editor, Julian Muller, decided that there was too much spice, so we cut it down when I reduced the book to reasonable size.

That's about it on research. It's just a matter of endless hours of probing, then of gaining the confidence of people. I never interview anybody without telling them what I'm doing—yet they frequently claim that they've talked too much. I always get them to okay their quotes.

N. In turning to the literature of our day—perhaps drama, also—how do you regard the quality of contemporary work?

■ *Lewis:* I think that a great many fine books are turned out today, just as they have been at any period. O'Hara is a splendid writer and depicts a valid portion of the contemporary scene. James Gould Cozzens is excellent. Herman Wouk's *Caine Mutiny* was tremendous, and *The Cruel Sea* was so tremendous I read it every year. (I also reread Dickens on a rough schedule.)

I can't read some of the moderns—I'm never quite sure of whether they're being experimental, careless, or lazy. I can't take Kerouac. He may be excellent, but he's not for me, but then I could never read Thomas Hardy—I thought he was a frightful bore, and the same goes for Galsworthy. He bored me to extinction.

I think that the state of literature today is rather healthy. I don't know if your best-seller lists are any criteria, but some contemporary literature of quality shows up on them—*Shoes of The Fisherman*, by West, is splendid, and O'Hara's *Elizabeth Appleton*. I thought Rechy's *City of Night* was interesting.

I'm not sure of what literature is, any more. I read, now, for only one purpose: for entertainment. If I'm not entertained, I don't like the book. I read a book a day; I have for about forty-five years, so perhaps I've grown increasingly difficult to keep entertained.

N. If you were to give advice to the young writer, what would that advice be?

■ *Lewis:* Just write. Many people are always going to write a book, and make noises about it, but never get around to it because the actual writing requires an awful lot of self-discipline. I don't say that everyone who writes books has to devote as much time as I do, and many people don't want to write for a living as I do.

Most writing comes from just sitting down and applying your seat to the typewriter chair. You can't wait for inspiration, though it's nice to have, but you can't depend on inspiration to carry you through the struggle.

I hate to give advice. I'm no oracle. I've done a lot of things in my time which were stupid, and I'm not sure that I've profited from my mistakes. Probably nobody is qualified to give advice on writing. The experiences a person accrues are important, probably the most important part of the battle, along with the willingness to work. I don't think much of writing schools or schools of journalism. I taught in one for a while, so I know. I think that some of those courses given at universities, especially some of the summer sessions where selling writers come in to discuss their work, are of limited value. The stimulation may be important, unless it goes off into the arty sort of thing that's all talk and no write.

But you can't teach writing. You can teach grammar. Perhaps you can even inspire an interest in reading, and this is terribly important, because anybody who wants to be a writer and doesn't read a great deal is not going to make it.

N. In looking over your own books could you pick out one that has given you an uncommon amount of pleasure?

■ *Lewis:* The book which gave me the most pleasure was my very first book, and it sold under two thousand copies. It was the story of a small town in Pennsylvania, a town called Aaronsburg. At the time I was doing promotion for the governor of the state, and ran across this town (population 321) that had a sign which said, "Founded by Aaron Levy in 1786." It astonished me that a Jew had been in Pennsylvania that early in history. I was probably ignorant for not knowing this, yet the town had obviously been named in his honor.

I stopped and talked to a minister in the town. He told me something of Levy's history, how Levy had given money and land to build a Lutheran church and to buy communion pewter. He had even brought them their first minister.

Well, we decided that we were going to have a pageant of some sort in this little town on a Sunday in October, 1949. (By the way, no Catholic, Jew, or Negro has ever lived in this town at any time. The town is seventh-generation descendants of original settlers, as homogenous a community as you'll find in America.)

On a Sunday afternoon in 1949 we brought 50,000 people to this town of 321 persons—Ralph Bunche, General Donovan, and Felix Frankfurter and other greats came to participate in the re-dedication of this community. A few years later I wrote a book titled *The Aaronsburg Story* which related this and subsequent events in the village. It was a moment of true achievement—sparking the celebration, participating in it, and finally seeing it in print.

This was more stirring to me than anything I've done since. Whatever I do, from that point on, is anticlimactic.

"There's very little humor being written now. . . . It may be the times we live in, but as terrible as times may be, I don't see the need for the let's-dance-on-the-casket sort of humor that does pop up. The novelist, the great novelist, may start popping up all over the place again."

A. J. Liebling
Interviewed in New York, December, 1963

A. J. Liebling

N. *The Most of A. J. Liebling*, published by Simon and Schuster in 1963, contains all the proof one needs of Liebling's vast command of style. Few writers at work today are as conscious of the delicacy and power of words. Few writers, for that matter, are at home in so many fields. Liebling, whether touring in bayou country, poised at ringside, analyzing a newspaper, or dining in France, is never out of his element.

Because of his high rank in the art of literary journalism, because his consistent though varied efforts contributed much to make *The New Yorker* what it is today, I'd like to ask Mr. Liebling to outline his career as he sees it.

■ *Liebling:* I'm of a second *New Yorker* generation really. I came on in 1935. White, Thurber, Wolcott Gibbs—the famous ones —were there already. I came straight from newspaper work and had the idea that *The New Yorker* was a bit of a butterfly, a little too elegant for me. Of course, Ross was the antithesis of elegance. He was, and remained, a newspaperman at heart. In the late 1930's, he realized that times had changed, that Eustace Tilley had better look for a job, and he hired a lot of newspaper writers like Joe Mitchell, Alva Johnston, Dick Boyer, Jack Alexander, and Mike Berger. We changed *The New Yorker* a great deal, I think.

People always speak of *The New Yorker* as one unchanging whole, and even speak of a *New Yorker* style which doesn't exist. In the late thirties we made the magazine unpretentious and irreverent. We got out and skinned or deshirted as many stuffed shirts as we could find. I look back on that era as the "golden period" of *The New Yorker*.

Then the war came along and *The New Yorker* changed again. But then, everything changed, and I think everyone changed a little bit, too. I went over to France in 1939 and got involved in quite a different way of life than I'd expected. Instead of doing profiles of hustlers and seal trainers and that sort of thing (showman at the fair), I covered the first year of the war in France and got chased out along with the French government when the country fell.

I decided that I must personally be revenged upon the Germans and that took up the next four years of my life. Of course, I didn't do anything to the Germans myself, but I watched other people doing things to them. It was a great satisfaction.

When I came back from the war, I started working on "The Wayward Press," a department Robert Benchley had handled between 1927 and 1937, before he went off to Hollywood. I revived this department in 1945 and had the great satisfaction (seeing I'd started as a newspaper reporter and had considered myself downtrodden for years) of telling off the publishers. I became the newspaperman's champion, because the newspaperman thinks he knows more than his publisher, and he's generally right.

Then I got back into my old ways of hanging around with prize fight managers and racing people and Broadway characters. I went down to Louisiana, the bayou country, and did the story of Earl Long, who—I finally decided—was the only civilized man in that forsaken region. It was a minority opinion, but after my articles came out, I got the support of the Long family, and this pleased me.

That's about it. My range is limited, I think. It embraces a half-dozen specialties like boxing, and the press, and the war, and French politics. I always find Broadway a great deal of fun, but now I find that I can only talk to Broadway characters of my own generation. I'm a fat old gentleman, now, and it just isn't natural to hang out with dancers and prize fighters. But I'm glad the managers live a long time—I can still hang out with them.

N. One of your most unforgettable "Wayward Press" series was the treatment you gave the *Chicago Tribune*. As you might expect, it caused a journalistic conflagration in Chicago. Could you describe how you wrote those pieces?

■ *Liebling:* I did them just from reading the late Colonel McCormick's column in the *Tribune*. He was such a marvelously bombastic old gentleman; he was just plain funny. He was as much an American phenomenon as Earl Long in Louisiana. The difference, to me, was that I didn't like McCormick. Everything had been handed to him on a silver platter. He was a great publisher only because he was handed a great paper. I simply didn't like the man at all. Yet I didn't attack him; I simply quoted him. He was so uproariously funny outside Chicago. Chicago people had been putting up with him for so many years, they finally became unconscious of him. Some liberal friends of mine in Chicago used to say that the Colonel had no influence any more, but I found that their minds had been shaped by him without their knowing it. They'd grown up inside this mental corset, which he laced up the back every chance he got.

When I simply reproduced and commented on the column to the rest of the country, even these friends thought he was terribly funny. He used to take those world-famous tours, to anywhere in the world, in his own B-17, and every time he left, he would reassure his readers that all precautions were being taken to protect his life. Otherwise Chicago couldn't have stood the strain of wondering about his safety. Then he would fly from capital to capital, praising Franco, or any other dictator who turned out a palace guard for him, and predicting great misfortune for any country whose ruler was too busy to talk to him.

Then I wrote a book that included some articles about the defensive attitude of so many Chicago people, which was true, and I received hundreds of letters of indignation from the very same persons who'd told me precisely what I was reporting. It all added up to an unhappy and ironic year in Chicago for me and (obviously) for my wife. In fact, I followed this with the short course in Nevada citizenship—the kind that takes six weeks.

In Nevada I got interested in a band of Piute Indians, whose reservation was being squatted on by some friends of Senator McCarron. I wrote a series of articles about the Piute's rights, and the wrongs done to them. I like Nevada very much, even if the Indians never did get their land back.

Reporting, by and large, is being interested in everyone you meet. It's surprising how often the most casual meetings turn up fascinating material. This goes for Egypt or a fight club in London. If you don't consider anybody as being beneath consideration, it's rewarding and it's fun.

N.   During the war, I read many of the pieces you wrote about the merchant marine. How did those develop?

■ *Liebling:*   I went to England in the spring of 1941. I did some pieces about the RAF, and the improvised munitions factories, and the kind of people the British were. Wherever you went in England, then, it reminded you of the speakeasy days in New York. The streets were dark and you would almost have to guess where the pubs were. Once you came in out of the dark, you might find Englishmen, Scots, Canadians, Aussies, Anzacs, and the girls in the services, and you were immediately accepted as a friend, just as you used to be in New York. The only analogy to the spirit of it, is the day of the speakeasy.

After seven months of this, I wanted to go home, and I wanted to go in a convoy. So I talked to members of the Norwegian shipping ministry which was in London, along with the Norwegian government. (Remember, there were seven governments in exile in London, and the place was livelier than it has been for generations. The exiles were much less stolid than the British.) The Norwegians put me on one of their ships, a tanker returning after having discharged its cargo. A tanker, when it's light, has no stability in the water. It rolls and it pitches, and this was the rough time of year. We left from London in December, and I dodged along the shore with the convoy that took us as far as Newcastle. Then we waited for another convoy to start us across. The Norwegians thought we were going to Brooklyn, but after we were five weeks out, the orders were changed to Houston. Then they were changed to Baton Rouge, and again to New Orleans, so I got to New Orleans six weeks after we'd started, and the United States was in the war.

That crew consisted of some of the nicest men I've ever met. None of the men was brilliant, but they were warm and good. In 1948, I went back to their home port, a little place in Norway called Arendal, and found that tanker—probably one of the slowest ships, and one of the best sitting targets in the war—had never been scratched. We had a great reunion.

N. You've also written some splendid articles on food. How did your interest in this area evolve?

■ *Liebling:* I happen to like food very much. I think that fact is obvious. I suppose the real interest in food began when I was a student in France. I had an opportunity to indulge my tastes (at that time the prices were moderate), so I used to spend a lot of thought on the menu and wonder whether I should have a good wine and simple food or good food and cheap wine. This posed serious daily problems, but I became well acquainted with a great range of foods. I became selective but not snobbish. Now, when I read obviously faked things about food, I get angry enough to write about food from the standpoint of pure enjoyment. I don't consider myself a gourmet. But I think the best qualification you can have for taking food seriously is a good big appetite, and I have that.

N. Your series of articles on Earl Long that were later published in book form, was a bizarre and effective job of reporting. How did you gather the material?

■ *Liebling:* To start with, I had a very good man in New Orleans helping me—Tom Sancton, a good reporter, born down there. Naturally, that made it easy for me to make contacts.

Earl Long was fascinating. He made so much more sense than his so-called respectable opponents. They were out-and-out racists. At one point, Long said to the racist leader, Leander Perez: "What are you going to do, Leander? The Feds have got the atom bomb." Earl knew it was inevitable that law and order would prevail in race relations, and he went that way. As a consequence, he got the only political licking of his life. He could and did do a lot of preposterous things, but nobody cared—he was a Long. But when he made a speech, and he said, "And gentlemen, you got to admit that a Nigger is a human being," they grabbed him and sent him off to an insane asylum. It was an Alice-in-Wonderland situation. He was right, but everybody treated him as if he was crazy, but he nearly licked them anyway. In the end he ran for Congress, after he was shut out for governor. He won, but he died a few days later.

I think he would have been a very refreshing presence in Washington. He was a very amusing man and he was a very sound man, even though he did like striptease girls. That was all right, too—it's just a matter of taste. Poor Earl just happened to get the word too soon. He knew the crinoline days were over.

N. How much time did you spend with Earl Long?

■ *Liebling:* Not much. I heard him; I had dinner with him once; listened to several of his speeches.

N. What were the circumstances of that rather famous "nothing but a pissant" statement he made?

■ *Liebling:* Well, he was speaking in Alexandria, and a local leader in Alexandria had been with Earl but had quarreled with him (as everybody did). His name was Camille something, and as Earl was speaking in the courthouse square, Camille came with a regiment of his children. He said he came because he heard that Earl was going to insult him, and he heckled Earl roughly. But Earl had the microphone, and Camille didn't, and when Earl had enough, he squashed him thoroughly. "Your Daddy was a fine man," Earl said on the mike, "but you're just nothing but a goddam little pissant."

I'd rather hear this kind of political oratory carried on, than the dull, platitudinous stuff speech writers are putting out today. Most political speeches might as well be advertising brochures, but you can be sure that no ghost writer ever wrote that line for old Earl.

N. Have you noticed—in the course of writing your "Way-ward Press" pieces—any definite improvement or decline in the quality of the American press over the past two decades?

■ *Liebling:* I'd say there is less competition and more uniformity. All papers use the press agencies and accept less brilliant writing. The *New York Times* and one or two other papers have held up. But most newspapers are much duller than they were twenty years ago. When we had the *New York World* papers, they would send their own men down to Florida, or to Ku Klux territory, or to Wyoming for even a fair story. Now you can't get a paper to investigate a real estate scandal down the block. The old fight isn't there any more.

N. I would like to discuss another of your favorite subjects: the prize fight.

■ *Liebling:* It's a great game. I used to box when I was a kid and for some time afterward, and I think there's more fun in boxing than in any other game. It's a sanctioned release of hostility. You feel good because you don't have to pretend anything (like being friendly with the fellow you plan to trick in a card game) and when it's over, you both feel much better.

I liked to watch men who were better than I was, just as some-one who fools around at the piano likes to hear a real pianist. Now, people who are antiboxing have never boxed. They think it's brutal. It isn't half as brutal as football. I bet I've seen a hundred football games in my life and 400 fellows carried off the field.

I've never seen a boxer carried out of the ring. And a lot of men walk around with football knees—even Eisenhower had one. There are more fatalities in automobile racing; more men drop dead on the golf links; and the middle-aged American male who plays tennis on Sundays keeps the channels open for junior executives coming on.

But boxing is the best. In Teddy Roosevelt's time it was the fashion. Teddy used to box in the White House, and the young men of that era wanted to be rugged fellows, so they boxed. Even when I was in college in the 1920's—I took a year or two at Columbia School of Journalism because I didn't want to go to work —we'd go down to the gym. Every afternoon you'd find three or four dozen fellows from law school, medical school, engineering, all down there to box for fun. No team to try for, no physical education credits, but great fun. You'd go down with a friend and see two perfect strangers and you'd break them up, just the way people used to do on dance floors. You'd change around and meet new fellows, and everybody had a good time. This is gone, of course. People watch boxing on television, and this is just silly.

Wherever you do find boxing and the people who understand it and enjoy it, it's still fun. I'm not speaking of the manipulators; but then, I don't think much of people who manipulate stocks, either, or who gather to set prices on electric irons. People who would rule out boxing because there are a few crooks in it, should first see about cleaning the crooks out of other lines that have no aesthetic appeal and no enjoyment value. I like boxing. It's like being nuts about a girl who's got a few primroses in her past. I happen to know and believe she's 95 per cent virtuous, and I hate to hear some smug, so-called authority judge her by that trivial 5 per cent.

N. I'd like to turn to a totally different area, perhaps a tender one. Can you draw a word-portrait of Harold Ross?

■ *Liebling:* Well, I've always thought of him as a man putting on a show and taking the best acts he could find to present what the old vaudeville people used to call a balanced bill. A certain amount of reporting, a certain amount of fiction. He would even read all the fashion notes before they went into the magazine.

Ross was an old-time reporter and he didn't have any pretensions about knowing a lot. When anybody wrote about a subject that was unfamiliar to Ross he would make them prove it all the way. He also thought that everything should be made so clear that even the silliest person could understand it, so this silly person could think, "Well, I'm sophisticated; I understand what's in *The New Yorker*," and he made us toe the line on that.

Ross used to work about eighteen hours a day. He was a good scout, but he didn't want you to think that he liked you all the way, so he would say something nice to you and then take it back. He had a great curiosity about all kinds of people. He was a lot smarter than some of the people who thought they were smarter than he. I would include my late, illustrious colleague James Thurber on this list. Thurber saw Ross as a Thurber character, and maybe Ross saw Thurber as a Ross character. They were probably fooling each other a great deal of the time, but Thurber wrote it first.

N. Now we enter the blue sky area. Looking from your vantage point, from the demands you place upon yourself regarding style and content, what do you most admire and deplore in today's literary world?

■ *Liebling:* Well, I can't regret the mere absence of more good books, of more good novels in particular. I think this is the age of the journalist and the historian. I don't think it's natural to turn inward and write novels about fine shades in human relationship. It seems abnormal to me, at this point in history, to do so, although it was fine in other periods.

But then, haven't there been great periods of novel writing, followed by centuries when nothing was done? The same is true for lyric poetry and every other type of writing. This seems to be the age of the journalist and the historian who are often one and the same.

There's very little humor being written now. I think everyone will agree with me on that. Again, it may be the times we live in, but as terrible as times may be, I don't see the need for the let's-dance-on-the-casket sort of humor that does pop up. The novelist, the great novelist, may start popping up all over the place again. I think Camus was a great young man, and there seemed to be a real revival in France after the liberation, but it petered out. Now they seem to have a completely manneristic school of young writers over there. Over here, we have not too many people who can really write. Sentences don't stand up as sentences, and paragraphs as paragraphs.

I think my friend Joe Mitchell on *The New Yorker* who writes very, very slowly, is one of the finest writers in America, one of the few who really fits words together. And I think very highly of Katherine Anne Porter's book, *Ship of Fools*, which was a popular success, then was denounced because some of it was unintelligible. I think it is a splendid piece of writing. She is one of the few truly gifted writers who writes carefully and doesn't make it seem at all labored. But I guess it doesn't matter greatly what I think of the troubled area of fiction. Most of my interest lies in reading historical books, books on concrete subjects, and old books.

N.   How would you appraise theater?

■ *Liebling:* I'm not good on theater. I like musical comedies. Saw a very good show in England last summer, *Oh What A Wonderful War*, a revue. There really isn't much theater, is there? At least, theater you can either enjoy or comprehend.

N.   If you were to give advice to the young writer, the young man or woman seriously interested in journalism, fiction, or any phase of creative writing, what would that advice be?

■ *Liebling:* First I would say that he must have, or develop, an intense curiosity about people, and an interest in people. I presume he would first start writing about whatever happens to be near him, physically or emotionally.

There's another "first"—he should be mad about books, almost all types of books, and the newspaper. There may be a declining number of newspapers, but they still offer the best way to view a lot of different situations and different people, and it helps to try to figure motivations.

But so much of it is practice. I've never been a creative writer, so I can't offer a blueprint. Once in Paris, when I was very young, I started to write a novel. I looked at it when it was two-thirds done and saw that it was nothing but a record of experiences. It was bad, and I junked the whole thing, because I felt that these very private experiences weren't nearly as important as the things that happen in public.

I'll discuss my own kind of work. You've got to be quick to spot motivations and to avoid any preconception of what the story is before you go out on it. You've got to have a capacity for the enjoyment of essential things. You've got to be able to feel the beauty of the place, the fun in the place. You've got to—and this is the hardest thing of all—you've got to draw people to you and make them "spill," which is what a detective does in a nastier way. But you've got to have this little trick; it's more than a trick: You've got to have the ability to draw people out. You're happy when you know you've got it, and you're afraid of losing it.

I don't know how you get it. I was amazed to find that I had it, because as a boy I was rather bashful and introverted. Even now, I like to read; I collect only a few friends. I used to think it a gross intrusion to ask somebody: "When did you first notice that your husband was dead?" or some damfool question like that.

Then I found that people concerned in accidents or news stories or even war are very much flattered that somebody should be interested in them. They're usually quite eager to tell you how things happened. But you musn't ever try to tell *them* how things happened. This is another fault of a great many reporters; they simply go around telling the victims what hit them.

There are things you can't tell any creative writer or journalist how to acquire. You've got to know the subject you're working on; you've got to document yourself enough to know what the people are talking about before you meet them; and you've got to have a sense of history; you've got to feel that nothing is unprecedented, and nothing is completely negligible, and nothing is exclusively all-important.

I could go on and on about this, but I think the writer should be conscientious about how he writes, and not say, "This is a way of life" more than four times in any one piece. He should have an "ear" to make sure he sounds right. He may be writing on a typewriter, but he ought to know the cadence, the smoothness of words, and use them to say, as nearly as possible, the precise shade of the precise thing, he wants to say.

What advice can you give? Well, in one kind of writing you've got to have the desire to tell what happened, and in another kind of writing, you've got to have the desire to tell somebody off. It happens that I have and like both jobs.

"What distresses me is the assumption that somehow or other 'democracy' means that everybody has to get into the act, that everybody must be cultured and take a serious interest in good art and good literature. . . . I don't see why interests shouldn't be completely voluntary."

Dwight Macdonald
Interviewed in New York, March, 1964

Dwight Macdonald

N. As critic, and as stylist, few figures in the literary world are rewarded with the esteem accorded Dwight Macdonald. Look, for example, at the number of times he is mentioned by the writers contained in this book—and further, to his continuing work for *The New Yorker* and *Esquire*—and still further (entering the royalty zone) to *Memoirs of a Revolutionist* and his brilliantly edited *Parodies*. To begin with I'd like to ask Mr. Macdonald to fill in at least a rough biographical sketch of his life and career as a whole.

■ *Macdonald:* I was born on Riverside Drive in New York City in 1906. I've always lived in New York, went to private schools there, Collegiate and then Barnard. From fourteen to eighteen I attended Phillips Exeter Academy. This was the most important educational part of my life; I had always known that I wanted to write, but this is where I began to write. They had an extremely good English department and a marvelous library, and I actually became a writer and critic while I was there.

I went to Yale and was graduated in 1928. At that time Yale really wasn't very much; I think it has improved a great deal since then. I got more out of Exeter. After finishing at Yale I got the naïve idea that I'd make a lot of money in retail trade, and retire at the age of thirty and write, so I enrolled in Macy's training course. They had a training squad for college graduates, and they paid me thirty dollars a week. At the end of six months I was graduated and they offered me the job of selling neckties at thirty-five dollars a week. They said they liked me very much, but they didn't think I was executive material. I certainly wasn't.

Then I did what I should have done originally. Through a friend, Wilder Hobson, who had been my roommate at Yale, and who was then at *Time*, I got an interview and took a test for getting a job there. I passed it, and became the first editorial employee of *Fortune*, which was just beginning in 1929. I was on *Fortune* all through the Depression, up to 1936, in fact. It was very educational for me because I did a great deal of writing. I was a staff writer and sometimes I'd do two or three short articles a month. I learned from *Fortune* how to deal with data and organize facts.

Then I resigned from *Fortune*. I really had had enough of it, and I was also becoming more and more left-wing. I wrote a big article in 1935–36, a four-part article on the United States Steel Corporation which was very critical of it. *Fortune* went along, but on the last article I began with a quotation from Lenin about monopoly capitalism being the last stage before socialism and therefore the steel corporation was leading us toward socialism. They balked at an acidulous profile I did of Myron C. Taylor, then the Steel Corporation chairman, and I resigned.

I was very political by that time. When I was at Yale I'd had no interest whatever in politics—I wasn't even a liberal, but at *Fortune*, when I saw the Depression and the reaction of the business community to the Depression, and then to Roosevelt, I came to realize how really incompetent big businessmen were, how stupid and provincial. This made me begin to think all kinds of basic thoughts about American society. Until the Moscow trials came along I was sympathetic to the Communists, but I decided that the trials were frame-ups and became a Trotskyite which I remained for six or seven years. I was a sympathizer for the most part, a member for only two years. In 1938 I became one of the editors of *Partisan Review*. Three of us from Yale, F. W. Dupee, George L. K. Morris, and William Phillips and myself joined forces with Philip Rahv, who were the old editors under the Communists. We took the magazine away from the Communists and ran it as an independent revolutionary socialist literary magazine. I stayed with this for six years, then resigned to start my own magazine called *Politics* in 1944.

Politics came out once a month, and I wrote at least a quarter of each issue, edited it, published it, and raised the money for it. I kept it up for five years, until 1949, when I became just plain tired of politics as a whole. Also, there was no hope for this kind of radical politics any more. The war was over, no revolutions had taken place, and the two big imperialist powers, the United States and Russia, had complete control of the situation, so there was no possibility of the fundamental revolutionary change that I, as a Marxist, favored. So I gave the magazine up. Then I had to make a living. I had been living partly on my savings from *Fortune* and my then wife had a small income. I became a staff writer on *The New*

Yorker, am still there, and three years ago I added the job as movie critic of *Esquire*.

N.   Are you still interested in politics?

■ *Macdonald:*   For many years I wasn't, but I think that politics has become more interesting again in the last five or six years. Not that there's anything fundamental to be done in this country; there is no chance of basic change. But I think the rise of the Negro movement is important; it concerns me very much, and I'm completely on the side of the Negro. The pacifist business interests me very much, too. But I don't write about politics. I did write quite a long article on poverty a year or so ago for *The New Yorker*, and this got quite a lot of attention because it was one of the first things written on that kind of poverty. I read in the paper the other day that reading it stimulated Kennedy to begin plans for the "war against poverty" that Johnson is now carrying out.

N.   To turn to a specific book you did, I'm curious to know how you put together that superb anthology of parodies.

■ *Macdonald:*   I've always been interested in humor—and in parodies in particular—and I suggested the idea of doing an anthology to Jason Epstein at Random House, my publisher and friend. He said, "Fine," and it took me about two and one-half years of on-and-off work to turn it out. I do a lot of speaking at colleges, and whenever I'd end up at Yale or Harvard or Wisconsin or somewhere else I'd take a day or two off and browse around in the stacks. This is the only way I know of doing an anthology, though of course, you begin with other anthologies. I wonder what the first anthologist ever did, the poor ——.

Well, in this case there was only one anthology that was any good—Walter Jerrold's one of English nineteenth century parody, published about 1907 by Oxford. But it was fun to do, and I suppose that if I'd taken five years I'd have had even more good stuff in it.

N.   One article you did that caused quite a furor was your piece on the *New York Times* book review magazine. Could you discuss your reasons for writing it?

■ *Macdonald:*   I've been angry at the *Times* book review section for about thirty years now. I mean, every time I read it I'd get irritated. Not that they'd ever injured me personally. They had asked me to review in the past, and I can't complain about their reviews of my books. My anger sprang from the fact that it's on such a low level and it should be so much better. I get angry rather easily, and I get personally angry when institutions or individuals aren't up to their job. This is how I felt about the *Times*. The chief villain of my *Esquire* series was Lester Markel, the fabulous editor of the Sunday sections. I had two interviews with him, and I must say that he couldn't have been more amiable or charming. We got along beautifully, except that I kept taking notes. I've found that people often make that mistake with me. We get along, and they say to themselves, "This fellow seems all right so I'll talk freely." They do, I take it down, it comes out, and Oh, God. I really liked Markel, yet everything he said confirmed my low opinion of his Sunday book review section. Americans are sure that if they can "sell" themselves personally to a journalist he will write favorably of them. But I can like a man and still think he is, professionally, a disaster. And print it, too.

N. Do you think that the book review situation in general has improved in the past few years?

■ *Macdonald:* Yes. There are two obvious examples. One is *The New York Review of Books*, which is a very hopeful thing. The reviews are too long, to say the least, but the level is high. The other is the remarkable renaissance of the *New York Herald-Tribune* book section. A year or so ago this was even worse than the *Times*—the same sort of stuff, but only half as much coverage. Now they have a new editor, as you know, and they have made great strides on their Sunday section, also. I think the *Tribune* book section is a very hopeful try.

N. I'll turn to the movies, now, into the field you cover for *Esquire*. What do you think of the quality of movies today?

■ *Macdonald:* I was fortunate in coming into the field three and one-half years ago, when movies were really getting interesting. It began with Ingmar Bergman, and then came the French new wave, the Italians, and Japanese. Movies are now an interesting, developing lively art form. What happened in movies was basically this: We had the primitive period, fifty years ago, when movies began—Griffith was the greatest, of course, and there were in the twenties the Russians and the Germans. The silent period ran up to 1930—Chaplin, Keaton, Erich von Stroheim, and Griffith. Murnau and Pabst in Germany and above all the great Russian school headed by Eisenstein, Pudovkin, and Douzhenko.

Then came sound and as so many experts predicted, it had a terrible effect upon the art of the cinema. In all countries, even Russia. Stalin came into power at the same time and imposed his socialist realism nonsense, outlawing all experiment as "formalism." The decline in Russia was so great that the Russians never have come back even to the level of Hollywood.

P

In this country, the great silent directors were completely out, and we had a long period of a rather mediocre sort of photographic stage play. Some good movies were made, but in general the medium wasn't interesting. It seems to me that only in the last four or five years has a whole new aesthetic been worked out. They have discovered, finally, how to use sound in a realistic and non-theatrical way, and the great directors, like Renoir and Truffaut, in France and Fellini in Italy have worked out new and original approaches to the film. I think I can safely say that movies are now more interesting than the stage or even the novel, and it's wonderful to be on the critical end of an art that is in flower.

A few years ago, at a party, you would talk about novels or plays, but now you constantly run into people who have recently seen a particularly good movie five or six times, and know every nuance. You can talk to someone for a half-hour about one scene in a Fellini film. Perhaps the movies are developing scholars as well as fans.

N.   How would you define your obligation as a movie critic?
■   *Macdonald:*   I think the main obligation I have is to myself to express what I think about the work I'm reviewing. I don't think the critic has any obligation to the public to try to figure out whether they'll like something or not, and explain it to them in those terms. If he does that, he's not writing criticism at all—he's turning out a tip sheet. (It's done this way in daily newspapers all the time.) The only obligation a critic has to the public is to make his ideas clear and to write as well as he can. It's up to them if they find something useful and persuasive in your work; if they don't it's too bad for them and too bad for you. As to approaching the work of art, I don't think that criticism should be "constructive." I think it's impertinent of a critic to second-guess the director of the movie, something which my friend the late James Agee, an excellent critic in other ways, persisted in doing. He always tried to show how it could have been better done. Agee was really a frustrated director. He would have made a very good director, too.

I think the obligation to a work of art is simply to relate it to other and similar works of art. I would say that the difference between a reviewer and a critic is in the inclusiveness of the standard by which works are judged. A reviewer judges a book or a play on the basis of the season. This may be a service to the public, but it leads to grotesque judgment because it tends to overestimate the book or the play which may be mediocre and yet look, on this narrow comparison, like a work of genius if the season is bad. The critic had to judge on a much broader standard.

I don't mean that the theater critic should go back for comparisons to Shakespeare and Greek tragedy, but he should at least go back to modern masters like Shaw and Ibsen. In the case of the movies which are, after all, quite young, I think it's perfectly legitimate to draw comparisons with anybody and anything in their history, beginning with Griffith and Chaplin. In fact, when it comes to some of the comedies that are made now—frank imitations, for instance, of Mack Sennett and Buster Keaton—I'm afraid the present variety must be discredited. For instance, Jacques Tati is so much like Keaton it seems weird—the same frozen business—but he hasn't the charm and magic Keaton had. He seems somewhat psychotic to me, and makes me uncomfortable.

N. How do you feel about the general level of criticism and review in all fields?

■ *Macdonald:* Well, we always have the inferior kind of hack criticisms that magazines like *The Saturday Review* or papers like the *New York Times* specialize in. But we also have some extremely good critics who write for the little magazines—and, of course, there's always Edmund Wilson.

As far as theater—well, Robert Brustein of the *New Republic* is good, but this is back to the little magazines. John Simon is good, in the *Hudson Review.* As for the newspaper reviewers, Walter Kerr is much the best of them; he actually seems to know something about theater. Unfortunately, there isn't much to criticize in theater—they have so little to work with.

Movie criticism—most unfortunate. Maybe the newspapers have to pay too much attention to local theater advertising.

The most insidious thing in movie criticism—and this applies just as much to France and England as it does to this country—is what I call the "insider" approach. You get the feeling that these critics accept everything that certain people do because they are part of an establishment. It's impossible to find criticisms of certain directors, certain producers, but actually nobody is perfect and the best people in the business make gaffes. There's a confusion now, for example—they think that any film that is the opposite of a Hollywood film is good. I've seen some terrible French noncommercial films.

N. Obviously, despite the fact that you spend a great deal of time at the movies, you read a great deal. What do you find in current literature that you most admire, and what, conversely, do you most deplore?

■ *Macdonald:* Well, I think that Faulkner was the last of the major twentieth-century novelists. We had the extraordinary outburst beginning with Dreiser, then after World War I with Anderson and Fitzgerald. I don't think we have had anything comparable to that, since.

I think we have two extremely talented novelists in Saul Bellow and John Updike. Both have done extremely good things. Norman Mailer is a great disappointment to me, at least recently, because he's turned from being a novelist into being some sort of man of action; he's living his life instead of writing it. He's of more interest right now to a psychiatrist than to the public because he's using his writing as some sort of therapy. His new novel running in *Esquire* degrades art to wish-fulfillment, and this is a shame because he has such a great talent.

You see, a whole historical period ended around 1930, sometime in the 1930's, the classical avant-garde that began with Rimbaud and James and Proust, then embraced Joyce, Eliot, Stravinsky, Picasso, and so forth. This period produced all of our really great works of art in every field.

Well, every movement has to come to an end, and it's extraordinary that this movement lasted almost fifty years. To some extent history intruded, because what happened in the 1930's was that the political thing came to the fore, and writers became very political. The Second World War didn't do much good because, unlike the aftermath of World War I, there was no flowering of the arts.

In other words, for a generation or two we haven't been able to create or invent a general movement, anything to approximate the classical avant-garde. There are very few current writers, painters, and musicians who are on the level of the antediluvian giants like Stravinsky and Picasso. Samuel Beckett, for example, is a peculiar sort of carry-over from Joyce. He was Joyce's secretary, but think of how limited he is compared to Joyce. His latest novel, *How It Is*, has been reduced to such a plane of abstraction, repetition, and minutia, there's almost no content left in it.

N. Now, if you were to give advice to the young writer, what would that advice be?

■ *Macdonald:* I think the most important thing a young writer must keep in mind is his way of making a living from writing. We've got to consider the relationship of the professional writer to the people who employ him. What he should try to do is use the magazine, or the publisher, or the producer, whomever he writes for, to meet his purposes and not their purposes.

A good example of this is William Faulkner's career in Hollywood. There was a time, you know, when he spent three or four months of each year in Hollywood, writing scenarios. I've seen some of these movies, and they're no better than the usual Hollywood film.

Now, Faulkner had no illusion about these scenarios. He did his work and led a very sober and nonparty life. He saved his money and went back to Oxford, Mississippi, to write good novels. He didn't try to reform movies, which he couldn't have done. He did a competent job but somewhere along the line kept himself detached, separated what he had to do from what he really wanted to do. No one was cheated. In other words, the young writer has to find, at some point, a way of making a living that coincides both with what he wants and with what a publisher wants. He can't expect to be subsidized. No one is in business for his health.

Sometimes, of course, it's best for the writer to work completely outside the field, far from the written word. At other times it's advisable to work as closely as possible in the field——for a magazine, as a critic, or some sort of journalist. Then the problem becomes one of keeping your talent your own. Edmund Wilson is a very good example of somebody who has made his living by writing all his life and who has also been able--in an extraordinary way—to do just what he wanted, and to be very well paid for it. His whole relationship with *The New Yorker* is an example of this. His writing for *The New Yorker* is not different from his other writing; he doesn't write *New Yorker* style. The subjects he takes up for them are the ones that interest him, even to writing boring articles about Indians. I don't know why he's so fascinated with Indians, but he got away with it, and now I hear he's writing a whole book on French Canadian culture.

N. Now I'm going to get personal. You have been alluded to as a snob, and I wonder what you might want to say in your own defense.

■ *Macdonald:* Well, it's true that I'm often accused of being a snob. But I'm not a social snob—I'm quite a democratic fellow, really. But I admit that I am a snob in an intellectual and cultural sense. I think it is important to stand up for certain standards and not to relax these standards at all, not even for the very worthy cause of democratizing culture or bringing a great many people into contact with great works of art. Mind you, I'm not at all against that. As many people as possible should take an interest in reading and writing and theater and good cinema and music. I'm not in favor of closing libraries or public art galleries, and I'm in favor of free education.

What distresses me is the assumption that somehow or other "democracy" means that everybody has to get into the act, that everybody must be cultured and take a serious interest in good art and good literature. I don't see any reason for making this assumption. I don't see why interests shouldn't be completely voluntary. It has nothing to do with real democracy. You can have two completely distinct cultures, as I think is actually the case right now. An elite culture, for people who care about these things, and a mass culture for people who don't. Both sides are happy.

But this business of making concessions to the public in order to interest them, I don't understand why this should be done at all. This is where real snobbishness comes in, it seems to me. The assumption is that you somehow cannot be a really dignified human being without deep cultural interests. I don't agree. I can respect somebody even if he hasn't the faintest interest in "culture."

Historically, a very small percentage of the population at any time—and I'm talking about Renaissance Italy and Periclean Athens and so forth—were really interested in art, music, sculpture, literature, history, and philosophy. I would say less than 20 per cent, and why isn't that a perfectly good state of affairs? In the past, up to 1800, it was not only just a small percentage of the people in general, but even a small percentage of the only people who had any contact with art (namely, the ruling classes) who were interested in culture. Seventy or 80 per cent of the population were peasants or other lower-class people who were completely outside the cultural marketplace. Only the upper classes—the clergy and the nobility—had anything to do with culture, and very often they were much more interested in hunting than they were in art.

Why is it necessary to have this broad diffusion? The avant-garde movement I just spoke about turned its back on the masses and on the cultural marketplace, which is precisely why they were able to create such great things. They appealed to a very small and sophisticated audience, and therefore they were able to be original, to be imaginative, to do the very best work they could do. They didn't have a lot of ignorant democratic louts looking over their shoulders and telling them they couldn't understand it.

When I was at Yale, I'd guess that less than 15 per cent of my classmates ever went to the library for any reason that did not relate to an assignment. I used to go to the library all the time because I was interested in books; I like to read books. But here were these sons of rich families who were paying a lot of money for their education, and they wouldn't read a word they didn't have to read. And if these rich boys, coming from homes with "every advantage" including books and educated parents, were still apathetic about culture, how can one expect any real interest from the great majority of Americans who never even finish high school? And why try to stimulate this interest artificially? I think it is the right of every American *not* to read books or go to museums or attend concerts. This is a free country, isn't it?

N. I shouldn't say this—but I couldn't agree with you more. My final question is really ethereal: If you could imagine yourself in the position of a critic or reader fifty or a hundred years hence, looking back to the work of Dwight Macdonald, how would you like to be regarded?

■ *Macdonald:* My God, what a question! I suppose I'd like them to think I was a good fellow, really—but it's more than that.

I would like them to think that I had some critical intelligence and that I wrote well. There might be some connection between the two; I think there is. I don't think you can conceive of a really good critic who doesn't write well. Bernard Shaw was the best all-around critic that we've had in the last century—the greatest practicing critic, that is.

On further reflection I don't care very much what posterity thinks of me. In fact, I don't have that concept at all. I want my work to be admired—but right now, not after I'm dead.

I'd like my work to communicate with some people who share my taste or come to share my taste. It isn't a question of how many people, either, because when I was running my little magazine *Politics*, which had a top circulation of a little over 5,000, I had the most satisfactory audience I've ever had. I got more letters than I could possibly answer, and even now, fifteen years after it folded, I seem to be better remembered for *Politics* than for my work for bigger magazines.

So I guess I don't care about either large audiences or posterity. After I'm dead, what possible pleasure could I get from having a chapter, or more likely a footnote, given to me in some history of American literature? I would trade all of that for more of the fun of success here and now: for more communication, more of making an effect on people's minds. Furthermore, these things work themselves out. I won't put anything over on posterity, I'm sure.

"This extreme use of words, of obscene words and obscene acts, the preoccupation with sex, has reached a point where it makes us look like Peeping Toms. I don't like to be made to feel like a Peeping Tom when I'm reading a book. I'm not a psychiatrist's couch—I'm a reader."

Helen MacInnes
Interviewed in New York, August, 1963

P*

Helen MacInnes

N. In recent years the suspense story has assumed a character its early practitioners would scarcely associate with the metier. The arts of sleuthing, the rambunctiousness of derring-do, have been blended with a studied, realistic approach to the temper and pace of the vast world of international relations. At the phalanx of this movement stands Helen MacInnes with a series of best-selling, critically acclaimed works like *Above Suspicion, Assignment in Brittany, Friends and Lovers, North from Rome, Decision at Delphi,* and *The Venetian Affair*. Since the construction of her novels must involve a great deal of research and planning, I'm going to ask her, first, how her latest, *The Venetian Affair*, was put together.

■ *MacInnes:* First of all, we have the difference between the plot and the theme that set me off on the plot. Shall I make the distinction?

N. By all means.

■ *MacInnes:* Underlying everything is the fact that I'm interested in international politics, in analyzing news, to read newspapers both on and between the lines, to deduct and add, to utilize memory. Why does this party behave in this way? What is its record? What is behind this story that goes deeper than this brief report?

The Venetian Affair sprang from events which were interesting and upsetting, which is a very good way to write. It means that the writer is moved. In April, 1961, a report appeared regarding the revolt of the French generals in Algeria. At that time a great many mixed reports came in, and our enemies claimed that our Central Intelligence Agency was at the bottom of it; some of our friends even began picking this up. The French never denied anything until the newsmen actually demanded the truth. I think this happened at a public luncheon for Ambassador Gavin, who had just arrived. They demanded to know what evidence was at hand for believing that the CIA had anything to do with the generals' revolt, and the French had to admit that there was no evidence at all.

I became interested in how a lie like this could be invented and grow to throw normal relations between countries out of kilter, create trouble between allies, and possibly change the course of history. I also discovered, through research, that there have been other dangerous lies, but that usually we have been able to cope with them because our ambassadors managed to move in on them before they became public. The minute the curious public gets onto one these, it increases the boiling of the pot. A recent example: In Canada, just before their last election, a letter was circulated—reportedly written by an American ambassador—that indicated American interference in the election. The ambassador denied writing this letter, and the Canadians discovered that it had in reality been mailed from London. It was a lie, but it could have caused a great deal of trouble.

But in 1961 I was traveling abroad, and the French generals–CIA affair preoccupied me. We traveled as far as Istanbul, but I was in Paris, Venice, and Greece. (My husband, you see, is a classical scholar—he is Gilbert Highet, Anthon Professor of Latin at Columbia University—and we do a lot of traveling in the Mediterranean, looking at ancient remains.) So when I got back to America in November, and this affair still haunted me, I began to think of what could have happened—how the President's visit to Europe would have been ruined had this lie gained strength, just as Eisenhower's visit was ruined by the U-2 affair. So I started from there—from what could have been done to build a lie into a really dangerous international incident.

Then, of course, I started with my characters and grew deeply interested in them. Every character has a plot of his own—his life, the ingredients of his life, the things that have happened to move him to act and react one way or the other. Bringing in the characters is like combining many plots under the umbrella of the main plot, which in this case is the danger of a big lie being used to disrupt international relations.

I don't know how well I've explained this. So many things are involved in writing a novel like *The Venetian Affair*.

N. Do you do a great deal of editing and rewriting?

■ *MacInnes:* Heavens, yes. I write in pencil, you know, and work on yellow unlined sheets—the cheapest paper—but the paper is inexpensive and crumples so nicely when I know a sheet is no good.

With this one I went through three 500-sheet packages of the yellow paper and thirty or more soft black lead pencils. I used all

1,500 sheets but ended up with less than 500 pencil pages, so I guess I did constant rewriting as I went along.

In a way it's like painting—you discover that you need a touch of red here, or yellow there, and I do this retouching as I go along. I'd love to write a 1,000-page manuscript, putting everything into it, but a writer must select, clarify, communicate. I don't dare underestimate the reader, and it's an insult not to communicate with him.

But despite all this rewriting and editing I simply can't call for outside help or advice while a novel is in progress. I never show anything to anyone—not even my husband—while I'm working on it. It would be a waste of their time, and dangerous for me because I'd try to change things according to their criticisms and the whole novel might be thrown off kilter.

N. If you were to give advice to the young novelist what would that advice be?

■ *MacInnes:* I'd say preparation comes first. You have to learn, before you write. Every novelist must be an individualist, of course, but you can't carry individualism to a point where you think you're the great discoverer—because you aren't. The world didn't begin when you were born, neither philosophy nor religion nor sex began the moment you came onto the earth. Preparation is best begun early in school. I didn't know this; at fourteen or fifteen, you don't know these things, but if you're lucky there's a teacher or a schoolmaster or someone in your family to encourage you. It's better if it comes from school, because I've noticed then when the family gets into the act they approach things from an adult point of view and supply too many frills and not enough basics. School should provide the education, and the family should help by being sympathetic.

The first thing is to read, read, read; there's plenty of good stuff in school libraries. We were made to do this and perhaps we grumbled at times. Every month we had to write a résumé of a novel we had read, and we had to read at least one novel a week. This, as well as taking a full load of subjects. I had three languages, science, mathematics, trigonometry, solid geometry, English literature, history, geography, etc.

I could bless these teachers now—I didn't have enough sense to bless them then. You have to be compulsory with children. In Scotland we did as we were told—at least, we did then—and we never had dropouts from school. You finished when you finished, and that was that. We knew we couldn't get anywhere in life unless we finished our work and finished school, so we stuck.

The habits we developed stayed with us. When I met my husband at college I was already skipping my lunch in order to buy novels, and when I went to London I joined a good book club. In order to afford this, I would walk rather than ride the bus, and eat apples and bread and cheese in my room, and make teas for myself, but I had to do these things in order to get to concerts and have books to read. I hadn't planned to marry a classical scholar when I went to Glasgow University. I was determined to go to work for the League of Nations, and I knew that the broader and the more intense my education was the better chance I had.

So my advice to the beginning writer would be to make sure of truly thorough preparation. None of it will ever be wasted, and without it you might be improperly armed.

N.   Where did you live after you were married, and when did you start writing?

■   *MacInnes:*   We lived at Oxford. My husband was a don at St. John's College, and we lived there for our first five years, though we did travel. We would translate books together, from the German, and made enough money to get away to France and Spain, or the Tyrol for mountain-climbing. We spent our honeymoon in Bavaria in 1932, just three or four months before Hitler came into power.

Our chief interest has always been literature, and we've always been wrapped up in music, art, and international affairs (which is really contemporary history.)

This is another thing for the writer: You have to know about past history or you have no frame of reference for what is happening now—how exaggerated or dangerous or relatively unimportant a current event might be. Unless you're going to write only about yourself and your family, a world enclosed by your garden wall, you must try to know and understand what has happened and what is happening.

I didn't start writing until we came to America. Before this I was occupied with learning to run a household, cook, how to run a baby, and helping my husband with translations that let us do some traveling.

In 1938 we moved across the Atlantic which is another energetic enterprise. I forgot to mention that I had also been doing some acting at Oxford—with the Oxford University Dramatic Society called the O.U.D.S., and with the Experimental Theater. I had leads, fortunately, and we did splendid things by Shaw, Cocteau, Pirandello, and Shakespeare, and I think this might have contributed a great deal to my preparation as a writer, too, because I learned so much about dialogue. If I may digress further, there was an earlier period at University College in London where I took a postgraduate course in librarianship. I was interested in bibliography and ancient manuscripts, and I was engaged to a man who was going to be a don at Oxford. There I learned a great deal—how to track down facts, how to work through bibliographies, how to check and countercheck, how to verify references. I have never, as a consequence, been intimidated by research.

Perhaps I didn't start writing until then because I fell into the trap of talking my ideas away. This is another danger to the young writer. The idea of sitting over a café table in Paris like Hemingway, talking about writing, sounds romantic, but it's actually insidious. After all, even Hemingway didn't do much writing during this talkative period. When a thing is talked out there's no private excitement left in your own mind.

In 1939 the war had broken out and we were in New York. My husband volunteered for service and I returned to analyzing news. Then one day my husband picked up a notebook I'd been keeping, the notes I'd jotted down all through the Nazi-Communist pact and those strange early weeks of the war, and he'd noticed that I had made prognostications of what was going to happen the next month, and the next, much of which had come true, and he evaluated this, and the style I was developing, and he said, "I think it's about time to write your novel." So I started to write—yellow paper, black pencils—while my husband finished some work of his own before going off into the Army. I wrote at night—our son was about six, and a six-year old boy fills up the daytimes quite thoroughly—but after eight o'clock at night I was free. I would sit down for at least four or five, often six hours and work. (I couldn't do that, now; I need more sleep.)

I suppose this would be another piece of advice to the young writer—don't complain about not being in a position to get eight hours of beautiful sleep, and being in a position to have no money worries. You can get along on relatively little sleep, and the struggle won't last forever, and I think there's actually more thrill, more reward, from smuggling time for writing during your earlier years.

So this is how I wrote *Above Suspicion*. I stopped most social life, stopped acting, stopped talking brightly about the art of writing a novel. I just stayed with the book, from eight in the evening until one or two in the morning, until it was finished.

N.   How did you react to this success?

■ *MacInnes:* Well, it was a bit startling. It was gratifying, of course, and it rather ensured the fact that I would go on writing. But even though I'm happy about what happens with a book after it's finished, my chief interest in it is while I'm writing it. It's the hardest possible work—you say "no" to the opportunity to do so many delightful things and live almost like a hermit. I'm lucky in that my husband respects these preoccupations; his own work as scholar, professor, critic, and writer involves similar periods of absorption, after all.

But, as I said, I'm grateful for success, and feel very happy about it, but it's rather after-the-fact, in a way. The keenest points of interest come in the writing of the book.

N.   You wrote two non-suspense novels, as I remember.

■ *MacInnes:* Yes. Both *Friends and Lovers* and *Rest and Be Thankful* were written between 1946 and 1948. *Rest and Be Thankful,* my first novel to be laid in America, had a Wyoming background. Peace was here, and I kept thinking, "We've got to be peaceful," and I wrote in this vein until I realized that our international world had gone terribly wrong again.

I returned to analyzing news and got more and more worried. One thing we must always remember is that the Cold War was started by Russia. Remember this, when we are told about "American imperialism." Remember that in 1945, America had ten million men and women under arms; she had the atomic bomb (no other country had), and if she had wanted to conquer the world she could have done it right then and there. Nothing could have stopped her.

So, even though I write fiction I had to return to the contemporary state of affairs and my peaceful novels rather went by the boards.

N.   Now, in turning to the literature and theater of our day, what do you find most to admire and deplore?

■ *MacInnes:* I read a great deal, of course, and my tastes run from Jane Austen to Dostoevsky and include a great deal that is contemporary. I must admit that I'm not too happy with some of contemporary literature. It has been fashionable among certain groups to applaud something simply because it contains a great deal of obscenity in words and actions, a violation of all standards of moral behavior. But the odd thing is, if you were to take away the dirty words and the dirty ideas you're left with little that is worth reading or even interesting or *able to stand alone.* I'm beginning to think that this is a very easy way to write—the writer doesn't have to work at his plot or his characters or any of the problems of our day or of our lives. Everything is going to be done from the view of his own sensuality, or from the sensuality of characters who are very much like him. It's all very private, and wickedly free of significance.

I cannot write this way because I don't admire it; I don't enjoy it. This extreme use of words, of obscene words and obscene acts, the preoccupation with sex, has reached a point where it makes us look like Peeping Toms. I don't like to be made to feel like a Peeping Tom when I'm reading a book. I'm not a psychiatrist's couch—I'm a reader.

These same writers, and their ardent appreciators, might tell us to look back to Rabelais, that he used a lot of obscenity too, and his works rate as literature. But Rabelais was totally different. Of course, he was sometimes obscene and bawdy, but what he said had value and still has value. His satire is still very pungent and true. What I'm objecting to is the use of obscenity *for the sake* of shock, just as I object to abstract art that's done *for the sake* of shock. It's not good enough. You can use shock methods to accomplish a mood or create a form, but shock, by itself, is never enough. In an even broader sense, I believe this material is out of step with our times. I feel that our times involve a perpetual test of character, a test of people, a test of standards, and I think that we must maintain solid and rather high moral standards. We must have a frame of reference to be able to decide what is right and what is wrong. To think that everything is relative, that nothing matters in the end, is an invitation to disaster.

"The really big things [the writer owes his subject matter and his public] would be in the realm of truth and accuracy, of course. This is taking the fact rather for granted that one must make the work interesting to the reader."

Jessica Mitford
Interviewed in San Francisco, August, 1963

Jessica Mitford

N.   There is no denying the news value of the Mitford family. For decades their highly individualistic behavior has amazed and amused a vast public on both sides of the Atlantic. Two of the daughters, however, have made notable contributions to the literature of our time: Nancy, with the incomparable comic style that sweeps both her novels and essays, and Jessica, with her more serious analyses of her own unique life and with American funeral practices. *Daughters and Rebels* is as lively an autobiography as one could hope to read, as Jessica combines "the Mitford touch" with ambition and dedication. *The American Way of Death*, one of 1963's important books, lowers the boom on our costly methods of disposing of loved ones. Both books are graced with style and keenness of observation, but in the latter we find the evidence of painstaking research.

First I'd like to discuss Miss Mitford's rather extraordinary upbringing in England.

■ *Mitford:* We weren't educated, you know. This is the thing that still annoys me. We were brought up in a large English country house, and my mother thought that school was an inappropriate thing for girls and that the uniforms would be too expensive. Consequently, we were never sent to school, but my mother taught us to read. She started us at five and by the time we were six, we had to be able to read the London *Times*. After that we were actually on our own, and we just knocked around in this large house, picking up what we could in the way of reading matter.

N.   You girls became quite political, didn't you?

■ *Mitford:* Yes. A lot of the family, particularly my sisters Diana and Unity, became Fascists during the time of the rise of Hitler, beginning back in 1933. Unity went to Germany, of course, rather a dreadful thing as it turned out, and Diana married the head of the British Fascists, Sir Oswald Mosley, who still carries on his odious activities. I decided to run away and join up with the other

side, so to speak, and after I reached the age of nineteen I never
really went home again.

N.   Your first, brief, and rather tragic marriage was to a brilliant young Communist sympathizer, was it not?

■ *Mitford:* This was at the time of the Spanish Civil War. I don't
think he was ever a Communist party member, but he went to fight
with the International Brigade in Spain. He was a vague relative
of mine, a second cousin, and I knew of his existence and of the
fact that he wanted to go off to Spain to fight. Finally I met him.
We ran off to Spain together and we were married. We went back
to England, and from there to America in 1939, just to see what it
was like. I never returned, but he went back during the war after
he enlisted in the RCAF. He was killed in 1941. I stayed on in
Washington.

N.   What did you do in Washington?

■ *Mitford:* I got various odd jobs—*very* odd, come to think of
it. Since I really wasn't trained for anything, I worked for a while
in the Office of Price Administration where I was classified as
"sub-eligible typist." The wages were $1,440 a year, on which I
supported myself and my daughter. I was so hopeless at the typing
that they finally let me be an investigator in the rationing and rent
control enforcement division. This turned out to be much easier
work as I didn't have to type. I had my own secretary, in fact, and
the new salary was a help, too, because I earned twice as much. I
met my present husband, Robert Treuhaft, in the OPA (he was
an enforcement lawyer), and in 1943 we were married and moved
to San Francisco. Later we moved to Oakland.

I had thought, when we came out here, of going to the University of California, but discovered that one had to have gone to
high school to qualify. To get into high school one had to have
gone to grammar school. Needless to say, I didn't pursue *that*.

Until I started writing, at the age of 38, I was rather occupied
with bringing up the children: my daughter Constancia Romilly
and our son, Benjamin Treuhaft. I also spent a lot of time doing
volunteer work for various civil rights organizations throughout
the 1950's.

N.   Now I'd like to turn to *The American Way of Death*, as I
mentioned, one of the truly notable best-sellers of 1963. How did
you become interested enough in American funeral practices to
write it?

■ *Mitford:* Well, my husband is a lawyer, and in the course of
his work he became terribly irritated by the depletion of small

estates of clients through funeral costs. In 1956 he, and a group of other men in Berkeley, California, began to organize The Bay Area Funeral Society, an organization devoted to assure low-cost funerals for those who wished them. This was its only objective. I thought it a worthy civic endeavor, but not terribly exciting.

Then he began bringing home trade magazines with lovely names like *Casket and Sunnyside, Mortuary Management* and—my favorite title of any magazine I've encountered—*Concept: The Journal of Creative Ideas For Cemeteries*. Now, actually having seen all these glorious titles, I could hardly fail to read them. The pages of these magazines opened up a whole new world to me. I discovered "Futurama," the casket style of the future, and the Practical Burial Footwear Company which offers "Fit-a-Fut Oxfords" with a slogan, "The finest . . . for those who care enough."

Naturally, the Fit-a-Fut Oxford doesn't show up on the foot of the deceased—it only shows on the bill for the survivors. Then there is an embalmer's aid called "Natural Expression Formers." A marvelous idea, because you can now state in your will the expression you would like to wear for your last ride.

Well, all these things were fascinating enough, but even more extraordinary was the vituperation with which the trade journals attacked clergymen and lay people working to simplify funerals. My curiosity became thoroughly aroused.

N. Wasn't a great deal of research involved?

■ *Mitford:* As a matter of fact, the book could never have come about if it hadn't been for my husband's help. He actually took months away from his law practice in order to help with the research. We traveled extensively, of course. For instance, we went to Evanston, Illinois, to investigate the National Foundation of Funeral Service. This is sort of a graduate school for morticians, where they teach all kinds of things like counseling the bereaved, business procedures, and how to sell vaults.

N. How did you first become aware of the difference between English and American funeral practices?

■ *Mitford:* Quite some time before I became interested in doing the book. I remember the first American funeral I ever went to. When the service was over, everybody got up and started walking toward the coffin. I couldn't understand what this was all about until I got up there—playing follow-the-leader, you know—and realized that I was supposed to look at the dead person who, by now, was a complete parody of his former self, rather ostentatiously made up, and lying in that ridiculous satin outfit. In England this procedure would be considered so weird and contrary to good taste, that it simply couldn't happen. Perhaps it isn't commonly known that this business of body-viewing is unique to the United States and Canada; in no other part of the civilized world is this sort of thing done.

N. How did the funeral industry respond to *The American Way of Death?*

■ *Mitford:* Well, Mr. Wilbur Krieger, whom we interviewed at length—he's the managing director of a lovely organization called National Selected Morticians—wrote a rather blistering attack. He claims the book is atheistic, and that it's an attempt to bring the Communist, godless sort of funeral to America to replace what he calls "our traditional American funeral." Ironically, there's nothing traditional about the American funeral; it's a brand new thing that was started in the last few years by the undertakers themselves—let's say in the last fifty years.

As for being atheistic, that's another bit of irony. The warmest reactions to the book have come from people like Bishop James Pike, head of the Episcopal Diocese here in California, and from ministers, priests, and rabbis. I should think they'd be quicker to spot atheism than a party like Mr. Krieger, whose self-interest is so clearly involved.

N. Do you feel that the various funeral organizations—and associated parties like the Florists Delivery Telegraph Association—were able to curtail the reviewing of your book anywhere?

■ *Mitford:* This is rather hard to assess. There were areas where the book was not reviewed, not even mentioned, and it may or may not have been due to pressure from the larger organizations or undertakers. Their lobbying ability is clearly seen on the state level in most states, so I imagine they could bring pressure to bear as far as newspapers are concerned.

For instance, in the state of California a law says that if a person has been cremated, the survivors may—under no circumstances—get possession of the cremated ashes. The ashes must be maintained in a cemetery or cremation center. You can see the financial gain from this because the niche, the urn, and the grave cost money. Thus the people who would like to privately bury the ashes of the deceased, or scatter them, are forbidden by California law to do so.

N. In other words you cannot keep Aunt Martha on the mantle in California.

■ *Mitford:* You cannot. As a matter of fact, one of the large cemeteries has put out a brochure explaining the importance of caring for cremated ashes, pointing out the dangers inherent in keeping Aunt Martha in the house. They point to the danger of burglary, or the loss of the ashes by *fire!* which I found a particularly odd thought.

The pressures spring, naturally, from the fact that a tremendous amount of money has been invested in all phases of the funeral industry. The funeral parlors of today are utterly wild in extravagance—wall-to-wall carpeting, concealed lighting, the finest in furniture, and piped music. And the last ride is apt to come in a rose-colored Cadillac—not black; the whole idea of the modern funeral is to negate death.

N. Isn't the epitome found at Forest Lawn, that much-publicized Disneyland for the dead?

■ *Mitford:* Forest Lawn has been covered over and over again, of course—and deservedly. Evelyn Waugh did it up in great style. Perhaps the final bit of madness, however, is *The Forest Lawn Coloring Book.* It's fascinating. You can buy it there or order it from the Forest Lawn Gift Shop. In it you'll find Michelangelo's "David"—the Forest Lawn version, with fig leaf attached (what color you do that portion, I don't know)—and bits of "The Last Supper," and so on. It's a terribly sacrilegious little item, I think, yet it's precisely what one would expect.

N. A short time ago, we spoke of pressures which could be brought to bear. The influence on state legislatures is apparent from some of the laws that exist, but isn't the Florists Telegraph Delivery Association another potent pressure group?

■ *Mitford:* Immensely potent. We ran onto this through the trade press, originally, when we kept seeing articles, advertisements, and editorials combating what they call "the menace of P. O." The "P. O." stands for "please omit flowers" which people often want to put in the death notice in the newspapers. Florists, who make 60 to 70 per cent of their annual revenue from the sale of funeral flowers, have conducted a hard-hitting and tremendously successful campaign against the right to put "please omit flowers" in the funeral notice. Their advertising appropriation must be important.

For example, in the San Francisco area, not one newspaper will carry "please omit flowers" in the funeral notice, even though the deceased may have expressed, in his will, the desire to have flowers omitted. Oddly enough, the newspapers are violating another California law, one which states that the decedent's wishes in regard to his funeral must be carried out in all respects.

I tested this out, myself. I called one of the metropolitan dailies and said that I was arranging a funeral for a friend's mother. I told the girl who was taking down the advertisement that I wanted the words, "please omit flowers." She said, "We're not allowed to do that; we're not allowed to say anything derogatory about anybody or anything." I said there was nothing derogatory in this notice—it's just saying "please omit flowers." She insisted, "You're being derogatory about flowers."

This was rather a puzzler, so I spoke about freedom of the press and the first amendment. So she got her supervisor on the line who said, "Well, we couldn't publish a notice like that; the florists would be right on our necks."

Now, a few papers, like the *New York Times*, will publish the "please omit flowers" statement, but these papers are few and far between.

N. I'd like to turn, now, to the American way of life. Having come here from England, what do you think of our vitality and our sense of direction?

■ *Mitford:* I lived through the depressing reign of McCarthyism—a frightening thing, of course, but I feel that we're snapping out of it rather completely despite the Birch types. For example, this extraordinary Negro movement which has caught up so many intelligent young white persons, too, is encouraging. I toured the South to do an article on the Negro movement for *Esquire*, and I found so much, even there, that is hopeful.

Here, at the University of California, I find that conformities are breaking down. I enjoy talking to the students, having them at the house, and they seem to be snapping out of the dull, student lethargy of "the silent fifties."

N. What obligation do you feel the writer owes his subject matter—on one hand—and his public, on the other?

■ *Mitford:* The really big things would be in the realm of truth and accuracy, of course. This is taking the fact rather for granted that one must make the work interesting to the reader. For example, the thing that really sort of bugged me, all the way through writing *The American Way of Death*, was the matter of accuracy. It's difficult, but one must be so exact. Getting the really accurate information on the costs of funerals is almost impossible to do—they're not properly maintained by any government agency. One of the things I hope might result from the book would be a government investigation of costs, and proper figures for what is spent on what the funeral industry calls, "the care and the memorialization of the dead." It's a fantastic sum, and I'm not really satisfied with the way we arrived at our final figure of $2 billion a year. I think it's too low, but we wanted to be on the conservative side, rather than the sensational.

But despite the hard work, and the grimness of the subject, I think I enjoyed writing *The American Way of Death*, and I hope it serves to reduce the cost of funerals.

"I am not opposed to any novel that depicts life as it is . . . but when we take only the most depraved and degrading aspects of our society to write about and ignore all the better elements, I think we're doing our country and our age an irreparable injury."

Ralph Moody
Interviewed in San Francisco, August, 1963

Ralph Moody

N. Occasionally a writer comes along who enters the scene with relatively little fuss, and yet, as years go by, builds a loyal audience. The sales of successive books rise, they assume a position on high school and college reading lists, and suddenly reviewers and critics discover that they have been giving a valid and talented writer very short shrift. This sums up, but in an oversimplified manner, the career of Ralph Moody, whose ingratiating studies of western life cover the years prior to, during, and after World War I—the settling-in period not covered by the shoot-'em-up epics of the Old West and big business look of the New West. In talking to Mr. Moody I would first like to ask him how he came to write the series that began with *Little Britches*.

■ *Moody:* Well, I can't call it a matter of compulsion, though I had aspired to be a writer from the time I was a youngster. But my schooling ended with the eighth grade, so I felt that I lacked the necessary education. On my twenty-first birthday my mother gave me a beautiful five-year diary which I kept up for only a week, but on the first page I outlined the program that I intended to follow in life. I wrote that I would marry early, have a large family, work hard, and save enough money by the time I was fifty that I could retire.

I would then go back to school and acquire sufficient education to enable me to write for publication. Ever since finishing grammar school I've been a compulsive reader, and since I was interested in writing it was only natural that I should read from the viewpoint of the author. When he had raised a particularly clear picture before my mind, brought a character alive for me, or moved me emotionally, I went back and read the material over again to find out how he had gone about it.

Then, when I was in my late forties our daughter signed up for creative writing at high school, thinking she had discovered a "snap course." She found it less of a snap than she expected, so she came to me one evening for help on a short story. I told her she had picked the wrong horse; that her father was an eighth grader, and that she would have to go to her educated mother for help. But she hung on, saying that I was the storyteller in the family, and that I must help her. Partly to put her off, partly because she had re-awakened my boyhood desire to become a writer, I told her I would try to get into an adult education class and see if I could learn something that might be helpful to her. The next day I joined a beginners' class in short-story writing at a San Francisco evening school. At our first meeting the professor handed out sheets of paper and told us, "Write me one concise sentence, stating your reason for wishing to become an author."

I had long believed that the small farm where a whole family worked together to make its living was the cradle of American independence and democracy. And I had been deeply disturbed at seeing small farmers driven from the land by the mass production methods developed in wartime agriculture, or obliged to compro-mise their independence by accepting government subsidies for not raising crops. So I knew what I wanted to write about, but was somewhat awed at the realization that I, an eighth grader, was attending class at a branch of the University of California. To keep from disgracing myself, I felt that I must produce in that one concise sentence the very finest English prose at my command, so I wrote, "I wish to become an author in order to preserve for posterity a record of the rural way of life in these United States before the advent of World War One."

Fortunately, I had a very excellent and understanding teacher. Before returning my paper he scribbled on one corner of it, "No, you don't either! You want to stir the emotions of your reader." Since then I have tried to do both—not through glamorization and sensationalism, but by presenting as simply as possible the people and the rural life I knew in my youth, and letting the actual situa-tions and reactions of the characters stir the emotions of the reader.

In the evening class, our assignment for the semester was to write a five-thousand-word story taken from our own experiences. Reaching back to the most exciting period of my life, I wrote of my first job away from home. That was the summer I was ten years old and worked as waterboy on a big Colorado cattle ranch where the cowhands taught me to do trick riding. I didn't try to write any fine prose, only to tell the story, but when my paper was re-turned the professor had again scribbled on the corner of a page. This time he wrote, "Don't let this go for a short story! Expand into a book."

It was 9:30 when we got out of class that evening, and I think I ran all the way back to my office. I got out my secretary's typewriter, rolled in a sheet of white paper, and sat down to write my book. Then I became overwhelmed by the realization that, even though my story had evidently pleased a college professor, I was still an uneducated man. All I knew about composition was what I had learned in the eighth grade, and I had no more idea how to write a book than the man in the moon.

For more than four hours I sat staring at that sheet of blank paper, barely conscious of its being there, for I was back once more in my boyhood, living it all over again as scene after scene rose vividly before my mind. In the story the teacher had told me to expand, I had chosen what I believed to be the only experience of my life worth writing about. But as I sat there remembering back, I became aware that there was nothing in that story to expand, that if I had a story worth telling it was of my father, not of myself. As a boy I had known only that I loved the tall, quiet man who was my father. As a man myself, sitting there and remembering back, I realized that he was a most unusual person.

I had been feeling sorry for myself because of my eighth-grade education, but he had never felt sorry for himself a moment, and his total schooling had amounted to only six weeks. Furthermore, he was born of deaf-mute parents in the backwoods of Maine, had no opportunity to learn spoken language until sent to visit relatives at the age of eight, and contracted tuberculosis in his early twenties. Yet, he had developed a clearer and more definite philosophy of life than any other man I had ever known. And without any preaching or obvious teaching, he passed it on to his children before he died at the age of thirty-seven.

Our sons, both well-educated men, were then in military service in Germany, but I had failed to teach them my beliefs as my father had taught me his, and it seemed rather late to begin such instruction. A man can hardly write to a grown boy, "Son, I am enclosing herewith an outline of the principles in which I believe, and of a way of life that produced self-reliant, industrious citizens, but which I feel we are losing sight of in the midst of our tremendous scientific, economic, and social advancement."

To write any such thing would be absurd, but our boys had always liked to have me tell them stories of what they considered to be the "olden times." It occurred to me that if I could tell them stories of my boyhood on paper, I might be able to let them see the way of life I believed to have been good, and learn from my father as I had learned from him, with no apparent preaching or teaching.

By two o'clock in the morning I had given up any idea of expanding the story I had written for class, or of trying to write a book for publication. Instead, I would write for my own sons the story of my boyhood from the age of eight to eleven, the three years I had really known my father. And to avoid problems of composition or the use of too many words I couldn't spell, I decided to write the story as though I were still ten years old and telling it verbally. I began pecking at the typewriter keys, and by daylight had six poorly typed pages lying face-down in the bottom drawer of my secretary's desk.

By the end of three months the drawer was full, and I was beginning to hope that some of the material might be worthy of publication. I wrapped the pages into a bundle, took it to the teacher, and said, "If you have time, will you look this over and see if there is anything here that's worth publishing? If you think there is, I'd like to employ a professional writer to put it into acceptable book form and submit it to a publisher."

A week later the professor brought the bundle to my office and told me, "What you need is a professional typist; you've written your own book." Then he suggested that I send it to a New York agent.

I did, and a few days later received a letter saying, "Manuscript received and read with pleasure. Have entitled it *Little Britches* and submitted to W. W. Norton & Co." In another two days I received a wire, "Your book taken by Norton contract in mail."

I had no sooner received the wire than I phoned the professor to tell him of my good fortune. During the conversation I remembered that he had returned the original story a week or so before Christmas, so asked if he could tell me the exact date. After referring to his records, he told me that it had been returned on December 15. By the merest of accidents, and only because I had stared in bewilderment at a blank sheet of paper for several hours, I had written the first page of my first book on December 16, 1948, the day I became fifty years old.

N.   How many copies of *Little Britches* have been sold to date?
■ *Moody:* I'm not sure. About 100,000 in the American trade edition, somewhat more in the book club edition, and somewhat less in the combined foreign editions.

N.   To go back to your early life, you had rather a rugged childhood, didn't you?

■ *Moody:* If so, I didn't realize it, and it was by no means unique. There were then thousands of other families in the same circumstances as ours, in fact, almost every one that homesteaded west of central Kansas. All hands pitched in gladly to scratch a living from the soil, and when families ran into bad luck, death, or sickness, the neighbors stood by to see them through—not with charity, but with a helping hand. Many another widow was left with as large and young a family of children as my mother's, but only the most shiftless accepted charity, and I never heard of a child starving. The children went to work early, at any respectable job they could find, and took pride in being able to carry their share of the family load. I doubt that any one was injured by it, either physically or mentally, and it made self-reliant, industrious men and women of them. Neither my brothers and sisters nor I ever felt that we were "deprived" of anything, and we certainly were not "underprivileged," for there were then no child labor laws to deny us the right to earn a living, and no government hand-outs to rob us of our self-respect.

There can be no reasonable denying that there is need of relief for the jobless in times of severe national depression, such as the early 1930's, or that laws were needed to correct the abuses of child labor in factories and workshops. But I think we have created an ever-growing class of professional indigents by our too-easy government hand-me-out policy and have brought about a frightening increase in juvenile delinquency through our unrealistically sentimental child labor laws.

N. Has the series that began with *Little Britches* come to an end?

■ *Moody:* Nearly. It will end with the book I'm working on now. This one is of the two years following World War I, when I was a Kansas farmer and cattle trader, and it takes me up to the time I married. From there on a man could only bore readers by writing of his own experiences—unless he had done something really outstanding in his business or profession, which I never have. I'm sure that the only reason there has been a demand for stories of my early experiences is because the circumstances of my youth took me into situations and environments which no longer exist. It seems that stories of those bygone days and situations kindle a pleasurable nostalgia in the older readers and excite the spirit of adventure in younger readers who have never had the opportunities for adventure that I had. I think all readers like to feel that they are taking part in adventures beyond the bounds of their own experience, and many have written of feeling so when reading stories of my boyhood. I'm sure it is because I myself relive the experiences as I write of them, and because I tell the stories in simple colloquial language. My most highly prized letter is from a little boy in northern Montana. He wrote, "Dear Littlebritches: There is nine of us in our school. Our teacher read your book and I like it becose you write such bad english I can understand it."

N. Are the books in the *Little Britches* series actually true stories?

■ *Moody:* They are true in that they are my own experiences, but since I use dialogue in them they are, of necessity, fictionalized to some extent, for no one could remember exact conversations for fifty years or more. Then too, if I mentioned all the people who took part in those experiences the reader would become totally confused by names and would not feel acquainted with anyone. So I sometimes combine several actual people into a composite character, and since he is composite he is, of course, fictional to a certain degree. Also, I occasionally change a name. For instance, I found it necessary to write of a man who was not an admirable character in any way but whose children are probably still living. Being true, what I wrote of the man was in no way slanderous, but if I had used his true name it might have reflected harmfully upon his children.

N. Aside from the autobiographical series, are there any other books you've particularly enjoyed writing?

■ *Moody: The Old Trails West* was tremendously enjoyable, probably because I've been fascinated by old trails since early boyhood. I have never tired of digging into their origins, the reasons for their establishment, and the stories of those who traveled over them, both animal and human. There's a lot of popular belief that American "pathfinders," such as John Charles Frémont, pioneered the trails by which civilization moved westward across this country. They didn't. It is doubtful that Frémont pioneered a single mile of those trails.

Migrating animals originally pioneered nearly all the routes by which our civilization moved westward, choosing the most direct course that would allow reasonably easy travel and provide abundant food and water. Long before the first Indians reached this continent—more than 25,000 years ago—these migration routes had been worn into deep trails. The Indians, being hunters, spread throughout the land by following the animal trails in search of game. Few of our frontiersmen traveled any great distance without following these long-established migration trails or being guided by local Indians.

Come On Seabiscuit was a labor of love. No other horse ever attained greatness with so many strikes against him. As far as I know, he was the only horse that Sunny Jim Fitzsimmons ever came close to ruining, but there appeared to be a personal antagonism between the man and horse which was harmful to both. When badly frightened, the colt proved to have amazing speed, but would not respond to Sunny Jim's usual training methods. Under punishment he became sulky, nervous, and unruly. In an effort to force from Seabiscuit what he would not willingly give, Fitzsimmons raced him so unsparingly as a two-year-old that his front knees were badly weakened and his disposition completely soured. Then Tom Smith, an old-time cowhand turned trainer, recognized the trouble and told his boss, "Get me that horse, Mr. Howard. He's got real stuff in him. I can improve him, I'm positive." How well Tom Smith kept his word is one of the greatest stories in American turf history. He gave the colt understanding and affection, and in appreciation Seabiscuit gave back every atom of his speed and heart. It was enough to bring him recognition as champion of his time, and his lifetime winnings topped those of any horse before him.

N. You were a Kansas rancher after the first World War; how did you happen to become a city dweller?

■ *Moody:* I fell in love with a city girl who wouldn't marry a rancher believing that rural people couldn't give their children the cultural advantages she wanted ours to have. I wanted the girl and a family more than I wanted to be a rancher, so went to Kansas City to see whether or not I could make a living in town. Almost by accident, I acquired an interest in a newly formed chain restaurant business, and was fortunate enough to have it prove successful. I devoted all my attention to the restaurant business until joining the evening writing class. For the next ten years I kept two desks in my office—a work desk and a play desk. My first half dozen books were written at the play desk, in stretches of five minutes to an hour, when my attention was not needed at the work desk. Five years ago I retired to devote my whole time to writing.

N. To move now toward the realm of theory—what are your impressions of the status of today's literature. What do you most admire, on the one hand, and what do you most deplore?

■ *Moody:* I think *To Kill A Mockingbird* was the finest novel produced in this country in many a year. It was beautifully written, the author handled a great deal of difficult material extremely well, and the book had deep perspective. I think there is considerable novel writing now being done in the United States that is harmful to our culture and degrading to us as a people, for too many of our young writers are failing "to hold the mirror up to life." I am not opposed to any novel that depicts life as it is, no matter how rough or raw it may be, but when we take only the most depraved and degrading aspects of our society to write about, and ignore all the better elements. I think we're doing our country and our age an irreparable injury. All of us—by the time we are in our late teens—know that some aspects of life are not lovely, but those with the sensitivity to be discerning know that a great deal of it is fine and noble. When in our literature and entertainment we make it appear smart and "chic" to be morally and ethically corrupt, but "square" to be honest and aboveboard, I think we are destroying the morals and character of our youth. I am not a particularly religious man, but I believe that we must turn back, that we must renew our faith in religion, ethics, and moral conduct before we will again advance culturally.

N. If you were to give advice to the talented youngster who's intent upon becoming a writer, what would that advice be?

■ *Moody:* Read! Read the classics or anything that you'd be proud to have written yourself, but read from the viewpoint of the author. Although lacking formal education, I found little difficulty in writing because I'd been a constant reader and had had the best teachers in the world—the authors of the classics. If reading is not almost compulsive to you, I think you may find successful writing next to impossible. I don't think one needs any unusual experience in order to write successfully, but he must have a sincere liking for people, the knack of understanding them, and the rare gift of being able to see problems from the other fellow's viewpoint. But above all, I would urge the budding author to learn by heart the advice that Shakespeare had his character, Hamlet, give to the players: "to hold, as 't were, the mirror up to nature; to show virtue her own feature, scorn her own image, and the very age and body of the time his form and pressure."

"The critic owes the book and the writer and the public the same degree of attention and sincerity that the writer gave the book. I can never take very seriously the book that's obviously merely rubbish, and calculated rubbish at that. . . ."

Hoke Norris
Interviewed in Chicago, March, 1964

Hoke Norris

N. Hoke Norris is literary critic of the *Chicago Sun-Times*. Along with the lively book page he assembles, and his own play in depth upon literary issues of the day, Norris is known for magazine pieces and books devoted to two towering problems: integration and censorship. The first, of course, is not truly a literary issue, yet enough top journalistic talents are involved with it to give it a strong literary cast. Norris published, a few years ago, a novel, *All The Kingdoms Of Earth;* he has published some thirty short stories in various magazines—both novel and short stories arising out of his experiences as a born and raised Southerner.

More recently, he published *We Dissent*, a striking collection of articles on integration by southern intellectuals of liberal persuasion. This book is a vital analysis of the serious racial issue in the South. It was edited by Mr. Norris, who also contributed an article to it. So my first question will be: How much have these dissenters actually influenced integration in the South?

■ *Norris:* Some of them have done a great deal. Ralph McGill, for example, can be almost single-handedly credited among the unofficial forces that made possible the integration of Atlanta schools, the University of Georgia, and Georgia Tech a peaceful one. Five years ago I would have firmly believed and said that any attempt to integrate schools anywhere in Georgia would be met with extreme violence. It came about with little violence because Ralph McGill was there and on the scene, and because they had a good mayor in Atlanta and a responsible chief of police. These men were determined that there should be no violence, and that the edicts of the court, the laws of the land, should be upheld in spite of all obstacles.

Among others who've shown the way in the South are Jonathan Daniels, on the Raleigh, North Carolina, *News and Observer;* Hodding Carter and his son on the *Delta Democrat-Times*, in Greenville, Mississippi; Harry Ashmore, when he was in Little

Rock during the crisis there; William C. Baggs on the *Miami News;* and in Norfolk, Virginia, Lenoir Chambers, editor emeritus of the Norfolk *Virginia Pilot.* They did a fine job of preparing people for eventual desegregation. Norfolk schools were closed for a while, but they were reopened when people discovered they couldn't get along without schools.

This, of course, will be the discovery everywhere in the South, because in no area, in this age, can we get along without schools, and Southerners have always believed in schools. At great expense and at personal sacrifice they've attempted to educate their children. They've built some fine universities; the University of North Carolina and the University of Georgia are two I know well, and I suspect they're finer than many of the large colleges to the north. In the South you find the classical tradition prevailing, whereas elsewhere in the big land-grant universities the classical tradition has been abandoned in favor of ballroom dancing or basket weaving or speedreading or some of the other absurd subjects that appear in their catalogs.

To return to your question, the book was prepared because we thought that unfortunately, quite unfortunately, the mass of people in the United States hear only the voices of violence in the South. We knew, all of us, that other important and influential voices were seldom heard, especially by those who only read newspaper reports or see television or hear the radio when violence occurs. For when there's violence there's news—without violence there is silence.

Many people have been speaking up for a long time. Even former Governor Collins of Florida, sensitive as the situation was there, spoke out quite frankly. He has a piece in the book about the necessity for law and order, and it prevailed in Florida as long as he had his way.

N. How would you compare the real state of integration in the North as opposed to the South?

■ *Norris:* Certainly the North isn't blameless. There's a considerable degree of segregation and widespread prejudice, in all northern areas. Every once in a while it is demonstrated, especially when Negro families try to move into new residential areas or into established pure white residential areas.

In the South the pattern of segregation is written into the laws. In the North they're not written into the laws and segregation can be more subtle and just as effective. The Negro in the North doesn't know what to expect—he doesn't know where he's going to be admitted or where he's going to be refused. In some ways he is more sure of himself in the South, which may be a negative virtue, but it always helps to know where you stand.

I was in Oxford, Mississippi, last fall for the unpleasantness on the campus of the University of Mississippi. On my return, when I began writing a series of stories on the occurrences there, I read in the newspaper that a group of Negro families had been made homeless by a fire and been given overnight haven in a church on Chicago's southwest side. It was a "white" church. And the church people were forced to take the homeless Negro families away because a white mob gathered outside and threatened violence. The damnyankee has no reason to be pious about the integration issue.

N. Do you think the patterns of violence will continue?

■ *Norris:* They won't disappear overnight, but I think actual violence will diminish. In fact, the University of Alabama is the only remaining large southern school that has remained segregated, although it, too, had the Autherine Lucy episode a few years ago.

I suspect that these things represent the dying struggle of the old Confederacy. There'll be episodes, of course, and it's a shame that such episodes overwhelm the fact that the desegregation of southern universities goes back to 1938, when people voluntarily or under court order began admitting Negro students. The Supreme Court, even before 1954, was preparing the nation for the ultimate decision that segregation is within itself per se discrimination. Gradually we're chipping away at the old equal-but-separate concept. (This had been the rule since the *Plessy* v. *Ferguson* case of 1896, I believe.)

N. Now I'd like to enter that second area where your interests are so definitely expressed—that confused world of censorship. You did an article for *The Evergreen Review* on one of Chicago's cases.

■ *Norris:* The case involved Henry Miller's *Tropic Of Cancer*. There are those who would attack the book and attack Miller, and those who would defend him, but Miller and his book became irrelevant, as the author and the book almost always do in these cases. It becomes not a matter of defending the author and his book, but of defending the rights of the people.

In this case the Chicago police and the police in some of our Chicago suburbs threatened the arrest of people if they sold a paperback edition of *Tropic Of Cancer*. In one instance there was an actual arrest of a bookseller in one of the suburbs who tended to object to what the police were doing in confiscating his books.

Subsequently Grove Press, on behalf of itself and others, brought suit in Superior Court of Cook County to restrain police

officers of Chicago and the suburbs from further interfering with
the sale of the book. There was a long and colorful trial—it lasted
two or three weeks. The case was tried before Judge Samuel B.
Epstein in the Superior Court of Cook County, at the end of which
Judge Epstein issued a momentous decision restraining the police
from further interference with the sale of the book. In his judgment
he made a classic statement of the Supreme Court's present position
in regard to censorship. I would hope that this statement could
serve, for all time, as judgment on such cases:

"The now accepted legal test of obscenity is whether (a) to the
average person, (b) applying contemporary community standards,
(c) the dominant theme of the material (d) taken as a whole,
appeals to prurient interests." No book, in other words, can be
considered in fragments; it must be considered as an entire work. To
further quote Judge Epstein: "The presence of a single objection-
able passage, the influence of the book on youth, the abnormal or
the erratic or the advocacy of unpopular theses no longer are
accepted as a legal test of obscenity," and furthermore, if the book
has any redeeming characteristics—that is, any social or artistic
significance—it cannot be held to be obscene.

Thus, by strong inference at least, only works obviously written
for licentious purposes may be subject to police action. The limitation is strict and precise insofar as a definition in law can be, and it
eliminates legal censorship of all but a few relatively insignificant
works.

This ruling of the Supreme Court was in force at the time the
cops picked up *Tropic Of Cancer* and tried to prevent its sale. The
cops should have known better. They were armed, in most cases,
with only their own dubious prejudices and so-called injured
sensibilities. They operated outside the law in confiscating the book,
in arresting one man, and in threatening others with arrest if they
insisted upon selling *Tropic Of Cancer*.

Unfortunately, the biggest trouble from censorship doesn't come
from the professionals. The police are just doing a job—a job, in
some cases, of which they're rather ashamed, but they've got to
make a living by enforcing what they presume is law. The biggest
difficulty comes from the amateurs—those who snoop in bookstores, look in one passage of the book, say page five of the paperback edition of *Tropic Of Cancer*, and fly into outrage and demand
that the bookseller not sell the book, and take it to the cops and
sign a complaint which results in an arrest. They are troublesome
people—here in Chicago and elsewhere.

I suspect this pattern exists all over the country. The schools have been subject to this sort of idiocy. Outraged parents appear before the school boards demanding the withdrawal of certain books. The books that always seem to appear on the outraged-parent list are *Catcher In The Rye*, by J. D. Salinger; *Brave New World*, by Aldous Huxley; and *1984*, by George Orwell. Add some of the works by John Steinbeck. There's such a unanimity in these lists as they appear throughout the country that I suspect the existence of a central clearinghouse of information. These people haven't really read the books; someone has told them they're bad books. Oddly enough, two of these—*1984* and *Brave New World*—are books that warn of just such a moral welfare state as the amateur censors would attempt to create if we let them.

The problem, as I see it, is totally ignored by the would-be censor. The problem is not to keep people from reading books, but to get them to read at all.

Some of the tongue-in-cheek things that pop up in the course of censorship are wonderful. *Field And Stream*, a magazine devoted to outdoor sport, had a review of *Lady Chatterley's Lover* that reads as follows:

"Although written many years ago, *Lady Chatterley's Lover* has just been reissued by Grove Press. This fictional account of the day-by-day life of an English gameskeeper is still of considerable interest to outdoors-minded readers, as it contains many passages on pheasant raising, the apprehending of poachers, ways to control vermin, and other chores and duties of the professional games-keeper. Unfortunately, one is obliged to wade through many pas-sages of extraneous material in order to discover and savor these highlights on the management of a midland shooting estate. In this reviewer's opinion the book cannot take the place of J. R. Miller's *Practical Game Keeping*."

This is a better review of *Chatterley* than appeared in most places.

N. How do you regard the censorship of textbooks—the move-ment that seems most organized in states like Texas, but still crops up on the local level almost everywhere?

■ *Norris:* They are the maintainers of the status quo, or the status quo ante, to be more precise about it—or what these organi-zations regard as the status quo. Naturally, any viable society changes every moment of existence, though we still have people fighting the American Revolution and the Civil War.

It's hard to know just what the textbook censors hope to accomplish. They apparently object to anything that has a relevance to our modern day and to the years we are moving into. Anything more startling or revolutionary than, say, McKinley, is likely to startle this group. They are a small minority, but they are vocal. The danger arises from their vocal activities, and from the fact that the ordinary citizen who doesn't go along with them doesn't do anything at all, thus lets them have their way. They get textbooks censored on very stupid grounds, especially in the South, which is very sensitive to change these days. And Texas is apparently sensitive to everything.

N. In terms of autobiography, could you describe where you were born, reared, and educated, and how you entered the field of literary criticism?

■ *Norris:* I was born and raised in North Carolina and was graduated from a small Baptist college there, Wake Forest, before the war. After the war I attended the University of North Carolina for a short while. I just didn't want to go back to work after four years in uniform. Then, later, I went to Harvard for a year, and to the University of Chicago. All my studies at these places pointed in one direction—literature. Not that they were all so-called literary subjects. As you know, astronomy and nuclear physics and public affairs and the history of the world—it's hard to mention a subject that doesn't somehow bear upon one's competence in literature. But specifically I suppose that I happened to be at the right place at the right time, for once. I'd written some short stories and published a novel, and was working for the *Sun-Times*. And when the literary job fell open there, I was it. And I am a Southerner. Apparently that helps these days when you want to write.

N. In looking at present day literature, what do you see that you most admire on one hand, and most deplore on the other?

■ *Norris:* I think I most admire those who can write and do so in the face of the most formidable of obstacles and temptations. By obstacles I mean the deadly grinding and ever-growing difficulties involved in making a living. It's just too expensive, these days, for one to take time off to write that book he wants to write. There's almost nowhere a writer can take his family, as there used to be, and live on, say, a thousand a year. By temptations I mean the superficial distractions that divert us all from our natural calling— the distraction of the car, television, high living. But also the temptation to make a killing in advertising, in public relations, in the movies, in TV. They do pay quite well, and they often destroy just as well. And so I suppose that I deplore most of all the loss of

Q*

writers for whom the obstacles and the temptations are too persuasive. This kind of thing creates a constant erosion that may account
for the present low estate of creative writing. We do have many
writers, but we don't have many extraordinarily good ones. We'll
never know how much civilization has cost us.

N.   Could you pick out highlights—your own highlights, either
from the standpoint of pleasure or significance—of books published
within the last few decades?

■ *Norris:*   After Hemingway, Fitzgerald, Faulkner, and Wolfe—
what? We still have John O'Hara, who's always a delight, a real
pro who writes in the European fashion, that is, one book after
the other—one *good* book after the other. And of course one must
mention J. D. Salinger, Norman Mailer and James Jones and above
all Nelson Algren. But after *them,* what? We have a group of writers,
Updike, Cheever, and the like, who haven't quite done it yet, haven't
written the books we may expect from them. We seem to be in a
period of waiting, and literary creation is a thing that can't be forced.
It dies in the hothouse. And so there remain the older books, by the
several writers that I mentioned—we can always go back and reread
them, while we wait. They are still the highlights of our time.

N.   If you were to give advice to the young writer—the serious
youngster with talent—what would that advice be?

■ *Norris:*   I can give it in one word: Write. For the writer there's
no substitute. Too many of us seem to entangle ourselves; we don't
write, we talk about writing. The young man to watch is almost
always the quiet, rather homely, retiring fellow seen alone in
corners at parties. He goes away and you forget him, and when his
picture appears on the jacket of a book, you wonder where you've
seen him before. The glib talker, the bright young man who's the
center of attention and chatter, he's really the one you ought to
forget. He's too much a part of the race to report it. The only
position from which to report an event is the close sidelines—sort
of half-in and half-out of the event. The wholehearted participant
is in no position to see anything but the face in front of his own.
The sideliner sees all the faces. And these qualities are born in us.
Which is perhaps another way of advising a would-be writer that
he should be very careful in his choice of genes. I don't mean to be
flippant. It's just that that's the way it is, and nobody can do a
thing about it.

N.   What would you hope to see emerge in the near future
in the world of publishing?

■ *Norris:*   Publishing does need some reform, but you won't get any significant reform in it until you've reformed the public. It'll come as news to nobody, I trust, to say that publishers, like all businessmen, are out to make a buck. They've got to publish books that'll sell. Since it's the public that they sell books to, it's up to the public to make its demands, and it does so by choosing the books it shall buy. Until the public taste is elevated above the meretricious and the factitious, we'll be inundated with meretricious, factitious books. And so we are led back to the root of all cultural evil, and all cultural good—education. Elevate the nation's literary tastes, and you elevate publishing, and writing too. Not alone publishers need the stimulus of demand. Writers do too. No man can continue writing long in a vacuum. If he knows that there's somebody out there after all, he'll seek the echo of his own private genius.

N.   What do you feel the literary critic or reviewer owes the books that are reviewed in his paper, the writer who has produced those books, and the public for which he writes?

■ *Norris:*   The critic owes the book and the writer and the public the same degree of attention and sincerity that the writer gave the book. I can never take very seriously the book that's obviously merely rubbish, and calculated rubbish at that—the quickie written in the morgue of some newspaper about some hot person or topic, the novel aimed directly at the movies, the thinly disguised biography or autobiography intended to get the bucks where they are, and quickly. Such books should be ignored, and can be. But the so-called serious book is another matter. The reviewer can tell the difference. The shabby quickie smells; read a passage here and there, and it betrays itself for what it is. The real book has a tone, a feeling, a weight—not that it's always a good book, but you do take another look at it. And review it. And before you review it, you read it. Some critics, I understand, don't bother to read the books they review. The jackets are very complete—or have an illusion of completeness—these days. Such reviewers are frauds, of course; they defraud alike public, writer, publisher, and reviewing medium. But it's a pleasure to see a good critic at work. He reads and rereads a book, he makes notes as he reads, he checks some passages over and over again, and then he does his best to give an honest assessment. More than that nobody can do.

N.   If you were to look back, say, from the vantage point of 2064 at Hoke Norris, what would you hope would be said about him?

■ *Norris:*   What a chilling question. And what a good one. I suppose that as man more and more loses faith in his own immortality, his existence upon earth becomes the more and more important. That's at the basis of our civilization, I suppose—our materialistic longing for comfort and luxury. If there's no future, the present becomes very important indeed. The serf who was saturated with his religion took, understandably, the opposite view. And out of this mundane approach, so to speak, has arisen not only our materialistic civilization, but our humanism as well. If we value our own lives, we must value the lives of others. And at the same time monuments have become more and more important—not in bronze or granite or marble, but in works. William Faulkner was once visiting a friend who'd collected all of Faulkner's works. Faulkner contemplated the shelf, and said after a moment, "That's not a bad monument for a man to leave." For myself I'd hope that some day —in 2064—somebody might come across one of my creations, that it would speak to him, that it would be my voice he would hear. I can only hope that it will speak to him truthfully and well.

"I suppose one's obligation is to tell the truth, even though it hurts, yet one must make this qualification: One can only tell the truth as one sees it, while nearly everybody else will see the truth differently."

Hesketh Pearson
Interviewed in London, England, October, 1963

Hesketh Pearson

N.   Hesketh Pearson is unique in his presentation of biography. Accuracy is never merely enough. His unique flair for presenting his subject in full dress and, for that matter, complete undress, enlarges our concept of man and of history by plunging us into the character, the color, and the humor of the given person, place, and event.

At the time of this interview *Henry of Navarre* was Mr. Pearson's most recent highly praised offering. Thus I'll begin the interview by asking him how he came to write it.

■ *Pearson:* I started being interested in Henry of Navarre at the age of twelve, when I read the exciting romances of Stanley Wayman and Alexandre Dumas. I then began to read every book on Henry that I could find—even those in French. (Nowadays I don't think my proficiency in French would carry me very far.)

Two years ago my wife and I went to France with two friends, Norman Hunter and his wife. Norman, of course, is a playwright, and while we were down in Navarre I suddenly infused the Hunters with my early hero worship of Henry of Navarre. The result was that Germaine, Norman's wife, suddenly asked me why I didn't write a play based on Henry's life. I told her that Norman was the playwright, I the biographer, but that I would write a biography of Henry, and Norman could write a play.

At once I started on my biography by rereading the many books I had read in my youth and several more I have come across more recently. The result was that I knew a great deal about Henry of Navarre before I started writing the book, and learned a great deal more as I proceeded with the book. It took me nine months to do my preliminary work, and about a year to write the biography.

Meanwhile I had provided all this background to Norman Hunter, and he has written an excellent play—quite up to successful things he's done like *Waters Of The Moon, A Day By The Sea, A Touch Of The Sun*, and *The Tulip Tree*. I hope his dramatization of Henry is as much of a hit.

494

Henry of Navarre was an extraordinary person, one the biographer can get lost in. He united France and made a nation of it. Before his time France was torn by civil wars between Catholics and Protestants and ruled by a degenerate series of kings. Henry not only brought peace and prosperity to the country, but saved it from the horror and ruin of civil war, then prevented the return of feudalism. At the time of his death he had even formulated a plan for a league of nations, an alliance basically to ward off the threat—the constant threat—of the Hapsburgs, but a genuine league nonetheless.

Henry was not dull, however; he exhibited a few of the vices of his predecessors, namely a fairly insatiable sexual appetite and a fondness for certain luxuries, but he was remarkably without prejudice and possessed of intelligence and a desire for fair play.

A man like Henry is really a triumphant figure for the biographer. He allows one to triumph and sin vicariously, but in a most satisfying manner.

N. To go back to the beginnings of your career, I wonder if you can explain how you originally became interested in the role of biographer?

■ *Pearson:* It's a little difficult to say, but I do remember that at the age of fourteen I wrote a paper for domestic consumption which I called "The Lightning." I discovered this many years later and was quite surprised to find that my interest in famous men went back to that early age. (This may explain why I did so badly in school in everything except history.)

Then, owing to my interest in Shakespeare, I became an actor and remained on the stage for many years though I was never cast for Shakespearean roles. I continuously ended up in modern things by Coward and Lonsdale and Shaw, so after a time I got fed up and decided to leave the stage. Then, if you please, I became an advertising consultant, and it was while I was working in advertising that my early interest in famous men returned to me.

At the age of thirty I decided to embark on a career as biographer. I started off with my own ancestor, Erasmus Darwin, because there were quite a few more or less private papers my mother and friends of the family could give me. Having finished *Doctor Darwin* I found myself so absorbed in this type of work that never again has there been a question of doing anything else.

N. If you were to look back over the many books you've done, could you pick any favorites?

■ *Pearson:* This would be awfully difficult, something like picking a favorite child. I suppose I still like my book on Sidney Smith

[*The Smith of Smiths*] better than any other, not only because it actually put me on the literary map but because the character of Smith appeals to me, perhaps more than anyone else in history.

Yet I must admit that two or three of my latest figures have appealed to me almost as much—Charles II, for example, and Henry of Navarre. Yet I can claim some resemblance to Sidney Smith whereas I'm not awfully like Charles or Henry, no matter how much I would like to resemble them in at least a few specific aspects. Perhaps I can simply state that I am in complete sympathy with Smith, thus he became my favorite biography but not my best.

I think that my best biography is that of Walter Scott [*Sir Walter Scott*] because within relatively minute dimensions I reconstructed a character of extraordinary complications which it had taken Lockhart some twelve volumes to exhibit. I not only read Lockhart's twelve volumes but every book written on the subject including twelve volumes of correspondence, and I think the result is entirely satisfactory.

Two others I like very much are my lives of Bernard Shaw and Oscar Wilde, both of whom did more to arouse my literary sense than any writers who ever lived, with the probable exception of Shakespeare. In the case of Oscar Wilde I felt I was able to make him the extraordinary character that he was, a wonderful wit and humorist and a charming man. His physical peculiarities, rather, sexual peculiarities, made it difficult to tackle him when I did because the prejudice against him then was so strong; a prejudice my book overcame.

N.   Another unforgettable book you wrote was *Lives of the Wits*, a collection of fairly brief biographies. Could you explain how this was written?

■ *Pearson:*   Well, one has to remember that I had already written quite a number of these people at full length—Wilde, Whistler, Sidney Smith, Shaw, Disraeli, etc. Therefore all I had to do was to take the essence of the long biographies and condense them as much as possible, transforming full length portraits to cameos. The two longer ones in the book, Sheridan and Dean Swift, were new to me, but I knew a great deal about them in advance. I had read so much about them that I felt I knew them as intimately as one can know a person you've never met.

Perhaps biographies should be brief—I believe they should be, in fact. You should be able to distill the essence of anybody with reasonable length, say three-hundred pages in the case of a long biography, thirty pages in the brief biography. Of course it is anything but easy, and I found it extremely difficult to extract, as it were, the cream from what I had already done. In my humble opinion I had already extracted all that was vitally necessary in writing the longer books. *Lives of the Wits* was a hard book to write, and I'm unusually grateful to find it appreciated.

N. In dealing with the lives of important persons, what do you feel the obligation of the biographer is toward the subject matter you're working with?

■ *Pearson:* I suppose one's obligation is to tell the truth, even though it hurts, yet one must make this qualification: that one can only tell the truth as one sees it, while nearly everybody else will see the truth differently. For example, I wrote a book on Oscar Wilde because I saw Oscar Wilde as a wonderful man, but shortly after my book was published St. John Ervine wrote a biography of Wilde, and he obviously thought Wilde was a horrible man. He is no doubt as honest as I am, but the points of view were so different we might easily have been writing about totally different men.

To me there is only one obligation of the biographer, and that is to tell the truth—no doubt the biographer himself will view the truth in some individual light, and each reader will add some interpretation of his own, but if he has presented the truth he has fulfilled his obligation to his subject, himself, and the public.

N. If you were to give advice to the talented youngster interested in writing biography or history or nonfiction of any type, what would that advice be?

■ *Pearson:* First and foremost he must want to do it above all things. Enthusiasm is absolutely the first requisite. After that I suppose he must have ability, and the patience to study everything he can lay his hands on pertinent to his subject. If by any chance he is dealing with a person whose memory is still alive, he should tackle each of his subject's contemporaries to find out what their knowledge and thoughts and reactions are. He should read every book on the subject, and every document; this means that his enthusiasm must be so intense that it more or less absorbs the whole of his time and thought. He cannot give very much time to pleasure, except to indulge in the necessary recreation that keeps him going on his job.

Enthusiasm brings out all the other necessary qualifications for the job—whether one becomes a biographer or a burglar. Now, I don't mean that his private life is much more important than anything else one does, but a large part of one's public life must necessarily be sacrificed. One has a family and friends who cannot be

completely neglected. But the public life really isn't important because one is too exhausted from work to enjoy much of it, anyway.

I find at my present age—but I am getting on—that three or
four hours of concentrated work in the morning finishes me for
the day. Other people are more fortunate; they can go on much
longer. But three hours of real concentration, intense concentration,
may be all one can put in—at least, I think so. I remember discussing
this subject with Shaw, who dealt, of course, with a totally different
kind of literature, but Shaw told me that after four hours he was a
spent man. I asked him how he managed to produce so much if he
worked only four hours a day, and he replied, "I don't only work
four hours a day, I work four, then rest, then put in another four
later." Well, I don't. I'm finished with four hours, and after that I
walk and read and map out my next day's work.

The intensity of one's ambition and absorption will necessarily
rule out those things which waste time and effort. But one cannot
rule out love and affection—these things are less replaceable than
one's career.

N. Could you state your objectives insofar as your career is
concerned? How would you like best to be appraised and remembered?

■ *Pearson:* I started life practically with no ambition at all except
to enjoy myself. Later, when on the stage, I became ambitious to
play Hamlet but this didn't last long. Underneath all my other
efforts, however, I can distinguish an unquenchable interest in
remarkable men dating from my school days and I can only assume
therefore that I was born with an ambition to re-create them in
prose.

It is therefore solely as a biographer, who has brought many
vital and entertaining men to life again so that readers feel they
have known them, that I would care to be remembered.

"When you walk out of the theater after seeing a play by Tennessee Williams, you want to go and take a bath. You feel absolutely worn out and dejected, as though you should, perhaps, go to church and sit down for five minutes and commune."

Basil Rathbone
Interviewed in Los Angeles, August, 1963

Basil Rathbone

N. Basil Rathbone really needs no introduction beyond the admission that he is *not* Sherlock Holmes. For generations he has appeared on the stage and in motion pictures as an actor of rare discipline and power, recently turning to a one-man show, *In and Out of Character*, which provides a compelling evening of theater. As much as possible this interview with Mr. Rathbone will concern itself with his remarkable stint as a writer. His autobiography, *In and Out of Character*, stands as one of the finest to emerge from a theatrical personality. But first, an answer to a question that seems to automatically come to mind when an actor's book is mentioned: Did he write it himself?

■ *Rathbone:* You mean, was there a ghost writer? There emphatically was not. I started out with a pack of legal-size paper and a piggyback pen. I used up two, then three, then four packs of paper with no help of any kind until I arrived at Doubleday, where wiser heads than mine resequenced certain portions of the book. I was willing and happy to have good editorial help from John O'Connor at Doubleday, but I wrote every word of the book myself.

I can't imagine how anyone could work with a ghost writer. No matter how good a ghost he is, I don't see how he can convey certain experiences because those experiences are so privately and intimately felt. Some part of them might be conveyed, but in the end the ghost writer is bound to put down what he thinks a person's feelings and reactions were.

The book was written all over the place because I travel a great deal with this one-man show. The two sustained opportunities I had to sit down and write and be alone—to literally not be bothered by anything or anyone—came in Los Angeles, here at the Hollywood Biltmore Hotel, when I was in California to make a picture. I was not asked to appear for something like two weeks, so I wrote during that stretch, and then there was an interval of ten days in Salt Lake City, Utah.

I'm not experienced as a writer. I've written plays which have not been produced—except for one, which was a failure, and should have been. Yet the book didn't take me more than six or eight weeks to write. It came very fast, once I had been persuaded to do it. You see, I hadn't intended to write my autobiography, but someone suggested the idea to Doubleday. I think the reason they thought it might be worth doing was because of my long and close association with Sherlock Holmes. I cover this in the book, and I probably disappoint quite a few people when I say that it was not the happy experience the radio and television and movie audience thinks it must have been. Sherlock Holmes became so important to me that he practically put me out of work, just as he did his author. Remember, poor Sir Arthur Conan Doyle eventually became so impatient with the success of Sherlock Holmes that he decided to kill him, and he did. But the public outcry was so great that he had to bring him back again.

Now, I wasn't in a position to kill Sherlock Holmes because I was under contract, and I had to fulfill that contract, but when the contract was over I would go to New York and managers would say, "I'd love to have you in this play, but your identification with Holmes is too powerful. We can't risk it. You would walk onto the stage as whomever, but nobody in that audience would think of you as anyone but Sherlock Holmes."

N. Could you go back over your career, at least roughly, in the pre-Sherlock Holmes era?

■ *Rathbone:* I suppose the most fortunate element in my background was the training I had with a Shakespearean company which is now known as the Stratford-on-Avon Players. This was organized and instituted by my cousin, Sir Frank Benson, who was knighted by King George V under exceptional circumstances at Drury Lane Theater. But I had my early training with this company, touring all over England, and I struck a great moment when Miss Constance Collier came to Stratford after the war in 1919 and saw me playing Romeo. She decided that she wanted me for a play called *Peter Ibbetsen*, which had been done in New York with Jack and Lionel Barrymore, and as neither Jack nor Lionel wanted to go to England I inherited Jack's part.

This did it for me. Overnight I turned from an actor known only to my own family and a small group of friends to a public figure. Within two weeks everyone knew who I was, wherever I went. This is interesting because I don't think the public appreciates what it is to be a young person and to be a success overnight.

So much of it must be attributed to good fortune, and so little to talent.

But actually—out of all the plays I've been in, and all the performances I've given—I think my most powerful recall is wrapped up in *Hamlet*. You may play *Hamlet* as often as you like, but you will never be satisfied with your performance because you will never have gotten it all. Here or there you may do some parts well one night, other parts on another night, but you'll never give a perfect performance. Hamlet is simply the most demanding role in theater.

Hamlet stands above all other plays in its awesome presentation of human relationships. I think it's the best ghost story ever written. It is one of the best melodramas ever written. We have a problem with Shakespeare—the schools approach him academically, and if there's anything Shakespeare was not, it was an academic. He wasn't even particularly well educated—no college or university training at all. Shakespeare was a humanitarian with a great gift and a great love of fellow man. This love and understanding gives him a rank—to compare fields of artistry—with Beethoven and Michelangelo.

This year, in 1964, we'll celebrate the 400th anniversary of the birth of Shakespeare—not for artistry, but for money—and we'll find out once again that Shakespeare was not only the greatest playwright of all time, but the best at the all important box office. Think of what his returns would have been if he'd only had a trust fund.

N. If I may digress, you spoke of the demands of playing *Hamlet*. In a movie version with Sir Laurence Olivier wasn't there a disturbing preface, "This is the story of a man who could not make up his mind?"

■ *Rathbone:* It disturbed me, too, and I disagree with it. Larry is a good friend of mine, and he's not here to defend his own point of view, but I have discussed this with him and told him that I disagree. If Hamlet was a man who could not make up his mind—well, make up his mind about what? Would you, or could you, have done other than what Hamlet did? This man is told that his uncle, now on the throne, killed his father. You go downstairs the moment the ghost tells you this and kill the king. So people, no end annoyed, say, "Why did you kill your uncle?" and you say, "My father's ghost told me to."

This would be rather skimpy motivation, wouldn't it? Without evidence, at that. Horatio wasn't there. No one was there. If you want to argue with Shakespeare that Hamlet was a man who could not make up his mind, I again say, make up his mind about what? He had to prove the king's guilt before he could kill him, and things don't knit together until that beautiful last scene. Oh, I could go on, but I think Hamlet is much more complex than a man who could not make up his mind.

N. Are there any motion picture roles you remember with particular fondness?

■ *Rathbone:* I can't forget *Anna Karenina*—with the magnificent Garbo, and Frederic March. I was proud to be in that picture. Proud because I was allowed to play a realistic part. They called me a "heavy," another bit of oversimplification. Anyone who's read the book couldn't possibly label as a "heavy" a man who had married a woman far younger than himself, a foolish and conservative man who should never have married Anna at all. Some of the real drama of the story was marred by censorship, unfortunately. We aren't quite as silly about censorship, now, but at that time we sacrificed some of the real poignancy of the story. But it was a splendid movie, and I'm glad that it's still being shown.

N. To take a general look at today's culture—literature and theater in particular—what do you find that you admire and deplore?

■ *Rathbone:* I don't think my opinion is more valuable than anyone else's, but I am awfully tired of the downbeat. I'm very tired of probing at the underbelly of everything. I recognize the fact that Ibsen wrote plays titled *Ghosts* and *The Master Builder*. They were plays about social changes in life. We had Freud. We've had too much of Freud interpreted and misinterpreted and too much dark at the top of the stairs. Surely there must be something to write about, to act about, to think about, that relates to pleasantness and is nice about people. I, personally, would sooner make a mistake in liking someone than a mistake in disliking someone. I'm not being Pollyanna about this. I just think that, while people obviously have failings, their failings aren't in such devastating proportion to their presence in theater and on the screen and even (now) on television. Besides, don't we have to accept their failings when we come across them?

Once in a while somebody has got to write an unpleasant play about a situation with which they've been closely associated, like *The Heiress*, a play in which I appeared and which was written by Mr. and Mrs. Goetz. Now, Mrs. Goetz herself had a situation very similar to the father-daughter relationship in *The Heiress*, and she wrote very feelingly about it. The play was terrifying in many aspects, but when you walked out of the theater you didn't feel utterly miserable.

When you walk out of the theater after seeing a play by Tennessee Williams, you want to go and take a bath. You feel absolutely worn out and dejected, as though you should, perhaps, go to church and sit down for five minutes and commune.

I don't understand this continuous point of the finger at everything that is unpleasant when there is validity and amusement from sources that are more representative.

I'll go back a long way, but what about Galsworthy's wonderful *Forsythe Saga,* filled with human beings? They all had weaknesses, and one was glad to feel sad about them. They didn't make one feel sick. Sadness, I fear, will do for me; I don't want to vomit.

N.   I'd like to return to your autobiography, now, to refer to what we might call a matter of selection. Did you leave a great many unpleasant events and unpleasant people out of it?

■ *Rathbone:*   Yes, I did. I suppose, like everyone else, I might revel in saying some very unpleasant things about prominent people I've met and played with in the theater, but I thought I'd leave that to someone else. There was one instance I couldn't ignore completely—a man I despised who was associated with a play I did on Broadway called *The Captive*—but I don't want to make an issue out of it.

I believe I did give one page to Errol Flynn, and on that page I said that Flynn had recorded his own life in a manner in which he undoubtedly wanted posterity to think of him. I didn't agree with Errol; I didn't agree with Errol Flynn's view of himself. I think he was a very interesting man, and in that page I pointed out why. Flynn definitely had what is called the death complex. He could no more avoid destroying himself than I can avoid getting up and jumping into the pool in a few minutes. But Flynn was great fun; we did three pictures together and never had an unhappy moment. It's so tragic that he destroyed himself so soon.

But you see, I'm not a writer by profession, and the importance of this book is its relationship to the theater. I also was determined to write the book to prove (at least to myself) that an actor can be a creative artist, not just an interpretive artist. There are a number of episodes in the book which are basically true, yet they are so changed and arranged that no one will be hurt by their disclosure. Rightly or wrongly, I think the positive things in and about one's life, and about the people you meet and the circumstances you get involved in, are usually the most important.

N.   In writing your autobiography did you feel any obligation to the public it would reach?

■ *Rathbone:* Well, I don't call it an autobiography; privately I refer to it as a reminiscence. It's not the dull sort of thing that begins, "I was born on such and such a date."

What I wanted to do was to give impressions of my career and, above all, the particular world which surrounded me. There are places in the book where I've thought about things and come up with opinions—for example, the relationship of the motion picture to theater, to radio, and to television.

I've tried, from my point of view, to let my readers know what these mediums of entertainment are and how they interact. For example, television is the least important art form because it borrows from everything. Radio is an art, silent pictures were an art, but the moment pictures talked the medium became a borrowed art. In the silent film you imagined their voices, in radio you imagined appearances because you had only the voice to go on, and these were art forms. Nobody uses their imagination watching television—unless it's the Hallmark Playhouse. The best that can be said for 90 per cent of the shows is that they're rather like sitting in a swirl bath, pleasant but hardly inspiring.

N.   What do you think of the future of American theater?

■ *Rathbone:* Well, it's distressing to realize that in the 1920's we had, in this country, over 400 repertory theaters—professional status. At a luncheon four or five years back this subject was being discussed by actors, producers, and other theater people in New York, and we discovered that we only had about seventeen.

But I'll tell you this about the theater. I think that much of the future of whatever theater we have is simmering, is being prepared, and is being worked at with enthusiasm and affection, in our colleges and universities, in community theater groups. It's amateur theater, and this is its problem, because the jump to the professional is such a long one.

In order to become a professional at anything—golf, tennis, baseball—you can't make a major league until you actually become a pro. You have to learn more than you can possibly learn by playing with it part-time, but God bless the colleges and the community theater for keeping theater alive at all.

"The hope for the future of the art of the drama in America lies, I think, in the development of nonprofit, subsidized community repertory theaters."

Elmer Rice
Interviewed in New York, August, 1963

Elmer Rice

N. *The Adding Machine, On Trial, Street Scene,* and *Dream Girl* are just four of the powerful and enduring dramas that have won immortality for Elmer Rice. In addition to being great plays, within the limits we normally ascribe to plays as drama, they brought innovations which added to the techniques and scope of American theater. Thus, since Mr. Rice's first play was produced in 1914, he has not only witnessed the drastic changes which have swept the so-called "modern" theater; he has been responsible for many of them.

I'd like first to ask him what the greatest changes have been in this half-century of his creation and attendance.

■ *Rice:* The changes have been mainly economic—the shrinkage of the professional theater. For example, the 1962–63 season found about thirty theaters in operation in New York City, what we call first class theaters, Broadway theaters. There were between fifty and sixty productions.

Now, in the 1926–27 season, there were seventy theaters and over 250 productions. The population was only two-thirds as large as it is now, and probably only one-third the number of tourists and convention delegates added their potential weight of attendance. This gives you an indication of the physical shrinkage. And you can match this up with the decline on the road—fewer road companies, fewer cities to play in. Chicago, for example, now has only two or three theaters. Fifty years ago Chicago had fifteen.

Not only are there fewer theaters, but the length of the run—both in New York and on the road—has been cut. My first play was produced in 1914, and three months after it opened in New York we opened a second company in Chicago which ran six months. Now, except for an occasional runaway hit, if Chicago can give you six weeks, you're lucky.

The same thing is true of stock companies. When I first was in theater, there were about 150 stock companies. I don't mean summer theaters, I mean winter theaters, all-year-'round theaters with a

508

permanent group of actors. I don't think there are a half-dozen permanent stock companies now.

So with one-night stands. A successful play would sometimes have four or five companies out playing every small town—six different towns in a week. This, of course, is the great change in theater, and it has mostly to do with the extremely high costs of maintaining the simplest show on Broadway or on tour.

N. What changes in what we might call the "character" of American theater have occurred during this same fifty years?

■ *Rice:* I would say that despite our good years and bad, our spurts and slumps, American theater has come of age. You see, we had very little native theater prior to 1920. We had produced little that was original and deep and significant. We did melodramas, farces, or imitations of European styles. But in the 1920's there was a great burst of creative writing in the theater—some twenty-five or thirty young playwrights came up at that time, and they produced a very substantial body of work. I don't mean that there were many great masterpieces—masterpieces, after all, are rare in any art. But a considerable, lively, indigenous, interesting group of plays put the American playwright, and the American theater, in command of its own resources for the very first time. We can't even call it a renaissance because it was unprecedented. Oddly enough, today there are more American plays done around the world than plays produced within any other given country, yet until the 1920's we hadn't created very much.

This lasted for about fifteen years. I think you can pinpoint the beginning with the production of Eugene O'Neill's *Beyond The Horizon* in late 1919, but until 1933 or 1934 writers, gifted writers, kept coming on to develop their work. Since then we have some good writers, of course, but never have they presented any collective impact. If we are to name a Golden Age of American Theater, it would have to be that extremely creative period.

But then, an age like this, an age of vitality and accomplishment and innovation, is not peculiar to theater. It's true of all the arts. Perhaps theater needs a certain sense of security for successful breeding. Since that particular Golden Age the world has not known any period of even relative security.

N. You used the word "innovation." You were responsible for a great many changes in the staging of drama, weren't you?

■ *Rice:* They weren't changes for the sake of changes—I simply had to find effective ways, new ways, of doing the things I wanted to do on the stage.

On Trial achieved much of its success through novelty. It was the first time in the theater that what is called the "flashback technique" was used. It was a courtroom melodrama, the trial of a murder case. A witness would take the stand and begin to testify, and the scene changed to show his testimony being enacted. This was in 1914, and it was probably the novelty of the flashback that kept it on Broadway for a year and that kept three companies on the road.

A few years later I did *The Adding Machine* which was one of the first expressionistic plays done in America.

In *Street Scene* the technical innovations were not as obvious as they were in the other plays. They weren't as formal. But *Street Scene* required a cast of fifty to play the seventy-odd characters interwoven in the action. This was a much larger cast than had been seen in a Broadway drama, and the mere physical action required some unique handling, plus a split-level set that facilitated entrances, exits, groupings, and simultaneous movement. For example, the first act alone had about one hundred entrances and exits, whereas the average play has perhaps ten or fifteen.

N. I'd like to return to the cost factor for a moment—to the scarcity of plays being done in light of costs. What relative comparison can you draw?

■ *Rice:* I can answer that very easily. In 1931 I produced two of my own plays, produced them with my own money because I had had a great success with *Street Scene* and I was willing to gamble. I produced *The Left Bank* for $8,000 and *Counsellor-At-Law* for $11,000. Today a similar production for *The Left Bank* would cost between $75,000 and $100,000 and *Counsellor-At-Law* from $125,000 to $150,000. This will give you some idea of what is involved in relative costs and consequent risks. Now, when you add to this the fact that profits are smaller because of higher operating costs, the risks are again increased. *Counsellor-At-Law* paid off its production cost in three weeks; today it would take six months. This makes it increasingly difficult to capitalize plays, to finance them, to get backing for them. It makes it increasingly difficult to keep a play running if it doesn't catch on immediately. At one time a play could be panned or dismissed by the critics, but it could be kept running until word of mouth or publicity made it an eventual success. Today, if it doesn't catch on immediately, it's done for.

N. Is this the reason for the development of the off-Broadway theater?

■ *Rice:* We always had an off-Broadway theater—groups willing to work experimentally, or in small theaters away from the Broadway pressure: for example, the Provincetown Players, the Washington Square Players, The Neighborhood Playhouse, Eva Le Gallienne's Repertory Theatre. Unfortunately, the costs of off-Broadway productions have gone up, too. I would say that they have tripled in the last eight to ten years. Once it cost only $3,000 or $4,000 to do an off-Broadway show; now it's closer to $15,000. It can't help but follow the Broadway pattern, so I don't think we can make a sharp distinction as you could some years ago.

N. Looking back—and this seems very elemental—could you single out some of the highlights of your career?

■ *Rice:* It's hard to pinpoint particular things—there's been such a continuance of activity. Of course, I was greatly pleased by the success of *Street Scene* which won a Pulitzer Prize. I was particularly pleased with its success because it barely got a production. It was turned down by practically every management in New York, and it was strictly by chance that it happened to be produced at all.

The Adding Machine has given me continuous satisfaction because it's being done somewhere in the world all the time.

Then, of course, there was the wonderful twenty-year period with The Playwrights Company—a happy, stimulating, productive period. Perhaps this stands out above all, because in many ways it matched all the excitement to be found in the 1920's. In 1937 Sidney Howard, Maxwell Anderson, S. N. Behrman, Robert Sherwood, and myself organized The Playwrights Company to produce our own plays. We went on for over twenty years, and on the whole it was a highly successful venture. We did somewhere between thirty or forty plays, many of them landmarks, two Pulitzer Prizewinners—*Abe Lincoln In Illinois* and *There Shall Be No Night*. There was *Joan Of Lorraine* and *The Eve Of St. Mark* and *No Time For Comedy*. I would say we had a very high standard of production, a very high percentage of hits, both in the critical and popular senses. You see, a primary reason for forming the company was to maintain integrity in production. We wanted to present our work with all the truth and honesty and integrity we felt the plays deserved. On the whole we succeeded very well. As a matter of fact, The Playwrights Company has never really had its just recognition. Now I understand that several graduate students are doing doctorate dissertations on The Playwrights Company, and that a book is being written about it, so it may get some of the recognition it deserves and never really had.

N. To return to *Street Scene*. You mentioned that it almost didn't reach Broadway.

■ *Rice:* That's right. It had been turned down by every manager in New York, and I despaired of having it produced at all. Then every director—or practically every director—turned it down. Finally William A. Brady decided to produce it, and I volunteered to direct it, even though I'd never directed a play. Fortunately, it turned out well. The notices were wonderful, it ran for a year and a half—over 600 performances—and we had three companies out on the road.

Then it had a long run in England, and now, of course, it's been done practically everywhere in the world. Recently a Greek producer told me he has had great success with it.

N. How important do you think a particular actor or actress is to a play? For example, it's hard for me to think of *Street Scene* without recalling Sylvia Sidney, and I can't conceive of *Dream Girl* without Betty Field.

■ *Rice:* There's no formula type to answer to that. There can't be. It would be dangerous to write a play that just one actor or actress could put across. This happens, of course, and there are plays and musicals and movies that will always be associated with personalities like Bolger and Bobby Clark and Danny Kaye. I suppose the same is true of *Private Lives*—Bankhead made an imprint on it that can't be forgotten, though twenty years from now, if it's done again, the memory of Bankhead won't be that strong.

You mentioned Sylvia Sidney in *Street Scene*, but she played in the movie version, not on the stage. She was splendid, but I don't identify her with *Street Scene*—Erin O'Brien Moore was magnificent in that role on Broadway, and if you'd seen her performance she would be the one you'd recall.

I was married to Betty Field at the time I wrote *Dream Girl*, and I think I wrote that play with Betty in mind. When it was finished I asked her to do it, and she was superb—but there was another great performance of *Dream Girl* by Lucille Ball, and it's been done, too, by Judy Holiday.

If a play is good enough, or a part is strong enough, it cannot be confined for all time to one part or one performer. A popular and/or colorful personality may claim it for a while, but it can only be temporary.

N. Your autobiography, *Minority Report*, was an unusual one in that you treated your own life, and the people who have woven themselves into the fabric of your life, with an unusual amount of candor. Can you answer the hardest question of all: Why did you write it as you did?

■ *Rice:* It's hard to say. It took me two years to write it, and before I started I did a lot of thinking. I tried to be wholly objective about myself, as aloof and detached as I could, and simply narrate what happened insofar as I could remember and how I felt about the things that happened. Of course, total objectivity about oneself is impossible—the ego won't allow it.

I think it's a candid book—I tried to make it honest. I didn't set out to shock anybody, and I certainly didn't mean to injure anyone. I glossed over a great many things I could have explored because they might have hurt people who are still living, or passed some sort of slight on the reputations of people who are dead.

I wrote it as I did to present my life, and the background of that life, primarily, I think, because I wanted to try to find out what, if anything, I had learned in seventy years of living.

N. If you were to give advice to the aspiring writer or playwright, what would the advice be?

■ *Rice:* Don't embark upon a playwright's career, unless you are prepared to cope with defeat, disappointment, and frustration. Even the experienced playwright has his share of discouragement. For the novices, the risks are enormous. Of the innumerable plays written every year, perhaps one in a hundred finds its way to production; of those produced, only one in six or seven has any real measure of success. For the lucky author of a Broadway hit, the rewards are staggering. But there is no foretelling what will succeed, nor is there any discernible relationship between merit and success. Write plays if you must—there is a need for good ones!—but don't feel sorry for yourself if your hopes are not realized.

N. How would you define the obligation of the playwright to the material he's using, on the one hand, and to his audience, on the other?

■ *Rice:* I think his only obligation is to himself, to write what he believes is the best he can produce. The other things are secondary or incidental. I don't think he should be concerned with his audience, though if he's a craftsman he will inevitably write plays that are produceable and actable. This is obvious: plays are written to be performed.

As far as themes are concerned, this is a matter of individual temperament or inclination or psychology. There are some writers who feel that they must identify themselves with their own times, and the problems of the world, and others who do not.

R

In short, I think the playwright's only obligation is one of integrity. He must have something he believes in, and express this belief with the full strength of his talent.

N.   As far as theater at present is concerned, what do you find that you most admire, and what do you most deplore?

■ *Rice:* I find little that is admirable in the present state of the commercial theater. American writers, actors, designers, and directors are as talented as any to be found anywhere in the world, but our theater does not allow them to realize their potentialities. Costs have risen to a point that makes it profitable, in the main, to offer only light entertainment.

Furthermore the theatergoer of moderate means has been priced out of the theater. There is no likelihood that costs or ticket prices will come down. The hope for the future of the art of the drama in America lies, I think, in the development of nonprofit, subsidized community repertory theaters. There is already a tendency in this direction.

"Corruption in this era comes in many forms, and in many disguises; and that, along with how it tends to blur distinctions between good writing and bad, is what I deplore."

Lillian Ross
Interviewed in New York, September, 1963

Lillian Ross

N.   Lillian Ross is one of the great realists of our time. In books like *Portrait of Hemingway*, *Picture*, and *The Player* she has examined our liveliest arts and artists discerningly, with enough candor to arouse occasional criticism, but above all with a driving honesty and comprehension. She obviously believes that if people are presented at all, they deserve to be shown as total entities, not as misleading fragments. Miss Ross has not escaped censure for this objectivity—certain critics and the fans of certain personalities have complained. With her first book of fiction, *Vertical and Horizontal*, we find the same attributes of total truth applying to fiction as well. The reader feels certain that characters like those she portrays exist; and further, that some characteristics of those persons may exist within us. Miss Ross, to go back to *Portrait of Hemingway*, which started off as a *New Yorker* profile, there were critics who objected to your presentation of Hemingway, weren't there?

■ *Ross:*   Yes, but I think it should be apparent to anyone who has read *Portrait of Hemingway* that I not only liked and admired Hemingway very much, but found him to be unique in a wonderful way. He was an extremely generous man—generous enough to co-operate fully with a young, unknown writer—and he was absolutely honest and forthright, without pretension of any kind. Also, he was a man of vitality, humor, and fun, and one who loved life. He expressed all that in many ways. These were just some of the things I tried to show in the profile. I tried to show Hemingway as he was—with spirit intact.

I loved the way he was and found him exciting, and I tried to present him that way. The profile was written ten years ago, and I tried then—just as I try now, for that matter—to exercise discretion, judgment, and taste in what I write, particularly with regard to an invasion of privacy. To be absolutely sure, I showed Hemingway and his wife the profile; I sent it to them in Cuba, where they were then living. They made one or two small corrections and returned it to me, and it was published.

Now, there was a certain kind of criticism of the profile. Many people didn't want Hemingway to be Hemingway, so they ascribed to my profile certain aspects of his personality, his way of talking, even the kind of vitality he had. I think that *they* were the people, mostly, who objected.

On the other hand, I received a number of letters from people who obviously enjoyed Hemingway's writings, and enjoyed him as he was, enjoyed the way he talked, enjoyed all he had to offer in humor and fun. It's been interesting, of course, in the ten years that have followed, to see people find, in the profile, what they were looking for.

Hemingway himself understood it. After the profile came out, and I received negative comment along with enthusiastic and positive comment, he wrote to reassure me. On June 16, 1960, he wrote that I shouldn't worry about the piece, that it was a matter of people getting things all mixed up. A number of times, he wrote about people he called, "the devastate people," those people who claimed that my article was "devastating." There were those, he said, who just couldn't understand his enjoying himself, and not being really spooky. They couldn't understand how he could be a serious writer, without being pompous. I think he himself summed it up very well.

I found the way he talked, the way he acted, and especially his humor, absolutely delightful. It was a great, refreshing relief to find a writer utterly without pretension.

N.   Which is a rarity, I understand.

■ *Ross:* I think so. Writers are very apt to take themselves too seriously and to pontificate about various matters. But Hemingway was a joyous and wonderful man and, from what I could see, he had such a good life with Mary and his work. He loved writing and respected what he did. There, too, he was unusual because many writers don't respect what they do.

N.   Now for *Picture*, which I've found to be the best study of Hollywood ever done, particularly where the production of a movie is concerned. In *Picture*, Louis B. Mayer and Dore Schary are two of the figures that emerge in glorious color. How did you find working with them?

■ *Ross:* I had a very good time in Hollywood. I lived out there for eighteen months while I did the series of articles, and it was while I was out there that I began to think in fictional terms for the structure of the story. In writing *Picture*, I think I was able to do something (or so I've been told) that was never done before:

namely, to tell a factual story in fictional form. *Picture* really takes the form of a novel. It was up to me to build the story, to show relationships, to use quotes, in the course of revealing how the movie was made. All those things I used in a so-called fictional form.

As I gathered the material, my association with all the leading characters became close. Most of them were friends before the book was written, and the key characters are still my friends—John Huston, the director; Gottfried Reinhardt, the producer; and their wives.

N. To turn to *The Player*—one of the important books of 1962. How did you put it together?

■ *Ross:* My sister Helen and I took four years to turn it out. I wouldn't have been able to do it myself because I don't think I'd have been able to sustain my enthusiasm for eight years. What we do in *The Player* is to present fifty-five self-portraits of leading actors—stage, movie, and television actors—of the English-speaking theater. We do have a few French, Italian, and German actors and actresses, but they have appeared in English-language movies or plays.

We feel that these fifty-five represent a cross-section. We used a special form for the pieces: each actor speaks in the first person singular, without questions or comments from the authors. What we try to do, is to give the actor or actress to the reader, as though he were on the stage, presenting himself to the audience, telling who he is, what he is, what he does, what he feels about what he does, how he feels about acting, how he works on a part, etc. Each of the pieces is the product of conventional interviews; Helen and I did not use a tape recorder because we prefer to listen carefully and take notes.

Each piece has a photograph, taken by me, because we wanted to have a natural, unretouched picture that matched the spirit of the pieces.

N. Now for your last book—*Vertical and Horizontal*. Here again your technique for coming to grips with the heart of the matter is very evident. What are your first comments regarding its reception?

■ *Ross:* The reviews have been wonderful—also the comment—so I have no complaint. To my surprise, the book has not been mis-understood. The reviewers talk about the humor, and they point out that Dr. Spencer Fifield (the leading character) is, when looked at deeply, a sympathetic character. He's cold; he finds it impossible to feel things the way most people can, and he tries to reach feeling through thought—which is just about impossible to do. And he's been understood.

Again to my surprise, I've had letters from psychoanalysts and other psychiatrists who say they like and enjoy the book, and it's been reviewed in some of their journals. The editor of the official psychosomatic journal said it was ideal reading for tired therapists and pointed out that there is something of my doctors in all of them.

N. I thought that psychiatrists might be annoyed—you didn't leave them unscathed. In fact, Dr. Blauberman looked rather foolish several times.

■ *Ross:* When some of the stories appeared in *The New Yorker*, I got letters and phone calls indicating that people receiving treatment were reading them, and talking about them, on the couch. Even one of the real doctors mentioned in the book, the writer of a paper called, "Chess, Oedipus and the Mater Dolorosa," which is mentioned by one of the fictional characters, turned out to be the person who reviewed the book for the *San Francisco Chronicle*. He gave it a favorable review.

N. Miss Ross, I'm sure that most readers associate you with *The New Yorker* where most of your work has originally appeared. How long have you been with the magazine, and how much have you done?

■ *Ross:* I haven't done too much, actually. It was my first real job, and I've been with them for fifteen years. We've talked about the major things I've written, although I do write a great many of "The Talk of the Town" stories that appear, unsigned, in the magazine. I've written "Reporter at Large" pieces, and "Profiles."

I love working at *The New Yorker*—it's the greatest place in the world for the writer, especially for the young writer, to develop and find himself, or herself; to get helpful and constructive guidance without interference; to develop his own original style. The editor of *The New Yorker*, William Shawn, is probably *the* editorial genius of our time. He's quiet, unassuming, and unpretentious, and doesn't seek publicity. But in a very firm way, over the past fifteen years—or even before Harold Ross, the original editor, died and Shawn became editor—he has been doing a great deal to mold the character of the magazine. *The New Yorker* keeps growing.

N. To turn to the realm of theory: What advice would you give the youngster who wishes to make a career of writing?

■ *Ross:* First of all, corny as it may sound—"To thine own self be true." Find what you are, and what you want to be, and what you want to say; then try to find the strongest and most direct line from your feelings and ideas, to what you write. Hold to what you know is true, no matter what is offered to you in the way of distraction.

N. In looking at today's literary product, what do you see that you most admire?

■ *Ross:* I read only a modest amount of contemporary fiction and nonfiction, but of what I do read, I find that *The New Yorker* seems to attract the most original and purest talent of our time, in both fields. J. D. Salinger is, in my opinion, the most powerful, the most interesting, and the most enjoyable writer to read. In the management of his life, he has, more than any other writer I know, attained the joys available to man and has kept himself free of any kind of interference with the expression of his sublime talent. He is uncorrupted. Corruption in this era comes in many forms, and in many disguises; and that, along with how it tends to blur distinctions between good writing and bad, is what I deplore.

N. If you were a critic in, say, 1999, looking back at the output of our age, how would you like it to be regarded?

■ *Ross:* I don't regard myself as a critic in 1964, so I find it impossible to imagine one in 1999, about myself or anybody else. Thirty-five years from now, it may well be that there won't *be* writers any more. The kind of people who felt drawn to writing in this century may want to be creating figure eights in space in the next.

N. A simple, very simple final question: What do you feel the writer's obligation is to his subject matter?

■ *Ross:* To be truthful, interesting, and attractive.

"It is an unhappy fact of life that most people *don't* know what they mean, and they *don't* know—really—what they want to say. Most verbal output—conversation, speech, or writing—is a spraying out of words on the ambiguous assumption that somehow or other these words will come together. . . ."

Leo Rosten
Interviewed in New York, September, 1963

Leo Rosten

N.   I'd like to open this interview by asking the simplest question of all: How would you outline your career? I know it's a more involved and complex career than most. Your writings have varied enormously, and so have your activities. Perhaps it would be better to approach it from the standpoint of a rough autobiography.

■ *Rosten:* Your simple question does involve a complex answer. I was raised in Chicago and attended the University of Chicago. I was interested in—everything. I studied in about seventeen departments before I settled down to graduate work in social science, with emphasis on politics and psychology. But I always wanted to write; I always assumed that I would be a writer; and after I began working for my degree I started to write.

My first pieces were articles about the psychology of politics. Then I tried fiction and collected the usual number of rejection slips. I used a pseudonym because I was working on a Ph.D. thesis, and I didn't want the university to think I was shirking my scholarly duties. I sold stories to *The New Yorker* for three years without any of my professors knowing I was doing so. This was a series about a night school for adults, based on experiences I had had as a teacher in a night school on Chicago's West Side. I called my hero Hyman Kaplan.

The stories caught on—so much so, that I felt like one of those writers you read about who awakens to find himself famous: telegrams, cables, long distance telephone calls, etc. Meanwhile, I was working on my Ph.D. thesis on the Washington Press Corps. These two extremely diverse activities were being conducted simultaneously, which may give you a clue as to the kind of writer, or person, I am. I love to work simultaneously on quite different subjects. When I'm writing a novel, for example, and tire of it, or begin to run dry, I switch to a serious article. Then I go back to the fiction, or to humor.

After my work in Washington, I landed in Hollywood—as a screenwriter. This was a sheer fluke. I soon discovered that I was more interested in the life—you might say the sociology—of this extraordinary community, than in writing screenplays. So I obtained a grant from the Rockefeller Foundation, and another from the Carnegie Foundation, and spent the next three years doing a quite serious book about Hollywood. I had twelve assistants, at one time or another. I loved every moment I spent on that research.

The book, *Hollywood: The Movie Colony*, appeared with really wonderful reviews, front page Sunday *New York Times* book section, front page Sunday *Herald Tribune*, superb coverage across the country, but the date was December 7, 1941! When historians of the future study this period, one of the things they may ask is: "What was the American public reading while Pearl Harbor was being bombed?" Well, they were *not* reading my book on Hollywood, because scarcely a copy was sold for the next months of the war.

I was called to Washington. I had been working for one agency or another during Roosevelt's administration. I became a deputy director of the Office of War Information. My job embraced the usual variety of tasks, mostly dealing with what might be called the psychology of propaganda and how to counteract Nazi propaganda to and in the United States. Fascinating work. I was sent overseas on special assignments for the Secretary of War, with the "assimilated" rank of colonel. After the war, I went back to Hollywood but for only two years. My children had already been raised in the golden sun and the lovely pagan outdoor world, so my strongest tie to California could be broken. We came to New York —it was time to. I'm a city boy, raised on city streets. I spend about half my time as special editorial adviser to *Look* magazine, the rest of my time writing and traveling. I love Europe. I get an enormous amount of pleasure, to say nothing of material, stimulation, and knowledge, out of travel. I always have a book or two simmering, not necessarily by intention.

I have a secret hobby. Some people like to fish, some to hunt, etc. I used to play chess, but I gave it up, because chess became an obsession, not a hobby. My hobby is writing melodramas—not murder stories, but novels of suspense, cliff-hangers. For ten years after I received my Ph.D., I wrote one melodrama a year, under a pseudonym, so as not to interfere with my allegedly more serious occupations. Instead of going off on a fishing trip, I would go into my study and begin writing a nice, violent, intrigue-laden melodrama. I would be lucky enough to sell it to the movies, and the money let me spend the rest of the year doing some teaching, some research, and writing the sort of things from which you can hardly expect to earn a living or raise a family. Serious things, for the more learned journals: analyses of politics or social life, or other unprofitable subjects.

N. I can't help wondering about the smash success of H*Y*M*A*N K*A*P*L*A*N. This must have been closely identified with you for many years, and I'm curious to know if you felt any resentment at being identified with him.

■ *Rosten:* No, I've always been terribly grateful. There were great pressures on me to write more Kaplan stories after the first book, offers from publishers, blandishments from magazines. I did write some more Kaplan stories, but they didn't satisfy me; I put them away. Periodically I would reread them and rework them, always with a vague feeling of discontent. I simply didn't think they were good enough to publish.

Twenty years passed. One day I picked up the draft of a story I had written five years earlier and, suddenly, everything fell into place, astonishingly so. This is an interesting problem that I can only describe in terms of the position from which you see your material, the stance, what military men call the "posture," in my case the curious and special viewpoint from which the subject matter is visualized or sensed. What I discovered in 1958 was that, at long last, I suddenly knew how I wanted to approach another book on Hyman Kaplan. It appeared about twenty-one years after the first one.

In the meantime, I'd written a book of travel sketches, which first appeared in *The New Yorker*, a series of ironic and amusing (I hope) pieces about all sorts of wacky places in the United States. I had also written half a dozen juicy melodramas, the most noted—or the most notorious—being *The Dark Corner* and *Sleep, My Love*.

Then I began to get interested in some of my wartime experiences, some of the people I'd met or observed. I'd always known I would write about them, but I'd never felt "on top of" the material. You know, writers sometimes use the expression "on top of the material" to mean that they can control it, bend it to the will, give it proportion, direction, climax. It's a subtle thing, but vital. If you lose yourself in the material, it gets out of hand. Characters can suddenly roar off on their own; you may think it's wonderfully funny or tragic, that it just couldn't be better, that you've written some of the greatest pages in the English language. A week later, you'll read it and wonder what on earth you thought you were doing! In that intervening week, your attitude has shifted (perhaps to normalcy) and now you're looking at what you wrote as a reader, not as the absorbed, lost, runaway-with creator.

As I said, for almost fifteen years I had been bubbling, or simmering, or vaguely preoccupied with a group of characters I had met during the war, in different places, under circumstances of stress or euphoria. Finally, I wrote a book about these things, a book in which I dared myself to try to bring off a story I felt very deeply, people and events that stirred up the very essence of the self, of myself, as a human being, no less than a writer. The technical challenge was enormous. I wondered whether I could bring off a story that shifted emotional gears, as it were, from chapter to chapter. That is, I hoped that in one chapter I could make people roar with laughter, then make them weep; I wanted to move from comedy to tragedy to fantasy to farce, moving from mood to mood without keying the story to one central story line.

The book was *Captain Newman, M.D.* It was terribly, terribly difficult to write.

N.   How did you feel about the critical and public acceptance of *Captain Newman, M.D.?* I recall my own reaction to it. The drastic shifts of mood were startling, at times, especially when you went from wild humor to actual pathos. It seemed a very mature and challenging book, one that kept the reader on his toes.

■ *Rosten:*   The response has been wonderful, all that an author can hope for. I'm told, for instance, that in some medical schools they are using *Captain Newman* as required reading for students of psychiatry. I've received any number of requests for permission to use chapters in teaching, in heaven knows how many anthologies, in courses on American literature, in training people in the treatment of emotional disturbances. The book's impact is not, I think, confined to Army life. The Air Force setting and the war heightened certain stresses, heightened internal conflict, which is at the heart of the story.

N.   But it was rooted in actual situations you encountered?

■ *Rosten:*   I think almost everything a man writes has some root in his experience. I'll contradict myself now: I have always enjoyed writing melodrama because it takes nothing out of me, emotionally —it's one form of writing that, for me at least, is sheer diversion, problem-setting and problem-solving; it doesn't spring from my own life. I don't have to hammer out basic truths about the human experience. Melodramas are play, the structuring of surprise, the plotting of the unexpected and its delights.

N.   Could you describe your own working processes?

■   *Rosten:*   I don't think people really believe that writing is, as it surely is, terribly hard work. I'm both pleased and annoyed when someone comments on something I've written by saying, "Oh, you write so easily." It pleases me to know that I so involved them in reading what I wrote, but it angers me that they think it was easy. I don't know any writer—any really good writer—who writes easily.

Nothing I've undertaken in my life, and I've undertaken a great many complex things, even begins to approach the demands you must make upon yourself when and while you're writing. If I were to tell you that chapters of *Captain Newman, M.D.* were rewritten ten, twenty, fifty times, would you believe me? But it's true. I don't mean that I changed a word or a phrase here and there—I mean totally rewritten. One chapter runs about 8,000 words and was rewritten at least fifty times, from first word to last, cut, expanded, reshaped, remolded.

Fiction involves so very many subtle and evasive variables. The very rhythm of a sentence, the mood struck by a word, the context, the momentum, the interplay between what is revealed and what is concealed, the atmosphere you're trying to create. You begin to monkey around with an exchange of dialogue, say; you sense somehow that something is wrong, but you don't exactly know what it is. The only way I can find out is to immerse myself in it, to see it and "hear" it on many levels, to hear it as the writer, as the reader, as the character talking, as the character responding, as an editor, as a critic, as an analyst, as a creator and re-creator.

You can spend days and days on a brief sequence. To an observer, this may seem silly, but it's anything but silly. The writer must live with the perplexing fact that his characters reveal themselves in every tiny thing they say or *don't* say, do or don't do, in the way they sigh, or grunt, or turn away, or cross their legs, in the pace of their speech, a gesture, a movement, a thought clumsily articulated, a phrase unfinished, an impassioned or restrained utterance.

In creating, you start with nothing but a blank, a very blank and unhelpful sheet of paper. You have to put something on that paper which communicates to a reader an entire and precise world, a world that lives inside your mind or your heart or both. You must double-check and triple-check the nuances of that world in terms of the *reader's* perspective. You have to put yourself in the position of the negative reader, the resistant reader, the reader who doesn't surrender control easily, the reader who is alien to you as a type, even the reader who doesn't like what you're writing. You must make sure you are communicating—really communicating—getting something from your mind and emotions into his.

I've been interested in this problem of communication for many years. I've done a certain amount of research in it, this immensely complex matter. And I've decided that people who communicate well—in words or sounds or visual images, in writing or in speech, in formal speeches or in simple twosomes—are people who first communicate truly and well *with themselves*. This means they really know what they want to say.

This may sound like a platitude, but bear with me. It is an unhappy fact of life that most people *don't* know what they mean, and they *don't* know—really—what they want to say. Most verbal output—conversation, speech, or writing—is a spraying out of words on the ambiguous assumption that somehow or other these words will come together, will achieve meaning, will say something greater than their several parts—and greater than the intent of the communicator.

Those who write well think clearly. They know what they want to say; they've thought it out and through. Communicating is hard. It's work—hard work.

The communicator segregates his material, organizing and proportioning and structuring it internally, trying it out on himself, seeing if it makes sense to him before he externalizes it for others. I've been a professional writer for about thirty years, and each time I start a new project, whether it's a thousand-word piece on Isaac Newton or a full-length novel, I think now it's going to be easier—that I've at last learned my techniques, can master my content, can readily bridge the gap between me and a reader.

Three weeks later, I'm beating my head against the wall wondering why the piece still doesn't come off to my satisfaction. What prevents me from getting what I want? Perhaps it's a matter of how and where to begin, or how to set the tone, or how to fuse the elements in the middle, or what to emphasize, when and how much, or where to put the "punch." I may take something that appears at the very end of the fortieth draft and discover that I ought to start there, with an arresting point, a dramatic hook. The process of viewing the material, of seeing what belongs where, is a mystery I never resolve once and for all. Everything one starts to write is new, tormenting, tantalizing, exciting, challenging.

Now, I don't mean to give the impression that the writer sits around torturing himself all day, every day. Some things solve or resolve themselves with marvelous abruptness. For example, I wanted to do a piece about what's wrong with New York. I love the city, but there are a lot of things wrong with it: the traffic, the dirt, the noise, the absurdly small taxis, the ghastly new apartment houses. I started to write a piece that had a tone of moral outrage. But it was wrong. It was so damned "virtuous." It sounded like a speech about civics at a political protest rally. Virtue is a hard thing to make interesting; evil is dramatic and colorful. So here I was, trying to write a piece about what's wrong with New York, and in my drafts I made certain points well, I thought. But one afternoon, while I was taking a walk, I suddenly realized what was still bothering me: I was posturing. The article was too solemn, too literal; it was earnest—and dull. Just dull because it dealt humorlessly with the *obvious*.

I said to myself, "Why not enlist humor, exaggeration, a bit of burlesque? Why don't I write this damn piece as though it's being written by a man who's *defending* the mayor, who thinks the city is wonderful, but who is an idiot? The facts he parades in defending the mayor and New York are so absurd that the reader roars." So I wrote this piece, which has become a rather celebrated spoof, as "An Open Letter to the Mayor." It's ostensibly written by a man who admires the mayor, but is barely literate; his brain is a bit under par; his argument is dead-pan—and delirious. Readers laughed, and the points were made more effectively, I think, than if I'd preached or inveighed.

Humor is extremely hard to write. I'd rather turn out ten melodramas than one piece that's funny. But this is a digression. I was using the New York piece as an example of the struggling, and the juggling, and the sudden "inspiration," that often goes into a relatively simple article.

N.   Do people ever ask you where your ideas come from?

■ *Rosten:* I'm sorry to say—yes. Like most writers, I'm afraid I can't explain where ideas come from. A writer lives and breathes and sees and hears. Perhaps he knows that all the facets of his life, his experiences, are materials he can use.

About five years ago I started a new project. I'd been reading biographies about, and the writings of, men whom we would all agree are great men, geniuses, landmarks in the history of the human race. I tried to discover where each of these giants had made his big breakthrough—established a theory, made a discovery, hit upon a new or revolutionary idea. What kind of person is an

Einstein or a Socrates or a Freud? What kind of man has the courage, the originality, the infantile directness to challenge the prevailing way of looking at things? I got excited about this.

I was invited to the University of California for a year as a visiting professor, and I spent most of that year reading and thinking about these men. Finally, I wrote a rather short paper called "The Creative Idea," which deals with creativity, the creative process, and moves from art to physics to philosophy. It will appear in a book of nonfiction due fairly soon.

N. Now I'll compound the felony. How did you get interested enough in the specific subject matter to write *Religions of America?*

■ *Rosten:* That is another example of the preservation of *directness*, or naïveté. I was taking a walk one day—about ten years ago—and I passed five or six churches, temples, synagogues. It occurred to me that I didn't know what went on inside a Baptist church, for example; or what a Presbyterian believes, as distinguished from a Quaker. I didn't know the religious orientation of a Christian Scientist or a Mormon, and where there'd be significant differences. I had some imprecise general ideas, as all of us do, I suppose.

It occurred to me that it would be fascinating to draw up a list of simple, direct questions, almost impertinent questions, and get—say—a Roman Catholic to answer these questions in so direct and simple a manner that I, a non-Catholic, could say, "Now I understand. Now I know what you believe." I started working with this idea at *Look*, and before we were done, we had run a series of nineteen articles: "What is a Methodist?" "What is a Jew?" "What is a Seventh-day Adventist?" I drew up all of the questions and commissioned someone from each faith to answer them. Then I would sit by the hour with the author examining the answers, making profound comments like, "This sentence isn't clear," or "I'm afraid I don't understand this point," or "This sounds like a professional theologian; it won't be clear to a lay reader."

The response to this series on religion astounded me. For instance, we got requests from the churches about whom these articles were written asking for a half-million reprints, say, for distribution to their own members! Many an article was called the clearest statement in English of what a particular religious group believed. That I hadn't expected. It's an interesting example of the "clarifier" at work, the man who says stubbornly, "I don't understand, and it's up to you to explain it to me so that I do understand."

When we decided to put all the articles into a book, it occurred

to me that many people don't know where to find the simplest,
most basic facts of religion. So I began to assemble elaborate
appendices: figures, tables, statistics, charts. I discovered that many
of the statistics and data printed about religious groups in the
United States are not very good, and are not even reliable! If you
ask, for example, how many Catholics there are in the United
States, you'd have a hard time getting a reasonably accurate answer.
Why? Well, suppose a child is born to Catholic parents in Boston.
He is baptized in his parish church, and is carried on the rolls of
this church. Later, his family moves away from Boston. Now,
Americans move about a great deal. How long will that one Catholic member be carried on the rolls of the Boston church? How
long will he be carried on the rolls of a second, a third, and a fourth
church he may attend in later years? It all depends on who records
the membership figures; how realistically these figures are kept and
changed.

Even supposedly obvious things, like how many persons in a
given faith obtain a divorce, are extremely hard to ascertain. Some
delightful paradoxes turn up. In Philadelphia, for example, the
divorce rate is lowest (of course) for Catholics. But the unofficial
separation rate is highest for Catholics! The Church's stand on
divorce doesn't mean that marital *stability* is higher amongst Catholics. I began to wonder what all the figures meant, what new
figures could be obtained.

I wrote to the people who take polls, like Gallup and Roper,
asking to see all they'd collected over the years regarding religion
in the United States. I discovered some amazing things. For example, Americans were asked to name the four gospels in the New
Testament, and a very small percentage could name even one. If
you ask Americans if they believe in a life after death, you get a
curious distribution of responses. In the end, we put into the appen-
dix just about every fact and figure I could lay my hands on, from
hundreds of sources, checked and double-checked. They are all in
the book, *Religions In America*. This is one volume to which people
can refer when they want to know if a Catholic believes that an
unbaptized baby will go to purgatory, or why Jews don't eat certain kinds of meat, or if a Christian Scientist believes that someone
hundreds of miles away can be healed by a practitioner, or what
the basic differences are between the Roman Catholic and Greek
Orthodox faiths. Many people must, as I did, wonder about the
religious makeup of the churches and synagogues they pass each
day; I think they can find the answers in this book.

N. Now we switch to the theoretical. What advice would you give the neophyte, the young writer, playwright, or poet who wants to play a significant role in the world of letters? What courses of study, what approach would you recommend?

■ *Rosten:* I think that there is no substitute for being educated. There is no substitute for prolonged involvement in the great ideas of the West, and in *the ways of using the mind.* I constantly run into this problem with college students—as I did with my own children: "What should I study?"

My answer sounds a bit Victorian, but it's based on a good deal of thought and teaching and study, and the experience of raising three children. My advice to the young might be summed up this way: You will never, during the rest of your life, possess the span of free time now available to you. I hope you will use this time to *study,* to learn, to enrich your mind and spirit with ideas which are important and which you might otherwise never know how to absorb, master and use. Begin with a strong, tough discipline in the use of your own language: courses in English and I don't mean courses in English literature, which is something different. Courses in the writing of English, if properly taught, are really courses in *reasoning,* in good thinking, in clear thinking, in the presentation and handling and arrangement of ideas. There just is no substitute for the discipline of learning how to use your own language. It is astonishing how few people in any society, and certainly in the United States, use their own language really well, as the wonderful, magical key it can be.

My second piece of advice is simply: get a background which has substance. You can read on your own, but there are some things you will find extremely difficult to study on your own. So take courses in philosophy to learn how the enduring problems of mankind have been analyzed or perceived by the greatest minds the human race has produced. There's nothing more exciting than the discovery of Socrates—how he thought, how he taught men to think. There are few things (to me, at least) as exhilarating and forever rewarding as reading Plato, or Montaigne. Anyone can read Montaigne with profit. His writings are merely the thought and observations of a man trying to understand himself. After all these hundreds of years his work remains fresh and pertinent because, as you read him trying to understand *himself,* you constantly grasp the truths he is writing about you.

Anyone who is not going to renounce the world we live in by turning to one of the symbolic arts—dance, painting, music—certainly has to learn the fundamentals about how our society works, how it is organized, how men are motivated. This means courses in politics, sociology, economics. I know no way of avoiding this. The subject matter may sound heavy to youngsters (it often is) but it can be just as exciting as the study of algebra can be—even if you're not a mathematician.

I have strong doubts about the wisdom of letting students choose what they want to study. Why not say: "These are the things you *have* to know to be educated."

To be educated simply means to be at home with ideas. I once tried to define wisdom, and said: ". . . wisdom is equanimity in the presence of intolerable or threatening ideas." The capacity to handle an idea that may upset you, that may fly in the face of everything you believe, that may seem dangerous or wicked or subversive. The *way* of approaching it, of handling it, of being at home with complexity or with novelty—these are the things you can learn in the course of learning other things. These are the ways I say we must learn, to use the precious instrument we call the mind.

N. In surveying literature and theater at the present time, what do you find admirable? What do you deplore? Where would you hope to see change?

■ *Rosten:* I think that the new freedom of the theater has led many to the silly conclusion that if a play is psychopathic, it is good; if it is aberrant, it is superior. I, for one, have little admiration for this point of view, or for the kind of drama that exploits distortions of human behavior. This has nothing to do with content, oddly enough; it concerns the *way* the content is treated. We do not *have* to emphasize the evil, the sick, the wacky, the eccentric, the psychopathic, to hold the attention of an audience. Nor need we make perversity or aberration the subject of admiration.

Let me quickly add that my last book, *Captain Newman, M.D.*, uses a psychiatric ward as its background. But I try to deal with recognizable human beings who are suffering and are being helped by other recognizable human beings trained in the problems of human emotion. I try to understand, not despise. I pity those who suffer—even if they are normal men and women.

At any rate, I have a squeamish feeling about the deliberate exploitation of sensational material, whether the sensational be about sex or marriage or the pathological side of human behavior—whenever I feel reasonably sure that sincerity, conviction, truth, if you will, have been sacrificed. Dostoevsky on crime and the nature of the criminal is redeeming because of how very much we learn from him, from his insight, from his compassion. He did not write in order to startle or shock, or to make you feel superior or bold or daring. A great novelist conscientiously uses material to form an important and *significant* story. For my taste, too much of our present theater is not inspired by creative honesty, but by a desire to deliberately commercialize the peculiar.

About the contemporary novel, I have somewhat different feelings. I often wonder if the great age of the novel isn't over. It may be that the novel, as a form, no longer serves the function it once did. The novelists of the eighteenth and nineteenth centuries were —for the most part—the best psychologists and the best sociologists we had. The novelist knew more about human behavior—the behavior of individuals, which is psychology, and the behavior of groups, which is sociology—than any of his contemporaries. You can read Balzac to learn a great deal about French society; you can read Dickens to learn a great deal about England, and about a wonderful gallery of "personality types" as the psychologists dub them.

But observe what has happened today. The growth of specialists, of technicians, of scientists in these fields, means that the psychologist, the psychiatrist, the psychoanalyst today know more about human behavior than most of the writers who write about it. This doesn't mean that a writer should run to the laboratory or the clinic for his material. But it does mean that a great many of today's *readers* are acquainted with nonfictional psychology, and are so absorbed in, and stimulated by, the factual that they're likely to regard a novel as pretty thin stuff. The reader has changed because of what he's been exposed to.

I think that a great many novels written today are not very good. Let me hasten to add that I think this is true of just about everything—most of the songs being sung aren't very good, nor the baseball games being played, nor the pictures being painted.

Why? Well, most of anything is of mediocre, if not inferior, caliber. There's an unfortunate, deplorable, but inescapable fact we must face: not many people are talented. One of the great things about democracy is that it gives the man with talent a chance to express that talent—no matter who his parents are, or where he comes from, or what his race or religion happens to be. He has an opportunity to express his own artistic or aesthetic propensities. But talent is rare, talent is scarce. I find myself reading far more nonfiction than I used to, and far less fiction—and not strictly from choice. I love fiction, but it seems to become less rewarding; nonfiction, to me, seems far more rewarding and exciting.

The novel suffers from being in competition with a whole world of materials that have only recently come into existence: space travel, the dramatic accomplishments of technology and science, the whole world of investigation of things like cells, the nature of color, the nature of light. From the satellite to the bathysphere, we are opening up enormous, enthralling domains of a kind that were once confined to the vision of a Jules Verne or an H. G. Wells. These new worlds are now being explored with infinitely more drama and detail than a writer can dream up, and it's inevitable that people prefer to read about these new areas. Simply by examining the content of popular American magazines, you see the decline of fiction over the past thirty years, and the rise of what might be called "fact pieces."

Having said all this, let me contradict myself: There is no substitute for the writer, the truly gifted writer, the book of infinite merit.

N. In closing I'd like to go back two years, to the speech you made at the National Book Awards presentation. I wonder if you could sum up a few of its central points.

■ *Rosten:* Well, it was an attempt to explore the free mind—an attempt to bring home to people what I consider the most precious part of life in America, our freedom to *inquire*, to talk, to debate, to argue, to disagree. It was an attempt to refute something that had been going on in the United States for some years—that terrible, terrible thing we got into in which people became suspect for their *ideas*, or what others alleged their ideas to be.

I'm not talking about the Communists or the Communist scare. I'm referring to what happened in a growing uneasiness, a suspicion of debate, really good debate, about the problems that exist. What I was trying to say in that address was that our nation is rich and great and strong because we make a distinction between ideas and dissent; between dissent and treason; between ideas and deeds. I tried to put into arresting form a kind of philosophy for the free man—the man who just can't tolerate dogma, political dogma, or repression. Freedom I hold sacred—it isn't simply something in a textbook or that you hear about on the day you go to vote.

I tried to point out that much of our life is dominated by what I call "mythology," and that if we are bold enough and honest enough to confront myths, they collapse. I tried to illustrate this with certain myths, such as "Facts speak for themselves." This is nonsense; facts don't talk at all; they have no meaning whatsoever until they are arranged, analyzed, or interpreted.

I'll give you another myth: "Always tell the truth." This sounds like a fine idea, but life would be intolerable if we went around telling people the truth all the time. How can you tell the truth to a girl about to go out on her first date, who says, "Daddy, how do I look?" She looks just awful. You're not going to say, "You look awful." How do you tell the truth to a wife who's just come home from a miserable day and bought a preposterous little hat; she puts on the hat, hopeful and glowing, and says, "How do I look?" Do you tell her the truth—that she looks absurd?

These are small matters, of course. There are larger ones, more dangerous ones that hide as myths. Take voting. Every time an election comes up, the worthy citizens of a community say, "Get out and vote. It doesn't matter who you vote for, but *vote*." This is madness. It *does* matter for whom you vote. I would prefer to tell people, "Don't vote unless you have taken the trouble to think a little, to explore the issues and the candidates. Let those who care, who have tried to inform themselves, vote. Don't you get into the act if you haven't exercised the obligation that comes with the privilege."

I don't see anything magical about numbers. I don't think you get a better decision if 10,000 people vote instead of 7,000. Perhaps those 7,000 have gone to the trouble of informing themselves; maybe they're clearer, maybe they know more about the issues and candidates—and care more.

Another dangerous myth: that the far Left and the far Right are opposites: that is, the Communists at the left end of the scale, and the Fascists or reactionaries at the right end, are opposed to each other. This idea stems from the way we traditionally distribute political opinions—along a straight line. There's no reason for this. If you take the ends of the line and tie them together to make a circle, you'd get a much more accurate picture. The far Left and the far Right are far more alike than either is like the middle. They both would cheerfully imprison or exile or kill people who disagree with them. It isn't surprising that extremist personalities find themselves just as comfortable at the far Left as they do at the far Right, and often switch—as they so notably did in Nazi Germany.

It's the middle position that is the hope of mankind. It's the middle that is reflective, that is never sure it's right, that believes that disagreement is important, that you must never punish a person for his faith or belief, that you never throw a person into prison without a trial.

I was trying, in that speech, to summarize what I felt the free man's creed must be. I tried to express this creed in two or three hundred words. I don't remember them at all. Had I known you were going to ask me this question, I'd have read the speech again, but it went something like this:

The purpose of life is not to be happy. I get angry when I hear people talk about happiness, happiness, happiness. It annoys me when I hear them say, "Have fun," or "I read a fun book," or "I had a fun time." I think this demeaning. There are things far more important and rewarding than fun, and I don't think the purpose of life is happiness. Happiness is what we hope for; it's what we want for our children, but happiness is not an *end* in itself, to be reached for and seized.

Happiness is what happens after you do other things; happiness is a by-product of the respect you pay to the self; of the doing of those things which make it possible for you to live in a world which, as a whole, is unhappy. To me, the purpose of life is to *count*, to matter, to amount to something, to do something as meaningfully as you can, to express your talents, whatever they may be, large or small. Happiness is to make an effort, to reach, to try and keep trying, knowing that at best, life is full of pain and conflict and suffering—so very much suffering.

If you want no pain, no conflict, pray for senility. Senile people are, presumably, happy. Or, go and get yourself injected with "happy juices" and you'll be "happy"—but what a way to live. There's a form of idiocy that is happy and blissful, free of pain and free of conflict, but it's also free of meaning. Much of life is going to be hard and full of pain—and lonely. There's an infinity of loneliness in the human experience. I think it inevitable. Thoughtful people, creative people, people who try, who care, people who are *concerned*, pay a price—but the rewards are indescribable. It is these rewards which are returned from respect for one's own values, one's own way of living—in trying to be incorruptible, at least in trying not to be corrupted. The state of internal contentment we call happiness means using the resources of the mind and the heart—as deeply and fully as you can. You have to be hard on yourself to do this; you have to deprive yourself of some ease and self-indulgence and painlessness; but the reward is all the greater because it comes from yourself, and it is greater than anything the world can give you.

"I think it's not only useful but almost essential for a writer to have other experiences . . . get a job in a grocery store, a lumber camp. Fish, be a secretary, a switchboard operator, go on the stage. But don't just confine yourself to writing."

Margery Sharp
Interviewed in London, England, October, 1963

Margery Sharp

N. "Her style is impeccable, her taste sublime, her humanity infinite." Thus did a Midwest reviewer recently sum up an appraisal of Margery Sharp which sweeps from *The Nutmeg Tree* to *Martha In Paris*, from *Britannia Mews* to *The Turret*. On both sides of the Atlantic, Miss Sharp commands a growing legion of fans which will never miss a word she writes. Her rare gift for fantasy that is never a step removed from life or the significance of life is apt to grant immortality to heroines named Julia, Martha, and—yes, Miss Bianca.

In talking to Miss Sharp I'd like to ask first about her own life and the beginnings of her interest in writing.

■ *Sharp:* I started writing in the classic way—poetry, or rather verse—and I can remember that my first published poem was on that extremely classic subject, "The Moon." I was in the sixth form in high school (that is, here, the top form). I used to write these verses to fill up magazines. You know, a short story very rarely ends exactly at the bottom of a page. There's a gap of three or four inches, and the editors at that time were always willing to buy a poem to fill in. I was paid ten and sixpence, half a guinea, for each. For a high school student this is a very rewarding sum, at least it was when I was doing it.

I had no idea of becoming anything except a writer—oh, possibly a painter, as you might gather from *Martha In Paris*. I have had a certain training in painting, but I never really got serious about it because if you paint you must do so full time and I couldn't afford that. But I wanted to write, and the fact that I had to earn a living probably turned me into a writer rather than a painter. I think I obtain something of the tactile pleasure a painter gets from slamming paint on canvas. I write everything in longhand two or three times, and I quite enjoy the physical sensations of dealing with pen and ink and paper.

N. What was your first published novel?

■ *Sharp:* The very first was called *Rhododendron Pie*. It's been out of print for decades, but I read it again the other day. It's not bad, not bad at all, but I do have the proportions wrong. I started out as though it were going to be a big book and it turned into a short one. I wouldn't make that mistake today.

The first book which met with any success at all was the second, *Fanfare For Tin Trumpets*. I was going in for rather *chichi* titles at the time. Now I call them things like *Martha In Paris* and *Martha, Eric and George*. Very *terre-à-terre*. But *Fanfare* had a nice little success, did me a lot of good, and I simply went on from there.

N.   How did your series of children's books enter the picture?

■ *Sharp:* I enjoy writing them immensely because they are a complete release of the imagination. The first of the Miss Bianca series was called *The Rescuers*. It was about the Prisoners Aid Association of Mice—mice are traditionally the prisoner's friend, you know—so I describe how the organization works with all its branches in various countries, the basic idea being the cheering of prisoners in their cells. You might say that it's national service stuff all mice go through. But then there are adventures when they feel prisoners have been wrongly imprisoned and should be released. It's fascinating to me, and I hope to the people who read the books.

I think a great deal of the success has been due to Garth Williams' illustrations. His technique is marvelous, but he shows the most wonderfully sympathetic imagination. For example, in one place I describe the chairman's chair as being made from walnut shells, so Garth Williams carpentered a walnut shell into a chair and then drew it.

N.   The stories have gone into a number of translations, haven't they?

■ *Sharp:* I'm delighted about this. For one thing, the foreign companies have told me that the stories are written in such good English they are a pleasure to translate. Then it's fascinating to see the questionnaires at the end of chapters, like the Dutch edition, for schools, where one question reads, "Why did they put Nils in the pocket closest to the poet's heart?" Answer: "Because they were both Norwegians." It's all very fascinating.

N.   To turn to your adult fiction—can you remember where the basic idea or thematic structure for a book like *The Nutmeg Tree* may have sprung from?

■ *Sharp:* More or less. I think that the basic idea was a theory that people often aren't bad but circumstances sometimes make them so. I think of Julia, particularly, a warm-hearted and completely amoral person who was perfectly good in her way, but if placed in a completely conventional society she looked bad. In fact, she *was* bad for them because she broke up all their patterns.

I know how *Britannia Mews* started. I was walking through a semislum stable that was being converted into these elegant little town-cottages, and I thought, "What a history that place has had from the day it was built!"—carriages and horses, then desolation, now cocktail parties and theater clubs.

Of course, it's remarkably easy to define where *Martha, Eric and George* sprang from, because it's a sequel to *Martha In Paris*. If you remember, Martha was a very headstrong, determined young woman who was going to paint and that was that. She was very annoyed at the prospect of having a baby; she didn't want the husband to go with it, didn't want the baby, and actually went out of her way and spent extra francs in taxi fare to leave the infant on its father's doorstep. Martha wondered why it should always be the woman who is saddled with a little illegitimate, so she reversed things. This reversal—beginning, of course, with the wonderful moment of discovery when Eric is handed his baby—made a natural springboard into the book.

But I sometimes feel that we had better not dig too deeply into the roots of novels to figure out where they come from. If it has come, wonderful, but let's not pull up the roots to examine them.

N. This magnificent place you live in—Albany House—has quite a history, hasn't it?

■ *Sharp:* Yes, and I think it's the nicest place in the world to live. Byron lived here, you know, and had the famous scene with Lady Caroline Lamb. At the other end of the scale we had William Gladstone adding a touch of respectability, and Montague Corry. There's no service, no elevators, no central heating, so it's very rugged but just as nice.

N. I'll turn toward the theoretical. If you were to give advice to the young and talented writer, what would that advice be?

■ *Sharp:* First of all I'd tell them never to think about the results. You must learn to write rather than be a writer. Write as well as you can. Don't think of what is wanted, what is popular, what will sell. Write what you want, and write as well as you can.

I think it's not only useful but almost essential for a writer to have other experiences. I think it would be terrible for a person of sixteen or seventeen to leave school and go home and say, "I'm going to be a writer" and sit down and write all day. Far better to

have a job, or as many jobs as possible. Do all sorts of things because you must first have actual experience to work with. Otherwise the things you write will be derived only from books, already
processed through someone else's minds. Don't get on a magazine
staff—get a job in a grocery store, a lumber camp. Fish, be a secretary, a switchboard operator, go on the stage. But don't just confine
yourself to writing.

Of course, when you actually are writing, you must regard
time as a sacred thing. Writing time, your treasured hours, dare not
be violated.

N. Do you feel that the writer has an obligation to the materials he uses in his work, on the one hand, and toward the public,
on the other?

■ *Sharp:* Well, there must certainly be an obligation to the
characters used. One cannot falsify them.

For example, I couldn't have made Martha be suddenly overcome with maternal love at the sight of her infant because it would
have been totally out of character. Nor could I reform Julia. Characters are shaped, you know, and live as truths.

I feel that I have an obligation to write good English and
another to be interesting to the reader. I can't remember who said
it, but someone stated that the cardinal quality of a novel is that it
should be interesting.

I think this really sums up its imperatives, because if it is to be
truly interesting the characters cannot be falsified and it must be
readable. If not stylistically pure, at least readable.

N. You maintain quite an active list of hobbies, don't you? I
mention this because I've heard your friends comment on the
schedule you keep.

■ *Sharp:* Well, I'm particularly fond of embroidery—gros point,
not petit point, which is too hard on the eyes. I find it relaxing and
agreeable, and I love to create my own designs. I designed that
coffee table of Henry VIII and his wives. I also find it useful, when
I'm traveling, to have a piece of embroidery with me because you
can get held up at airports for two hours or two days, and when
you embroider the time passes quickly. I did part of that chair
flying to the Argentine—a two-day flight, very boring so far above
everything.

I'm fond of gardening—I have a little garden in the country.
And I swim and draw. But I haven't enough time. All I want is
time—I would like to live two or three lives concurrently.

I have always thought that a jobbing gardener must lead an

interesting life, going from house to house, working for several people, visiting each family once per week and getting to know them. And I have always thought that it would be nice to be the lady in a troupe of adagio dancers—the one they fling through the air. I've always thought it would be delightful to be flung about like that, though probably it would be grueling—not able to eat for several hours beforehand, then only sole. Perhaps I should have been both a jobbing gardener *and* an adagio dancer. I might not have had time to write a word, but I'd have had a splendidly exciting life.

N.   How would you define your own objectives insofar as your career is concerned? What satisfied you most? What would you still like to accomplish that you haven't already done?

■ *Sharp:* I think that of all I've written what I'm best satisfied with—though not completely, don't think that for a moment—are the three books with Martha in them—*The Eye Of Love*, *Martha In Paris*, and *Martha, Eric And George*.

What I should like to achieve in the future, of course, is a novel as good as *Emma*, and a play as good as *The Cherry Orchard*. But that's talking of miracles.

"There is an unfortunate tendency in America to look at writing as though it's a continuous sporting event, an athletic contest in which you win one week and lose the next. Everything goes up and down. The writer himself can't afford to believe that."

Irwin Shaw
Interviewed in New York, February, 1964

Irwin Shaw

N. The strong talents of Irwin Shaw are spread across a wide canvas. As a reviewer my most vivid associations are divided between the desperate courage of *Bury The Dead*, the dramatic continuity of *The Young Lions*, and the poignant sensitivity of *Two Weeks In Another Town*. But first, in discussing his career, I'd like to go back to where he was born, reared, and educated, and how his interest in writing first developed.

■ *Shaw:* I'm a native New Yorker. I was born in New York and grew up in Brooklyn and I was educated in Brooklyn from beginning to end, including Brooklyn College. I think it was Year One when I first knew I wanted to write. At college I wrote a column for the school newspaper and plays for the dramatic society. Then I went to work as a professional writer, doing radio serials (which I quit as soon as I could).

All this goes back a long time, because *Bury The Dead* was done in 1936. I had just turned twenty-three when the play was first presented. Since that time I've written many more plays, a great many short stories, some movies, and four novels. A lot of people erroneously think that *The Young Lions* started it all, but I've been a professional for thirty years now, and I'm reaching that terrible moment when I have to start thinking about renewing copyrights. Believe me, this didn't bother me when I started writing.

Up to the end of 1963 my most recent work had been the writing and producing of a movie entitled *In The French Style*. It's playing throughout the world at the moment. I should say I co-produced it, but I wrote it alone. I had a play on Broadway last season, *Children From Their Games*. It was a failure, but I intend to redo it, perhaps in England, after some drastic revisions. I hope to bring it back to the United States some time in the next year or two because I like the play, even if the critics didn't. I made a lot of mistakes in it, so it didn't get a fair shake the first time around. This year (1964) I should have three books published—a travel book about the Mediterranean, entitled *In the Company of Dolphins;* a book of ten short stories, to be called, *Love on A Dark Street;* and a short novel I've just about finished, *The Lineaments of A Summer Day. In the Company of Dolphins* is the result of a trip I took by boat a couple of summers ago.

I'm going to start working on a novel this year, and perhaps another screenplay.

N. To go back to the first big impact of Irwin Shaw—*Bury The Dead.* It was a rather intense social document, wasn't it?

■ *Shaw:* Well, it was play about war, a play against war. In fact, in the program, the time was put down as the second year of the war beginning tomorrow night. It was written in 1935 and put on in 1936. I saw that some kind of war was coming. You didn't have to be a prophet in 1935 to know there was going to be a war. You weren't sure of who would be on which side, but you (or maybe I should shift to "me") were horrified by the idea of another war. This was the background for writing the play.

Actually, by the time the war broke out, my feelings were completely changed, because everybody on our side—by "our side" I mean the British, the French, the Russians, and ourselves—had fumbled away the chance of stopping the war. There was nothing left for anybody to do (I thought) but go and fight and win it, to try to avoid another one. This may be the position we're in now. In fact, after *Bury The Dead* I did a play called *The Gentle People,* an allegory in which I pointed out that if, in the world of today, we are faced with unscrupulous men, unscrupulous powers, personal and genocidal murderers, the only way to survive is to fight back. This point was not made in *Bury The Dead.* And since that time, though I like *Bury The Dead* as a play, my politics have changed to such a point that I don't approve of the politics of *Bury The Dead.* Even so, I let it be published, and acted in colleges and drama classes. I don't allow it on the public stage because, as I mentioned, the politics of the play no longer satisfy me. It's a curious thing, but this can happen as politics change, a person matures, and the world turns on its axis.

N. You mention that your politics have changed.

■ *Shaw:* Well, I'm still against war. I was a soldier myself for three years and three months, and if I saw that we were being attacked I'd know that the only way to survive would be to fight back and win. *Bury The Dead* was an appeal to the conscience not to fight.

It wasn't a completely pacifist plea, but I've heard it called that.

S

Actually, the stupidity that caused World War II and the death of thirty million people could have been avoided if we'd treated the Germans and Japanese with good hard sense before the war became inevitable. I'd like to think of *Bury The Dead* as a protest against stupidity as well as a pacifist plea.

N. I'd like to return to *The Young Lions*, with its wide range of characters and locations and its prewar and wartime actions. How much of it was based upon your own experiences?

■ *Shaw:* I think just about all writers will give the same answer to a question about any novel. Most will say, "It's a mixture of both," which is true. Some incidents can be related exactly as they occurred; some can be used as springboards for similar incidents; some you combine. Some characters you combine. Some people you meet you divide and they turn into three or four other characters. There's no rule I can figure out, but I did see just about every place I described in the book, except Berlin. I saw Africa, England, Germany, France—maybe not at the moment I describe them in the book, but I was there. On the other hand, I also talked with a great many people who had been in all these places in the time span I used, so I think I was able to start writing *The Young Lions* with a fair sense of reality.

N. As contrast, could you discuss the travel book, *In the Company of Dolphins?*

■ *Shaw:* The approach to this one is of joy, of sheer pleasure. Ever since I was a kid, and poor, I wanted to do something like this. I lived in the Sheepshead Bay section of Brooklyn, and at that time people used to dock pleasure boats there. I used to yearn to get on one and go somewhere, just anywhere. Finally, a couple of summers ago, my wife, my son (eleven), and I rented a boat and went from Saint Tropez to Venice, all around the Mediterranean, down the coast of Italy, visiting various islands, then to Corfu and the Dalmatian coast, Yugoslavia, and finished in Venice. *Holiday* magazine asked for five or six thousand words and I wrote 30,000 words simply because I had such a good time doing it and writing about it. It's a gentle, quiet little book, but somehow it was very satisfying to write. It extended the pleasure of the summer to the typewriter. Since then I've added another 25 per cent to the book, putting in things that I felt I didn't have the space for in a magazine piece.

N. You mentioned that you're at the point of renewing copyrights. Can you look back on your career, now, to pick out the highlights?

■ *Shaw:* I'm loath to pick out highlights. A writer thinks about his whole career; he doesn't think about the success or failure of any particular work except at the time it's happening.

When I look back there are things I don't like at all—things I've done, I mean. And there are things I like very much, even if they haven't been as popular as, say, *The Young Lions*. I haven't reread *The Young Lions* since it was published. I don't know why, but I've never reread any of my novels since they were published.

I'm not particularly fond of one novel I wrote—I won't mention its name—but there are others I like very much. The same goes for short stories. Through the years you can pick out things you like. But to pit one against another, or admit that I do—I try to avoid it, publicly *and* even in the privacy of my own mind.

There is an unfortunate tendency in America to look at writing as though it's a continuous sporting event, an athletic contest in which you win one week and lose the next. Everything goes up and down. The writer himself can't afford to believe that. The writer should feel he's going to win or lose fifty years after he's dead, not during any short spurt of success or failure. A success or failure in the literary world today is capricious, very often mistaken. Good things are panned, bad things are praised. For example, F. Scott Fitzgerald died thinking he was an absolute failure. Today he's one of the icons of American fiction. His best book—better than *The Great Gatsby* in my opinion—was *Tender Is The Night*. It got disgracefully bad reviews when it came out. He never recovered from the panning. In fact, he went so far as to try to rewrite it, taking into account the critics' attitudes toward it. But it happened that the critics of the book were all wrong, and Fitzgerald was right. Malcolm Cowley brought this revised edition out as a literary curiosity a few years ago, and it was nowhere nearly as good as the original.

N. Do you feel that the writer has an obligation to his material, on the one hand, and to the public, on the other?

■ *Shaw:* The writer has only one obligation—to stay alive and try to please himself.

N. If you were to look at American writing today, what would you choose to most admire, and what would you most deplore?

■ *Shaw:* Well, in the field of American fiction there's nothing much I deplore. The whole thing seems to be wide open. When I say "wide open" I mean it seems any man can write any way he wants, and if he has some talent, he'll be published and noticed. The public can make a choice. There seems to be absolute freedom in publishing today.

The theater is another thing. The theater is being crippled most of all by the financial lunacy of putting a play on Broadway. I have a feeling that a great many good plays are either not written, or not produced, or when produced are not given a fair chance because the commercialism of Broadway is the overriding factor of the American theater. Until we beat this I think our theater is going to become more and more puny, less adventurous, and in-finitely less rewarding for the writer who works in the medium.

The short story situation has deteriorated, too. A great many magazines have folded, and many more no longer print fiction, so the short story writer is stuck with a very limited choice of plat-forms. When I began writing short stories in 1934 there were five times the number of magazines than are published today that used short stories. But where does the fiction writer go for his bread-and-butter money now?

From an artistic point of view, the novelist or nonfiction writer is as free as his talent will permit him to be. He seems to have no other barriers. It's rough, however, if he wants to specialize in the theater or the short story.

N. Do you think the rather large invasion of British theater—strong plays and revues with relatively small, sharp casts—will have any influence upon American theater?

■ *Shaw:* I hope so. Take the way the British are developing actors—men like Peter O'Toole and Albert Finney and Paul Scofield. Now, in my own time in the American theater, in the late 1930's and the early 1940's, we showed up with two talents like that. We had Marlon Brando and Montgomery Clift. Neither of them was the result of an academy or method (though Brando since worked with method actors in the Actor's Studio). But I don't think either Brando or Clift has really lived up to his first promise.

Maybe this thing goes in a peculiar rhythm, a national rhythm which is very hard to figure out. The London theater does give its actors an advantage in training. The movie industry is located in London, too, so that an English actor theoretically can (and often does) work in a movie during the day and act on the stage in the evening. The same thing goes for France—both theater and motion picture production facilities are centered near Paris.

In the United States we always have had this division between the movies in Hollywood and the theater in New York. People have to uproot themselves when they go from one to the other.

The same is happening in television. Television is moving out to California and skimming off the cream of the crop of young actors who never get back to New York to do a play. So how do we develop O'Tooles and Finneys?

At the moment the. British theater is having a brilliant renaissance, due not only to the quality and appeal of their actors, but to the emergence of playwrights like Pinter and to the acceptance of Ionesco, a Frenchman well liked in England, plus the work of such brilliant veterans as Laurence Olivier, who now selflessly spends more or less all his time in a new theater outside London.

It's odd, but the British theater is more loyal to its heroes than the American theater. The American theater public is probably the most fickle public in the world. What you did last year doesn't count—it's what you do this year, this week, this minute. You're only as successful as your last performance or your last play, and if you have a cold on Wednesday night, God help you.

No matter how much respect an American actor or playwright or writer has earned, the last-minute thing seems to destroy all memory. Hell, a critic first wrote that I was washed up when I was twenty-four years old.

N.   How do you feel about the art of criticism in America?
■ *Shaw:* My feeling about the criticism in America could be more or less wrapped up in one name: Edmund Wilson. He's the only critic I take seriously. Other people in other fields are not too bad. Harold Clurman is an acute judge of the theater except that he loves theater so much (he's a director, himself) that his judgments are apt to be too gentle. He's very perceptive, but he doesn't get angry. Wilson doesn't get angry, either, but he marshals his case like a great prosecuting attorney when he wants to break down pretense or show that some movement is going in the wrong direction.

Aside from Wilson, I know of no critic of fiction who consistently makes any sense to me. The theater critics in New York are pleasant journalists, none of them as intrinsically important as he thinks. It's the newspapers they write for that carry the weight, and if you lose the *Times* and the *Tribune*, almost always you might as well shut up shop. But almost any English major or transferee from the sports page, given the same space in the same two papers, would be just as influential. The people who write about novelists are scattered, belong to no school, set no standards; thus whether their reviews are good or bad seem the result of chance. In general, my feeling about critics, even when I get good reviews or outrageously bad reviews for a book, is that the critics are generating no real authority. It's like chatting with people at a cocktail party—there's no depth, no searching. And, of course, there's a deplorable amount of log-rolling in certain groups—a "you say I'm good, I'll say you're good" private school. This doesn't do the art of criticism any good.

Oddly enough, the British literary reviews are, in general, worse than ours, and they don't have the massive example of Wilson to lead them on. And the log-rolling there is shamefully blatant. Maybe this just isn't the age for criticism.

N.   If you were to give advice to the young American writer who possesses both talent and dedication, what would that advice be?

■ *Shaw:*   There's absolutely no answer to that question, is there? You can say "Write well" but that's like telling a girl "Be Beautiful." If she's not beautiful she's not going to come off beautiful, no matter how hard she tries, and if a writer isn't both talented and ambitious he's not going to write well. I'd simply say, "Apply yourself—work." And even that isn't necessarily good advice because we have at lot of industrious fifth-rate writers, and we have one or two very lazy writers who are first-rate.

I believe in talent for writing, just as I believe in it for a sprinter. You're born with—you have within you—the capacity to run the hundred yards in 9.2, and if you only have the capacity to run the hundred yards in 9.7 you're not going to get it down to 9.2. There's a lot of training you can do, but there's a limit beyond which training cannot help, a limit determined by God-given abilities.

I've taught writing courses, but I don't think I've helped anybody very much. It's a way of stimulating young people to try something new, to see what they can do, but it shouldn't be necessary and I don't think it is. I don't think writers become writers because they go to college or take a course. A writer is a man who is born with talent and who fights all out to use his talent to the utmost.

N.   You've also done a great deal of writing for motion pictures. Could you express your satisfactions and dissatisfactions with that medium?

■ *Shaw:*   I guess the first real satisfaction I've felt after many years of on-and-off writing for movies came with my last picture, *In The French Style*, with Jean Seberg. It was based on my own stories, I was my own co-producer, and whatever virtues or failures the picture has belong to me, plus my co-producer, Robert Parish, who directed it. For the first time I had the feeling that I could use the medium as I wished, and I would like to do one picture every two years on this same basis.

I plan to do a movie from an old short story I wrote, "The 80-Yard Run," which first appeared in *Esquire* in 1938 or 1939 and do it the same way. I'd like to write the script, co-produce it, and film it in New York and in the Middle West a year or so from now.

I like the movies as a medium to work in, when I'm my own boss. But when I had to worry about a studio or producers it became a troublesome medium. The dissatisfactions are tremendous, because the final thing is liable to bear very little resemblance to anything you actually wrote.

In Europe, for example, especially in France, the young intellectuals are much more concerned about the movies than they are about theater. The same goes for Italy. I think there's some of this feeling in London (though, as I mentioned, the British theater is enjoying a renaissance). But even in England the young intellectuals are taking movies seriously. Even some of the starts of the theatrical renaissance, like John Osborne, have not just remained in the theater. Osborne did the magnificent *Tom Jones* and is planning other films. I have a feeling that he must have enjoyed writing that script, working on the movie, and perhaps determining at just which point he'll divide his time between the theater and movies.

I'm too far gone as a short story writer and a novelist to be able to divide my time equally with movies, but I would like to keep my hand in. I think that a writer is at his best, stimulated and keyed up and challenged, when he has a hand in many media. Even if subject matters never interact or interplay he's bound to grow, and growth is everything.

"I . . . dislike the growing obsession with the pornography of violence, with the deliberate cultivation of all those parts which exist in all of us, which all of us nevertheless regret. It seems to me that if this becomes the substance of art, it will kill art as a serious force in our spiritual lives."

C. P. Snow
Interviewed in London, England, October, 1963

C. P. Snow

N. Lord Snow—known best in America, of course, as novelist C. P. Snow—has gathered such a loyal audience of readers and critics that he now threatens to assume both the distinction and the danger of becoming the center of a cult. Frankly, I hope this does not happen for some time: there is too much to be enjoyed and gained in the rich sweep of Snow's work before we split into partisan groups that ignore the whole of his output to fight guerilla battles over commas and hidden meanings. C. P. Snow is one of the important novelists of our time in the philosophical sense; this is evidenced by the heed paid to phrases like "establishment" and "two cultures," but he is also one of our most entertaining and rewarding writers. In appraising the significant novels of the past decades we cannot omit books like *Homecoming, Time of Hope*, and *The Affair*.

In talking to Lord Snow I would like to begin with the rough outline of life we call biography.

■ *Snow:* I was born in a Midland town called Leicester, which is something like Lancaster, Pennsylvania, or perhaps Columbus, Ohio. My parents were poor, and I had to make my own way at a very early age. By luck and good judgment I ultimately found my way to Cambridge University, where I became what we call a "don"—Americans would use the term "professor." This was during a ten-year period just before the war.

During the war I played some part in apportioning the use of scientific personnel for the British government. This rather interrupted my literary career which had begun quite early in life. Though I was trained as a scientist I had always wanted to be a writer, and I started writing novels in the early 1930's. I didn't start to work seriously on my series of novels until after World War II although I published the first one in 1940. There simply wasn't the time—nor, perhaps, the place—for them. But life is odd, and owing to the things I had been doing during the war I found myself caught up in other activities afterward. I became a civil service commissioner, and I also found myself a director in charge of personnel for one of our largest industrial companies. This triple thread I maintained for some time, though writing was the predominant interest during that time. I gave up being a public servant in 1960. I'm still a director of the English Electric Company, but I've been writing fairly continuously for the past thirteen years.

N. The word "establishment" has been kicked around for the past ten or fifteen years on both sides of the Atlantic, but I have a feeling that (in America, at least) the public is apt to confuse and oversimplify its meanings. We're apt to think of conservative versus liberal, which I don't think is exactly right.

■ *Snow:* It isn't that at all. Insofar as the concept has any meaning (and there's some doubt whether it has), we would refer to the fact that there are a relatively small number of people in Great Britain who are concerned actively with running it, but they are not the people one would normally think of. The "establishment" is largely composed of civil servants, administrators, some industrialists, some academics, some people like the editor of the *Times*, and so on. It's a fairly complex body, perhaps fifty thousand strong, and its enemies say they all know each other. This is not true, of course. The stereotype is much simpler than the actual reality, insofar as the reality exists.

The conservative-versus-liberal interpretation is quite wrong. There are many people of strong liberal conviction—including myself—who would certainly mingle with the "establishment" and perhaps assume an active part in the scheme of things. And there are, likewise, many persons of strong conservative sympathies who could no more be members of the "establishment" than a pop singer.

N. During the past few years there's been a diminishing of publicity surrounding "the angry young men." What has happened to them? Are they angry middle-aged men or aren't they angry any more?

■ *Snow:* I think they may be angry, but I think the world outside England, and to some extent England herself, misinterprets them totally. The general idea—certainly held in Eastern Europe and to some extent in America, too—was that they were rebels against society. This is quite untrue. You don't make yourself a rebel by being rude or even by taking off your tie. You make yourself a rebel by doing something to protest seriously against the society in which you're living. The angry young men have never done that—at least, most of them have never done that.

They seem to have felt—and I think that in part they were right—that after the war the limits of English society became rather more definite. It was harder for someone who was born in modest circumstances, as I was, to make his way right through society in (say) 1950 than it was for us in 1930. This did give rise to a certain amount of frustration. But it didn't produce a movement of serious social protest. The "angry young men" were never that. I never believed in them in social terms for a moment, and I believe in them even less at the present time.

N. More recently you have become deeply involved in the controversy of the "two cultures." Could you explain what this is, and what your role in the controversy has been?

■ *Snow:* What I've said—and I've said this in chorus with many others, but I think my name has been more closely attached to it, by chance as much as anything, is that if our two cultures cannot communicate we are in great danger. The two cultures, of course, are the scientific, on the one hand, and the literary, on the other. This lack of communication is sharper in England than it is anywhere, although it is obvious in the United States and it is obvious to some extent all over the world.

The danger of the division is obvious when you see it in action. For instance, Sir Lawrence Bragg recently said in the *Times* that the difficulty with people who have not had any kind of scientific education is this: they just take the view, "I've had a liberal education, I don't understand anything about the latest scientific discoveries, therefore, they can't be part of a liberal education, q.e.d."

This is not the view that any sensible person ought to take. There are too many aspects of the sciences which affect and will affect both the course of our lives and the way we think about ourselves. Therefore we must have some communication both ways. Neither scientists, on the one side, nor literary intellectuals, on the other, can possibly regard themselves as adequately educated unless they can communicate across this obvious—but unnecessarily wide—gulf.

N. I'd like to turn to your own writing, now, but the first question may seem rather oblique. A reviewer—perhaps because he reads too much—seldom remembers individual characters in novels. But for some reason I can't forget a creation of yours named Sheila —and I think she was in *Homecoming*—because it was the most impressive study of a neurotic woman I've come across. How did you come to create her?

■ *Snow:* I'm glad you mentioned her because I think she's one of the three best characters I've done—in some ways the best. I can't pretend that she didn't have some origin in real life, my life. I think that all characters do spring from some personal acquaintance, some involvement, however slight, with the fabric of one's life. You begin with something that had some impulse in life and add to it from other sources and blend it into something usually quite different from the original. But Sheila, of course, was someone I knew, someone I was in love with—this is obvious, I think, in the book—yet she became, in writing the book, both more than and less than the real Sheila.

N. To turn to the theoretical, how do you feel about the obligation of the novelist? This is a two-pronged thing, actually, because I'm referring to the novelist's obligation to his material and to his public.

■ *Snow:* In the ultimate sense the two obligations become one, of course. You simply have to work as hard as you can, with all the talent you have, with worthwhile subject matter. And let us hope you have enough discrimination to choose worthwhile subject matter. The two extremes of failure—the worthwhile badly presented, or the trivial served up beautifully—still represent failure.

I think the epitome of success can be wrapped up in the single word "communication." I'm afraid that the 'writer who doesn't feel he has to communicate with his public, who doesn't want to reach a wide public, is usually fooling himself and certainly fooling the public. I've never been a great believer in making the commonplace incomprehensible. This is one of the occupational diseases of Western art. I think you've got to consider what you want to say, think about it as deeply and in as complicated a manner as you like (or as comes naturally to your temperament) but when you write it you've got to make it as interesting, as capable of being understood, as your talent will possibly allow.

N. In looking at today's world of letters and the theater—and since you travel so broadly in England and America, Europe and Russia, your world is a broad one—what do you most admire and what do you most deplore?

■ *Snow:* I passionately dislike two things. I dislike art trickling away into a kind of gifted insanity, an esoteric nonsense. This is an easy way out for art. Art has always had this temptation, and some of its most gifted practitioners are drawn to extremes almost beyond their will. This I dislike.

I also dislike (and England and America are the two greatest culprits) the growing obsession with the pornography of violence, with the deliberate cultivation of all those parts which exist in all of us, which all of us nevertheless regret. It seems to me that if this becomes the substance of art, it will kill art as a serious force in our spiritual lives. There is some assurance in knowing that when the pornography of violence goes too far there will be a revolt against it, but aren't we intelligent enough and discriminating enough to stop the nonsense before it goes too far?

N.   Do you think that the pornography of violence represents our own standards of morality, perhaps an apathy?

■ *Snow:* I think we are overpessimistic about moral apathy. To an extent it exists, but on the other hand I would have thought that over the past three hundred and five hundred years we have changed immeasurably—despite all the horrors we've seen, despite all we know about how ineffective the conformist can be in a hideous situation like the Nazi regime. In the United States and in Great Britain there is an extraordinary reservoir of moral concern. Remember, the Italian of the Renaissance wouldn't have been terribly worried if he saw someone starving in the streets. This was simply a fact of life. You and I are so constructed, so conditioned, that we can't accept such a sight. I think we underrate ourselves.

I remember going to the American Midwest, visiting American colleges, and finding a general concern for the welfare of the world—not just a nation or a portion of the world, but the whole world. This attitude exists, and it must be encouraged. The future is not all black. Portions of it can be individually hideous, but there is no reason why it should be socially hideous.

N.   Conversely—what would you call the high points of present-day culture?

■ *Snow:* The most obvious high point is the fact that there's never been so much skill at hand. We are educating far more people; greater numbers have the chance to use a literary talent that, in a less literate society, would go unexpressed (except, perhaps, for telling stories to one's children). Until fairly recently we were an illiterate society—few of the persons who would have been good writers had a chance to come through.

In addition, we are developing certain skills, certain truly professional talents to a very high point—to a higher point than they've ever been developed. Technological advances· in printing, for example, mean that thousands of titles of books can be produced very cheaply. The writer has the potential of a greater audience than he's ever been able to consider. It's at his disposal if he's willing to work conscientiously to get it. If he truly wants to communicate.

God knows we're bad, and sometimes we act as though we have little sense, but I don't think we're worse or have less sense than our forefathers. We simply have to assimilate and use our abilities and accomplishments and have a bit of faith and hope.

N. If you were advising the talented youngster who wishes to make a career of writing, what would that advice be?

■ *Snow:* First of all I would tell him to learn and know. To experience all he can of the actual world, the real world, where people live and work for a living and raise children and experience all the joy and uncertainty and tragedy that goes into life.

He should move in literary circles only when he has to. Some contact is necessary, professionally, but the person who sets himself up as a writer before he's written is living in a state of delusion. Of course, many people like to lead the writing life who haven't the capacity to become a writer.

He should discover his talent, his temperament, his interests, and then not give a damn. Forget the fashion—ignore the fashionable.

He should cultivate a good heart. This is difficult for a writer, because part of a writer's skill is his ability to peer into the very blackest, as well as the not-so-black, sides of himself and his fellow man. But he cannot let this overwhelm him. This is an all-too accessible pitfall for the writer, and it has destroyed many talents.

N. Recently you and your wife had a rather long visit in Russia. What is your impression of the art that has come, and is to come, from the Soviets?

■ *Snow:* I believe they are going to produce some really fine literary art—probably very quickly, perhaps in the very next decade. They have, of course, produced some fine art in recent times, but the West has been quite stupid about accepting it. Sholokhov, in my view, is probably the best novelist of the last forty years. *And Quiet Flows The Don*—and I am prepared to argue this point —is, I think, the peak of the realistic novel in my time, the great achievement of Soviet literature. It was written over thirty years ago.

All too many Soviet writers and poets aren't known in the West. This has been because the West has only wanted to get from Russia its dissident voices, the grumblings and complaints of those who are not a part of society, who are not easily assimilated into society. The West has been bad in not exerting itself to get a fine reproduction of Soviet literature. They had done better by us. For instance, ask any Russian in Russia who are their four best living novelists. He will certainly say Sholokhov first—good, he is well

known in the West. He will almost as certainly go on to mention
Leonid Leozov and Konstantin Fediv. Leozov, who is a writer of
extreme originality hasn't, so far as I know, been translated into
English for thirty years. Fediv has never been translated into
English.

Another, Alexander Tvardovsky is the most famous living poet
in the Soviet Union. He is also the editor of *Novy Mir*. The man
who has sponsored the talents of the new literary generation, such
as Solzhenitsyn. Tvardovsky is both as writer and man one of the
most important figures in the world. So far the West has managed
to translate one short story of his, and one lyric poem.

N.   My final question relates to your own work—to the series
of novels that have made such strong impressions over the past few
decades. How would you define your own objective in planning
and writing them?

■ *Snow:*   What I was trying to say—what I am still trying to say
—is that the tension between man and society, as felt by someone
living very actively in that society, springs from two sources: the
pressures of understanding the society and making it go, and the
necessity for making peace with his lonely soul. In all our world,
East and West, gulfs exist between the human who lives quite alone,
the person who is contracting out, and the person who is too easily
absorbed into activity, who has lost touch with his own experience.

In the West I think I'm probably best known for those novels
in which Lewis Eliot is living actively in society—the novels that
could be called "political" in a sense. My own feeling is that people
will ultimately value some of the other books more.

"The things I'm personally bored with, like the antinovel—all the "anti" brigade, the dirt brigade, the sicks and the beats—I don't deplore because they have their value; they're trying things out, keeping literature alive and moving. Good things get thrown up eventually, even out of the silliest new movement."

Mary Stewart
Interviewed in Edinburgh, Scotland, November, 1963

Mary Stewart

N. The series of novels that Mary Stewart has so triumphantly produced as best-sellers is hard to define. They are not mysteries, though elements of mystery are always involved. They are not suspense stories, though the threat or promise of danger often obsesses the reader. Nor are they whodunits, in the classic sense of that word, for the arts of sleuthing are usually incidental to the action. But however her skilled blending of romantic background, thorough characterization, and logical plotting is defined, millions of readers have been gloriously entertained by *Madam, Will You Talk?*, *Wildfire At Midnight*, *Thunder On The Right*, *Nine Coaches Waiting*, *My Brother Michael*, *The Ivy Tree*, *The Moon-spinners*, and *This Rough Magic*.

In talking to Miss Stewart I'd like to begin with basic auto-biography—where she was born and reared and how her interest in writing first developed.

■ *Stewart:* I was born in Sunderland in the county of Durham, which is in the north of England. Both of my parents are still living. My father, a Church of England clergyman, is now retired. I don't remember Sunderland, actually. I was only a baby when we left. The first home I remember is a little agricultural village called Trimdon where we lived for the first seven years of my life. I don't recall a time when I wasn't interested in writing. I believe I could put words on paper when I was a little over three years old. When we left the parish of Trimdon, I had already written several exercise books full of fairy stories.

I didn't have many toys. Trimdon was a remote place, and my parents were poor, and I suppose I was driven in on myself to make my own amusements. This was probably a very good thing. I remember hours spent in the attic of the old vicarage, with a cheap exercise book, a pencil, and my three toys. I had a little rubber horse, a tin elephant, and a small rubber cat that whistled when you pressed it. I remember those three creatures very distinctly. They used to sit around me on the floor when I wrote my stories, and the stories were always about them. They were my first characters.

N. A bit of Winnie-the-Pooh.

■ *Stewart:* But hardly as successful. I can't remember any of the stories; I'm afraid they've gone with the wind. My mother did save a book of poems when we left Trimdon, and I must take a look at them. The best thing, a book of fairy stories I illustrated, has been lost. You see, my first ambition, even before writing, was to be an artist. I can't remember a time when I didn't try to draw. I would draw my stories, then write to match the pictures. I think I took the writing part of it very much for granted.

N. What was your educational program?

■ *Stewart:* I went to the village school when I was very small, and when we moved from Trimdon to a larger parish, I was sent away to boarding school. I attended Skellfield School which was then a girls' public school. (Actually, a private school; the English terminology is misleading.)

After the boarding school in Yorkshire, I went to Durham University and read English Language and Literature for three years. Then, since I planned to be a teacher, I took a year's diploma in education.

N. Did you teach?

■ *Stewart:* Yes. I taught for two years; this was just at the beginning of the war. Then I was asked by my university at Durham to go back to lecture. I very happily packed my bags and returned to Durham, which I loved. I took lodgings and lectured for four years in English.

N. And that was where you met your husband.

■ *Stewart:* He was a lecturer in geology at Durham. He's now head of the Geology Department at the University of Edinburgh. We actually met at a victory dance at the end of the war in 1945. It was VE night, and I was to leave Durham the next day. But after meeting him that night, I decided not to go to work in London. I stayed on, and we married three months after we met. It was a quick business, very painless.

N. Has your rather deep knowledge of Greece and the Mediterranean as a whole, come from traveling with him?

■ *Stewart:* No. This is a bit of misinformation that has crept into some biography of me. My husband hasn't visited Greece yet. I usually go there in the spring or in autumn, when it isn't too hot, and so far, he hasn't been able to get away at the right time. But he has promised to go with me this next spring. I want to show Greece off to him because I know he'll love it, and I'll see a lot of new aspects of it through his eyes. We did travel in the Pyrenees together; that was the setting for *Thunder On The Right*. But the one background that I owe entirely to him is the Scottish one for *Wildfire At Midnight*. We traveled every inch of Scotland together.

N. There seems to be some confusion, on the part of critic and reviewer, in defining your stories. Can you do it?

■ *Stewart:* Heavens, no. I realize there's a fashion, now, for categorizing books, and I find this extraordinarily difficult and irritating. I'm always asked to classify, but all the available definitions have specific meanings that somehow don't fill the bill. I find myself calling my books "thrillers" for want of a better word, but it isn't the one I like. The same with "mysteries." People expect a detective story or a whodunit, and my books certainly aren't that. They're not really mysteries, because the mystery element isn't nearly as important as other aspects. "Entertainments" might be a good word, but it's clumsy. I'd rather just say that I write novels, fast-moving stories that entertain.

To my mind there are really only two kinds of novels, badly written and well written. Beyond that, you cannot categorize. If a book is well written and well characterized, it can use what you can call suspense materials—what, in another hand, could even be cheap material—and it will be a good book. I'm not talking about me, here. I'm thinking about Graham Greene. Look at all the suspense elements he uses. There's no difference in kind, really, in quality, between Greene's serious novels and his "entertainments." They are all superbly written, and if they serve different purposes, we can't say that one is less good than the other.

I certainly don't put myself in Greene's category. But I do think that the treatment, and what is in the writer himself, matters more than the material. The writer himself is the difference. As for me, I suppose I do the best I can with material that excites me. Can't I say that I just write stories? "Storyteller" is an old and honorable title, and I'd like to lay claim to it.

N. As a writer do you feel an obligation to the reader, on one hand, and to the material you use, on the other?

■ *Stewart:* Yes, I think I do feel a sense of obligation, but I'm not sure to whom. I certainly never think of pitching a story to any particular audience, to any age level, or type of reader. In fact, I don't think about the reader at all—I'm merely concerned with doing the best I can.

Did you say an obligation to one's material? Perhaps that's the key. Perhaps, at the back of my mind, there's the thought that I don't want anyone to be the worse for having read anything I've written. That's a silly, rather priggish way of putting it. But I don't want anyone made troubled or unhappy by anything I've written; perhaps "depressed" and "hurt" are better words. This may sound as though I don't think people should read things which are depressing, but this isn't true, either. Perhaps, after all, "injured" is the word I want, yet it isn't quite right.

I rather think that the hero or heroine of a novel should observe certain standards of conduct, of ethics, a somewhat honorable behavior pattern. I know that I can't go along with anyone I don't admire. It would be difficult for me to expect readers to go along with an antihero I created. I don't like the antihero. He fails, to my mind, because it is terribly hard to identify oneself with someone whose views run counter to everything one believes to be right. I think what this age needs is exactly the opposite. We need a hero, a hero-pattern—not the old type flag-waving-stiff-upper-lip hero, but some living pattern of rightness that fits our time. Something positive. If we haven't got one, let's create him. It's happened before. Nature follows art.

N. In creating your characters, would you say that they are drawn altogether from the imagination or are they rooted in your own experience?

■ *Stewart:* I think the actual writing of the novel determines my characters. The plot is drawn up before I start, of course, and certain scenes and specific actions are planned. But I do find, as the characters develop and the plot thickens, that I've landed certain people in situations where they're supposed to do something no longer in character. Then I have to alter the situation. The people have solidified, assumed a quality quite different from the sketch I'd started with. In cases like this one might say that the characters move me. I have to respond to their reality, otherwise the story would be false.

But are they complete blueprints of real people? No. I would say that they are 99 per cent created, but that doesn't mean that my people aren't put together out of memories and things observed in real people. One must take more nuances of character from real life than one realizes. My people may be more composite than meets my eye.

N. This is a difficult question, perhaps an impossible one. Could you pick any one of your novels and describe its genesis, from the basic plot idea, to its final shape as a novel?

■ *Stewart:* You're right, this is almost impossible to answer. The book that's freshest in my mind is *This Rough Magic,* of course, because it's the most recent. But it took me almost two years to write it because of various interruptions, and I can't truly analyze how it grew. I can't help but think of an experiment we used to do at school, in science class, where we hung a thread into an alum solution, and the crystals began to cling to the thread until they bunched together like rather startling grapes. I suppose all writers work differently, but my stories grow in much that same pattern. It starts with a basic idea; then things I read, and hear, and remember, cling to that central idea, until I have the nucleus of a book. Most of its conformation occurs subconsciously.

For instance, take *My Brother Michael,* which was written after I'd visited Greece two or three times and was wildly in love with it. I longed to set a book there, to re-create certain places for myself and other people. So I looked around for the sort of thing that could logically and dramatically happen to people in Delphi or on Parnassus (curious, lovely, wild country). The idea, the key idea, became the plot of the hidden statue. Then I decided what sort of people I wanted to put there, and when I thought I had a rich enough cast, I sat back and figured out how they would react to certain events. If the writer knows his characters well enough, most of the incidents in the novel will outline themselves.

N. When your novels first began appearing—and with such marked success—can you remember your own reactions to this success? And to the quality of the reviews?

■ *Stewart:* The reviews varied greatly, of course, as they still do. On the whole, reviewers have been very kind. The best ones, the most valuable ones, are where the reviewer can actually appraise the book as a whole, not just as a story that moves from "a" to "b" to "c." By which I mean, it's so much more satisfying to find a reviewer who deals with an entire book, with what the author tried to do, and with what overall success, than just with details of the plot.

I wish one did not sometimes feel that too many rather young people are let loose on one's books, people neither trained nor experienced. I suppose, if it comes to that, they've got to get experience somewhere, but to have them let loose on us is a bit difficult, at times.

Even if you can see that a reviewer doesn't know his job, superficial criticism can be irritating. Destructive, too. I don't mean to sales—I mean to oneself. If someone has judged your book deeply and fairly, and thinks it's bad, fair enough; that can be helpful. But you get the reviewers who are concerned with their own image and not the book, trying to be flip and clever at the author's expense. You know the kind of thing—a whole review leading up to a wise-crack. That is silly and cruel and irresponsible. It does such a lot of real damage. Nobody's really self-confident, and writers never, ever are. Do you know, I feel the better for having said that? Most reviewers do a good job, and one is grateful to them. Some of them I feel I know, and I look forward to hearing from them, as though the review were a kind of open letter.

You asked me how success took me. I was terrified. The first time my photograph appeared with a "new writer" caption underneath, I burst into frightened tears. I felt as though I couldn't bear to have anyone else see this, or read the book.

N.   But you've gotten over that?

■ *Stewart:*   You'd be surprised; I'm still frightened. I suppose it's inevitable. The more success one has, the more there is at stake. People expect more, and there's the dreadful feeling, each time, that I've fallen short of what I tried to do. Toward the end, when I'm rewriting and revising, I feel so terrified that I just won't let it out of the house. Then the publisher takes it from me, rather forcibly, and the forthcoming publication becomes a terrible inevitability.

N.   If you were to give advice to the younger person who wanted seriously to write, what would that advice be?

■ *Stewart:*   I think the best advice I've ever heard given to would-be writers came from Samuel Johnson, when he said, "If you want to be a writer, write. Write all the time." One must simply write so much every day, bad or good, and tear up the bad. Someday, something worth keeping will be turned out.

The great mistake would be to wait for "inspiration." This doesn't exist, to "fall like a spark from heaven" as Arnold put it, to set you off writing. I make myself write so much every day of my life whether I want to or not. I've sat before a sheet of blank paper for an hour, or a sheet with one sentence on it that's crossed out, thinking I'm never going to get going, that I should get up and go out into the garden or into Edinburgh, anything to get away from that awful sheet of paper and the frustration. Then suddenly, there it was, something happened, and I was writing. I suppose you could call *that* a spark from heaven, but the point is, you've got to be there at your desk, and working, *before* it comes. It doesn't really fall from heaven—only from your study ceiling.

N.   In looking at the literary output of today, would you

point to what you most admire, and to what you most deplore?
■ *Stewart:*   When I'm asked a question like that I can never think
of names, even of my favorites. As a general thing I suppose I
admire craftsmanship, good writing. With Graham Greene—I know
I've mentioned him before, but he always comes to mind first because he's the maestro—with him you read the first sentence, and
you think, "Here we go again, here's a man who can't put a foot
wrong." It's pure delight. You can't ask for his sort of genius
everywhere, but you can demand professionalism, sweat and blood
and time and the ability to stand back from one's work and assess
it, and accept criticism and put it right where it goes wrong. I like
to like the writer—to feel that this is a man with intelligence,
humor, and passion, who's in control every minute.

Salinger, now. I admire Salinger very much. He writes like an
angel, and you go right along with him as naturally as breathing. I
did find the last one sagging a bit (*Raise High The Roofbeam,
Carpenters*) and I hope he doesn't get bogged down with the Glass
family, though *Franny and Zooey* was marvelous. I've a feeling
poor Salinger is paying for having written one of the best things of
our time. He's stuck with that magnificent *Catcher In The Rye* and
it's going to be terribly hard to match it.

I admire James Baldwin, too. Not the last book; that was a
mistake, but *Another Country* and *Giovanni's Room*. I like historical novels—some, that is. Especially those that add some insight
into what's happening *now*. Mary Renault, Margaret Irwin, Jay
Williams.

One novelist I admire very much is Pamela Hansford Johnson. I
think she's first-rate, another writer you're safe with, from the very
first sentence. Francis King is another fine writer who doesn't seem,
to me, to be rated highly enough. He's beautifully disciplined, with
a habit of getting the reader by the entrails. Agony to read, but
terribly good. *The Dark Glasses* impressed me very much. It's set in
Corfu. So is my newest book, *This Rough Magic*, and I can tell you
that I wouldn't want anyone to read them side by side. A writer
like Francis King makes me feel about an inch high. I'm afraid this
is rather haphazard. I'm reading one of Aubrey Menen's just now.
I always read him with pleasure, like drinking dry champagne. I
think a man to watch is Robert Shaw—only two books so far, and
both first-class. John Masters is another who handles exciting
material wonderfully well. *The Deceivers* and *Bhowani Junction*
are both classics.

Mysteries? I don't read many nowadays. I read Ian Fleming, of course, but who doesn't? I admire him very much—he writes beautifully. I don't envy him, though; I can see him getting farther and farther out on a limb for plots, though I may be wrong. I hope he's not going to do a Conan Doyle on us. I hope he isn't seriously trying to kill James Bond. What would life be without him? Alastair MacLean—he's done something very difficult: pulled away from a rather overrated first best-seller and gotten better and better. I like William Haggard and Eric Ambler; and there's Gavin Lyall, who's only written one book, so far, but it's excellent. On the whole, I now find that detective novels bore me. Except for Rex Stout. He does such a lovely job, and, of course, I adore Archie Goodwin.

You asked me what I deplored in modern literature (not the same as disliking). There are a lot of highly rated writers whose work I dislike or by whom I am bored, but that doesn't mean I deplore what they're doing. Personal tastes oughtn't to count in a general appraisal of what's going on in literature. The things I'm personally bored with, like the antinovel—all the "anti" brigade, the dirt brigade, the sicks and the beats—I don't *deplore* because they have their value; they're trying things out, keeping literature alive and moving. Good things get thrown up eventually, even out of the silliest new movement, even if it's only in the countermovement that's bound to follow. It's interesting to watch it go on. In the theater, too—all this zany stuff, the theater of cruelty and so on, at least things are alive and working. We've already got some first-rate playwrights out of it: Robert Bolt, Peter Schaffer, John Whiting.

I'd rather not mention names I *don't* admire. It's only personal taste, and writers are too exposed and too vulnerable.

N. Looking back on your own output, can you pick out a novel as a particular favorite? And conversely, the one you least like?

■ *Stewart:* The least favorite is simple: *Thunder On The Right.* I detest that book, I'm ashamed of it, and I'd like to see it drowned beyond recovery. It's overwritten. It was actually the second book I wrote, and for some strange reason I went overboard, splurged with adjectives, all colored purple. As far as a favorite is concerned, I'd be torn between *The Moon-spinners* and *This Rough Magic.* Perhaps this choice comes up only because they're my last two. I think any writer is closer to his latest work. Perhaps the ego demands that we feel that our latest is the best—constant improvement and all that.

Another difficulty about picking a favorite is the difference between the books that are episodic like *The Moon-spinners* and *Wildfire At Midnight*, and those built around a more complex core, like *The Ivy Tree* and *Nine Coaches Waiting* and *This Rough Magic*. The former, the *Thirty-Nine Steps* sort of thing, are fairly easy to write—they take about a year. The latter take eighteen months or more and cause no end of difficulty. I'm a muddled thinker, really, and when I get gummed up, I have a dreadful time untangling myself.

N.   How did you come to write *This Rough Magic?*

■ *Stewart:* Well, in the spring of 1962 I went to Corfu, an island I had not visited before. I found it very different in character from everything else on the Greek mainland, and in the Aegean Islands. Much richer, beautiful in a fertile, flowering sort of way. The Corfu setting actually suggested the theme of the book.

Now, this will refer to your previous question about the genesis of a novel. Corfu is rumored to be the island on which Shakespeare's play *The Tempest* was set. Prospero was supposed to have lived there, and the Neapolitan ship was wrecked on Corfu. The title *This Rough Magic* comes, of course, from Prospero's abdication speech, and this suggested, to me, the *Tempest* theme which is woven through the book.

The new knowledge of Corfu was added, of course, to my previous experiences in Greece, so even a brief stay of a couple of weeks gave the book some rather solid ground. I'm lucky in having a good visual memory, almost like a movie camera. When I start describing something in a book, I find myself putting down things I didn't know I'd caught. I'm a sponge, a happy thing for a writer to be.

N.   We spoke before of the worthwhileness of characters, of the attributes the central character should have. Are you aware, in creating your heroines, of any duplication?

■ *Stewart:* I suppose there must be some. The heroines in my novels tell their own stories, you know, so I have to create young women each time who are susceptible to experience and sensitive enough to record it. There's bound to be a sameness in their style, too. I do give them different backgrounds, different physical attributes and temperaments, but it could be that a pattern does emerge because the heroine has to be the sort of person who interests me. I have to like her. I have to live in her. I do try to put myself into these bodies and minds, and think and act the way they would, but to some extent they are bound to like the things I like —I mean, the important things. They have the same general values.

When my heroine is very young, like Nicola in *The Moon-spinners*, perhaps I haven't been able to put the clock back far enough. Perhaps my own judgment and comment colors her with too much maturity. I know my own irony creeps in. Irony isn't something one acquires when young. I suppose it's me standing back to watch.

N. What ambitions do you have as far as the future is concerned?

■ *Stewart:* Very few or very many—it all depends upon how ambitious you think ambitions should be. I want to keep writing, of course—a new novel every eighteen months or so, good ones if possible. I'd like to write a play, and I have a historical novel in mind that excites me. I enjoy living here in Edinburgh, adore husband and friends, anticipate new trips to the Continent and a return trip to America. And I love gardening.

Basically, my ambition is to go on living as quietly and happily as I do now, and to do some good work.

"I am made sad by picking up novels by young Americans to find that they are long wails and laments. To myself I have occasionally described them as the "crybaby school." . . . It is absolutely amazing, the number of American novels coming out in which the writers are doing very little more than feeling sorry for themselves."

Irving Stone
Interviewed in Los Angeles, August, 1963

Irving Stone

N.   Irving Stone is one of the few writers whose books are best-sellers at release time and remain on best-seller lists for months and even years. His novels find their way into costly bindings, even into limited editions. One reviewer called Mr. Stone our foremost "histo-biographer," claiming that the Stone novels invariably treat a notable person in breadth and depth and favor the audience with a carefully researched picture of social and historical conditions as they truly existed. Thus the man, and his times, come together in terms of mutual influence.

Two of Mr. Stone's novels that invariably spring to mind are *The Agony and The Ecstasy* and *Lust For Life*. The latter was published several years ago and I don't believe it has ever really been out of print. The former, only a few years old, promises to set the same record. But to begin I'd like to ask Mr. Stone about the writing of *The Agony and the Ecstasy*—its conception, and what was involved in the writing.

■   *Stone:* I'd be pleased to tell that story, but before I do I must thank you for the compliment of saying that *Lust For Life* was published several years ago. This year is its thirtieth anniversary. It seems incredible to me that so much time has passed. One of the gratifying things about *The Agony and The Ecstasy* is that it was only the second truly big book I've written about an artist after *Lust For Life* was released. It came twenty-seven years later, and there—almost intact, not only in America but in England and in Europe and in the rest of the world—was the *Lust For Life* audience waiting for *The Agony and The Ecstasy*. Nothing could make a writer happier than to have a waiting audience, unless it's to know that this audience has not been disappointed. Most gratifying, of course, is the fact that *Agony* seems to have lived up to expectations.

N.   I probably regard *Lust For Life* as being fairly recent because *I'm* fairly recent. As a matter of fact, *Lust For Life* came to me about five years ago in a beautifully done Heritage edition.

■ *Stone:* Yes, that Heritage edition had 150 Van Gogh paintings and watercolors and drawings, each of them dropped in at the exact spot in the text where I described Vincent drawing or painting, whether he was out in the woods, in the fields, or in his studio. This is exactly what Doubleday has done in the illustrated edition of *The Agony and The Ecstasy,* not always, but whenever possible. For example, when you're reading about Michelangelo carving the Moses or the David or painting the Sistine vault, the magnificent marble sculptures are right at hand for you to look at, and the great paintings from the Sistine Chapel to study.

N. How many years of research and writing went into *The Agony and The Ecstasy?*

■ *Stone:* The research and writing—full time—was four and one-half years, but before that, while I was finishing another of my books, *Men To Match My Mountain,* the story of the opening of the Far West, I spent a full year of evenings and Sundays reading about Michelangelo. Also, I engaged the man who founded the Italian Department at UCLA to translate into English for the first time—and this is unbelievable, really, considering their importance —the full body of Michelangelo's letters. I needed these, of course, because I wanted to hear Michelangelo's interior monologue. It's very difficult to know how a man sounds when he's talking to himself, yet it's important to know. The closest you can get is by reading five or six hundred of his letters—then, when he's angry or when he's ecstatic or when he's joyous or when he's frustrated, he's inclined to write the letters in exactly the same way he's been thinking. You begin to hear the flow of his own words, in thoughts and fragments of thought and nuance. That's why Mrs. Stone and I—by the way, Mrs. Stone is the editor on all of my books—took the 600 letters after the novel was published and converted them into an autobiography of Michelangelo we titled *I, Michelangelo, Sculptor.* The title sprang from the fact that whenever Michelangelo wrote to his family or his friends, from Rome or Carrara or Bologna, he always signed the letter, "I, Michelangelo, Sculptor in Rome" or in Bologna, as though his family wouldn't know he was a sculptor.

N. You actually spent a great deal of time in Italy, didn't you, during the construction of this book? I'm using the word "construction" because a novel this large and complex seems to be built as well as written.

■ *Stone:* I agree with the term. I feel as though it was constructed. As soon as *Man To Match My Mountain* was finished and sent to press we sold our home in Beverly Hills, took a child under each arm, and went to Italy. We put our son in school in Geneva, then rented a home in Fiesole that was within twenty minutes of walking from the spot where Michelangelo was born. I walked to Settignano every day for a year. We lived there, and in Florence, then moved to Rome for another year. As you know, half of Michelangelo's life was spent in Rome, and half his work created there. Then we spent months in places like Carrara in the marble quarries with the Carrarini, men who carved that marble out of the mountainside, and we spent additional months in Siena and Bologna, wherever Michelangelo lived and worked. In fact, wherever he spent the rich years of his life we spent at least some time of our own.

N. To flash back to *Lust For Life*. Did the writing of that novel follow approximately the same pattern?

■ *Stone:* Yes, but in many very different aspects. You must remember that I was very young when I wrote *Lust For Life*. I said I wouldn't write it because I was only twenty-three at the time and I had just stopped teaching at the University of California. I thought the story was so big and so great that it should be written by a Thomas Mann, an experienced novelist. I hadn't yet written a novel, but the story of Van Gogh and his brother Theo so got into my blood that I found myself dreaming about them at night, and I couldn't write anything else during the day because what we call master scenes, the great scenes of crisis, of confrontation, were writing themselves in the back of my mind. Now, at that time I was flat broke, as all young writers are, and I needed money to go to Europe to follow the trail of Van Gogh.

I was supporting myself after a fashion by writing murder and detective stories. I would take one day a week and start at eight in the morning. By six at night I'd have a second draft that I would drop in a mailbox. The editor of a pulp magazine would have it the next morning; he'd put a check for $30 or $40 or $50 in the mail (I got a penny a word); I'd get the check the next day. That's how I was making a living. But in order to go on the trail of Van Gogh, to travel through England, Holland, Belgium, and spend a long time in France, I knew I needed money. So I sat down and wrote six straight murder stories in six days. I sold five of the stories, and when I put the money together I found that I would have enough to live on in Europe for six months provided I spent only two dollars a day, including food, lodging, and transportation. I literally walked across the face of Europe, straight down from

Holland, through Belgium, and all the way from Paris to Arles to St. Rémy to Auvers-sur-Oise, where Vincent lived and where he finally died.

N. In dealing with subjects as complex as Van Gogh, and again, of course, Michelangelo, you bring a great deal of color into the life of your subject but at the same time inspire the reader with trust in the accuracy of all you picture. Do you feel any special obligation to your subjects, and again, to your reader?

■ *Stone:* My obligation is absolute, and I follow it in this sense. I find all of the letters that have been written by the subject, or to him; all of the diaries, the journals, all the comments that have been made about him. I follow the trail, as I did with Van Gogh, and find hundreds of people who knew him, including the Dr. Felix Ray who took care of Vincent when he cut off his ear in Arles, the Monsieur and Madame Denis with whom Vincent lived. (They were still running a bakery up in the coal mining region.) I interviewed these people, read and reread the letters and documents, and walked across the earth where Vincent lived and worked and died. I felt the quality of the sunshine, the rain, the cold, the wind, and the snow. I smelled the flowers and the trees. I came to know sensually the ambient, the area where he lived and worked. After this, of course, came the real problem—the actual point of your question:

Is there always complete documentation?

Of course not. Even if there were endless documentation it would be impossible to know what a man thought inside his own mind, what he felt inside his own heart, through years and years when he was embittered and hungry and frustrated. This is where the novelist's creative imagination has to take over, and this raises the great question:

Do you push your character around, and distort history, or do you study your character so carefully, identify with him so totally and with such honesty, that when you come to that point where documentation leaves off, and you must put yourself inside the heart and the mind of this man or woman, can you think and feel as he (or she) would have, in given circumstances?

This is the creative part of the book, and if you are honest, if you are sincere, if you have worked hard, if you are determined to be true and to achieve exact identity and to plumb the depths of a man's feelings, I think you have a good chance of doing the job proudly.

N. Do you think, as you write, of the public you're writing

T*

for? Do you ever feel that in the transmission of accuracy, or truth, into actual text, that you translate or modify for the reader? Or would this be an unconscious thing?

■ *Stone:* It's both conscious and unconscious. For example, one of my conscious approaches is typographical. I dislike reading a heavy solid black page of type, so I'm always conscious, when working on my manuscript, to break up my pages. Wherever possible it seems germane to work in as much dialogue as possible, so that the reader's interest is held not only by the things that are taking place, the development of character and the plot, but that his eye is fascinated and his attention is absorbed and delighted by the physical appearance of the page. I don't know any other writer who thinks and worries about this, but I do.

But your question is a great deal more serious and more profound than that. In its nether sense, perhaps, you are asking, "Does an author make concessions to hold a reader's interest?" I don't think so. I spent my early years being trained as a dramatist. I stage all of my scenes in a novel as though they were taking place under a proscenium. I see these things being acted out. I hear every word, I visualize every movement, and I attempt, through my own inner force, my feeling for the people, my own warmth, my own love, to so project these characters and what they are thinking, feeling, saying, doing, that the reader becomes identified with them and cannot be disinterested. He must be fascinated because a fascinating life is being played out in front of him.

N. This is a rather abrupt change in subject, but I'm curious as to how many copies of *The Agony and The Ecstasy* have been sold and in how many languages it appears in translation.

■ *Stone:* I don't know the total number of editions in this country because Doubleday doesn't print the number in the book. I know that we have sold, hardbound only, about 400,000 copies in bookstores. The book clubs have distributed four or five million copies. The paperback, at ninety-five cents, has passed two million in sales, and this is within a few months. We've had what you would call "absorption" in America, probably the greatest absorption of any of my books.

Last September I went out for the State Department on the Cultural Exchange, touring Western Europe, Yugoslavia, Poland, Czechoslovakia, and the Soviet Union. To my delight I found the book selling in almost every European nation, and doing well. It was being translated and is now out in the Soviet Union and Poland and Yugoslavia, which indicates that there can be and must be these bridges of books, and art, and thought, between writers of every nation.

N. *The Agony and The Ecstasy* also won, as I recall, the "big" Florentine award—The Golden Lily.

■ *Stone:* Yes, I'm very proud of that. I'm not a prize winner; it's not part of my luck. I've won the Christopher Award and one or two others, but I don't have many prizes on record. I'm particularly proud of what the Florentines call their Giglia d'Oro, Golden Lily, because it's the only decoration they have for foreigners, and to quote their citation, ". . . for distinguished service to our Renaissance city." I believe there are only three Americans who have it, and a few non-Italian Europeans have received it. If I am going to be decorated by only one place in the world, and apparently that's all I'm ever going to mark up and I'm content, I think I would make Florence my very first choice.

N. I'd like to turn to your most recent book, *The Irving Stone Reader.* What does this book contain, and why was this anthology published?

■ *Stone: The Irving Stone Reader* is actually an attempt to give the public a full range of the variety of works that have filled my last thirty years. For example, there are a few of the key chapters from *Lust For Life* which I wrote in 1931, and a few of the germinal chapters from *The Agony and The Ecstasy*, which I wrote in 1961. There are important chapters from all eleven of my big biographies—Jack London's *Sailor On Horseback, Immortal Wife, The Passionate Journey, The President's Lady*, and so on. Between them we use a dozen of my short articles and short biographies which have appeared in American magazines. The real concept behind the book was to attempt to show growth. I think an author is interesting only in terms of his growth. What was he when he started? What were his values? What was his sense of perception? How much did he understand about people and fate and the universe and God? What sympathy did he have, and how much understanding? Then, the interesting thing is to watch him work ahead for five, ten, twenty, thirty years, to see if he grows; to see if he becomes a better writer, not only in terms of style and characterization, but to see if he gains a more profound knowledge of the human fate, the human condition; to see what he can contribute to the world in terms of understanding and beauty and penetration. This is a very rugged test for any author, and I'm curious, now, to see what the critics will say: to see whether I grew forward or regressed in thirty years.

N.   One theoretical question: What advice would you give the young writer? How do you think he should live and train? I know there's no absolute prescription, but what do you believe the primary objectives should be?

■ *Stone:* I've been asked this question many times over the years, and I think many elements are involved in the only true answer I can give. I think anyone who wants to be a very good writer should be a very good reader. He should read through the history of American literature. He should read Dostoevsky and Zola and Balzac and all of the Italian and Russian and French so that he knows what is contained in world literature, has a sense of the structure of a novel, how big and how intertwined and how profound it can be.

Secondly, my whole concept of the writer is that he or she really wants to become a writer, if this is his whole life, he must be determined to be nothing else. He cannot hold a job during the day and write in the evenings and on Sundays because there's just not enough time. He cannot go out and earn money to buy himself all the things he would like because these things are not going to help him write books or even stories. I think my cardinal piece of advice for a writer would be to say to himself, "I am going to be a writer and I am going to write. I am going to start at eight o'clock every morning of my life, Saturdays, Sundays, the Fourth of July, and New Year's, and I will work until twelve or one o'clock, and then I'll take a long walk or a swim or get an hour of air and I'll go back and work until six o'clock. If my mind isn't functioning while I'm at my desk, if I'm not getting anything good on paper, I won't walk away or listen to records or watch television or start a conversation; I'll stay there until my mind clears, until my ideas focus, until the words and the sentences begin to come through."

In other words, a writer is a man who sits himself down at his desk 365 days of a year and writes 365 days of a year, pours out of him everything he can think of. Studying the structure of short stories, plays, novels, but always writing and never saying, "I'll write later, ten or twenty years from now when I have the money or when I have the experience or when I have the leisure." Because that's too late. The time is now for any young writer to begin—eight o'clock tomorrow morning, and never, never stop until they bury you.

N.   How would you describe your own working habits?

■ *Stone:* I can describe them very simply. I'm a bourgeois, I come from bourgeois people. My people were shopkeepers. I get up at the same time every morning, try to be at my desk by eight-thirty, go to work as quickly as I can after glancing at the sports page to see if the Dodgers won or lost the night before, and then I work straight on until it's twelve-thirty or one o'clock. I have a cheese sandwich and a cup of tea and then I get an hour's exercise. I go back and work until six o'clock. In front of me are pads of paper, pens, pencils. Now that I am more prosperous than I was at the beginning I even have a dictating machine which I use for notes, the organization of books, and character descriptions. There's nothing romantic about my working processes and I don't believe in inspiration. I believe that you get to your desk, you stay there, you work, you think of nothing else. You write and you write, and in the end you write something good.

N.   What is the major novel you're working on now?

■ *Stone:*   Shortly I'll take you out to my desk, which is an unholy mess because it's covered with a couple of hundred pages of manuscript and a thousand pages of research notes. I'm trying to write a big biographical novel about a wonderful gal named Abigail Smith, daughter of a clergyman, who fell in love with a young and rather unpromising lawyer in Braintree, near Boston. His name was John Adams. They married, they participated in the beginning years of America prior to the Revolution, they fought in the Revolution and created, in good part, the American republic and the American democracy, and they made it work. This is probably the most amazing story of a woman in all of American history. One night as we were driving to dinner, I told my friend, Clifton Fadiman, about it and he said, "Irving, Abigail was an enormously talented woman." There was a pause, then he turned to me with wide eyes as though he had thought of it for the first time, and added, "You know, she was a genius." She was. For fifty to sixty years she sustained John Adams through such miseries and treacheries and defeats as no man has ever encountered, and sustained him through the fabulous successes and the great contributions that grace our world today. It's a big story, and at the moment I'm buried under hundreds of pages of my own writing and notes from other books, but I'm beginning to see the architectural plan for the novel.

This is something important for writers, by the way. Books have structural form, the way houses and bridges and cathedrals do, and until you resolve a structural form—a solid base, with every segment of the novel assigned its co-ordinated position, its own organic function—you're not getting a good book. The materials have to be fitted to the proper spaces and the proper rooms of the architectural blueprint.

N.   In looking at the current literary scene, perhaps considering the last few decades, what individual trends or books would you pick out to either applaud or deplore?

■ *Stone:* I wish you'd given me some warning. If I'd had an hour I could name four or five novels I like very much. I read a great deal. Publishers send me their first novels, and I try to buy a great many so that I can keep up with what's going on.

There are many talents I respect a great deal. James Baldwin is one, Herbert Gold is another, Lloyd Morris is another, and there are more. However, I think I come from a different tradition. I was born into a world that had hope. I have a passionately optimistic nature. I think that the world can be good and can be creative and even possibly can be saved. So I am made sad by picking up novels by young Americans to find that they are long wails and laments. To myself I have occasionally described them as the "crybaby school." Their mothers hated them or their fathers didn't take proper care of them, they were neglected as children. It is absolutely amazing, the number of American novels coming out in which the writers are doing very little more than feeling sorry for themselves. Now, I don't want to be superficial about this. I know it is part of our times. I know it's confusion, the sense of being lost, that young people have. I know it has been created by two wars, by the Depression, by the threat of atomic warfare, but in spite of all this I regret the "crybaby school" and deplore it because it seems to be totally negative, a destructive point of view. All the things they fear may happen, but I think they'll happen faster if we have only the kind of person who fears them, and not the kind of person who says, "Maybe they'll happen but I'm going to work and fight to make sure they don't."

N.   Another change in subject: In dedications in your books, and from your own mentionings, I find that you work in very close concert with Jean Stone, your wife. Could you explain this arrangement?

■ *Stone:* Easily. All authors have their editors. The editors are usually in publishing houses, and many of them are quite great. I have my editor in my own house, and it came about through a natural sequence of events. I met my wife Jean back in 1931 after I'd finished *Lust For Life*. I was sending it around to a series of seventeen of the biggest publishers in America, and they were all rejecting it on the grounds that they could not sell a book about an unknown Dutch painter to an American public in times of a depression. After I had known my then-fiancée for about two years, I said, "You know, if we cut it a little, maybe 10 per cent, we might have a better chance. Would you take a look at the manuscript to see if you could cut it without hurting the actual structure of the book?" She said, "I don't know, I've never cut any manuscripts. I've never even *read* any manuscripts, so how would I know what to take out?" I told her that I couldn't tell her in advance, that she must sit down and read the whole manuscript, then go back to the beginning to sweat out a phrase here, a sentence there, and even a paragraph somewhere else, to watch for redundancies, and so forth.

She stayed at the beach that summer, and I had been invited out by her parents. In the evenings and on weekends she cut *Lust For Life*, learning as she went along, but she did cut about 10 per cent of the manuscript. Now, I can never be sure whether it was this particular cutting or simply fate, but we sent it to our eighteenth publisher and he accepted it. Naturally, we got married. We were waiting to marry until I had some money, but when *Lust For Life* was accepted I told Jean that she now had two jobs: wife and editor.

From that time forward I gave her all my manuscripts. I have what might be called a weakness in writing—I'm overblown. The less polite word is long-winded. My manuscripts have a tendency to come out anywhere from a quarter to a half million words in length, to 350,000. I'm always afraid that I haven't said something exactly the way I wanted to say it, that the reader wouldn't understand it totally, so I say it four times in four different ways. Mrs. Stone goes to the heart of the matter and gets the one way that's best, or weaves together the best elements of all the versions. To give you an example, my final manuscript of *The Agony and The Ecstasy* was 1,800 pages. By the time Jean got through cutting—and of course I work with her—we had brought it down to 1,200 manuscript pages. In other words we had thrown out the less interesting third, and we were now at a manageable length to go to press. Also, in the very beginning, Mrs. Stone and I edited the Van Gogh letters, which we published as a book called *Dear Theo*, an autobiography just as *I, Michelangelo, Sculptor* is an autobiography of Michelangelo. She's really a very great editor.

N.   In other words, you've got a co-histo-biographer.

■ *Stone:* That's an amusing line, and you used it in the beginning, and I wanted to comment on it. A number of years ago someone asked me to define myself and my work. I had a very bad time and I finally came up saying, "What I write is bio-history." You see, that's exactly the reverse of histo-biographer, but they mean the same thing: bringing history to life in terms of the tremendous human stories that have made that history.

N. This is an art form you've more or less developed by yourself, isn't it?

■ *Stone:* There have been isolated works before mine. A great biographical novel called *The Romance of Leonardo Da Vinci* was published back in the 1880's, and Gertrude Atherton wrote a biographical novel about Alexander Hamilton called *The Conqueror,* I believe, a really wonderful book published in 1906. But those are the only two cases that I know of, and neither of them was exactly the kind of novel I meant to present in my biographical novels. I guess one might say that in 1934, when *Lust For Life* was finally published, the contemporary biographical novel came into a new life of its own. Today it's impossible to pick up any literary magazine without seeing a half-dozen books published very proudly as Biographical Novels.

If this is something I launched I'm afraid I succumb to the sin of pride, because I think the biographical novel, honestly and conscientiously done, is important.

"I want to entertain and . . . be entertained. I don't want to be preached at, I don't want to be sickened, and whenever either occurs I'll close the book or leave the theater. The hell with it."

Robert Lewis Taylor
Interviewed in New York, March, 1964

T*

Robert Lewis Taylor

N. At least two of Robert Lewis Taylor's books should be a part of everyone's reading experience. The joy of youth, the pleasure of discovery, the imperatives of growth, have seldom been so superbly dramatized as they are in the Pulitzer Prize winning *The Travels of Jaimie McPheeters* and *A Journey To Matecumbe*. Midway between the bumptious exhilarations of early Twain, and the bittersweet sophistication of early Salinger, Mr. Taylor has established—with consistent stylistic grace—a firm position in American letters.

First I'd like to go to the beginning, to discuss where Robert Lewis Taylor was born, reared, and educated, and how his interest in writing developed.

■ *Taylor:* I was born in southern Illinois, which is a rather strange land, being neither South nor North. But it's a pretty good place to grow up, and I'm afraid that I myself had some of the characteristics of the boys I write about. Oddly enough, my mother and father are still living in Carbondale.

I went to college, first of all at the local college, Southern Illinois University, then to the University of Illinois, and secured the usual A.B. Then I was very lucky because my grandmother provided me with a certain amount of money, saying that I could take my choice: I could either go on for further degrees or go traveling.

I thought this over for five minutes, maybe ten, and I went traveling. I spent a year knocking around in Europe, then a year in Tahiti, just having a good time. I began to write, for reasons I've totally forgotten. Maybe I needed money. I wrote short stories for the old *American Boy Magazine*. I thought I could perpetuate life in Tahiti by doing this, but they only had two ships a month—one coming from Auckland and one coming from San Francisco, and they converged at Tahiti. Between the time that you wrote the piece and got the check, a rather modest check, at that, two months went by, and in that period you lived a pretty lean life.

My grandmother had not provided much money to live on, just to travel on, and eventually the word came from home that it might be well to move on.

I went to New Zealand and Australia and up to Samoa and Honolulu and got a job as a free-lance writer for the morning paper, the *Honolulu Advertiser*, and made enough to live for a while. I also had a job as night desk clerk and bouncer for the Army-Navy YMCA in Honolulu, and it was a very tough job. I didn't bounce anywhere near as many as bounced me.

Because of the little pieces for the *Advertiser* and a few small successes with *The American Boy* I had delusions of grandeur and thought I should be a reporter, so I came on to New York. It didn't work out. It was the middle of the Depression, and I walked all around town and had some very cheery refusals from the *Daily News*, the *Times*, the *Herald Tribune*, and all, so I returned to my homeland and shortly thereafter, in 1937, got a job with the *St. Louis Post-Dispatch*.

The head man there, at the time, was Roy Alexander, who is now the head man at *Time* magazine, and Roy had had this experience early in his reporting career. He had gone to Southern Illinois to cover some type of mine problem, and had come away with the impression that the natives were the toughest people on earth. (This did not include me, of course.) When I told him where I was from, he said, "Do you know a man named Colonel Bob Davis?" and I said, "Yes, he's an old friend of my father's and of mine." He asked me if I would be offended if he called Bob Davis to ask him about me, and I said, "Not at all." So he called, and Davis, who is a rollicking fellow, said, "Oh, yes, I know Louie Taylor. He's the meanest son-of-a-bitch that ever grew up in this town." Roy said, "Thank you very much," hung up, and hired me.

After three years of working there and liking it very much, I left to go to *The New Yorker*. Harold Ross had come to like the feature pieces I'd been doing for the *Post*, and he hired me to replace their reporter-at-large man, Morris Markey, when he left. I went out to New York scared stiff (I still am) and began to write these pieces. But having a mercenary side I decided that more money could be made by writing "Profiles," so I switched over to these and wrote them for some years, up until the beginning of the war, when I enlisted in the Navy as a Lieutenant j.g.

I was in this country and abroad and wound up with the rank of lieutenant commander, which was just the normal progression that came with getting older. Then I began to write books for

Doubleday, and since that time I've been writing books off and on and suffering a bit more with each one. I'll probably go on doing just this for some time, I hope.

N. Could you describe some of your "Profile" work at *The New Yorker?* How many did you do, and how did you write them?

■ *Taylor:* At one time I was told that I had written as many Profiles as anybody. I think I wrote ten a year, and a Profile is a very fine piece to write because it goes into practically everything about a person. (It's not a Profile at all, it's a full-faced view, even an X-ray.) Some of the Profiles I wrote—such as the one on Percy Grainger—could scarcely have been more fun to do, even though I've always been terribly exacting with myself about Profiles. To me, each should be a piece of perfection.

In the case of Percy Grainger, the Australian pianist and composer, my wife and I became quite friendly with him and his wife, who lived in White Plains. Percy was a great eccentric. He never cut the grass. A neighbor, a dentist, came over and said very timorously, "Would you be awfully offended if I cut your grass for you?" Percy wasn't offended at all. I even went down on one recital trip with him to some nearby (thank God!) place because he always walked. Unless it was clear across the country, Percy walked to save money. He sent all of his money to nineteen starving relatives in Australia. He was a wonderful little man, and we walked on the Pike; he had his bag with him. When we got there he went to sleep on top of the piano, there was some mixup, and they drew the curtain. There was Percy, atop the piano. They pulled the curtain back, got him up, and he played rather well, but in the middle of the performance he got up and moved the piano. The piano was not situated to suit him, and four or five times he got up and moved it rather than call on a stagehand.

On the way to this performance, weirdly enough, some woman had a piano delivered to her and left it on her doorstep. She called to Percy, who probably looked like an itinerant fruit picker, to ask him to help. Well, he helped and I helped, and she gave us a quarter, and we took it and went on down the road. I loved that man. He's dead now, and I'm sorry about that.

You may remember from the news stories that he wanted to send back his remains to Melbourne, Australia, to be installed in the Percy Grainger Museum, where he had gathered up a great many manuscripts and stuff from other composers, gifts from friends like Delius. He wanted to send back his body, but we have some kind of rule that you cannot do such a thing, so as a corollary in the will he stated, "If this is difficult I would like the meat stripped off the bones and the bones sent back." This they did. In a way it was a fitting last event because everything he did was unusual, and often very funny.

But as to Profiles in general, what you do is spend about a month or two doing legwork on a one- or two-part Profile, then another few weeks writing it. The first I ever wrote was about Willie Hoppe, and I was anxious to get this in because it meant about twice as much money as for a reporter-at-large piece. I had all my notes in a briefcase and went to the Strand Billiard place on Broadway where I used to shoot pool with Bunny Berigan. He was a wonderfully odd sort of fellow, a great trumpeter, and we never exchanged words; we just met and played pool, and both of us could play rather well.

I put this damned briefcase down on a nearby table, and when we finished shooting pool it was gone. I was petrified with fear. Bunny and I went out and looked in all the ash cans. His theory was that the thief would throw the material in an ash can and keep the briefcase. We couldn't find it. I was so scared that I went back to *The New Yorker* office and, with the charwoman cleaning around me, put the whole piece together from memory. By some strange chance I don't think I missed anything that had been in the notes.

N. What was your reaction to the terrific popular and critical success of *Jaimie McPheeters?*

■ *Taylor:* Frankly, I was astounded. I just wrote this book by thinking back through my own childhood. I'd been a handful, really, and my aunt, who was Dean of Women and head of the English Department at the local university (a rather large one, now, with ten or twelve thousand students) was after me all the time, hammer and tongs, but I eluded her and everyone else in somewhat the same way my boy in *Jaimie* did. I drew on my recollections and made up a lot of adventures and leaned fairly heavily on some research that some men at Yale made available. I thought it was just a book, a book people might like and my kids might enjoy, but I was dumbfounded at what happened. Bewildered, in fact.

N. In *Jaimie* and *Matecumbe* and any of your other books, for that matter, do you assume a definite objective or obligation?

■ *Taylor:* I do have a motive, an objective. It's a simple one. I, myself, am so bored by being lectured at, tutored, preached to, and the like, that I simply want to provide entertainment. This is hard to do, in our sensitive age, because people's feelings seem so absurdly easy to hurt.

I don't like to use the word "egghead," but I was bored with reading the kind of book in which you had to go back and read the paragraph over in order to find out what the writer was talking about. I was bored with messages of all kinds—right, left, and center. I was more or less loafing at the time I started *Jaimie*, and I thought it would be fun to write a book that would be fun (for me, at least) to read. I decided I'd like to write three or four books of a generally similar format, using a boy (myself) as the protagonist. I know a little bit about that kind of boy, so after *Jaimie* I let a year or two go by and started *A Journey To Matecumbe* which took the same type of boy but used a different area as background. Now I've finished a third book about a boy—but again, with a different background—which Doubleday will publish in September. It's titled *Two Roads To Guadalupe*. I've lived in Mexico off and on; my wife and I spent the entire winter there and most of last year, driving a car around everywhere in the little corners of Mexico, places where it isn't safe. But I enjoyed it all. We lived in Mexico City for the last few months, and I worked on the book there.

Again, I have a boy, a boy and a relative, his half-brother, who start from Missouri as members of the Missouri First Volunteer Regiment. When they get down to Mexico they diverge and have some adventures. Well, I've finished the research and I've finished the writing and now, while I await publication, I'm convinced (as usual) that the book is dreadful. If it turns out to be better than that I'll be delighted.

N.   Before we started taping, you mentioned that you were taking your children to Europe for a year to (as you put it) "remove some pressures." Could you go into that more thoroughly?
■ *Taylor:*   They're in a wonderful school, but it seems to me that all the private schools in New England are in the most unhappy position of having to make a record to keep up their reputations. At the end of the year they must say, "so many of our boys went to Princeton, so many here, so many there." And the pressure is put on the students to make sure that a proper percentage go here and there.

It seems to me that this is a period in a child's life when he should be having a good time. I think Kent is better off than most private schools, and they have a fair amount of organized entertainment, but the pressure is there, and we are taking our boy out. He feels that he's been accepted at Stanford (he'll finish Kent this year) and our daughter is a second-year student at Kent. We're going to Spain and France; we've entered both children in the University of Madrid's special courses for foreign students. To me it seems very important, right now, to learn Spanish—this strikes me as the coming language. It's the predominant language in most of our hemisphere, but very few Americans learn it. We've all been taught some French, but I don't see how French can possibly be regarded as the language of the future. Spanish is important.

So they'll attend the University of Madrid for the fall term, then we'll go to Granada, to another very good university, for further study. And for a year at least the pressures will be off them.

N. Now, to turn to the area of theory and opinion, I wonder if you could look at today's literature and theater in terms of the elements you most admire and those you most deplore.

■ *Taylor:* I assume you want the truth even if it might get me jailed. First and foremost, I'm sick of messages. I am sick of being told that I am responsible for minority problems. I'm not responsible for them at all. I have no feeling about them other than the knowledge that I can't solve them, and I'm awfully tired of hearing that I should go out and solve them. I have every hope that these great problems will be solved, but I haven't got the magic formula.

I would like to branch out now into the field of pure entertainment. This will probably make me even more unpopular, but I like a book to have a beginning, a middle, an end, and something of a plot. This business of the obscure seems to me to be riding high. If you don't understand it you're supposed to have a guilty feeling that you should understand it; therefore go ye and search through a program of responses.

This strikes me as being completely phony.

I saw a motion picture yesterday that struck me as having no artistic merit at all. I like to go to movies because it's dark and I can hide and nobody can find me. But at this movie—and I won't publicize it by naming it—I have a feeling that the crowd came to see the sexual scenes that had been described with such delicious shock by the reviewers. The sexual scenes weren't that good; you and I have both imagined better ones. They made sex ugly.

Now, I want to tell a story if I can entertain people, and I'm really pleased that my "kid books" are on a great many required reading lists in schools all over the country. I get a lot of exceedingly literate letters from teachers who thank me for writing my kind of book, a book they can pass to their children and say, "Read this because you might have some fun, and whether you know it or not you'll absorb some facts about, say, Florida, or the wagon train perils, the gold rush, San Francisco, etc."

I want to entertain and I want to be entertained. I don't want to be preached at, I don't want to be sickened, and whenever either occurs I'll close the book or leave the theater. The hell with it.

In the United States we're apt to get our messages mixed up, or get hysterical about trivial as well as major issues—I'm not neglecting those awful Beatles. So we get hysterical about problems of class and color, and wallow in our hysteria while we do very little to solve the real problems. There's a saturation point. People are angry today, in a sense they have never been angry in this country before, and this disturbs me. If the anger paid off, fine, but it just seems to lead to hysteria and violence without anyone becoming the wiser or the better for it.

N.   If you were to give advice to the talented youngster who really wants to write, what would that advice be?

■ *Taylor:* First of all I'd tell him to read all the old classics—particularly those he finds entertaining. He needn't study the style; he'll absorb a certain amount of it. And when he starts to write he should avoid imitating anyone. No imitations of Steinbeck or Capote or whomever. The style he writes will be an amalgam of all he's read, especially what he's loved, but he'll begin shaping his own.

Stick to this style no matter what. I've had many a classic row with *The New Yorker* and with book publishers about doing things my way. I've stuck to my guns, however, and I've been right at least as often as I've been wrong.

I think he should write his way and write to entertain. If he amuses and entertains himself, no doubt he will entertain some other people, too. I'm delighted to say that my son is a great reader; I talk to him about books, and the things he likes about books seem to be the things I like, and the freshness of his approach seems to add validity to my outlook. He likes the good things about a book. I have no idea as to whether or not he'll be a writer, and I don't think this matters. From reading, from the books he loves, and the books he discovers, he will have an immeasurable companionship all his life, and this is a wonderful thing.

N.   Is there anything on any subject you'd like to add?

■ *Taylor:* I think I've talked myself into enough trouble for one day.

"It is always hard work, sitting alone at a typewriter. It's lonely and it's difficult and you're scared. You can't ever be quite sure of where you're going. . . . But in referring to the way in which society now treats writers, I think it deals with them perhaps too kindly, certainly too seductively.

Diana Trilling
Interviewed in New York, March, 1964

Diana Trilling

N. In the purest of sentences, with the keenest of thought and analysis, Diana Trilling keeps building an audience commensurate with critical praise. Together with E. B. White, and a scant handful of other writers, she prevents the essay from sliding into the limbo of an unpracticed art. In this interview we will touch upon many of the subjects which excited and provoked that brilliant collection titled *The Claremont Essays*, but I'll start by asking for a resumé of her life, and how her interest in writing developed.

■ *Trilling:* I'm that rarest of creatures, a born and bred New Yorker, and I've lived here all my life except for my college years at Radcliffe in Boston. I started to write rather by accident. During the war I wrote a column of fiction reviews for *The Nation*. I hadn't written at all before that; I had quite different plans for life.

N. You are the wife of Lionel Trilling?

■ *Trilling:* That's right. I had planned to be a singer, then I became ill and couldn't sing for a while. I was casting about for something to do and quite by accident stepped into reviewing. It really was an accident because a call came from *The Nation* asking my husband if he knew of anyone who could write little unsigned notes on the minor books that were coming out. So I said to my husband, "Why don't you suggest me?" and he looked a bit appalled, then rallied and hesitantly agreed to. I tried it, and within a short time these little reviews had developed into a column called "Fiction in Review" in *The Nation*. That was back at the beginning of the war, and I stayed on *The Nation* for the next seven or eight years, and I guess I covered almost all the fiction that came out during that period. In that time I also did some other free-lance writing, but then I got to the point where I felt that I had read as many novels as I could, that I couldn't bear to read any more; so I gave up the column and concentrated on free-lance writing, and that's what I've done ever since.

N. I'd like to discuss *The Claremont Essays*. As penetrating and well written as they are, it would be interesting to see where your interest in that wide range of subjects sprang from, if you can' break things down into particulars.

■ *Trilling:* Some of the essays are political and demonstrate an old interest in politics, the politics of liberalism, if we can use that word any more. It certainly doesn't mean what it once did, and this concerns me very much. I suppose I've had some hope that I could rescue that word from the corruptions it's undergone and restore it to a more traditional meaning. I've wanted to distinguish the liberalism that's been so dominant in this country in recent years, what I prefer to call "progressivism," from the meaning the word once had. So when I write, I put liberalism in quotes, or I hyphenate it with progressivism. I do everything possible to try to distinguish the generally mindless liberalism of our time from the sterner liberalism of the nineteenth century or even the earlier decades of this century.

The Alger Hiss piece was of course a natural for anyone interested in this field. It was suggested to me by *Partisan Review* and I was frightened to death to take on the assignment because at the time it was *the* case, in the intellectual-liberal community especially. I thought it was too big to tackle, until I found the small angle from which I chose to approach it.

When it came to the Oppenheimer piece, it was my suggestion to *Partisan Review* because I thought that, having done the Hiss case, I should do the Oppenheimer case too.

The third political piece in the book is the most recent. I wrote it while the book was going to press with the rest of the essays. This was the essay on the Profumo case. As the situation of Profumo and Ward had developed, I had become increasingly distressed by the hypocrisies and confusions involved in it, and in particular by the role of the Labour Party in the whole affair. Then, too, I felt it had got to be so much Ward's case, not Profumo's or Christine Keeler's, and I wanted to write about that.

Of the so-called literary pieces the one I myself like best is the one called *The Other Night At Columbia.* It's the least formal essay in the book, and I suppose that's why I so much enjoyed writing it. I wrote it easily enough, but its publication brought me an enormous amount of trouble. It had the worst reception of anything I've ever written, at least among the people I know best. They thought it was condescending, patronizing, genteel. Every irony that I intended seemed to have been missed by this section of readers. But curiously enough, it was not lost on the people who didn't know either me or my husband. Strangers caught every irony in it, but anyone who knew us, who had some previous image of us, felt that the piece violated this image and that I was being condescending in my sympathy for the "beats." Well, I had certainly gone to their performance, their poetry reading, in a spirit of condescension. But when I got there I was deeply moved by the whole performance; I had another sense of what was going on in these people, both a human and a social sense which was very moving to me. That was what made me want to write the piece, to make a correction in my own prejudgment and to complicate my view of a phenomenon like the beats. The ambiguity I was trying to explore was my own ambiguity about respectability, and I think the piece makes that clear. But the people who had a preconception of my attitudes toward respectability wouldn't recognize this.

This demonstrates so clearly to me the degree to which people read what they intend to on a page. They don't want you to change their opinions, and, if they know you, certainly not their opinions of *you*. Of course there must have been *some* failure of communication on my part. I'm bound to have had some responsibility for the misreading, but I think it was small. I can't feel that the failure could possibly have been extreme if so many people I *didn't* know found in it exactly what I assumed I had put into it. I've worried over that piece a great deal, trying to find where I failed. But even when it came to republishing it in my book, when I had the chance to make alterations in it, I couldn't find anything I wanted to change except a tiny little phrase here and there. I had to leave it for people to take wrongly if that's what they prefer to do.

Now, the trouble with publishing a book of essays is the way some of them become dated before publication time. But I feel that each essay, written in the heat of some issue or other, would suffer from rewriting—it would be a little dishonest. All through the book I let things stand virtually as I first wrote them, without benefit of hindsight.

N.   I was interested in your views on Margaret Mead. I have always suspected her of oversimplifying some matters, despite her brilliance.

■ *Trilling:*   Yes, I think she does oversimplify, not when she is reporting from the field, but when she moves the situation into politics, for example, or into society in general. And she seems to me to be particularly confused in the book I was dealing with, *Male and Female*. As I try to say in that essay, she is a woman who has peculiarly lived on the gains of feminism, so I find it strange for her to be disavowing that advantage. But I don't think she was writing a "femalist" book in any very simple way. But somehow she was being influenced by a current of thought at that particular time which was both antifeminist and utilitarian—social-utilitarian, I mean.

You understand, of course, that I wasn't expecting from Miss Mead any final answers to the problem of woman's role in society. That was perhaps her mistake in conceiving the book; she was trying to solve the unsolvable. I think women have a very tough time in our society and that they are really quite remarkable to do as much as they do, meeting all the changing demands made of them, dividing their energies in the way they must. If they have any professional life at all, that is. And by and large, I don't believe they're the least bit interested in dominating men. On the contrary. I've written in a more popular vein on this subject in various mass-circulation magazines, and I have stated my feeling, rather strongly, that women, far from asking men to relinquish their role as leaders, are doing everything in their poor powers to restore to men the strengths of which they are robbed in our modern world. I think what most women are saying is, "We want to work with such qualities of leadership as we ourselves have. We want to work alongside men who are neither excluding us nor deferring to us because we are women."

I don't believe it's fair to characterize American women as a nation of "Moms," and accuse them of destroying the masculinity of their sons. Of course they make mistakes all over the place. So do men. But I can't think of American women as being so hungry for power that even their affection is an instrument for their ascendancy. They're all *for* men—terrifically for them. They want men to fulfill themselves, to be as masculine as they can possibly be. This masculinity, after all, is essential to their own happiness as women.

Actually, as a sidelight on this topic, one of the most interesting things I've observed is the fact that virtually every successful lady writer I know is a very good cook. Why? They all say, "It's an art." But I suspect that they feel as I do, that running their homes well is as much their job as writing, and they are pleased to run them well. I'm as pleased when I'm told that I cooked a good dinner as when I'm told I've written a good essay, maybe even more. And I think this is true of almost all the professional women I know; they pride themselves on the fact that their professional concerns don't alienate them from their domestic lives.

N. Now, in dealing with the serious subject matter you cover, do you feel a sense of obligation—first, to the material you work with, and second, to the public that will read you?

■ *Trilling:* I feel a terrific sense of obligation to the material I'm dealing with. And doesn't that imply an obligation to the public? I think it does.

For example, to go back to book reviewing (and I did an enormous amount of it in my time; I don't do much of it any more), I think the first responsibility of the critic is to the book, to the object as it really is. I hate reviewing which is primarily directed to the glorification of the reviewer at the expense of the object under examination.

Of course, we all do show ourselves off when we review a book. It would be a pretty dull affair if we didn't. But there is a considerable difference between using a book one is reviewing as an occasion for speculation and excursion or even perhaps for self-definition and using it for doing one's own private dance on the author's grave. Obviously the critic brings himself to any estimate of a book; but the book makes the objective context within which he works, and he must respect this context even if he despises it.

Of course when you come to something like the Oppenheimer case, there's more objective context than you perhaps counted on. I read every word of that testimony at least twice—a terrific amount of work. I felt I just had to go over some things again and again, and I actually wrote my first draft after one reading of the testimony; then I read the testimony all over again and wrote a whole new piece. I found my first version had still retained prejudices I had brought with me to my first reading.

I can't say that I read every book I review more than once, but if I'm doing an essay on a book I certainly do.

As for an obligation to the public apart from the obligation of honesty—well, don't you think that most writers feel that they have a dozen people standing in back of them at the typewriter when they're writing? You may not be able to name them, you don't allow them actually to type for you or move to the forefront of your mind, but I think we always have some special group of people we're writing for, and if we feel they are satisfied, we're satisfied. It's a subtle thing, but I don't think we do anything without that omnipresent audience: it might be certain of our friends whom we particularly respect; or perhaps it's writers we may not even know but whom we especially admire.

There's another aspect to this, and I don't know if I can formu-

late it. I've recently had the feeling of wanting to be *freer* than
I've so far been as a writer, and maybe this means I want to get
rid of that little gallery at my shoulder; perhaps I'm going to
change my invisible audience. Whether this means that I will be
writing more fictionally than I have been, I don't know. I don't
mean writing fiction, mind you, just more fictionally. But I want
to write as if I were pushing away that dozen people who have
always surrounded my typewriter; I want to write something that's
just me. I don't feel I've done that, yet—that I've written something
of which I can say, "This is entirely, truly myself." I hope some day
I'll have that feeling.

N.   In looking at today's cultural world—perhaps literature, in
particular—what do you see that you most admire? Conversely,
what do you most deplore?

■ *Trilling:* I'm afraid it's easier for me to talk about what I
deplore. I deplore, very much, the enormous subjectivity, the personal posturing and stance-taking in current writing, and the refusal
to look outward to the world and see society in all its complexity
and variousness and concreteness. And I hate the softness and the
self-pity that accompany this limitation of vision. I miss society,
particularly in fiction; but fiction and criticism on its highest level
(it's literary criticism I'm talking about now) seem to me to be
becoming assimilated to each other in some odd unhappy way.
Thus the speculating mind, the judging mind, is at work in fiction
at the cost of the observation of reality.

You see, I think society gets far more interesting all the time. It
can seem overwhelming, and it may be destroying the individual,
but this doesn't diminish its interest.

I totally agree that this is a world in which the individual is
having a desperate time holding his head above water, but this
doesn't mean that the forms of society are less fascinating. As the
class structure (I'm now talking about American society) breaks
down, we find sensibility, morality, and the criteria of taste substituting for the old criteria of birth and hereditary privilege. But
surely this is no less interesting than the earlier form of our social
organization, these new terms in which people woo and win social
power.

Things as diverse as political attitudes or interior decoration
or forms of cookery are all ways in which what once would have
been called "class" are now being demonstrated. It isn't class in the
old hereditary sense, but it certainly is something just as interesting
and just as much to be observed and used by the writer. But, un-

happily, it isn't being reported on, no record is being kept of these new substitutes for the old class codes.

I remember spending a holiday in one of the suburban areas not far from New York where a great many literary, theatrical, and musical people live. It seemed to me, just from snooping around during those few days, that there was as strict a class judgment being exercised on the basis of such things as on which side of the house someone was planting her flowers, or whether the right herbs were being grown, or what kind of lawn people had, or what kind of windows they put in their houses, as Lily Bart's friends submitted her to in Edith Wharton's *House of Mirth*.

I've spent many summers in Connecticut, and I watch it going on there too. Among the people I've known in Connecticut, if a social or political discussion is going on and you don't have the currently appropriate liberal attitude, you can feel yourself totally ostracized for such a transgression against the rules of your section of society! The codes are very strong in these things—whether it is what canapes you serve with cocktails or what position you take at the PTA—and wherever there are codes you have something worth examination, surely by the novelist, but also by the writer in any category.

To turn, finally, to things I admire. Well, I can't come up with too much, at least in fiction. I have a high regard for a writer like Saul Bellow in his recent books. I liked *Lolita* very much. I have an extraordinarily high regard for Norman Mailer, perhaps more for that which is intended than for that which is yet accomplished; I think the intention is a major one, but I'm afraid he's mythologized himself so much that people are judging the personality more than they are the work. Salinger, Baldwin, Updike. They are all so talented in their various ways. But I get so tired of that same old message—that life is empty and meaningless and futile, that the personality cannot develop or find fulfillment in our society. Self-pity makes such a dead-end road for a writer.

Take Salinger, for example—think what it tells us about a present generation of adolescents that they can't read *Huckleberry Finn*, but they all discover themselves in Holden Caulfield. Is that nature imitating art? I'm afraid it is. I don't mean that the artist has the duty to create a generation of romantic heroes. But I really do exercise a choice in protests, and I don't think that self-pity, even when it is intended to protest a world inhospitable to youth and sensitivity, constitutes any kind of rebelliousness that will get us anywhere.

N. If you were to give advice to the talented youngster who wanted to write, what would that advice be?

■ *Trilling:* I think I'd not give any. I don't know what advice one can give a writer except, "Just do your work and try not to be too successful too fast."

Does that last sound odd? I mean it very seriously. I don't know why anyone is any longer justified in talking about the unappreciated artist. It is always hard work, sitting alone at a typewriter. It's lonely and it's difficult and you're scared. You can't ever be quite sure of where you're going. I have the greatest sympathy for the writer sitting at his desk alone. But in referring to the way in which society now treats writers, I think it deals with them perhaps too kindly, certainly too seductively.

A writer becomes fashionable and glamorous so terribly fast these days. Once he's become a public personality, once he lets himself become *too* public a personality so that he's busy all the time being on radio panels and television programs and having his picture in the fashion magazines, he's straying from his job, and he's bound to be engaging in things that are destructive to time and talent and development.

But how could you say this to someone who's just beginning? They wouldn't know what you were talking about. To say to someone who thinks that just publishing a line is wonderful, "Beware of publishing too much, too quickly, too easily; beware of being too celebrated," can't possibly make sense. But I wish it did.

N. Could you possibly sum up your own objectives, as far as your career is concerned?

■ *Trilling:* I don't know. I sometimes get a feeling of terrible strain about the quick passage of time; there's so much I want to do. Obviously, there must be something I want to accomplish or I wouldn't feel that way, and yet if you ask me what my objective is I can't answer—I don't know.

My fifteen-year-old son said to me the other day, "Do you realize that Cassius Clay is a Black Muslim, and do you know that Patterson has challenged him to a fight—that Patterson says he'll fight for no purse, just to vindicate his view of the Negro against the Black Muslim view?"

Well, first thing I knew I was gathering the clippings. I'd have to write about this. It's so extraordinary, of course, to have trial by combat on a racial or religious issue. Probably I'll never get to writing the piece, something will come around that will excite me even more. And even if I did write it, I'd not suppose I was going to change the world by it. But that's the kind of thing that happens to me all the time—I get excited about something and feel I simply have to write about it. That's all the artistic or intellectual program I have, and I simply don't think about it in any exalted way—it's just the job I have to do. But maybe these objectives, coming one at a time, are all I need to keep me busy the rest of my life.

"The writer, like the artist, the priest, and the doctor, must have a purpose, perhaps even a mission. The writer cannot afford to be false or inaccurate. Within his means he must strive for reality as opposed to unreality, for truth as opposed to untruth, for perspective as opposed to distortion."

Laurens van der Post
Interviewed in London, England, November, 1963

Laurens van der Post

N. With the release of *A View Of All The Russias*, Laurens van der Post achieved the ultimate recognition he had long deserved. By leaping above the level of the travel book to portray Russian life and art, by penetrating to the soul (or the various souls) of the Russian as men of private belief and public destiny, he produced an epic of journalism that ranks with de Tocqueville and Adams and all the great writing travelers whose mission has been the assessment of a nation. Ironically, van der Post had displayed the same power of observation in writing about his native South Africa and of his experiences during World War II, for his life has been carved of contrasts and conflicts.

In talking to Mr. van der Post I would like to go back to the beginning—and the rough outline of autobiography.

■ *Van der Post:* I don't suppose one can take a South African origin casually. My mother's family had been in South Africa almost since the European beginning. It was an extremely long-lived family, and throughout my childhood I seemed to be in living contact with the past—the remote past—of my country. From my grandfather, for example, I heard an account of a battle in which he fought against the British in 1848. I could virtually orchestrate that battle because it was made so clear to me.

My family was a pioneering family. They were always on the edge of the frontiers of that great movement from the south of Africa north into the interior. You will recall that the white man moved from south to north, the black from north to south, both exterminating the helpless, primitive Bushman caught in the center. My own grandmother, for example, was one of few survivors of a Zulu massacre in the interior. Now, all these things were communicated to me, and I had an immense sense of belonging to Africa in a way that was rooted and infinite and timeless.

On the other hand, my father was born in Holland, and though he had a French mother and a Dutch father, his was a family of rather notable lineage. He brought to Africa the fresh impact of

European civilization, though he identified himself completely with Africa. This created, in me, a sort of double awareness—an awareness of Africa which was very deep, and a more nervous awareness of Europe. All my life I've been aware that a balance had to be struck between these two poles of being. If I add the enormous primitive content of Africa, I might say that I was buffeted between *three* separate and distinct cultures.

You see, one of the first languages I spoke was a black one, and as a child I faced two great problems. One was that my people had been conquered by the British just a few years before I was born. I know to the full the bitterness of what it means to be a member of a conquered race. There was an enormous resentment of this fact and a constant awareness of it. My father, a prominent Boer statesman, refused, for six years, to take the oath of allegiance to England, and for this reason he could not return to his own part of Africa. Though I liked the English people without reservation, I had inherited this bitterness.

The second problem was the fact that I loved the black peoples of Africa. The great characters of my childhood, the real and fairy-tale characters, were Hottentots and Bushmen and Zulus. It was a great shock to me, when I was sent away to school from the part of Africa where I was born, to find that I was being educated into something which destroyed the sense of common humanity I had shared with the black people. I was divided from them and could not take these friendships with me into the years that lay ahead.

These, I think, are the raw materials of my spirit. All the conflicts and tensions that came later resemble, or hold, for me, in a dramatic, almost Greek form, the fundamental issues in living. I haven't finished with these things yet. There is still some turmoil within, but one has to come to terms with life.

When I was nineteen I joined two friends, a great South African poet named Roy Campbell and a South African novelist now living in England named William Plomer in launching a magazine in Africa which was called *The Lash of a Whip*. We attacked the prejudices of South Africa, and it wasn't too long before things were made so unpleasant for us we had to leave. Plomer and I went to Japan. He stayed there for three years before coming to England. I stayed a much shorter time, then went back to Africa because I felt that was where I belonged, where the struggle had to go on.

If I may digress a moment. William Plomer wrote a tremendous novel titled *Turbott Wolfe*, which was published in 1926, when he was only twenty. For the first time in South African literature the black man appears as a human being in his own right. Until then the black people were absent from South African literature, just as the working man is absent from the novels of Jane Austen. (You can read Austen from end to end without finding servants or farm laborers. They don't exist; they don't enter the imagination.) The literature of South Africa inhabited a similarly sealed world. Psychologically, and in the deepest sense of the word, the South African did not see the black people. The great and good Olive Shriner, who wrote *The Story Of An African Farm* (in a sense the beginning of modern South African literature) saw the black man, but she saw him only as an ethical problem. She admitted that the white man was treating him badly, but she did not recognize him as a human being with his own living personality. She didn't attempt to find what went on in his mind and his heart, but she knew, on principle, that he was getting a raw deal.

Suddenly, with Plomer's novel, a host of Zulu characters entered the imagination. The question of intermarriage arose, all the things people never spoke about. This rang an enormous bell for me, for I shared this view of life's inequities; thus the magazine was started.

My return to South Africa may not have been politic, but it was the only course I could follow. It's where the struggle had to go on. It also induced another type of awareness. The stay in Japan had acquainted me with the cultures, the civilizations of the peoples of the Far East. I would say, now, that my imagination walks a long beat: from Africa to the East, Africa to Europe, Africa to America, Africa to Russia. In *The Seed and The Sower* I combined much of this world. It was natural, to me, to make the principal character a British officer, another major character a South African, and still others a Japanese officer, and a Dutch girl. It interested me very much that one of our leading British reviewers found it extraordinary that one man could write about all of these and make each character valid and credible. The fabric of my life may be unusual, but all of it reflects against the African experience. As I sit here now, for example, everything is referred, in my mind, back to the African experience.

N. You've fallen into some disfavor with the South African government, haven't you?

■ *Van der Post:* Yes, I have. I think I am one of the writers actively on their blacklist. I simply can't think of a government more in the wrong, more dreadfully in the wrong, than the South

African government. Yet I must say in all honesty that they have never repressed me, never tried to stop me from saying what I do about South Africa. And I pull no punches. I tell them that they have let down the whole of South African history, the whole of our tradition. I say this quite openly, but they have never quashed me. This is important to remember when one refers to South Africa as a police state, because if South Africa were totally a police state they would have been more repressive. I hate their guts, I say so, and they don't try to stop me from saying so.

N.   You had a rather astonishing military career.

■ *Van der Post:*   I think everyone who sees action has an astonishing military career—it's so contrary to living. I've never written much about mine. Looking back on it, now, I simply wonder how and why I'm alive. I was put into all sorts of situations that now seem impossible. My involvement was with the Japanese rather than the Germans, and it started long before the war began. In 1926 I found myself in South Africa defending two Japanese against the color bar. They were journalists who wanted a cup of tea, and a woman wouldn't give it to them because she said she wanted no colored persons in her establishment. I told her that if she refused them I would leave. I made friends with these journalists, and afterward obtained an invitation from the Japanese government to go to Japan. I learned Japanese—if I hadn't I'd have been killed when I was a prisoner of war, interned by the Japanese. But that is a very long story, and enough of it is contained in *The Seed and The Sower* to make it unnecessary to relate here.

N.   Before we turn to your views on writing, I'd like you to sum up your recent and extensive journey in Russia. As a Westerner you came closer to what we might call the "heart" of the Soviet Union than any writer with whom I'm acquainted.

■ *Van der Post:*   I spent very nearly three months constantly traveling within Russia, from one end to another. Perhaps this is a reflection on the limitations of consciousness, but all the time I was in Russia I didn't realize what was happening to me. It was only when I began writing that I realized what an impact the journey had made. This is the fascinating thing about writing, why I love it above all things; it's a fusion and a release of awareness with that which is only subconsciously observed.

Friends had remarked that I'd stay in Russia only twenty-one days. My journey lasted eighty-nine days, for which I'm thankful because of my deep interest in Russia. It's difficult to summarize what one felt during such a long journey over such a vast country, but two things, that are almost thematic in value, impressed me in a powerful way.

The first is the fundamental Europeanism of the Russian people. They don't feel that they belong to the East; they are European. In other words they belong to the complex of the European spirit of which you in America and we in Africa are a part. This association is both obvious and subtle—ethnic, in one sense, and spiritual in another.

The other thing that impressed me is the Russians' lack of fear regarding Europe. They are afraid of what we call the East. This is the thing that has terrorized much of Russian history. When these things are considered it is not surprising that the Russians are in such close communication with us. I don't mean communication in the sense that we send telegrams to each other, but communication in the real sense of the word—that they read European literature written in English.

Longfellow, to my amazement, is now much more of a Russian poet than he is an American one. My American friends seem rather ashamed of Longfellow, but not the Russians. Over and over again a Russian would say to me, "Are you interested in poetry? Listen to this . . ." and they'd start reciting something in Russian. The only words I could understand were things like "Minnehaha." Shakespeare is perhaps the greatest Russian poet today—no, I take that back; Robert Burns is Russia's favorite. He has been translated into Russian on an incredible scale. People sing "Auld Lang Syne" and recite Burns in Russian at the drop of a hat. One example:

I arrived in Siberia, and before breakfast the first morning a man recited Burns to me. His choice: "For a' that, an' a' that,/It's comin yet for a' that,/That man to man the world o'er/Shall brithers be for a' that."

You know, I think we must never lose sight of this. However difficult our political patterns are, however difficult our cultural patterns, the greatest lesson I've learned from my extensive travel is that in his heart the modern man has a greater sense of brotherhood than he's ever had before, and a greater potential for living in peace. We may loathe the Russian government and the Russian system, but we cannot help but love the Russian people.

N.   This may reduce itself to mechanics, but I wonder if you can describe how you write.

■ *Van der Post:* I wish I knew the answer to that one. I was trying to explain it to my daughter, and the only thing I could say to her was that first of all it's a question of following what I call "the bird." There's a tremendous process in which you beat about the bush to get the bird to fly. And there's an awful feeling that no matter how much you beat the bush there is no bird—it won't come out.

In the process of writing, everything is important—color, smell, scenes, wherever life has taken you, whatever you've felt. Nothing is unimportant to me. Perhaps I'm a fool about this because many modern writers feel that the only thing that matters is what one thinks about things.

In many respects this is the least important element to me. It isn't what we, ourselves, think. It's what manifests itself in what we see and smell and feel. The physical is as important, to me, as the mental, and this is where I part company with so many modern writers on the modern scene. Not with the poets, because I think the poets are on my side. I think of the poet I happen to love particularly, who means a great deal to me because he has transcended, in his own life, many of the things I would like to transcend. He also happens to be a friend of mine, T. S. Eliot. He started in America, and he lives in England, yet he expresses, I think, all that is best in the human spirit. In a strange way he takes the best of America and the best of Britain. He's the man, incidentally, the young Russian poets follow.

Now, I still haven't told you how I write. Perhaps I don't know.

N.   Here we enter the area of theory. How would you evaluate a writer's obligation in treating the raw material he uses, on the one hand, and the public he writes for, on the other?

■ *Van der Post:* I don't know if writers think about this consciously, but they must basically possess a very deep feeling of belonging to life and humanity. The writer, like the artist, the priest, and the doctor, must have a purpose, perhaps even a mission. The writer cannot afford to be false or inaccurate. Within his means he must strive for reality as opposed to unreality, for truth as opposed to untruth, for perspective as opposed to distortion. If you are false you are a bad writer, technically, and an inept one, spiritually. You've got to be—I can't say "dead accurate"—you've got to be "living accurate."

N.   What advice would you give the young writer who wants to work conscientiously with his talent and within his profession?

■ *Van der Post:* The first thing I would say is: "If you want to write, for God's sake write." That's the only way to learn how to do the job.

This makes it sound so simple—God knows it's not. It's very

difficult, and I've gone through the process, all the processes, myself. You start off as a writer, you know that you're the sort of person who could only be employed by yourself, and yet you're often unemployable, not only to the outside world but even to yourself. This is a terrible thing to face up to. You've got to become employable to yourself, and this takes time. But once you discover that you are self-employable the reward is virtually infinite: you find that by being different, by not belonging, you belong to more people than you could possibly belong to in any other profession. This is an exquisite discovery. You're manic with power, then depressed with obligation, but the self who employed you is suddenly worthy.

As for me, I hate what I've written. Once I've written it I never want to see it again. Yet it's given me a bond, a way of behavior, a way of living, a sense of communication, and nothing can compare with it.

N. The final question concerns the present state of the arts—literature, theater, poetry—whatever, in your sphere of observation, invites comment. What do you most admire? And what do you most deplore?

■ *Van der Post:* I'll have to start negatively, with the art form I love the most, the one which gives me the greatest portion of joy—the novel. I don't know if the same situation exists in the United States, but here the modern novel can hardly be sold at all. Publishers are in despair, and people talk about the novel as they used to speak of the theater before the war. They say the novel is dead.

I think that the real thing which is happening in art—in the novel, in theater, and, perhaps, in all forms of art—the thing which still strikes sparks, that lives, that sells, is the breakaway from the pattern of art. The pattern that existed before the war. The articulate, conscious, cerebral form of expression that existed before the war. People still go on writing them, but I think there's a tremendous feeling of deception in this approach to life.

I could point this out in science, and in other fields, but in art, where we usually sense these changes and trends long before anyone else senses them, I think the public feels a profound disillusionment. What is dead, actually, is this one type of novel, this one type of art.

Today—and what is terribly interesting—it is the profound rejection of the obvious, the material, the physical levels of reality. The public, when confronted with the same old form, seems to say, "Well, we know this, we've heard this, and we're tired of it; we want something else." Thus there's a turn to natural imagery, a return, if you will, to symbolic thinking as if, in this natural symbolism of the human spirit, the new meaning of our lives is to be found.

You'll find this in painting, for instance; people couldn't care less about the physical world. The painting that's gripping everybody, the young in particular, is the abstract painting of images that takes place within their own spirit and their own mind. Sometimes there's this difficulty: it's so private, so interior, it cannot be communicated. Sometimes there is nothing to be communicated. But at its best, people find that this purity of expression corresponds to all other kinds of symbolism and imagery.

We may think this belongs to one portion of the world, or only to our Western world, but this isn't true. Not long ago I went to Japan, and more recently to Russia (which is cut off from the world in so many senses) and I found that the reaction of young people everywhere is the same. This is why I think the future of literature is a literature where there is—for the moment, at least—an absorption in natural symbolisms which will be exaggerated, and in a sense untrue, because of overcompensation. But it will lead to a much greater welding of what I call "the world without" and "the world within" and this can't help but be terribly exciting.

When this happens I think we'll happily endure a renaissance of the novel, of literature as a whole, of poetry, painting, music, sculpture, everything.

One of the most difficult points in life—one of the most painful, if we can call it that—is the period of transition. Before we can possess the new faith we must lose faith in the old. And it's a dangerous moment, a moment of great peril in civilization, because this is where the devil finds a playground. This is where the established forces give battle and fight with every weapon including the threat of annihilation, the oncoming new era. (After all, they've everything to lose.) This is where, too, carelessness and opportunism can masquerade as development, or sincerity, or truth. One crosses a very dark street to attain the new.

At the moment the return to the natural instinctive images of life is obvious. It is obvious in the theater, in painting, in writing, and when it occurs and completes its process in all phases of life, we shall have the birth of truly modern man. For in a sense we are a hangover, a remnant of the renaissance. The modern man, with a few rare exceptions, doesn't exist—he has yet to be born. We live, technically, in a modern age, but it is only now that the modern spirit is being fashioned.

This is where I have my great quarrel, not personally, with the critics of the moment. I think this is where we have the decadence of modern criticism; it's rational, overly conscious criticism completely incognizant of this deep, underlying process taking place in the sensibility of modern man.

I find this age, this transition of art, terribly exciting. I think we are on the verge of a tremendous breakthrough into rejoining the two essential poles, the two very necessary opposites in the spirit of modern man.

Then we'll see something.

"Much contemporary literature, and much literature at any time, seems totally thoughtless—the authors don't write as though they had a brain; they fail to take seriously all the beautiful and painful and thoughtful things that great writers deal with—in tragedy and in comedy. Those two things add up to all there is."

Mark Van Doren
Interviewed in New York, July, 1963

Mark Van Doren

N.   In an age of specialization in all our arts, the name of Mark Van Doren stands out as representing the opposite of specialization. He's a poet of a stature which could entitle him to the title, if we used the title, of our Poet Laureate. He's an essayist, short story writer, critic, and recently Mr. Van Doren concluded a long career at Columbia College as a professor in the fullest sense of the word. If all his other books were to disappear, *Collected and New Poems,* published in 1963, would present all the proof we need of Mr. Van Doren's sensitive genius. But now it seems advisable to talk to Mr. Van Doren in terms of his own career, his life, and his attitude toward the creative arts, beginning where most of man's affairs begin, all the way back to the time of birth.

■ *Van Doren:* Let me say first, that among all these careers of mine you were kind enough to mention, the career of poet has always been to me the central one. That has been my continuing interest all the way along. My teaching was connected with that, my short stories are associated; they are poems in a sense, too. You forgot to mention the play, *The Last Days of Lincoln,* which I hope to produce before long. As to chronology, I'm sixty-nine years old, and I was born in Illinois, in the east-central region, on a farm between Danville and Urbana. My family moved when I was six into Urbana because there were five sons, and my family wanted us to have better schooling. We went to the University of Illinois at Urbana, where I got a Bachelor's and a Master's degree. Then I came to New York, as my brother Carl had before me. He was nine years older than I. I began teaching at Columbia and stayed there until I retired four years ago. My criticism, which you mentioned, almost entirely grew out of my teaching. The book on Shakespeare which I wrote, I finished after teaching Shakespeare for fifteen years to the undergraduates at Columbia College. *The Noble Voice* and other such books had the same origin.

But the teaching itself, I always thought, bore a very direct relationship to my poetry. I can't explain that very well, but to me the poetry has been the central thing, and that's why I'm so happy to hear you speak well of the book that has just come out. I published a *Collected Poems* twenty-four years ago, in 1939, but since that time, I have published several individual volumes, and in recent years I have written many new poems that appear for the first time in this book.

I have lived in New York, but now in Connecticut, on a farm my wife and I have had for forty years. I still return to Illinois rather frequently; my family is still there, although they've dwindled over the years. In fact, I'll be at the University of Illinois this coming September at the invitation of the president to speak to the incoming students. I don't know what I'm going to say to them yet; I'll just trust to luck.

N. I've run into three or four of your former students. They're adults now, but they still remember you with great fondness from their days in Columbia. There must have been something special in your philosophy of teaching, or your approach, to make such strong and favorable impressions.

■ *Van Doren:* I really have never had a theory about teaching. I just did it. I always had great respect for my students. I never despised a student, or thought of some as being worse than others. I always proceeded on the assumption that they were all equal, that they were just one student, so that no matter how many there were in the class—and in later years there were hundreds—I still talked to them as if they were one, and believed that they could understand anything I could possibly say. I never talked down to them, never suggested that I didn't think they were exactly like myself. And this paid off in the kind of answering respect they had for me and the subject. After all, if I do have a philosophy of teaching it's this: The subject is more important than either the teacher or the student. The teacher isn't the thing, it's the subject. Say it's Shakespeare, for example—of course he is more important than the teacher. Some teachers, however, try to get in front of their subject, try to be brighter and more impressive than the subject, and they play up to that sort of vanity in the student, too.

I think there should be no vanity whatever in instruction. There should be nothing but respect for the third thing which is present, and that is the ever-vital, ever-important subject.

N. Now, to turn to a slightly different subject, I would like to hear any comment you might have and any observations regarding the state of American letters as a whole.

■ *Van Doren:* I don't know what to say about all that. I'm

occasionally asked this question, but I am never sure that I have any opinions regarding the state of the arts at the moment. I'm not being evasive. I simply think about what I am doing, and what other individuals are doing, rather than about the state of the drama or of fiction or of poetry.

As to fiction, I'm afraid I agree with a great many people these days who wish that the fiction of our time tried harder to tell stories about people, instead of being psychological, sociological, philosophical, and everything else. The notion that a short-story writer is first of all a storyteller seems to have withered, and we hear a novelist praised for his style, or his ideas, or his psychological understanding, rather than for his story. But it remains true that the story is everything in fiction. I think this explains the disappearance of much of the audience for serious fiction. Many of us are taking up the detective story, or science fiction, or the western, because they at least tell stories.

N. And they offer entertainment.

■ *Van Doren:* Entertainment—you use the word, and I'm glad, because it's such an important word. The most entertaining of all writers is Shakespeare, and we tend to forget this. We tend to forget that he meant his works to interest us at the level of the story. There is nothing more exciting than reading or watching one of Shakespeare's plays.

Entertainment, to me, is not a light word; it is a very great word. It covers all that literature should do. Every now and then you hear that a book is "merely entertaining." I don't like the word "merely," because the only thing that can be entertained is the mind. Artists don't entertain our eyeballs or our thumbs or our big toes—they entertain our minds. If we remembered that, I think we would be in a better state. I guess I am answering your question, after all.

N. Yes, and you've led right into the next question, too: In regard to the fledgling artist, the student or post-student whose aspirations are definitely in the fields of fiction, poetry, drama, what do you think his preparation should be?

■ *Van Doren:* First of all, he should study what other accomplished men have studied. He should get the best liberal education he can, and I mean, by that, the education designed for men generally considered, as human beings. Intellectual education, which liberal education really is at bottom (people don't talk seriously about liberal arts these days; they are something to "take" if you can't think of anything else) remains the great and central part of education. It is the thing that frees the mind to do whatever the mind has the capacity to do. It makes a man out of a child. A good college education makes more difference in the life of the individual who obtains it than anything else ever does. The four years transform him. The parents think so, at any rate, because they usually don't recognize him when he comes home. He is a man, not a child, and he is thinking about things they never heard of before. Thinking is what does it.

Much contemporary literature, and much literature at any time, seems totally thoughtless—the authors don't write as though they had a brain; they fail to take seriously all the beautiful and painful and thoughtful things that great writers deal with—in tragedy and in comedy. Those two things add up to all there is.

My advice to an ambitious young writer is to get the best education he can. He will learn the tricks of writing, if that is the word for them, in the course of trying, in the course of studying masterpieces he wants to imitate. Above all, he should have something in his head. He should have ideas; he should find out what the great themes have always been in stories, what makes a story really powerful, what makes some stories more powerful than others. And never should he get too far from the soul of man, which is the basic concern of all art. Do I sound too serious?

N.   No. To me you hit all the important points, and I'm glad to see the emphasis shifting a little away from the scientific education, back to some recognition of the liberal arts and philosophy.

■ *Van Doren:* Philosophy—I'm glad you mention that. Philosophy shouldn't be just a course in a college, it should be what the whole college is trying to give the student. It should be trying to make him more philosophical, more serious. And when I say more serious, I hope you don't think I mean solemn. The best sign of a person who is serious is his humor. You can't take seriously people who have no sense of humor. You can't quite believe them.

N.   I can't trust them.

■ *Van Doren:* You don't trust them to know what life is really about, to have perspective. Humor is probably the most precious thing in any art. It was what made Robert Frost a great poet; he was a great poet anyway, but the humor in him proved it. Shakespeare, too. Humor has a definite relationship to warmth, and to love. The difference, for example, between humor and satire is very deep. A satirist is usually a hater, but a humorist is a man who —though he sees all the shortcomings in himself and others, certainly, beginning with himself—finds a perspective that makes

U*

him pity and love, makes him free to point out all the discrepancies between what is and what ought to be; but in the long run he has mercy. Something like the gods. You know, the gods smile, they don't weep, and the smile of the gods is one of the most beautiful of all expressions.

N. Mr. Van Doren, I wonder if we could switch to one facet of your writings I know very little about; your work as a playwright.

■ *Van Doren:* Well, *The Last Days of Lincoln* is a book, and it will be produced within a year, I hope. The play is very important to me because Lincoln has always been for me a man of endless fascination. I never tire of talking about him. I wanted to get him into a play, and I hope I have. The play is partly in verse, incidentally; Lincoln speaks prose, and everybody else speaks verse. He is the best poet, but you can't imagine him speaking verse, can you?

N. Then there's your autobiography.

■ *Van Doren:* Yes, that came out four or five years ago. When I was first asked to write it I said, "No, I can't write a book about myself." It sounded like an act of vanity. Then I began making notes for it and realized that it wouldn't be primarily about myself at all, it would be about everything and everyone else: the places I'd been, the books I'd read, the teachers I'd had, the students I'd taught, the woman I married, my children, friends, places, times, events.

In other words, one begins to take stock of the times one has lived in, and that is really what an autobiography has to be about. The reader takes stock of the author because of the way the author talks about and cares about everything around him and may grow irritated to hear him talk only about himself. We learn by indirection; we learn that is, more about a person by the way he loves and hates, appreciates and dismisses, than by what he has to say about himself.

N. Now that *New and Collected Poems* has been issued, bringing you up to date in that department, at least, I was wondering what you're doing right now.

■ *Van Doren:* Well, I'm not teaching any more, but this spring I was invited to Harvard to teach a summer term, and I've just come back from there to our farm in Connecticut. I really enjoyed the session because both my wife and I were fascinated with life at Harvard, which is really a very special thing. There is nothing like it anywhere, except in England. Much as I liked it, however, I think it's the only experiment of the sort I'll make. I think I'm really through with teaching now. Much as I've enjoyed it, I think I deserve a rest—forty years is long enough.

N. This brings up another point, Mr. Van Doren, not related to the arts, particularly, but to life itself. You say you are sixty-nine. Now, I know so many men that age, or near that age, who are forced to retire due to company laws, and who are going into their retirement years rather resentfully because they have no interests, no hobbies, nothing really to do. Is there any comment you can make on this state of affairs?

■ *Van Doren:* This is a familiar question, not easy to answer. I'm sorry for anyone who retires and has nothing to do. It seems to me he should have prepared for this, got to reading, or making, or building things. He should have a plan for the rest of his life. In my own case there was no problem because I had lived a double life. As a matter of fact, I can now let a whole day pass without doing anything at all, and I love that.

I think that some men are forced to retire too early. They are perfectly capable of going on, and if their business has been their whole life they *should* go on, unless they are in their dotage and don't know it.

Finally, I think that a more flexible policy in regard to retirement should be maintained by companies. They should not dismiss their senior employees on the basis of a rule that says "Sixty-five and out." Each person should be considered individually.

N. Now, if you would, I would like you to read some of your poems, perhaps new ones that have appeared for the first time in *New and Collected Poems.*

■ *Van Doren:* Thank you. This first one, a very short one, was published as a Christmas card a few years ago.

> Eternity's low voice,
> That no one yet has heard,
> Sings peace be with you, children
> Of man, beast, worm, and bird.

The significance of this for me, if that isn't too big a word for so short a poem, is this: These days when we speak about the possible end of the world, most of us think of it only as the end of men. I think of it as the end of birds, too, and animals, too, and all living things. To me they are as important as we are. We came last, as a matter of fact, to join them. Thus we want to prevent the end of the world on behalf of all living things, as well as ourselves.

Another poem, "Variation on Disaster," calls to mind certain possibilities that exist.

> The stone lifted
> A little flaming salamander, startled by broad light,
> Darts away among wet leaves.
>
> The hay cut,
> A spider web, that danced between the blowing stalks
> Has to be built again.
>
> The tree felled,
> Four blue eggs roll out of a robin's nest.
> No young this year.
>
> The basket overturned,
> A mouse's brood—run, run—so many mouthfuls
> For the scampering cat.
>
> The earth quakes
> And villages fall; but rise again when all the dead
> Have namesakes: the new children.
>
> History, a hundred feet
> Above high tide, comes in unnoticed; customs drown
> So painlessly, nobody weeps.

In that last stanza I am referring to something that isn't called a custom unless one is aware of it; I have in mind a total change in habit, a total change in belief. It is a slower, but a more shocking change, than change through catastrophe.

Here is a very short one again. In recent years I have been writing very short poems. I don't know exactly what this means, but maybe I've simply learned how to say things quickly. This is titled "Born Equal." Equality is a principle I take very seriously, for I consider it the basis of all sound political and religious life. There are some who think it pointless to talk about the equality of men, but I don't think so, not any more than Lincoln did, or Jefferson. I really believe it, and I think these men meant what they said when they claimed that all men are born equal. This is a dialogue:

"Born equal? When so many—
Look 'round you—are inferior?
In God's name, who believes"—
"None but the superior."

It is usually the better person—and I hope I'm not patting myself on the back—who can understand the doctrine of equality.

Here's a longer one, a narrative which I think explains itself
perfectly. It's called "The First Snow of the Year."

The old man, listening to the careful
Steps of his old wife as she came,
Up, up, so slowly, then her slippered
Progress down the long hall to their door—

Outside the wind, wilder suddenly,
Whirled the first snow of the year; danced
Round and round with it, coming closer
And closer, peppering the panes; now here she was—

Said "Ah, my dear, remember?" But his tray
Took all of her attention, having to hold it
Level. "Ah, my dear, don't you remember?"
"What?" "That time we walked in the white woods."

She handed him his napkin; felt the glass
To make sure the milk in it was warm;
Sat down; got up again; brought comb and brush
To tidy his top hair. "Yes, I remember."

He wondered if she saw now what he did.
Possibly not. An afternoon so windless,
The huge flakes rustled upon each other,
Filling the woods, the world, with cold, cold—

They shivered, having a long way to go,
And then their mittens touched; and touched again;
Their eyes, trying not to meet, did meet;
They stopped, and in the cold held out their arms

Till she came into his; awkwardly,
As girl to boy that never kissed before.
The woods, the darkening world, so cold, so cold,
While these two burned together. He remembered,

And wondered if she did, how like a sting,
A hidden heat it was; while there they stood
And trembled, and the snow made statues of them.
"Ah, my dear, remember?" "Yes, I do."

She rocked and thought: he wants me to say something.
But we said nothing then. The main thing is,
I'm with him still; he calls me and I come.
But slowly. Time makes sluggards of us all.

"Yes, I do remember." The wild wind
Was louder, but a sweetness in her speaking
Stung him, and he heard. While round and round
The first snow of the year danced on the lawn.

Here's a much shorter poem which is about something that may
strike you as slight, but no subject is really slight to me. This is
about an experience that everyone has had while waiting for a frog
to croak—you know, when you're near a pond the frog makes
noise, you talk about it, and you wait, but the frog takes its own
time and doesn't know or care whether you're waiting. There's
such a frog under an old building that I use as a study on my farm.
A stream runs under the building, and the frog lives down there,
and once in a while I hear him.

Under this building
A small stream runs,
In the dark, and noiseless
Save for a frog—
Listen, that lets me
Know he is there.
Now now; he is waiting;
He takes his time.

I must not wait;
He will never begin.
It is not for me
His intervals are,
It is not to me
He says what he says,
Or to anyone warm—
Ah, there he is.

Anything that is true is interesting to me, and I have faith that it's interesting to everybody else. I spoke to you of the play I wrote about Lincoln. Of course, it involved the war over which he presided, and in recent years I've been writing a few short poems about the Civil War, about things that particularly interested me as I pursued the Civil War in so many dozens of books.

One thing that always absorbed me was "What happened when a battle began?" especially in the woods. All the animals and birds must have been scared to death, must have retreated to safety, somewhere, and perhaps didn't know how. Thus the poem:

> Suddenly commencing—
> Boom, swish! Boom, swish!—
> Artillery over the mountain:
> Hell in the high woods.
> We looked at one another, startled. Then
> Here came the birds,
> More startled—bullets themselves, flying
> So wild, so near,
> We almost could have caught them. Almost.
> No, too fast, too utterly shot forth
> By fear. A naked speed;
> Nestless, now and
> Forever.

Then there's another Civil War poem dealing with a very familiar theme—the theme of related men, one on one side, one on the other, who meet in battle. You often hear about brother and brother doing this. This is a son and a father, and it's a dialogue:

> "Boy, I have dreamed of this.
> But the other way around.
> I was the wounded one,
> And you, the good, the strong—"
>
> The son looked into the father's
> Eyes, then shut his own.
> "And so with me." His whisper
> Might have been heard at home.
>
> There was no war between them.
> In them two armies touched:
> Enemies so earnest,
> Encounter was a tryst;

The laying on of glances
That made their love complete.
But oh, the separation,
And marches in the night.

"My boy, I prayed we never
Would meet until peace again."
"So I," as the waves of battle,
Eddying, washed on.

Here's one that's not about anything at all, but came as the
result of driving once through a city in the United States—a city
I got lost in, lost in the shabbier parts. You know, when you go
through cities you usually see the best part, but seeing this shabbi-
ness, in a part of a city I probably wasn't supposed to be, made me
angry. It made me angry that so many people had to or did live
this way.

I went among the mean streets
Of such a city
As should have moved my wrath;
But it was pity.

I did not count the sad eyes,
There were so many.
I listened for the singing;
There was not any.

O thieves of joy, O thoughtless
Who blink at this,
Beware. There will be judgment,
With witnesses.*

You know, we talk so much about standards of living and
conduct and the lack of poverty and the equality of privilege, but
sometimes I'm afraid that this talk is awfully quick, and cheap,
perhaps some sort of magic salve that covers a problem—not a cure
for the problem itself.

*Poems quoted by Mr. Van Doren are reprinted by courtesy of Hill
& Wang, publishers of *Collected and New Poems 1924–1963* by Mark
Van Doren, 1963, $10.00.

"To me, much of modern fiction seems to be fragmented, obscure, filled with phony symbolisms, not really fiction at all. It's been my experience that a writer who can't make things clear to his readers either doesn't know what he wants to say, or has something to say that is totally unimportant."

Jerome Weidman
Interviewed in New York, August, 1963

Jerome Weidman

N. Jerome Weidman has established a firm position in the world of letters with twenty-three books, none of which has been lightly dismissed at publication time, none of which will be totally forgotten in years to follow. *I Can Get It For You Wholesale*, *The Enemy Camp*, and *The Sound Of Bow Bells* are three that spring immediately to mind in terms of critical and popular success, but also by virtue of Weidman's tendency to "pioneer" in areas of American life writers have seldom penetrated. In talking to Mr. Weidman, however, I'd like to discuss *Back Talk*, not a novel, but a particularly stimulating and entertaining collection of essays released in 1963. How did you come to write it?

■ *Weidman:* As you know, a novelist, short story writer, and playwright deals constantly with matters of the imagination. I don't mean that he doesn't deal with actual facts, but facts can only furnish raw material. Thus, these facts, together with whatever opinions he has, must be expressed through characters in the novel or the story or the play. So he never puts it on the line himself.

Every now and again, a man who works with fiction feels the impulse to speak directly in his own person, not through John Jones, a character he has created. The opportunities for doing this in print are rather limited for a man who is essentially a writer of fiction, yet every now and again a magazine editor will come along and ask for a special piece beyond the realm of fiction, or a friend will want an introduction for a book, or an anthologist will want something for a collection. In this way, over the course of years, the novelist puts together a number of nonfiction pieces, some of which become important to him, perhaps only because they break the confines of his work.

Strictly speaking, the novelist's function is not to deal with facts. He deals, so to speak, with the secret labyrinths of the human heart, and all those other places that have neither place names nor house numbers. So when the chance comes to do a nonfiction piece he grabs it, quite eagerly. I have not yet met the novelist who didn't welcome the opportunity to write a nonfiction piece. Including, of course, myself.

I've done factual pieces, introductions, all the things I mentioned, and it occurred to me, at this stage of my career, that it might be interesting to see exactly what I've turned out over the past twenty-five years that adds up to creditable nonfiction. Above all, I was interested in seeing if I've changed any of my beliefs and opinions over the years, and if I have changed, if the change is for the better. We like to progress, you know, not regress.

I was pleasantly surprised to find that most of the opinions I had expressed twenty-five, twenty, and fifteen years ago regarding books, people, and so on, hadn't changed. I was chagrined to find myself sounding off, sometimes, on things I knew little about, but for the most part I was pleased with the consistency. So what I did in *Back Talk* was to collect these various pieces, some dealing with close literary friends like Somerset Maugham, some dealing with heroic figures like Eleanor Roosevelt, some dealing with the problems of raising two boys, others with life in the suburbs, in the country, and the fun of returning to live in the city, and put them together for whatever sense they make.

It's a very opinionated book—not gospel, but opinion—and that's why I called it *Back Talk*, though I would like to elaborate upon that for a moment, if I may.

I remember, as a boy in school, a current events class. The teacher used to give us assignments to cover certain current events of the day. At the time—I think it was in the sixth or seventh grade —Joseph Conrad was visiting this country. Obviously, kids our age were not going to cover actual events; we were to read newspaper reports, then issue a summary to the class. I "covered" Joseph Conrad's visit in this way. The reason I remember this obscure little event was his answer to a reporter who asked him why writers took the trouble to write introductions to their books. His answer, not in these words, of course, was that it was the only opportunity the writer gets to talk back to his critics.

In a way *Back Talk* resurrects my favorite nonfiction pieces, and my fondest sustained opinions, and it also talks back to critics.

N. One of the essays in the book, the piece on Somerset Maugham, was particularly impressive. Could you elaborate upon that?

■ *Weidman:* Well, I met Maugham twenty or thirty years ago. Richard Simon of Simon & Schuster—he's now dead—was my publisher then, and he knew that I admired Maugham's work. When

Maugham was visiting in this country, well before the war, Simon and his wife arranged a small dinner party in their home on Eleventh Street and invited me. They didn't tell me that the guest was Somerset Maugham. I liked Maugham from the moment I met him, and started and maintained a correspondence. It was one of those extremely satisfying things—ideas, discussions, a great deal of give-and-take.

Then, during the war, Maugham lived in this country, part of the time in New York and the rest of the time in a house Nelson Doubleday built for him on his North Carolina estate. As I recall, Maugham's funds were frozen in England, and he was living on a rather limited budget. To help him out, somebody cooked up the idea of bringing out a sampler of his work, an anthology. Maugham asked me if I would make the selections and write the introduction; this delighted me, of course.

Now, twenty-five years later, I reread the introduction and, because I still believe what I said, I've included it. I've also included a companion piece, an introduction to a biography of Maugham by Carl Pfeiffer that I did very recently. Oddly enough, I wrote the latter after I'd virtually forgotten the existence of the former. Yet when I compare the two pieces I find that they dovetail as a forward glance and a backward glance at the same person.

N.   How do you glance at Maugham?

■ *Weidman:* In my opinion, Maugham is the modern Maupassant. He is, without doubt, one of the greatest storytellers of all time. He's fallen out of fashion a bit, lately, because he specializes in what is regarded as an old-fashioned story: quaint, with a beginning, a middle, and an end. Maugham's stories deal with recognizable human emotions. Meanings and events are crystal clear. A Maugham story is written with the same cool, dispassionate approach to human nature that Maupassant possessed. This is much more effective in conveying genuine compassion for the trials and tribulations of human beings than breastbeating.

Maugham has written ninety-one short stories. I think at least a dozen of them will live and be read a century from now. As far as his novels go, I think at least two of them are great novels, *Of Human Bondage* and *Cakes and Ale.* The latter may seem frivolous to some people, but it is nevertheless almost the perfect novel. It's a superb piece of work. And we might have to rank *The Moon and Sixpence* right along with these two. And we might even have to add two or three of the finest comedies of manners of our time, *Our Betters, The Circle,* and *The Constant Wife.* It all adds up to quite an achievement, an achievement many modernists cannot bear gracefully.

To me much of modern fiction seems to be fragmented, obscure, filled with phony symbolisms, not really fiction at all. It's been my experience that a writer who can't make things clear to his readers either doesn't know what he wants to say, or has something to say that is totally unimportant. Purposeful obfuscation, lack of clarity, marks the second-rate. I've never had trouble understanding what Dickens meant, or Thackeray, or Tolstoy.

Another reason for the modernist's dismissal of Maugham is the fact that a great many short story writers of today turn out things that are called novels that really aren't novels at all. They are short story writers who are told by their publisher, "Now do a novel." These writers are under the impression that if a short story runs twenty pages, all they have to do is write four hundred pages and presto—there's a novel. This just isn't true. A novel must be built from the ground up, and have within it its own coiled tension just as a short story should. Accumulating pages doesn't make a novel, no matter how it's classified in bookstores.

N.   I'd like to turn—more generally, now—to your own career. The point where we call for autobiography with feeling.

■ *Weidman:*   Well, as you know, most writers start writing inadvertently. They're not self-conscious about it at all. There are some writers who set out to become writers, but it's been my experience that genuinely talented writers sort of fall into it. They don't take courses in "How to become a writer." At a certain point in their lives, just as water will ultimately find its own level, a talented writer will begin to write. The motivation he feels at that particular moment could spring from an overwhelming emotional experience or from economic necessity—it doesn't make any difference.

Next, it seems to me that the early writings of any writer are unplanned. I don't mean that the individual piece of work is unplanned, but that the overall structure and pattern of his life's work has not yet taken shape.

I'm taking a long look into my career because I didn't plan things very well, for a very long time. As a kid I wrote stories that excited me at the particular moment, and novels that were clear in my own mind. But after I had written about a dozen volumes, and was well into my thirties—pushing forty, in fact—I suddenly began to take stock of my career. I think most people do this when they approach forty; it's the now-or-never hour of life.

I looked back at the work I had done, and forward to the work I had in my notebooks, and it suddenly occurred to me that a pattern was beginning to emerge. I thought that if I would just pat it a little, like a meatball, I'd have something, be something.

Every man sees life through his own peculiar lens. Every writer writes through his own peculiar lens. After all, the only thing a writer has to offer is his own personality as it emerges through his work. I saw that my lens was New York City. I was born and reared here, it's the part of the world I know best and feel the most comfortable in. This is where my roots are, and even though I have traveled in all parts of the world, and written a good deal about those places, I always wrote about them as a New Yorker seeing them. Some instinct—perhaps some inability—kept me from trying to pretend that I was an Australian or an Englishman or a Frenchman. I'm simply a New Yorker.

Thus at forty I decided that it was a good thing to set my work within that particular framework, to view my time as I have seen it through the lens of New York City. I hate to sound like a Rotarian, and I'm not running for office, but New York is the Mecca of the Western World, and I think it's fortunate for me that New York is the tool I have been given to work with.

I don't mean to draw comparisons, but some time ago I read Zweig's excellent biography of Balzac, and I discovered that Balzac had made somewhat the same discovery about himself. He never set out to write the *Comédie Humaine*. He was a very busy hack writer who turned out novels about people in Paris, about people in the country, about clergymen, about doctors, and I think he even wrote the first novel about a boarding house. He just wrote the way a vacuum cleaner sucks in lint. But in his middle years it occurred to him that he was giving a portrait of France, so he started dividing up the books into scenes of country life, scenes of city life, scenes of military life, and so on, and that's how the *Comédie Humaine* came into being.

But at the very beginning I wrote, like most writers do, without pattern. Scott Fitzgerald once said that you never know when you're living in history, and it's absolutely true. Young people accept what happens to them with complete equanimity.

I wrote *I Can Get It For You Wholesale* very late at night. I had a job as a delivery boy during the day, I was going to Law School at New York University at night, and I'd get home to the apartment in the Bronx where I lived with my parents about eleven and work until three in the morning. I wrote a chapter a night for thirty nights. I finished the novel and sent it off, and when it was purchased by Simon and Schuster I was terribly excited, but it didn't occur to me that there was anything unusual about this. Years later, when I looked back, I thought of how fortunate I had been, but at that age I took it in stride. Everything that's followed has fallen into some sort of progression, perhaps the most notable one being the thing I've talked so long about, my affinity for New York, for New York scenes and characters.

N.   But haven't you rather broken the mold of the novelist with your work in theater?

■ *Weidman:* My theatrical experiences have been, I think, commonplace in the sense that I've not yet met a writer who wasn't stage-struck. As a matter of fact, this is a curious thing about a majority of writers—when you get to know them you learn that they all started out as playwrights. I don't know what the fascination is, but I know that I share it.

I made one or two stabs at working in the theater, but it's an intensely co-operative medium, and I couldn't seem to work out very well. I'd get started, a project would seem to be taking shape, then it would fizzle out, but in order not to waste the material, I would convert it into short stories or into a novel. Then one day a producer named Bobby Griffith and his partner, Hal Prince, came to me and said, "Look, we've got the rights from Mrs. LaGuardia to do a show about the late mayor, and we think you'd be the ideal person to write it because you were a contemporary of his." By this they meant that I had grown up in New York at the time he was mayor.

Well, I *had* lived through this colorful period in New York; it was part of the lens I used in my work, and since Fiorello LaGuardia had been one of my great heroes, I became excited. In fact, *Fiorello!* turned out to be a very happy experience. It was hard work because a musical show involves so many talents—composer, lyricist, director, choreographer, and so on. With a person like George Abbott, who directed it and who worked with me on the book, you're dealing with a man who is almost like a painter with a palette—each of the persons in the show is just so much paint on the palette, and he's got to put the thing together into a picture.

After working on *Fiorello!*, the same group, naturally, wanted to do something else. As it happened, the same producer owned the rights to Sam Adams' novel *Tenderloin*. So this came next.

By this time I felt that I sort of knew my way around a bit in the world of musical theater, and I wanted to do something on my own. Quite a while ago I had decided that I wanted to do a musical version of my first novel, *I Can Get It For You Wholesale*. From time to time I tried to sell this idea to producers, not very strenuously, and no one thought much about it until I ran into David Merrick. Merrick had a property he wanted to convert for the stage, and we talked about it, and I said, "Yes, it's interesting and I might want to do it, but you know how writers are—they really only want to do the thing that's at the top of their minds at the moment." He asked me what was on my mind, and I told him that I was working on the libretto for a musical version of *I Can Get It For You Wholesale*. He asked me if the rights were available and I said "yes"; he asked me if I had a composer and lyricist lined up, and I said "no."

The upshot was that Merrick bought *Wholesale*, sight unseen, and introduced me to Harold Rome. I had known Harold socially for a number of years, but we had never worked together, and as soon as I told him what I had in mind he got quite excited. He knew the novel, wanted to do it, and we did do it. It was a wonderful and happy experience.

I do find that working in the theater is very exciting, a great relief after working on a novel and a short story. You see, the novelist and the short story writer live a very lonely existence. I'm not pleading for sympathy—I like my lonely existence. You are alone in a room with a pad and a pencil for a long stretch of time, and when you've finished what you're working on, you put it into an envelope and mail it to your agent, or if you live in New York, as I do, you just walk down the street and leave it at your agent's office. That's the end of it. You see galleys and things like that, but there's really no human contact.

In the theater, on the other hand, you're involved with highly articulate, highly talented, highly volatile people all the time. Spending a few hours with them every day is a rather stunning contrast to the hours you've been cooped up with pen and pencil. It's stimulating and exciting, though I suppose a writer couldn't spend all his time with them or he'd get nothing written. The balancing act, again, as far as both hours and talent are concerned.

N.   To turn to the theoretical: If you were to give advice to the talented youngster who sincerely wants to write, and write well, what would that advice be?

■ *Weidman:* Start writing. Don't take courses. Just write. And get an agent in New York. It is almost impossible today for a new young writer to get a hearing, or viewing, without the professional guidance of a New York literary agent.

N. Now, in looking about you at today's literature and theater, could you point out what individual things or trends you most admire? And, conversely, which you most deplore?

■ *Weidman:* I deplore what I have always deplored—arty obscurantism. I admire what I have always admired—clarity, grace, and fecundity, all harnessed to the service of the truth. As between a writer who has written one or two "brilliant" things and a writer who has written a dozen "good" things, I prefer the latter. He is a worker, and I understand and admire workers.

N. My final question concerns a critical flurry that came up not too long ago. You, as well as other Jewish writers, were criticized by a group of religious leaders for presenting Jews in an unfavorable light. Could you comment on that?

■ *Weidman:* Well, those scars on my forehead were put there during this controversy, yet I have almost nothing to say about it that hasn't already been said before.

I am a Jew, and I understand Jews because I have lived with them all my life. They are my material and I'm going to write about them. The accusations that are occasionally made against Jewish writers, and I'm not the only one, that we present Jews in an unfavorable light, are absolute nonsense.

If you look at all these books very carefully, mine and the others, you will occasionally find an unattractive character. But there will be an unattractive character on any street corner in the United States, along with all the nice people.

Now, I have published twenty-three books. Three of them deal with Jews, yet the theory persists in certain quarters (usually official Jewish quarters) that I write exclusively about Jews and that I invariably choose disreputable characters. This is absolutely untrue, on every ground including statistics. Yet the inaccuracy is nothing to get angry about, because I think this sort of reaction is true within any ethnic group. There are always people who will object to your portraying any member of that group in an unfavorable light. It's as simple as that.

Now, it's true that in the world we live in there is a great deal more anti-Semitism than there is, for example, anti-Indianism, and therefore a Jew who is portrayed in a book as an unfavorable character will probably loom as a larger figure than, say, a disreputable Indian. Yet as long as the writer is working honestly, and in perspective, and holding his special lens to life, he cannot turn his back

on his material simply because certain members of his ethnic group
protest.

N. If you were to look back, now, at the total of your career,
what would stand out as highlights?

■ *Weidman:* My two favorites among all my books are *The
Hand of the Hunter* and *The Third Angel.* I was pleased to receive a Pulitzer Prize for *Fiorello!* but I thought these two novels
deserved the prize in the years of their publication. In other years
when I have published novels I thought the books that received
the awards were superior to mine. In the years of *The Hand of the
Hunter* and *The Third Angel*—no.

"I'd say, in short, that the satisfying novel—the so-called serious novel that pleases the novelist now and tomorrow and the day after, and stands a chance of being read a year from now—has to be faithful to the issues and characters the novelist creates."

Morris L. West
Interviewed in New York, June, 1963

Morris L. West

N.   Timing is always important, but nothing in literary history matches the release of Morris L. West's *The Shoes of the Fisherman* during the final illness of a beloved Pope. The novel, of course, deals with the election of a new Pope and the immediate problems he faces. More significantly, West probes deeply at the heart of modern Catholicism, working realistically with opposing elements of liberalism and conservatism within the Church as well as the continued need for modification.

Critically, this book was highly acclaimed, with West honored, as he had been previously, with *The Devil's Advocate* and *Daughter of Silence*, for his willingness to deal with provocative themes.

In talking with Mr. West I'd like to ask for the customary summary of background—the chronology of birth and events.

■ *West:* I'll cut this short because birth, after all, is a matter of being acted upon; one really has very little to say about it, which may be a good thing because we might gum things up by declining the pleasure.

I was born in Melbourne, Australia, in 1916, and educated at schools of the Christian Brothers order. I joined the order as a postulant when I was fourteen, and left twelve years later without taking the final vows.

I served in Army Intelligence during World War II. After the war I became a partner in a recording and transcription business which I left because, when I analyzed things, I realized that I wanted to write my own stuff, not write what sponsors wanted.

During a stay in Italy I roamed the back streets of Naples, posing as a seaman on the run. As a result I wrote *Children of the Sun*, really a study of street urchins who roam that impoverished city and their benefactor, Father Borelli. This book was published in England in 1957 and sold quite well. As far as American publication was concerned, *The Crooked Road* appeared in 1957 and *Backlash* in 1958. I don't think they racked up any phenomenal sales records.

In 1958 I returned to Italy as Vatican correspondent for *The Daily Mail*. I suppose I functioned rather as a blotter, soaking up background with intensity and, I hope, discrimination, because this period was responsible for *The Devil's Advocate*, *Daughter of Silence*, and *The Shoes of the Fisherman*.

N. Since all I've written and said about *The Shoes of the Fisherman* is in the realm of praise, we're not going to have much of a chance to argue. One thing I am wondering, however, is if you have had, or if you expect to have, any unfavorable reaction from Catholic clergy and from Catholic laymen?

■ *West:* In a book like this, one always lays one's head on the block. So much ground for controversy is largely a matter of semantics, and there is always, at the back of the mind of the pastoral clergy, the thought that somehow or other the free expression of even a mutually accepted truth can give scandal.

This, I think, is a great mistake, and I feel that it has caused great harm within the Church. The failure to estimate the value of human judgment and to recognize the influence of the Holy Ghost, which works in the individual as well as in the Church, is deplorable.

However, we have had considerable Catholic reaction to this book, and so far it has been favorable. We have been advised that in certain, shall we say, conservative areas, there will be some rather rigorous criticism. However, this really has nothing to do with whether the book is (per se) conformable or not to Christian doctrine. This is a book written specifically from the point of view of a believing Christian and a believing Catholic. Yet what it does attempt to do is to explore the true ground of Christian belief, ". . . to strip off the historic overlay," as I have Karyl say in the book. The accretions of practice, and sometimes of superstition, overlay the true rock of belief. And these are really the things that divide us. All too often, however, there are people inside and outside the Church who are not truly aware of this, or who are afraid of seeing the naked rock on which they stand because it can be wonderful and frightening at the same time.

N. I wanted to ask you whether or not I was being presumptuous in going beyond the book in one respect, in that I found the moral issue you raised not only concerned the Catholic faith, but applied to Western civilization as a whole.

■ *West:* I think this is a true statement of the aim of the book, which is to point out that, to boil everything down, survival for the human race, war or peace, justice or injustice, is at base a moral issue.

You are having a problem in America at this moment, the immense conflicts of integration. Unfortunately, everybody understands in his heart, but comparatively few people are prepared to admit to themselves in so many words that to give justice to the Negro involves personal sacrifice. A sacrifice of an attitude of security. A sacrifice of prejudice, a sacrifice possibly even of possession. If a Negro moves next door, and the value of your house goes down, this is a necessary contribution on the part of the individual to his survival in a peaceful society.

You can't have it both ways. We in Australia are vitally preoccupied with our future relations with Southeast Asia. We are an appendage of Southeast Asia, we're in this orbit. We have to live with Southeast Asia, yet we, eleven million people, are cultivating the vast illusion that we should remain a white continent with a political practice which excludes all Asians from residence in our country on the grounds that such immigration would constitute an economic danger. We don't say color, of course. Actually we practice a color bar.

I was in Hong Kong recently, and I saw an advertisement in the local paper—a very big ad for a film called *The Tunnel* which described the escape of several Germans from the East to the West and which lauded their courage and their endurance for reaching out for freedom in spite of all dangers. Right next to it, in the same paper, was a laconic account of how two junk-loads of refugees from the China coast had been turned back under police guard. There was no question about their being hungry for liberty or courageous strugglers for an ideal; they were simply Chinese, so the moral issue became different.

My point is that, at bottom, it is the same moral issue, and you get back to the old story that if a man is dying on your doorstep, while you on the inside of the house are replenished with food, you are dying, too—although you don't know it.

N. Another thing that interested me very much in *Shoes* was the way you dealt with the fact that the Church must identify itself with native populations in Asia and South America and Africa to rid itself of its identity with colonialism and occupation.

■ *West:* This presents an enormous problem, and it goes beyond the simple identification with imperialism. In Japan, for example, it boils down to an identification with everything that is foreign. The Japanese word for foreigner is "gigen" and it means, literally, "outside man." Christianity is identified, and has been, historically, since the Portugese first came to Japan, with the outside man. Even those missionaries who came back to Japan after a stay abroad, who return to the country with considerable enlightenment and good will, are hampered by the fact that certain details of their practice and their attitude—things they themselves take for granted—constitute an affront and a barrier to the Japanese. For example: The Japanese is a scrupulously clean person. He doesn't wash himself in a bath. He bathes for pleasure, and washes himself outside the bath.

Now, if you go into a Catholic Church there's a holy water stoop outside. You put your finger into the holy water and bless yourself with it—a simple sacramental practice pleasing to people and possibly useful to them. In Japan, the native reacts violently against this practice—it's dirty. You can see how this may constitute a hideous barrier, not only to his understanding of religion, but to his understanding of the West. I was in a little church called Takaduchi. It was rather like being among the early Christians, for these very poor people had found in the Christian faith a comfort and a belief and a ground for existence. And here was a gift, given to the mission by an Australian. It was a rather hideous statue of the Sacred Heart, all different colors and monstrous to look at.

N. We have them here, now, in bird baths.

■ *West:* I know. I've seen some of them. Now, the interesting point was that Christ was shown in this statue with a beard. Historically the Christ was bearded. But to the Japanese the bearded man again represents a foreigner. There's another word for foreigner which means "bearded hairy man," and it goes all the way back to the first visitors to Japan who were Dutch and Portuguese sailors and who were hairy and smelly. Now, this apparently small psychological barrier can be built up in the mind of a very subtle person like the Japanese to become a whole fence which cannot be crossed, not only between Christianity and Japan, but between East and West.

N. Do you feel, then, that some of the traditions of the Church could probably be done away with without sacrificing the essence of faith, to bring the Church closer to the comprehension of the people of a given nation?

■ *West:* Most certainly. But rather than baldly "do away with them," they should be analyzed in relationship to a particular country or area. Many outward manifestations and demonstrations of faith are embellishments that may be useful in a Latin country, for example, and distasteful in Asia. This attitude goes right to the root of ecumenism.

Every Church, every religious body, every national body, has certain attitudes which it regards distinctively as being necessary to its existence, whereas actually they are not. We find this at all levels. For example, your government feels that to give up the offshore islands of Quemoy and Matsu would plunge the world into war. Now, these islands are a running sore in the political situation in Southeast Asia. I'm not saying that America cannot surrender them without grave danger to Formosa, without creating a dangerous attitude of mind throughout the Far East, but one must never regard this nonessential fact as being essential to the preservation of liberty and the Constitution in America. They may be, but they are not, of the essence of the situation.

People say, in regard to the Negro question, that ". . . if you've been down South you see people living in depression, without education. They don't know how to use a privy; they don't know how to do this or that or the other thing." This is incidental. It is accidental to a situation. The essence of the situation is that such persons have the right to be educated, to be given opportunity to grow into a normal civilized state.

This is the case all around the world. It reminds me of a story—if I'm not talking too much?

N. Not at all.

■ *West:* When I was recently in Saigon and Hong Kong, I met two Americans who were fighting with the "chopper" groups in South Vietnam. They, as you know, have had a very rough time. They've been cut off by the Viet Cong, and it's a very brutal, unhappy war for everyone concerned. Now one of these men, a major, told me what had happened to him the previous week. He had planned a strike which was to take place on Monday morning, and everything was right—Intelligence, wind, even the enemy positions were favorable to the attack. He called up the local South Vietnam commander who said, "I'm sorry, Major, we can't fight on Monday. I've consulted my book of omens, and Wednesday is the only day we can fight this week."

Now, men die because of these things, but they exist. You know, it's not only on the side of the Americans or the British or the Australians that errors are made. They're made by everyone. Yet the only way to break down the kind of deadly superstition I just mentioned is by patience and education, with understanding coming first. You can't spit in the eye of the man who has consulted his book of omens; he represents millions of people who think the same way in Southeast Asia. You've got to respect him first, then understand him, and then try very patiently and painfully to get down to the common rock on which we stand.

N. To change the subject, Mr. West, I was impressed, in *The Shoes of the Fisherman*, with your apparent deep knowledge of the inner workings of the Vatican. How did all this come about?

■ *West:* To begin with, I was twelve years as a teaching Brother in a religious order, so I had a very wide background of religious education and philosophy, of Church history of theology. I've lived and worked in Italy, first in Naples, then in Rome, and I've visited that country rather often. The atmosphere is rather like a skin to me; I still have many friends in the Church around the Vatican and in high places in Rome. It's rather interesting, I believe, that one critic has attacked me on the grounds that my knowledge is too simple, that my treatment of the complexities of the Vatican is too simple. This is true, but unfortunately I didn't want to write a Vatican *Advise and Consent* which nobody would read. Not everyone knows what a camelingo is, and what the various Italian terms mean, and the identity of various Curia officials, and if I used all these terms the book would become totally unintelligible. I had to simplify while preserving the essential spirit of the place, and of the ceremonies, and of the novel, and I'm sure it makes no difference to eternal truth whether the Pope does or does not invoke the Holy Ghost at the beginning of the consistory.

N. What has your reaction been to American reviews as a whole, not only regarding *Shoes* but also the two previous novels that have appeared in the past few years?

■ *West:* Well, let me say that in this country I am constantly surprised by the high level of education, not only in the literary field, but in all normal fields of intellectual intercourse. I find that this country is most stimulating, and it can be equally stimulating when you're in opposition—when you're under fire—as well as when you're being praised.

I have no complaints at all about American critics. I find them enlightened and, in the main, just. And even when they haven't been just I find them very agreeable fellows to have a drink with.

N. Now I'd like to ask one of those inevitable questions about your theories or philosophies regarding the novel. In your case, while you maintain a high level of entertainment, you always bite off large themes—issues more important to the world as a whole than the predicament of your characters. What would you say the objectives of the serious novelist should be?

■ *West:* Well, first of all I don't think any writer should waste

x

his time on a novel that won't be read. In other words, as important as his theme or themes might be, if it's not entertaining enough
to keep the reader's attention it might as well not be published.
Yet a serious novel must have a theme; it may not be at all religious or political or even moral, but it must have a conflict between persons or ideas, and the conflict or the issue at stake should
be big enough to reach out beyond the novel into areas of life or
thought the reader can identify himself with, or sympathize with.

Not all novels are written with these integrities, as you no doubt
know very well. There are far too many potboilers and cheap
books that offer a superficial bit of entertainment but offer nothing
to bring the reader back to the book again—or make him want to
keep the book. Some of them are very successful, yet I wonder if,
in the long run, even the wealthy writer of bad novels feels very
proud of himself.

I'd say, in short, that the satisfying novel—the so-called serious
novel that pleases the novelist now and tomorrow and the day after,
and stands a chance of being read a year from now—has to be faithful to the issues and characters the novelist creates. If he cheapens
his book through some expediency, he hurts himself, and this is a
private hurt that must be harder to bear than relative obscurity or
poverty.

N. Now, as far as the beginning novelist is concerned—the
youngster who is seriously intent upon making a career of writing
—what advice would you give?

■ *West:* I think this would come in several parts, but the reader
must remember that all advice is a personal thing, sometimes good,
sometimes bad, but always personal. Perhaps the best way to take
or dismiss advice depends upon the private evaluation of the person
giving it.

I should think that the first thing the young writer should do
is to read everything, and read all the time. Poetry, philosophy,
economics, Sears Roebuck catalogs, history, novels. Reading that's
good, bad, and indifferent, but infinitely varied.

He should also travel as far as his feet, his time, and his finances
will carry him.

He should submit everything he sees, hears, reads, or believes to
a most searching examination, as if his salvation depends upon it,
as indeed it does.

He should write one book, again, good, bad, or indifferent, to
prove to himself that he can fill 350 pages with a connected composition, that he has enough stamina to finish the course. The world

is full of writers who have "not quite finished" a book for twenty years.

Finally he should set out to share, observe, and record the experience and the vision of this very wonderful world.

N.   In looking at the culture of today—the performing as well as the literary arts—how would you evaluate the state of affairs?

■ *West:* To take theater first; it is a mess. Everyone wants to write the play; the star, the director, the producer, the designer, and sometimes the backer. Until the dignity of the writer is restored in the theater, until the actor relearns to take direction, and until the director learns that his function is to direct what is written and not to rewrite it, theater will go on being a mess. It will go on being at the mercy of the featherbedders and the emotionally unstable.

As for the novel, I think the novel is the healthiest literary art form at present, especially in America. Its forms are diverse, the level of execution is extraordinarily high, and things are being said with vigor, passion, and considerable art.

N.   I realize that you've just finished a long session of work, and that you probably haven't resolved the backwater incurred by *The Shoes of the Fisherman.* Yet I wonder what plans you have for your next novel?

■ *West:* It involves two years of study, actually. I'm learning Japanese, and I'm beginning to learn Siamese. I've been backed on a two-year study of Buddhism, Shintoism, and Confucianism so that I can prepare myself in a small way for what I hope will be a real contact with the Far East. I have no intention of doing another novel about Europe. I feel that *Shoes* sums up everything I can say at this stage of my development about Europe, which is basically the history of the Catholic Church and its ramifications and its divergences and its failures and its triumphs.

Now I want to enter into the great dialogue between East and West, to try first to understand it, then to dramatize it, if possible, in a novel. But this is so important that one cannot approach it shallowly or simply, as a writer of thrillers might. I think one must prepare himself thoroughly, with study and education, and this is what I am trying to do.

"I do think this endless harping on sex in novels is preposterous. The endless overt, overconscious frankness of detail gets obsessive. It isn't that one is shocked; it's hard to be shocked any more, but one gets bored. The variations of sex may be infinite, but not the patience of the reader."

Emlyn Williams
Interviewed in New York, September, 1963

Emlyn Williams

N. Emlyn Williams serves with distinction in three capacities: as playwright, actor, and author. He need only have *written* such plays as *The Corn Is Green* and *Night Must Fall* to have won immortality. Yet he has made an indelible impression upon generations of theatergoers by starring in these plays as well as in the works of other playwrights. His frontal assault on the literary scene came a few years ago when *George*—the autobiography of his early years—was acclaimed in England and in the United States as one of the most lyric, lucid, and revealing autobiographies written in recent times.

In talking to Mr. Williams I'd like to ask him, first, if there will be a sequel to *George*. Frankly, I've been hoping for one.

■ *Williams:* You know, *George*, and that's the name I grew up with, by the way, finished in 1927. It doesn't go any further for two reasons: I don't think my life after that time is as interesting, nor could I be as honest in presenting it.

With *George* I could be quite candid. Partly, of course, because my parents were no longer alive. Though I hope I give a very affectionate picture of them, it's not the sort of thing my mother would have enjoyed reading at all. She would have been very distressed by it, really, if only because of the way I discuss my father.

After we reach the age of twenty-one, autobiography becomes difficult. So many people are alive who would have to play a part in it. They are sensitive and vulnerable and might take a dim view of whatever objective or subjective honesties you employed. To avoid hurting them it would be like writing with one's hands tied behind one's back, and this would not be physically comfortable; besides, presumably, entailing holding the pen between one's teeth!

N. Then there won't be a sequel?

■ *Williams:* No. I knew at the time there wouldn't be. It wouldn't be interesting, even if I could bring myself to write it. You see, as you remember at the end of the book, I went into the theater. Somehow a book about the theater tends to be more superficial than the account of a more ordinary life. It's a series of plays, some of which are successful, some of which fail. The best you can come up with are anecdotes about well-known actors and actresses. Quite often the anecdotes that are really fascinating can't be used. They'd be in bad taste. Others, even the affectionate ones, are too private, too special, to use. So you'd be left with a bad book.

I put my pen away after writing *George*. I hope to take it out again, some day, to write a novel. But I can't do that until I feel I really have something to write about, and that "something" hasn't come to me yet. I suppose that if someone told me that my wife and children would be sent to a concentration camp in three weeks unless I finished a novel in that time, I would write one. But it wouldn't necessarily be a very good one.

I'd rather wait. It seems to me that altogether too much writing is turned out that doesn't have a theme, or serve a need, and I'd rather not be another culprit.

N.   To retrace a bit of the material in *George*. You were born and reared in Wales?

■ *Williams:*   Yes. And you know, I must emphasize this because people from outside of England think of Wales as a mere section of England with minor differences. This isn't so. Welsh is a language completely different from English. I was brought up speaking Welsh and learned English as a foreign language. Now, English is the language of business, of commerce, but in the smaller towns and in many rural areas, Welsh is spoken more than English. Even the B.B.C. has a Welsh department which gives the news and many other programs in Welsh.

In schools, of course, the learning of the two languages fits one admirably well for the study of other languages, French, etc. The structure of Welsh and English is different. Welsh is not a dialect, like the Yorkshire accent, or (in America) the Brooklyn accent. Welsh is as different from English as Russian is.

N.   Was yours a mining town?

■ *Williams:*   No, my home was in the country. My father was a miner for a time, and I wrote a play about a miner called *The Corn Is Green*. Oddly enough, three or more films in which I've appeared, like *The Citadel* and *The Stars Look Down* were about miners, and in the end, I almost believe I've been a miner myself. Actually, I've never been down in a mine, and I have no intention of starting.

My father was a miner for a short time, but then, he was all sorts of things. Sailor, publican, and so on. But I grew up in the northern, more agricultural part of Wales; the mines are south. But to show how all impressions of Wales are blurred, even the works of Welsh writers, I'm constantly fending off compliments on *How Green Was My Valley* which I did not write. It's a beautiful book, and I would love to take credit for it, but it isn't mine.

N.   *The Corn Is Green* was heavily autobiographical, wasn't it?
■ *Williams:* Yes. This becomes quite clear when you read *George.* It's based upon my schoolmistress, but it's broadly adapted for theater. The part about the boy in the play who has an affair with a girl in the village, which results in the illegitimate child adopted by the school nurse is, I hasten to say, all fiction.

When I wrote the play I was apprehensive of what my teacher, Miss Cooke, would think. I set it back in time (1890), because I thought that the actual conditions (1916) weren't dramatic enough, weren't extreme enough. I wanted to show how a boy was helped by this teacher (which, indeed, I was) but the total actuality didn't lend itself to theater. So, instead of writing it about a boy and a schoolmistress in 1916, when conditions in schools were really very good, I set it back to 1890 when conditions were primitive, and a lot of poor people simply never went to school, never learned to read and write. It worked. I was nervous about her seeing the play, but she reacted marvelously. She took my picture of her—a loving picture, but critical, too, because she was a clumsy, forthright character, her major defect in the play—as a tribute to all teachers. I had dedicated the play to her, but she insisted that the American edition be dedicated, "To S.G.C. and all teachers." She was a very generous woman.

But I talk as though she's gone, as though I hadn't seen her for years. Actually, I saw her two weeks ago. I went to stay with her in Leeds, Yorkshire, when she celebrated her eightieth birthday. She's still tremendously active.

N.   How would you describe her effect upon your career?
■ *Williams:* She was a tremendous influence, a great driving force. She was terribly interested in what your mind was like, and it was a challenge to do well in her eyes because she was immensely critical. She was not—how can I put it?—a "loving character" in the sense that she would tell you you were wonderful. She would tell you you were good only if you had done something that came up to scratch. She also planned consistently. She was determined that I should have a tremendous advantage over lots of people. Of course, with the two languages I spoke, I had an advantage when it came to studying French, Latin, and Italian, both in accent and

structure of grammar. She planned it so I got to Oxford through a scholarship. She prepared me three or four years for this scholarship without my being aware of exactly what she was doing. But when it came, I had all the qualifications. She had groomed me, as they say in theater, for this thing.

Nor was I the only one she helped. She constantly hears from former pupils, both boys and girls, who owe much of their success to her efforts.

N. *George* left you at Oxford, as I recall, more than a bit mixed up, with theater and classes competing for your attention.

■ *Williams:* I was at Oxford for three years. Took up tutoring. I knew in my heart that I wanted to go into the theater, but there were no obvious encouragements. I was already writing plays, and in the end this pushed me into the theater because I wasn't the obvious type for an actor. In those days the matinee idol, the John Barrymore type, was the thing. I wasn't beautiful. Today, with actors like Albert Finney dominating the scene, I'd fit. We've gotten over the handsome stereotype.

Life opened up for me at Oxford, perhaps too widely, and I neglected my studies, concentrating on acting, writing and, as my mother would have called it, gadding about. Finally, I reached a point where I couldn't catch up, so I left Oxford under a cloud and took what they call "schools" (exams, actually) a year later, when I was already on the stage. I got my degree, the Master of Arts you normally leave Oxford with. I was just a year late. But I don't really think I could have done things any differently, obsessed as I was with theater.

N. Since much of the time you've conducted both careers simultaneously, it may be impossible to separate them completely. But let's regard you only as a playwright, for the moment, and discuss the feelings you have in regard to the obligations the playwright should impose upon himself.

■ *Williams:* I suppose I have the commonplace, old-fashioned attitude that you should simply entertain your audience. I don't mean play down to them. You hope your audience is an intelligent one. Keep them fascinated, interested, moved, and amused. This is your ultimate goal. You can't think of this every second you're writing; you are writing for your own satisfaction, too, needless to say.

There is always a part of me that seems to sit back in the audience, all the while I'm writing, passing some sort of judgment on what I'm doing. This isn't deliberate. I never lose the feeling of watching it from the audience. I know that many playwrights work without the sense of audience, but I can't do it. After all, the play, if it's produceable, is destined for the audience, for those people who sit there like children, sometimes very sophisticated children, and you've got to hold them to whatever it is you're doing, a comedy or a very serious play. At the same time that you hope for their intelligence and receptiveness, you've got to consider this "span of attention" business.

N. What do you feel about an actor's obligations to an audience?

■ *Williams:* I think they're very much the same, really: to hold the audience, to keep it interested in what you're saying, to convince them that what you're saying is inimitable, that it's never been said before. I don't mean by another player, but by anyone before that very moment. Just as we're talking now, whether I'm being interesting or not, the things I'm saying are being said for the first time, to you. Whatever glibness, whatever flowing quality is required in a play, is the product of talent and knowledge and rehearsal, but it must never sound rehearsed.

N. *The Corn Is Green* was a great hit. It ran throughout the war in London with Dame Sybil Thorndike and yourself as stars. It furnished a great vehicle in America for Ethel Barrymore. Its roots are heavily autobiographical. Was *Night Must Fall* similarly based upon reality?

■ *Williams:* No. Well, in a way it was based upon two or three people I knew; parts of them, particularly one who was a pathological liar. *Night Must Fall* was a gruesome, very gruesome play, an amalgam of two or three famous English murder cases. One, a boy who murdered his mother for insurance. This was too awful to use, intact. I had to twist it so that she wasn't his mother, but a horrible old woman who had not legally adopted him. He had insinuated his way into her affections. Then there was the case of a man who had murdered a woman and left the body in a trunk for several months. He couldn't do anything about it because his mind was paralyzed. The play wasn't based on any one person or any one event, the way *The Corn Is Green* was developed.

N. Could you describe the theatrical experiences you've enjoyed most?

■ *Williams:* The parts I've enjoyed most have been in plays I haven't written. Both the Edgar Wallace plays I appeared in, *On the Spot* and *The Case of the Frightened Lady*, were very happy experiences.

I wrote *Night Must Fall* for myself because I was determined to play a star part. Nobody was offering me a good one! I did, for something like thirty months, and it led to a pattern, a series of plays I wrote and appeared in: *The Light of Heart, The Morning Star,* and *The Wind of Heaven.*

Then I was in a play by Terence Rattigan called *The Winslow Boy.* This was a wonderful, marvelous part. I played the lawyer in it, and realized then that I enjoyed it more than my own plays because I could never relax in my own plays. You never relax, anyway, but when it's your own, you keep thinking, "How is it going?" or, "Is it all right?" even when you aren't on stage. You should forget it, because you've quite enough to do as an actor, but somehow you can't.

In *The Winslow Boy* I could think to myself, "I've got this fine part, the play is fine, and I don't have to worry." It was almost like a vacation. *And Months Thereafter* is another play which fascinated me. And this past year, I played Bob Scofield in *A Man For All Seasons* in New York—a difficult, fascinating, exhilarating play to be in.

In 1951 I started a new career. It happened so gradually that I was caught up in it before I realized it was happening. It began when I was asked to do a bit at a concert—what they call an "all star matinee" at Drury Lane and a "benefit" in America—but they asked me to do a scene from *Night Must Fall.* A great many actors were doing scenes, big scenes, from plays they had been in. I said, "Now, really, I'm too old to play *Night Must Fall* during the week and so presumably too old to play it on Sunday!"

At the time I was reading a biography of Dickens. I had always loved his things and I thought, "Well, why not impersonate him, because Dickens was tremendous on his tour of America, doing his readings." So I tried about six minutes of *Bleak House,* and it went so well for me that I sat down and thought, "Well, I should try to work an evening out of Dickens, doing my own adaptations—it's rich territory." Gradually, I did learn pieces. I tried them out on friends; some worked and some didn't. Some were all right, but not next to certain others because you had to have variety for an evening, rather like a review. All that piecing together and discarding was fascinating work, and I've been at it ever since, between plays. I'll be touring America again with it through late 1964, ending 1965.

It was a challenge—I'd never held the stage by myself before—but it's so easy to put together. No assembling of cast, no wardrobe and scenery difficulties. And it's always fresh to me because, as I said, I do it between plays.

N. To move to the theoretical, what do you think of the present state of the novel, perhaps writing as a whole, and the theater?

■ *Williams:* That's very broad, isn't it? I'm not very good with generalizations; I don't think about the "state of anything" very often because I'm wrapped up in a play I'm doing at the moment. I do think this endless harping on sex in novels is preposterous. The endless overt, overconscious frankness of detail gets obsessive. It isn't that one is shocked; it's hard to be shocked, any more, but one gets bored. The variations of sex may be infinite, but not the patience of the reader.

Theater suffers from a different problem; we might call it the deliberate propagation of obscurity. I think it's maddening to see a play you simply can't understand, when it's just a flood of words. One gets irritated and bored because one's time is being wasted. But the obscure can make tremendous theater, if the playwright is skillful enough to interest the audience and hold it. *The Caretaker* is rather extreme, but I found it absorbing, haunting. Some of it is difficult, but you accept that in view of its marvelous quality.

N. If you were to give advice to the young playwright or writer who is serious about a career, what would that advice be?

■ *Williams:* First of all, I would hope that he would look inside himself to find out what there is in him that is absolutely true and is going to be different from the next playwright. By the next one, I mean the next-door playwright who is writing a play which will be individual with him. Obviously, the best plays are expressions of individuality which are going to fascinate other people because they will strike a new note. Tennessee Williams did this with *A Streetcar Named Desire,* for example. This was an extraordinary experience because it was something that sprang from within himself, people he knew about, and he wrote that play as nobody else would. The thing is to try not to imitate other playwrights. This is always a problem, being oneself; even in real life, isn't it? Be yourself—because if you aren't, you'll be just like everybody else, and you'll pass unnoticed—stereotyped and artificial.

I rather imagine the same advice would apply to the young novelist—the insistence upon originality, honesty, reality. You didn't ask me about young actors, but here we enter an area where everything is grist to the mill. Here foreign languages, reading, study, training, observation—everything enters in. The more intensive and extensive the training, the better, because I think that even the intangible thing called "style" is really a matter of development.

But for the playwright, the novelist, or the actor, the most important thing is originality. Without that quality, however well trained we might be, we're doomed to go through life as understudies—not a bright prospect!

GEORGE ALLEN & UNWIN LTD

London: 40 Museum Street, W.C.1

Auckland: 24 Wyndham Street
Bombay: 15 Graham Road, Ballard Estate, Bombay 1
Bridgetown: P.O. Box 222
Buenos Aires: Escritorio 454–459, Florida 165
Calcutta: 17 Chittarajan Avenue, Calcutta 13
Cape Town: 68 Shortmarket Street
Hong Kong: 44 Mody Road, Kowloon
Ibadan: P.O. Box 62
Karachi: Karachi Chambers, McLeod Road
Madras: Mohan Mansions, 38c Mount Road, Madras 6
Mexico: Villalongin 32–10, Piso, Mexico 5, D.F.
Nairobi: P.O. Box 4536
New Delhi: 13–14 Asaf Ali Road, New Delhi 1
Ontario: 81 Curlew Drive, Don Mills
Philippines: 7 Waling-Waling Street, Roxas District,
Quezon City
Sao Paulo: Caixa Postal 8675
Singapore: 36c Prinsep Street, Singapore 7
Sydney: N.S.W.: Bradbury House, 55 York Street
Tokyo: 10 Kanda-Ogawamachi, 3-Chome, Chiyoda-Ku

THE HUMAN SPIRIT

Edited by Whit Burnett

Demy 8vo   2 5s net

Contributions by Graham Greene; Jacquetta Hawkes; C. E. M.
Joad; D. H. Lawrence; C. S. Lewis; Katherine Mansfield;
W. Somerset Maugham; Albert Schweitzer and others.

There is more to the human spirit than its capacity to triumph
over adversity and come through resplendent. Sometimes the
human spirit is filled with doubt; at other times it may be a
questing, or a wondering, or a playful thing; occasionally, it is
filled with the purest joy. But that 'spirit' which we know to
distinguish man from all other living creatures is common to us
all, to all nations and classes and creeds.

In this anthology, forty different personalities—from desert
naturalists to priests and philosophers, from explorers and air
pilots to teachers and scientists—set forth their most intense
personal observations and experiences, and the thoughts provoked by the deepest crises of their lives. In fact, fiction and
reflection, forty different human beings reveal in a profoundly
personal way what for them are the most significant aspects of
living.

What does it mean to be forever lonely, as was Thomas Wolfe?
To face death as a prisoner of war, as did Sidney Stewart, tor-
tured and starving? To gain one's sight after many years as did
John Howard Griffin and for the first time to gaze upon the face
of the woman you have married and of your child, and to find
them almost unbearably beautiful? What does it mean to feel at
peace with the world, confident of a kind of rightness in it all,
to come back from death, as Jesse Stuart did, and feel that man
is not a lost creature, but that in him and in him alone, by the
grace of something, lies all the past and future? Here is the
evidence of the great variety of spiritual crisis, of inspiration and
of the joy of life. It reveals the indomitable courage of the
human spirit in daring and doing, at moments of being, sharing
and living, feeling and wondering.

THIS IS MY PHILOSOPHY

Edited by Whit Burnett

Demy 8vo   *Third Impression*   2 5s net

Each selection in this book is a statement of personal philosophy by one of the world's leading thinkers. The contributors are twenty eminent living philosophers, scientists, statesmen, authors, historians, educators, sociologists, and theologians. Each has selected from his own writings (or has written especially for this book) an expression of his approach to ·life, his work, and our present-day world.

Here are the matured reflections of men who have lived a full and busy life and have achieved wisdom with their years. What is man's relation to the world to-day? To history? To society? To death? To God? To country? What is thinking? What is our civilization coming to? Can the East and West find a philosophy of life in common? How does the Christian ethic stand up in an atom-splitting world? What is mankind's greatest present need?

These are some of the questions treated in a book of many points of view; a challenging collection of seasoned reflections on the biggest and most fundamental problems, conflicts, and concepts of man to-day.

I BELIEVE

Demy 8vo   *Fifth Impression*   2 5s net

H. G. Wells, Bertrand Russell, Lancelot Hogben, E. M. Forster, Julian Huxley, Beatrice Webb, H. J. Laski, Rebecca West, W. H. Auden, Emil Ludwig, Thomas Mann, Jules Romains, Jacques Maritain, Sir Arthur Keith, Albert Einstein, Pearl Buck, Stuart Chase, Lin Yutang, Hendrik van Loon, James Thurber, J. B. S. Haldane.

This collection of credos is not set out that readers may choose from among them, but rather that they may share the fundamental faith in freedom and intelligence that is the inspiration of them all.